# Lecture Notes in Computer Science    **15564**

Founding Editors

Gerhard Goos
Juris Hartmanis

AF166270

The series Lecture Notes in Computer Science (LNCS), including its subseries Lecture Notes in Artificial Intelligence (LNAI) and Lecture Notes in Bioinformatics (LNBI), has established itself as a medium for the publication of new developments in computer science and information technology research, teaching, and education.

LNCS enjoys close cooperation with the computer science R & D community, the series counts many renowned academics among its volume editors and paper authors, and collaborates with prestigious societies. Its mission is to serve this international community by providing an invaluable service, mainly focused on the publication of conference and workshop proceedings and postproceedings. LNCS commenced publication in 1973.

Houbing Herbert Song · Roberto Di Pietro ·
Saed Alrabaee · Mohammad Tubishat ·
Mousa Al-kfairy · Omar Alfandi
Editors

# Network and
# System Security

18th International Conference, NSS 2024
Abu Dhabi, United Arab Emirates, November 20–22, 2024
Proceedings

 Springer

*Editors*
Houbing Herbert Song ⓘ
University of Maryland
College Park, MD, USA

Saed Alrabaee ⓘ
United Arab Emirates University
Abu Dhabi, United Arab Emirates

Mousa Al-kfairy ⓘ
Zayed University
Abu Dhabi, United Arab Emirates

Roberto Di Pietro ⓘ
King Abdullah University of Science
and Technology
Thuwal, Saudi Arabia

Mohammad Tubishat ⓘ
Zayed University
Abu Dhabi, United Arab Emirates

Omar Alfandi ⓘ
Zayed University
Abu Dhabi, United Arab Emirates

ISSN 0302-9743          ISSN 1611-3349 (electronic)
Lecture Notes in Computer Science
ISBN 978-981-96-3530-6          ISBN 978-981-96-3531-3 (eBook)
https://doi.org/10.1007/978-981-96-3531-3

This Springer imprint is published by the registered company Springer Nature Singapore Pte Ltd.
The registered company address is: 152 Beach Road, #21-01/04 Gateway East, Singapore 189721, Singapore

If disposing of this product, please recycle the paper.

# Preface

The International Conference on Network and System Security (NSS) is an annual event that explores both theoretical and practical aspects of network and system security. The 18th edition, designated NSS 2024, was held from November 20 to 22, 2024, in Abu Dhabi, UAE. The conference was organized by Zayed University in Abu Dhabi and was co-located with the 10th International Symposium on Security and Privacy in Social Networks and Big Data (SocialSec 2024).

The review process for NSS 2024 involved 62 submissions. On average, each member of the Technical Program Committee (TPC) was assigned three submissions to review, with each paper assigned to a minimum of four reviewers. To ensure anonymity, the submission process was structured so that the reviewers could not see the authors' names. Likewise, the reviewers remained anonymous to other members of the TPC and the paper authors. The management of the review process was conducted through EasyChair. At the beginning of the process, reviewers were required to declare any conflicts of interest regarding the submissions. The EasyChair system was set up to prevent TPC members (including the TPC chairs) from viewing either reviewer assignments or the reviews for any papers where they had a conflict of interest. In cases where one TPC Co-Chair had a conflict, discussions about those papers were held and decisions were made by the other two TPC Co-Chairs who did not have conflicts. The selection process was competitive. After engaging in interactive discussions and careful deliberation, the TPC chose 21 full papers for presentation at the conference.

The NSS 2024 conference and the co-located SocialSec 2024 hosted three invited talks for participants from both conferences. The speakers included Mohamed Al Kuwaiti, Head of the UAE Cyber Security Council; Lin Zhiqiang from Ohio State University, USA; and Nir Kshetri from the University of North Carolina-Greensboro, USA.

The Technical Program Committee (TPC) of NSS 2024 selected one paper for the Best Paper Award; the winner received a certificate and a gift kindly sponsored by Zayed University.

The NSS 2024 Technical Program Committee (TPC) was co-chaired by Saed Alrabaee from United Arab Emirates University, UAE; Roberto Di Pietro from King Abdullah University of Science and Technology, KSA; and Houbing Herbert Song from the University of Maryland, Baltimore County, USA. They were responsible for selecting the TPC members and overseeing the selection of the papers included in this volume. The organization of NSS 2024 and the co-located SocialSec 2024 was led by Omar Alfandi from Zayed University, UAE; Saed Alrabaee from United Arab Emirates University, UAE; and Mousa Al-Kfairy from Zayed University, UAE, who served as the joint General Chair and Co-Chairs for both conferences.

The conferences were made possible thanks to the professional efforts of several individuals. Huwida Said, Samia Loucif, Abdallah Tubaishat, and Feras Al-Obeidat from Zayed University, UAE, Dhcya Mustafa, Hashemite University, Jordan, and Maui antonio

Caprolu, King Abdullah University of Science & Technology, KSA were the Publicity Co-Chairs. The Publication Chair was Mohammad Tubishat from Zayed University, UAE, along with Thangavel Murugan from United Arab Emirates University, UAE. April Maramara from Zayed University, UAE served as the Web Chair. Additionally, the Technical Program Committee (TPC) received guidance from a Steering Committee chaired by Yang Xiang from Swinburne University of Technology, Australia.

We would like to express our gratitude to everyone who contributed to the success of NSS 2024. We thank all members of the Organizing Committee for both NSS 2024 and the co-located SocialSec 2024 for their professionalism and support provided to the TPC and all participants of both conferences. Lastly, we extend our thanks to all authors who submitted to NSS 2024 and to all conference participants for making NSS 2024 such an enjoyable experience.

November 2024

Houbing Herbert Song<br>
Roberto Di Pietro<br>
Saed Alrabaee<br>
Mohammad Tubishat<br>
Mousa Al-kfairy<br>
Omar Alfandi

# Organization

## General Chair

Omar Alfandi                    Zayed University, UAE

## General Co-chairs

Saed Alrabaee                   United Arab Emirates University, UAE
Mousa Al-kfairy                 Zayed University, UAE

## Program Committee Chairs

Saed Alrabaee                   United Arab Emirates University, UAE
Roberto Di Pietro               King Abdullah University of Science and
                                    Technology, KSA
Houbing Herbert Song            University of Maryland, Baltimore County, USA

## NSS Steering Committee

Yang Xiang                      Swinburne University of Technology, Australia
Elisa Bertino                   Purdue University, USA
Robert Deng                     Singapore Management University, Singapore
Dieter Gollmann                 Hamburg University of Technology, Germany
Xinyi Huang                     Hong Kong University of Science and
                                    Technology, China
Kui Ren                         Zhejiang University, China
Ravi Sandhu                     University of Texas at San Antonio, USA
Wanlei Zhou                     City University of Macau, China

## Publicity Co-chairs

Huwida Said                     Zayed University, UAE
Samia Loucif                    Zayed University, UAE
Abdallah Tubaishat              Zayed University, UAE

Feras Al-Obeidat            Zayed University, UAE
Dheya Mustafa               Hashemite University, Jordan
Maurantonio Caprolu         King Abdullah University of Science &
                            Technology, KSA

## Publication Chairs

Mohammad Tubishat           Zayed University, UAE
Thangavel Murugan           United Arab Emirates University, UAE

## Web Chair

April Maramara              Zayed University, UAE

## Local Organizing Committee

Rima Grati                  Zayed University, UAE
Nadia Dahmani               Zayed University, UAE
Sarra Almessabi             Zayed University, UAE

## Sponsorship Co-chairs

Fatma Taher                 Zayed University, UAE
Mousa Al-kfairy             Zayed University, UAE
Yaser Khamayseh             Zayed University, UAE
Dina Tbaishat               Zayed University, UAE

## Registration Chair

Abeer Alhasan               Zayed University, UAE

## Technical Program Committee

Martin Andreoni             Technology Innovation Institute, UAE
Pietro Tedeschi             CY4GATE S.p.A., Italy

| | |
|---|---|
| Sven Dietrich | City University of New York, USA |
| Yazan Alahmed | Al Ain University, UAE |
| Nisha Madathil | UAE University, UAE |
| Muhusina Ismail | UAE University, UAE |
| Omar Darwish | Eastern Michigan University, USA |
| Kyungbaek Kim | Chonnam National University, South Korea |
| Samer Khamaiseh | Miami University, USA |
| Claude Fachkha | Concordia University, Canada |
| Edwin Dauber | Widener University, USA |
| Christoforos Ntantogian | Ionian University, Greece |
| Bo Luo | University of Kansas, USA |
| Paria Shirani | University of Ottawa, Canada |
| Wenjia Li | New York Institute of Technology, USA |
| Claudio Ardagna | Universita' degli Studi di Milano, Italy |
| Sergio Pastrana | Universidad Carlos III de Madrid, Spain |
| Khaled Shuaib | Al Ain University, UAE |
| Lianying Zhao | Carleton University, Canada |
| Christos Xenakis | University of Piraeus, Greece |
| Kuo-Hui Yeh | National Yang Ming Chiao Tung University, Taiwan |
| | |
| Adel Abusitta | Polytechnique Montréal, Canada |
| Nora Cuppens-Boulahia | Polytechnique Montréal, Canada |
| Mahmoud Khasawneh | Al Ain University, UAE |
| Nikos Salamanos | Cyprus University of Technology, Cyprus |
| Kallol Krishna Karmakar | University of Newcastle, Australia |
| Elias Bou-Harb | Louisiana State University, USA |
| Dima Alhadidi | University of Windsor, Canada |
| Irfan Ahmed | Virginia Commonwealth University, USA |
| Josep Domingo-Ferrer | Universitat Rovira i Virgili, Spain |
| Matthew Edwards | University of Bristol, UK |
| Helei Cui | Northwestern Polytechnical University, China |
| Dheya Mustafa | Hashemite University, Jordan |
| Chan Yeob Yeun | Khalifa University, UAE |
| Inah Omoronyia | University of Glasgow, UK |
| Azadeh Tabiban | Concordia University, Canada |
| Chiara Boldrini | Consiglio Nazionale delle Ricerche, Italy |
| Wenjuan Li | Education University of Hong Kong, China |
| Yunsheng Wang | California State Polytechnic University Pomona, USA |
| | |
| Weizhi Meng | Technical University of Denmark, Denmark |
| Mengyuan Zhang | Vrije Universiteit Amsterdam, Netherlands |
| Xingliang Yuan | University of Melbourne, Australia |

# Contents

## System Security and Prevention

## Network and Infrastructure Security

## Blockchain and Smart Contracts

## Data Security

# Authentication and Security

# How to Accomplish Key and Communication Compression Over Authentication Channels

## Proxy Re-authentication and Its Instantiations

Yoshiro Matsuoka[1], Sohto Chiku[1]([✉]) [ID], Keisuke Hara[1,2] [ID],
and Junji Shikata[1] [ID]

[1] Yokohama National University, Yokohama, Japan
`chiku-sohto-tw@ynu.jp`, `shikata-junji-rb@ynu.ac.jp`
[2] National Institute of Advanced Industrial Science and Technology, Tokyo, Japan
`hara-keisuke@aist.go.jp`

**Abstract.** The Internet of Things (IoT) has widespread applications covering from tiny wearable devices to large industrial systems. When building authentication channels among IoT devices for security enhancement, one of the biggest challenges is how to reduce the size of keys and authentication tags in systems since they do not have rich resources (such as, memory and bandwidth) in many cases. Although many solutions have been introduced to address this challenge so far, to the best of our knowledge, we do not have a solution to compress the size of keys and authentication tags *simultaneously* in a cryptographic manner.

In this paper, as a core primitive to solve this problem, we propose a new cryptographic protocol called *proxy re-authentication*. In proxy re-authentication, we realize key compression by converting a (authentication) tag generated with a sender's private key into another one so that a receiver can verify with his own private key through a proxy. In other words, in the systems equipped with proxy re-authentication, each user is required to have only its own key to communicate with other users. Moreover, in this protocol, it is possible to realize a compression of the size of tags by aggregating tags based on the idea used in aggregate message authentication. We provide two constructions of proxy re-authentication: one is based on the hardness of the computational Diffie-Hellman problem over cyclic groups and the other is based on the hardness of the learning with rounding problem over lattices. Then, we show that these constructions are practically efficient by implementing them.

**Keywords:** Proxy Re-Authentication · Key and Communication Compression · Diffie-Hellman Problem · Learning with Rounding Problem

## 1 Introduction

The Internet of Things (IoT) is a system of billions of smart devices connected to the Internet and takes charge of collecting, exchanging, or processing data.

H. H. Song et al. (Eds.): NSS 2024, LNCS 15564, pp. 3–20, 2025.
https://doi.org/10.1007/978-981-96-3531-3_1

The popularization of IoT has reduced business costs, improved service quality, and helped people live and work more. However, despite its convenience, some security problems remain significant challenges for IoT in practical applications. Especially, as a specific issue in IoT devices, they do not have abundant resources (such as, memory and bandwidth) for implementing protocols for security.

Among the security challenges on IoT, in this paper, we focus on the challenge on how to build authentication channels involving IoT as efficient as possible. Foremost, we consider message authentication code (MAC)-based (not signature-based) methods for gaining more efficiency.[1] A prominent approach to reduce the communication cost in MAC-based authentications is *aggregate message authentication code* (aggregate MAC) which is introduced by Katz and Lindell [13]. This primitive allows multiple authentication tags to be aggregated into one shorter tag that still suffices to convince a verifier that each signer indeed signs appropriate messages. Katz and Lindell [13] proposed a simple and efficient mechanism to realize authentication aggregation using existing MAC schemes.

While we can reduce the communication costs by using aggregate MAC, conventional (aggregate) MAC requires us to share a (common) secret key between a sender and a receiver. This implies that, if the number of communicating parties increases, each device must hold these additional keys for authentication. This drawback makes saving the storage in IoT devices challenging. For example, this must be a matter of concern in the IoT setting since the number of devices increases at an astonishing rate. To the best of our knowledge, in such authentication scenarios, we do not have a solution to compress the amount of keys stored in each device.[2] Hence, in this paper, we tackle the following important question:

> *How can we accomplish key and communication compression over authentication channels?*

## 1.1   Our Contribution

In this paper, as a core primitive to solve the above question, we propose a new cryptographic protocol called *proxy re-authentication*. More precisely, we give the following technical contributions.

**Formalization of Proxy Re-authentication.** Firstly, inspired by the previous works [3,13], we propose a formalization of proxy re-authentication which is capable of key and communication compression. In proxy re-authentication, in addition to senders and receivers, we prepare an additional (semi-trusted) entity called *proxy*. Roughly, the proxy with re-authentication keys is responsible for transforming senders' authentication tags into another one that can be verified

---

[1] We believe that this setting is reasonable by considering situation where IoT devices are given their own (secret) MAC keys during manufacturing.

[2] In this paper, for convenience, we sometimes call compressing the amount of keys stored in each device as *key compression*.

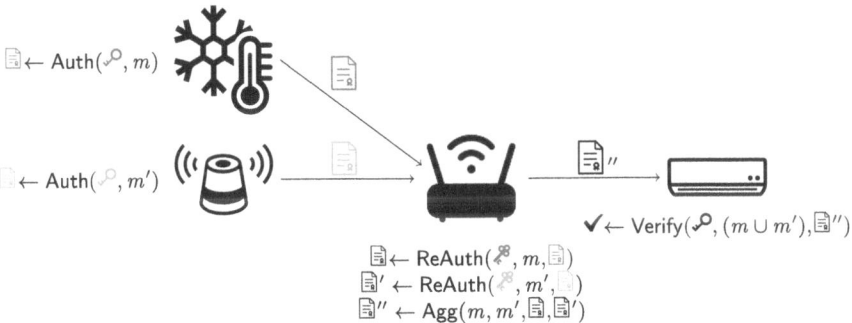

**Fig. 1.** System overview of proxy re-authentication.

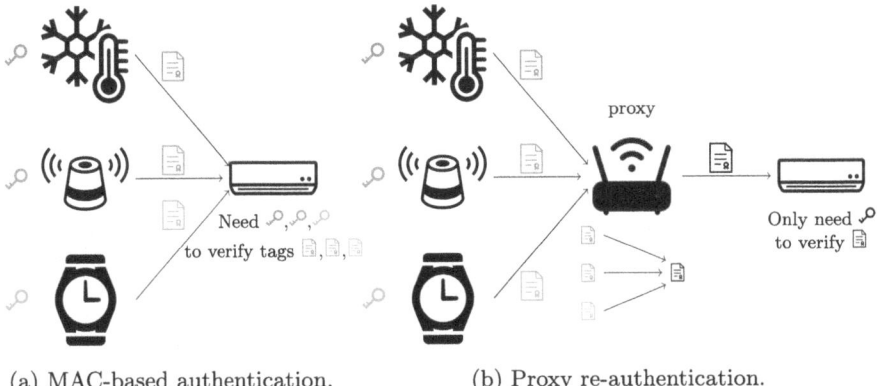

(a) MAC-based authentication.          (b) Proxy re-authentication.

**Fig. 2.** Comparison between a conventional MAC-based authentication (Fig. 2a) and our proposed proxy re-authentication method (Fig. 2b).

by a receiver as shown in Fig. 1.[3] Moreover, in this protocol, it is possible to compress authentication tags by aggregating them based on the idea used in aggregate MAC. Regarding security aspects, we define existential unforgeability under chosen message attacks which guarantees security against users and a proxy. Especially, it is required that a proxy cannot forge (fresh) signatures for new messages which are not created by signers, while it has additional re-authentication keys.

In Fig. 2, we provide an overview of the difference on authentication procedures by the (conventional) MAC-based method and proxy re-authentication method. As seen in the left figure (Fig. 2a), in the MAC-based authentication, a (right) verifier has to have all (left) senders' secret keys to verify authentication tags sent by them. This requires a verifier to prepare large storage. Conversely, in the proxy re-authentication (Fig. 2b), a verifier only needs its own secret key

---

[3] We assume that a proxy is an entity (e.g., base station) who has rich resources (such as, computational power, storage, and bandwidth).

to verify all authentication tags thanks to a proxy converting all tags into ones that can be verified under the verifier's key.[4] We can see that, the more users there are in the system, the greater this benefit becomes.

**Concrete Constructions of Proxy Re-authentication.** Based on our formalization of proxy re-authentication, we propose two concrete constructions of proxy re-authentication in the random oracle model. One is based on the computational Diffie-Hellman (CDH) assumption over cyclic groups and the other one is based on the learning with rounding (LWR) assumption over lattices. Our CDH-based construction is shown in Sect. 4 and our LWR-based construction is shown in Sect. 5. Furthermore, to show the practical efficiency of our proxy re-authentication schemes, we implement and evaluate our schemes in Python. In particular, regarding the main high-level operations in the proxy re-authentication scheme from the CDH assumption (resp., the LWR assumption), the authentication time is 62.73 μs (resp., 487.4 μs), the re-authentication time is 65.65 μs (resp., 483.7 μs), the two message aggregation time is 1.308 μs (resp., 0.2871 μs), and the verification time is 87.17 μs (resp., 663.9 μs). While it is a proof of concept, you can see that both of our schemes have the potential to provide an efficient solution. We note that, while the LWR-based scheme is slightly inferior on efficiency than the CDH-based scheme, this scheme can provide a post-quantum solution.

## 1.2 Overview of Our Constructions

In this section, we provide the technical overview of our constructions. To construct proxy re-authentication, we dive into the mathematical structures of specific PRF construction based on CDH or LWR assumption.

**CDH-Based Construction.** Let $H : \{0,1\}^* \to \mathbb{G}$ is hash function modeled as a random oracle. Now, the PRF based on the CDH assumption is expressed as $F_{\mathsf{CDH}}(k, x) := H(x)^k$, where $x \in \{0,1\}^*$ and $k \in \mathbb{Z}_p$. Then, we can observe that $F(k_1 + k_2, x) = H(x)^{k_1+k_2} = H(x)^{k_1} \cdot H(x)^{k_2} = F(k_1, x) \cdot F(k_2, x)$, where $x \in \{0,1\}^*$ and $k_1, k_2 \in \mathbb{Z}_p$. Based on this construction, we can transform an authentication tag from the sender Alice to the receiver Bob as

$$\mathsf{sk}_{\mathrm{Alice}} \in \mathbb{Z}_p, \quad \mathsf{sk}_{\mathrm{Bob}} \in \mathbb{Z}_p, \quad \mathsf{rk}_{\mathrm{Alice} \to \mathrm{Bob}} := \frac{\mathsf{sk}_{\mathrm{Bob}}}{\mathsf{sk}_{\mathrm{Alice}}},$$

$$\mathsf{Auth} : \mathsf{t}_{\mathrm{Alice}} = H(m)^{\mathsf{sk}_{\mathrm{Alice}}},$$

$$\mathsf{ReAuth} : (\mathsf{t}_{\mathrm{Alice}})^{\mathsf{rk}_{\mathrm{Alice} \to \mathrm{Bob}}} = \left(H(m)^{\mathsf{sk}_{\mathrm{Alice}}}\right)^{\mathsf{sk}_{\mathrm{Bob}}/\mathsf{sk}_{\mathrm{Alice}}} = H(m)^{\mathsf{sk}_{\mathrm{Bob}}}.$$

To aggregate two or more tags, by using the multiplicative homomorphism of cyclic groups $g_1^k \cdot g_2^k = (g_1 \cdot g_2)^k$, we have

$$\mathsf{Agg} : \mathsf{t}_{m_1} \cdot \mathsf{t}_{m_2} = H(m_1)^{\mathsf{sk}} \cdot H(m_2)^{\mathsf{sk}} = (H(m_1) \cdot H(m_2))^{\mathsf{sk}} = \mathsf{t}_{m_1 \cup m_2}.$$

---

[4] In the authentication channel using proxy re-authentication, we assume that a verifier can know that which user sends a (converted) tag (e.g., a sender includes an identity information in a corresponding message).

**LWR-Based Construction.** The core idea of our LWR-based construction is the same as the above CDH-based construction. Let $H : \{0,1\}^* \to \mathbb{Z}_q^n$ be a hash function modeled as a random oracle and $\lfloor \cdot \rfloor_p$ is a rounding function with modulus conversion. Now, the PRF based on the LWR assumption is expressed as $F_{\mathsf{LWR}}(k, x) := \lfloor \langle H(x), k \rangle \rfloor_p$, where $x \in \{0,1\}^*$ and $k \in \mathbb{Z}_q^n$. Then, we can observe that $F_{\mathsf{LWR}}(k_1 + k_2, x) = \lfloor \langle H(x), k_1 + k_2 \rangle \rfloor_p = \lfloor \langle H(x), k_1 \rangle \rfloor + \lfloor \langle H(x), k_2 \rangle \rfloor = F_{\mathsf{LWR}}(k_1, x) + F_{\mathsf{LWR}}(k_2, x)$, where $x \in \{0,1\}^*$ and $k_1, k_2 \in \mathbb{Z}_q^n$. Based on this construction, we can transform the authentication tag from the sender Alice to the receiver Bob as

$$\mathsf{sk}_{\text{Alice}} \in \mathbb{Z}_q^n, \quad \mathsf{sk}_{\text{Bob}} \in \mathbb{Z}_q^n, \quad \mathsf{rk}_{\text{Alice} \to \text{Bob}} := \mathsf{sk}_{\text{Bob}} - \mathsf{sk}_{\text{Alice}},$$

$$\mathsf{Auth} : \mathsf{t}_{\text{Alice}} = \lfloor \langle H(m), \mathsf{sk}_{\text{Alice}} \rangle \rfloor_p,$$

$$\mathsf{ReAuth} : \mathsf{t}_{\text{Alice}} + \lfloor \langle H(m), \mathsf{rk}_{\text{Alice} \to \text{Bob}} \rangle \rfloor_p = \lfloor \langle H(m), \mathsf{sk}_{\text{Bob}} \rangle \rfloor_p = \mathsf{t}_{\text{Bob}}.$$

Thanks to the rich structure over lattices, this naive construction can get over the above functionality problem. However, this construction has a subtle point in proving its security. More precisely, we cannot simulate the challenger in the security game on reducing to solve the LWR problem. Specifically, to prove the security by reducing to the LWR problem, it seems that we have to change the behavior of the random oracle as the challenger picks $r \leftarrow \mathbb{Z}_q^n$ and computes $H(m) := r \cdot \mathbf{a}$, where $\mathbf{a}$ is a part of a instance of the underlying LWR problem. However, the entropy of randomness is decreased and we fail to prove security by this change. Therefore, we modify the above LWR-based construction so as not to lose the functionalities of re-authentication as follows.

$$\mathsf{Auth} : \mathsf{t}_{\text{Alice}} = \lfloor \langle \mathbf{a} \cdot H(m), \mathsf{sk}_{\text{Alice}} \rangle \rfloor_p,$$

$$\mathsf{ReAuth} : \mathsf{t}_{\text{Alice}} + \lfloor \langle \mathbf{a} \cdot H(m), \mathsf{rk}_{\text{Alice} \to \text{Bob}} \rangle \rfloor_p = \lfloor \langle \mathbf{a} \cdot H(m), \mathsf{sk}_{\text{Bob}} \rangle \rfloor_p = \mathsf{t}_{\text{Bob}}.$$

When aggregating two or more tags, we use the additive homomorphism of inner products $\lfloor \langle x_1, k \rangle \rfloor_p + \lfloor \langle x_2, k \rangle \rfloor_p = \lfloor \langle x_1 + x_2, k \rangle \rfloor_p$ and have

$$\mathsf{Agg} : \mathsf{t}_{m_1} + \mathsf{t}_{m_2} = \lfloor \langle \mathbf{a} \cdot H(m_1), k \rangle \rfloor_p + \lfloor \langle \mathbf{a} \cdot H(m_2), k \rangle \rfloor_p$$
$$= \lfloor \langle \mathbf{a} \cdot (H(m_1) + H(m_2)), k \rangle \rfloor_p = \mathsf{t}_{m_1 \cup m_2}.$$

## 1.3   Related Works

**Proxy Re-signature.** In a proxy re-signature scheme, a (semi-trusted) new entity called *proxy* is introduced and it can transform a someone's signature on a message into an another party's signature on the same message. As the security requirement, we do not allow a proxy can generate (fresh) signatures for any party by itself. The notion of proxy re-signature was first introduced by Blaze et al. [5] and Ateniese and Hohenberger [3] gave the first formal definition for it. After these seminal works, a lot of proxy re-signature schemes have been proposed from various assumptions [8,11,14,17]. From another perspective, more advanced proxy re-signature schemes (such as, identity-based setting [17], attribute-based setting [15], and threshold setting [20] ones) were proposed so far.

**Aggregate Message Authentication Codes.** Aggregate message authentication codes (MAC) enable simple and efficient authentication aggregation for existing MAC schemes first proposed by Katz and Lindell [13]. Aggregate MAC can reduce the size of MAC tags on multiple messages to a short aggregate tag. As the security requirement, we consider an adversary who may adaptively corrupt various senders and learn their secret keys, and require security to hold also in such a setting. After that, a lot of constructions with additional functionalities are considered [10,12,16,19].

**Homomorphic Proxy Re-authenticators.** Homomorphic proxy re-authenticators (HPRA) [9] is a primitive that adds security and verifiability guarantees to multi-user data aggregation scenarios. It allows users to authenticate their data under their own keys and a proxy can transform these MACs and evaluate arithmetic circuits (functions) on the inputs so that the resulting MAC corresponds to the evaluation of the respective function. The difference between HPRA and our PRA is as follows: their HPRA scheme needs bilinear groups since it requires two strong security notions of "input privacy" and "output privacy", whereas ours can be realized on (non-bilinear) cyclic groups. Furthermore, we show that our PRA can be realized in a post-quantum manner under the LWR assumption. Finally, our constructions are more efficient than HPRA since it focuses on only aggregation.

## 2   Preliminaries

In this section, we recall some notations and computational assumptions used in this paper.

**Notation.** $\mathbb{N}$ denotes the set of positive integers. $\emptyset$ denotes the empty set. PPT stands for probabilistic polynomial time. For $n \in \mathbb{N}$, we denote $[n] :=$ $\{1, 2, \ldots, n\}$. $x := y$ denotes that $x$ is defined by $y$. $y \leftarrow \mathcal{A}(x; r)$ denotes that a PPT algorithm $\mathcal{A}$ outputs $y$ on input $x$ and randomness $r$. We simply denote $y \leftarrow \mathcal{A}(x)$ when $\mathcal{A}$ uses uniform randomness. $\mathsf{poly}(\lambda)$ denotes a polynomial in $\lambda$. We write $\mathsf{negl}(\lambda)$ to denote a negligible function in $\lambda$. We say that a function $f(\lambda)$ is negligible in $\lambda$ if $f(\lambda) = o(1/\lambda^c)$ for every $c \in \mathbb{Z}$, and we write $\mathsf{negl}(\lambda)$ to denote a negligible function in $\lambda$. $x \leftarrow_\$ \mathcal{X}$ denotes an element $x$ is sampled uniformly at random from a finite set $\mathcal{X}$. We use $\lfloor \cdot \rfloor$ to denote rounding a real number to the largest integer which does not exceed it. For integers $q$ and $p$ where $q \geq p \geq 2$, we define the function $\lfloor \cdot \rceil_p : \mathbb{Z}_q \to \mathbb{Z}_p$ as $\lfloor x \rceil_p = i$, where $i \cdot \lfloor \frac{q}{p} \rceil$ is the largest multiple of $\lfloor \frac{q}{p} \rceil$ that does not exceed $x$.

### 2.1   Computational Diffie-Hellman Assumption

In this section, we introduce the computational Diffie-Hellman (CDH) assumption.

**Definition 1 (Computational Diffie-Hellman Assumption).** *Let $\mathbb{G}$ be a group of prime order $p$. We say that the CDH assumption holds if for any* PPT *adversary $\mathcal{A}$,*

$$\mathsf{Adv}_{\mathbb{G},\mathcal{A}}^{\mathsf{cdh}}(\lambda) := \Pr\left[D = g^{ab} \;\middle|\; \begin{array}{c} g \leftarrow\!\!\$\; \mathbb{G} \\ a, b \leftarrow\!\!\$\; \mathbb{Z}_p \\ D \leftarrow \mathcal{A}(g, g^a, g^b) \end{array}\right] \le \mathsf{negl}(\lambda).$$

## 2.2 Learning with Rounding Assumption

In this section, we recall the "learning with rounding" (LWR) problem [2,4], which are like "derandomized" versions of the usual LWE problems, in the sense that the error terms are chosen deterministically.

**Definition 2 (Learning with Rounding Assumption).** *Let $n \ge 1$ and $q \ge p \ge 2$ be integers. For a vector $\mathbf{s} \in \mathbb{Z}_q^n$, define the* LWR *distribution $L$ to be the distribution over $\mathbb{Z}_q^n \times \mathbb{Z}_p$ obtained by choosing a vector $\mathbf{a} \leftarrow\!\!\$\; \mathbb{Z}_q^n$ uniformly at random and outputting $(\mathbf{a}, D = \lfloor \langle \mathbf{a}, \mathbf{s} \rangle \rceil_p)$. We say that the* LWR *assumption holds over $L$, if for any* PPT *adversary $\mathcal{A}$,*

$$\mathsf{Adv}_{L,\mathcal{A}}^{\mathsf{lwr}}(\lambda) := \left| \Pr\left[\mathsf{coin} = \widehat{\mathsf{coin}} \;\middle|\; \begin{array}{c} \mathbf{a} \leftarrow\!\!\$\; \mathbb{Z}_q^n \\ \mathbf{s} \leftarrow\!\!\$\; \mathbb{Z}_q^n \\ D_0 = \lfloor \langle \mathbf{a}, \mathbf{s} \rangle \rceil_p \\ D_1 = \mathbb{Z}_p \\ \widehat{\mathsf{coin}} \leftarrow \mathcal{A}(\mathbf{a}, D_{\mathsf{coin}}) \end{array}\right] - \frac{1}{2} \right| \le \mathsf{negl}(\lambda).$$

# 3 Formalization of Proxy Re-authentication

In this section, we present a new cryptographic primitive called *proxy re-authentication* that enables key and communication compression simultaneously. In authentication channels using message authentication codes (one of the major conventional authentication techniques), two parties have the same common secret key. Then, a sender must use the secret key to generate a tag and a receiver must use the same secret key to verify the tag. In the proxy re-authentication scheme, sender and receiver hold different secret keys respectively, and instead of exchanging them directly, the sender first sends a message and an authentication tag to an intermediate entity called proxy. The proxy then transforms the tag from the sender and sends it to the receiver. When the receiver gets the tag, it was already converted to one under the receiver's secret key, and thus the receiver can verify it using his own secret key without having to share a secret key between two parties. The specific method where a proxy transforms the tag is to use a new re-authentication key (created based on the sender's and receiver's secret key), the sender's tag, and the message.[5] In the following, we provide the formal syntax and security definitions of proxy re-authentication.

---

[5] We assume that re-authentication keys are generated by some key generation authority (holding senders' and receivers' secret keys).

## 3.1   Syntax

**Definition 3 (Proxy   Re-Authentication).** *A   proxy   re-authentication scheme* PRA *consists of the following PPT algorithms:*

Setup$(1^\lambda) \to$ pp: *The setup algorithm takes as input a security parameter* $1^\lambda$, *and outputs a public parameter* pp. *Moreover, we assume* pp *is implicitly provided as input to the following algorithms.*

KeyGen(pp) $\to$ sk: *The key generation algorithm takes as input a public parameter* pp, *and outputs a user secret key* sk.

ReKey$(\text{sk}_i, \text{sk}_j) \to \text{rk}_{i \to j}$: *The key transformation algorithm takes as input two secret keys* $\text{sk}_i$ *and* $\text{sk}_j$, *and outputs a re-authentication key* $\text{rk}_{i \to j}$.

Auth(sk, $m$) $\to$ t: *The authentication algorithm takes as input a user secret key* sk *and a message* $m$, *and outputs an authentication tag* t.

ReAuth$(\text{rk}_{i \to j}, M, \text{t}_i) \to \text{t}_j$: *The re-authentication algorithm takes as input a re-authentication key* $\text{rk}_{i \to j}$ *(transforming from the user* $i$'s *tag* $\text{t}_i$ *into the user* $j$'s *tag* $\text{t}_j$), *a set of messages* $M$, *and an authentication tag* $\text{t}_i$, *and outputs an transformed authentication tag* $\text{t}_j$.

Agg(t, t') $\to$ t̂: *The aggregation algorithm takes as input two authentication tags* t, t', *and outputs an aggregated authentication tag* t̂.

Verify(sk, $M$, t) $\to 1$ *or* 0: *The verification algorithm takes as input a user secret key* sk, *a set of messages* $M$, *and an authentication tag* t, *and outputs* 1 *(means "accept") or* 0 *(means "reject").*

*Correctness.* *We say that a proxy re-authentication scheme* PRA *is correct if:*

1. *for all* $\lambda \in \mathbb{N}$, pp $\leftarrow$ Setup$(1^\lambda)$, sk $\leftarrow$ KeyGen(pp), *and* $m \in \mathcal{M}$, *it holds that*

$$\Pr[\text{Verify}(\text{sk}, m, \text{Auth}(\text{sk}, m)) = 1] \geq 1 - \text{negl}(\lambda).$$

2. *for all* $\lambda \in \mathbb{N}$, pp $\leftarrow$ Setup$(1^\lambda)$, $\text{sk}_i \leftarrow$ KeyGen(pp), $\text{sk}_j \leftarrow$ KeyGen(pp), *and* $m \in \mathcal{M}$, *it holds that*

$$\Pr[\text{Verify}(\text{sk}_j, m, \text{ReAuth}(\text{ReKey}(\text{sk}_i, \text{sk}_j), m, \text{Auth}(\text{sk}_i, m))) = 1] \geq 1 - \text{negl}(\lambda).$$

3. *for all* $\lambda \in \mathbb{N}$, pp $\leftarrow$ Setup$(1^\lambda)$, sk $\leftarrow$ KeyGen(pp), $m, m' \in \mathcal{M}$, t, t' $\in \mathcal{T}$, *if* Verify(sk, $m$, t) $= 1 \wedge$ Verify(sk, $m'$, t') $= 1$, *it holds that*

$$\Pr[\text{Verify}(\text{sk}, \{m, m'\}, \text{Agg}(m, m', \text{Auth}(\text{sk}, m), \text{Auth}(\text{sk}, m'))) = 1] \geq 1 - \text{negl}(\lambda).$$

## 3.2   Security Definition

In this section, we give the security definition of a proxy re-authentication scheme. Similar to (standard) signature schemes, it is required that proxy re-authentication schemes satisfy existential unforgeability against chosen-message attacks (EUF-CMA security). Here, proxy re-authentication schemes must be secure not only against adversaries outside the protocol but also against a semi-trusted proxy. In other words, the user's secret key information must not be leaked from the re-authentication key when the proxy performs the tag transformation in the re-authentication algorithm. In the following, we provide the formal definition of EUF-CMA security for proxy re-authentication.

**Definition 4 (EUF-CMA Security).** *We consider the following experiment* $\mathsf{Expt}_{\mathsf{PRA},\mathcal{A}}^{\text{EUF-CMA}}(\lambda)$ *between an adversary $\mathcal{A}$ and the challenger[6]:*

**Initialize:** *The challenger first executes* $\mathsf{pp} \leftarrow \mathsf{Setup}(1^\lambda)$. *Next, it prepares three lists* $\mathcal{L}_{crpt}, \mathcal{L}_{uncrpt}, \mathcal{L}_{auth} := \emptyset$ *and a counter* $N := 0$. *Finally, it sends* $\mathsf{pp}$ *to* $\mathcal{A}$.

**Query Phase:** *When $\mathcal{A}$ makes a query, the challenger answers as below[7]:*

    **Uncorrupted Key Query:** *When $\mathcal{A}$ makes an uncorrupted key query, the challenger runs* $\mathsf{sk} \leftarrow \mathsf{KeyGen}(\mathsf{pp})$ *and returns* $\mathsf{sk}$ *to $\mathcal{A}$. Then, it updates* $\mathcal{L}_{uncrpt} \leftarrow \mathcal{L}_{uncrpt} \cup \{(N, \mathsf{sk})\}$ *and* $N \leftarrow N + 1$.

    **Corrupted Key Query:** *When $\mathcal{A}$ makes a corrupted key query, the challenger runs* $\mathsf{sk} \leftarrow \mathsf{KeyGen}(\mathsf{pp})$ *and returns* $\top$ *to $\mathcal{A}$. Then, it updates* $\mathcal{L}_{crpt} \leftarrow \mathcal{L}_{crpt} \cup \{(N, \mathsf{sk})\}$ *and* $N \leftarrow N + 1$.

    **Key Transformation Query:** *When $\mathcal{A}$ makes a key transformation query on $(i, j)$, if $(i \in \mathcal{L}_{crpt} \wedge j \in \mathcal{L}_{uncrpt}) \vee (i \in \mathcal{L}_{uncrpt} \wedge j \in \mathcal{L}_{crpt})$, the challenger returns $\bot$ to $\mathcal{A}$. Otherwise, the challenger extracts $\mathsf{sk}_i$ and $\mathsf{sk}_j$ from $\mathcal{L}_{crpt}$ or $\mathcal{L}_{uncrpt}$, and computes* $\mathsf{rk}_{i \to j} \leftarrow \mathsf{ReKey}(\mathsf{sk}_i, \mathsf{sk}_j)$. *Finally, it returns* $\mathsf{rk}_{i \to j}$ *to $\mathcal{A}$.*

    **Authentication Query:** *When $\mathcal{A}$ makes an authentication query on $(i, m)$, if $i \notin \mathcal{L}_{uncrpt}$, the challenger returns $\bot$ to $\mathcal{A}$. Then, if $(i, m, \mathsf{t}) \in \mathcal{L}_{auth}$, the challenger returns $\mathsf{t}$ to $\mathcal{A}$. Otherwise, the challenger extracts $\mathsf{sk}_i$ from $\mathcal{L}_{uncrpt}$, executes* $\mathsf{t} \leftarrow \mathsf{Auth}(\mathsf{sk}_i, m)$, *and returns $\mathsf{t}$ to $\mathcal{A}$.*

    **Re-Authentication Query:** *When $\mathcal{A}$ makes a re-authentication query on $(i, j, m, \mathsf{t}_i)$, the challenger checks whether $i, j \notin [N]$ holds. If this is the case, then it returns $\bot$ to $\mathcal{A}$. Otherwise, the challenger extracts $\mathsf{sk}_i$ and $\mathsf{sk}_j$ from $\mathcal{L}_{uncrpt}$ or $\mathcal{L}_{crpt}$ and computes* $\mathsf{rk}_{i \to j} \leftarrow \mathsf{ReKey}(\mathsf{sk}_i, \mathsf{sk}_j)$. *Then, it computes* $\mathsf{t}_j \leftarrow \mathsf{ReAuth}(\mathsf{rk}_{i \to j}, m, \mathsf{t}_i)$ *and returns $\mathsf{t}_j$ to $\mathcal{A}$.*

**Forgery:** *When $\mathcal{A}$ outputs $i^*, m^*, \mathsf{t}^*$ as forgery, the challenger outputs*

$$
\begin{cases}
1 & ((i^*, \cdot) \in \mathcal{L}_{uncrpt} \wedge (i^*, m^*, \mathsf{t}^*) \notin \mathcal{L}_{auth} \wedge \mathsf{Verify}(\mathsf{sk}_{i^*}, m^*, \mathsf{t}^*) = 1) \\
0 & (otherwise)
\end{cases}
$$

*We say that a proxy re-authentication scheme* $\mathsf{PRA}$ *is EUF-CMA secure if for any PPT adversary $\mathcal{A}$, it holds that*

$$
\mathsf{Adv}_{\mathsf{PRA},\mathcal{A}}^{\text{euf-cma}}(\lambda) := \Pr\left[\mathsf{Expt}_{\mathsf{PRA},\mathcal{A}}^{\text{EUF-CMA}}(\lambda) \Rightarrow 1\right] \leq \mathsf{negl}(\lambda)(\lambda).
$$

## 4 Proxy Re-authentication Over Cyclic Group

In this section, we give a construction of proxy re-authentication $\mathsf{PRA}^{\mathsf{CDH}}$ based on the CDH assumption in the random oracle model and its security proof.

---

[6] Since $\mathcal{A}$'s ability does not change even considering the output of Aggregated tags, one must contain a pair of $(m, \mathsf{t})$ that is not queried to authentication oracle, we define excluding aggregated tags are not outputted by $\mathcal{A}$ in forgery.

[7] $\mathcal{A}$ can make the following queries polynomially many times.

## 4.1   Construction

In this section, we provide the description of our CDH-based proxy re-authentication scheme $\mathsf{PRA}^{\mathsf{CDH}}$.

$\mathsf{Setup}(1^\lambda)$: Let $\mathbb{G}$ be a cyclic group with prime order $p$. The setup algorithm picks a hash function $\mathsf{H} : \{0,1\}^* \to \mathbb{G}$ modeled as a random oracle and outputs $\mathsf{pp} = (\mathbb{G}, p, \mathsf{H})$.

$\mathsf{KeyGen}(\mathsf{pp})$: The key generation algorithm picks $\mathsf{sk} \leftarrow^\$ \mathbb{Z}_p$ and outputs $\mathsf{sk}$.

$\mathsf{ReKey}(\mathsf{sk}_i, \mathsf{sk}_j)$: The key transformation algorithm computes $\mathsf{rk}_{i \to j} = \frac{\mathsf{sk}_j}{\mathsf{sk}_i}$ and outputs $\mathsf{rk}_{i \to j}$.

$\mathsf{Auth}(\mathsf{sk}, m)$: The authentication algorithm computes $h_m = \mathsf{H}(m)$ and $\mathsf{t} = h_m^{\mathsf{sk}}$ and outputs $\mathsf{t}$.

$\mathsf{ReAuth}(\mathsf{rk}_{i \to j}, M, \mathsf{t}_i)$: The re-authentication algorithm computes $\mathsf{t}_j = \mathsf{t}_i^{\mathsf{rk}_{i \to j}}$ and outputs $\mathsf{t}_j$.

$\mathsf{Agg}(\mathsf{t}, \mathsf{t}')$: The aggregate algorithm computes $\hat{\mathsf{t}} = \mathsf{t} \cdot \mathsf{t}'$ and outputs $\hat{\mathsf{t}}$.

$\mathsf{Verify}(\mathsf{sk}, M, \mathsf{t})$: The verification algorithm first extracts $M = \{m_0, \ldots, m_l\}$. Next, it computes $h_M = \prod_{i=0}^{l} \mathsf{H}(m_i)$ and $\mathsf{check} = h_M^{\mathsf{sk}}$. It outputs 1 if $\mathsf{t} = \mathsf{check}$, and it outputs 0 otherwise.

**Correctness.** Standard correctness for the verification algorithm trivially holds. Thus, we first show that the re-authentication algorithm is correct. For all $m \in \{0,1\}^*$, $\mathsf{sk}_i \in \mathbb{Z}_p$ and $\mathsf{sk}_j \in \mathbb{Z}_p$, a re-authentication key is computed as $\mathsf{rk}_{i \to j} = \frac{\mathsf{sk}_j}{\mathsf{sk}_i}$. Now, it holds that

$$\mathsf{t}_i^{\mathsf{rk}_{i \to j}} = \mathsf{t}_i^{\frac{\mathsf{sk}_j}{\mathsf{sk}_i}} = \left(\mathsf{H}(m)^{\mathsf{sk}_i}\right)^{\frac{\mathsf{sk}_j}{\mathsf{sk}_i}} = \mathsf{H}(m)^{\mathsf{sk}_j} = \mathsf{t}_j.$$

Next, we show that the aggregation algorithm is correct. For all $m \in \{0,1\}^*$, $m' \in \{0,1\}^*$ and $\mathsf{sk} \in \mathbb{Z}_p$, the authentication tags are computed as $\mathsf{t} = h_m^{\mathsf{sk}}$ and $\mathsf{t}' = h_{m'}^{\mathsf{sk}}$, where $h_m = \mathsf{H}(m)$ and $h_{m'} = \mathsf{H}(m')$. Now, it holds that

$$\hat{\mathsf{t}} = \{\mathsf{H}(m) \cdot \mathsf{H}(m')\}^{\mathsf{sk}} = \mathsf{H}(m)^{\mathsf{sk}} \cdot \mathsf{H}(m')^{\mathsf{sk}} = \mathsf{t} \cdot \mathsf{t}'.$$

## 4.2   Security Proof

In this section, we show that $\mathsf{PRA}^{\mathsf{CDH}}$ is EUF-CMA secure in the random oracle model based on the CDH assumption.

**Theorem 1.** *Suppose the hash function $\mathsf{H}$ is a random oracle. Under the CDH assumption, $\mathsf{PRA}^{\mathsf{CDH}}$ is EUF-CMA secure in the ROM. Formally, if there exists an adversary $\mathcal{A}$ that breaks the EUF-CMA security of $\mathsf{PRA}^{\mathsf{CDH}}$, there exists an adversary $\mathcal{B}$ that breaks the CDH assumption such that*

$$\mathsf{Adv}_{\mathsf{PRA}^{\mathsf{CDH}}, \mathcal{A}}^{\mathsf{euf\text{-}cma}}(\lambda) \leq 2e(1 + Q_{\mathsf{Auth}})\mathsf{Adv}_{\mathbb{G}, \mathcal{B}}^{\mathsf{cdh}}(\lambda),$$

*where $e$ is the napier number and $Q_{\mathsf{Auth}}$ is the maximum number of queries $\mathcal{A}$ makes to the authentication oracle.*

*Proof.* To prove the theorem, we consider the following sequence of games $\mathsf{hyb}_i$ for $i \in \{0, 1, 2\}$. We define the advantage of $\mathcal{A}$ in $\mathsf{hyb}_i$ as $\epsilon_i := \Pr\left[\mathsf{hyb}_i^{\mathcal{A}}(\lambda) \Rightarrow 1\right]$.

$\mathsf{hyb}_0$: This is the original security game. By definition, we have

$$\epsilon_0 = \mathsf{Adv}_{\mathsf{PRA}^{\mathsf{CDH}}, \mathcal{A}}^{\mathsf{euf\text{-}cma}}(\lambda).$$

$\mathsf{hyb}_1$: In this game, we add some abort conditions to each query. Specifically, the challenger answers as below to each query from $\mathcal{A}$:

- When $\mathcal{A}$ makes a random oracle query on $m$, the challenger returns $h_m$ if $(m, h_m, \cdot, \cdot) \in \mathcal{L}_{\mathsf{H}}$. Otherwise, the challenger flips a coin $d \in \{0, 1\}$ which yields 0 with probability $1 - \delta$. Then, the challenger picks $r \leftarrow_\$ \mathbb{Z}_p$ and returns $h_m = g^r$ to $\mathcal{A}$. Moreover, the challenger updates $\mathcal{L}_{\mathsf{H}} \leftarrow \mathcal{L}_{\mathsf{H}} \cup \{(m, h_m, r, d)\}$.
- When $\mathcal{A}$ makes an authentication query on $(i, m)$, the challenger searches an entry $(m, h_m, r, d) \in \mathcal{L}_{\mathsf{H}}$ and extracts $\mathsf{sk}_i$ from $\mathcal{L}_{crpt}$ or $\mathcal{L}_{uncrpt}$. If $d = 0$, the challenger aborts the game and outputs 0. Otherwise, it computes $\mathsf{t} = (g^{\mathsf{sk}_i})^r$ and returns $\mathsf{t}$ to $\mathcal{A}$.
- When $\mathcal{A}$ outputs $(i^*, m^*, \mathsf{t}^*)$ as its forgery, the challenger searches $(m^*, h_{m^*}, r, d)$ from $\mathcal{L}_{\mathsf{H}}$. If $d = 1$, the challenger aborts the game and outputs 0. Otherwise, it works as in $\mathsf{hyb}_0$.

The advantage of $\mathcal{A}$ in $\mathsf{hyb}_1$ is equal to the advantage of $\mathcal{A}$ in $\mathsf{hyb}_0$ conditioning on the game does not abort. Therefore, we have $\epsilon_1 = \epsilon_0 \cdot \Pr[\neg\mathsf{abort}]$. Let us estimate the probability $\Pr[\neg\mathsf{abort}]$. The probability that the game does not abort in authentication queries is $\delta^{Q_{\mathsf{Auth}}}$. Also, the probability that the game does not abort in the forgery phase is $1 - \delta$. Hence, the overall probability that the challenger does not abort in $\mathsf{hyb}_1$ is $\Pr[\neg\mathsf{abort}] = \delta^{Q_{\mathsf{Auth}}} \cdot (1 - \delta)$. This value is maximum when $\hat{\delta} = \frac{Q_{\mathsf{Auth}}}{1 + Q_{\mathsf{Auth}}}$, and thus we have $\Pr[\neg\mathsf{abort}] = \frac{1}{e(1 + Q_{\mathsf{Auth}})}$ for sufficiently large $Q_{\mathsf{Auth}}$. Therefore, we have

$$\epsilon_0 \leq e(1 + Q_{\mathsf{Auth}}) \cdot \epsilon_1.$$

$\mathsf{hyb}_2$: In this game, we modify the behavior in responding to re-authentication queries. Specifically, we change the response to a re-authentication query depending on whether $\mathsf{sk}_i$ and $\mathsf{sk}_j$ (corresponding to inputs $i$ and $j$) are contained in $\mathcal{L}_{uncrpt}$ or $\mathcal{L}_{crpt}$. When $\mathcal{A}$ makes a re-authentication query on $(i, j, m, \mathsf{t}_i)$, the challenger responds as follows:

(1) If $i \in \mathcal{L}_{crpt} \wedge j \in \mathcal{L}_{crpt}$, the challenger extracts $\mathsf{sk}_i$ and $\mathsf{sk}_j$ from $\mathcal{L}_{crpt}$. Then, the challenger computes $\mathsf{t}_j = \mathsf{t}_i^{\frac{\mathsf{sk}_j}{\mathsf{sk}_i}}$ and returns $\mathsf{t}_j$ to $\mathcal{A}$.
(2) If $i \in \mathcal{L}_{crpt} \wedge j \in \mathcal{L}_{uncrpt}$, the challenger extracts $\mathsf{sk}_i$ from $\mathcal{L}_{crpt}$ and checks whether $\mathsf{Verify}(\mathsf{sk}_i, m, \mathsf{t}_i) = 1$ holds. If not, the challenger returns $\mathsf{t}_j \leftarrow_\$ \mathbb{G}$ to $\mathcal{A}$. Otherwise, (that is, if $\mathsf{t}_i$ is valid,) the challenger makes an authentication query on $(j, m)$, receives $\mathsf{t}_j$, and returns $\mathsf{t}_j$ to $\mathcal{A}$.

(3) If $(i, m, t'_i) \in \mathcal{L}_{auth}$, the challenger checks whether $t'_i = t_i$ holds. If not, the challenger returns $t_j \leftarrow_\$ \mathbb{G}$. Otherwise, the challenger makes an authentication query on $(j, m)$ and retrieves $t_j$. Then, the challenger returns $t_j$ to $\mathcal{A}$.

(4) If $j \in \mathcal{L}_{uncrpt}$, the challenger returns $t_j \leftarrow_\$ \mathbb{G}$ to $\mathcal{A}$.

In (1), (2) and (3), we can easily see that the challenger returns a correct authentication tag $t_j$ if the input $t_i$ is correctly generated. Thus, we need to show that $\mathcal{A}$ cannot distinguish the change in the case (4). To show this, in the following, we show that one can construct a PPT algorithm $\mathcal{B}_1$ that solves the CDH problem using $\mathcal{A}$. Upon receiving $(\mathbb{G}, g, g^\alpha, g^\beta)$, $\mathcal{B}_1$ initializes $N := 0$ and $\mathcal{L}_H, \mathcal{L}_{uncrpt}, \mathcal{L}_{crpt}, \mathcal{L}_{auth} := \emptyset$ and sends a public parameter $pp = (\mathbb{G}, p)$. When $\mathcal{A}$ makes a random oracle query on $m$, $\mathcal{B}_1$ picks $r \leftarrow_\$ \mathbb{Z}_p$. With probability $1 - \delta$, $\mathcal{B}_1$ computes $h_m = (g^\beta)^r$ and updates $\mathcal{L}_H \leftarrow \mathcal{L}_H \cup \{(m, h_m, r, 0)\}$. Otherwise, $\mathcal{B}_1$ computes $h_m = g^r$ and updates $\mathcal{L}_H \leftarrow \mathcal{L}_H \cup \{(m, h_m, r, 1)\}$. When $\mathcal{A}$ makes an uncorrupted key query, $\mathcal{B}_1$ picks $a \leftarrow \mathbb{Z}_p$, implicitly sets $sk_N = \alpha \cdot a$, and updates $\mathcal{L}_{uncrpt} \leftarrow \mathcal{L}_{uncrpt} \cup \{(N, a)\}$ and $N = N + 1$. When $\mathcal{A}$ makes an authentication query on $(i, m)$, $\mathcal{B}_1$ searches $(m, h_m, r, d) \in \mathcal{L}_H$. If $d = 0$, $\mathcal{B}_1$ aborts the game. Otherwise, $\mathcal{B}_1$ computes $t = (g^\alpha)^{ar}$ and returns $t$ to $\mathcal{A}$. When $\mathcal{A}$ makes a re-authentication query on $(i, j, m, t_i)$, if the query is matched to the case (4), $\mathcal{B}_1$ searches $(m, h_m, r, d) \in \mathcal{L}_H$ and extracts $a$ from $(i, a) \in \mathcal{L}_{uncrpt}$. If $d = 1$, $\mathcal{B}_1$ checks $(g^\alpha)^r \cdot g^{ar} = t_i$ or not. If so, $\mathcal{B}_1$ runs the authentication query by itself. Otherwise, (that is, if $(g^\alpha)^r \cdot g^{ar} \neq t_i$,) $\mathcal{B}_1$ returns $t_j \leftarrow_\$ \mathbb{G}$ to $\mathcal{A}$. If $d = 0$, $\mathcal{B}_1$ computes $D = t_i^{-ar} = (h_m^{a\alpha})^{-ar} = ((g^{r\beta})^{a\alpha})^{-ar} = g^{\alpha\beta}$ and outputs $D$ as its solution of the CDH problem. Therefore, we have

$$|\epsilon_2 - \epsilon_1| \leq \mathsf{Adv}^{cdh}_{\mathbb{G}, \mathcal{B}_1}(\lambda).$$

Finally, to show $\epsilon_2 = \mathsf{Adv}^{cdh}_{\mathbb{G}, \mathcal{B}_2}(\lambda)$, we construct a PPT algorithm $\mathcal{B}_2$ that solves the CDH problem using $\mathcal{A}$. The responses of $\mathcal{B}_2$ to $\mathcal{A}$'s queries are the same as in the above reduction $\mathcal{B}_1$. When $\mathcal{A}$ outputs a forgery $(i^*, m^*, t^*)$, $\mathcal{B}_2$ searches $(m, h_m, r, d) \in \mathcal{L}_H$ and extracts $a$ from $(i, a) \in \mathcal{L}_{uncrpt}$. If $d = 0$, $\mathcal{B}_2$ computes $D = (t^*)^{-ar} = (h_m^{a\alpha})^{-ar} = ((g^{r\beta})^{a\alpha})^{-ar} = g^{\alpha\beta}$ and outputs $D$ as its solution of the CDH problem. Therefore, we have

$$\epsilon_2 = \mathsf{Adv}^{cdh}_{\mathbb{G}, \mathcal{B}_2}(\lambda).$$

Putting everything together, we obtain

$$\mathsf{Adv}^{euf\text{-}cma}_{\mathsf{PRA}^{CDH}, \mathcal{A}}(\lambda) \leq 2e(1 + Q_{\mathsf{Auth}}) \cdot \mathsf{Adv}^{cdh}_{\mathbb{G}, \mathcal{B}}(\lambda).$$

Since the CDH assumption holds over $\mathbb{G}$ and $Q_{\mathsf{Auth}}$ is some polynomial in $\lambda$, $\mathsf{Adv}^{euf\text{-}cma}_{\mathsf{PRA}^{CDH}, \mathcal{A}}(\lambda) \leq \mathsf{negl}(\lambda)$ holds, that is, $\mathsf{PRA}^{CDH}$ satisfies EUF-CMA security. $\square$

## 5   Proxy Re-authentication Over Lattice

In this section, we provide a proxy re-authentication scheme $\mathsf{PRA}^{\mathsf{LWR}}$ based on the LWR assumption in the random oracle model and its security proof.

## 5.1   Construction

In this section, we provide the description of our LWR-based proxy re-authentication scheme $\mathsf{PRA}^{\mathsf{LWR}}$. The core idea is the same as one of our CDH-based scheme.

$\mathsf{Setup}(1^\lambda)$: Let $n \geq 1$ and $q \geq p \geq 2$ be integers. The setup algorithm picks a hash function $\mathsf{H} : \{0,1\}^* \to \mathbb{Z}_q$ modeled as a random oracle and a vector $\mathbf{a} \leftarrow\!\!\!\$\ \mathbb{Z}_q^n$. Then, it outputs a public parameter $\mathsf{pp} = (\mathsf{H}, \mathbf{a}, n, p, q)$.

$\mathsf{KeyGen}(\mathsf{pp})$: The key generation algorithm picks $\mathsf{sk} \leftarrow\!\!\!\$\ \mathbb{Z}_q^n$ and outputs $\mathsf{sk}$.

$\mathsf{ReKey}(\mathsf{sk}_i, \mathsf{sk}_j)$: The key transformation algorithm computes $\mathsf{rk}_{i \to j} = \mathsf{sk}_j - \mathsf{sk}_i$ and outputs $\mathsf{rk}$.

$\mathsf{Auth}(\mathsf{sk}, m)$: The authentication algorithm first computes $h_m = \mathsf{H}(m)$ and $\mathsf{t} = \lfloor \langle \mathbf{a} \cdot h_m, \mathsf{sk} \rangle \rceil_p \in \mathbb{Z}_p$. Then, it outputs $\mathsf{t}$.

$\mathsf{ReAuth}(\mathsf{rk}_{i \to j}, M, \mathsf{t}_i)$: The re-authentication algorithm first extracts $M = \{m_0, \ldots, m_l\}$. Then, it computes $h_M = \sum_{i=0}^l \mathsf{H}(m_i)$ and $\mathsf{t}_j = \mathsf{t}_i + \lfloor \langle \mathbf{a} \cdot h_M, \mathsf{rk}_{i \to j} \rangle \rceil_p$ and outputs $\mathsf{t}_j$.

$\mathsf{Agg}(\mathsf{t}, \mathsf{t}')$: The aggregation algorithm computes $\hat{\mathsf{t}} = \mathsf{t} + \mathsf{t}'$ and outputs $\hat{\mathsf{t}}$.

$\mathsf{Verify}(\mathsf{sk}, M, \mathsf{t})$: The verification algorithm first extracts $M = \{m_0, \ldots, m_l\}$. Then, it computes $h_M = \sum_{i=0}^l \mathsf{H}(m_i)$ and $\mathsf{check} = \lfloor \langle \mathbf{a} \cdot h_M, \mathsf{sk} \rangle \rceil_p$. It outputs 1 if $\mathsf{t} = \mathsf{check}$, and it outputs 0 otherwise.

**Correctness.** Standard correctness for the verification algorithm trivially holds. Thus, we first show that the re-authentication algorithm is correct. For all $m \in \{0,1\}^*$, $\mathsf{sk}_i \in \mathbb{Z}_q^n$ and $\mathsf{sk}_j \in \mathbb{Z}_q^n$, a re-authentication key is computed as $\mathsf{rk}_{i \to j} = \mathsf{sk}_j - \mathsf{sk}_i$. Now, it holds that

$$
\begin{aligned}
\mathsf{t}_j &= \mathsf{t}_i + \lfloor \langle \mathbf{h}_m, \mathsf{rk}_{i \to j} \rangle \rceil_p = \lfloor \langle \mathbf{a} \cdot h_m, \mathsf{sk}_i \rangle \rceil_p + \lfloor \langle \mathbf{a} \cdot h_m, \mathsf{rk}_{i \to j} \rangle \rceil_p \\
&= \lfloor \langle \mathbf{a} \cdot h_m, \mathsf{sk}_i \rangle \rceil_p + \lfloor \langle \mathbf{a} \cdot h_m, \mathsf{sk}_j - \mathsf{sk}_i \rangle \rceil_p \\
&= \lfloor \langle \mathbf{a} \cdot h_m, \mathsf{sk}_i \rangle \rceil_p + \lfloor \langle \mathbf{a} \cdot h_m, \mathsf{sk}_j \rangle \rceil_p - \lfloor \langle \mathbf{a} \cdot h_m, \mathsf{sk}_i \rangle \rceil_p \\
&= \lfloor \langle \mathbf{a} \cdot h_m, \mathsf{sk}_j \rangle \rceil_p.
\end{aligned}
$$

Next, we show that the aggregation algorithm is correct. For all $m \in \{0,1\}^*$, $m' \in \{0,1\}^*$ and $\mathsf{sk} \in \mathbb{Z}_q^n$, the authentication tags are computed as $\mathsf{t} = \lfloor \langle \mathbf{h}_m, \mathsf{sk} \rangle \rceil_p$ and $\mathsf{t}' = \lfloor \langle \mathbf{h}_{m'}, \mathsf{sk} \rangle \rceil_p$, where $h_m = \mathsf{H}(m)$ and $h_{m'} = \mathsf{H}(m')$. Now, it holds that

$$
\hat{\mathsf{t}} = \lfloor \langle \mathbf{a} \cdot (h_m + h_{m'}), \mathsf{sk} \rangle \rceil_p = \lfloor \langle \mathbf{a} \cdot h_m, \mathsf{sk} \rangle \rceil_p + \lfloor \langle \mathbf{a} \cdot h_{m'}, \mathsf{sk} \rangle \rceil_p = \mathsf{t} + \mathsf{t}'.
$$

## 5.2   Security Proof

In this section, we show that $\mathsf{PRA}^{\mathsf{LWR}}$ is EUF-CMA secure in the random oracle model based on the LWR assumption.

**Theorem 2.** *Suppose the hash function $\mathsf{H}$ is a random oracle. Under the LWR assumption, $\mathsf{PRA}^{\mathsf{LWR}}$ is EUF-CMA secure in the ROM. Formally, if there exists an adversary $\mathcal{A}$ that breaks the EUF-CMA security of $\mathsf{PRA}^{\mathsf{LWR}}$, there exists an adversary $\mathcal{B}$ that breaks the LWR assumption such that*

$$
\mathsf{Adv}_{\mathsf{PRA}^{\mathsf{LWR}}, \mathcal{A}}^{\mathsf{euf\text{-}cma}}(\lambda) \leq 2 \cdot \mathsf{Adv}_{L, \mathcal{B}}^{\mathsf{lwr}}(\lambda).
$$

*Proof.* To prove the theorem, we consider the following sequence of games $\mathsf{hyb}_i$ for $i \in \{0, \ldots, 4\}$. We define the advantage of $\mathcal{A}$ in $\mathsf{hyb}_i$ as $\epsilon_i := \Pr\left[\mathsf{hyb}_i^{\mathcal{A}}(\lambda) \Rightarrow 1\right]$.

$\mathsf{hyb}_0$: This is the original security game. By definition, we have

$$\epsilon_0 = \mathsf{Adv}_{\mathsf{PRA}^{\mathsf{LWR}}, \mathcal{A}}^{\mathsf{euf\text{-}cma}}(\lambda).$$

$\mathsf{hyb}_1$: In this game, the challenger picks a secret information $\mathbf{s}^* \leftarrow_{\$} \mathbb{Z}_q^n$ at the beginning of the game. This change cannot be distinguished from the $\mathcal{A}$'s perspective. Therefore, we have

$$\epsilon_1 = \epsilon_0.$$

$\mathsf{hyb}_2$: In this game, we change the behavior in responding to uncorrupted key queries. Specifically, the challenger picks $\mathbf{s}' \leftarrow_{\$} \mathbb{Z}_q^n$ and implicitly sets $\mathsf{sk}_N = \mathbf{s}' + \mathbf{s}^*$. Then, it updates $\mathcal{L}_{uncrpt} \leftarrow \mathcal{L}_{uncrpt} \cup \{(N, \mathbf{s}')\}$. This change cannot be distinguished from the $\mathcal{A}$'s perspective. Therefore, we have

$$\epsilon_2 = \epsilon_1.$$

$\mathsf{hyb}_3$: In this game, we change the behavior in responding to authentication queries. Specifically, when $\mathcal{A}$ makes an authentication query on $(i, m)$, if $(m, h_m) \notin \mathcal{L}_{\mathsf{H}}$, the challenger picks $r \leftarrow_{\$} \mathbb{Z}_p$ and updates $\mathcal{L}_{\mathsf{H}} \leftarrow \mathcal{L}_{\mathsf{H}} \cup \{(m, h_m := r)\}$. Otherwise, the challenger extracts $r := h_m$ from $\mathcal{L}_{\mathsf{H}}$. Then, the challenger extracts $\mathbf{s}'$ from $\mathcal{L}_{uncrpt}$ and computes $\mathbf{t}_i = \lfloor r \cdot \langle \mathbf{a}, \mathbf{s}^* \rangle \rceil_p + \lfloor r \cdot \mathbf{a}, \mathbf{s}' \rangle \rceil_p$. Now, the authentication tag for the index $i$ should be $\mathbf{t}_i = \lfloor \langle r \cdot \mathbf{a}, \mathbf{s}^* + \mathbf{s}' \rangle \rceil_p = \lfloor r \cdot \langle \mathbf{a}, \mathbf{s}^* \rangle \rceil_p + \lfloor r \cdot \mathbf{a}, \mathbf{s}' \rangle \rceil_p$. Thus, since $\mathsf{hyb}_2$ and $\mathsf{hyb}_3$ is identical from the $\mathcal{A}$'s perspective, we have

$$\epsilon_3 = \epsilon_2.$$

$\mathsf{hyb}_4$: In this game, we change the behavior in responding to re-authentication queries. Specifically, when $\mathcal{A}$ makes a re-authentication query on $(i, j, m, \mathbf{t}_i)$, the challenger responds as follows:

(1) If $i \in \mathcal{L}_{crpt} \wedge j \in \mathcal{L}_{crpt}$, the challenger extracts $\mathsf{sk}_i$ and $\mathsf{sk}_j$ from $\mathcal{L}_{crpt}$. Then, it computes $\mathsf{rk}_{i \to j} = \mathsf{sk}_j - \mathsf{sk}_i$ and $\mathbf{t}_j = \mathbf{t}_i + \lfloor \langle \mathsf{H}(m) \cdot \mathbf{a}, \mathsf{rk}_{i \to j} \rangle \rceil_p$ and returns $\mathbf{t}_j$ to $\mathcal{A}$.

(2) If $i \in \mathcal{L}_{crpt} \wedge j \in \mathcal{L}_{uncrpt}$, the challenger extracts $\mathsf{sk}_i$ from $\mathcal{L}_{crpt}$ and checks whether $\mathsf{Verify}(\mathsf{sk}_i, m, \mathbf{t}_i) = 1$ holds. If so, the challenger executes an authentication query on $(j, m)$, receives $\mathbf{t}_j$, and returns $\mathbf{t}_j$ to $\mathcal{A}$. Otherwise, the challenger picks $\mathbf{t}_j \leftarrow_{\$} \mathbb{Z}_p$ and returns $\mathbf{t}_j$ to $\mathcal{A}$.

(3) If $(i, m, \mathbf{t}_i) \in \mathcal{L}_{auth}$, the challenger executes an authentication query on $(j, m)$, receives $\mathbf{t}_j$, and returns $\mathbf{t}_j$ to $\mathcal{A}$.

(4) Otherwise, (that is, if $i \in \mathcal{L}_{uncrpt}$,) the challenger picks $\mathbf{t}_j \leftarrow_{\$} \mathbb{Z}_p$ and returns $\mathbf{t}_j$ to $\mathcal{A}$.

In (1), (2) and (3), we can easily see that the challenger returns a correct authentication tag $t_j$ if the input tag $t_i$ is correctly generated. Thus, we need to show that $\mathcal{A}$ cannot distinguish the change in the case (4). To show this, in the following, we show that one construct a PPT algorithm $\mathcal{B}_1$ that solves the LWR problem using $\mathcal{A}$. Upon receiving $(\mathbf{a}, D = \lfloor \langle \mathbf{a}, \mathbf{s} \rangle \rceil_p)$, $\mathcal{B}_1$ initializes $N := 0$, $\mathcal{L}_\mathsf{H}, \mathcal{L}_{uncrpt}, \mathcal{L}_{crpt}, \mathcal{L}_{auth} := \emptyset$. and implicitly sets $\mathbf{s}^* := \mathbf{s}$. Then, $\mathcal{B}_1$ sends $\mathsf{pp} = (\mathbf{a}, n, p, q)$ and answers to each query from $\mathcal{A}$ as follows: When $\mathcal{A}$ makes a random oracle query on $m$, $\mathcal{B}_1$ picks $r \leftarrow_\$ \mathbb{Z}_q$, computes $h_m = r$, and returns $h_m$ to $\mathcal{A}$. When $\mathcal{A}$ makes an authentication query on $(i, m)$, if $(m, h_m) \notin \mathcal{L}_\mathsf{H}$, $\mathcal{B}_1$ picks $r \leftarrow_\$ \mathbb{Z}_p$ and updates $\mathcal{L}_\mathsf{H} \leftarrow \mathcal{L}_\mathsf{H} \cup \{(m, h_m := r)\}$. Otherwise, $\mathcal{B}_1$ extracts $r := \mathsf{H}(m)$ from $\mathcal{L}_\mathsf{H}$. Then, $\mathcal{B}_1$ extracts $\mathbf{s}'$ from $\mathcal{L}_{uncrpt}$, computes $\mathbf{t} = \lfloor r \cdot \langle \mathbf{a}, \mathbf{s}^* \rangle \rceil_p + \lfloor \langle r \cdot \mathbf{a}, \mathbf{s}' \rangle \rceil_p$, and returns $\mathbf{t}$ to $\mathcal{A}$. When $\mathcal{A}$ makes a re-authentication query on $(i, j, m, t_i)$, if the query is matched to the case (4), $\mathcal{B}_1$ extracts $(m, h_m = r)$ from $\mathcal{L}_\mathsf{H}$ and $\mathbf{s}'$ from $\mathcal{L}_{uncrpt}$ respectively, and if $t_i/r - \lfloor \langle \mathbf{a}, \mathbf{s}' \rangle \rceil_p = D$, $\mathcal{B}_1$ aborts the game and outputs $\widehat{\mathsf{coin}} = 0$ as its guess for the LWR problem. Otherwise, it outputs $\widehat{\mathsf{coin}} \leftarrow_\$ \{0, 1\}$. Therefore, we have

$$|\epsilon_4 - \epsilon_3| \leq \mathsf{Adv}^{\mathsf{lwr}}_{L, \mathcal{B}_1}(\lambda).$$

Finally, we bound $\epsilon_4$ by a similar argument as above. To this end, we construct a PPT algorithm $\mathcal{B}_2$ that solves the LWR problem using $\mathcal{A}$. Upon receiving $(\mathbf{a}, D = \lfloor \langle \mathbf{a}, \mathbf{s} \rangle \rceil_p)$, $\mathcal{B}_2$ initializes $N := 0$, $\mathcal{L}_\mathsf{H}, \mathcal{L}_{uncrpt}, \mathcal{L}_{crpt}, \mathcal{L}_{auth} := \emptyset$ and implicitly sets $\mathbf{s}^* := \mathbf{s}$. Then, $\mathcal{B}_2$ sends $\mathsf{pp} = (\mathbf{a}, n, p, q)$ to $\mathcal{A}$ and answers to each query from $\mathcal{A}$ as the above reduction $\mathcal{B}_1$. When $\mathcal{A}$ outputs $(i, m, \mathbf{t})$ as its forgery, $\mathcal{B}_1$ extracts $(m, h_m = r)$ from $\mathcal{L}_\mathsf{H}$ and $\mathbf{s}'$ from $\mathcal{L}_{uncrpt}$ respectively, and if $t_i/r - \lfloor \langle \mathbf{a}, \mathbf{s}' \rangle \rceil_p = D$, $\mathcal{B}_2$ outputs $\widehat{\mathsf{coin}} = 0$ as its guess of the LWR problem. Therefore, we have

$$\epsilon_5 = \mathsf{Adv}^{\mathsf{lwr}}_{L, \mathcal{B}_2}(\lambda).$$

Putting everything together, we have

$$\mathsf{Adv}^{\mathsf{euf\text{-}cma}}_{\mathsf{PRA}^{\mathsf{LWR}}, \mathcal{A}}(\lambda) \leq 2 \cdot \mathsf{Adv}^{\mathsf{lwr}}_{L, \mathcal{B}}(\lambda).$$

Since the LWR assumption holds over $L$ now, $\mathsf{Adv}^{\mathsf{euf\text{-}cma}}_{\mathsf{PRA}^{\mathsf{LWR}}, \mathcal{A}}(\lambda) \leq \mathsf{negl}(\lambda)$ holds, that is, $\mathsf{PRA}^{\mathsf{LWR}}$ satisfies EUF-CMA security.                                        $\square$

## 6   Experimental Result

In this section, we show that our proposed schemes are highly efficient to be applied in the real world. To show this, we implement a proof of concept of our schemes in Python 3.7.13. Specifically, to implement our CDH-based scheme, we use Charm 0.50 [1] (which is a framework for prototyping mathematical groups-based cryptosystems) and the Weierstrass curve [18] over a 256-bit prime field[8]

---

[8] This is the elliptic curve domain parameters recommended by National Institute of Standards and Technology (NIST).

**Table 1.** Evaluation of Time Performances ($\mu$s)

| Operation | PRA$^{\text{CDH}}$ (Sect. 4) | PRA$^{\text{LWR}}$ (Sect. 5) |
|---|---|---|
| Key Generation | 1.704 | 483.3 |
| Key Transformation | 62.49 | 484.8 |
| Authentication | 62.73 | 487.4 |
| Re-Authentication | 65.65 | 483.7 |
| Aggregation (2 Messages) | 1.308 | 0.2871 |
| Verification (Aggregated Tags) | 87.17 | 663.9 |

**Table 2.** Evaluation of Space Performances (bytes)

| Element | PRA$^{\text{CDH}}$ (Sect. 4) | PRA$^{\text{LWR}}$ (§ 5) |
|---|---|---|
| Secret Key | 56 | 24280 |
| Re-Authentication Key | 56 | 23960 |
| Tag | 56 | 32 |
| Aggregated Tag | 56 | 32 |

as a cyclic group which gives 128-bit security [6]. Moreover, regarding our LWR-based scheme, we implement with parameter ($\log q = 10, \log p = 8, n = 608$) which set for 128-bit security [7]. The experimental platform is performed on a personal computer running 64-bit Ubuntu 22.04 LTS with AMD Ryzen 5-3600 CPU@3.50GH and 8 GB of RAM.

Table 1 presents a comparison of the costs in microseconds, associated with the main cryptographic operations among our schemes. We executed these experiments in 50 different runs of 10 times each, and the average timing was taken for each operation. We use the Python module `timeit` for these measurements. The CDH-based scheme (resp., LWR-based scheme) is very efficient from a computation time perspective, requiring a total of 151.208 microseconds (resp., 1.15159 ms) for main cryptographic operations, such as authentication, aggregation of two messages, and verification (which are the processes performed by the user).

Table 2 compares the space costs in bytes, associated with the main variables among our schemes. We use the Python module `pympler` for these measurements. The size of the information that a user needs to handle in the CDH-based scheme is 112 bytes (indicating that it is very efficient regarding the space cost). On the other hand, the size of the information that a user needs to handle in the LWR-based scheme is 2.4 KB (indicating that it is not as good as the CDH-based scheme, but efficient enough).

## 7  Conclusion

In this paper, we proposed a new cryptographic authentication scheme called *proxy re-authentication*, aiming at enabling key and communication compression over authenticated channels, which are difficult to achieve in conventional authentication schemes. In proxy re-authentication, the key compression is achieved by introducing a mechanism to convert a sender's tag to a receiver's one through a proxy. Moreover, the communication compression is achieved by aggregating multiple tags based on the idea of aggregate MAC. We propose two proxy re-authentication schemes based on the CDH assumption over cyclic groups and the LWR assumption over lattices. Furthermore, to show the practical efficiency of our proxy re-authentication schemes, we implement and evaluate our schemes in Python.

Our work leaves an important open question. It would be interesting to construct a proxy re-authentication scheme based on a wide variety of existing (standard) MACs.

**Acknowledgements.** This research was in part conducted under a contract of "Research and development on new generation cryptography for secure wireless communication services" among "Research and Development for Expansion of Radio Wave Resources (JPJ000254)," which was supported by the Ministry of Internal Affairs and Communications, Japan. This work also was in part supported by JSPS KAKENHI Grant Numbers JP22K19773, JP24K20776, JST-CREST JPMJCR22M1, and JST-AIP JPMJCR22U5.

# References

1. Akinyele, J.A., et al.: Charm: a framework for rapidly prototyping cryptosystems. J. Cryptogr. Eng. **3**(2), 111–128 (2013). https://doi.org/10.1007/s13389-013-0057-3

2. Alwen, J., Krenn, S., Pietrzak, K., Wichs, D.: Learning with rounding, revisited. In: Canetti, R., Garay, J.A. (eds.) CRYPTO 2013. LNCS, vol. 8042, pp. 57–74. Springer, Heidelberg (2013). https://doi.org/10.1007/978-3-642-40041-4_4

3. Ateniese, G., Hohenberger, S.: Proxy re-signatures: new definitions, algorithms, and applications. In: Atluri, V., Meadows, C., Juels, A. (eds.) ACM CCS 2005: 12th Conference on Computer and Communications Security, pp. 310–319, Alexandria, Virginia, USA, 7–11 November 2005. ACM Press (2005). https://doi.org/10.1145/1102120.1102161

4. Banerjee, A., Peikert, C., Rosen, A.: Pseudorandom functions and lattices. In: Pointcheval, D., Johansson, T. (eds.) EUROCRYPT 2012. LNCS, vol. 7237, pp. 719–737. Springer, Heidelberg (2012). https://doi.org/10.1007/978-3-642-29011-4_42

5. Blaze, M., Bleumer, G., Strauss, M.: Divertible protocols and atomic proxy cryptography. In: Nyberg, K. (ed.) EUROCRYPT 1998. LNCS, vol. 1403, pp. 127–144. Springer, Heidelberg (1998). https://doi.org/10.1007/BFb0054122

6. Chen, L., Moody, D., Randall, K., Regenscheid, A., Robinson, A.: Recommendations for discrete logarithm-based cryptography: elliptic curve domain parameters (2023). https://doi.org/10.6028/NIST.SP.800-186. https://tsapps.nist.gov/publication/get_pdf.cfm?pub_id=935198

7. Cheon, J.H., Kim, D., Lee, J., Song, Y.: Lizard: cut off the tail! A practical post-quantum public-key encryption from LWE and LWR. In: Catalano, D., De Prisco, R. (eds.) SCN 2018. LNCS, vol. 11035, pp. 160–177. Springer, Cham (2018). https://doi.org/10.1007/978-3-319-98113-0_9

8. Chow, S.S.M., Phan, R.C.-W.: Proxy re-signatures in the standard model. In: Wu, T.-C., Lei, C.-L., Rijmen, V., Lee, D.-T. (eds.) ISC 2008. LNCS, vol. 5222, pp. 260–276. Springer, Heidelberg (2008). https://doi.org/10.1007/978-3-540-85886-7_18

9. Derler, D., Ramacher, S., Slamanig, D.: Homomorphic proxy re-authenticators and applications to verifiable multi-user data aggregation. In: Kiayias, A. (ed.) FC 2017. LNCS, vol. 10322, pp. 124–142. Springer, Cham (2017). https://doi.org/10.1007/978-3-319-70972-7_7

10. Eikemeier, O., et al.: History-free aggregate message authentication codes. In: Garay, J.A., De Prisco, R. (eds.) SCN 2010. LNCS, vol. 6280, pp. 309–328. Springer, Heidelberg (2010). https://doi.org/10.1007/978-3-642-15317-4_20

11. Fan, X., Liu, F.-H.: Proxy re-encryption and re-signatures from lattices. In: Deng, R.H., Gauthier-Umaña, V., Ochoa, M., Yung, M. (eds.) ACNS 2019. LNCS, vol. 11464, pp. 363–382. Springer, Cham (2019). https://doi.org/10.1007/978-3-030-21568-2_18

12. Hirose, S., Kuwakado, H.: Forward-secure sequential aggregate message authentication revisited. In: Chow, S.S.M., Liu, J.K., Hui, L.C.K., Yiu, S.M. (eds.) ProvSec 2014. LNCS, vol. 8782, pp. 87–102. Springer, Cham (2014). https://doi.org/10.1007/978-3-319-12475-9_7

13. Katz, J., Lindell, A.Y.: Aggregate message authentication codes. In: Malkin, T. (ed.) CT-RSA 2008. LNCS, vol. 4964, pp. 155–169. Springer, Heidelberg (2008). https://doi.org/10.1007/978-3-540-79263-5_10

14. Libert, B., Vergnaud, D.: Multi-use unidirectional proxy re-signatures. In: Ning, P., Syverson, P.F., Jha, S. (eds.) ACM CCS 2008: 15th Conference on Computer and Communications Security, pp. 511–520, Alexandria, Virginia, USA, 27–31 October 2008. ACM Press (2008). https://doi.org/10.1145/1455770.1455835

15. Luo, F., Al-Kuwari, S., Susilo, W., Duong, D.H.: Attribute-based proxy re-signature from standard lattices and its applications. Comput. Stand. Interfaces 75, 103499 (2021). https://doi.org/10.1016/j.csi.2020.103499. https://www.sciencedirect.com/science/article/pii/S092054892030386X

16. Sato, S., Shikata, J.: Interactive aggregate message authentication scheme with detecting functionality. In: Barolli, L., Takizawa, M., Xhafa, F., Enokido, T. (eds.) AINA 2019. AISC, vol. 926, pp. 1316–1328. Springer, Cham (2020). https://doi.org/10.1007/978-3-030-15032-7_110

17. Shao, J., Cao, Z., Wang, L., Liang, X.: Proxy re-signature schemes without random oracles. In: Srinathan, K., Rangan, C.P., Yung, M. (eds.) INDOCRYPT 2007. LNCS, vol. 4859, pp. 197–209. Springer, Heidelberg (2007). https://doi.org/10.1007/978-3-540-77026-8_15

18. Standards for Efficient Cryptography Group: SEC 2: Recommended Elliptic Curve Domain Parameters. Standards for Efficient Cryptography Group (SECG), January 2010. https://www.secg.org/sec2-v2.pdf

19. Wagner, E., Serror, M., Wehrle, K., Henze, M.: When and how to aggregate message authentication codes on lossy channels? In: Pöpper, C., Batina, L. (eds.) ACNS 2024. LNCS, vol. 14584, pp. 241–264. Springer, Cham (2024). https://doi.org/10.1007/978-3-031-54773-7_10

20. Yang, P., Cao, Z., Dong, X.: Threshold proxy re-signature. J. Syst. Sci. Complexity 24(4), 816–824 (2011)

# Enhancing Network Security Through Vulnerability Monitoring

Ryan Williams$^{(\boxtimes)}$, Anthony Gavazzi, and Engin Kirda

Northeastern University, Boston, MA, USA
{williams.ry,gavazzi.a,e.kirda}@northeastern.edu

**Abstract.** In modern cyberattacks, adversaries no longer focus solely on individual computer systems but instead establish an initial foothold within a company's network, advancing through compromised assets in a process known as lateral movement. Detecting lateral movement is challenging due to diverse infection vectors, making network traffic monitoring prone to false positives and negatives. Security patches, while crucial, can create a false sense of security. To address these issues, we introduce PATCHCANARY, a framework for augmenting source patches for CVE-identified vulnerabilities, allowing precise monitoring of modified functions. We propose the idea of "patch and monitor" as a new approach to vulnerability patching, enhancing lateral movement attack detection. Evaluation on 108 CVEs across 75 real-world programs demonstrates PATCHCANARY's capability to automatically augment source patches for 95.9% of CVE-triggering paths while incurring a minimal 712 ms compile-time overhead, on average.

**Keywords:** Intrusion Detection · Network Security · Program Repair

## 1 Introduction

Today, in a typical attack campaign, bad actors often have a concrete security-sensitive objective in mind, such as accessing a top developer's machine to steal a popular project's source code, accessing all of an important executive's files, or reading a database that stores customer credit card data [16]. While such data breaches often start with a single compromised system in an organization, the initial compromised asset is usually not the attackers' ultimate destination. Rather, after breaking into a web server, email account, employee device, or any other low-value starting location, the attackers will move "laterally" from the initial cyber "bridgehead" (i.e., foothold) that they have established to reach their intended target, or to opportunistically locate a target that is of value.

*Lateral movement* is when attackers acquire access to an asset within a network and are then able to spread their reach from that asset to others within the same environment. Today, the initial compromise itself in an organization seldom causes significant damage [49]. As a result, if an organization's security team can detect the lateral movement before the attackers are able to reach

H. H. Song et al. (Eds.): NSS 2024, LNCS 15564, pp. 21–38, 2025.
https://doi.org/10.1007/978-981-96-3531-3_2

a more security-sensitive target, the data breach can potentially be mitigated. Unfortunately, advanced attacks succeed because current security controls lack the ability to detect the malicious activity as it moves laterally across a network.

A typical organization's network has a security perimeter (e.g., a firewall or a security monitor) that separates and defines what is "inside" and what is "outside" the organization with respect to its security policies. Assets that are outside the security perimeter are called the "top half," and assets that are inside are called the "lower half." Hence, in order to compromise an asset within the organization, an attacker must first move vertically. That is, the initial attack needs to occur from the outside, and an asset that is inside needs to be compromised. This direction of the attack is often called North-South traffic. Once the attacker has established a bridgehead, however, they can now move laterally (or horizontally) within the network to reach their objective. This direction of the attack is often called East-West traffic.

In the attacks that are observed today, there are two main techniques that a threat actor uses to move laterally [37]. The first approach consists of the attacker stealing credentials belonging to unsuspecting users, and then using them to move laterally within the organization. In the second approach, the attacker deploys internal scanning to discover the network topology around the initial established bridgehead. Typically, the attacker scans for open ports that are listening for incoming traffic, and attempts to identify network services that suffer from (often known) vulnerabilities. Once a vulnerable network service has been discovered (e.g., a vulnerable internal print spool service), the attacker can exploit this weakness to move laterally within the organization and compromise another asset.

Because of the substantial consequences posed by data breaches, to date, there has been much research in the area of intrusion detection and prevention. These techniques focus on learning the characteristics of attacks and identifying similar attacks in the future [11,33,39,45,52], or learning what legitimate activity looks like and flagging anything that does not match what was learned as malicious [12,13,34]. In contrast, in this paper, we introduce a novel, deception-based approach that aims to detect vulnerability-based lateral movement attempts whenever an attacker attempts to compromise a vulnerability on a host that has already been patched.

When new CVEs (Common Vulnerabilities and Exposures) are disclosed, network managers and system administrators typically apply an available patch and then stop worrying about the initial flaw so that they can focus on other tasks at hand [30]. However, even if a vulnerability is patched and cannot be compromised anymore during a lateral movement attempt, the attacker may still remain undetected on the network, can wait, and can try other vectors of compromise including other vulnerabilities that exist in the organization. Thus, although patching a vulnerability is important for preventing a potential attack, it does not contribute at all to the detection of any attempts to compromise the vulnerability.

To bridge this gap and allow vulnerability patching to become a powerful contributor to the detection of lateral movement attacks, we propose the novel idea of "patch and monitor" as an alternative to the traditional mindset of "patch and move on." That is, besides patching the vulnerability, we propose an automated approach that also inserts code to monitor the section of vulnerable code that was disclosed by a given CVE, and that allows the network manager or system administrator to *detect* when an attacker is attempting to compromise this patched vulnerability as an early warning system for lateral movement within the organization.

This work makes the following contributions:

- We develop PATCHCANARY, a novel system to semi-automatically generate and insert monitors to augment source patches;
- We propose the novel idea of "patch and monitor" as an alternative to the traditional "patch and move on" paradigm;
- We systematically evaluate PATCHCANARY on 75 real-world programs and 108 known CVEs. In our evaluation, we find that PATCHCANARY is able to successfully report potential indicators of compromise on patched vulnerabilities while incurring minimal overhead.

## 2   Background

While most existing security tools focus on detecting attacks coming from outside of a *security perimeter*, or monitor a specific type of artifact such as network traffic [32,45,52], in contrast, we aim to provide a finer granularity of control over monitoring systems and the vulnerability-based attack that is being launched. By providing a novel approach of monitoring individual functions in a program, we can tell how an attack is being attempted while being agnostic in terms of the source of compromise. For example, although monitoring an Apache web server for any anomalous traffic may provide insights on external actors attempting to gain access to the system, monitoring specific functions in Apache that were found to be vulnerable previously, and that were patched, provides a powerful method to detect indicators of a larger compromise [16]. In our approach, because we monitor individual functions, the overhead incurred is low enough (see Sect. 5) to consider all inputs as untrusted, regardless of source.

In practice, when patches are released, the most information provided along with it is a changelog that states what the patch fixes. Once the patch is applied, the effect–if any–is opaque to the user [54]. By inserting monitors, however, we are also provided with some insight as to the efficacy of the patch that was provided. If the patch came from an untrusted source, or if the network manager is simply interested in knowing if the patch is actually blocking any attempted exploitation, the monitors will provide that level of information.

While other detection systems may rely on classifying anomalous behaviors [7,47] that are all prone to false positives, PATCHCANARY is able to monitor functions and their parameters concretely. Hence, we can insert monitors into a system to look specifically for executions that pass input that is known to trigger a vulnerability from a CVE. This also means that the incurred overhead of running systems with monitors that were inserted will be negligible compared to running machine learning-based solutions, or an intrusion detection system (as we show in Sect. 5). Because PATCHCANARY is implemented as a compiler pass in Clang, the overhead is confined to this monitor injection step.

## 2.1  Threat Model

We consider two threat models that both include an attacker who intends to compromise a high-value asset on a network. Note that this could be an attack from outside the security perimeter, or from within the network. PATCHCANARY operates agnostic to the source of the attack, as we intend to insert monitors that are not only looking for potential breaches, but also internal lateral movement.

In the first threat model, an attacker armed with a standardized exploit, scans the Internet for vulnerable devices. The attacker may use a vulnerability search engine such as Shodan [3], or randomly scan the IP address space. The attacker commandeers any device that replies to their probes and is vulnerable to the exploit, which can then be used as a foothold. In the second threat model, we consider an attacker who already has access to a node on the local network. In this instance, the attack would be more difficult to detect with traditional methods because there are no typical indicators of compromise. Instead, the signal the attacker generates may resemble normal traffic if it is passing between two trusted nodes on a network, as opposed to coming from a source outside the security perimeter.

In both threat models, the attacker most likely does not need to directly compromise every device; compromised devices may in turn become vectors of infection, as it is common in Internet worms and IoT botnets. The source of the attack is less important in our use case as we are more interested in first detecting a signal that may indicate not only compromise, but lateral movement. With both of our threat models, we consider any input to functions with monitors to be *untrusted*. This allows for detection of malicious input even from an otherwise trusted source.

## 2.2  Objectives and Goals

PATCHCANARY's goal is to provide a foundation to augment publicly-available patches with simple monitoring functionality. It explicitly aims to provide feedback on the efficacy of potentially untrusted patches, and provide early indicators of compromise regardless of the source. The purpose is to move from the current traditional mindset of "patch and move on" to our proposed "patch and monitor". We do not claim that PATCHCANARY captures data flows to every possible vulnerability, nor that it cannot be bypassed in individual cases by a skilled, motivated attacker. Its defined goal is to provide a mechanism for determining the efficacy of applied patches, and tracking inputs to monitor for early signs of compromise and lateral movement.

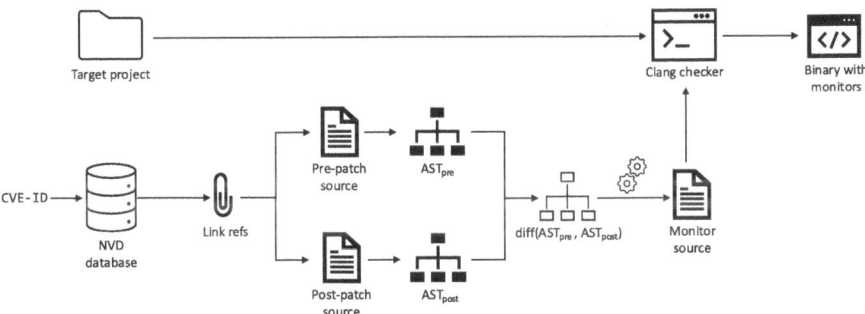

**Fig. 1.** High-level overview of PATCHCANARY's workflow where the two inputs are a target application and a CVE-ID corresponding to a vulnerability the analyst is interested in generating a monitor for.

# 3   System Workflow and Design

## 3.1   System Overview

In this section, we present an overview of PATCHCANARY. Figure 1 shows an overview of PATCHCANARY's workflow. At a high-level, PATCHCANARY is implemented as a Clang plugin to be used as a standard pass at compilation time, and as a LibTooling-based [4] standalone tool that can be used to perform analyses without full compilation. We chose to implement PATCHCANARY at this level due to the flexibility that the Clang API provides for performing source-level transformations using the underlying abstract syntax tree (AST).

Functionally, PATCHCANARY first looks up CVE disclosures for the target program, $\mathcal{P}$, and finds those that have a source patch file linked. Next, we create a set, $\mathcal{F}$, of functions that are modified in the patch file. This is necessary for knowing where to insert the monitors later. The next step is *trigger inference*, which aims to determine what input(s) will trigger the vulnerability disclosed in the CVE. This information is then used to generate a monitor that checks for the given critical input(s), and reports when there was an attempted exploit. The monitors are then inserted into the functions that were patched, and compilation continues to produce an augmented, patched program, $\mathcal{P}'$.

## 3.2   Patch Lookup

The first step in PATCHCANARY's workflow is to find a patch for a CVE that is of interest for monitoring. Given a target CVE, PATCHCANARY looks up details assigned to it using cve-search [1], which allows for efficient, local queries for known CVEs. PATCHCANARY then parses the CVE data in the output of cve-search for CVEs that have patches linked through version control systems (e.g., GitHub), pulls the patches via their commit hash, and saves them locally. For our evaluation, we filtered for CVEs that had a higher risk associated with

**Table 1.** Parameters for Gathering Target Vulnerabilities

| Parameter | Description |
|---|---|
| cvss | >= 7.0 |
| exploitabilityScore | >= 8.0 |
| impactScore | >= 6.0 |
| vulnerable_product | $\neg$(cpe:2.3:o $\wedge$ cpe:2.3:h) |
| access.vector | NETWORK |
| access.complexity | LOW |
| access.authentication | NONE |
| references | Includes URLs |

exploitation (e.g., buffer overflows, remote code execution, etc.). This is found using the exploitability metrics provided by NIST vulnerability scoring system (CVSS). We also only look at patches for codebases that are C/C++-based as our tool is built on Clang. This resulted in targeting a total of **108** CVEs across **75** applications. The details of the query parameters used in cve-search are shown in Table 1. After obtaining the patch associated with the target program, PATCHCANARY parses the patch file to find which functions are modified in the patch, and saves them in a set, $\mathcal{F}$, which is used in the subsequent steps.

### 3.3  Patch Semantic Parsing

This step involves parsing the pre-patch and post-patch source files, generating their Abstract Syntax Trees (ASTs), and computing the differences between these ASTs to find the constraints introduced by the patch. The process begins by parsing both the pre-patch and post-patch versions of the source code to generate their respective ASTs. The ASTs provide a structural representation of the source code, highlighting the syntactic elements and their hierarchical relationships. By comparing the pre-patch and post-patch ASTs, we can compute the differences (diffs) that pertain to the exact changes introduced by the patch. Once the AST diffs are computed, we analyze these differences to extract the relevant constraints. These constraints typically correspond to new conditions, type modifications, or other logical changes added by the patch. By encoding these constraints symbolically using a tool such as Z3, we can formalize the logical conditions that the patch introduces. Next, the extracted constraints are used to generate the necessary monitoring conditions that will be inserted into the patched functions.

---

**Algorithm 1.** Patch Monitor Generation

---

**Input:** Source of pre-patch and post-patch source files
**Output:** Binary with inserted monitors
 1: **Input:** $AST_{pre}$, $AST_{post}$                                      ▷ Abstract Syntax Trees
 2: `diffs` ← computeDiffs($AST_{pre}$, $AST_{post}$)
 3: **for** each `diff` in `diffs` **do**
 4:     **if** `diff.type` == ConditionAddition **then**
 5:         $condition$ ← extractCondition(`diff`)
 6:         **if** $condition$ == semanticInvariant($AST_{pre}$, $AST_{post}$) **then**
 7:             $monitor$ ← generateDirectMonitor($condition$)
 8:         **else**
 9:             $inverse$ ← generateInverseCondition($condition$)
10:             $monitor$ ← generateMonitor($inverse$)
11:     **else if** `diff.type` == TypeModification **then**
12:         $typeChange$ ← extractTypeChange(`diff`)
13:         $monitor$ ← generateTypeMonitor($typeChange$)
14:     **else if** `diff.type` == Modification **then**
15:         $modification$ ← extractModification(`diff`)
16:         $monitor$ ← generateModificationMonitor($modification$)
17:     **else**
18:         `diff` ← `"<unknown>"`
19:     insertMonitor($monitor$, `diff.location`)
20: compileBinaryWithMonitors()

---

## 3.4  Monitor Generation

The monitor generation phase involves creating runtime monitors that can detect potential exploit attempts of the patched vulnerabilities. Our approach leverages symbolic execution to derive the necessary conditions from the patched code. The encoding of the vulnerability condition as constraints is then passed to the Z3 theorem prover to find a set of input values that satisfy these constraints.

**Symbolic Encoding.** For each identified change, we encode the corresponding patched code segment as symbolic constraints using a symbolic execution engine. These constraints represent the logical conditions introduced by the patch.

**Condition Generation.** Based on the symbolic constraints, we generate the conditions that need to be monitored at runtime. If a condition addition is detected, we generate both the direct condition and its inverse. For type modifications and other changes, appropriate monitoring conditions are derived.

When the theorem prover returns `satisfiable`, we can then return the constraints and concrete value(s) that were used. This ensures that the runtime monitors are precise and can effectively detect attempts to exploit the vulnerabilities addressed by the patches. The steps of monitor generation are outlined in Algorithm 1.

```
1 int test(int a, int b)
2 {
3   return a + b;
4 }
```

```
1 int test(int a, int b)
2 {
3   if (a < b)
4   {
5     return a + b;
6   }
7 }
```

**Fig. 2.** Example of a simple patch that will be detected via the semantic parsing and used as conditions in the monitor.

To illustrate this process, consider the example in Fig. 2. In this example, the patch introduces a new condition: if (a < b). The condition (a < b) is encoded as a symbolic constraint using Z3. The constraint represents the logical condition added by the patch. Both the direct condition and its inverse are generated from the symbolic constraint. $DirectCondition : (< a\ b)$, $InverseCondition : (\geq a\ b)$. The generated inverse monitor is now able to detect an attempted exploit of the patched vulnerability, and is ready for insertion into the patched function.

### 3.5   Monitor Insertion

Finally, given a program $\mathcal{P}$, the set of target functions, $\mathcal{F}$, and the monitors, $\mathcal{M}$, PATCHCANARY is able to insert monitors inside the functions modified in the patch during compilation time, outputting an augmented, patched program, $\mathcal{P}'$. When inserting the augmented source patch for $\mathcal{P}$ that takes input $y$, we require that $\mathcal{P}'$ satisfies the following property: $\forall y, \mathcal{P}(y) = \mathcal{P}'(y)$. That is, the monitors we insert do not alter the control flow of the program. Instead, they passively monitor, and report alerts to the administrator.

Once we have generated the necessary monitors, $\mathcal{M}$, PATCHCANARY parses the AST of the program using our Clang checker. PATCHCANARY's compiler passes statically traverse the AST and find the target functions, $f \in \mathcal{P}$, along with their respective monitor(s), $\mathcal{M}_f$, that we wish to insert. Once it has the location of those function definitions, PATCHCANARY uses the program's AST to find an appropriate insertion point within the function, $\mathcal{P}_f$, for the monitor code generated in the previous step.

## 4   Implementation

Our PATCHCANARY prototype is built as a set of Clang compiler passes, along with a standalone, LibTooling-based tool for a simpler user interface. The monitor generation component utilizes Z3 [38] for finding the conditions that trigger a vulnerability. Our patch lookup component is based on *cve-search* [1], which allows us to perform more complex queries on CVEs from the NVD database locally. Building PATCHCANARY on Clang and LibTooling [4] provides us access to a powerful set of APIs for analyzing and modifying source files in the C language family. Using this framework allows us to create PATCHCANARY without the need for re-implementing various functionalities like all our operations on a program's AST.

## 5   Evaluation

To evaluate the prototype of PATCHCANARY, we conducted: ($i$) an evaluation on the completeness of monitor generation (Sect. 5.2); ($ii$) tests to show the correctness and usability of the augmented patches generated including a real-world use case deployed on a production system (Sect. 5.3); ($iii$) performance measurements to show the practicality of using PATCHCANARY (Sect. 5.4), and ($iv$) case studies detailing monitor generation for specific CVEs (Sect. 5.5).

### 5.1   Experimental Setup

For our evaluation, we aimed to select a diverse and representative set of vulnerabilities. We focused on the C language family due to its widespread use and the high prevalence of vulnerabilities in C-based applications. Our dataset was automatically collected from the National Vulnerability Database (NVD) [5], where we filtered out vulnerabilities that require specific devices to trigger as well as those whose behaviors cannot be directly observed. We further concentrated our dataset based on Common Weakness Enumerations (CWEs). The focus was on CWEs with well-known triggers, ensuring a meaningful and consistent evaluation of PATCHCANARY's effectiveness. From this, we selected 108 real-world vulnerabilities to test the efficacy of PATCHCANARY. The vulnerabilities are from 75 applications which include media encoding libraries, messaging systems, PHP, and the Linux kernel.

All experiments below were performed on an Ubuntu 20.04 workstation with a quad-core Intel i7 @ 3.00 GHz and 16 GB of RAM.

### 5.2   Monitor Generation Completeness

To evaluate the effectiveness of our monitor generation process, we analyzed the completeness of the monitors generated for the 108 example CVEs. We focused on two key metrics:

- **Successful Monitors**: Monitors that were fully generated and able to detect potential exploit attempts;
- **Unknown Monitors**: Monitors that were partially generated or incomplete where a condition and/or variable to monitor could not be inferred.

We collected data on the number of successful and unknown monitors for each instrumented file. Across the 108 vulnerable projects targeted, PATCHCANARY generated a total of 782 monitors. This is because we consider a monitor to be

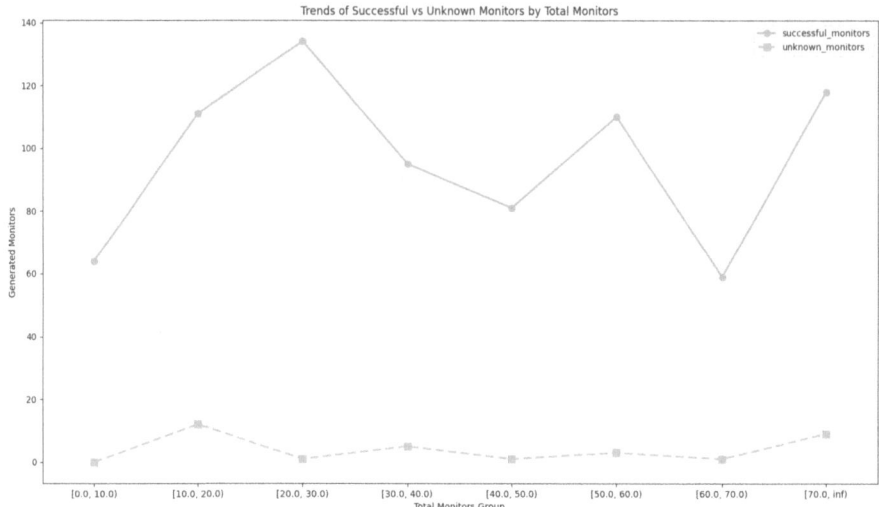

**Fig. 3.** Trends of successful versus unknown monitors grouped by the number of monitors needed for a given patch. E.g., for a CVE that required 100+ monitors for a patch, we have 9 cases where we are unsuccessful in generating the given monitor.

each inserted code block that detects a given pattern. In the case of a simple patch, we may see only one monitor; whereas a more complex one may have hundreds. Of the 782 total monitors, 750 of them were complete and the remaining 32 were unable to be inferred. That is, PATCHCANARY was able to generate source-level monitors for 95.9% of the target CVEs. The overall distribution of successful and unknown monitors as well as their relation to patch complexity is shown in Fig. 3.

### 5.3   Augmented Patch Correctness

For all of the CVEs that we evaluated against, we require an evaluation on the efficacy of the augmented patches. The program that is now patched with monitoring functionality, $\mathcal{P}'$, must meet the following two properties: ($i$) any triggers that the original patch would defend against must remain unmodified; and ($ii$) when an input is passed that would otherwise trigger the vulnerability, the monitor must report the blocked attempt.

To test these properties, we compiled all of our codebases with the augmented patches, $\mathcal{P}'$. Next, we manually verified that the unpatched codebase, $\mathcal{P}$, was indeed exploitable with the triggering inputs. We then took the known inputs that trigger the given CVEs for each target, and manually attempted to trigger the vulnerability in $\mathcal{P}'$. We consider an augmented patch correct only when these tests are passed. In all of the test cases where a monitor was generated, the vulnerability described in the CVE was no longer exploitable, and on each of the attempts, a report was logged from the monitors. Thus, our evaluation found that all generated patches are correct.

To illustrate real-world efficacy, we compiled a patched version of OpenSSH where we monitored the functions modified for the CVE-2021-28041 patch. We ran ssh-agent on a developer workstation for two weeks without any reported errors or issues from the users. Over the course of this two week-long experiment, we ran ssh-agent with various keys and agent forwarding, to attempt to exercise as many code paths as a typical user might, and show that PATCHCANARY does not inadvertently introduce any new bugs. While we do not claim that this test is complete in that it covers all execution paths in the binary, it does provide evidence of the usability of PATCHCANARY on production software.

### 5.4   Performance Evaluation

**Macro-performance Tests.** For our 108 evaluation targets, we measured the compile-time overhead of using PATCHCANARY. Because PATCHCANARY is built on Clang to provide source-level transformations, the incurred overhead is confined to the compilation stages. The monitors that we insert are currently simple checks (value, range, type, etc.) and do not impact the runtime of the target program. Runtime would see a performance degradation, however, if we were to insert complex monitors throughout the target program. In the case of PATCH-CANARY, though, we are only inserting monitors which perform passive reporting, and do not alter the control flow of the system. On average, the time for monitor generation and insertion across all of our tests was 712 milliseconds. The distribution of the compile-time overhead measurements are shown in Fig. 4.

**Runtime Performance Tests.** For this test, we took each of our codebases and manually triggered each of the CVEs we evaluated. This was done both with the regular patched program, $\mathcal{P}$, and that with augmented patches, $\mathcal{P}'$. We measured the time it took for each respective codebase to handle the vulnerability-triggering input, with the goal of determining the overhead incurred by PATCH-CANARY's monitoring functionality being invoked. On average, PATCHCANARY imposed an additional 0.75 μs of runtime. It is worth noting, however, that this overhead incurred is primarily due to PATCHCANARY's monitors writing out alerts to log files, which is extra I/O operations. In the case of non-malicious input being passed, there is no extra overhead incurred as PATCHCANARY's monitors are never triggered.

### 5.5   Case Studies

We have shown at a high-level how PATCHCANARY automates the process of monitor generation (see Sect. 3). Next, we provide two case studies for selected CVEs to illustrate in more detail how PATCHCANARY works. Here, we cover an example from an instance where PATCHCANARY is able to fully generate a monitor, and one where some component of the monitor could not be inferred, thus the monitor could not be generated.

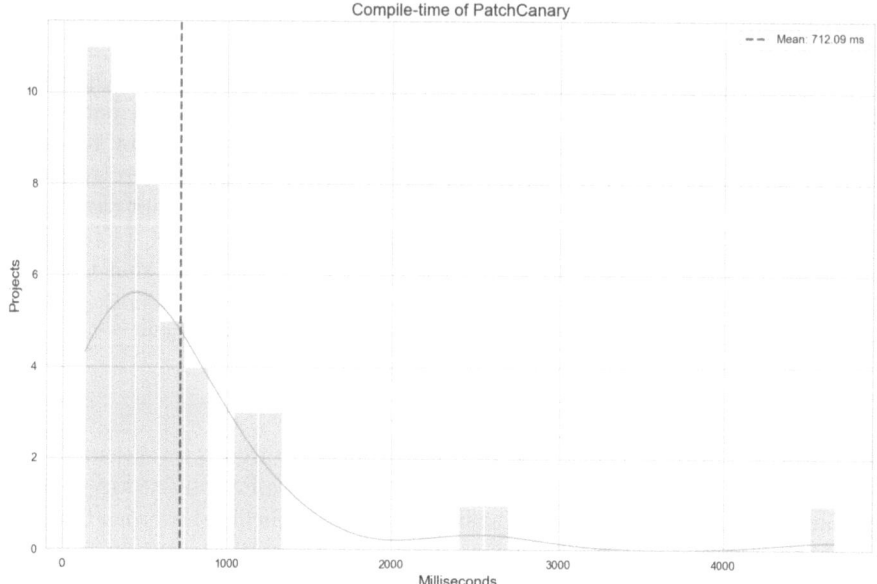

**Fig. 4.** Time for PATCHCANARY to generate and insert monitors.

**FFmpeg (CVE-2020-12284).** For this instance of generating a monitor for CVE-2020-12284, PATCHCANARY was able to fully automate the process. That is, PATCHCANARY was able to determine the target variable and its value to monitor for, as well as the constraint on the value that would trigger the vulnerability. The necessary constraints for triggering the vulnerability were inferred from the diff of the ASTs before and after applying the patch. When parsing the respective ASTs, PATCHCANARY found that the function `cbs_jpeg_split_fragment` had a modification (addition type) that checked the length of a variable. This missing length check from the original code is what caused the heap-based buffer overflow vulnerability outlined in the CVE. PATCHCANARY was able to automatically generate a monitor that would check the length of the variable, and log an alert if the length was greater than the constraint.

**Linux Kernel (CVE-2017-13715).** When running PATCHCANARY on CVE-2017-13715, the monitor generation was semi-automated. That is, PATCHCANARY was only able to determine where the modifications happened in the codebase, but was unable to infer the necessary constraints for the monitor. The `__skb_flow_dissect` function was properly identified as the target function to monitor, but the modifications to the function were unable to be handled by PATCHCANARY. The modifications consisted of replacing the statement `return true` with `goto out_bad`, which is a pattern we were unable to generate the appropriate constraints for automatically.

# 6    Limitations and Future Work

While our approach to monitor generation for patched code introduces significant improvements in detecting potential exploit attempts, there are several limitations that need to be addressed. First, the reliance on symbolic execution and constraint solvers, such as Z3, can introduce performance overhead, especially for large and complex codebases. This overhead can affect both the compilation time and the runtime performance of the instrumented binaries. Second, our current method assumes that the differences between pre-patch and post-patch versions can be effectively captured and encoded as symbolic constraints. However, certain subtle changes or complex logical conditions may not be fully represented, potentially leading to incomplete monitoring coverage.

We envision PATCHCANARY to be most useful in a community-driven way, much like how YARA signatures work, where signatures are crowdsourced and shared among users [6]. The key insight here is that independent analysts can contribute patches with monitors to our open source project that can then be used by other users in their organizations.

Techniques from the domain of automated program repair can also be used in conjunction with PATCHCANARY. While orthogonally related, a useful future work may be to use PATCHCANARY to augment patches that are automatically-generated or synthesized to not only provide monitoring, but to show that the patch is actively mitigating a threat. To the best of our knowledge, there is currently no standard way of measuring the efficacy of security patches. Using PATCHCANARY, it would be possible to measure every exploit attempt for a specific vulnerability, giving system administrators a measurable indicator that the patches they applied are actively working in their described way.

# 7    Related Work

In this section, we briefly survey previous related research. We start by looking at previous research in detecting network attacks and lateral movement in particular, and then continue by surveying research on program patching.

## 7.1    Attack Detection Research

**Intrusion Detection.** Intrusion detection techniques generally fall into two main categories: *misuse*-based and *anomaly*-based techniques. Misuse-based techniques [11,33,39,45,52] focus on learning what known attacks look like, and identifying attacks with the same characteristics in the future. Misuse-based techniques range from building signatures of known attacks [45,52] to leveraging machine learning to identify similar attacks [33]. Anomaly detection techniques [12,13,34] focus on learning what the normal activity on a network looks like and flag anomalies as potential attacks. More recently, research in intrusion detection has started focusing on specific types of attacks, developing more specialized systems, for example to detect web-based attacks [31], botnet infections [22,23], or malicious file downloads [40,43,44]. Compared to previous work in this domain, PATCHCANARY is different because it monitors inputs targeting patched vulnerabilities.

**Alert Correlation.** Intrusion detection systems are designed to provide information about a single attack, but modern attacks usually unfold across a number of steps [46]. The field of *alert correlation* [15,51] focuses on analyzing the alerts intrusion detection systems, and provide higher-level information on attempted intrusions. A number of approaches have been proposed to provide effective alert correlation [15,27,29,50,51].

**Lateral Movement Research.** Despite the importance of lateral movement attacks, the research in this space is very limited. Ho et al. [25] study lateral phishing, a type of lateral movement in which attackers progressively compromise machines in a corporate setting by sending spearphishing emails from an initial compromised account to further the breach. Fawaz et al. [19] propose a system that builds a graph from the network connection between hosts in a network to detect lateral movement attacks; and, *Latte* [35] focuses on a graph-based representation to model a network for detecting lateral movement attacks. In this paper, we take an alternative approach to this existing research [42,48], and propose the first monitor-based system that can detect an attacker within an organization who is trying to exploit known vulnerabilities as part of a typical lateral movement attempt.

### 7.2   Program Patching

The challenging task of program patching and modification has been extensively studied [24,26,28,56,59]. For example, BinSurgeon [20], and AutoFix-E [55] allow users to write patches using templates or source code annotations. Duan, et al. [17] proposed OSSPATCHER, which patches vulnerable open source mobile applications with source patches. The work on *honey-patches* [8] presented a way to reformulate security patches in a way that misleads or frustrates potential attackers. Furthermore, techniques in the area of program repair [21,36,41,57] seek to minimize user effort to efficiently fix bugs in software. Other tools work assume that patches are available publicly, or from the analyst [2,9,14]. Binary-rewriting [10,18,53,58] and hot-patching at runtime [9,14] are also viable patching techniques; however, we focus on precisely targeting individual functions that can be monitored to catch early indicators of compromise. These techniques are solely concerned with applying a fix to a program, while PATCHCANARY's focus is on monitoring the functions those patches modified.

## 8   Conclusion

In this paper, we propose the idea that monitoring even attempted exploits against patched vulnerabilities provides invaluable information for revealing the presence of an attacker in an organization, and we introduce PATCHCANARY, a framework for augmenting source patches to monitor for early indicators of compromise. By specifically targeting known-vulnerable functions from CVE disclosures, PATCHCANARY is able to precisely inject monitors that watch for specific data flows to the functions that were modified in the patch. To allow vulnerability patching to become a powerful contributor to the detection of lateral movement attacks, we propose the novel idea of "patch and monitor" as an alternative to the traditional mindset of "patch and move on." Evaluation on 75 real-world programs shows that PATCHCANARY is able to automatically augment source patches for 95.9% of the target vulnerable paths to monitor for potentially malicious input while incurring minimal overhead.

# References

1. cve-search - a tool to perform local searches for known vulnerabilities, November 2021. https://github.com/cve-search/cve-search
2. kpatch, October 2021. https://github.com/dynup/kpatch
3. Shodan, January 2021. https://www.shodan.io/
4. Libtooling is a library to support writing standalone tools based on clang (2022). https://clang.llvm.org/docs/LibTooling.html
5. The mission of the CVE program is to identify, define, and catalog publicly disclosed cybersecurity vulnerabilities, October 2022. http://cve.mitre.org
6. Yara - the pattern matching swiss knife for malware researchers, June 2022. http://virustotal.github.io/yara/
7. Ahmed, M., Mahmood, A.N., Hu, J.: A survey of network anomaly detection techniques. J. Netw. Comput. Appl. **60**, 19–31 (2016)
8. Araujo, F., Hamlen, K.W., Biedermann, S., Katzenbeisser, S.: From patches to honey-patches: lightweight attacker misdirection, deception, and disinformation. In: Proceedings of the 2014 ACM SIGSAC Conference on Computer and Communications Security, pp. 942–953 (2014)
9. Arnold, J., Kaashoek, M.F.: Ksplice: automatic rebootless kernel updates. In: Proceedings of the 4th ACM European conference on Computer Systems, pp. 187–198 (2009)
10. Arras, P.A., et al.: SaBRe: load-time selective binary rewriting. Int. J. Softw. Tools Technol. Transfer **24**, 1–19 (2022)
11. Barbara, D., Wu, N., Jajodia, S.: Detecting novel network intrusions using Bayes estimators. In: Proceedings of the 2001 SIAM International Conference on Data Mining, pp. 1–17. SIAM (2001)
12. Bhuyan, M.H., Bhattacharyya, D.K., Kalita, J.K.: Network anomaly detection: methods, systems and tools. IEEE Commun. Surv. Tutor. **16**(1), 303–336 (2013)
13. Chandola, V., Banerjee, A., Kumar, V.: Anomaly detection: a survey. ACM Comput. Surv. (CSUR) **41**(3), 1–58 (2009)
14. Chen, Y., Zhang, Y., Wang, Z., Xia, L., Bao, C., Wei, T.: Adaptive android kernel live patching. In: 26th {USENIX} Security Symposium ({USENIX} Security 2017), pp. 1253–1270 (2017)
15. Cuppens, F., Miege, A.: Alert correlation in a cooperative intrusion detection framework. In: IEEE Symposium on Security and Privacy (2002)

16. DeGonia, T.: Cyber kill chain model and framework explained, March 2020. https://cybersecurity.att.com/blogs/security-essentials/the-internal-cyber-kill-chain-model

17. Duan, R., et al.: Automating patching of vulnerable open-source software versions in application binaries. In: NDSS (2019)

18. Duck, G.J., Gao, X., Roychoudhury, A.: Binary rewriting without control flow recovery. In: Proceedings of the 41st ACM SIGPLAN Conference on Programming Language Design and Implementation, pp. 151–163 (2020)

19. Fawaz, A., Bohara, A., Cheh, C., Sanders, W.H.: Lateral movement detection using distributed data fusion. In: 2016 IEEE 35th Symposium on Reliable Distributed Systems (SRDS), pp. 21–30. IEEE (2016)

20. Friedman, S.E., Musliner, D.J.: Automatically repairing stripped executables with CFG microsurgery. In: 2015 IEEE International Conference on Self-Adaptive and Self-Organizing Systems Workshops, pp. 102–107. IEEE (2015)

21. Goues, C.L., Pradel, M., Roychoudhury, A.: Automated program repair. Commun. ACM **62**(12), 56–65 (2019)

22. Gu, G., Perdisci, R., Zhang, J., Lee, W.: BotMiner: clustering analysis of network traffic for protocol-and structure-independent botnet detection (2008)

23. Gu, G., Porras, P.A., Yegneswaran, V., Fong, M.W., Lee, W.: BotHunter: detecting malware infection through ids-driven dialog correlation. In: USENIX Security Symposium (2007)

24. Heinricher, A., Williams, R., Klingbeil, A., Jordan, A.: Weldr: fusing binaries for simplified analysis. In: Proceedings of the 10th ACM SIGPLAN International Workshop on the State of the Art in Program Analysis, pp. 25–30 (2021)

25. Ho, G., et al.: Detecting and characterizing lateral phishing at scale. In: 28th USENIX Security Symposium (USENIX Security 2019), pp. 1273–1290 (2019)

26. Huang, Z., Lie, D., Tan, G., Jaeger, T.: Using safety properties to generate vulnerability patches. In: 2019 IEEE Symposium on Security and Privacy (SP), pp. 539–554. IEEE (2019)

27. Janakiraman, R., Waldvogel, M., Zhang, Q.: Indra: a peer-to-peer approach to network intrusion detection and prevention. In: WET ICE (2003)

28. Jiang, J., Xiong, Y., Zhang, H., Gao, Q., Chen, X.: Shaping program repair space with existing patches and similar code. In: Proceedings of the 27th ACM SIGSOFT International Symposium on Software Testing and Analysis, pp. 298–309 (2018)

29. Kannadiga, P., Zulkernine, M.: DIDMA: a distributed intrusion detection system using mobile agents. In: SNPD-SAWN (2005)

30. Kim, B.C., Chen, P.Y., Mukhopadhyay, T.: The effect of liability and patch release on software security: the monopoly case. Prod. Oper. Manag. **20**(4), 603–617 (2011)

31. Kruegel, C., Vigna, G.: Anomaly detection of web-based attacks. In: ACM SIGSAC Conference on Computer and Communications Security (CCS) (2003)

32. Lazarevic, A., Ertoz, L., Kumar, V., Ozgur, A., Srivastava, J.: A comparative study of anomaly detection schemes in network intrusion detection. In: Proceedings of the 2003 SIAM International Conference on Data Mining, pp. 25–36. SIAM (2003)

33. Lee, W., Stolfo, S.: Data mining approaches for intrusion detection (1998)

34. Lee, W., Xiang, D.: Information-theoretic measures for anomaly detection. In: Proceedings 2001 IEEE Symposium on Security and Privacy. S&P 2001, pp. 130–143. IEEE (2000)

35. Liu, Q., et al.: Latte: large-scale lateral movement detection. In: MILCOM 2018-2018 IEEE Military Communications Conference (MILCOM), pp. 1–6. IEEE (2018)

36. Long, F., Rinard, M.: Automatic patch generation by learning correct code. In: Proceedings of the 43rd Annual ACM SIGPLAN-SIGACT Symposium on Principles of Programming Languages, pp. 298–312 (2016)

37. Mitre: Mitre ATT&CK. https://attack.mitre.org/

38. de Moura, L., Bjørner, N.: Z3: an efficient SMT solver. In: Ramakrishnan, C.R., Rehof, J. (eds.) TACAS 2008. LNCS, vol. 4963, pp. 337–340. Springer, Heidelberg (2008). https://doi.org/10.1007/978-3-540-78800-3_24

39. Mukherjee, B., Heberlein, L.T., Levitt, K.N.: Network intrusion detection. IEEE Netw. **8**(3), 26–41 (1994)

40. Nachenberg, C., Wilhelm, J., Wright, A., Faloutsos, C.: Polonium: tera-scale graph mining and inference for malware detection. In: SIAM International Conference on Data Mining (2011)

41. Nguyen, H.D.T., Qi, D., Roychoudhury, A., Chandra, S.: SemFix: program repair via semantic analysis. In: 2013 35th International Conference on Software Engineering (ICSE), pp. 772–781. IEEE (2013)

42. Noureddine, M.A., Fawaz, A., Sanders, W.H., Başar, T.: A game-theoretic approach to respond to attacker lateral movement. In: Zhu, Q., Alpcan, T., Panaousis, E., Tambe, M., Casey, W. (eds.) GameSec 2016. LNCS, vol. 9996, pp. 294–313. Springer, Cham (2016). https://doi.org/10.1007/978-3-319-47413-7_17

43. Rahbarinia, B., Balduzzi, M., Perdisci, R.: Real-time detection of malware downloads via large-scale url−> file−> machine graph mining. In: ACM ASIA Conference on Computer and Communications Security (ASIACCS) (2016)

44. Rajab, M.A., Ballard, L., Lutz, N., Mavrommatis, P., Provos, N.: CAMP: content-agnostic malware protection. In: ISOC Network and Distributed Systems Security Symposium (NDSS) (2013)

45. Roesch, M., et al.: Snort: lightweight intrusion detection for networks. In: LISA, vol. 99, pp. 229–238 (1999)

46. Shen, Y., Stringhini, G.: Attack2vec: leveraging temporal word embeddings to understand the evolution of cyberattacks. In: USENIX Security Symposium, pp. 905–921 (2019)

47. Steinwart, I., Hush, D., Scovel, C.: A classification framework for anomaly detection. J. Mach. Learn. Res. **6**(2), 211–232 (2005)

48. Tian, Z., et al.: Real-time lateral movement detection based on evidence reasoning network for edge computing environment. IEEE Trans. Industr. Inf. **15**(7), 4285–4294 (2019)

49. Tripwire: The MITRE ATT&CK Framework: Lateral Movement. https://www.tripwire.com/state-of-security/mitre-framework/the-mitre-attck-framework-lateral-movement/

50. Valeur, F., Vigna, G., Kruegel, C., Kemmerer, R.A.: Comprehensive approach to intrusion detection alert correlation. IEEE Trans. Depend. Secure Comput. **1**(3), 146–169 (2004)

51. Vasilomanolakis, E., Karuppayah, S., Mühlhäuser, M., Fischer, M.: Taxonomy and survey of collaborative intrusion detection. ACM CSUR **47**(4), 55 (2015)

52. Vigna, G., Kemmerer, R.A.: Netstat: a network-based intrusion detection approach. In: Proceedings 14th Annual Computer Security Applications Conference (Cat. No. 98EX217), pp. 25–34. IEEE (1998)

53. Wang, R., et al.: Ramblr: making reassembly great again. In: NDSS (2017)

54. Wang, S., Wen, M., Chen, L., Yi, X., Mao, X.: How different is it between machine-generated and developer-provided patches?: an empirical study on the correct patches generated by automated program repair techniques. In: 2019 ACM/IEEE

International Symposium on Empirical Software Engineering and Measurement (ESEM), pp. 1–12. IEEE (2019)

55. Wei, Y., et al.: Automated fixing of programs with contracts. In: Proceedings of the 19th International Symposium on Software Testing and Analysis, pp. 61–72 (2010)

56. Williams, R., Ren, T., De Carli, L., Lu, L., Smith, G.: Guided feature identification and removal for resource-constrained firmware. ACM Trans. Softw. Eng. Methodol. (TOSEM) **31**(2), 1–25 (2021)

57. Wong, W.E., Gao, R., Li, Y., Abreu, R., Wotawa, F.: A survey on software fault localization. IEEE Trans. Software Eng. **42**(8), 707–740 (2016)

58. Xie, J., Fu, X., Du, X., Luo, B., Guizani, M.: Autopatchdroid: a framework for patching inter-app vulnerabilities in android application. In: 2017 IEEE International Conference on Communications (ICC), pp. 1–6. IEEE (2017)

59. Zhang, X., Zhang, Y., Li, J., Hu, Y., Li, H., Gu, D.: Embroidery: patching vulnerable binary code of fragmentized android devices. In: 2017 IEEE International Conference on Software Maintenance and Evolution (ICSME), pp. 47–57. IEEE (2017)

# AndroPROTECT: Hardening the Android API Against Fingerprinting

Gerald Palfinger[✉][iD]

Graz University of Technology and A-SIT Secure Information Technology Center
Austria, Inffeldgasse 16a, 8010 Graz, Austria
gerald.palfinger@a-sit.at

**Abstract.** To protect user privacy, Android has been hardened to prevent apps from tracking users across apps. In particular, starting with Android 10, third-party apps have been restricted from accessing various non-resettable device identifiers. However, non-unique information accessible to apps can still be combined to create a fingerprint. Therefore, fingerprinting allows apps to circumvent these privacy protections. To address this problem, we introduce the AndroPROTECT patch creation pipeline. Essentially, AndroPROTECT automatically creates patches for the Android API to harden it against fingerprinting attempts. AndroPROTECT starts with a set of information sources that have been automatically detected to provide information which can be used for fingerprinting. From this set, it automatically generates patches that modify the values which can be obtained by third-party apps. AndroPROTECT creates patches for various types of information sources present in the API, in particular, for methods, fields, and content providers. The resulting patch package can be applied to individual apps without requiring modifications of the operating system. In our experiments, a total of 989 information sources were patched automatically, representing more than 95% of the detected information sources. By testing the patch package against a set of popular Android apps, we show that the created patches can be applied with minimal impact on compatibility compared to repackaging an application.

**Keywords:** Fingerprinting protections · Android · Privacy

## 1 Introduction

Mobile apps provide a wide range of services and capabilities, often at no (direct) cost to the users. To generate revenue from these free apps, developers frequently depend on personalised advertising [32]. To deliver targeted advertisements, mobile apps collect personal information from the devices they run on [16,29]. This enables them to track their users across different apps. While this practice allows app developers to offer their services for free, it significantly compromises the privacy of users [30]. To counter this and enhance user privacy, several protections have been added to Android over the years. For instance, with Android

6, the permission system has been revamped to give the user control over access to data sources considered privacy sensitive, such as contacts or photos. These so-called dangerous permissions require the user to give explicit consent before an app can access the protected data. Over the years, more permissions have been added and some existing ones are now considered dangerous. In addition, with Android 10, access to user-unresettable identifiers has been restricted for third-party apps [3]. Conversely, apps are encouraged to use a resettable identifier such as Google's advertising ID. Despite these attempts by the operating system vendors to limit access to identifiable information, apps still collect, or sometimes start to collect, data about the devices they run on [17]. In particular, apps can still combine user- and device-specific information to create a fingerprint that can be used as replacement for a unique identifier [19,35]. This effectively circumvents the protections that have been implemented by the operating system vendors.

This paper introduces the AndroPROTECT patch creation pipeline to address this problem. AndroPROTECT creates patches that modify the Android API to reduce its fingerprintability. In particular, it alters the data returned by information sources that have been found to provide fingerprintable information. It supports methods, fields, and content providers, covering the main information sources accessible via the API. The patch creation pipeline is fully automated, from discovering fingerprintable information sources to creating and applying patches. The compiled patch package can be applied to individual apps without requiring any changes to the system itself. Thereby, it eliminates unwanted side effects on the operating system itself or other trusted apps. While there have been some approaches to detect fingerprinting by smartphone apps [13,33], to the best of our knowledge we are the first to introduce a solution that protects a mobile operating system from both first- and third-party fingerprinting. More details on our contributions are provided below.

*Contributions.* The main contributions of this paper are as follows:

1. We propose a patch creation pipeline that automatically creates patches for methods, fields, and content providers of the Android API. These patches aim to reduce the fingerprintability of the API.
2. We collect fingerprintable information sources of the Android API and use our patch creation pipeline to automatically create a patch package for the identified information sources. The created patch package can be applied to individual apps, reducing the number of fingerprintable information sources available to them.
3. We evaluate the created patch package on different devices to assess how it reduces the information that is available to create a fingerprint. We test it against real-world fingerprinting libraries and analyse the compatibility of the patch package by evaluating it against a set of popular apps.

*Outline.* The remainder of the paper is structured as follows: In Sect. 2 this paper continues with background knowledge on app patching and related publications. Afterwards, in Sect. 3 we present our methodology on how to reduce the fingerprintability of the Android API. Subsequently, in Sect. 4 we evaluate our methodology by measuring its coverage and by testing it against real-world apps and an automated testing framework. In Sect. 5 we discuss our methodology and its limitations. Finally, with Sect. 6 we conclude this work.

## 2    Background

This section introduces relevant background on the approaches available for modifying the app runtime. Afterwards, it continues by highlighting related work.

### 2.1    Altering the Application Runtime

To reduce the fingerprintability of the Android API by modifying the information it provides, we need to alter the app runtime or the app package. Some approaches rely on modifying the system, either by gaining root or by deploying a modified system image. However, modifying the system affects the entire device and increases the device's vulnerability to attack. Alternatively, apps can be executed within a container app. While no changes to the system are required, the container app has to request any permission that an app may need in advance. The container resides in the same process as the app, so it is generally unable to prevent the app from using a pre-requested permission. Furthermore, this approach will break some operating system integrations and change the signature of the app package reported by the system, which in turn will break signature checks. Finally, modifications can be applied directly to the app package. This approach allows the executable code and resources contained in the package to be modified. To install the modified package on a device, it must be repackaged and re-signed, which also breaks signature checks, similar to running inside a container. Common to all three approaches is that they can usually be detected using remote attestation, either by checking the signature of the app or the bootloader state [28]. For AndroPROTECT, we selected the A2P2 patching pipeline [7] to patch the app package directly. This approach allows us to generate app-agnostic patches, which can be applied to individual app. As it is applied to the app package, no modification of the system is required, eliminating unwanted side effects on the operating system and other apps. In addition, patches could be modified or disabled for individual packages if required.

### 2.2    Related Work

Fingerprinting allows uniquely identifying a user across different domains without requiring access to a unique identifier. As browsers do not expose a unique identifier, fingerprinting has received particular interest in this domain [20]. Similarly, with recent iterations of the major mobile operating systems, the app sandbox has become more restrictive. For example, with Android 10 access to unique identifiers has been removed for third-party apps [3]. Therefore, fingerprinting can be used as a replacement for unique identifiers in mobile apps.

*Smartphone Fingerprinting.* Wu et al. [35] have shown that it is possible to create a device fingerprint of Android devices by combining information from sources available to third-party apps. Similarly, Kurtz et al. [19] have shown that the same is feasible on iOS by collecting information from 29 different sources.

Torres and Jonker [33] analysed the data collection practices of third-party tracking and ad libraries on Android. These libraries collect information from many different sources which could be combined to create a fingerprint. Likewise, in [13], Heid et al. present an analysis environment for identifying iOS libraries that collect fingerprintable data. The authors used a dynamic approach on a jailbroken iOS device to detect fingerprinting activity in a number of apps.

In [25], a framework for systematically detecting fingerprintable information sources on Android is presented. It automatically invokes methods, queries fields, and dumps content providers of the system. Similarly, using OCScraper [24] it is possible to systematically search for fingerprintable information sources on iOS.

Meng et al. [21] analysed how pre-installed privileged apps and services handle access to unique identifiers. They show that many vendor apps leak unique identifiers through various channels, such as system settings or properties.

Kollnig et al. [17] analysed the impact of Apple's improved privacy policies. They found that collecting the advertising ID is prevented when requested. However, many apps still collect information that can be used to create a fingerprint.

*Emulator Detection using Fingerprinting.* As fingerprinting allows for detecting different device models, Jing et al. [15] have used it to detect emulators used in malware analysis and differentiate them from real devices. They use data collected from the file system, system properties, and a small subset of methods from the API. Similarly, Kondracki et al. [18] use the API to collect static device information and user configurations, some of which are protected by a permission. Conversely, CamoDroid [9] provides an extension for the Android emulator to mimic a real device. It tries to imitate a real device by simulating user data, input, and sensor values. In addition, it also changes some of the information returned by the API, in particular device information in the `android.os.Build` class and network information available through the `TelephonyManager`.

*Fingerprinting Protections.* To the best of our knowledge, there is limited work in the literature on protecting mobile operating systems from fingerprinting. However, in the context of browsers, several strategies have been proposed to protect against fingerprinting. For instance, FPGuard [10] uses heuristics to detect fingerprinting attempts and modifies the information returned to the fingerprinting website. PriVaricator [23] uses different randomisation policies to change the information obtainable by websites. Similarly, the FP-Block extension [34] also randomises the data provided by fingerprintable information sources. This is done only across different domains to reduce breakage. The JShelter [27] extension aims to reduce the fingerprintability by altering the JavaScript API. In particular, the extension restricts or changes certain methods and properties and is able to simulate certain sensors. Similarly, both the Tor browser [26] and Firefox [22] have implemented measures to counteract fingerprinting.

*Automatic Patch Creation.* AppSealer [37] automatically creates patches to mitigate component hijacking in Android apps. OSSPatcher [8] adapts security patches for open source components to automatically apply them to existing Android apps. On the Android kernel level, Vulmet [36] is an automated tool to adapt upstream fixes and convert them to a format suitable for hot patching. CocciEvolve [11] is an automatic patch creation tool for replacing deprecated function calls from Android apps. Similarly, AndroEvolve [12] builds on CocciEvolve to improve successful patch creation and readability. However, none of the presented approaches can be directly applied to reduce the fingerprintability.

# 3   Methodology

In order to reduce the fingerprintability of the information sources of the Android API, we use a three-step approach. First, we search the API for information sources that could potentially be used to create a fingerprint and collect values from a reference device. This is done by using an automated tool to compare different devices and collect the information sources that differ between them. The result of this step is then used to automatically generate patches that change the return values of the identified information sources based on the reference device. Finally, the generated patches are applied to individual apps. These three steps are discussed in more detail in the following sections.

## 3.1   Preparation

**Detecting Fingerprintable Information Sources.** To detect fingerprintable information sources and collect reference values, we use an adapted version of the AndroPRINT framework [25]. The framework collects the return values of method calls, retrieves the contents of fields, and queries the contents of content providers. Thereby, it retrieves all essential information sources accessible to a third-party app via the Android API. Essentially, AndroPRINT uses a list of all known methods and constructors in the Android API as its starting point to find fingerprintable information sources. For the purposes of this paper, these lists have been updated to reflect the latest Android version (Android 14). From the list of constructors, the framework begins to create objects of the classes of the Android API using reflection. It then proceeds to invoke methods and query fields on the created objects. If it receives an object of primitive type when invoking a method or querying a field, it saves the value for comparison. Conversely, if it retrieves a value which is an object of a complex class, it additionally invokes the methods and queries the fields of the received object recursively. For this paper, we improved the memory usage of AndroPRINT to allow using an unlimited exploration depth for returned class values.

In addition to methods and fields, the framework also retrieves the values provided by content providers. Essentially, the content provider architecture allows access to data provided by system services. During the retrieval of fields and return values of methods the framework collects all strings that begin with the `content` scheme. When the framework has finished collecting return values and fields, it then attempts to access all content-URIs it has encountered. While many of the content providers require permission from the user, such as the contacts or calendar providers, some of the system-provided content providers can be accessed without user consent. All data accessible through content providers that do not require user consent are thus dumped for comparison.

Finally, the framework is executed on different smartphones and the collected data are then analysed to identify fingerprintable information sources to be patched. For this purpose, the retrieved data is first cleansed. More specifically, this involves removing duplicates, such as removing calls to methods that return the same value despite having different parameters or being invoked on different objects. The collected, cleansed and sorted values of a device are subsequently compared with all other devices analysed during the analysis. All values that are identical on all analysed devices are removed, as they cannot be used to differentiate between the devices. Conversely, each value that is different on at least one device is retained and its source is marked as fingerprintable.

**Collection of Reference Values.** The framework stores the textual representation of an object by invoking `toString()` or, for arrays and collections, by invoking the `Arrays.deepToString()` method. In addition to storing the textual representation of return values and fields, we adapted AndroPRINT to probe if a retrieved object can be either serialised or exported as an Android parcel[1]. This allows our patching pipeline to restore the return value of a method or the contents of a field for non-trivial object types that cannot be easily restored from the textual representation. In case it can be exported, the framework saves the serialised content or the parcel to a file. When the framework encounters an array or a collection, it first tries to serialise it. Since most collection types implement the `Serializable` interface, the retrieved object can be serialised directly, provided the content of the collection is also serialisable. If the framework fails to serialise the object, it then tries to create parcels. For arrays and collections, it has to create a parcel object for each element of the array or collection. The array or collection will be recreated at runtime by the patch which unmarshalls each parcel and adds it to an array or collection of the corresponding type.

For content providers, in addition to dumping the textual representation of each entry, the modified framework also dumps the entire content of each provider into a table of a SQLite database. This database allows us to create patches for content providers more easily than using the textual representation. In particular, we can use helper classes of the Android API to create a cursor object that can be used as a drop-in replacement for the cursor returned by the content provider interface, as discussed in more detail in Sect. 3.2.

---

[1] The Parcel API provides a format for storing flattened data or references to remote objects that can be obtained using the Binder IPC mechanism. For the purposes of this paper, we will focus on using parcels to export return values as flattened data.

**Collection of Auxiliary Data.** In addition to exporting the return values of methods, the content of fields, and the rows and columns of content providers, we also dump information about all constructors available on the device using the Reflection API. In particular, we need to get information about the type of the constructor parameters. This is required to create patches for the constructors of a class, allowing us to change the value of non-static fields during object creation.

## 3.2   Automatic Creation of Patches

**Methods.** The automated patching pipeline creates a patch in the A2P2 format [7] for each method that has been found to return information that can be used for fingerprinting. The method signature and the value collected from the reference device are used to create the patch. In particular, the patching pipeline uses the value from the reference device to create the return value of the patch method. If the value is of a primitive type, or if it is a common data class used in the Android API, AndroPROTECT uses the textual representation of the return value to recreate it. Conversely, if the return value is of complex type, it uses either the serialised representation or the parcel, depending on the type of the reference value. The patching pipeline adds the serialised representation of the return value or the parcel to the resources of the patch project. When an app invokes a method that has been patched, the patch reads the object from its serialised representation or unmarshalls the parcel to recreate the return value.

Some of the methods found to provide fingerprintable information are not part of the public API. While many of these hidden methods have been restricted for third-party apps, some have only been greylisted and are thus still accessible via reflection [6]. However, A2P2 can only patch classes and methods that are public. To circumvent this problem, we use A2P2 to patch the Reflection API. In particular, the patching pipeline creates a patch for the `invoke` method of the `java.lang.reflect.Method` class. The patched method compares whether the signature of the method to be invoked matches a fingerprintable method. In case the method signature matches, the patch invokes the patched version of the method to return the modified return value. Otherwise, the original implementation of `invoke` is called, which subsequently invokes the original method.

**Fields.** In addition to the return values of methods, fields can also hold information that can be used to create a fingerprint. When creating patches, it is necessary to distinguish between static and non-static fields. Static fields can already be modified at app startup, while non-static fields can at the earliest be changed when the corresponding object is created.

*Static Fields.* Static fields can be accessed without a corresponding class object. Therefore, any static field that contains fingerprintable information must be changed before it can be accessed by an app. To achieve this, a patch is created to register a new content provider in the app's manifest. By setting a high value for the `initOrder` [4] attribute, the content provider gets initialised early in the app startup process. The `onCreate` method is invoked when the content provider is initialised. This method allows for setting the values of static fields to their reference value before the app's own code is executed. However, it is not possible to set all fields directly. Fields marked as final, in particular, cannot be changed. Nevertheless, this limitation can be overcome by using the reflection API. Specifically, our patching pipeline retrieves the reflected representation of the field, allowing it to access the field's access modifiers. By negating the final modifier, it is possible to make the field writable and change its value. For instance, this encompasses the final values in the `android.os.Build` class, which contain information about the device and the operating system.

*Non-static Fields.* In contrast to static fields, the values of non-static fields are stored as part of a particular object. Therefore, non-static fields cannot be set during app startup. As this is the earliest option, AndroPROTECT generates a patch for the constructors of the corresponding class to modify the values of non-static fields. More specifically, patches for non-static fields first invoke the original constructor. Afterwards, the patches alter the value of the fields in the received object of the class before it is passed to the app's code. As classes can have multiple constructors taking a different number of parameters, a patch has to be created for each of them. To do this, the patching pipeline require the signature of each constructor to create a valid patch method. During the preparation phase, this information was retrieved from a device using reflection. In particular, an app iterated over all accessible classes of the programming interface and dumped the signature of all constructors. This information is now used by our patching pipeline to create patches for all constructors of a class if a non-static field needs to be modified for a particular class.

**Content Providers.** On Android, content providers serve as an interface for accessing structured data. Not all content providers are protected by a permission. For instance, the settings content providers which are part of the system provide access to user-influenced settings without requiring a permission. In general, content providers can be accessed using a URI with the scheme `content`. When a valid URI is used to access a content provider, the system returns a cursor object that enables access to the provider's content as rows and columns.

When an app requests access to a content provider that has been found to provide access to fingerprintable data, the cursor returned to the app is exchanged by our patch. Content providers can be accessed using the content resolver class. Therefore, a patch has been developed to modify the content resolver's behaviour. When an app invokes the `query` method to request access to a specific content provider, the content URI provided by the app is examined. If the URI corresponds to a content provider that has been identified to contain fingerprintable information, the cursor returned by the method is modified. In particular, our patch package includes a SQLite database which gets added to the app's resources. This database contains a table for each fingerprintable content provider. If an app accesses such a content provider, we return a cursor to the corresponding table in the database. Our implementation preserves any projection requested by the app and honours the query arguments passed to the method. For any other content URI, our patch invokes the original method.

**Additional Measures.** Besides patching the sources found by AndroPRINT, we also prevent apps from accessing information in the /proc directory. This part of the file system has been found to contain information allowing apps to infer various events [31]. Additionally, it also contains information about the device, such as memory or CPU details. Thus, we created patches for methods allowing to read files. Whenever an application accesses a file in the /proc path, the file handle is replaced with the reference file. To collect the reference values, we created an app which retrieves all accessible files in the /proc path. Additionally, we also prevent apps from accessing the ad ID by removing the AD_ID permission.

### 3.3   Application of Patches

Finally, once the patches have been generated, they are compiled into a patch package. Our patching pipeline uses the static rewriting backend of A2P2 to create the patch package due to its better compatibility with different devices, architectures, and newer versions of Android. Furthermore, the static rewriting backend has lower overhead in terms of both app size and runtime speed [7]. The patch package created in this step can be applied to any Android app package. During patching, A2P2 unpacks the original app package, rewrites the code contained therein to include the patches, and finally repacks and re-signs it.

## 4   Evaluation

In this section, we evaluate our approach. Firstly, the test setup is detailed, followed by an evaluation of the number of successfully patched information sources. Afterwards, the efficacy of the created patch package is examined by testing it on different devices against the reference device. Finally, the compatibility of the patches is evaluated by testing it using a set of popular apps.

### 4.1   Test Setup

The evaluation focuses on the latest version of Android, which was version 14 at the time of writing. To collect the reference values for patch generation, a Google Pixel 6 Pro was used. To identify sources of fingerprintable information, the AndroPRINT framework was executed on various devices from different manufacturers. Our experiments focus on API calls that can be invoked either without a permission or with a normal permission which are granted at install time. We focus on these types of sources because access to them cannot be denied by the user. In contrast, access to information requiring dangerous permissions can already be denied by the user via Android's permission system.

However, in case an app refuses to run without a specific dangerous permission, AndroPROTECT is also able to create patches for them automatically. Furthermore, AndroPROTECT can be used to restrict the information accessible through permission-protected APIs, instead of granting holistic access to all data of a certain type, which is typically the case with most dangerous permissions.

## 4.2   Coverage

As our patching pipeline is fully automated, the coverage of the different information sources in the Android API is an important metric to evaluate its efficacy. The following sections provide an analysis of the coverage.

**Content Providers.** In total, five content providers were found to provide fingerprintable information. All of them have been successfully patched by AndroPROTECT. Therefore, our reference database contains five tables for each of the detected content providers respectively. In total, the reference database contains 441 entries. By far the most fingerprintable entries were found in the `settings` content providers. In addition to some constants, these providers mainly contain system settings that can be customised by the user of the device. The `settings` provider is divided into three sub-providers. In particular, these are `settings/global`, `settings/secure`, and `settings/system`. The reference table for the `settings/global` content provider contains 221 entries. It includes, for example, the user-settable device name, the boot count, and radio settings. For the `settings/secure` provider, the reference table contains 130 different entries. These include, among various others, accessibility settings, input method and autofill service, and lock screen settings. Finally, the `settings/system` provider holds 47 entries. This provider primarily contains information about media and notification settings, including, for instance, set notification tones or vibration settings. The `media/internal/audio/media` content provider contains information about ringtones, notification, and alarm sounds. The reference table obtained from our test device contains 42 different entries. As well as various data about the sounds, this table also contains a `date_modified` column. On unpatched devices, this column corresponds to the time of the first boot of the device for the pre-installed sounds. Finally, the `service-state` provider contains information about the mobile network, such as the type of data network or the number identifying the network operator. As our reference device had a single SIM card installed, this provider contains one entry.

**Methods and Fields.** A condensed representation of the number of detected fingerprintable methods and fields found, and the patches generated for them, is depicted in Table 1. In total, 895 methods and 139 fields were found to provide fingerprintable information. Out of these, 4 methods and 20 fields could not be patched because the corresponding class did not exist in the public Android API. Additionally, 4 methods could not be patched because the return type is hidden. For one class containing a non-static field, the corresponding constructor could

**Table 1.** Overview of the API coverage. The table commences with the number of methods and fields detected to provide fingerprintable information, and provides a rationale for why some of them could not be patched.

|  | Methods | Fields | Total |
|---|---|---|---|
| **# Detected fingerprintable methods & fields** | **895** | **139** | **1034** |
| – Corresponding class not found on reference device | 4 | 20 | 24 |
| – (Return) Type not existing | 4 | 0 | 4 |
| – No constructor found | – | 1 | 1 |
| – Exception type not existing | 0 | – | 0 |
| – No reference value found | 10 | 5 | 15 |
| **= Automatically created patches** | **877** | **113** | **990** |
| + Manually defined reference values | 3 | 0 | 3 |
| – Blocklisted information sources | 8 | 1 | 9 |
| **= Created patches** | **872** | **112** | **984** |
|  | 97.4 % | 80.6 % | 95.2 % |

not be found. For all methods that declare exceptions, the corresponding class could be resolved. However, 10 methods could not be invoked and 5 fields could not be retrieved on the reference device. Therefore, AndroPROTECT was able to create patches for 877 methods and 113 fields automatically. Furthermore, reference values were manually defined for 3 methods based on values obtained from other devices. 8 of the methods and 1 field required patching to be block-listed due to their negative impact on certain apps (see below). Thus, a total of 872 methods and 112 fields were patched by AndroPROTECT.

*Public and Hidden Sources.* Out of the 872 patched methods 748 are instance methods from 211 different classes. Of these, 662 methods are part of the public API and could thus be directly patched via A2P2's patch commands. For the remaining 86 hidden methods, our framework had to create a patch for the reflection API to redirect invocations to the patched version of the method. Additionally, our framework created patches for 124 static methods in 70 classes. 111 of the static methods are publicly accessible, while the remaining 13 methods are hidden. In total, AndroPROTECT created patches for 773 public and 99 hidden methods. Out of the total of 112 patched fields, 84 are non-static fields from 22 classes. The other 28 fields are static and are modified across 5 different classes. As the fields are set either at app startup or at object creation using the Reflection API, we do not differentiate between public and hidden fields. A listing of the patched methods grouped by their package can be found in Appendix A.

*Blocklisting.* As discussed above, some methods and fields had to be block-listed. In particular, eight methods and one field have been be blocklisted as they caused problems or crashes in a range of apps. Changing the value of the non-static field `uiMode` in the class `Configuration` resulted in excessive flickering in the UI, rendering the affected apps unusable. On smartphones, this field allows to detect whether night mode is on. Furthermore, it can be used to detect if the app is running on a TV or VRR headset, for example. Additionally, the `getAllNetworks()` and `getActiveNetwork()` methods of the `ConnectivityManager` have been blocklisted. These methods allow to query all available networks or the active network respectively. Patching them resulted in connectivity issues in some apps. The method `getConfiguration()` of the `Resources` class has been blocklisted because unmarshalling an old `Configuration` object caused problems in some apps. Nevertheless, our framework was able to create patches for some of the methods and fields within the `Configuration` class. Moreover, the method `getText()` of the class `TextView` has been blocklisted as it caused apps to retrieve incorrect text from text views. In the class `DisplayManager` the method `getDisplays()` has been blocklisted as the return value could not be deserialised correctly, resulting in an empty array being returned. This issue was detected during our efficacy tests as the return value differed from that of the reference device. Additionally, it caused a problem in an app which expected at least one display to be returned. This resulted in a crash of the app with an `ArrayIndexOutOfBoundsException`. Furthermore, two methods in the `WindowManager` class have been added to the blocklist. Specifically, the methods `getCurrent-` and `getMaximumWindowMetrics()` have been blocklisted due to the `windowInsets` parameter being null in the collected reference values. In the compatibility tests, this caused five apps to crash with a `NullPointerException`. Finally, we also excluded the method `getCallingUid()` of the `Binder` class as it caused problems in certain security checks.

### 4.3   Efficacy

This section presents the results of an evaluation of the efficacy of our approach. Initially, we apply the patches to real-world fingerprinting libraries, demonstrating the effectiveness of the patches. Subsequently, we compare different devices against the reference device using AndroPRINT to test the correctness.

**Fingerprinters.** For this section, we applied our patch package to two demo apps of fingerprinting libraries, namely FingerprintJS Android and TrustDevice. The patched apps were installed on a Google Pixel 7a running Android 14. The FingerprintJS demo app calculates a local device ID based on information obtained from the device. Depending on the chosen stability level, the app chooses different information source to calculate the fingerprint. On the test device, the patched application computed the same fingerprint as on the reference device on all stability levels. The app collected information about, for example, the ringtone, locale and language information, input devices, and sensors. Additionally, it retrieved the battery size via a hidden API and collected information about the CPU from `/proc/cpuinfo`. The app also gathered various user-adjustable settings from the settings content providers, such as accessibility settings, font sizes, and UI animation settings. All of the retrieved information sources that differed between the devices were patched by AndroPROTECT.

The TrustDevice demo app collects device information in a JSON structure, which can be sent to a backend for fingerprint calculation. We compared this JSON from the test device with the reference device. The collected data were found to be identical, and therefore, cannot be used to create a fingerprint. The app retrieved information about, for example, installed applications, locale and language information, or device size and resolution. Similarly to FingerprintJS, it also collected information from the settings content providers and accesses, for example, information sources returning data about the CPU, battery, and sensors. Additionally, TrustDevice used a native library to check the root status of the device. Native binaries are currently not supported by AndroPROTECT. However, as our test devices were not rooted, the information returned by those checks did not differ between devices. Furthermore, hiding the root status is out of scope of this paper, as there are other solutions, such as MagiskHide, available.

**Same Manufacturer Setup.** The test was conducted using a Google Pixel 7a running Android 14. A total of 24 of information sources differed between the test and the reference device. In particular, the return values of five methods were different because they were blocklisted. Furthermore, there were differences in the values obtained from three fields and three methods. Our framework was unable to create a patch for them because the class did either not exist in the public API or it did not have a constructor. These include, for example, the hidden method `getVolumes()` of the `StorageManager` class. Five methods have been successfully patched and return the same values as the reference device. However, they are printed differently from the reference device. Four of these methods return an object of the `Set` or `Hashtable` type. For those, the order in which they are printed using the `toString()` method differs from the reference device. The fifth method returns an object of type `PersistableBundle`. After unmarshalling the parcel containing the return value, its contents are printed differently. In particular, for bundles contained within the bundle, only the size is printed, whereas on the reference device the contents of the sub-bundles were printed. Additionally, the value of two fields has changed after being set at startup. This can generally occur with non-final fields. To prevent changes to non-final fields, it would be necessary to check each memory access. However, this would result in a significant performance overhead. For four methods, no reference value was available to create a patch. This occurs when the return value cannot be parsed and there is no serialised version or package of it available. Finally, the return values of two methods are now different as a result of patching. Specifically, these two methods return information from the stack trace. The values now differ as they also contain methods from the patching framework.

All content providers that were found to provide fingerprintable information have been successfully patched. As confirmed in this test, the patched cursors provide only access to the reference values. However, it is noteworthy that the cursor returned for the `service-state` provider reports the columns in a different order compared to the reference device. Nevertheless, the values therein are the same as on the reference device.

**Different Manufacturer Setup.** For this setup, we used a Samsung Galaxy S24 Plus running Android 14. In total, 14 information sources that were not present in the previous case study were found to be different. This includes an additional method which was blocklisted. Furthermore, for two fields and three methods its class or a constructor could not be found in the public API. A patch was generated for five methods. However, the parcel used to assign the return value of one method did not contain all the member variables of the return class. As a result, some of the values in the `toString()` method differed between the test and the reference device. Two more methods returned a deserialised time object that reported a slightly different time when printed. The remaining two methods returned an object of a class that contained two additional fields that were not present on the reference device. These fields are included in the output of the `toString()` method of the class. As they were unassigned, no value was printed other than the name of the additional fields. Finally, for three methods returning a complex object, no pre-defined value was available.

## 4.4   Application Compatibility

As our approach modifies the runtime environment of apps, we assess the compatibility by testing them on popular apps. Since the patches are applied to individual applications, they do not affect other apps or the operating system. The compatibility tests were conducted on a Google Pixel 7a running Android 14. In particular, the tests were performed using the top six apps from 21 different categories of the Google Play Store. One of the apps was exclusively available for Android TV devices, rendering it incompatible with our test device. There were an additional five apps listed in two categories, resulting in a total of 120 distinct apps available for testing. To prepare the test environment, the Android Debug Bridge (adb) was used to automatically install and launch the patched app. In addition, the UI Monkey [5] was used to automatically execute events on the running app. The apps are compared in three different configurations. Firstly, the apps are executed without any modifications to identify any incompatibilities with the test device. Secondly, the patching pipeline of A2P2 is used to re-sign the app. No additional patches are applied in this test, i.e. an empty patch package is used. This enables the detection of any problems that may arise when the app is repackaged with a different signing certificate. Finally, the complete patch package is applied. Three apps already exhibited problems even when executing unmodified. Two of them closed on the loading screen, while one displayed a popup stating that critical app data were missing. Thus, 117 apps could be run on our test device.

*Compatibility with Repackaging:* Two out of the 117 apps could not be patched as the patching framework could not re-sign the patched app package. The remaining 115 were successfully patched and installed. Out of those, a total of nine crashed with an exception when being patched with an empty patch package. Five of them crashed due to an `IncompatibleClassChangeError`. Although some apps were obfuscated, upon inspecting the stack traces, it appeared that all of them crashed on the same line in the `DrawScope` class of Android's Compose UI framework. It appears that this problem is caused by smali/dexlib2[2], which is a dependency of A2P2. The remaining four apps were terminated due to failing signature checks. During the tests, another six apps were terminated prematurely. Two of these apps displayed an error message indicating that a file was corrupted. The remaining four apps just terminated.

*Compatibility with Patches:* Out of the remaining 100 apps which are compatible with our test device and A2P2, five terminated during runtime when patched with the full patch package. In particular, one of these apps crashed when accessing a method of the `TimeZone` class. Another app crashed while reading a file in the `/proc` folder while the third app closed because it was unable to access a resource stored in the app bundle. One app displayed an error message indicating that a device ID cannot be retrieved while another app crashed in a method called `getDeviceSerialNumber`. Additionally, two apps appeared to have network connectivity problems during the tests. Furthermore, AndroPROTECT generated patches for some UI classes in the API, resulting in visual differences in some UI elements. For instance, some buttons had a different background colour, while switches had a different size. Despite these visual differences, we manually confirmed that the affected UI elements remained clickable.

# 5   Discussion and Future Work

Using our patch creation pipeline, we created patches for a large number of methods, fields, and content providers. Our evaluations demonstrate that AndroPROTECT was able to successfully patch the majority of the detected fingerprintable information sources automatically. Furthermore, we have shown that the patches are effective on devices from different manufacturers and remain compatible with most apps.

   As AndroPROTECT utilises A2P2 to generate the patch package, it inherits the limitations of A2P2. Specifically, apps have to be re-signed with a different key. Some apps verify the signature to prevent malicious changes to the app. Unfortunately, these checks also affect our non-malicious patches. Although in-process signature validation could be removed using A2P2, it is not possible to bypass signature checks on the backend using attestation [7]. However, Ibrahim et al. [14] report that less than 0.1% of the examined apps use such checks. Furthermore, both A2P2 and the AndroPRINT framework do not support native code. Thus, our approach also focuses on the main Java API.

   Our approach relies on AndroPRINT [25] to detect fingerprintable information sources in the Android API. As AndroPRINT compares the information

---

[2] https://github.com/iBotPeaches/Apktool/issues/3616.

obtained from different devices, the exhaustiveness of the result is dependent on the diversity of the devices. Our set of fingerprintable information sources was created using devices from various manufacturers, but testing more devices may reveal some additional sources. However, since our approach is automatic, creating patches for newly found information sources is straightforward. Additionally, some information may only be accessible when providing specific parameters. While AndroPRINT parses constants from the API documentation to enhance its coverage, it can only use a small subset of parameter combinations. Nevertheless, to our knowledge, AndroPRINT provides the most comprehensive coverage of fingerprintable information sources in the literature. Like AndroPRINT, our research is centered on the mitigation of fingerprinting through data obtained directly from the API. However, it should be noted that our approach does not extend to the protection against fingerprinting utilizing side-channel information. As protection against this particular form of fingerprinting requires a different methodology, we leave this as future work.

In our experiments, we chose a reference device and used its values to replace the information provided by fingerprintable sources. This enabled us to test it against fingerprinting applications and to check if fingerprinting apps report the same values across devices and whether the patches were applied correctly. To prevent browser fingerprinting, previous research has suggested randomising the returned information across different domains [34]. A comparable approach could be followed with AndroPROTECT by utilising the reference values from different devices to patch different apps.

Research on browser fingerprinting has shown that newer browser versions generally provide a greater number of fingerprintable information sources [2], despite efforts to improve privacy. Although no research has been conducted to compare the fingerprintability of Android versions, it can generally be assumed that new APIs can introduce new fingerprintable information sources. Since our pipeline is fully automated, it can easily be applied to new versions of Android.

## 6   Conclusions

In this paper, we introduced the AndroPROTECT automatic patch creation pipeline. AndroPROTECT automatically creates patches to reduce the fingerprintability of the Android API. From a list of automatically gathered information sources and their reference values it generates a patch package. It modifies the information returned by methods, fields, and content providers, making them ineffective for fingerprinting purposes. In our experiments, AndroPROTECT was able to generate patches for the majority of the detected information sources automatically. Our evaluations demonstrated that the generated patch package can be applied to apps with minimal impact on compatibility. Furthermore, the patches can be applied to individual apps without requiring modifications to the device. This ensures that the patches do not have any unintended side effects on the system or on other trusted apps. The patch creation pipeline of AndroPROTECT is fully automated, enabling it to be applied to future versions of Android without the need to manually write patches for new information sources by hand.

**Disclosure of Interests.** The authors have no competing interests to declare that are relevant to the content of this article.

## A  Methods and Fields Patched

Table 2 provides a more comprehensive overview of the number of methods and fields that have been patched across the API's base packages. It shows that the fingerprintable sources of information are distributed across various packages and classes. Some of the methods and fields of these packages are described in the following paragraph to illustrate what kind of information sources have been patched. The highest number of methods was patched in the `android.view` package. These allowed, for instance, querying installed input devices, and view-related settings, such as input timeout or scroll speed. The methods from the `android.icu` package return information related to the locale set by the user, such as time format, weekdays, or currency. In the `android.widget` package, various methods and fields have been patched. These include information sources that report the colours of widgets and effects, text sizes, and scroll speed. 59 patches for methods of the `android.telephony` package have been created. Prior to patching, these methods provided information about the network country, operator, MMS user agent, or roaming and data settings. The generated patches for the methods and fields of the `android.os` and `java.io` packages change information regarding the build information, storage sizes, and user accounts. The patched information sources of the `android.content` package reported information about default colours, the display, and some of the installed packages. Methods from the `android.net` and `java.net` packages allowed querying WiFi settings, network usage, or buffer sizes. The created patches for the methods of the `android.app` package change the reported values of the user-set night mode times, launcher icon sizes, and wallpaper ID and colours. Furthermore, AndroPROTECT created patches for methods in the `android.media` package which returned information about the user-set ringtone, media volumes of different streams, and codecs. Information sources in the `android.text` packages reported information about the locale, timezone, and text-specific layout sizes.

**Table 2.** Overview of the number of methods and fields patched across the base packages of the Android API.

| Package (# Classes) | # Methods | # Fields | Total |
|---|---|---|---|
| android.view (23) | 112 | 1 | 113 |
| android.icu (19) | 99 | 5 | 104 |
| android.content (20) | 53 | 37 | 90 |
| android.graphics (21) | 73 | 4 | 77 |
| android.widget (21) | 61 | 12 | 73 |
| android.net (17) | 62 | 5 | 67 |
| android.os (13) | 42 | 24 | 66 |
| android.telephony (8) | 59 | – | 59 |
| android.text (12) | 48 | 2 | 50 |
| android.app (16) | 40 | 7 | 47 |
| android.media (16) | 41 | – | 41 |
| java.util (7) | 35 | – | 35 |
| java.text (5) | 24 | – | 24 |
| android.provider (12) | 22 | – | 22 |
| android.hardware (8) | 18 | – | 18 |
| android.bluetooth (1) | 16 | – | 16 |
| java.net (4) | 14 | – | 14 |
| android.util (1) | – | 12 | 12 |
| java.lang (3) | 6 | 1 | 7 |
| android.location (2) | 6 | – | 6 |
| android.nfc (2) | 6 | – | 6 |
| android.system (1) | 5 | – | 5 |
| android.appwidget (2) | 4 | – | 4 |
| android.preference (2) | 3 | 1 | 4 |
| libcore.util (1) | 4 | – | 4 |
| android.telecom (1) | 3 | – | 3 |
| android.webkit (3) | 3 | - | 3 |
| java.time (2) | 2 | 1 | 3 |
| android.speech (1) | 2 | – | 2 |
| com.android (1) | 2 | – | 2 |
| javax.net (1) | 2 | – | 2 |
| android.accounts (1) | 1 | – | 1 |
| android.drm (1) | 1 | – | 1 |
| android.security (1) | 1 | – | 1 |
| android.service (1) | 1 | – | 1 |
| java.io (1) | 1 | – | 1 |
| Total | 872 | 112 | 984 |

# References

1. Proceedings of the 20th International Conference on Security and Cryptography, SECRYPT 2023, Rome, Italy, 10–12 July 2023 (2023)
2. Akhavani, S.A., Jueckstock, J., Su, J., Kapravelos, A., Kirda, E., Lu, L.: Browserprint: an analysis of the impact of browser features on fingerprintability and web privacy. In: Liu, J.K., Katsikas, S., Meng, W., Susilo, W., Intan, R. (eds.) ISC 2021. LNCS, vol. 13118, pp. 161–176. Springer, Cham (2021). https://doi.org/10.1007/978-3-030-91356-4_9
3. Android-Developers: Privacy changes in android 10 - restriction on non-resettable device identifiers (2019). https://developer.android.com/about/versions/10/privacy/changes#non-resettable-device-ids/
4. Android-Developers: <provider> - android:initorder (2023). https://developer.android.com/guide/topics/manifest/provider-element.html/#init
5. Android-Developers: Ui/application exerciser monkey (2023). https://developer.android.com/studio/test/other-testing-tools/monkey
6. Android-Developers: Restrictions on non-SDK interfaces - android developers (2024). https://developer.android.com/guide/app-compatibility/restrictions-non-sdk-interfaces/
7. Draschbacher, F.: A2P2 - an android application patching pipeline based on generic changesets. In: Availability, Reliability and Security – ARES, pp. 1:1–1:11 (2023)
8. Duan, R., et al.: Automating patching of vulnerable open-source software versions in application binaries. In: Network and Distributed System Security Symposium – NDSS (2019)
9. Faghihi, F., Zulkernine, M., Ding, S.H.H.: CamoDroid: an Android application analysis environment resilient against sandbox evasion. J. Syst. Archit. **125**, 102452 (2022)
10. FaizKhademi, A., Zulkernine, M., Weldemariam, K.: FPGuard: detection and prevention of browser fingerprinting. In: Samarati, P. (ed.) DBSec 2015. LNCS, vol. 9149, pp. 293–308. Springer, Cham (2015). https://doi.org/10.1007/978-3-319-20810-7_21
11. Haryono, S.A., et al.: Automatic android deprecated-API usage update by learning from single updated example. In: ICPC 2020: 28th International Conference on Program Comprehension, Seoul, Republic of Korea, 13–15 July 2020, pp. 401–405 (2020)
12. Haryono, S.A., et al.: AndroEvolve: automated Android API update with data flow analysis and variable denormalization. Empir. Softw. Eng. **27**(3), 1–31 (2022). https://doi.org/10.1007/s10664-021-10096-0
13. Heid, K., Andrae, V., Heider, J.: Towards detecting device fingerprinting on iOS with API function hooking. In: European Interdisciplinary Cybersecurity Conference – EICC, pp. 78–84 (2023)
14. Ibrahim, M., Imran, A., Bianchi, A.: SafetyNOT: on the usage of the SafetyNet attestation API in Android. In: Mobile Systems – MobiSys, pp. 150–162 (2021)
15. Jing, Y., Zhao, Z., Ahn, G., Hu, H.: Morpheus: automatically generating heuristics to detect Android emulators. In: Annual Computer Security Applications Conference – ACSAC, pp. 216–225 (2014)
16. Kollnig, K., Shuba, A., Binns, R., Kleek, M.V., Shadbolt, N.: Are iPhones really better for privacy? A comparative study of iOS and android apps. Proc. Priv. Enhancing Technol. **2022**, 6–24 (2022)

17. Kollnig, K., Shuba, A., Kleek, M.V., Binns, R., Shadbolt, N.: Goodbye tracking? Impact of iOS app tracking transparency and privacy labels. In: Conference on Fairness, Accountability, and Transparency – FAccT, pp. 508–520 (2022)

18. Kondracki, B., Azad, B.A., Miramirkhani, N., Nikiforakis, N.: The droid is in the details: environment-aware evasion of android sandboxes. In: Network and Distributed System Security Symposium – NDSS (2022)

19. Kurtz, A., Gascon, H., Becker, T., Rieck, K., Freiling, F.C.: Fingerprinting mobile devices using personalized configurations. Proc. Priv. Enhancing Technol. **2016**, 4–19 (2016)

20. Laperdrix, P., Bielova, N., Baudry, B., Avoine, G.: Browser Fingerprinting: a Survey. ACM Trans. Web **14**, 8:1–8:33 (2020)

21. Meng, M.H., et al.: Post-GDPR threat hunting on android phones: dissecting OS-level safeguards of user-unresettable identifiers. In: Network and Distributed System Security Symposium – NDSS (2023)

22. Mozilla-Corporation: Enhanced tracking protection in firefox for desktop (2023). https://support.mozilla.org/en-US/kb/enhanced-tracking-protection-firefox-desktop/

23. Nikiforakis, N., Joosen, W., Livshits, B.: PriVaricator: deceiving fingerprinters with little white lies. In: International Conference on World Wide Web – WWW, pp. 820–830 (2015)

24. Palfinger, G.: OCScraper: automated analysis of the fingerprintability of the iOS API. In: International Conference on Security and Cryptography – SECRYPT [1], pp. 433–441

25. Palfinger, G., Prünster, B.: AndroPRINT: analysing the fingerprintability of the Android API. In: Availability, Reliability and Security – ARES, pp. 94:1–94:10 (2020)

26. Perry, M., Clark, E., Murdoch, S., Koppen, G.: The design and implementation of the tor browser - cross-origin fingerprinting unlinkability (2019). https://www.torproject.org/projects/torbrowser/design/#fingerprinting-linkability

27. Polcák, L., Salon, M., Maone, G., Hranický, R., McMahon, M.: JShelter: give me my browser back. In: International Conference on Security and Cryptography – SECRYPT [1], pp. 287–294

28. Prünster, B., Palfinger, G., Kollmann, C.: Fides: unleashing the full potential of remote attestation. In: Proceedings of the 16th International Joint Conference on e-Business and Telecommunications, ICETE 2019 - Volume 2: SECRYPT, Prague, Czech Republic, 26–28 July 2019, pp. 314–321 (2019)

29. Razaghpanah, A., et al.: Apps, trackers, privacy, and regulators: a global study of the mobile tracking ecosystem. In: Network and Distributed System Security Symposium – NDSS (2018)

30. Shklovski, I., Mainwaring, S.D., Skúladóttir, H.H., Borgthorsson, H.: Leakiness and creepiness in app space: perceptions of privacy and mobile app use. In: Conference on Human Factors in Computing Systems – CHI, pp. 2347–2356 (2014)

31. Spreitzer, R., Kirchengast, F., Gruss, D., Mangard, S.: ProcHarvester: fully automated analysis of procfs side-channel leaks on android. In: Asia Conference on Computer and Communications Security – AsiaCCS, pp. 749–763 (2018)

32. Statista: Most popular app monetization methods by publishers from the united states as of december 2023, September 2023. https://www.statista.com/statistics/1119916/app-monetization-methods-united-states-app-publishers/

33. Ferreira Torres, C., Jonker, H.: Investigating fingerprinters and fingerprinting-alike behaviour of android applications. In: Lopez, J., Zhou, J., Soriano, M. (eds.) ESORICS 2018. LNCS, vol. 11099, pp. 60–80. Springer, Cham (2018). https://doi.org/10.1007/978-3-319-98989-1_4

34. Torres, C.F., Jonker, H., Mauw, S.: *FP-Block*: usable web privacy by controlling browser fingerprinting. In: Pernul, G., Ryan, P.Y.A., Weippl, E. (eds.) ESORICS 2015. LNCS, vol. 9327, pp. 3–19. Springer, Cham (2015). https://doi.org/10.1007/978-3-319-24177-7_1

35. Wu, W., Wu, J., Wang, Y., Ling, Z., Yang, M.: Efficient fingerprinting-based android device identification with zero-permission identifiers. IEEE Access **4**, 8073–8083 (2016)

36. Xu, Z., et al.: Automatic hot patch generation for android kernels. In: USENIX Security Symposium, pp. 2397–2414 (2020)

37. Zhang, M., Yin, H.: AppSealer: automatic generation of vulnerability-specific patches for preventing component hijacking attacks in android applications. In: Network and Distributed System Security Symposium – NDSS (2014)

# Privacy and Encryption

# Optimizing Privacy-Preserving Continuous Authentication of Mobile Devices

David Monschein$^{(\boxtimes)}$ (iD) and Oliver P. Waldhorst (iD)

Institute of Data-centric Software Systems (IDSS), Karlsruhe University of Applied Sciences, Karlsruhe, Germany
`{david.monschein,oliver.waldhorst}@h-ka.de`

**Abstract.** In response to the rise of identity theft, continuous authentication based on user behavior (e.g., background sensor data) is emerging as a promising solution. However, in the context of distributed mobile applications, the processing of sensitive data raises serious concerns about user privacy. Existing methods employing homomorphic encryption address this, but face issues with increased network traffic and latency. Therefore, we introduce a novel approach that extends homomorphic encryption-based authentication systems to ensure efficient, continuous, and privacy-preserving authentication. It uses a modern homomorphic encryption scheme and an analysis process that leverages machine learning methods. In the first step, behavioral data is preprocessed on the clients' mobile devices prior to encrypting it and sending it to the server. The server then performs an analysis with neural networks on the encrypted data, which serves as the basis for the authentication decision. We conducted an experiment using real mobile devices and a public dataset to validate our approach's effectiveness, demonstrating competitive authentication accuracy, 32% reduction in network traffic, and over 68% reduction in latency compared to existing research.

**Keywords:** Behavioral Authentication · Machine Learning · Mobile Applications · Homomorphic Encryption · Latency Optimization · Traffic Optimization

## 1 Introduction

In recent years, numerous cases of identity theft, data breaches, and unauthorized access have increased the demand for secure and privacy-preserving authentication methods. In particular, distributed applications with mobile clients require robust authentication, as mobile devices are inherently susceptible to theft, loss, and compromise due to their portability and widespread use. Here, continuous authentication by means of user behavior analysis [33] provides a powerful framework. It leverages the wealth of behavioral data generated on mobile devices through diverse sensors, location data, and interactions [36] to verify the user's identity throughout the application's usage. However, integrating this concept into client-server applications [8] (e.g., social networks or mobile banking services) while protecting user privacy is challenging. The reason for this is that behavioral data (e.g. location data) contains sensitive details and must be processed by the server, as clients cannot be trusted for secure data processing.

As a result, several approaches have emerged that enable the analysis of behavioral data while protecting the user's privacy [39]. In particular, methods relying on homomorphic encryption (HE) [40] are promising, because they prevent the misuse of sensitive information with certainty [39]. These methods involve the mobile client applying HE to behavioral data before sending it to the server. The server then utilizes the homomorphic properties to perform the analysis on encrypted data and finally derives an authentication decision in exchange with the client. In this process, the current behavior is compared to the baseline data of the legitimate user. By ensuring that the server only possesses encrypted data, the confidentiality of sensitive data is maintained throughout the whole authentication process.

However, there are three crucial problems (**P1-P3**). On the one hand, HE results in ciphertexts that comprise a significantly larger amount of data compared to the raw information. Consequently, the arising network traffic increases substantially, which is especially problematic for mobile devices with low network bandwidth (**P1**). On the other hand, HE is limited in the operations supported on encrypted data and highly demanding in terms of computational effort [39]. Therefore, the analysis of encrypted behavioral data causes high latencies for authentication processes (**P2**) and is constrained in its complexity (**P3**). The high latencies result in reduced system responsiveness, which can negatively impact user satisfaction, while the constrained complexity limits the system's ability to recognize more intricate usage patterns. This affects the usability and security characteristics of the respective mobile application.

There are three groups of approaches that try to tackle these problems. The first one makes use of HE schemes that limit the server-side analysis to addition operations [5,6,15,37]. As a consequence, the complexity of the behavioral analysis is constrained and may reduce the authentication accuracy in comparison to ML-based strategies [39]. The second group of approaches combines HE with ML-based behavior analysis [22,24]. Despite excellent authentication accuracy, these transfer raw behavioral data over the network, which is difficult for mobile devices to handle. Additionally, the computational effort involved leads to high latencies. The third group consists of approaches that rely on techniques other than HE for privacy protection [14,17,35,39]. However, these are either vulnerable to attacks on security and privacy [34,38], suffer from increased latency or low recognition rates [39].

In this paper, we propose an approach for privacy-preserving continuous authentication of mobile clients using HE and ML-based analysis of user behavior. To address existing problems, it ensures appropriate latency and network traffic characteristics. Specifically, we employ the Cheon-Kim-Kim-Song (CKKS) HE scheme [10], which has been researched extensively for the application of ML methods to encrypted data [29]. In contrast to existing strategies, we utilize an

ML-based analysis procedure that involves both the client and the server. More precisely, the raw behavioral data is first preprocessed on the client's device with ML techniques. Subsequently, the result of the preprocessing is encrypted and transferred to the server. In this way, the amount of data to be sent can be greatly reduced. In addition, the ML strategies used for preprocessing operate on raw data, which means that they are not limited by the supported HE operations and associated computational load. Finally, the server performs the second part of the ML-based analysis on encrypted data using the homomorphic properties. The analysis result serves as the basis for the authentication decision.

The key contributions can be summarized as follows:

(i) Reducing the required network traffic by preprocessing behavioral data on the client device with ML techniques prior to encryption and transmission to the server (P1).

(ii) Improving authentication latency through a reduction in the number of operations on encrypted data involved in the behavioral analysis performed by the server (P2).

(iii) Enabling the unrestricted use of ML methods within the preprocessing of behavioral data. Thus, the complexity of the behavioral analysis can be increased while maintaining adequate latencies (P2, P3).

In a comprehensive experiment, we evaluated the accuracy, latency, and network traffic characteristics of our approach using a recent dataset [32] that contains behavioral data collected on mobile devices. In doing so, we used three mobile devices to simulate authentication processes. First, we showed that the accuracy of the authentication is close to related work that does not provide any privacy protection. Second, we proved that the preprocessing on the client device is able to reduce the network traffic by 32%. Lastly, we demonstrated that the latency of the authentication can be cut by up to 68% when using our analysis procedure, which offloads preprocessing tasks to the client.

The remainder of this paper is organized as follows. Section 2 introduces related work and its shortcomings. Section 3 describes fundamental concepts, followed by our approach in Sect. 4 and Sect. 5. Section 6 presents the evaluation. Section 7 summarizes key aspects and outlines future work.

## 2   Related Work

The first category of related approaches adopts HE but relies on schemes that only support addition operations. Baig et al. [5,6] proposed multiple protocols for privacy-preserving authentication which are based on the Pallier HE scheme [25]. The behavior analysis relies on distance metrics to enable low latencies for authentication. Wei et al. [37] presented a protocol for the authentication of internet of things devices that also uses the Pallier HE scheme in combination with distance metrics. Govindarajan et al. [15] developed a protocol that uses distance metrics but adopts the DGK HE scheme [12]. Despite authentication latencies of less than a second, these approaches encounter significant challenges. Compared to the CKKS scheme that is used by our approach, both the Pallier HE scheme and the DGK HE scheme are limited to addition operations on encrypted data, which severely limits the complexity of server-side behavioral analysis. This can lead to reduced authentication accuracy [39]. Furthermore [5,15], and [6] do not provide a detailed evaluation of the required network traffic.

The second category includes approaches that combine HE with ML-based analysis for privacy-preserving user authentication. Loya et al. [22] came up with an authentication that utilizes the CKKS HE scheme and simple ML models to analyze keystroke data. Monschein et al. [24] apply the CKKS scheme for privacy-preserving authentication of mobile devices. Their approach makes use of multiple behavioral data sources and neural networks to derive authentication decisions. Nevertheless, both approaches suffer from high volumes of network traffic involved due to sending raw behavioral data from the clients to the server. In addition, the use of ML models on encrypted data leads to authentication latencies averaging more than five seconds. For these reasons, the practical applicability of these approaches is limited.

The third category comprises approaches that use techniques other than HE to protect user privacy within the authentication process. The method of Vassallo et al. [35] aims to remove sensitive details from behavioral data. Smart-CAMPP [16], on the other hand, applies format-preserving encryption. Evaluations of the accuracy of these approaches showed promising results, but the guarantees in terms of security and privacy are much weaker compared to HE-based solutions [20,34,39]. Domingo-Ferrer et al. [14] use private set intersections to compute similarities of behavioral data, e.g., in terms of physical locations. However, the analysis only supports the calculation of similarity scores and is time-consuming, which leads to high latencies. Moreover, approaches for privacy-preserving authentication are summarized in [17,39]. Yet, they face problems regarding network traffic, authentication latency, or authentication accuracy.

## 3  Foundations

### 3.1  Homomorphic Encryption

Homomorphic encryption (HE) [40] is a cryptographic technique that allows computations to be performed on encrypted data without having to decrypt it first. There are various HE schemes that differ in terms of the operations supported and the computational effort involved. For example, the Paillier cryptosystem [25] and DGK [12] only support the addition of ciphertexts (encrypted data). This imposes major restrictions on their usability, which led to the development of fully homomorphic encryption (FHE) schemes [40]. These support an arbitrary number of successive additions and multiplications to be performed on ciphertexts.

Current HE applications focus on the Cheon-Kim-Kim-Song (CKKS) [10] FHE scheme, which is designed for real-number arithmetic. More precisely, it supports approximate arithmetic as it introduces small error terms during the encryption process and upon some operations [10]. Consequently, accurate calculations with CKKS require careful consideration of the error introduced during encryption. Due to its efficiency, it is currently the state-of-the-art HE scheme. With CKKS, each ciphertext consists of multiple slots, while each slot can hold a single numerical value. The number of slots (*slot count*) depends on configuration parameters and typically exceeds 2048. Nevertheless, the ciphertexts comprise a substantially larger amount of data compared to raw numerical values. Furthermore, CKKS is an asymmetric encryption scheme, which means that it uses a key pair consisting of a public key and a secret key. On the one hand, the public key is used for encryption and operations on encrypted data. On the other hand, the secret key is used to decrypt ciphertexts. The numerical operations supported on the encrypted data are limited to slot-wise additions and multiplications. Additionally, the slots within a ciphertext can be rotated, i.e. the content is shifted to the right or left.

### 3.2  Privacy-Preserving Machine Learning

The range of operations supported and the efficiency of FHE schemes allow ML techniques such as neural networks to be applied to encrypted data [39]. This is very attractive for cloud computing scenarios [41], as providers can offer ML services with enhanced data privacy. However, there are limitations due to the computational complexity and the types of operations required. In particular, the training of ML models on encrypted data is currently not feasible [29], and inference times tend to be significantly higher than on raw data. For these reasons, neural networks are initially trained on unencrypted data and then transformed to perform the numerical operations necessary for inference on encrypted data. There are several approaches that speed up inference times through intelligent mapping of the data to the ciphertexts and efficient scheduling of operations [3,13]. Despite these optimizations, designing neural networks with reduced complexity is essential to maintain acceptable inference times [39]. Additionally, well-established activation functions that require computing a maximum of two numbers (e.g., ReLU [4]) are not supported. As a result, a common fallback is to use polynomial approximations of these activation functions [13].

## 4  Approach Overview

Next, we introduce all the building blocks of our approach for optimizing network traffic and latency of privacy-preserving authentication of mobile clients within client-server-based systems. The underlying authentication protocol was adopted from prior work [24]. It is important to note that within the considered threat model, clients may attempt to authenticate as another user, while the server could misuse acquired sensitive information for various purposes (e.g., profiling).

First, the *enrollment* is responsible for collecting baseline data that serves as a reference for legitimate behavior (see Sect. 5.1). Once an initial baseline is established, continuous authentication based on user behavior can be used. We assume that the times at which user authentication is triggered are predefined (e.g., at a fixed frequency). The process that is executed for each behavior-based authentication is summarized in Fig. 1.

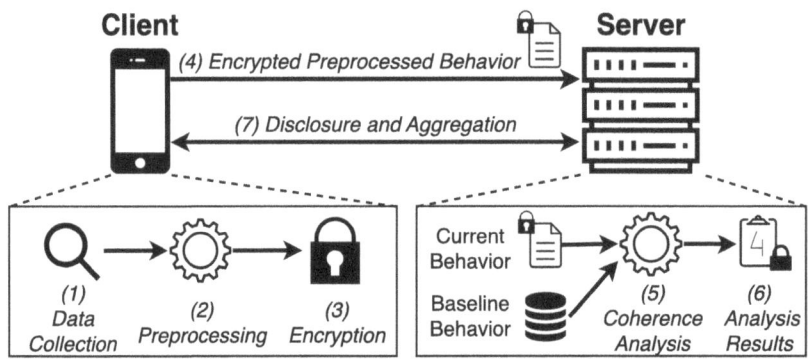

**Fig. 1.** Overview of our approach for privacy-preserving authentication of mobile clients with a two-stage ML-based analysis

At first, it is necessary to collect data that reflects user behavior within the client part of the mobile application. Common data sources that have proven to be suitable for behavior-based authentication include sensor data (e.g., accelerometer) [2,32,33], touchscreen interactions [2,19,33] and location data [2,33]. Each time an authentication process is triggered, the data collection component provides the preprocessing with the behavioral data that was collected since the last authentication (1). In the following, we refer to the periods between two authentications as *segments* of the overarching usage session.

Next, the preprocessing extracts a set of features from the raw behavioral data and then maps the output to a vector of fixed length for each data source (*behavior vector*) (2). The mapping is accomplished by ML techniques, specifically neural networks with LSTM layers [18]. The feature extraction and the structure of the ML models are explained in Sect. 5.2.

The behavior vectors are encrypted using the CKKS HE scheme [10] (3), as it is the most suitable for the use of ML methods on encrypted data [27,29]. Afterwards, the encrypted behavior vectors are transferred to the server (4). As the vectors represent a compressed version of the behavioral data, our approach reduces the amount of data that needs to be encrypted and sent. More details on the encryption and the transmission to the server are presented in Sect. 5.3.

The server then determines separately for each encrypted behavior vector whether it matches the user's baseline data. To this end, the behavior vector is used with behavior vectors collected in previous sessions (baseline) as input for an ML model that performs the *coherence analysis* (5). Recall that all behavior vectors received by the server are encrypted. Therefore, the server can not gain any insights about the behavior, which guarantees user privacy. However, ML model inferences on encrypted data are associated with high computational load (see Sect. 3.2). Hence, the ML models used are lightweight. Their structure is described in Sect. 5.4.

Since the inferences of the ML models are performed on encrypted data using the properties of HE, the results of the coherence analysis (6) are still encrypted. The server does not have access to the secret key and therefore cannot decrypt them by itself. But as it must know the analysis results to make a sound authentication decision, we apply a method that discloses them to the server by an exchange with the client (7) while protecting confidentiality and integrity [7]. Subsequently, the server needs to aggregate the plain results, namely one per data source considered. To do so, we use a compact decision tree, which determines the overall probability of an attacker being present. Additional information on the disclosure and the aggregation of the individual results is provided in Sect. 5.5. Finally, the probability can be used to make the authentication decision. In case the user is authenticated successfully, the behavior vectors are added to the database containing the baseline vectors.

# 5    Continuous Authentication Framework

## 5.1    Enrollment

During the enrollment, behavioral authentication is not available because we lack a baseline of legitimate behavior. There are two ways to obtain such baseline data. The first option is to actively prompt users to perform certain actions. At the same time, the behavior is recorded and saved for subsequent use as a baseline. The second option is to fall back to conventional authentication factors during the enrollment (e.g., passwords). After a sufficient amount of data has been collected, the system can switch to behavior-based authentication. Our approach is independent of the enrollment type, requiring only a specific amount of data to form a baseline, as outlined in Sect. 5.4.

## 5.2    Preprocessing

Figure 2 illustrates the steps involved in preprocessing, which makes up the first stage of our analysis.

For each data source, the raw behavioral data consists of a matrix of numeric values. The rows of the matrix represent the collected data points and the columns reflect the corresponding attributes. For instance, a gravity sensor provides the gravitational force acting on the device along the x, y, and z axes as columns of the matrix. The first step of the preprocessing is the feature extraction which converts the matrix of raw behavioral data into another matrix with each column representing a feature and each row representing one series of features. For feature extraction, we rely on existing literature [19, 28]. For instance, we group sensor data within fixed time intervals and then calculate peak values, percentiles, and spectral energy [28].

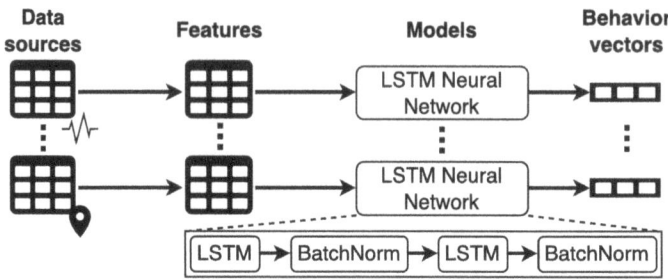

**Fig. 2.** Outline of all steps involved in preprocessing behavioral data

Following the feature extraction, each feature matrix is used as input for a neural network that outputs a vector of fixed length (*behavior vector*). To do so, we rely on long short-term memory layers (LSTM) [18], as these are effective in capturing temporal dependencies and patterns within behavioral data [1]. The concrete structure of the models is inspired by the autoencoder architecture [21] and comprises two LSTM layers, each followed by a batch normalization layer (see Fig. 2). The size of the LSTM layers can be varied, which can be useful when considering different data sources. In addition, the size of the second LSTM layer determines the size of the behavior vector, which in turn affects the network traffic required. Details on the training of the models are presented in Sect. 5.6.

### 5.3   Encryption and Transmission

Prior to sending data the behavior vectors to the server, they need to be encrypted by the client using his public key. As mentioned before, we use the CKKS HE scheme, where each ciphertext has a fixed number of slots, each of which contains a numeric value (see Sect. 3.1). For this reason, there are several ways to map the behavior vectors to ciphertexts. Our goal is to minimize the number of ciphertexts required because these determine the arising network traffic. Therefore, we store the behavior vectors one after the other in the slots of the ciphertexts. A new ciphertext is only established if a behavior vector does not fit into an existing ciphertext.

As a result, the number of ciphertexts required depends on the size of the behavior vectors and the slot count of the ciphertexts. After the encryption has been completed, the ciphertexts are transferred to the server.

### 5.4   Coherence Analysis

Once the server receives the encrypted behavior vectors from the client, it initiates an ML-based analysis to verify that the current behavior matches the known behavior of the legitimate user. Here, all data sources are evaluated separately, which means that the individual behavior vectors must first be isolated from the joint ciphertext. This is accomplished by using multiplications to separate and extract the individual vectors from the encrypted data. Next, the server applies an analysis process to each encrypted behavior vector.

To this end, the server first samples a configurable number (*history size*) of encrypted behavior vectors from previous sessions (baseline data). By default, the most recent behavior vectors are selected, although other sampling methods can be utilized (e.g., random sampling). Together with the current encrypted behavior vector they are used as input for the second stage of our analysis, which consists of one neural network per data source. Therefore, the history size determines the minimum extent of the baseline data required for behavior-based authentication. The structure of the neural networks is simple, as it involves four consecutive dense layers [4]. The number of units of the first three layers is configurable, while the last layer consists of one unit which outputs the probability of an attacker being present. As the neural networks need to be carried out on encrypted data, commonly used activation functions are not available (see Sect. 3.2). Consequently, we use $x^2 + x$ as activation function for the first three layers as recommended by existing work [13]. The last dense layer has no activation function since we can apply it to the plain data later. In order to optimize the execution time of the ML inferences we use existing techniques that minimize the number of HE operations required [3,13]. The process for training the ML models is explained in Sect. 5.6.

Finally, we end up with one ciphertext per behavior vector received, which contains the result of the respective neural network inference. However, these results cannot be interpreted as such, because they can only be decrypted with the secret key of the client. As a result, we require an exchange between the client and the server to disclose the computed results securely, which is explained in the following Sect. 5.5.

## 5.5   Disclosure and Aggregation

For disclosing the results of the neural networks, we adopt the strategy of Baumstark et al. [7], which basically adds another layer of encryption to CKKS ciphertexts before sending them to the client. Thereafter, the client decrypts the ciphertext using his secret key, but there remains another level of encryption, which prevents him from manipulating and inspecting the analysis results. Thus, the integrity and the confidentiality of the results are protected [7]. To avoid multiple exchanges, we combine all analysis results into one ciphertext before disclosing them.

The server ends up with one numerical value per data source. These values correspond to the results of the neural network inferences on the encrypted data. At this point, we catch up with the activation function, meaning that we apply the sigmoid function $\sigma(z) = \frac{1}{1+e^{-z}}$ to all results. This normalizes them to values between 0 and 1, representing the attack probability.

Ultimately, we need to aggregate the probabilities that we obtain for the different data sources. To do so, we implement a decision tree, which is trained together with the other ML models as described in Sect. 5.6. The final result constitutes an aggregated probability of whether the current client is an attacker, which can be used to make an authentication decision. If the user is successfully authenticated, the encrypted behavior vectors received from the client are added to the baseline data. Therefore, it is possible to incorporate changes in the user's behavior and thus prevent them from leading to incorrect decisions over time.

## 5.6   Model Training

Our approach relies on a composite neural network for each data source, consisting of the preprocessing part and the coherence analysis part. On top of that, a decision tree is required to aggregate the results obtained for the different data sources. To train the models we chain both analysis stages, which is demonstrated in Fig. 3.

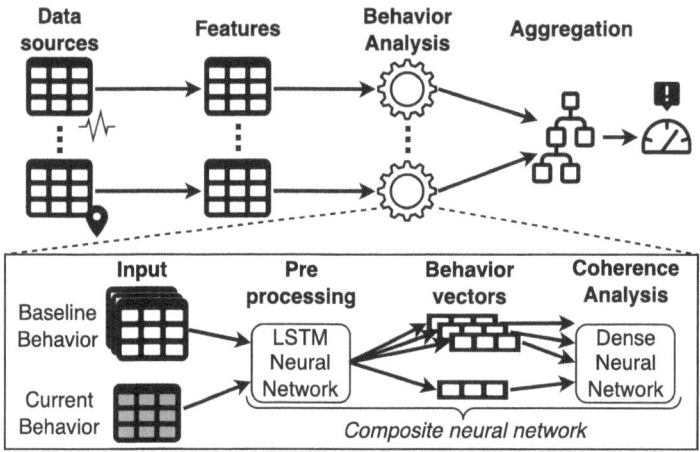

**Fig. 3.** Illustration of the training process of the ML models

Before the ML models can be trained, proper input data must be prepared. This is done separately for each data source. Initially, features are extracted from the raw data as described in Sect. 5.2. Next, we split the user sessions into segments that span a fixed period of time (e.g., one minute). Then we generate an input sample out of each segment by attaching a predefined number of segments from previous sessions (baseline behavior). The number of segments used as a baseline depends on the history size introduced in Sect. 5.4. However, with this strategy, we can only generate samples for the case of a legitimate user being present. For this reason, we artificially generate additional samples that represent an attack by keeping the baseline data the same and replacing the current segment with that of a different user. To make the attack as sophisticated as possible, we look for another user's segment that is similar to the original segment. This is realized by using the Earth mover's distance [26] as a metric that quantifies the similarity of two segments.

Lastly, the generated samples, which include both legitimate use and attacks, are used to train a composite neural network per data source consisting of pre-processing and coherence analysis. Once the training is complete, the decision tree used to aggregate the results is trained based on the output of the neural networks. In the final step, the composite neural network is divided into the two distinct parts, which can then be deployed on the client and the server.

# 6   Evaluation

## 6.1   Evaluation Setup

Our evaluation examines the characteristics of our approach from three different perspectives. The first is the accuracy of authentication, which is critical to ensuring adequate security. The second is the amount of network traffic involved, which must be manageable even for mobile devices that tend to have slower network connections. The third is the latency of the authentication process, which is essential for fast and responsive user access. As a result, we can assess whether our approach is making the intended contributions.

*Dataset Description.* To obtain insights about these three aspects we setup and test our approach using the BehavePassDB dataset [32]. It contains behavioral data collected on mobile devices of real users. In a controlled environment, users were requested to complete four different tasks, e.g., reading through a text or swiping through pictures. While the users were completing the tasks, touch gestures and background sensor data (magnetometer, accelerometer, gyroscope, and gravity sensor) were captured. Overall, the dataset comprises 81 users and also covers attack scenarios, making it a popular benchmark. More specifically, it includes random and skilled imposter scenarios. In a random imposter scenario, the attacker uses a different device and has no information about the legitimate user's behavior. On the other hand, in a skilled impersonation scenario, the attacker uses the legitimate user's device and attempts to mimic legitimate behavior [32]. Moreover, the dataset is split into three subsets:

- **Training Set:** Contains behavioral data from 51 users divided into multiple sessions per user/task. However, it does not include any attacker scenario.
- **Validation Set:** Covers behavioral data from 10 users with two sessions per user/task and incorporates random as well as skilled imposter scenarios. In addition, labels are attached to the sessions which represent the ground truth of whether an attacker was present or not.
- **Test Set:** Includes behavioral data from 20 users with two sessions per user/task and both types of imposter scenarios. The labels are not publicly available and insights about accuracy metrics require uploading predictions to a challenge platform[1].

---

[1] https://codalab.lisn.upsaclay.fr/competitions/3564.

*Experiment Setup.* We use the BehavePassDB [32] to simulate a continuous authentication setting where authentication is triggered every minute during the usage sessions. Accordingly, we first split the user sessions from all subsets of the dataset into segments of one minute. We then use the data of each segment to perform an authentication process. In doing so, the client carries out the preprocessing, encrypts the resulting behavior vectors, and sends the encrypted data to the server. Subsequently, the server executes the coherence analysis, performs the disclosure, and aggregates the results (see Fig. 1). The baseline data needed for the coherence analysis is explicitly referenced in the BehavePassDB dataset for each session [32]. To evaluate the characteristics of our approach in practice, we run the experiment on three different mobile devices that act as clients: an *iPhone 13 Pro*, a *Google Pixel 7 Pro*, and a *Samsung Galaxy S22*. As hardware for the server, we use a Microsoft Azure D8_v5 cloud system, which comprises 8 vCPUs and 32 GB RAM.

*Authentication Framework Configuration.* Before running the experiment, we need to train the ML models required for preprocessing, coherence analysis, and aggregation. To do so, we use the procedure from Sect. 5.6 and the ML framework Keras [11]. Moreover, for training the ML models, we rely on the training set. The validation set is used to select the models with the best performance. The layer configurations of the neural networks are (cf. Sect. 5):

– **Preprocessing**: The first LSTM layer has 144 units and the second LSTM layer has 128 units. Thus, the size of the behavior vectors corresponds to 128 numerical values.
– **Coherence Analysis**: The history size equals three segments that are used as baseline input (see Sect. 5.4). In addition, the first dense layer has 196 units, the second one has 96 units and the third one has 32 units.

The decision trees for aggregating the results from multiple data sources are implemented using XGBoost [9]. Furthermore, we slightly extend them, so that they are able to receive an arbitrary number of results for each data source. Accordingly, we can not only aggregate results within one segment but within an entire session. In total, we establish 12 neural networks (two per data source) and one decision tree (cf. Sect. 5.6). To run the neural networks on mobile devices during preprocessing, we make use of Tensorflow.js [31].

Apart from the ML models, we employ Microsoft SEAL [30] as HE library. We select parameters for the configuration of CKKS that have been tested for machine learning inferences on encrypted data [3,13]. With this configuration, each ciphertext consists of 4096 slots. To optimize the inference times of the coherence analysis on the encrypted data, we use Microsoft EVA [13].

*Metrics and Measurements.* In order to quantify the effectiveness of our approach, we perform several measurements within the experiment. These can be broken down according to the aspect of our approach that is to be investigated:

1. **Accuracy:** Since we can use our approach to predict the labels of the sessions within the test dataset, we get reliable information about the accuracy

by submitting the results to the official platform. We obtain the area under the curve (AUC) metric [4], broken down by task and scenario. The AUC metric quantifies a classification model's ability to discriminate between positive and negative classes, offering a comprehensive assessment of its performance. Furthermore, validating our approach against the test set has two key advantages. First, the results show whether our ML models generalize well and second, the accuracy can be easily compared to related work. In this way, we are able to substantiate *contribution (iii)* of our approach.

2. **Network Traffic:** The authentication process of our approach involves two exchanges between the client and the server. The first one for sending encrypted behavioral data to the server and the second one for the disclosure of the analysis results. We only measure the amount of bytes that need to be transferred in the first exchange, as the disclosure process was already evaluated extensively [7]. In addition, we compare the results to the transmission of raw behavioral data to confirm *contribution (i)*.

3. **Latency:** The authentication latency depends on the execution times of the individual components. Within the experiment, we record each authentication process and collect the completion times for all components executed by the client and the server. In this way, we are able to calculate the overall latency. Here, we exclude the process for the disclosure, as it has already been tested thoroughly [7], and the time required for transmission, as it heavily depends on the network connection. Additionally, by running the experiment on different mobile devices, we gain insights into the latency in real-world scenarios. Along with comparisons to the latency of related strategies, we can support *contribution (ii)* and *contribution (iii)* of our approach.

Besides, we repeat the whole experiment ten times to obtain robust results. For authentication accuracy, we considered the median value of the results achieved, as it provides a more reliable central tendency and reduces the influence of outliers. For all other aspects, we considered the full set of measurements from each run to ensure that the full range of data was included in our analysis.

## 6.2  Authentication Accuracy

We investigated the authentication accuracy of our approach on the test set of the BehavePassDB [32]. Table 1 shows the AUC scores for the different tasks of the dataset and the scenario considered. It differentiates between a mixed case scenario, which considers both attack scenarios and legitimate use, a random case scenario, which only considers random attackers and a skilled case scenario, which only considers skilled attackers (see Sect. 6.1). The table also includes the results of a reference implementation published with the dataset [32]. The reference implementation currently achieves the best results of any related work, but lacks support for any privacy protection.

Our approach achieves slightly lower AUC scores across all tasks compared to the reference implementation. However, we provide strong protection of user privacy. Furthermore, our approach ranks second among all studies that have

**Table 1.** AUC scores for different tasks and attacker types compared to reference implementation [32] (MC = Mixed Case, RC = Random Case, SC = Skilled Case)

| Method | Task 1 - Keystroke | | | Task 2 - Text Reading | | |
|---|---|---|---|---|---|---|
| | MC | RC | SC | MC | RC | SC |
| Reference | 77.5586 | 86.3828 | 68.7344 | 71.4141 | 77.0156 | 65.8125 |
| *Our approach* | 75.8711 | 85.8594 | 65.8828 | 69.4219 | 76.4531 | 62.3906 |
| | Task 3 - Gallery Swiping | | | Task 4 - Tapping | | |
| Reference | 72.8867 | 81.0859 | 64.6875 | 69.8594 | 78.5000 | 61.2188 |
| *Our approach* | 67.4297 | 77.7578 | 57.1016 | 61.0430 | 69.4375 | 52.6484 |

benchmarked their predictions. Beyond that, all AUC scores indicate that the dataset poses a difficult challenge, as they are significantly lower compared to the performance of behavior-based authentication on other datasets [23,33]. This is due to the fact that the dataset accounts for strong attackers and that there is a very limited number of sessions per user. To summarize, the results indicate that our analysis approach is able to keep up with the state of the art technologies in terms of authentication accuracy. In addition, our strategy for training the ML models (see Sect. 5.6) has proven to be effective.

### 6.3   Network Traffic

We examined the network traffic generated across all subsets of the dataset (see Sect. 6.1). As mentioned before, we focus on the traffic generated by the transfer of the encrypted behavioral data. It turned out that we always need to transfer about **442 KB**, which is the size of a ciphertext with our CKKS configuration. The reason for this is that we end up with a maximum of six behavior vectors, and each of them consists of 128 numeric values. Therefore, all behavior vectors fit into a ciphertext that has 4096 slots.

On the contrary, if we were to send the encrypted form of the raw behavioral features to the server, we would have to transfer about **656 KB** of data on average (min: 442 KB, max: 1327 KB). Thus, the mean saving in network traffic equals 214 KB, which corresponds to a **32.62% reduction**. Additionally, there would be room to extend the size of the behavior vectors without increasing network traffic.

In summary, our approach is able to reduce the size of the encrypted behavioral data in our experiment by **32%**. As we consider continuous authentication environments, this is even more important, because we save network traffic on each authentication process. Consequently, the load on a mobile device's network connection can be greatly reduced.

## 6.4    Authentication Latency

We measured the execution times of the individual components of our approach per authentication process. Since we consider three different client devices, we obtain three distributions for the execution times of each component executed by the client device. It follows that we get only one distribution for the components executed by the server. Figure 4 shows all distributions of the execution times as box plots, broken down by component and hardware on which it was executed. In addition, it includes the distribution of the overall latency per client device.

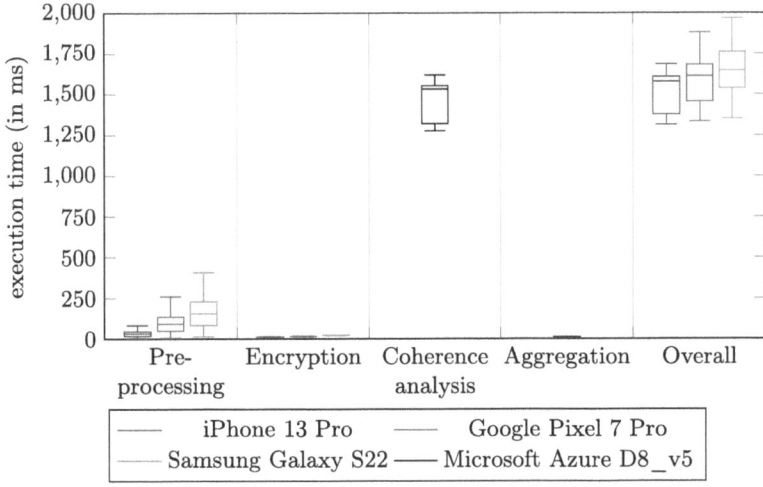

**Fig. 4.** Visualization of the execution times in the experiment, broken down by the individual components of our approach and by the hardware used

It becomes clear that the overall latency is dominated by the coherence analysis. On average, it needs about 1.4 s for execution. This is because the inferences of the neural networks on encrypted data involve a high computational effort [29]. The execution time of the preprocessing, which is performed on the client device, depends on the hardware it is running on. For the iPhone, it takes 32.42 milliseconds (ms) on average, while on the Google Pixel 7 Pro it needs 94 ms on average and on the Samsung Galaxy S22 it requires about 159 ms on average. The encryption of the behavior vectors also takes longer on the Google Pixel 7 Pro and the Samsung Galaxy S22, but is negligible on all mobile devices with an average execution time of 10.97 ms (iPhone 13 Pro), 13.33 ms (Google Pixel 7 Pro) and 20.76 ms (Samsung Galaxy S22). The same applies to the aggregation task that is carried out by the server, which requires on average 7.17 ms to complete. In total, the latency of an entire authentication process did never exceed two seconds. More precisely, the mean latency of an authentication amounts to **1.642 s** on the Samsung Galaxy S22, **1.571 s** on the Google Pixel 7 Pro and **1.506** seconds on the iPhone 13 Pro.

In comparison to related work that combines HE with ML for user authentication, these results represent a significant enhancement. Loya et al. [22] and Monschein et al. [24] benchmarked the analysis of encrypted behavioral data and achieved average execution times of 14.21 and 5.16 s, respectively. Despite they are using different datasets, their setting is similar and it is to be expected that our approach delivers consistent results for different environments. The reason for this is that the latency of our approach is not sensitive to the amount of behavioral data generated, since the preprocessing is done on unencrypted data. Figure 4 emphasizes that mobile devices can accomplish this task efficiently. Therefore, it can be stated that our approach is able to cut the latency of the authentication **by at least 68%** compared to existing strategies.

# 7    Conclusion and Future Work

In this paper, we presented an innovative approach that improves the latency and network traffic characteristics of privacy-preserving authentication involving homomorphic encryption and machine learning techniques. It targets client-server-based applications [8] with mobile clients and utilizes behavioral data, such as touchscreen gestures and sensor data, to authenticate users. In this context, it addresses shortcomings of existing work by reducing network traffic and latency while preserving accuracy and analytical complexity. It employs an analysis that makes use of machine learning techniques and the Cheon-Kim-Kim-Song (CKKS) homomorphic encryption scheme [10]. In the first stage, raw behavioral data is preprocessed on the client's device using neural networks. As a result, we significantly reduce data transmission requirements. For the second stage, the server performs inferences of machine learning models directly on the encrypted data, leveraging the homomorphic properties of the CKKS scheme [13]. Here, we avoid a lot of expensive operations on encrypted data through the preceding preprocessing step which leads to improved authentication latency.

The evaluation is based on the recent BehavePassDB dataset [32], which was specifically designed for building and testing behavior-based authentication systems. We set up an extensive experiment in which we simulated authentication processes on three popular mobile devices. First of all, our approach demonstrated comparable authentication accuracy to methods that do not consider user privacy and ranked second out of all the studies that evaluated their performance on the same dataset. Second, we showed that our analysis procedure is able to reduce the network traffic for transferring encrypted behavioral data by 32%. Lastly, we observed a significant improvement of at least 68% in terms of authentication latency compared to systems that process all behavioral data in encrypted form on the server side.

While our proposed approach has shown promising results, there are several avenues for future research and improvement. It has to be investigated whether the preprocessing has an impact on the security characteristics of the authentication, as it may be easier to forge preprocessed data instead of raw behavioral data. In addition, our strategy could be rolled out to cloud computing services that build on the combination of homomorphic encryption and machine learning to improve their latency and network traffic requirements. Finally, we are planning an evaluation within a real-world mobile application, which is intended to substantiate the practical applicability.

**Acknowledgments.** This work was supported by the projects KIWI (16KIS1142K) funded by the German Federal Ministry of Education and Research (BMBF), the state projects bwNET2020+/bwNET2.0 funded by the Ministry of Science, Research and Arts Baden-Württemberg (MWK), and the aura.ai project co-funded by the European Union through the Interreg Upper Rhine program.

**Disclosure of Interests.** The authors have no competing interests to declare that are relevant to the content of this article.

# References

1. Acien, A., Morales, A., Monaco, J.V., Vera-Rodríguez, R., Fiérrez, J.: TypeNet: deep learning keystroke biometrics. IEEE Trans. Biometrics, Behav. Identity Sci.**4**, 57–70 (2021)
2. Acien, A., Morales, A., Vera-Rodríguez, R., Fiérrez, J.: MultiLock: mobile active authentication based on multiple biometric and behavioral patterns. In: Proceedings of the 1st International Workshop on Multimodal Understanding and Learning for Embodied Applications, Nice, France, pp. 53–59 (2019)
3. Aharoni, E., et al.: HeLayers: a tile tensors framework for large neural networks on encrypted data. In: Proceedings of the 23rd Privacy Enhancing Technology Symposium, Lausanne, Switzerland, pp. 325–342 (2023)
4. Alzubaidi, L., et al.: Review of deep learning: concepts, CNN architectures, challenges, applications, future directions. Big Data **8**(1), 53 (2021)
5. Baig, A.F., Eskeland, S., Yang, B.: Privacy-preserving continuous authentication using behavioral biometrics. Springer Inf. Secur. **22**, 1833–1847 (2023)
6. Baig, A.F., Eskeland, S., Yang, B.: Novel and efficient privacy-preserving continuous authentication. MDPI Cryptogr. **8**(1), 3 (2024)
7. Baumstark, P., Monschein, D., Waldhorst, O.P.: Secure plaintext acquisition of homomorphically encrypted results for remote processing. In: Proceedings of the 48th IEEE Conference on Local Computer Networks, Daytona Beach, FL, USA (2023)
8. Berson, A.: Client/Server Architecture. McGraw-Hill, New York (1992)
9. Chen, T., Guestrin, C.: XGBoost: a scalable tree boosting system. In: Proceedings of the 22nd ACM SIGKDD International Conference on Knowledge Discovery and Data Mining, San Francisco, CA, USA, pp. 785–794 (2016)
10. Cheon, J.H., Kim, A., Kim, M., Song, Y.: Homomorphic encryption for arithmetic of approximate numbers. In: Proceedings of the 23rd International Conference on Theory and Application of Cryptology and Information Security, Hong Kong, China, pp. 409–437 (2017)
11. Chollet, F., et al.: Keras (2015). https://keras.io
12. Damgard, I., Geisler, M., Kroigard, M.: Homomorphic encryption and secure comparison. Appl. Cryptogr. **1**(1), 22–31 (2008)

13. Dathathri, R., Kostova, B., Saarikivi, O., Dai, W., Laine, K., Musuvathi, M.: EVA: an encrypted vector arithmetic language and compiler for efficient homomorphic computation. In: Proceedings of the 41st ACM SIGPLAN Conference on Programming Language Design and Implementation, London, UK, pp. 546–561 (2020)
14. Domingo-Ferrer, J., Wu, Q., Blanco-Justicia, A.: Flexible and robust privacy-preserving implicit authentication. In: Proceedings of the 30th IFIP TC 11 International Conference on ICT Systems Security and Privacy Protection, Hamburg, Germany, pp. 18–34 (2015)
15. Govindarajan, S., Gasti, P., Balagani, K.S.: Secure privacy-preserving protocols for outsourcing continuous authentication of smartphone users with touch data. In: Proceedings of the 6th IEEE International Conference on Biometrics: Theory, Applications and Systems, Washington, DC, USA, pp. 1–8 (2013)
16. Hernández-Álvarez, L., de Fuentes, J.M., González-Manzano, L., Hernández Encinas, L.: SmartCAMPP - smartphone-based continuous authentication leveraging motion sensors with privacy preservation. Elsevier Pattern Recognit. Lett. **147**, 189–196 (2021)
17. Hernández-Álvarez, L., de Fuentes, J.M., González-Manzano, L., Hernández Encinas, L.: Privacy-preserving sensor-based continuous authentication and user profiling: a review. MDPI Sens. **21**(1), 92 (2021)
18. Hochreiter, S., Schmidhuber, J.: Long short-term memory. Neural Comput. **9**(8), 1735–1780 (1997)
19. Karanikiotis, T., Papamichail, M.D., Chatzidimitriou, K.C., Oikonomou, N.C.I., Symeonidis, A.L., Saripalle, S.K.: Continuous implicit authentication through touch traces modelling. In: Proceedings of the 20th IEEE International Conference on Software Quality, Reliability and Security, Macau, China, pp. 111–120 (2020)
20. Lacharme, P., Cherrier, E., Rosenberger, C.: Preimage attack on biohashing. In: Proceedings of the International Conference on Security and Cryptography, Reykjavík, Iceland, pp. 1–8 (2013)
21. Li, P., Pei, Y., Li, J.: A comprehensive survey on design and application of autoencoder in deep learning. Appl. Soft Comput. **138** (2023)
22. Loya, J., Bana, T.: Privacy-preserving keystroke analysis using fully homomorphic encryption & differential privacy. In: Proceedings of the IEEE International Conference on Cyberworlds, pp. 291–294 (2021)
23. Monschein, D., Waldhorst, O.P.: SPCAuth: scalable and privacy-preserving continuous authentication for web applications. In: Proceedings of the 46th IEEE Conference on Local Computer Networks (LCN), pp. 281–286. Virtual Conf. (2021)
24. Monschein, D., Waldhorst, O.P.: mPSAuth: privacy-preserving and scalable authentication for mobile web applications (2022). https://arxiv.org/abs/2210.04777
25. Paillier, P.: Public-key cryptosystems based on composite degree residuosity classes. In: Proceedings of the 17th IACR Eurocrypt Conference, Prague, Czech Republic, pp. 223–238 (1999)
26. Pele, O., Werman, M.: Fast and robust earth mover's distances. In: Proceedings of the 12th IEEE International Conference on Computer Vision, Kyoto, Japan, pp. 460–467 (2009)
27. Podschwadt, R., Takabi, D., Hu, P., Rafiei, M.H., Cai, Z.: A survey of deep learning architectures for privacy-preserving machine learning with fully homomorphic encryption. IEEE Access **10**, 117477–117500 (2022)

28. Preece, S.J., Goulermas, J.Y., Kenney, L.P.J., Howard, D.: A comparison of feature extraction methods for the classification of dynamic activities from accelerometer data. IEEE Trans. Biomed. Eng. **56**(3), 871–879 (2009)

29. Pulido-Gaytan, L.B., Tchernykh, A., Cortés-Mendoza, J.M., Babenko, M., Radchenko, G.: A survey on privacy-preserving machine learning with fully homomorphic encryption. In: Proceedings of the Latin America High Performance Computing Conference, Guadalajara, Mexico, pp. 115–129 (2021)

30. Microsoft SEAL (release 4.1), January 2023. https://github.com/Microsoft/SEAL

31. Smilkov, D., et al.: Tensorflow.js: machine learning for the web and beyond. In: Proceedings of the Machine Learning and Systems, Stanford, CA, USA, pp. 309–321 (2019)

32. Stragapede, G., Vera-Rodriguez, R., Tolosana, R., Morales, A.: BehavePassDB: public database for mobile behavioral biometrics and benchmark evaluation. Pattern Recognit. **134**(C) (2023)

33. Stylios, I., Kokolakis, S., Thanou, O., Chatzis, S.: Behavioral biometrics & continuous user authentication on mobile devices: a survey. Inf. Fusion **66**, 76–99 (2021)

34. Topcu, B., Karabat, C., Azadmanesh, M., Erdogan, H.: Practical security and privacy attacks against biometric hashing using sparse recovery. EURASIP Adv. Signal Process. (2016)

35. Vassallo, G., Van hamme, T., Preuveneers, D., Joosen, W.: Privacy-preserving behavioral authentication on smartphones. In: Proceedings of the 1st Inter4national Workshop on Human-Centered Sensing, Networking, and Systems, Delft, Netherlands, pp. 1–6 (2017)

36. Wang, C., Wang, Y., Chen, Y., Liu, H., Liu, J.: User authentication on mobile devices: approaches, threats and trends. Comput. Netw. **170** (2020)

37. Wei, F., Vijayakumar, P., Kumar, N., Zhang, R., Cheng, Q.: Privacy-preserving implicit authentication protocol using cosine similarity for internet of things. IEEE Internet Things J. **8**(7), 5599–5606 (2021)

38. Wu, Y., et al.: Attacks and countermeasures on privacy-preserving biometric authentication schemes. IEEE Trans. Depend. Secure Comput. **20**(2), 1744–1755 (2023)

39. Yang, W., Wang, S., Cui, H., Tang, Z., Li, Y.: A review of homomorphic encryption for privacy-preserving biometrics. MDPI Sensors **23**(7), 3566 (2023)

40. Yi, X., Paulet, R., Bertino, E.: Homomorphic encryption. In: Homomorphic Encryption and Applications, pp. 27–46. Springer, Cham (2014). https://doi.org/10.1007/978-3-319-12229-8_2

41. Zhao, E.M., Geng, Y.: Homomorphic encryption technology for cloud computing. Procedia Comput. Sci. **154**, 73–83 (2019)

# PPDL: Efficient Dropout-Resilient Aggregation for Privacy-Preserving Decentralized Learning

Ali Reza Ghavamipour[1]([✉])[iD], Benjamin Zi Hao Zhao[2]([✉])[iD], and Fatih Turkmen[1]([✉])[iD]

[1] University of Groningen, Groningen, The Netherlands
{a.r.ghavamipour,f.turkmen}@rug.nl
[2] Macquarie University, Sydney, Australia
ben_zi.zhao@mq.edu.au

**Abstract.** Decentralized learning (DL) offers a novel paradigm in machine learning by distributing training across clients without central aggregation, enhancing scalability and efficiency. However, DL's peer-to-peer model introduces unique challenges in protecting machine learning models against inference attacks and privacy leaks. By forgoing central bottlenecks, DL demands privacy-preserving aggregation methods to protect data from 'honest but curious' clients and adversaries, maintaining network-wide privacy. Privacy-preserving DL faces the additional hurdle of client dropout, clients not submitting updates due to connectivity problems or unavailability, further complicating the aggregation. In this paper, we propose three secret sharing-based dropout resilience protocols for privacy-preserving DL. We evaluate the efficiency, performance, and accuracy of these protocols through experiments on open datasets MNIST, Fashion-MNIST, SVHN, and CIFAR-10. We also compare our protocols with traditional secret-sharing solutions including a scenario that contains up to 1000 clients. Evaluations show that our protocols significantly outperform conventional methods, especially in scenarios with up to 30% of clients dropping out and model sizes of up to $10^6$ parameters. Our proposals demonstrate significantly high efficiency with larger models, higher dropout rates, and extensive client networks, highlighting their effectiveness in enhancing decentralized learning systems' privacy and dropout robustness.

## 1 Introduction

Machine learning (ML) has become a pivotal component in numerous applications, including pattern recognition, medical diagnosis, and credit risk assessment. The effectiveness of a machine learning model is heavily dependent on the availability of large volumes of data. The conventional method of training a machine learning model involves collecting a dataset on a central server and conducting the training process on this server. However, centralization poses difficulties when the data is distributed over numerous devices or among a workforce that are located in different geographical regions. This issue is compounded by growing concerns over data privacy. To address these challenges, researchers have suggested alternative approaches to centralized learning under the umbrella term Collaborative Machine Learning (CML). CML enables the training of machine learning models directly on local devices to enhance privacy (by maintaining data locality) and offload compute demand (away from the central server) [27].

Federated Learning (FL) [30], a key example of CML, has garnered notable interest across academia and industry. It decentralizes the training process across multiple clients, ranging from mobile devices to data centers, under the coordination of a central server. Clients locally update the model using their data, then share these updates with the server, which aggregates them for distribution. While FL facilitates training in novel contexts, it relies heavily on a central server, introducing risks like a single point of failure and challenges in maintaining model integrity and data privacy [7].

Decentralized Learning (DL) [4, 22, 24, 28] emerged as a popular, scalable, and communication-efficient alternative to traditional CML algorithms. Unlike FL methods, DL operates without a central aggregator, thereby mitigating integrity and privacy risks associated with the central server in FL, and more importantly avoiding a (potentially untrusted) single point of failure. DL achieves global model training through on-device aggregation of model parameters, facilitated by peer-to-peer exchanges among clients [21]. This process, akin to gossip-based algorithms in random networks eliminates the need for centralized aggregation. In DL, each client plays an active role in updating its model using both local data and updates from its peers, leading to improvements in model accuracy and faster convergence.

As we have established, the practice of sharing model updates instead of raw datasets mitigates privacy concerns related to the centralization of data for learning. Unfortunately, CML retain risks of private information leakage [6, 41], as a passive adversary can infer sample membership [36, 47] and reconstruct training data [29] from the shared updates of honest users. Moreover, DL systems are especially susceptible to said privacy risk, as the architecture of DL requires all clients to share their updates with every other client for aggregation, thereby providing any client the opportunity to launch the aforementioned privacy attacks [33].

To mitigate these privacy concerns, secure aggregation is proposed to prevent the aggregator(s) from inferring private data from local model updates [13, 17–19, 37]. However, implementing secure aggregation faces implementation challenges because of client dropout (as depicted in Fig. 1). The issue of Dropout arises when a client fails to submit its model updates or cannot participate in the secure aggregation procedure due to poor network connections, energy constraints, or temporary unavailability. Such dropout can disrupt the secure aggregation process, necessitating a restart of the round, potentially leading to a Denial of Service (DoS) effect on model training.

In this work, we introduce three novel secret sharing-based protocols designed for privacy-preserving aggregation within decentralized learning environments.

These protocols enable dropout-resilient aggregation, merging clients' local models into a global model while ensuring the privacy of individual data contributions. Our approaches not only effectively mitigate privacy risks posed by 'honest but curious' clients but also uphold the integrity of the learning process despite varying levels of client participation, thereby enhancing dropout resilience. The underlying techniques are inspired by their proven effectiveness in federated learning. However, our contribution lies in adapting and refining these techniques to address the unique challenges of secure decentralized learning. This adaptation extends their applicability and enhances the privacy and security framework of the learning process, especially by incorporating mechanisms for dropout resilience. To validate the effectiveness of our proposed protocols, we conducted a comprehensive evaluation across multiple datasets, demonstrating their robustness and scalability in diverse learning scenarios.

## 2    Related Work

Research on privacy-preserving and dropout-resilient FL is extensive, yet studies tackling similar issues in DL are notably fewer [33]. In this respect, PPDL stands out as the first to directly address dropout challenges in the realm of privacy-enhanced DL.

In the context of FL, various strategies have been developed for performing privacy-preserving aggregation with a limited outlook on resiliency to client dropout. Most existing works focus on combining federated training with Differential Privacy (DP) [12], Homomorphic Encryption (HE) [15], and secure Multi-Party Computation (MPC) [10]. Since dropout has an impact on the privacy protection mechanism employed in the aggregation method, highlighting the differences between these methodologies in terms of privacy guarantees, efficiency, and the implementation challenges is important.

Approaches employing homomorphic encryption result in significant performance overheads [40]. This technique requires all clients to either share a common secret key or hold shares of a secret key [1,45]. These shares must be generated through complex multi-party protocols or distributed by a trusted third party [40], which results in prohibitive overheads for large-scale CML systems [46]. Moreover, supporting dropout resilience in conjunction with homomorphic encryption poses an additional challenge, as it requires sophisticated mechanisms to handle the potential discontinuity in participation without compromising the security or the integrity of the aggregated model updates [39].

As a more scalable and dropout-resistant alternative, MPC has been proposed [8]. In this model, users' data is masked, with the seeds for generating these masks securely distributed among the users through a threshold secret-sharing scheme to manage client dropouts. An improvement on this approach, [2] replaces the complete communication graph with a $k$-regular graph (i.e., every vertex having a degree of $k$), reducing communication overhead. A DP-based FL method has been introduced where noise is added to each client's locally trained model before aggregation [16], effectively masking the data distribution of the

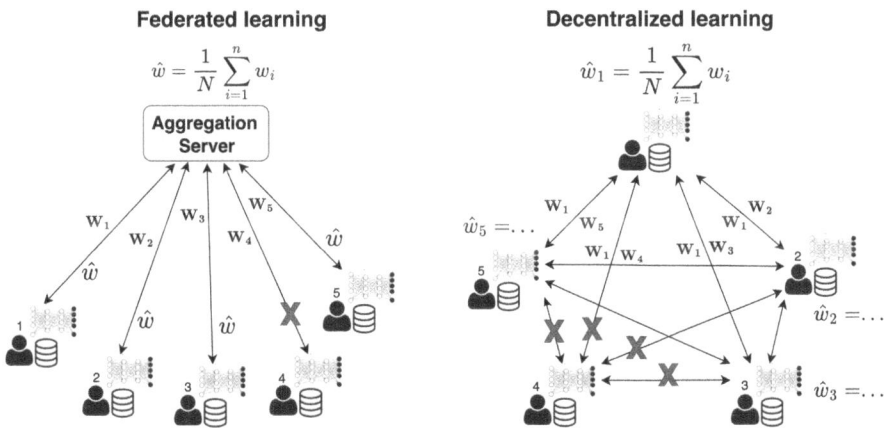

**Fig. 1.** Collaborative learning system in a federated and decentralized manner when Client 4 has dropped out.

clients. However, this method requires careful balancing between the level of privacy maintained and the impact on the model's performance due to perturbation.

Guo et al. [20] pioneered the application of differential privacy in decentralized learning through the introduction of LEASGD, which enhances a stochastic gradient descent algorithm with privacy protection and noise reduction strategies. While this method effectively maintains privacy at the model level, there is a competing trade-off in the utility of the model. Further advancing the field, Bellet et al. [3] devised a fully decentralized algorithm for training personalized ML models, embedding differential privacy to safeguard individual data privacy. Further, Xu et al. [43] presents $D^2$-MHE, a secure and efficient framework for decentralized deep learning that employs advanced homomorphic encryption techniques for the private updating of gradients. This method notably decreases communication complexity and provides robust data privacy safeguards. It emphasizes training models in an encrypted format, leveraging sophisticated cryptographic schemes such as Brakerski-Fan-Vercauteren (BFV) and Cheon-Kim-Kim-Song (CKKS). Despite its advantages in guaranteed protections of client updates, [43] remains burdened by inefficient computation and does not address functional implications of client dropout in deployment as we do with PPDL.

## 3    Preliminaries

In this section, we provide the necessary background on decentralized learning, and introduce the building blocks used to provide privacy of updates and resilience against dropouts in PPDL.

## 3.1   Learning in a Decentralized Setting

In a decentralized learning framework, each participant, denoted as $c$ within the user subgroup $C$, establishes communication links directly with a designated subset referred to as their neighbors $\mathbf{N}(c)$. These links can be either static, established at the outset, or dynamic, subject to change over time. The ensemble of users forms an undirected graph represented by $G = (C, \cup_{c \in C, \ c' \in \mathbf{N}(c)}(c, c'))$, where the vertices represent the users and the edges denote the connections among them [28].

In this environment, each participant $c$ possesses a unique dataset $D_i = \{(x_i, y_i)\}_i$ that is sampled from an undisclosed distribution $\xi_i$. When these individual datasets are amalgamated, they form a comprehensive global dataset $D$ characterized by the distribution $\xi$. Initially, every participant is equipped with a common set of initial model parameters, labeled as $w^0$.

The objective of the training endeavor is to discover the optimal set of parameters, represented by $\mathbf{w}^*$, for the machine learning model. $\mathbf{w}^*$ aims to minimize the expected loss function over the global dataset $D$.

$$\mathbf{w}^* = \arg\min_{\theta} \frac{1}{|\mathbf{N}(c)|} \sum_{n_i \in \mathbf{N}(c)} \underbrace{\mathbb{E}_{s_i \sim D_i}\left[\mathcal{L}\left(\theta; s_i\right)\right]}_{\mathcal{L}_i}$$

For every client $n_i$ within the network, $\mathbb{E}_{s_i \sim D_i}\left[\mathcal{L}\left(\theta; s_i\right)\right]$ determines the expected loss associated with the dataset $D_i$ of that specific client, with $s_i$ representing a sample drawn from $D_i$. Consequently, the goal of this formulation is to identify the model parameters $\theta$ that lead to the minimization of the average expected loss across all clients in the network.

---

**Algorithm 1:** Decentralized Learning Protocol

---

   **Input** : Initial model parameters $w_c^0$ for $c \in C$
             User local training data: $X_c$ for $c \in C$

1  **for** $t \in [0, 1, \ldots]$ **do**
2     **Local optimization step:**
3     **for** $c \in C$ **do**
4         Sample $x_c^t$ from $X_c$
5         Update parameters: $w_c^{t+\frac{1}{2}} = w_c^t - \eta \nabla_{w_c^t}(x_c^t, w_c^t)$
6     **Communication with neighbors:**
7     **for** $c \in C$ **do**
8         **for** $u \in \mathbf{N}(c) \setminus \{c\}$ **do**
9             Send $w_c^{t+\frac{1}{2}}$ to $u$
10           Receive $w_c^{t+\frac{1}{2}}$ from $u$
11     **Model updates aggregation:**
12     **for** $c \in C$ **do**
13         $w_c^{t+1} = \frac{1}{|\mathbf{N}(c)|} \sum_{c \in \mathbf{N}(c)} w_c^{t+\frac{1}{2}}$

---

We summarize the decentralized training of ML models in Algorithm 1. The process unfolds through a sequence of stages until a specified termination point (e.g., convergence). Initially, each client $c$ performs gradient descent on their unique model parameters, leading to the generation of an interim model update, denoted as $w_c^{t+1/2}$. Subsequently, these clients exchange their interim model updates $w_c^{t+1/2}$ with their network neighbors ($\mathbf{N}(c)$), while also receiving updates from these neighbors.

Following the exchange, clients aggregate the updates received from their neighbors with their own. This aggregation typically involves averaging the model updates to modify their local model state, expressed mathematically as $w^{t+1} = \frac{1}{|\mathbf{N}(c)|} \sum_{c \in \mathbf{N}(c)} w_c^{t+1/2}$ that signifies the collective adjustment based on the aggregated updates.

In this study, we assume that the clients exhibit full connectivity, which implies that every client is directly connected to all other clients within each subgroup. This full connectivity framework ensures that every client can directly exchange information with every other client in its subgroup, facilitating a comprehensive and synchronous training process across the network.

## 3.2   Shamir's Secret Sharing

Shamir's Secret Sharing (SSS) Scheme [35] allows a secret $s$ to be divided into $n$ pieces, known as shares, using a $t$-out-of-$n$ scheme. Any group of $t$ or more shares can be used to reconstruct the secret $s$. The process is as follows:

- To generate shares from a secret $s$, by using the function $Ss.Share(s,t,n)$, $t-1$ random positive integers $a_1, \ldots, a_{t-1}$ are selected from a finite field $\mathbb{Z}_P$, with $a_0 = s$ representing the secret. Let $f(x) = a_0 + a_1 x + a_2 x^2 + \cdots + a_{t-1} x^{t-1}$ mod $P$ be a polynomial with coefficients from $\mathbb{Z}_P$, where $\mathcal{U} = \{u_i | u_i \in [1, P]\}$ is a set of $n$ random numbers and $0 < t \leq n < P$. The shares are then $\{(u_i, s_i)\}_{u_i \in \mathcal{U}} = \{(u_i, f(u_i))\}_{u_i \in \mathcal{U}}$.
- To reconstruct the secret $s$ from shares using $Ss.Recon(\{(u_i, s_i)\}_{u_i \in \mathcal{U}}, t)$, any subset of $t$ shares can be used for the recovery of $s$ through Lagrange interpolation. Since $a_0 = s$, the secret is efficiently found as $s = a_0 = f(0) = \sum_{j=0}^{t} f(u_j) \prod_{i=0, i \neq j}^{t} \frac{u_i}{u_i - u_j}$ mod $P$.

Moreover, SSS method inherently supports operations that resemble additive homomorphism, allowing for the direct combination of secrets. If the index $i$ and the corresponding element $u_i$ of any share in the set $\{(u_i, s_i)\}_{u_i \in \mathcal{U}}$ for a given secret $s$ match the index and element $v_i$ in another set $\{(v_i, s_i')\}_{v_i \in \mathcal{V}}$ for a different secret $s'$, the secrets can be seamlessly combined. The combined secret $s + s'$ can be efficiently reconstructed by applying the reconstruction function $Ss.Recon$ on these merged shares.

The security of Shamir's $t$-out-of-$n$ secret sharing ensures that for any two sets of shares $U, V$ both less than threshold $t$, the output of $Ss.Recon(V)$ is indistinguishable from $Ss.Recon(U)$, thereby maintaining the confidentiality of the secret $s$.

### 3.3    Diffie-Hellman Key Agreement Protocol

The Diffie-Hellman (DH) key agreement protocol [23] is structured around probabilistic polynomial-time (PPT) algorithms, as outlined below:

**Parameter Generation:** $(\mathbb{G}', g, q, H) \leftarrow$ DHParam($\kappa$): Given a security parameter $\kappa$, this algorithm generates a cyclic group $\mathbb{G}'$ of prime order $q$ and a generator $g$ of the group, and specifies a hash function $H$, such as SHA-256, for hashing purposes.

**Key Generation:** $(s, g^s) \leftarrow$ DHGen($\mathbb{G}', g, q$): This algorithm selects a secret key $s$ from the integer group $\mathbb{Z}_q$ and computes $g^s$ as its corresponding public key.

**Key Agreement:** $s_{a,b} \leftarrow$ DHAgree($s_a, g^{s_b}$): For a secret key $s_a$ and a public key $g^{s_b}$, generated by another party's secret key $s_b$, this algorithm produces the shared secret key $s_{a,b} = H((g^{s_b})^{s_a})$, leveraging the hash function $H$ for the final key derivation.

The security of the DH key agreement protocol, when deployed to protect against honest-but-curious adversaries, relies on a fundamental cryptographic principle known as the Decisional Diffie-Hellman (DDH) assumption [9]. This assumption secures the protocol by rendering it computationally difficult to differentiate between instances of the DH exchange and random group elements.

## 4    Problem Definition

Recall that in a collaborative learning setting, an honest client aims to obtain an aggregated model update that integrates local models trained on other clients' private datasets. The hidden aggregation of these updates helps mitigate privacy risks to client datasets in two main ways. First, it protects individual local models from malicious scrutiny by obscuring specific details, preventing adversaries from identifying and exploiting exact data sources. Second, it reduces the impact of any single client's input by merging contributions from multiple clients into the aggregated model.

In FL, a central server collects model updates from clients before distributing the aggregated results back to them. This centralized approach ensures that only the server can access each client's individual updates. However, in DL, the absence of a central server elevates privacy risks, as updates must be shared directly between clients for aggregation [33]. These risks can be mitigated by implementing secure aggregation schemes.

Moreover, when secure aggregation is implemented in a collaborative learning setting, client dropout poses a significant challenge [8]. Clients may exit the aggregation process before sharing their model updates due to latency, network connectivity issues, or unexpected shutdowns. This can occur before they share their updates with any other clients or after having distributed them to everyone. Since dropout is a prevalent concern in deployed systems, designing systems resilient to client dropouts up to a certain threshold is vital.

This work presents privacy-preserving DL algorithms that are resilient to dropout, ensuring the model remains accurate and operationally efficient.

### 4.1 Threat Model

The threat model considered in this paper encompasses a landscape dominated by non-malicious yet curious clients operating under the assumption of an honest majority. While adhering to the established protocols of the system, these 'honest-but-curious' clients want to obtain or infer additional information about their peers through the interactions of DL. Their approach does not involve transmitting incorrect or manipulated data; instead, they aim to derive as much insight as possible from the communication flows inherent in the learning process. Adding to this complexity, we consider the scenario where a semi-honest client may collude with others. This collusion aims to pool resources and shared insights to enhance their collective ability to infer private information beyond what is intended through the system's interactions.

Therefore, the threat model underscores the need for advanced mechanisms to manage individual curiosity-driven inference attacks and collaborative efforts among semi-honest clients. These mechanisms are vital for providing robust privacy assurances when deployed in realistic environments, protecting private local data against these enhanced potential privacy risks.

## 5   Approaches

In this section, we introduce three distinct approaches for implementing secure aggregation in DL environments, emphasizing the incorporation of dropout resilience.

### 5.1   SA Using Shamir's Secret Sharing

This method allows clients to work together to build a shared model vector, $W$, enhancing resilience against dropout by enabling the model's reconstruction even if some clients do not contribute. Each client participates in the aggregation process by supplying vectors made up of field elements from a field of size $q$. This arrangement aligns with the objectives of the decentralized model. The approach not only addresses the complexities of distributed computation but also introduces an effective mechanism for managing client dropout. It ensures the confidentiality and integrity of the model aggregation process, eliminating the need for a centralized server.

In this approach summarized in Algorithm 2, each client $P_i$ generates $n$ shares for each element of their input vector $w_i$, adhering to a predetermined threshold $t$. The threshold $t$ should exceed the number of semi-honest clients to protect the integrity and confidentiality of the aggregation process. Next, each client distributes one share to the other clients while retaining a share for itself. Subsequently, clients aggregate the shares of the secret value received from

---

**Algorithm 2:** PPDL-NV: Secure Aggregation via Shamir's Secret Sharing for PPDL

---

**Input** : $n$ clients $C_0, C_1, \ldots, C_n$ each with a local training dataset $D_i$, for $i = 0, 1, \ldots, n$
Number of global iterations $R_g$
Shamir's threshold $t$ (e.g., $t = (n/2) + 1$)

**Output:** A globally trained model $\mathbf{w}$ for each client

1 **for** $r = 1$ **to** $R_g$ **do**
    // Initialization step
2     All clients start with the same initial model $\mathbf{w}^0$.
3     **for** $i = 0$ **to** $n$ **do**
4         Train local model: $\mathbf{w}_i \leftarrow \text{LocalUpdate}(\mathbf{w}^{r-1}, D_i)$
5         Generate and distribute $n$ shares of $\mathbf{w}_i$, denoted as $[\![\mathbf{w}_i]\!]_j$ for $j = 0, 1, \ldots, n$, to all clients, including itself
6         Receive shares $[\![\mathbf{w}_j]\!]_i$ from all other clients
7         Aggregate own share with received shares from other clients:
        $[\![\bar{\mathbf{w}}]\!]_i = \sum_{\substack{j=0 \\ j \neq i}}^{n} [\![\mathbf{w}_j]\!]_i + [\![\mathbf{w}_i]\!]_i$
8         Transmit $[\![\bar{\mathbf{w}}]\!]_i$ to all other clients and receive $[\![\bar{\mathbf{w}}]\!]_j$ from them
9         **if** *total shares received* $\geq t$ **then**
10             Perform Shamir Reconstruction to obtain $\bar{\mathbf{w}}$ and update global model: $\hat{\mathbf{w}}^r = \frac{1}{n}\bar{\mathbf{w}}$

---

others with their own and broadcast the cumulative value to all participants. Once sufficient shares of these combined values are collected, every client can reconstruct the aggregated value.

Although this approach inherently tolerates dropouts, the inefficiency of traditional Shamir's Secret Sharing in a decentralized setting primarily stems from the extensive number of secret values that need to be shared. These secret values correlate directly with the number of model weights, resulting in excessive communication and computation overheads.

Improvements to this inefficiency can be achieved by utilizing Packed Shamir Secret Sharing [14], a drop-in adaptation of Shamir's Secret Sharing in all three of our proposed approaches. Packed Shamir Secret Sharing significantly improves communication and computation efficiency by including multiple values within a single share. The packed secret sharing method has the capacity to split $k$ secret values into $n$ shares while requiring at least $t + k$ shares to recover the secret. Despite these improvements, this proposed scheme's naive application, still observes the vector size for secret sharing still correlating with the model's parameter size. The packing only lowers the per-client communication burden, particularly with large-scale models.

**Security Analysis.** In this part, we explore the security features of the PPDL-NV algorithm in detail:

**Theorem 1.** *The PPDL − NV protocol, which utilizes SSS to distribute model updates as n shares within a finite field $\mathbb{F}_q$ among clients, ensures security against semi-honest adversaries and exhibits resilience to client dropout in the honest majority setting.*

*Proof.* In PPDL-NV protocol, Shamir's Secret Sharing (SSS) ensures the confidentiality of model updates. Each element of a model update $s$ is divided into $n$ shares within a finite field $\mathbb{F}_q$ (assuming $n < q$), according to $A(x) = \sum_{i=0}^{t-1} a_i x^i$, where $a_0 = s$ and the coefficients $a_i$ are randomly and uniformly chosen from $\mathbb{F}_q$. This approach utilizes unique, non-zero points $x_i$ in $\mathbb{F}_q$, ensuring each share $v_i = A(x_i)$ contains part of the secret without fully disclosing it.

The security of SSS stems from the fact that a polynomial of degree $t − 1$ can only be uniquely determined by any $t$ distinct evaluations $(v_i)$, making it mathematically infeasible to reconstruct $s$ from fewer than $t$ shares. This is due to there being $q^{t-1}$ potential polynomials that could correspond to any given set of $t − 1$ shares, preserving the secrecy of $s$.

This mechanism also underpins the protocol's resilience to client dropout, as the threshold $t$ can be adjusted to maintain confidentiality despite partial participation. In essence, for any subset of $t − 1$ shares, the distribution of potential secrets remains uniform, ensuring no leakage of information about $s$.

For reconstruction, the protocol employs Lagrange polynomials $L_i$ for each share $i$, calculated as $L_i = \frac{\prod_{j \neq i}(X - x_j)}{\prod_{j \neq i}(x_i - x_j)}$, where $L_i(x_i) = 1$ and $L_i(x_j) = 0$ for all $j \neq i$. This enables the secure computation of $A(0) = s = \sum_{i=1}^{t} v_i L_i(0)$ from precisely $t$ shares. □

## 5.2   SA Using LWE-Based Masking

As we mentioned previously, packed secret sharing significantly improves the communication efficiency of PPDL-NV, however, the quantity of values that need to be secret shared still directly correlates to the size of the model update vector. To address this limitation in our second proposal, we draw inspiration from the work of Stevens et al. [38] and propose the use of a dropout-resilient Differentially Private (DP) secure protocol grounded with the Learning With Errors (LWE) assumption for a decentralized learning setting. This second approach which we call PPDL-LWE, each client generates a one-time pad of equal length to their model parameters and broadcast it to all other clients. Utilizing SSS, clients collaboratively sum their masks and then subtract each client's mask from the aggregated model updates value, thereby enhancing both the efficiency and security of the process.

As illustrated in Algorithm 3, clients share a public $m \times n$ matrix $A$, where each element of the matrix is from the finite field $\mathbb{F}_q$. Each client $i$ independently generates a secret vector $s_i$ of size $n$ and an error vector $e_i$ of size $m$, both derived from the same distribution. The client then computes a vector $b_i = A \cdot s_i + e_i$,

---

**Algorithm 3:** PPDL-LWE: Secure Aggregation via LWE-Based Masking for PPDL

---

**Input**  :  $n$ clients $C_0, C_1, \ldots, C_n$ each with a local training dataset $D_i$, for $i = 0, 1, \ldots, n$
Number of global iterations $R_g$
Public $m \times n$ matrix $A$ over finite field $\mathbb{F}_q$

**Output:** A globally trained model $\mathbf{w}$ for each client

1  **for** $r = 1$ **to** $R_g$ **do**
       // Initialization step
2  |    All clients start with the same initial model $\mathbf{w}^0$.
3  |    **for** $i = 0$ **to** $n$ **do**
4  |    |    Train local model: $\mathbf{w}_i \leftarrow \text{LocalUpdate}(\mathbf{w}^{r-1}, D_i)$
5  |    |    Generate secret vector $\mathbf{s}_i$ of size $n$
6  |    |    Generate random noise vector $\mathbf{e}_i$ of size $m$
7  |    |    Compute masking vector $\mathbf{b}_i \leftarrow A \cdot \mathbf{s}_i + \mathbf{e}_i$
8  |    |    Mask model parameters: $\mathbf{h}_i \leftarrow \mathbf{w}_i + \mathbf{b}_i$
9  |    |    Transmit $\mathbf{h}_i$ to all clients
10 |    |    Receive $\mathbf{h}_j$ from all other clients
11 |    |    Distribute $[\![\mathbf{s}_i]\!]$ to all clients
12 |    |    Collect $[\![\mathbf{s}_j]\!]$ from all clients
       |    |    // Using Secret Sharing for aggregation
13 |    |    Compute $\mathbf{s}_{\text{sum}} \leftarrow \sum_j \mathbf{s}_j$
14 |    |    Aggregate masked model parameters: $\mathbf{H}_{\text{sum}} \leftarrow \sum_j \mathbf{h}_j$
15 |    |    Compute aggregated model update: $\mathbf{W}_{\text{sum}} \leftarrow \mathbf{H}_{\text{sum}} - A \cdot \mathbf{s}_{\text{sum}}$
16 |    |    Update global model: $\hat{\mathbf{w}}^r \leftarrow \frac{1}{n}\mathbf{W}_{\text{sum}}$

---

where $A$ is the public $m \times n$ matrix. This forms an LWE sample with the pair $(A, b_i)$, where $b_i$ effectively serves as a one-time pad to mask the client's model update $w_i$, resulting in a masked vector $h_i = w_i + b_i$.

Next, clients transmit $h_i$ to other clients and subsequently compute the aggregation of the received vectors, $h_{\text{sum}}$, through vector addition. The $h_{\text{sum}}$ is composed of $w_{\text{sum}} + As_{\text{sum}} + e_{\text{sum}}$, where $e_{\text{sum}}$ is the added noise that satisfies the $(\varepsilon, \delta)$-DP criterion, and $w_{\text{sum}} + e_{\text{sum}}$ forms the noisy aggregated value of the model updates from other clients. Therefore, to eliminate $As_{\text{sum}}$ from $h_{\text{sum}}$, clients only need to compute $s_{\text{sum}}$. To determine $s_{\text{sum}}$ without disclosing the individual $s_i$ values, clients collaboratively use the SSS protocol, as introduced in Sect. 5.1. Finally, each client, using the shared matrix $A$ and $s_{\text{sum}}$, computes $h_{\text{sum}}$ as the aggregated value.

To ensure this protocol's effectiveness, two key points are crucial for balancing privacy and performance. First, protecting the confidentiality of individual error vectors $e_i$ is essential, leveraging the LWE assumption for privacy. By aggregating these vectors into a cumulative noise $e_{\text{sum}}$ via discrete Gaussians, the protocol achieves differential privacy, offering a precise yet privacy-aware estimation of $w_{\text{sum}}$. Second, the dimension of the secret vector $S$ plays a vital role in enhancing security. Stevens et al. [38] emphasize the importance of keeping $S_i$'s length at a minimum of 710 for robust security, regardless of the secret input vector $w_i$'s dimensionality. These elements are critical in creating a strong decentralized learning framework that effectively addresses privacy and efficiency challenges. Beyond the specific focus of adversarial robustness, adversarial training has been shown to increase the generalization, and thus the model performance on regular binaries too.

**Security Analysis.** In this subsection, we discuss the security provided by PPDL-LWE algorithm in detail:

**Theorem 2.** *In settings with an honest majority, the $PPDL - LWE$ protocol is secure against semi-honest adversaries by leveraging the LWE assumption for the encryption of model updates and utilizing SSS for the secure aggregation of clients' secret vectors. This protocol exhibits resilience to client dropout, ensuring the confidentiality and integrity of the DL process.*

*Proof.* The cornerstone of the $PPDL - LWE$ protocol's security lies in its employment of the LWE assumption, a principle positing that distinguishing between genuine LWE samples $(A, A \cdot s_i + e_i)$ and random pairs from the same distribution is computationally infeasible for any polynomial-time adversary. Here, $A$ represents a publicly known matrix, $s_i$ is a secret vector selected by the client, and $e_i$ is an error vector with elements drawn from a discretized Gaussian distribution. The distribution's parameters are chosen to maintain the encryption's integrity while enabling efficient decryption by legitimate entities.

The intractability of the LWE problem, rooted in the computational complexity of solving certain lattice problems deemed hard for quantum computers, underpins the protocol's resistance to quantum attacks. Without exact knowledge of $s_i$ and $e_i$, decryption of the encrypted model update $h_i = w_i + A \cdot s_i + e_i$ by adversaries is rendered impractical. This encryption model ensures that data confidentiality is upheld, even in the face of semi-honest clients who follow the protocol yet attempt to extract additional information.

Further enhancing the protocol's security is the application of SSS for aggregating the secret vectors $s_i$ into a collective sum $s_{\text{sum}}$. The SSS mechanism necessitates a predetermined number of shares to reconstruct any individual secret vector, thereby precluding semi-honest clients from independently accessing or inferring another's secret vector. The collaborative computation of $s_{\text{sum}}$, essential for decrypting the combined encrypted vectors $h_{\text{sum}}$, intrinsically protects against the potential disclosure of sensitive data to semi-honest participants during the aggregation phase.                                                    □

## 5.3   SA with Pairwise Masking

Building on the principles of the previous approach, the third proposed protocol emphasizes masking clients' model parameters before transmission to other clients. This method introduces a novel aspect where clients engage in pairwise sharing of a seed for a pseudo-random number generator (PRNG) [5,31], allowing each client to produce a shared vector tailored to the desired size locally. This technique addresses the unique challenges of secure aggregation by incorporating principles akin to those explored by Bonawitz et al. [8] in their work on Federated Learning. It offers a refined solution for enhancing privacy and security in decentralized learning environments.

In this protocol, each client $C_i$ generates a unique pairwise mask for their vector relative to every other neighbouring client $C_j$. The collective result of combining these masked vectors $\mathbf{y}_i$ is the aggregation of the original inputs, effectively concealing the individual vectors $\mathbf{w}_i$. The generation of these masks is facilitated by a PRNG, which uses a result derived from each client's public keys, exchanged during the initial steps of the protocol. This mechanism guarantees a secure and agreed-upon method for mask generation, ensuring the confidentiality of the data during the aggregation process.

$$y_i = w_i + \sum_{j:i<j} \mathrm{PRNG}(s_{i,j}) - \sum_{j:i>j} \mathrm{PRNG}(s_{j,i})$$

The Diffie-Hellman key exchange protocol provides a robust method for generating a common seed for a PRNG, essential for creating pairwise masks in secure communications. After generating and exchanging public keys $g^{a_i} \mod q$, each client uses their private key $a_i$ in conjunction with the received public keys from other clients to generate a shared secret seed $s_{i,j}$. This seed initializes the PRNG, allowing each pair of clients to agree on a complementary sequence of random numbers for mask generation, facilitating secure and pairwise synchronized communications across the network.

Similar to earlier approaches, we tackle the issue of clients dropping out after broadcasting their mask vector. A straightforward approach is having the remaining clients remove the dropout mask and resend the updated vector. However, this brings us a new challenge: more clients may drop out during this recovery phase before sharing their seeds, requiring additional recovery phases for these new dropouts. As a result, this approach could trigger a cascade of recoveries, possibly equaling the total number of clients and complicating the process.

To circumvent this issue, we employ the threshold secret sharing protocol introduced in Sect. 5.1, where users distribute a share of their private key to all other clients. In the case of a client dropping out after sending its masked model update vector, remaining client utilizes the SSS to reconstruct the dropout's private key. This enables the recalculation and removal of the dropout's mask from the aggregated value. While this solution necessitates additional steps for seed recovery and mask recalibration, it ensures the integrity of the aggregation process is maintained, even in the event of client dropouts.

**Security Analysis.** In this subsection, we detail the security measures implemented by the PPDL-PW algorithm:

**Theorem 3.** *PPDL-PW protocol, under the Decisional Diffie-Hellman (DDH) assumption, establishes a secure protocol for exchanging keys and masking model updates. This protocol ensures the confidentiality and integrity of decentralized learning processes, bolstered by the indistinguishability of shared secrets and enhanced with Shamir's Secret Sharing (SSS) for dropout resilience.*

*Proof.* Given a cyclic group $\mathbb{G}$ of order $q$ with generator $g$, the DDH assumption (as described in Sect. 3.3) states that for any polynomial-time adversary, distinguishing between tuples $(g^a, g^b, g^{ab})$ and $(g^a, g^b, g^c)$, where $c$ is chosen uniformly at random from $\mathbb{Z}_q$, is computationally hard. This assumption is crucial for securing the key exchange phase, ensuring shared secrets $g^{ab}$ are indistinguishable from random and protected against eavesdropping.

Following key exchange, the protocol uses a PRNG seeded with Diffie-Hellman derived shared secrets $s_{ij} = g^{a_i a_j}$ to generate cryptographic masks for obfuscating model parameters $w$. The security of this masking relies on the assumption that the hash function $H$, applied to $s_{ij}$ for randomness extraction, produces a uniformly random string that serves as a secure PRNG seed. These masks ensure confidentiality through computational secrecy, predicated on the DDH problem's hardness.

In the aggregation phase, clients compile masked model updates without exposing individual contributions, preserving privacy and integrity. This is achieved by each client $C_n$ aggregating the received masked updates $\sum y_i^{(w)}$, where $y_i^{(w)} = w_i + \sum m_{ij}$, leveraging the computational indistinguishability of the masks from random due to the secure PRNG process.

Moreover, integrating Shamir's Secret Sharing (SSS) with a defined threshold enhances the protocol's security against dropout. It leverages the uniform randomness and indistinguishability of shares to preserve confidentiality and integrity, even amid client dropouts. This strategic addition ensures the aggregation process remains secure despite network variability, reinforcing the protocol's robust security framework and its efficiency in decentralized settings.

---

**Algorithm 4:** PPDL-PW: Secure Aggregation with Pairwise Masking and Diffie-Hellman (DH) Key Exchange

---

**Input** : $n$ clients $C_0, C_1, \ldots, C_n$ each with a local training dataset $D_i$,
for $i = 0, 1, \ldots, n$
Number of global iterations $R_g$
Common base $g$ and prime $q$ for DH key exchange

**Output:** A globally trained model $\mathbf{w}$ for each client

1 **for** $r = 1$ **to** $R_g$ **do**
    // Initialization step
2     All clients start with the same initial model $\mathbf{w}^0$.
3     **for** $i = 0$ **to** $n$ **do**
4         Train local model: $\mathbf{w}_i \leftarrow \text{LocalUpdate}(\mathbf{w}^0, D_i)$
5         Generate private key $a_i$ and compute public key $g^{a_i}$
6         Exchange public keys $g^{a_i}$ with other clients
7         Distribute shares of $a_i$ using SSS to each client
8         **for** *each client $C_j$ where $j \neq i$* **do**
9             Receive public key $g^{a_j}$ from client $C_j$
10            Compute shared secret $s_{i,j} = (g^{a_j})^{a_i}$
11            Generate pairwise masks $\text{PRNG}(s_{i,j})$
12         Generate personal mask $b_i$ using PRNG
13         $\mathbf{y}_i \leftarrow \mathbf{w}_i + b_i$
14         **for** *each client $C_j$ where $j \neq i$* **do**
15            **if** $i < j$ **then**
16               $\mathbf{y}_i \leftarrow \mathbf{y}_i + \text{PRNG}(s_{i,j})$
17            **else**
18               $\mathbf{y}_i \leftarrow \mathbf{y}_i - \text{PRNG}(s_{j,i})$
19         Broadcast $\mathbf{y}_i$ to all other clients
20     Initialize an empty vector $\mathbf{V}$ for aggregation
21     **for** *each received masked vector $\mathbf{y}_j$ from clients* **do**
22         $\mathbf{V} \leftarrow \mathbf{V} + \mathbf{y}_j$
23     **if** *a client $C_k$ drops out* **then**
24         Collect shares of $a_k$ from remaining clients to reconstruct $a_k$
25         **for** *each client $C_j$ where $j \neq k$* **do**
26            Compute shared secret $s_{j,k}$ and $s_{k,j}$ using $a_k$
27            Adjust $\mathbf{V}$ by removing the mask contributions;
28     $\hat{\mathbf{w}}^r \leftarrow \frac{1}{n}\mathbf{V}$;

---

# 6  Evaluation

In this section, we conduct a set of experiments to demonstrate the robustness and efficiency of our proposed protocols.

## 6.1   Experimental Setup

We implemented the protocols in Python, utilizing the Pytorch framework for model training [34]. All experiments were conducted on a local compute cluster with an Intel Xeon Gold 6150, Nvidia V100 GPU, and 128 GB RAM.

**Datasets.** For our assessment, we utilized four widely recognized datasets in deep learning: MNIST [26], Fashion-MNIST [42], SVHN [32], and CIFAR-10 [25], all partitioned into subsets that are independent and identically distributed (IID). We divided the training data into smaller subsets (generally in equal sizes) and distributed these among the clients at random. The MNIST dataset is comprised of 60,000 training images and 10,000 testing images of handwritten digits in grayscale, with each image measuring $28 \times 28$ pixels. Fashion-MNIST offers a dataset for a 10-class fashion item classification challenge, including 60,000 training images and 10,000 testing images of fashion items. Derived from Google Street View images of house numbers, the SVHN dataset contains 99,289 color images in ten categories, with a training set of 73,257 images and a testing set of 26,032 images, each standardized to $28 \times 28$ pixels. CIFAR-10 presents a varied set of 50,000 training and 10,000 testing color images distributed over ten unique categories, with each image depicting one category.

**Model.** We implemented tailored model architectures to address the unique characteristics of our datasets: a CNN for CIFAR-10 and SVHN and a two-layer MLP for MNIST and Fashion-MNIST. The CNN architecture features two convolutional layers with a kernel size of $3 \times 1$ per layer, followed by three fully connected layers, with 384 neurons in each hidden layer and 10 neurons in the output layer. This structure is designed to effectively process and learn from the complex image data presented by CIFAR-10. The model is optimized with a learning rate of 0.002 and a batch size of 128, incorporating Group Normalization (GN) alongside max pooling and dropout rates between 0.2 to 0.5, culminating in a fully connected output layer. The MLP model is comprised of two fully connected layers with 100 and 10 neurons, respectively. This model is optimized with a learning rate of 0.01 and a batch size of 128.

## 6.2   Classification Accuracy

A comprehensive accuracy comparison of different aggregation methods we presented in Sect. 5 is provided in Table 1. The experiments involve four datasets (MNIST, CIFAR-10, SVHN, and Fashion-MNIST) and the number of users set at 50 and 100. The aggregation methods compared include baseline DL without privacy-preserving aggregation, PPDL-NV, PPDL-LWE, PPDL-PW, and DLDP (Differentially Private Decentralized Learning [11]).

For both groups of 50 and 100 users, DL consistently achieves the highest accuracy across all datasets, serving as a benchmark for the effectiveness of decentralized learning without privacy-preserving constraints. PPDL-NV and

PPDL-PW closely match the DL's accuracy with minimal losses, indicating their capability to maintain high accuracy while offering privacy-preserving benefits. Specifically, PPDL-NV demonstrates accuracies of 96.52% and 96.11% for MNIST, closely following DL's 96.56% and 96.24% for groups of 50 and 100 users, respectively. This pattern of minimal accuracy reduction persists across other datasets, underscoring the efficiency of these methods in balancing privacy with performance.

**Table 1.** Accuracy comparison of different aggregation method in Decentralized learning

| # of users | Dataset | DL | PPDL-NV | PPDL-LWE | PPDL-PW | DLDP |
|---|---|---|---|---|---|---|
| 50 | MNIST | 96.56% | 96.52% | 89.12%($\epsilon = 9.25$) | 96.22% | 89.85%($\epsilon = 9.25$) |
| | CIFAR-10 | 74.46% | 73.98% | 62.12%($\epsilon = 11.31$) | 73.9% | 62.74%($\epsilon = 11.31$) |
| | SVHN | 92.92% | 92.61% | 83.03%($\epsilon = 11.00$) | 91.82% | 83.07%($\epsilon = 11.00$) |
| | Fashion-MNIST | 87.48% | 87.22% | 83.01%($\epsilon = 11.00$) | 86.92% | 83.19%($\epsilon = 11.00$) |
| 100 | MNIST | 96.24% | 96.11% | 88.60%($\epsilon = 9.33$) | 96.11% | 89.12%($\epsilon = 9.33$) |
| | CIFAR-10 | 71.24% | 71.02% | 62.21%($\epsilon = 11.58$) | 71.20% | 62.56%($\epsilon = 11.31$) |
| | SVHN | 92.12% | 92.03% | 82.47%($\epsilon = 11.00$) | 91.23% | 82.97%($\epsilon = 11.00$) |
| | Fashion-MNIST | 87.13% | 87.02% | 82.21%($\epsilon = 10.610$) | 87.12% | 82.91%($\epsilon = 10.61$) |

PPDL-LWE and DLDP, however, exhibit a noticeable decrease in accuracy due to their rigorous privacy constraints, as evidenced by their accuracy figures and $\epsilon$ values. In the CIFAR-10 dataset, PPDL-LWE's accuracy dips to 62.12% for 50 users and 62.21% for 100 users, a significant reduction from DL's 74.46% and 71.24%. This decline in performance is echoed across the board, with PPDL-LWE and DLDP consistently posting lower accuracies in exchange for stronger privacy guarantees denoted by their respective $\epsilon$ values. For instance, in the SVHN dataset, DLDP's accuracy is 83.07% for 50 users and 82.97% for 100 users, compared to DL's more robust 92.92% and 92.12%.

In conclusion, PPDL-NV and PPDL-PW strike a good balance between privacy preservation and accuracy, closely matching the benchmarks set by the baseline DL. Meanwhile, PPDL-LWE offers strong privacy guarantees by combining differential privacy and masking techniques for DL, achieving a level of accuracy comparable to that of DLDP.

### 6.3 Impact of Client Number and Dropout on Computational Overhead

Figure 2 presents a comparative analysis of the three privacy-preserving aggregation methods for DL in terms of computation time when the number of clients and dropout ratio change. This examination is based on a single iteration of the learning process, with the model parameter count set at 50,000. Additionally, we note that 20% of the network clients are considered semi-honest, adding another layer of complexity to the privacy-preserving mechanisms employed.

As the number of clients increases from 10 to 1000, we observe a notable increase in computation times for all evaluated methods. PPDL-NV, despite leveraging packed Shamir secret sharing, experiences a significant rise in computation time, which varies from 12.22 s to 694.79 s. This increase underscores both the method's computational demand and its robustness in handling complex calculations. On the other hand, PPDL-LWE stands out for its exceptional efficiency, with computation times only ranging from 0.16 to 16.43 s as the number of clients grows. This efficiency highlights PPDL-LWE's potential for scalability in large-scale applications where computational resources are a critical consideration.

PPDL-PW stands out for its unique response to network conditions. At a 0% dropout rate, it maintains constant computation times of 0.71 s irrespective of the number of clients, showcasing unparalleled efficiency in stable conditions. However, its computation times increase linearly with the number of clients and dropout rates as network instability grows, peaking at 49.50 s for 1000 clients at a 30% dropout rate. This behavior points to a direct sensitivity to dropout rates, a characteristic not as pronounced in the other methods, where increases in computation time remain relatively unaffected by variations in dropout.

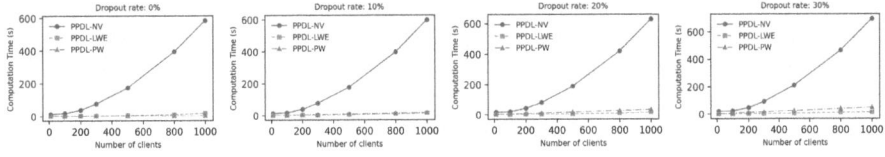

**Fig. 2.** Implications of increasing the number of clients on the efficiency of protocols.

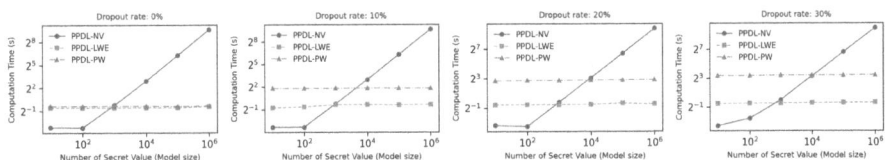

**Fig. 3.** Implications of increasing the number of model parameters on the efficiency of protocols.

## 6.4   Impact of Model Size on Computational Efficiency

The scalability of PPDL-NV, PPDL-LWE, and PPDL-PW in response to increasing model sizes and varying dropout rates is illuminated through a closer examination of their computational performance, as depicted in Fig. 3. PPDL-NV's computational times escalate significantly with model size, increasing from 0.11 s for 10 secret values to 760.58 s for 1,000,000 secret values at a 0% dropout rate. This trend intensifies under a 30% dropout rate, where computational times further surge to 983.88 s for 1,000,000 secret values, indicating a profound sensitivity to both increased model size and higher dropout rates. In contrast, PPDL-LWE exhibits extraordinary resilience to these factors, with computation times only slightly increasing from 0.66 s for 10 secret values to 0.73 s for 1,000,000 secret values, even at a 30% dropout rate. This negligible variation suggests unparalleled stability across model size and network reliability dimensions.

PPDL-PW, on the other hand, while demonstrating a modest increase in computation time with model size, reveals a more nuanced sensitivity to dropout rates. For example, at a 0% dropout rate, computation times increase slightly from 0.76 s for 10 secret values to 0.77 s for 1,000,000 secret values. However, as the dropout rate reaches 30%, computation times for PPDL-PW rise more noticeably, from 0.76 s for 10 secret values to 11.25 s for 1,000,000 secret values. This pattern suggests that while PPDL-PW is somewhat resilient to model size increases, its efficiency is more significantly impacted by higher dropout rates, especially as the model size grows.

These numerical comparisons reveal the critical interplay between model size and dropout rates in decentralized learning environments. PPDL-NV, though scalable to a degree, faces substantial challenges in maintaining computational efficiency with larger model sizes and higher dropout rates. PPDL-LWE stands out for its robustness, showing minimal impact from either increasing model sizes or varying dropout rates, making it a highly reliable choice for large-scale applications. PPDL-PW occupies a middle ground, offering reasonable scalability and efficiency but with a noticeable decrease in performance under higher dropout rates and larger model sizes.

### 6.5   Computation Overhead Comparison

In addition to evaluating our proposed approaches, we also compare our protocols with two homomorphic encryption-based DL aggregation protocols, namely $D^2$-MHE [44] and Paillier-HE [44], to provide a comprehensive analysis of computational overhead across different privacy-preserving mechanisms when applied to the MNIST and CIFAR-10 datasets. Table 2 illustrates the comparative computational demand for one iteration among various approaches, including PPDL-NV, PPDL-LWE, PPDL-PW, along with the aforementioned homomorphic encryption-based schemes.

The $D^2$-MHE scheme capitalizes on recent advancements in homomorphic encryption, explicitly employing the Brakerski-Fan-Vercauteren (BFV) framework, aiming to minimize computational costs while securely updating gradients in a decentralized training context. On the other hand, Paillier-HE represents a classical approach to homomorphic encryption, adapted here for decentralized settings. The performance data for both $D^2$-MHE and Paillier-HE were adopted from the study [44], eschewing direct implementation for these comparisons.

**Table 2.** Computational overhead of one iteration of various privacy-preserving approaches (Seconds)

|         | PPDL-NV | PPDL-LWE | PPDL-PW | $D^2$-MHE | Paillier-HE |
|---------|---------|----------|---------|-----------|-------------|
| MNIST   | 20.93   | 0.24     | 0.21    | 26.2 [44] | 59.54 [44]  |
| CIFAR10 | 513.18  | 0.24     | 0.21    | 62.19 [44]| 106.42 [44] |

We maintained identical model architectures and configurations across all evaluated protocols to ensure a fair and accurate comparison.

For the MNIST dataset, PPDL-NV's method exhibits a relatively high computational overhead at 20.93 s, which dramatically increases to 513.18 s for the more complex CIFAR-10 dataset, indicating its less favorable scaling with data complexity. In stark contrast, PPDL-LWE and PPDL-PW methods demonstrate exceptional efficiency, with negligible overheads of 0.24 and 0.21 s, respectively, for both datasets. This stark efficiency highlights their suitability for decentralized scenarios where minimizing computational burden is crucial. However, the $D^2$-MHE and Paillier-HE approaches present significantly higher computational times. For MNIST, $D^2$-MHE stands at 26.2 s, escalating to 62.19 s for CIFAR-10, while Paillier-HE jumps from 59.54 to 106.42 s, respectively. These results reflect the inherent computational overhead associated with HE techniques, particularly Paillier-HE's intensive modular exponential operations and the collaborative decryption process among multiple users, which, despite its privacy advantages, results in considerable computational overhead.

### 6.6   Computational and Communication Complexity

In this section, we derive the computational and communication complexities associated with each of the proposed PPDL protocols.

**PPDL-NV Computational Complexity:** PPDL-NV protocol, employing Packed Shamir's Secret Sharing, has a computational complexity that unfolds across a few key steps. Initially, clients generate packed shares of their local model update $w_i$ with a complexity of $O(nT/K)$, leveraging the efficiency of packing multiple elements per share for $n$ clients, $T$ as the threshold, and $K$ as the packing factor. The aggregation of shares from $n - 1$ peers follows a linear complexity of $O(n)$, thanks to the simple addition of packed shares. The final, most complex phase is the reconstruction of the aggregated value from shares, at $O(nT^2/K)$, due to polynomial interpolation for unpacking. The protocol's overall complexity is thus primarily determined by this reconstruction phase, leading to an $O(nT^2/K)$ complexity.

**Communication Complexity:** This protocol's communication complexity arises from two key operations: share distribution and aggregated share broadcasting. Each client sends their packed shares to $n - 1$ others and receives an equivalent number from every other client, resulting in a communication complexity of $O(n^2)$. This stems from the need for each of the $n$ clients to interact with all others. The aggregation step, involving each client broadcasting their aggregated share to all, also reflects an $O(n^2)$ complexity due to the peer-to-peer exchange among $n$ participants. Thus, the protocol's overall communication complexity remains $O(n^2)$, underscored by the extensive interactions necessary for decentralized aggregation.

**PPDL-LWE Computational Complexity:** The computational complexity for each client is primarily shaped by generating random vectors ($O(m)$), matrix-vector multiplication ($O(mn)$), and leveraging packed Shamir's Secret Sharing ($O(nmT/K)$ for sharing and $O(nT^2/K)$ for reconstruction). Given $m$ exceeds the length of the secret vector $s$, the initial vector generation simplifies to $O(m)$. The subsequent operations, particularly the reconstruction of packed secret shares, culminate in a dominant $O(nT^2/K)$ complexity. Thus, the overall client-side complexity is effectively summarized by $O(nmT/K + nT^2/K)$.

**Communication Complexity:** In PPDL-LWE protocol, the communication complexity for each participant is derived from a series of direct, peer-to-peer exchanges. Specifically, every client sends their encrypted gradient vector of size $m$ to $k-1$ peers and receives an equivalent number of encrypted vectors from others, leading to a communication load of $O(km(k-1))$. Additionally, the aggregate mask, also of size $m$, is computed using multi-party computation and subsequently distributed among $k-1$ peers, adding $O(mk(k-1))$ to the communication cost. Secure aggregation, facilitated through SSS, requires each client to distribute secret shares of their vector $s$ to all $k-1$ other clients, contributing $O(k^2n)$ to the overall complexity. Therefore, when accounting for both sending and receiving operations in this decentralized scenario, the communication complexity for each client effectively scales as $O(k^2 m + k^2 n)$.

**PPDL-PW. Computational Complexity:** It is defined by two primary operations: $O(n^2)$ for generating $t$-out-of-$n$ Shamir secret shares for the privacy key across $n$ participants, reflecting the quadratic nature of polynomial computations required for secure share distribution, and $O(mn)$ for the linear complexity associated with generating pseudorandom values for each participant, where $m$ denotes the size of the input vector. Furthermore, secret reconstruction, particularly exigent during participant dropouts, demands a computational complexity of $O(n^3)$ due to the intricacies of polynomial interpolation. To enhance computational efficiency, our work incorporates packed Shamir's Secret Sharing, effectively reducing the complexity to $O(nmT/K)$ for share generation and $O(nT^2/K)$ for reconstruction, with $T$ representing the threshold for reconstruction and $K$ the number of secrets integrated into each polynomial.

**Communication Complexity:** Initially, each participant exchanges a single public key with every other participant, resulting in $n(n-1)$ total public key exchanges across the network. Concurrently, secret shares of the privacy key are distributed similarly, with each participant sending and receiving a secret share to and from each of the $n-1$ other participants, doubling the count of exchanges and reinforcing the quadratic component of the communication complexity. Additionally, each participant broadcasts a masked data vector of size $m$ to all $n-1$ other participants, further contributing to the communication load with $m(n-1)$ units of data sent by each participant. The overall communication complexity per participant is $O(n^2 + mn)$, reflecting the quadratic growth from pairwise key and secret share exchanges ($n^2$ for large $n$) and the linear growth from broadcasting masked data vectors ($mn$).

## 7    Conclusion

This study delves into the challenges and necessities of privacy preservation and efficiency in decentralized learning environments. We introduce three novel protocols designed for secure aggregation that directly address DL's unique challenges, such as heightened risks of information leakage and data integrity issues in the face of variable client participation. These protocols represent a significant advancement in the field, aiming to set new standards for security and operational efficiency in decentralized systems. Additionally, exploring mechanisms for dropout resilience significantly strengthens the learning process against disruptions caused by client dropouts, thus greatly enhancing the system's overall reliability and effectiveness.

Through rigorous experimental evaluation across various datasets and scenarios, we have empirically validated the comprehensive effectiveness of our proposed methods. Our experiments, testing our protocols over diverse datasets to ensure robustness and generalizability, demonstrate their computational efficiency and resilience to network fluctuations while preserving privacy. The results of the experiments clearly reaffirm the feasibility of successfully implementing privacy-preserving decentralized learning at scale. It provides valuable insights into optimizing aggregation protocols to balance the trade-offs between privacy, accuracy, and efficiency. This work lays the groundwork for future progress in developing more efficient decentralized learning architectures.

## References

1. Aono, Y., Hayashi, T., Wang, L., Moriai, S., et al.: Privacy-preserving deep learning via additively homomorphic encryption. IEEE Trans. Inf. Forensics Secur. **13**(5), 1333–1345 (2017)
2. Bell, J.H., Bonawitz, K.A., Gascón, A., Lepoint, T., Raykova, M.: Secure single-server aggregation with (poly) logarithmic overhead. In: Proceedings of the 2020 ACM SIGSAC Conference on Computer and Communications Security, pp. 1253–1269 (2020)
3. Bellet, A., Guerraoui, R., Taziki, M., Tommasi, M.: Personalized and private peer-to-peer machine learning. In: International Conference on Artificial Intelligence and Statistics, pp. 473–481. PMLR (2018)

4. Beltrán, E.T.M., et al.: Decentralized federated learning: fundamentals, state of the art, frameworks, trends, and challenges. IEEE Commun. Surv. Tutor. **25**, 2983–3013 (2023)

5. Blum, M., Micali, S.: How to generate cryptographically strong sequences of pseudo random bits. In: Providing Sound Foundations for Cryptography: On the Work of Shafi Goldwasser and Silvio Micali, pp. 227–240 (2019)

6. Boenisch, F., Dziedzic, A., Schuster, R., Shamsabadi, A.S., Shumailov, I., Papernot, N.: When the curious abandon honesty: federated learning is not private. In: 2023 IEEE 8th European Symposium on Security and Privacy (EuroS&P), pp. 175–199. IEEE (2023)

7. Bonawitz, K., et al.: Towards federated learning at scale: system design. Proc. Mach. Learning Syst. **1**, 374–388 (2019)

8. Bonawitz, K., et al.: Practical secure aggregation for privacy-preserving machine learning. In: Proceedings of the 2017 ACM SIGSAC Conference on Computer and Communications Security, pp. 1175–1191 (2017)

9. Boneh, D.: The decision Diffie-Hellman problem. In: Buhler, J.P. (ed.) ANTS 1998. LNCS, vol. 1423, pp. 48–63. Springer, Heidelberg (1998). https://doi.org/10.1007/BFb0054851

10. Canetti, R., Feige, U., Goldreich, O., Naor, M.: Adaptively secure multi-party computation. In: Proceedings of the Twenty-Eighth Annual ACM Symposium on Theory of Computing, pp. 639–648 (1996)

11. Cheng, H.-P., et al.: Towards decentralized deep learning with differential privacy. In: Da Silva, D., Wang, Q., Zhang, L.-J. (eds.) CLOUD 2019. LNCS, vol. 11513, pp. 130–145. Springer, Cham (2019). https://doi.org/10.1007/978-3-030-23502-4_10

12. Dwork, C.: Differential privacy. In: Bugliesi, M., Preneel, B., Sassone, V., Wegener, I. (eds.) ICALP 2006. LNCS, vol. 4052, pp. 1–12. Springer, Heidelberg (2006). https://doi.org/10.1007/11787006_1

13. Fereidooni, H., et al.: SAFELearn: secure aggregation for private federated learning. In: 2021 IEEE Security and Privacy Workshops (SPW), pp. 56–62. IEEE (2021)

14. Franklin, M., Yung, M.: Communication complexity of secure computation. In: Proceedings of the Twenty-Fourth Annual ACM Symposium on Theory of Computing, pp. 699–710 (1992)

15. Gentry, C.: A Fully Homomorphic Encryption Scheme. Stanford university (2009)

16. Geyer, R.C., Klein, T., Nabi, M.: Differentially private federated learning: a client level perspective. arXiv preprint arXiv:1712.07557 (2017)

17. Ghavamipour, A.R., Turkmen, F., Jiang, X.: Privacy-preserving logistic regression with secret sharing. BMC Med. Inform. Decis. Mak. **22**(1), 1–11 (2022)

18. Ghavamipour, A.R., Turkmen, F., Wang, R., Liang, K.: Federated synthetic data generation with stronger security guarantees. In: Proceedings of the 28th ACM Symposium on Access Control Models and Technologies, pp. 31–42 (2023)

19. Ghavamipour, A.R., Zhao, B.Z.H., Ersoy, O., Turkmen, F.: Privacy-preserving aggregation for decentralized learning with byzantine-robustness. arXiv preprint arXiv:2404.17970 (2024)

20. Guo, S., Zhang, T., Xu, G., Yu, H., Xiang, T., Liu, Y.: Topology-aware differential privacy for decentralized image classification. IEEE Trans. Circuits Syst. Video Technol. **32**(6), 4016–4027 (2021)

21. Hegedűs, I., Danner, G., Jelasity, M.: Gossip learning as a decentralized alternative to federated learning. In: Pereira, J., Ricci, L. (eds.) DAIS 2019. LNCS, vol. 11534, pp. 74–90. Springer, Cham (2019). https://doi.org/10.1007/978-3-030-22496-7_5

22. Hegedűs, I., Danner, G., Jelasity, M.: Decentralized learning works: an empirical comparison of gossip learning and federated learning. J. Parallel Distrib. Comput. **148**, 109–124 (2021)

23. Hellman, M.: New directions in cryptography. IEEE Trans. Inf. Theory **22**(6), 644–654 (1976)

24. Koloskova, A., Stich, S., Jaggi, M.: Decentralized stochastic optimization and gossip algorithms with compressed communication. In: International Conference on Machine Learning, pp. 3478–3487. PMLR (2019)

25. Krizhevsky, A., Hinton, G., et al.: Learning multiple layers of features from tiny images (2009)

26. LeCun, Y.: The MNIST database of handwritten digits (1998). http://yann.lecun.com/exdb/mnist/

27. Li, T., Sahu, A.K., Talwalkar, A., Smith, V.: Federated learning: challenges, methods, and future directions. IEEE Signal Process. Mag. **37**(3), 50–60 (2020)

28. Lian, X., Zhang, C., Zhang, H., Hsieh, C.J., Zhang, W., Liu, J.: Can decentralized algorithms outperform centralized algorithms? A case study for decentralized parallel stochastic gradient descent. Adv. Neural Inf. Process. Syst. **30** (2017)

29. Luo, X., Wu, Y., Xiao, X., Ooi, B.C.: Feature inference attack on model predictions in vertical federated learning. In: 2021 IEEE 37th International Conference on Data Engineering (ICDE), pp. 181–192. IEEE (2021)

30. McMahan, B., Moore, E., Ramage, D., Hampson, S., y Arcas, B.A.: Communication-efficient learning of deep networks from decentralized data. In: AISTATS, pp. 1273–1282 (2017)

31. Narayanan, A., Shmatikov, V.: Robust de-anonymization of large sparse datasets. In: 2008 IEEE Symposium on Security and Privacy (SP 2008), pp. 111–125. IEEE (2008)

32. Netzer, Y., Wang, T., Coates, A., Bissacco, A., Wu, B., Ng, A.Y.: Reading digits in natural images with unsupervised feature learning (2011)

33. Pasquini, D., Raynal, M., Troncoso, C.: On the (in) security of peer-to-peer decentralized machine learning. In: 2023 IEEE Symposium on Security and Privacy (SP), pp. 418–436. IEEE Computer Society (2023)

34. Paszke, A., et al.: PyTorch: an imperative style, high-performance deep learning library. Adv. Neural Inf. Process. Syst. **32** (2019)

35. Shamir, A.: How to share a secret. Commun. ACM **22**(11), 612–613 (1979)

36. Shokri, R., Stronati, M., Song, C., Shmatikov, V.: Membership inference attacks against machine learning models. In: 2017 IEEE Symposium on Security and Privacy (SP), pp. 3–18. IEEE (2017)

37. So, J., et al.: LightSecAgg: a lightweight and versatile design for secure aggregation in federated learning. Proc. Mach. Learn. Syst. **4**, 694–720 (2022)

38. Stevens, T., Skalka, C., Vincent, C., Ring, J., Clark, S., Near, J.: Efficient differentially private secure aggregation for federated learning via hardness of learning with errors. In: 31st USENIX Security Symposium (USENIX Security 2022), pp. 1379–1395 (2022)

39. Tian, H., Wen, Y., Zhang, F., Shao, Y., Li, B.: A distributed threshold additive homomorphic encryption for federated learning with dropout resiliency based on lattice. In: Chen, X., Shen, J., Susilo, W. (eds.) CSS 2022. LNCS, vol. 13547, pp. 277–292. Springer, Cham (2022). https://doi.org/10.1007/978-3-031-18067-5_20

40. Truex, S., et al.: A hybrid approach to privacy-preserving federated learning. In: Proceedings of the 12th ACM Workshop on Artificial Intelligence And Security, pp. 1–11 (2019)

41. Wen, Y., Geiping, J., Fowl, L., Goldblum, M., Goldstein, T.: Fishing for user data in large-batch federated learning via gradient magnification. arXiv preprint arXiv:2202.00580 (2022)
42. Xiao, H., Rasul, K., Vollgraf, R.: Fashion-MNIST: a novel image dataset for benchmarking machine learning algorithms. arXiv preprint arXiv:1708.07747 (2017)
43. Xu, G., Li, G., Guo, S., Zhang, T., Li, H.: Privacy-preserving decentralized deep learning with multiparty homomorphic encryption. arXiv preprint arXiv:2207.04604 (2022)
44. Xu, G., Li, G., Guo, S., Zhang, T., Li, H.: Secure decentralized image classification with multiparty homomorphic encryption. IEEE Trans. Circuits Syst. Video Technol. **33**, 3185–3198 (2023)
45. Zhang, C., Li, S., Xia, J., Wang, W., Yan, F., Liu, Y.: {BatchCrypt}: efficient homomorphic encryption for {Cross-Silo} federated learning. In: 2020 USENIX Annual Technical Conference (USENIX ATC 2020), pp. 493–506 (2020)
46. Zhang, L., Xu, J., Vijayakumar, P., Sharma, P.K., Ghosh, U.: Homomorphic encryption-based privacy-preserving federated learning in IoT-enabled healthcare system. IEEE Trans. Netw. Sci. Eng. **10**, 2864–2880 (2022)
47. Zhao, B.Z.H., et al.: On the (in) feasibility of attribute inference attacks on machine learning models. In: 2021 IEEE European Symposium on Security and Privacy (EuroS&P). IEEE (2021)

# Credential Issuance Transparency: A Privacy-Preserving Audit Log of Credential Issuance

Edona Fasllija$^{(\boxtimes)}$ , Jakob Heher , and Stefan More

Graz University of Technology and Secure Information Technology Center Austria
(A-SIT), Graz, Austria
{edona.fasllija,jakob.heher,stefan.more}@iaik.tugraz.at

**Abstract.** Digital identity ecosystems are rapidly transforming the landscape of identity management. Self-Sovereign Identity (SSI) promises to enhance the individual's agency over their identity; and related concepts form core parts of the EU's upcoming eIDAS 2.0 regulation. Yet, this privacy-preserving technology must become *less* privacy-preserving for one overlooked party – credential issuers. Issuers are trusted to validate users' attributes and attest to them. Thus, a compromised or misbehaving issuer is an immense threat, being able to issue credentials that allow them to impersonate anyone.

We address this concern by introducing Credential Issuance Transparency (CIT), a transparency framework for the issuance of identifying credentials. We take concepts from the Web PKI's Certificate Transparency (CT), such as using public append-only logs, but adapt them to a privacy-preserving SSI world. In contrast to CT, the public logs of CIT disclose no information about a credential or its subject. Still, genuine subjects can monitor the log to discover mis-issued credentials that would allow an attacker to impersonate them; and empowered by non-interactive zero-knowledge proofs, verifiers can mandate correct logging.

CIT is practical. It adds a neglectable overhead of less than 2 ms to credential showing. Daily monitoring for mis-issuance requires less than 1 GB of data to be downloaded, and less than 10 s of computation to be invested. This makes CIT an important step towards SSI's organizational acceptance and real-world feasibility.

**Keywords:** self-sovereign identity · transparency logs · credential issuance · unlinkability · non-interactive zero-knowledge proofs

## 1 Introduction

Digital identities play a pivotal role in our daily interactions. They facilitate a secure online environment and foster trust in digital interactions. However, as Microsoft's Chief Identity Architect Kim Cameron aptly identified almost 20 years ago – the internet was built without an identity layer [5]. This absence of a standardized framework for managing digital identities in the foundational design of the internet has led to a diverse range of fragmented solutions for digitally identifying and authenticating individuals. Today, centralized solutions that enable users to use a single set of credentials across multiple services are commonly in use [32]. However, credential-based approaches under the banner of Self-Sovereign Identity (SSI) have emerged, promising to enhance privacy and restore user agency.

The European Union, recognizing this trend, is looking to incorporate SSI paradigms into the eIDAS 2.0 regulation [12]. This regulation thrusts many of the technology's challenges into the spotlight of forced practicability, with vision giving way to viability.

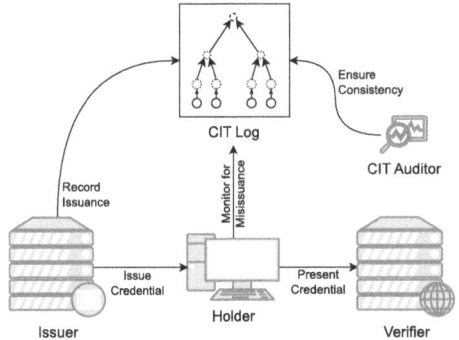

**Fig. 1.** Credential Issuance Transparency architecture

**Challenge.** A crucial open research area of such a privacy-preserving technology is the need for *transparency*. By allowing public visibility into both theories and practices of operation, corruption risks can be reduced, shortcomings can be noticed, and reputation-based penalties can be inflicted.

In computer science, such enforced transparency is not a novel concept; it is used to great effect in the Web PKI, where *Certificate Transparency* (CT) should serve as a safeguard against misbehavior by certificate authorities [20]. However, it is not clear how to translate such technologies to a privacy-preserving world. On the web, malicious actors commonly crawl certificate issuance audit logs – which are public by design – to discover target hosts for scanning campaigns [22,25,30]. In a credential ecosystem, which holds highly sensitive personal information, such information leakage must be avoided at all costs.

**Contributions.** We introduce *Credential Issuance Transparency* (CIT), a privacy-preserving audit logging mechanism for the issuance of identifying credentials. CIT takes CT's append-only log concept, but fully blinds the log entries, removing all sensitive information from them while retaining public auditability of the log's append-only nature as well as user discoverability. Instead of the publicly visible domain name, we rely on a randomly blinded commitment to obscure the credential subject's identity.

By also borrowing CT's trust model, we rely on truthful verifiers to enforce a logging mandate; in order for a credential to be accepted, it must have been logged in an appropriate manner. Here, our log entries' blinded nature introduce an additional validation challenge. We overcome this by employing non-interactive zero-knowledge proofs (NIZKPs) to demonstrate the claimed log entry's consistency with the presented credential.

CIT (illustrated in Fig. 1) thus allows users to monitor for issuance of any identifying credentials that could serve to impersonate them. Such an auditing framework is crucial in bringing self-sovereign identity principles closer to acceptability in legislative circles.

**Outline.** We first introduce relevant concepts (Sect. 2). In Sect. 3, we list involved entities and concepts; formally describing our system's design goals and threat model. In Sect. 4, we introduce CIT, its building blocks, and the issuance, showing, and validation processes. We particularly emphasize the importance of the unlinkability of user identifiers present in the log and zero-knowledge proofs for binding credentials and maintaining user privacy. In Sect. 5, we evaluate CIT's performance and practicability. Finally, we discuss possible adjustments to the protocol and related work in Sect. 6.

## 2   Background

### 2.1   Credential Schemes

A *credential* is a declaration about a *user* (or *holder*) made by an *issuer*. It may encompass various *attributes*, such as the user's name, physical characteristics, group affiliations, or other personal details that the issuer has verified. Users holding a credential can present it to a *verifier*. If the verifier trusts the issuer, this convinces the verifier that the user possesses the claimed attributes. The combined procedures for issuing and presenting a credential constitute a *credential scheme*.

Traditional credential schemes often adopt a centralized structure, where the issuer's server stores all user information. In contrast, user-centric digital identity paradigms such as Self-Sovereign Identity (SSI) enable individuals to independently handle digital attestations of their identity attributes and cryptographic keys for authentication. This is often done on users' personal devices, such as mobile phones, through a so-called "wallet" application. Such attestations contain cryptographic evidence of integrity, commonly in the form of a digital signature created by the issuer. This signature renders the information verifiable by machines. This concept led to the common term "verifiable credentials" (VCs) being used for the associated attestations [31]. We further describe the VC presentation process in Appendix A.

SSI concepts are seeing adoption in the European Union's eIDAS 2.0 regulation that introduces a "European Digital Wallet" [12] capable of receiving, storing, and showing digital credentials with high levels of assurance.

## 2.2   Transparency Logs

Transparency logs are a reliable mechanism for storing and showcasing information. They ensure that all users can independently confirm they are viewing the same entries irrespective of their role. This functionality is pivotal in maintaining integrity and trust within a system as it significantly reduces the chances of tampering or misrepresenting data.

These logs were initially introduced in the Web PKI. Here, they serve to record all certificates issued by Certificate Authorities (CAs). This allows mistaken or malicious certificate issuance to be detected. The resulting system is called Certificate Transparency (CT) [20].

Recognizing the potential of these transparency logs, developers have started applying them in various other ecosystems. Notably, they are now used to offer tamper-proofing in diverse sectors such as key transparency, binary transparency, and data access transparency [1,18,19,33].

When incorporated effectively in a responsive cycle, transparency logs can significantly enhance the speed of detecting and responding to any wrongdoing. This is because any changes or additions to the log can be immediately observed and scrutinized, thereby enabling swift action against potential security threats.

## 2.3   Merkle Hash Trees

Transparency logs organize their entries in a cryptographically verifiable data structure, specifically in a Merkle Hash Tree [23]. A Merkle Hash Tree is a form of tamper-evident history tree [8] that stores data at the leaves of a binary tree. A forest consisting of three such trees is depicted in Fig. 2. Each Merkle tree consists of leaf nodes (solid border), intermediate nodes (dotted border), and a root node (dashed border). Every non-leaf node is formed by concatenating the hash of its two child nodes, and hashing the result. Thus, each non-leaf node constitutes a commitment to the contents of its children, and transitively the children of its children. Consequently, each tree's root node is a commitment to the entire tree's contents.

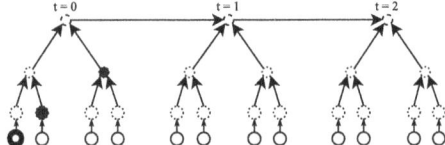

**Fig. 2.** A time-based forest of merkle trees.

The integrity of merkle threes is protected by two cryptographic proofs (as further described in Appendix B): An *inclusion proof* persuades external entities that a leaf is part of the log. A *consistency proof* proves that the log is append only by demonstrating that the published root hashes are consistent.

Based on these proofs, the concept of *verifying a log* generally involves four steps: (i) confirming entry inclusion, (ii) ensuring consistency in log growth, (iii) validating uniformity across user views, and (iv) scrutinizing entries for potential malfeasance. The first three checks verify the correct conduct of the log operator, while the last check strives to guarantee the reliability of log entries and detect indications of malicious actions. *Ensuring the accuracy* of log entries is equally crucial as *recording* them to derive security benefits from transparency. Any system aiming to enhance security through transparency logs must incorporate one or more entities responsible for validating the correctness of log entries.

In the CT use case, Certificate Authorities (CAs) submit their newly issued certificates to the CT Log. Upon acceptance of a certificate, the log issues a signed timestamp that serves as future evidence of submission. TLS clients or browsers can subsequently mandate that all certificates must be accompanied by such a signed timestamp to be deemed valid. Domain owners can actively monitor the logs, regularly requesting all new entries to check for unexpectedly issued certificates for the domains under their responsibility.

It is worth noting that the fundamental infrastructure of applications where these transparency logs are used remains largely unchanged. Instead, this paradigm offers a mechanism to monitor and audit the activities to swiftly identify and exclude authorities engaging in improper practices.

### 2.4 Zero-Knowledge Proofs

Zero-Knowledge (zk) proofs are cryptographic techniques that enable a *prover* to demonstrate their knowledge of information fulfilling certain properties to a *verifier* without disclosing the actual information [15]. Zero-Knowledge Succinct Non-Interactive Arguments of Knowledge (zkSNARKs) are short-proof constructions that do not require any back-and-forth interaction between the prover and the verifier. In this work, we will use zkSNARKs to prove that a certain privacy-preserving record, which is contained in a transparency log, corresponds to – and would be discoverable using – a particular privacy-sensitive piece of information.

## 3 Assumptions and Goals

### 3.1 Participating Actors

We now introduce our system's entities and their roles.

**Credentials and Users.** A *credential* is a data structure containing claims regarding a particular data subject. This data subject is commonly called the *user* or the *holder*. They operate a *user device* implementing a *wallet* application, which stores credentials on their behalf, and can present them to services.

**Verifiers.** The *(credential) verifier*, also known as the *service provider*, is a party requiring the user to prove or reveal certain attributes about themselves. The user achieves this by *presenting* a credential. There are many different service providers, which may offer wildly disparate services. An internet message board, a virtual storefront, a health provider's appointments software, a bank's online banking application, and a government bureau's web portal, are very different kinds of service providers, with different needs.

Many service providers share a need to (re-)identify users. If a user visits a message board, they should have the ability to edit messages they have previously sent; if they visit a storefront, they should be able to see their pending orders; and so forth. It is, therefore, commonly desirable that the credential presentation results in a *trusted persistent identifier* for the user.

**Credential Issuers.** The *credential issuer* is the party that issues credentials to users. They also store additional information that lets them authenticate users, such as password digests, shared secrets, or public keys.

Each service provider must decide whether it will trust a given credential. This decision almost always includes verifying that a trusted issuer issued the credential. In choosing this policy, the service provider determines to which issuers it will delegate the responsibility of actually verifying that the attributes contained in the credential accurately describe the user holding the credential.

We now outline actors not already involved in typical credential systems.

**Log Provider.** The *log provider* is an untrusted party that maintains a public append-only audit log containing chunks of information known as *log entries*. This role is primarily concerned with providing storage of information, and ensuring that this information remains publicly available; a responsibility that none of the traditional actors may wish to assume. The role is untrusted; it does not obtain any information that is not public, and can be cryptographically prevented from modifying or retracting information.

**Auditor.** *Auditors* ensure that the Log Provider strictly appends and maintains global consistency. In other words, Auditors are tasked with uncovering any misbehavior of the Log Provider. Any auditor can detect a cheating log provider, and can irrefutably prove that they cheated. Since any member of the public can operate an auditor, requiring no additional access or privileges, log providers must assume that the data they publish is monitored and audited at all times. This, combined with a robust gossip scheme of the observed log fingerprints, ensures they operate faithfully. Any interested party can act as an auditor; no particular access is required.

**Monitor.** *Monitors* routinely query the data published by the log provider and ensure internal consistency within individual trees. By verifying that the content of the log remains free from inconsistencies, monitors assist in identifying misconduct by the log provider. In doing so, monitors also process individual log entries and can detect mis-issuance. Monitors may also act as mirrors of the log, and offer search and notification services.[1]

---

[1] See Sect. 6.2 for a discussion of the privacy implications of such delegation.

## 3.2   Mis-issuance

In this work, we address a particular type of misbehavior by a credential issuer: the issuance of *legitimate* credentials to *illegitimate* recipients. We are not concerned with the issuer lying about someone's age; we are concerned about them attesting that someone is me even though they are not.

We thus limit ourselves to a particular class of credential, which we will call *identifying credential*. We define this as a credential which, when shown to a particular verifier, will result in that verifier learning some trusted, stable, persistent, unique identifier of that user towards that verifier. Note that these identifiers (or *pseudonyms*) are not necessarily global; the same user may have different pseudonyms towards different verifiers. However, multiple showings by the same user at the same verifier will result in the same pseudonym; this makes the pseudonym suitable for re-identification.

This is a common class of credential; it is used in both OpenID Connect [27] and SAML [24], the most widely used authentication protocols on today's internet. These stable pseudonyms are commonly derived from some private global user identifier (which we'll call userId) only known to the issuer. A naive example of this, commonly used in OpenID Connect's pairwise pseudonymous identifiers, is pseudonym derivation as $H(verifier\|\text{userId})$ for some cryptographic hash function $H$.

With these preliminaries in place, we now define *mis-issuance* in the context of this work as follows: an issuer surreptitiously issues a credential based on a victim's userId to some malicious collaborator, who is not the victim. The collaborator may be the issuer themselves. This credential allows the collaborator to impersonate the user towards verifiers, as presenting the credential will result in verifiers associating the victim's pseudonym with the collaborator.

Our work allows the victim to detect such missuance, allowing them to take appropriate reputation-based action against the issuer. This parallels the efforts of the certificate transparency system to allow website administrators to detect mis-issued TLS certificates. However, certificate transparency concepts do not trivially translate to the credential context; the content of credentials is private, and the user's global identifier is doubly so.

## 3.3   Threat Model

Users, issuers, auditors, and log providers may all act maliciously, attempting to subvert the protocol's intent. We identify the following challenges.

A malicious Log Provider might seek to present different views of the transparency log to different entities. This might serve to avoid disclosing a mis-issued credential to the user, while convincing a verifier that it was logged correctly.

A malicious or compromised issuer might cooperate with, or be, an imposter acting as a user – thus, it might issue a credential allowing this *malicious* user to impersonate another *genuine* user. This is the core challenge that our work mitigates; we consider an issuer that might try to hide the issuance from discovery via the public log, such as by not submitting it, or not submitting it correctly.

We assume that the verifier is motivated to defend against such imperson-ation. This is a natural assumption; if the verifier wanted to arbitrarily grant access to imposter users, they could already do so without involving the issuer.

A malicious auditor – a role that requires no particular authorization – might attempt to learn private information about the user. For example, it might try to enumerate a particular user's credentials.

Finally, collaborating verifiers might attempt to correlate multiple credentials issued to the same user; something that scoped pseudonyms schemes typically aim to prevent. In the scope of this work, we must not enable this via the logged information. The augmented version of any given credential scheme should be as unlinkable as the base version.

### 3.4  Goals

Certificate Transparency offers an inspirational example of such public audit logging being both practicable and practical. Yet, it cannot be translated directly to the credential context; there are multiple challenges, which we outline here.

Fundamentally, *a credential's contents are not public.* By contrast, in certifi-cate transparency, certificates' contents are public. Thus, we cannot simply log the entire credential, as certificate transparency does.

The blinding mechanism we employ needs to be able to solve two challenges. First, *user discoverability.* Given an entry in the credential log, a user should be able to determine whether this entry corresponds to their userId. Second, *verifier verifiability.* Given a credential and a log entry, the verifier needs to be able to determine whether the log entry corresponds to this credential.

Additionally, the following privacy requirements need to be met. First, *cre-dential privacy.* Given all public information, including the public log entry, it is infeasible to determine any claims contained within the credential.[2] Second, *credential unlinkability.* Given two credentials and their associated log entries, it should be infeasible to determine whether they correspond to the same userId.[3]

## 4  Credential Issuance Transparency

This section describes our Credential Issuance Transparency scheme. It is based on append-only logs, cryptographic blinding, and zero-knowledge proofs. It enables genuine users to detect credential mis-issuance while not compromis-ing the privacy properties of the underlying credential scheme.

### 4.1  Building Blocks

We utilize some of the previously-described building blocks unchanged, and make some assumptions regarding the underlying credential scheme.

---

[2] We assume that the entire credential contains sufficient entropy to prevent brute force attacks.

[3] We assume that the existing credentials, without logging, have this property.

**Append-Only Logs.** We assume that an append-only, tamper-evident log, as described in Sect. 2.2, exists. It features efficient proofs of inclusion and consistency, allowing us to ensure the integrity of the recorded information in the log. We assume that auditors have the capability to identify log misbehavior, such as altered logs or split-view attacks. This may necessitate connecting the public snapshots of the log to some form of transparency overlay [7]. We also assume that the log provider can somehow identify authorized credential issuers, preventing the log from being rendered unusable by garbage data.

**Pseudonyms.** We assume that users' stable pseudonyms can be deterministically computed with knowledge of the verifier's identity in addition to some secret global userId, which is only known to the user and issuer. In particular, we assume that this userId is known to the user. In a user-centric identity model, we find this assumption to be reasonable.

**Zero-Knowledge Proof System.** We assume that some trusted procedure has been used to globally initialize a non-interactive zero-knowledge proof system. This allows any user to prove zero-knowledge statements over disclosed or undisclosed inputs to any verifier. Such setup could employ multi-party computation, or some other scheme to ensure its compliant execution. Regardless of how this is done, it only needs to be done once, and the resulting parameters can be used globally.

Under these initial assumptions, we now introduce our protocol.

## 4.2   Protocol

To solve these challenges, we propose our *Credential Issuance Transparency* protocol for privacy-preserving credential issuance audit logging. Its log entries consist of the hash digest of the user's credential and a blinded commitment to the referenced userId. Knowing their userId, a user can then test whether a given entry corresponds to them by simple trial calculation. To satisfy verifiability, we supply verifiers with a non-interactive zero knowledge pre-image proof. Thus, they can verify that the blinded userId in the log entry equals the userId underlying their learned pseudonym, without learning that userId.

We now formalize this intuitive explanation.

Let $C(n, v)$ is a deterministic commitment function; $n$ is a nonce, and $v$ is the input. Given $n$ and $v$, $C(n, v)$ is easy to obtain. At the same time, even given $n$ and $C(n, v)$, $v$ is hard to determine. Additionally, given $n_1$, $C(n_1, v_1)$, $n_2$, and $C(n_2, v_2)$, it is hard to decide whether $v_1 = v_2$.

Let $P(s, u)$ be the pseudonym derivation function; $s$ is some service ID, and $u$ is the user ID. Given $s$ and $u$, $P(s, u)$ is easy to obtain. Yet, given $s$ and $P(s, u)$, $u$ is hard to determine. Additionally, given $s$, $s'$, $P(s, u)$, and $p'$, it is hard to determine whether $p' = P(s', u)$ or not.

Let $H$ be a cryptographic hash function, with the standard properties.

We now augment the credential issuance process as stated in Protocol 1. Steps marked with + are newly introduced by our protocol. The user can then verify that $C(n, \mathsf{userId})$ and $H(x)$ are correct, and that the append proof is valid.

- The issuer creates credential $x$ based on user ID userId.
+ The issuer samples a random nonce $n$, then sends a signed log entry $l :=$ $(n, C(n, \text{userId}), H(x))$ to the log provider.
+ The log provider appends $l$ to the append-only audit log, then returns a signed append-proof to the issuer.
- The issuer returns credential $x$, the log entry, and the append proof to the user.

**Protocol 1.** Issuance Process

The showing process is augmented as stated in Protocol 2. Once again, steps marked with + are added by us. In this process, the verifier convinces itself that the credential has been correctly appended to the public log; due to its append-only nature, the credential cannot be removed once appended.

- The verifier with verifier ID $s$ prompts the user to prove their identity.
- In response, the user shows identifying credential $x$.
+ They also show the log entry $(n, C(n, \text{userId}), H(x))$
  and its append proof.
- The verifier verifies the credential's provenance.
  It learns pseudonym $p := P(s, \text{userId})$ as a result.
+ The user provides a NIZKP of the statement
  $c = C(n, \text{userId}) \land p = P(s, \text{userId})$. The user does not reveal userId.
+ If necessary, the verifier may query a consistency proof from the log provider to validate the inclusion proof.
+ The verifier checks that $H(x)$ in the log entry matches the provided credential.
+ The verifier checks the NIZKP, and compares the revealed inputs $n$, $s$, $c$ and $p$ against the expected values.
+ The verifier can now be confident that the issuance of $x$ was correctly logged.

**Protocol 2.** Showing Process

Finally, in Protocol 3 we introduce a discovery process by which the user can discover all credentials issued for its userId.

+ The user requests all new audit log entries since the last time the process was run.
+ For each entry $(n, C(n, \text{userId}'), H(x))$, the user trial calculates $C(n, \text{userId})$ and compares this against $C(n, \text{userId}')$.
+ If the values match, this entry corresponds to a credential that was issued for the user's identity
+ The user compares $H(x)$ against the values for its known pseudonyms. If no match is found, this credential was mis-issued.

**Protocol 3.** Discovery Process

### 4.3   Analysis

We now argue that our protocol solves the challenges outlined in Sect. 3.4, and thus also addresses the threats discussed in Sect. 3.3.

**User Discoverability.** Assuming that the credential has been correctly appended to the log, the user will necessarily encounter its entry. Once the user encounters the entry, the trial calculation will succeed.

**Verifier Verifiability.** In a scenario where the identity provider has mis-issued a credential, both it and the user the credential was issued to are not trustworthy. Therefore, it falls to the verifier to verify whether the credential has been correctly appended. In order to be *correctly appended*, three criteria need to be met. 1. The log entry needs to be contained in the log. 2. The hash digest in the log entry needs to match the credential. 3. The commitment in the log entry needs to match the userId used for the pseudonym.

After performing the verification steps in Sect. 4.2, the verifier can be assured of all three requirements. 1. It has performed the inclusion check as described in Sect. 2.2. Therefore, the log entry is contained in the log. 2. It has verified that the hash digest of the credential is included in the log entry. 3. It has verified the user-provided NIZKP. Thus, it is assured that the userId committed to in the log entry is the same userId used in the pseudonym derivation.

**Credential Privacy.** The log entry makes $H(cred)$ publicly available. If $cred$ has sufficient entropy, it is infeasible to find $cred$ from this value.

Additionally, the log entry makes the pair $(n, C(n, \text{userId}))$ publicly available. However, assuming that userId has sufficient entropy, it is infeasible to find userId from this pair. Additionally, we note that, if userId did not have sufficient entropy, the pseudonym derivation $P(s, \text{userId})$ would not be privacy-preserving.

**Credential Unlinkability.** Given that the credentials in question are already known, only the two pairs $(n_1, C(n_1, \text{userId}_1))$ and $(n_2, C(n_2, \text{userId}_2))$ are learned from the log entry. Due to our security assumptions regarding $C$, this does not allow an adversary to decide whether $\text{userId}_1 = \text{userId}_2$.

## 5   Evaluation

To demonstrate the feasibility and practicability of CIT we provide a proof-of-concept evaluation based on the Trillian framework.[4] Trillian is a generalization of the tamper-evident log employed by Certificate Transparency, and it accommodates logs of arbitrary data. We use SHA-256 hashes, and commit to userId using $C(n, \text{userId}) := \mathsf{SHA}(n\|\text{userId})$. We similarly derive pseudonyms using $P(s, \text{userId}) := \mathsf{SHA}(s\|\text{userId})$. In both cases, $\|$ is concatenation.

Further, we evaluate the NIZKP proving the relation between the log entry $l$ and the user's pseudonym $p$. For the implementation of the NIZKP we utilize the gnark zk-SNARK library[5] [4].

---

[4] https://github.com/google/trillian.
[5] https://github.com/consensys/gnark.

To ensure the practicability of CIT, two criteria must be met: (i) Logging of issued credentials should not introduce significant delays to the credential issuance and verification process, and (ii) the underlying log storage layer should not impede scalability for broader deployments.

## 5.1   ZKP Proof

While our CIT concept is described on a generic level, the concrete choice of ZKP proof system and implementation is important to assess the feasibility and to evaluate the performance and security. Thus, we provide a concrete instantiation of CIT's NIZKP. To do so, we implement the statement $c = C(n, \mathsf{userId}) \land p = P(s, \mathsf{userId})$ in the form of a gnark circuit [4]. Paraphrased, this states that the commitment $c$ (in the log entry) and pseudonym $p$ (which the verifier will use) correspond to the same userId. This circuit is compiled into a Rank-1 Constraint Systems (R1CS) by gnark. As the proving scheme, we utilize Groth16 [16] on the BN254 elliptic curve. We choose Groth16 for its better performance over, e.g., PLONK [13]. Groth16 uses a circuit-specific trusted setup,[6] but this is not a downside as our system uses the same circuit for all entities in the system. BN254 provides 102 bits of security [17, Table 8]. We benchmark three different commitment functions, demonstrating their impact on the performance. Specifically, we apply the SHA-256, SHA3, MiMC hash functions [2,9,10]. While the SHA family is commonly used in practice, we additionally chose MiMC as representative of a family of ZKP-friendly hash functions. Implementing a ZKP proof on a ZKP-friendly function results in a smaller circuit and, thus, better performance.

## 5.2   Performance Results

We analyze the overhead of employing CIT in a real-world scenario and conclude that doing so would be practical.

**Logging.** We identify three key areas of concern when analyzing CIT's impact on performance.

First, a monitor – i.e., the user – must download all log entries that were appended since the last check. In Web PKI Certificate Transparency, a solution that is deployed in practice, Bingyu Li et al. report an average size of 5.93 KB for log entries, and an average growth rate of 7,778,870 records per day, resulting in 43.99 GB of new log content per day [21]. This makes it practically challenging for anyone except well-supported enterprises to run a CT monitor. In stark contrast, due to only storing blinded data, Certificate Issuance Transparency log entries are constant size – 96 *bytes* in our implementation.[7] Even assuming the monumental growth rate of CT, this results in only 746 MB of log content per day; certainly feasible for users to keep up with on a home internet connection.

---

[6] i.e., the trusted setup of verifier- and prover-key must be redone if the circuit changes.
[7] 32 bytes SHA-256 userId commitment, 32 bytes random blind, 32 bytes SHA-256 credential hash.

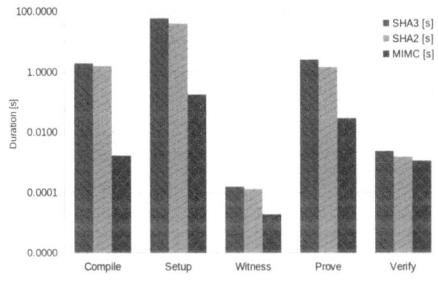

**Fig. 3.** NIZKP Evaluation

**Table 1.** Evaluation Results

| | | BN254 | | |
|---|---|---|---|---|
| | | MiMC | SHA256 | SHA3-256 |
| | security | 102 bit | | |
| | #constraints | 1322 | 170157 | 235032 |
| initiation | compile policy [s] | 0.002 | 1.541 | 1.891 |
| | setup (gen. keys) [s] | 0.176 | 39.134 | 58.189 |
| prepare | gen. witness [s] | 0.00002 | 0.0001 | 0.0002 |
| | prove statement [s] | 0.028 | 1.444 | 2.515 |
| show | verify proof [s] | 0.001 | 0.002 | 0.002 |

Second, the user must go through all downloaded entries and trial calculate to test the userId commitment. In our implementation using SHA-256, hardware acceleration allows for a hash rate of upwards of 3 million hashes per second on consumer hardware [11]. Even discounting various operating system overhead, performing such verification on the 8 million records per day reported by Bingyu Li et al. would clearly be feasible for home users.

Third, the entry must be submitted to the log, and an append proof must be obtained. Both involve negligible transfers of data. Merkle Tree append proof size is logarithmic in the number of elements in the tree; assuming SHA-256 hashes, day-long epochs, and the CT append rate reported by Bingyu Li et al., append proofs would be less than 1 KB each.

We conclude that, even at the scale of worldwide adoption (comparable to CT's), monitoring Certificate Issuance Transparency logs would remain feasible for end users on common home PCs. Additionally, the logging operations introduced by CIT do not add any perceptible overhead to the issuance process.

**Proofs of Logging Correctness.** To evaluate our ZKP implementation, we perform several benchmarks on an office laptop with an Intel i7-8550U CPU. The results of this evaluation are given in Table 1 and visualized in Fig. 3. We divide the steps into three phases: i) the initiation phase is only performed once for the whole system and comprises the (trusted) setup and the compilation of the circuits, ii) the preparation phase is performed once for each nonce-userID-spID tuple and can be pre-computed by the user, and iii) the showing phase is performed by the verifier on each credential showing. We note that the showing phase is fast enough that caching at the verifier is not useful, but possible.

## 6   Discussion

In a given application scenario, it might be desirable to tweak the functionality of our protocol. We discuss potential avenues for doing so; allowing the trading of privacy for performance alongside various axes.

## 6.1   Identifying Credentials

Our work is limited to auditing the issuance of *identifying credentials*, which produce a stable pseudonym for the user at a particular verifier. We have done this because for this class of credential, the intuitive concept of "mis-issuance" can be defined rather plainly, by tying it to the pseudonym in question.

Of course, not all credentials are identifying credentials. I might be issued a credential that only includes my date of birth. We might also want to audit mis-issuance of such credentials. However, I almost certainly share a date of birth with some other legitimate credential subject. If a date-of-birth credential for my date of birth is issued to them, this is not mis-issuance. Yet, from my point of view, the two cases are indistinguishable; it is not even clear how to define "mis-issuance" in this context.

Finally, we turn to a third case: identifying credentials being used in contexts where the identifying information – the pseudonym – is not used by the verifier. For example, this may be achieved by not selectively disclosing the pseudonym. At first, a path forward seems apparent in this scenario: perform issuance audit logging as usual, but instead of disclosing the pseudonym, extend the NInowZKP in Sect. 4.2 to prove consistency with the undisclosed pseudonym contained in the credential. While the details might vary based on the pseudonym derivation method used, this seems intuitively possible. Yet, this hope, too, is fleeting. After all, consider a scenario where the issuer, cooperating with some malicious user, issues a modified credential to that user containing otherwise identical claims, but a bogus pseudonym derived from a non-existent userId. The issuer then faithfully records this credential in the audit log. Since the only information the verifier makes use of in this scenario is non-identifying information – not the pseudonym – this credential is *functionally equivalent* to a genuine credential. Clearly, the modified credential was also *mis-issued*; yet, since the identifying attributes are not used by the verifier, this mis-issuance is functionally equivalent yet hard to capture in a rigorous definition.

**Other Uniquely Identifying Information.** In this work, we have focused on "a pseudonym" as the unique identifier of a user towards a given verifier. One might reasonably argue that no specific pseudonym is necessary to define "mis-issuance"; after all, if someone else is issued a credential containing my first name, last name, and date of birth, isn't this also clearly mis-issuance? It is not clear that this is the case; *identity* is a hard concept to pin down. "Data twins", people sharing both the same name and the same date of birth, are not unheard of. However, if one is convinced that they have identified such a uniquely identifying combination of attributes, the concepts of this work can be extended seamlessly by substituting the combination of these attributes for a pseudonym.

## 6.2   Delegating Log Monitoring

Our base scheme, described in Sect. 4.2, requires interested users to monitor all new additions to the audit log, and trial calculate to test whether the addition matches their own userId. This may not be desirable for some users. While the effort expended to perform this monitoring is not excessive, it may nevertheless be desirable for users to delegate this duty to professional *monitors*. Such a monitor could process the log just once, and notify each user only of the log entries that concern them.

This delegation can be supported by a slight adjustment to our protocol, and at a trade-off in NIZKP performance. Our current protocol publicly logs a commitment to userId, in the form of $C(n, \text{userId})$. Knowing userId, the user can test each log entry. However, delegating monitoring to a third party would then also require userId to be disclosed to the third party. This allows the user to be de-anonymized at SPs globally. Even if the monitor is trusted to perform monitoring, disclosing such sensitive data is not desirable.

Thus, if delegation should be supported, instead of logging a commitment to userId, a commitment to $H(\text{userId})^8$, i.e., $C(n, H(\text{userId}))$, can be logged instead. This allows a third-party monitor to operate only with knowledge of $H(\text{userId})$. This knowledge permits the monitor to determine whether a given log entry corresponds to the underlying user, as desired; but it does not allow it to perform any other operations on the userId, nor does it allow it to learn the userId. Of course, the NIZKP provided to the verifier also needs to incorporate this additional operation. This corresponds to a 50% increase in system setup and proof generation time compared to our existing benchmarks in Sect. 5.

### 6.3  Anonymity Versus Monitoring Efficiency

Another venue for improving monitoring efficiency is trading off some of the user's anonymity for a corresponding decrease in entries to be monitored. For $n$-bit userIds, this is achieved by choosing a parameter $p$ from 0 to $n$, and treating the first $p$ bits of the user's userId as public information. The audit log can then effectively be fragmented into $2^p$ different audit logs. Each user only needs to monitor one of these logs, which contains $2^{-p}$ times as many entries as the unparameterized log. The correct assignment of the entry to a particular log can be verified as part of the existing NIZKP by simply revealing the first $p$ bits of the userId input. This does not induce significant overhead. However, such a parametrization comes with a commensurate reduction in anonymity, as the user base is split into $2^p$ disjoint anonymity sets.

### 6.4  Related Work

We examine research associated with transparency overlays and digital (verifiable) credentials regarding the underlying data structures and sanitization mechanisms employed.

In *Certree*, Saramago et al. suggest a system that adds transparency to certification systems of academic credentials [28]. Their approach enhances transparency in the issuance process by leveraging metadata about each individual certification stage, such as a course completed towards a degree, recorded in a

---

[8] or, in practice, $H(\text{``}LOG\_KEY\text{''}\|\text{userId})$ to provide domain separation.

blockchain. However, at the same time, their approach requires all credentials to be made public. This allows tracking all users' credentials and related activities through on-chain data, as user addresses (hash of their public key) are included in the metadata for each credential.

*Zk-Cert* maintains the transparency of certifying academic credentials systems provided by Certree while significantly enhancing privacy by implementing zero-knowledge proofs [29]. Their approach employs a blockchain as a verifiable data registry with robust timestamping capabilities. A group of smart contracts systematically records cryptographic commitments of all issued credentials in an incremental Merkle Tree, and zero-knowledge proofs enable subjects to demonstrate ownership over these commitments without disclosing them.

Chase et al. propose and formalize their *credential transparency framework (CTS)* for remote (possibly cloud-based) credential management systems (CMS) [6]. CTS adds transparency guarantees by logging every time a credential management service provider *presents* a credential on behalf of a user to an honest verifier, in such a way that the user can then audit all the presentations made on their behalf, without the remote CMS being able to manipulate or omit any presentation without detection. This cloud-based CMS maintains a Strong Accumulator (SA) data structure that stores commitments of credential presentations' contexts and a zero-knowledge set (ZKS) of the number of uses of the user's credential. The framework is compatible with credential management systems of varying degrees of privacy-preservation. By taking this approach and abstracting each credential presentation as a "showing", they ensure that incorporating logging guarantees does not introduce substantial additional privacy leakage beyond what the credential presentation already discloses.

Goldwasser et al. address the lack of accountability of anonymous credentials that restricts their practical applications in real-world scenarios [14]. They present an *anonymous verifiable logging scheme* that allows decentralized inspectors to enforce accountability for anonymous credential users. This scheme guarantees that the user's activities are recorded and encrypted using a key that is unique to the user. A third-party auditor that possesses the user's log decryption key, can subsequently access and assess the user's actions to ascertain compliance to regulations. They adapt the issuing protocol by including a log encryption key chosen by the user and the auditor in the credential. They associate the log entries of anonymous credential presentations with the credential user identified during issuance so that a comprehensive log of all the user's activities at honest verifiers can be retrieved. Importantly, this retrieval doesn't compromise the privacy of other users.

Zk-creds, besides employing general-purpose zero-knowledge proofs as a basis for anonymous credentials, proposes to eliminate the requirement for credential issuers to secure signing keys by issuing credentials to a public bulletin board [26]. By doing so, every issued credential is observable and the issuance process is auditable. A user can use her credential by showing a membership proof that the credential is present in the issuance list. Membership proofs are realized through

Merkle Forests rather than a single Merkle Tree for an improved tradeoff between proving and verification time.

### 6.5    Future Work: Multi-show Unlinkability

Our approach described in this work has one log line correspond to one issued credential. The user then provides this log line, and a traditional inclusion proof, to verifiers when showing the credential. This prevents *multi-show unlinkability*, where multiple instances of showing the same credential cannot be correlated. Current eIDAS 2.0 implementations do not provide this property. However, more advanced cryptographic schemes such as BBS+ do [3].

It may be possible to adopt our approach to work in such schemes without compromising multi-show unlinkability. We believe this might be achieved by a two-step process: first, by replacing the credential hash $H(x)$ with a blinded commitment; and second, by showing a NIZKP that merely proves that a correct log line exists in a given tree instead of disclosing the particular line. We do not pursue this idea further in this work.

**Acknowledgments.** This work was supported by the European Union's research and innovation programme under grant agreements № 101020416 (ERATOSTHENES) and № 101168311 (LICORICE).

## A    Verifiable Presentations

A Verifiable Credential (VC) showing process begins with a verifier sending a credential presentation request to the user. This request generally includes a nonce to prevent replay attacks and asks for the disclosure of certain attributes from one or several of the user's credentials. It also includes additional parameters and constraints, such as a timestamp for expiration and revocation-related requirements, or a list of trusted issuers for each identity attribute.

Verifiable Presentation (VP) refers to a process involving individuals, or "users", who use their credentials to disclose identity attributes to "verifiers" or relying parties. Upon receiving the presentation request, the user's digital wallet application automatically searches for stored credentials that include the requested attributes and meet the requirements specified in the request. With the user's consent, the wallet app creates a cryptographic proof of the correctness of these attributes and sends them, along with the proof, to the verifier.

To avoid showing excessive information, VPs with a privacy emphasis selectively disclose specific attributes to the verifier. VPs also contain some form of blinded cryptographic evidence originating from the credential, indicating that the displayed subset of attributes is genuinely derived from a credential endorsed by the corresponding issuer. These proofs may be built using a variety of technologies, such as Merkle hash trees (Sect. 2.3) or zero-knowledge proofs (see also Sect. 2.4). The verifier can then automatically check the proof, and verify that the credential was issued by an issuer that it trusts. It thus trusts the authenticity of the identity attributes claimed by the user, allowing them to be used to provide services to them.

# B    Merkle Hash Tree Security

It is possible to link multiple hash trees trees together to form an incrementally growing forest. Each append batch consists of a single Merkle Tree. The root hash of the previous Merkle tree forms part of the input to the new tree's root hash. Thus, the new root hash also doubles as a commitment to the previous root hash; and, transitively, as a commitment to the previous tree's contents, as well as any other previous trees' root hashes and contents. This gives us two categories of cryptographic proofs: *inclusion proofs* and *consistency proofs*.

An *inclusion proof* persuades external entities that a leaf is part of the log. It consists of a path within the Merkle Tree, extending from the leaf containing the relevant data to the root hash embedded in the published fingerprint. A *Merkle audit path* is computed for an inclusion proof and consists of the set of missing nodes that are essential for calculating the tree's root. If the computed root from the audit path aligns with the actual root, it serves as evidence that the leaf in question is present in the tree. In Fig. 2, the inclusion proof for the bolded node is depicted with a dark background.

On the other hand, a *consistency proof* proves that the log is append-only by demonstrating that the published root hashes are consistent. Consistency proofs enable external entities to confirm that the log strictly appends, ensuring that the log reflected by a fingerprint at an earlier point in time is a precursor of the log indicated by a fingerprint at a subsequent time. A consistency proof contains a subset of intermediary nodes in the Merkle Tree that are essential for linking the two root hashes. Entities within the system share the observed log snapshots using so-called "gossiping" mechanisms that ensure that all parties have the same view of the log at the point of time of the snapshot.

# References

1. Al-Bassam, M., Meiklejohn, S.: Contour: a practical system for binary transparency. CoRR **abs/1712.08427** (2017)
2. Albrecht, M., Grassi, L., Rechberger, C., Roy, A., Tiessen, T.: MiMC: efficient encryption and cryptographic hashing with minimal multiplicative complexity. In: Cheon, J.H., Takagi, T. (eds.) ASIACRYPT 2016. LNCS, vol. 10031, pp. 191–219. Springer, Heidelberg (2016). https://doi.org/10.1007/978-3-662-53887-6_7
3. Au, M.H., Susilo, W., Mu, Y.: Constant-size dynamic k-TAA. In: De Prisco, R., Yung, M. (eds.) SCN 2006. LNCS, vol. 4116, pp. 111–125. Springer, Heidelberg (2006). https://doi.org/10.1007/11832072_8
4. Botrel, G., Piellard, T., Housni, Y.E., Kubjas, I., Tabaie, A.: Consensys/gnark: v0.9.0, February 2023. https://doi.org/10.5281/zenodo.5819104
5. Cameron, K.: The laws of identity (2005)
6. Chase, M., Fuchsbauer, G., Ghosh, E., Plouviez, A.: Credential transparency system. In: International Conference on Security and Cryptography for Networks (2022)
7. Chase, M., Meiklejohn, S.: Transparency overlays and applications. In: Proceedings of the 2016 ACM SIGSAC Conference on Computer and Communications Security (2016)

8. Crosby, S.A., Wallach, D.S.: Efficient data structures for tamper-evident logging. In: USENIX Security Symposium (2009)

9. Dang, Q.: Secure hash standard (SHS), 06 March 2012

10. Dworkin, M.: SHA-3 standard: permutation-based hash and extendable-output functions, 04 August 2015

11. ECRYPT VAMPIRE: Measurements of hash functions, index by machine (2024). https://bench.cr.yp.to/results-hash.html

12. European Parliament, Council of the European Union: Regulation (EU) 2024/1183 of the European Parliament and of the Council of 11 April 2024 amending Regulation (EU) No 910/2014 as regards establishing the European Digital Identity Framework (eIDAS 2) (2024)

13. Gabizon, A., Williamson, Z.J., Ciobotaru, O.: PLONK: permutations over Lagrange-bases for oecumenical noninteractive arguments of knowledge. IACR Cryptol. ePrint Arch. (2019)

14. Godtschalk, L.: Accountability and access control using anonymous credentials (2022)

15. Goldwasser, S., Micali, S., Rackoff, C.: The knowledge complexity of interactive proof-systems (2019)

16. Groth, J.: On the size of pairing-based non-interactive arguments. In: Fischlin, M., Coron, J.-S. (eds.) EUROCRYPT 2016. LNCS, vol. 9666, pp. 305–326. Springer, Heidelberg (2016). https://doi.org/10.1007/978-3-662-49896-5_11

17. Guillevic, A., Singh, S.: On the alpha value of polynomials in the tower number field sieve algorithm. IACR Cryptol. ePrint Arch. (2019)

18. Hicks, A., Mavroudis, V., Al-Bassam, M., Meiklejohn, S., Murdoch, S.J.: VAMS: verifiable auditing of access to confidential data. CoRR **abs/1805.04772** (2018)

19. Hof, B., Carle, G.: Software distribution transparency and auditability (2017)

20. Laurie, B., et al.: Certificate transparency v2.0. RFC **9162** (2021)

21. Li, B., et al.: Certificate transparency in the wild: exploring the reliability of monitors. In: CCS. ACM (2019)

22. Marquardt, F., Schmidt, C.: Don't stop at the top: using certificate transparency logs to extend domain lists for web security studies. In: LCN. IEEE (2020)

23. Merkle, R.C.: A digital signature based on a conventional encryption function. In: Pomerance, C. (ed.) CRYPTO 1987. LNCS, vol. 293, pp. 369–378. Springer, Heidelberg (1988). https://doi.org/10.1007/3-540-48184-2_32

24. OASIS Security Services TC: Security assertion markup language (SAML) v2.0 technical overview (2008). https://docs.oasis-open.org/security/saml/Post2.0/sstc-saml-tech-overview-2.0-cd-02.html

25. Roberts, R., Levin, D.: When certificate transparency is too transparent: analyzing information leakage in HTTPS domain names. In: WPES@CCS. ACM (2019)

26. Rosenberg, M., White, J., Garman, C., Miers, I.: zk-creds: flexible anonymous credentials from zksnarks and existing identity infrastructure. In: IEEE Symposium on Security and Privacy (2023)

27. Sakimura, N., Bradley, J., Jones, M.B., de Medeiros, B., Mortimore, C.: Openid connect core 1.0 (2014). https://openid.net/specs/openid-connect-core-1_0.html

28. Saramago, R.Q., Jehl, L., Meling, H., Estrada-Galiñanes, V.: A tree-based construction for verifiable diplomas with issuer transparency. In: IEEE International Conference on DAPPS (2021)

29. Saramago, R.Q., Meling, H., Jehl, L.N.: A privacy-preserving and transparent certification system for digital credentials. In: International Conference on Principles of Distributed Systems (OPODIS) (2023)

30. Scheitle, Q., et al.: The rise of certificate transparency and its implications on the internet ecosystem (2018)
31. Sporny, M., Longley, D., Chadwick, D.: Verifiable credentials data model v1.1 (2022). https://www.w3.org/TR/vc-data-model/
32. Zwattendorfer, B., Zefferer, T., Stranacher, K.: An overview of cloud identity management-models. In: WEBIST (1). SciTePress (2014)
33. Melara, M., Blankstein, A., Bonneau, J., Felten, E., Freedman, M.: CONIKS: bringing key transparency to end users. In: 24th USENIX Security Symposium, USENIX Security 2015, Washington, D.C., USA, 12–14 August 2015, pp. 383–398 (2015). https://www.usenix.org/conference/usenixsecurity15/technical-sessions/presentation/melara

# Decentralized Data Usage Control with Confidential Data Processing on Trusted Execution Environment and Distributed Ledger Technology

Shota Tokuda[1]([✉]) [iD], Shohei Kakei[1] [iD], Yoshiaki Shiraishi[2] [iD],
and Shoichi Saito[1] [iD]

[1] Nagoya Institute of Technology, Nagoya, Japan
`s.tokuda.570@nitech.jp`, {`kakei.shohei,shoichi`}`@nitech.ac.jp`
[2] Kobe University, Kobe, Japan

**Abstract.** Data utilization process can produce new value from a variety of data sources. Personal data is one of the valuable data sources, but its utilization has yet to reach its full potential due to the risk of data leakage. This paper proposes a decentralized data processing framework that leverages data usage control with trusted execution environments (TEEs) and distributed ledger technology. This framework allows data consumers to implement their data processing codes for flexible data utilization while data providers can control the use of data in those codes. Through this data usage control, data providers can control data disclosure or usage deadlines while preventing data leakage. We evaluate the proposed framework from both theoretical and practical perspectives. The results show that the proposed framework meets confidentiality requirements of provided data and that the prototype system using Intel SGX and Hyperledger Fabric can process small amounts of data, such as personal data, in acceptable time. While not suited for frequent data processing, it illustrates the potential for collecting and using personal data in advance, for example, to support disaster response.

**Keywords:** data utilization · data usage control · trusted execution environment · distributed ledger technology

## 1 Introduction

With the development of Internet of Things (IoT) devices and cloud technology, a variety of data are expected to be collected and utilized. Information about building conditions obtained from IoT sensors can be used to improve the evacuation process, such as in the event of a fire [22]. In addition, personal data, such as location information, can be used for decision-making during natural disasters and epidemics [18,21]. Location information obtained from mobile phones can help set up appropriate evacuation shelters and provide supplies during natural

H. H. Song et al. (Eds.): NSS 2024, LNCS 15564, pp. 127–144, 2025.
https://doi.org/10.1007/978-981-96-3531-3_7

disasters. If evacuee attribute information, such as medical history and physical characteristics, could be obtained in addition to this location information, it would be possible to provide evacuation guidance that provides the optimal evacuation route for each individual. The protection of privacy is crucial when using such personal data. The General Data Protection Regulation (GDPR) [5] is a law on personal data protection in the EU that came into effect in 2018, setting out principles to process personal data. Compliance with these laws and regulations ensures that data are provided and used securely. However, anonymizing data to protect privacy makes it difficult to obtain accurate information and can make it difficult to calculate the optimal evacuation route.

Park et al. [13] introduced a concept of data usage control to continuously monitor digital resources in dynamic distributed environments. Data usage control is a concept that extends general access control and allows for more detailed data control after data are provided. In recent years, some research has been conducted on methods to enforce compliance with data usage control in decentralized environments [2,3,7]. This research uses a trusted execution environment (TEE) and blockchain technology to achieve compliance with usage conditions through data usage control. In data sharing that involves data processing, verifying data processing is crucial to preventing data misuse. Some frameworks verify data processing before providing data to prevent data misuse [9,20]. However, this verification has not been adequately discussed because the method is assumed to be performed properly by assumption or relies on a single point of failure in these studies. With a data processing verification method that relies on a single point of failure, data could be misused if the central authority verifying data processing was compromised.

This paper proposes a data usage control method that ensures that provided data are used as intended by data providers while ensuring the flexibility of the data processing implemented by a data consumer. We also introduce a data processing framework that uses TEE and distributed ledger technology (DLT) to realize the proposed method. In this framework, data consumers implement data processing codes according to the templates specified by the framework. The template contains codes for communication with data providers and data usage control, and the security baseline for data processing is assured by verifying that the implemented source code is compliant with the template. In addition, data flow analysis is performed on the data processing code to prevent unintended leakage of provided data. These protection measures for provided data are carried out with a smart contract to ensure the integrity of the verification and analysis process.

The contributions of this paper are as follows:

- We propose a data usage control method that balances with the flexibility of the data processing. The template used by data consumers to implement data processing apps includes a module for data usage control, and data consumers can describe arbitrary algorithms under some restrictions in the data processing code. In this method, in order to prevent unauthorized acquisition of provided data, data providers can verify the data processing code implemented by the data consumer and know before providing data whether provided data will be disclosed or not.

– We propose a decentralized data processing framework that realizes the proposed data usage control method. The framework ensures the confidentiality of provided data by leveraging the integrity of TEE applications and the confidentiality of data being processed. In the proposed framework, data processing is verified by using a smart contract with permissioned DLT, so that data processing code implemented by a data consumer can be kept secret from data providers while the results of the code verification are presented to the data providers. Data processing using the proposed framework can handle not only scenarios that use pre-implemented and fixed apps, but also scenarios that require dynamic trust relationships to be established between data providers and consumers.

– We evaluated the security of the proposed framework and showed what threats it can counter. In addition, we implemented a prototype of the framework using Intel SGX and Hyperledger Fabric to demonstrate its feasibility and scalability.

## 2 Background

An example of a data utilization model is one in which data providers deposit data with a central authority, such as a broker, and data consumers gain insights through the central authority. This model forces data providers to trust that the central authority will not misuse their data. If this central authority is compromised, the data could be misused. As the data infrastructure develops, the types and volumes of data handled increase, but the risk of data leakage increases, creating a dilemma [19]. This dilemma requires the infrastructure to make a choice: accept the risk and increase the scale of the service, or avoid the risk and limit the scale to handle a smaller amount of data. This risk can be reduced by using a decentralized approach that exchanges data directly between data providers and consumers without aggregating data in a central authority.

Research has been conducted on data utilization using TEE and DLT to ensure data confidentiality. PrivacyGuard [20] uses TEE and blockchain technology to control data access and usage. This system manages data usage policies on-chain, and data processing is performed off-chain, protected by a TEE enclave. PrivacyGuard assumes that operations requested by data consumers are ratified in advance by a trusted third party. Therefore, the prevention of data misuse in this system was based on a single third party. This assumption is sufficient when data consumers only use programs ratified in advance. However, in scenarios where programs are implemented by data consumers, it is necessary to apply to the third party for each data processing, and such scenarios are outside the scope of PrivacyGuard. To address such a variety of scenarios, it is not sufficient to simply assume that an external third party has approved operations in advance, and it is necessary to verify a program within a system.

PrivacyGuard does not verify data processing in the system. However, Lei et al. proposed TrustControl [9], which incorporates this verification into remote

**Fig. 1.** Data processing scenario for facility visitors in the event of a disaster.

attestation. This method verifies the processing code with an external authentication server and decides to provide data based on the verification results. This code verification ensures that provided data are processed as expected by the data provider. TrustControl assumes that the authentication server for verification is sufficiently secure; however, because it is a single point of failure, a data provider must trust the server. If the verification depends on a single point of failure, the data can be misused if that server is compromised. Therefore, it is important to verify that data processing is independent of a single point of failure.

## 3    Motivation and Requirements

### 3.1    Motivating Scenario

Figure 1 shows a hypothetical scenario that uses data acquired from personal smartphones to provide evacuation guidance during disasters in a facility. In this scenario, a facility manager quickly guides visitors to evacuation sites by transmitting evacuation instructions through a smartphone app in the event of a disaster. The facility manager assesses damage information and directs evacuation routes; however, a uniform evacuation route is inconvenient for facilities used by a variety of people. For example, facility managers may need to direct them to other routes because wheelchair users cannot evacuate using stairs. Furthermore, if the facility manager records information on the health status, age, and other attributes of visitors, this information can be used for lifesaving activities by the first responder at evacuation sites. Thus, from the perspective of disaster risk reduction, facility managers should collect information on visitor attributes prior to a disaster. However, such attribute information must be handled carefully in terms of privacy. Therefore, it is necessary to have a mechanism to ensure the confidentiality of provided data by prohibiting access by facility managers during normal times and allowing facility managers to obtain only information on evacuation routes and first responders to gain only information

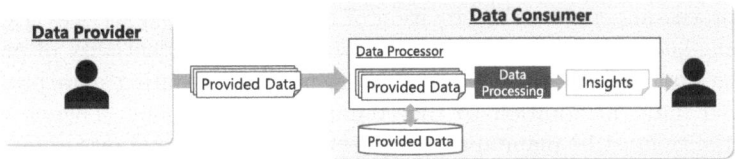

**Fig. 2.** Our assumed data processing model.

on lifesaving activities in the event of a disaster. In addition, controls on expiration dates are necessary to prevent the continuous use of the provided attribute information.

Considering the risk of data processing relying on a central authority, as described in Sect. 2, this research assumes a decentralized data processing model in which data providers and data consumers exchange data directly. The data processing model assumed in this study is shown in Fig. 2. In the assumed model, a data provider (e.g., visitor) provides data directly to a data processor of a data consumer (e.g., facility manager), and the data consumer temporarily stores provided data (e.g., personal data) until required. When the provided data are required (e.g., when a disaster occurs), consumers obtain only insights (e.g., route information and information necessary for lifesaving activities) from the provided data.

### 3.2 Threat Analysis

We assume that the goal of an adversary is to expose provided data in order to compromise the privacy of data providers. As a data consumer, an adversary can use the data provided for data processing. The assumed threat model focuses on the point of data leakage from the data processor and data store, and the adversary can take three approaches: compromise of the data processor and data store, misuse of the data processor, and substitution of the data processor. First, the adversary attempts to obtain provided data from the memory during data processing performed or temporarily stored provided data. Second, the adversary attempts to obtain provided data because of an unauthorized data processor. Third, the adversary substitutes the data processor after data acquisition and attempts to obtain provided data through an unauthorized data processor.

We assume that there is no exploitation of vulnerabilities, such as TEE side-channel attacks, and that servers used for remote attestation are trustworthy. Furthermore, in the proposed method, the distributed ledger network assumes that there are sufficient participants to maintain security.

### 3.3 Requirements

We defined three requirements based on the threat model.

**Req. 1: Provided data in the data processor and stored data cannot be obtained by data consumers.** The use of personal data as provided data in data processing enables the provision of more fine-grained services. However, when using such data, it is important to ensure the confidentiality of provided data. The provided data may be leaked from memory during data processing and stored data, in addition to the communication channel. Therefore, data confidentiality must be maintained during the data processing performed by the data processor and stored data against adversaries attempting to compromise the data processor and the data store.

**Req. 2: Data providers can make data provision decisions based on the data processor programmed by data consumers.** Data consumers can gain more flexibility in data processing by making the data processor programmable by data consumers. However, data providers should verify the data processor in advance to determine what data processing will be performed, as there is a possibility of data misuse during data processing. This verification prevents the unintended disclosure of data during data processing by adversaries who try to misuse the data processor. This verification should be independent of a single point of failure because if a single external organization performs the verification, this organization will not be properly verified if it is compromised.

**Req. 3: Provided data are used in the data processor in accordance with the agreement and conditions presented by data providers to the data consumer.** It is important to ensure that data consumers use provided data in accordance with usage conditions in order for data providers to be able to control how their data are used. Temporarily stored data must also be used in accordance with the conditions presented by the data providers. The conditions are assumed to include the data processor used, location, expiration date, and number of uses. Compliance with the conditions prevents the acquisition of provided data by adversaries who maliciously substitute data processors.

## 4    Design

### 4.1    Proposed Data Usage Control Method

The proposed data usage control method assures that provided data in a data processing app is used in accordance with usage conditions agreed to by data providers. In addition, data providers can verify whether the provided data are disclosed in the data processing. This method is characterized by the flexibility it provides for data processing implemented by data consumers while preventing unauthorized use or unauthorized acquisition of provided data.

#### 4.1.1    Overview

Figure 3 shows an overview of the proposed data usage control method. This section describes the proposed method using the terms used in XACML [12] and IDS [4]. In this method, a data consumer must implement data processing apps according to a specified data processing app template. This template contains codes for data acquisition and temporary data storing, and only the data processing part can be implemented by data consumers. It also contains a policy

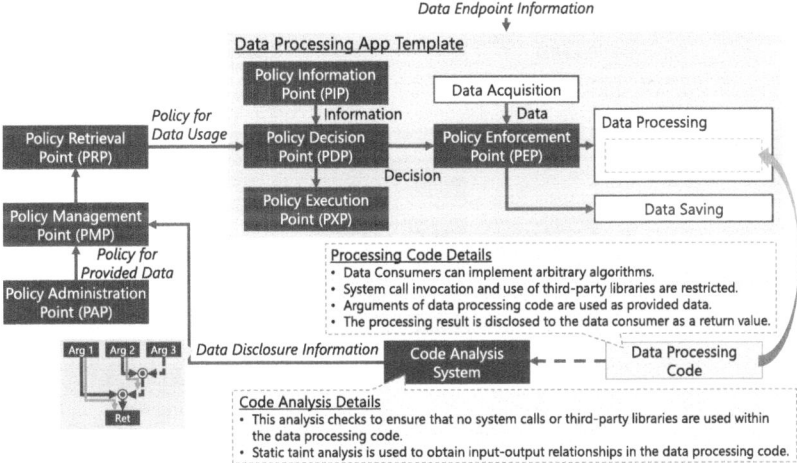

**Fig. 3.** Overview of proposed data usage control method. The PEP controls the use of data while intervening in the flow of data, based on the decision of the PDP. The decision will be based on the information from the PIP and PRP. The PRP provides usage conditions derived from the details of the data processing code and the policy from the PAP. The PXP performs additional actions for policy compliance under the PDP.

decision point (PDP) that makes a decision on data usage based on a data usage policy provided by the policy retrieval point (PRP). The decision on the PDP is made using information from the policy information point (PIP). Examples of information that can be obtained from the PIP include location or time information, which can be used for data usage control. The policy enforcement point (PEP) allows data processing and saving based on the decision of the PDP. The PEP intercepts the flow of data obtained from the data endpoint and requests the PDP to check the data usage policy. The policy execution point (PXP) performs actions as directed by the PDP. An example of this action is the deletion of expired provision data. The PRP acquires the instantiated data usage policy from the policy management point (PMP), which manages the policies created by the policy administration point (PAP). The PMP uses data disclosure information in the data processing code to calculate usage conditions contained in the data usage policy. This information allows the PMP to confirm whether or not each input data is disclosed in the data processing. Details of the data processing code and analysis method are explained in Sect. 4.1.2.

## 4.1.2 Processing Code Analysis

The proposed method employs data flow analysis to follow the flow of provided data in data processing. However, it could be difficult to analyze accurately in general. Therefore, the proposed method allows data consumers to implement only the data processing code, with the restriction of not using system calls and

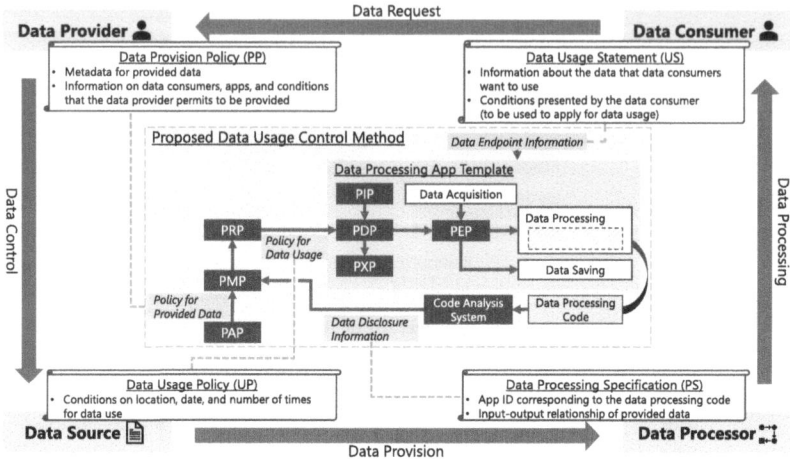

**Fig. 4.** Data model for proposed data usage control method.

third-party libraries that would make data flow analysis difficult. Then, data flow analysis is performed by static taint analysis while maintaining code brevity through template compliance. It can be seen from the analysis that the provided data will not be disclosed unless any part of the provided data is returned from the data processing code.

The proposed method uses static taint analysis for data flow analysis of the data processing code within the code analysis system shown in Fig. 3. Static taint analysis is a type of data flow analysis, which is an analysis method that analyzes source code to trace data transitions within a program and verify whether or not data leaks have occurred. This analysis labels defined information sources, called *taint source*, and propagates the labels among the variables. Then, when a labeled variable reaches a defined point, called *taint sink*, the data corresponding to that label is found to be disclosed. In the taint analysis of the proposed method, the arguments of the data processing code are set as taint sources and the return value is set as a taint sink. By performing taint analysis in such a setting, it is possible to check whether provided data will be disclosed.

## 4.2   Decentralized Data Processing Framework

### 4.2.1   Data Model for Proposed Data Usage Control Method

This section describes the information held by each entity that is necessary to realize the proposed method. Figure 4 shows the relationship between the information and the proposed method. These four types of information are used to manage provided data and data processing codes, and to present requests and conditions. Data endpoint information to be input into the data processing app is represented by a *data usage statement* (US). The US contains information about provided data to be used and how the data will be used. It is also used when applying to data providers for data usage (details are given in Sect. 4.3).

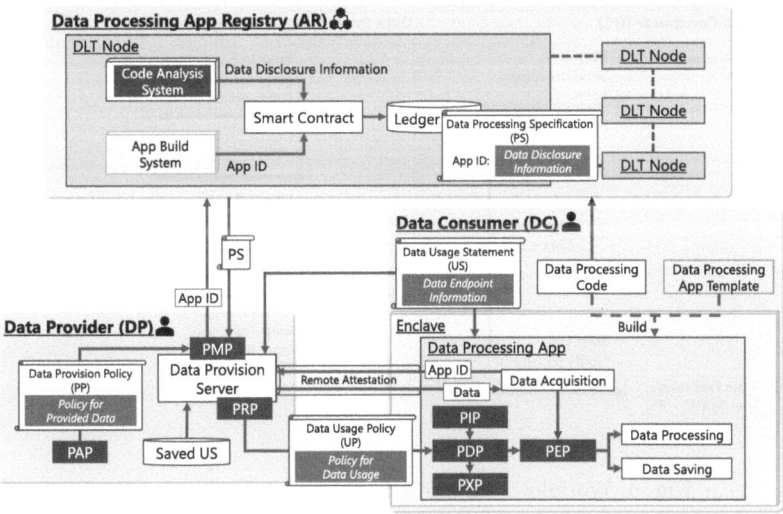

**Fig. 5.** Overview of proposed data processing framework.

The policy created by the PAP is described as a *data provision policy* (PP) and contains information about the provided data and the conditions for each provided data. Data disclosure information in data processing is managed as a *data processing specification* (PS) and presented to the PMP. The PMP creates a *data usage policy* (UP) based on this information and provides it to the PDP via the PRP.

### 4.2.2 Overview of Proposed Framework
Figure 5 shows an overview of the proposed framework. In this framework, data providers, data consumers, and a data processing app registry exist as entities.

**Data Provider (DP):** This entity provides the data it owns to the data consumers. This framework assumes that more than one data provider exists.

**Data Consumer (DC):** This entity obtains data from the DP and processes the data in the data processing app. The data processing app is implemented by a data consumer.

**Data Processing App Registry (AR):** This entity verifies and analyzes the data processing code sent from DCs and stores information on data disclosure in data processing. This entity comprises multiple organizations.

In the proposed framework, the data processing app runs in a TEE enclave, ensuring the integrity of the app and the confidentiality of provided data during processing. In addition, the analysis of the data processing uses a smart contract in the permissioned DLT. This analysis could be performed by the data provider; however, it would be an arduous work. The data consumer may not want to disclose the data processing code to data providers. To address this, the analysis

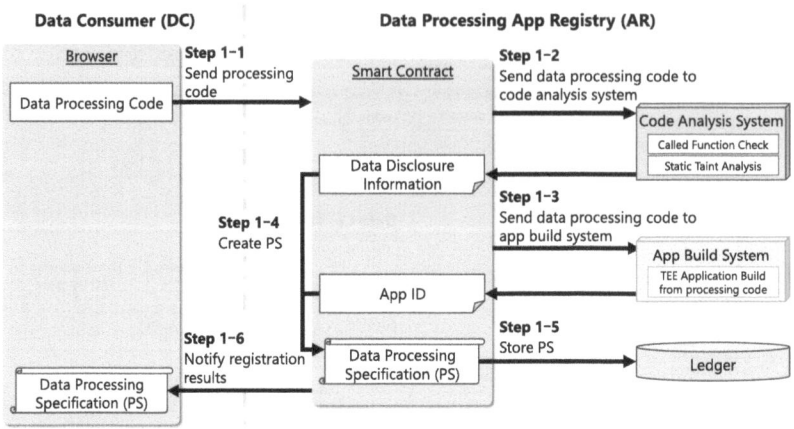

**Fig. 6.** Workflow of phase 1 in the proposed framework.

in the proposed framework is performed using permissioned DLT so that the data processing code is not disclosed to anyone other than the authorized entities that comprise the AR. In addition, smart contracts ensure the integrity and fault tolerance of the analysis process.

The data provision server obtains the PS using the ID of the data processing app obtained through remote attestation. To make the PS retrievable using the app ID, it is necessary to link the processing app code to the data processing app disclosure information with the app ID, and record it in distributed ledgers. The app ID is calculated at build time. To match the ID recorded in the AR with the ID of the app executed by the DC, the framework employs the same environment for app build system and DCs with container technology.

This method allows data providers to control the use of data by presenting usage conditions as a UP to data consumers. In this framework, the usage conditions can include the geographic location where the data will be used, the expiration date, and the number of times the data will be used. Geographic location and date information can be obtained from external servers via the PIP. Although the discussion of using an external server is outside the scope of this study, embedding server certificates in data processing apps may address the issue of server impersonation. The access count condition is realized by decrementing and storing the number of available times after data processing. Compliance with this condition is guaranteed because this decrementing processing is specified in the template.

### 4.3   Proposed Protocols

**Phase 1:** This phase registers for data processing apps (Fig. 6). In Step 1–1, the DC implements the data processing code and sends it to the AR using the DC's browser. Upon receiving it, the AR executes the smart contract to obtain

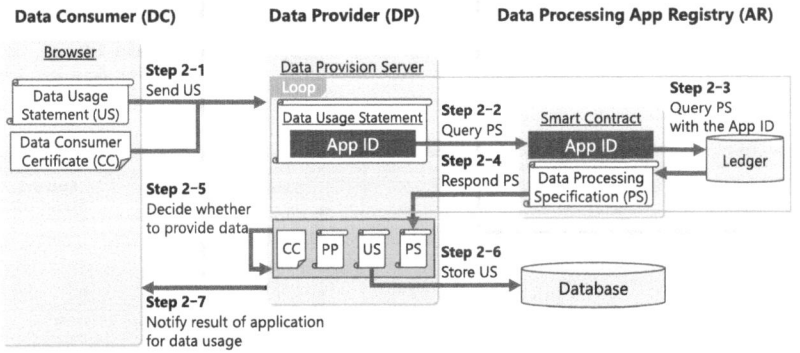

**Fig. 7.** Workflow of phase 2 in the proposed framework.

a PS. First, the smart contract analyzes the data processing code using the code analysis system (Step 1–2). This system verifies the format of the data processing code, including checking called functions, and then static taint analysis is used to obtain the input-output relationship of provided data. Then, the app build system generates an app ID for the data processing code (Step 1–3). Finally, the smart contract stores the PS that contains the data disclosure information and app ID in ledgers (Steps 1–4, 1–5). The AR responds to the DC's browser with the registration results (Step 1–6).

**Phase2:** This phase applies for data usage (Fig. 7). The DC obtains a data consumer certificate (CC) from the certificate authority (CA) operated by the AR before applying. The DC sends the US to a data provision server to apply for data usage (Step 2–1). After the data provision server authenticates the DC with the CC, the DP queries the AR for the PS using the app ID contained in the US, and the AR responds with the PS obtained using the smart contract (Steps 2–2, 2–3, 2–4). The DP can repeat steps 2–2 to 2–4 for multiple AR nodes to ensure the integrity of the PS. Next, the data provision server makes data provision decisions based on the obtained the CC, PP, US, and PS (Step 2–5). In this provision decision, the DP uses the CC to authenticate the DC. The DP then uses the PP to check if the DC and the app are authorized. In addition, the DP checks whether the data will be disclosed using the PS, and decides based on the PP whether to provide data under the conditions of use such as count, location, and duration described in the US presented by the DC. If data provision is permitted, the DP stores the US (Step 2–6). Finally, the data provision server notifies the DC of the result of an application for data usage (Step 2–7).

**Phase 3:** This phase processes data (Fig. 8). First, the DC obtains an app certificate from the CA. This certificate contains the information required for remote attestation, including the app ID. The DC's data processing app running in the enclave requests data to the data provision server through remote attestation (Step 3–1). The data provision server verifies the data processing app

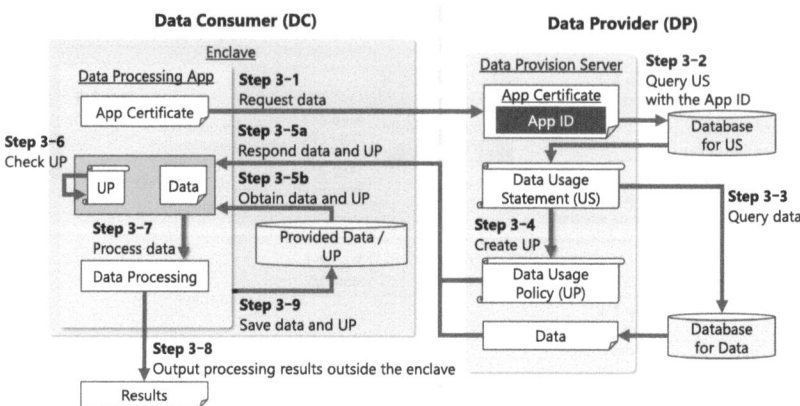

**Fig. 8.** Workflow of phase 3 in the proposed framework.

with the app certificate and retrieves the stored US using the app ID included in the certificate (Step 3–2). The data provision server creates a UP and obtains data based on the US (Steps 3–3, 3–4). The data provision server sends the data to the DC along with the UP in the form of a so-called sticky policy [14] (Step 3–5a). The data processing app verifies the received UP for the location and date before data processing (Step 3–6). Data processing is performed only when the usage conditions are satisfied (Step 3–7). The results were output outside the enclave (Step 3–8). Finally, the data processing app checks the number of times specified by the UP and saves provided data and the UP (Step 3–9). In Step 3–5a, the data processing app retrieved the data from the data provision server; however, if the cached data are available, the DC retrieves from the stored data and the UP (Step 3–5b). The stored data and the UP are encrypted using TEE sealing so that stored data cannot be obtained outside the enclave or from other enclave apps.

## 5    Evaluation of Proposed Framework

### 5.1    Security Evaluation

In this section, we evaluate whether the data processing framework incorporates the proposed data usage control method to satisfy the requirements defined in Sect. 3.3. We show that the proposed framework satisfies the three requirements and is able to address each of the threats.

Req. 1 is that provided data cannot be obtained by data consumers from data processors or data stores. In the proposed framework, data leakage does not occur during data processing using a TEE to run the app in the enclave. In addition, provided data are encrypted and transported from the DP to the data processing app through remote attestation, and the encryption key is protected in the enclave. This prevents the acquisition of provided data from outside the communication channel. Cached data are prevented from being loaded from anywhere other than the app concerned by using TEE sealing. This framework can address the threat of compromise of the data processor and data store because it can protect the confidentiality of provided data in the series of data flows described above.

Req. 2 is the verification by DPs for a data processor implemented by a DC before data are provided. In this framework, the source code of the data processor implemented by the DC is sent to the AR and verified using the smart contract. By receiving the PS, the DPs can know in advance the input/output relationship of the data during data processing and prevent unintended data disclosure. There is no single point of failure for this verification using DLT to compose an AR. This framework can address the threat of misuse of data processor through this verification.

Req. 3 is that provided data are used in accordance with the apps and conditions agreed upon by the DPs. In this framework, DCs can store provided data and conditions using TEE sealing. The presented usage conditions are stored together with the provided data, and the app loads and complies with these conditions. These usage conditions guarantee integrity through TEE sealing, and compliance with the usage conditions is ensured by the integrity of the enclave program. The framework can address the threat of substitution of the data processor by ensuring compliance with usage conditions through the use of TEE sealing.

## 5.2   Runtime Performance Evaluation

We implemented a prototype of the proposed data processing framework. This prototype uses SGX as a TEE and Gramine-SGX [16] as a data processing app execution environment. Gramine-SGX is a library OS that protects the entire process with enclaves. Hyperledger Fabric version 2.4 was used as the DLT for an AR. We used Pysa [11], a static taint analysis tool developed by Meta, to analyze the data flow in data processing. Each entity of the prototype ran on an Intel Core i5-10210U CPU (4 cores, 8 threads, 1.60 GHz). Intel SGX SDK version 2.17.100.3 was used for the DC. The data processing app was implemented in CPython version 3.6.9 on the Gramine-SGX framework version 1.3.1.

We evaluated the runtime performance of the prototype and demonstrated that each phase ran within a realistic execution time. In the performance evaluation scenario, there is one DC and AR consists of five organizations, with one DP in the data usage application phase and changing the number of DPs in the data processing phase. The DC, DPs and AR were run in the same local area network (LAN), and API servers outside the LAN were used for data usage control and remote attestation. In addition, five Hyperledger Fabric peer nodes used by the AR were run in the same machine.

We measured a performance in the app registration phase and the data usage application phase. The data processing app source code of approximately 5KB was used to register the app. The execution time of the subsystems in each phase was measured. The execution time is presented in Fig. 9. In this measurement,

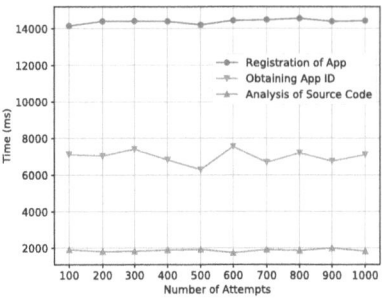
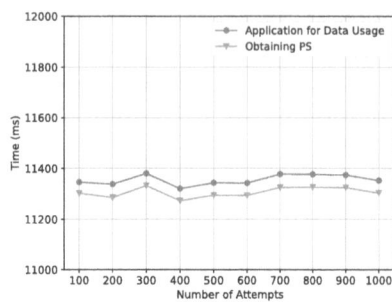

(a) Registration time and subsystem execution time for registration.

(b) Application time and PS obtaining time.

**Fig. 9.** Execution time for app registration phase and usage application phase.

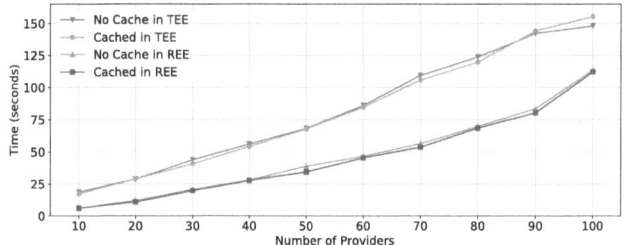

**Fig. 10.** Data processing time in TEE and REE.

the app registration phase took approximately 14,427±318 ms and the data usage application phase took approximately 11,430±165 ms.

Using approximately 1KB of randomly generated test data, we measured a performance of the data processing phase with and without caching. This data set represents the number of available hospital beds, and this data processing searches linearly through the data on available beds provided by each hospital to find the hospital with the most available beds. We measured and compared a data processing performance outside an enclave. Figure 10 shows the measurement results of the data processing phase. This figure shows that the difference in execution time between a TEE and a rich execution environment (REE) increases with the number of DPs. On average, the processing time in a TEE was 176% longer than that in a REE, which was maintained at a realistic level. Because a TEE app's startup time is independent of the number of DPs, we consider that this increase in the difference in execution time can be attributed to TEE sealing.

# 6   Related Work

In this section, we introduce related work on data processing or sharing of personal and medical data, etc. We classified them according to the requirements described in Sect. 3.3, and the results are shown in Table 1. The black circles in Table 1 indicate that our requirements are met, and the white circles represent the requirements that are not mentioned in each paper.

Basile et al. [2] proposed a decentralized data usage control architecture using a TEE and blockchain. This study extended the existing Solid access control mechanisms to enable data usage control. Havur et al. [8] proposed a decentralized architecture for data usage control based on combining SPECIAL and Solid. This study also proposed a framework for evaluating different personal data processing architectures, demonstrating the effectiveness of the architecture. Ayoade et al. [1] proposed a decentralized data management system using blockchain technology and smart contracts. In this system, data confidentiality is ensured using TEE sealing to store the data. Valadares et al. [17] focused on the use of sensitive data obtained from smart meters and proposed a solution for sharing data while protecting privacy using FIWARE and SGX. This solution ensures the integrity and confidentiality of the data. Ramahlosi et al. [15] proposed a blockchain-based data security model that uses smart contracts to process data. The system stores the data on the blockchain to ensure data integrity.

PrivacyGuard [20] performs verification before providing data processing while controlling data usage. PrivacyGuard assumes that an external trusted source has ratified data processing in advance and then uses remote attestation to verify that destination data processing matches ratified data processing before providing data. TrustControl [9] proposed a remote attestation method for the ARM TrustZone that incorporates processing verification by the data provider using an attestation server. These frameworks prevent data misuse by verifying data processing; however, this verification relies on trusting a single external source. Felde et al. [6] proposed MECT, an SGX-based architecture for trusted remote policy enforcement. MECT uses a multi-enclave approach in which data

**Table 1.** Comparison of related works based on requirements.

| Related Work | Decentralized | Req. 1 | Req. 2 | Req. 3 | Notes |
|---|---|---|---|---|---|
| Basile et al.[2] | ● | ● | ○ | ● | |
| Havir et al.[8] | ● | ● | ○ | ○ | No verification mechanism for data processing. |
| Ayoade et al.[1] | ○ | ● | ○ | ○ | |
| Valadares et al.[17] | ○ | ● | ○ | ○ | |
| Ramahlosi et al.[15] | ○ | - | ○ | ○ | |
| PrivacyGuard[20] | ○ | ● | ◑ | ◑ | Data processing verification by data providers relies on a single point of failure. |
| TrustControl[9] | ○ | ● | ◑ | ○ | |
| Felde et al.[6] | ● | ● | ● | ○ | Data processing verification by data providers does not rely on a single point of failure. |
| Proposed | ● | ● | ● | ● | |

● = fulfills completely; ◑ = fulfills partially; ○ = does not fulfill;

consumers implement a data processing code according to a template, and data providers verify this code and provide data. This verification is independent of a single point of failure, because it is performed by the data provider itself. However, MECT does not incorporate data usage control mechanism, and it is not possible for the data provider to control the data after it has been provided.

## 7    Discussion

The time-related data usage control in the proposed framework is based on querying an external trusted server to obtain an accurate time, as described in Sect. 4.2.2; however, it is also possible to obtain the time in the local environment. A method has been proposed to obtain accurate time in the local environment of SGX [10] and is expected to be applied to the framework presented in this paper to allow time-based data usage control to be completed in the local environment. Felde et al. proposed D-GATE [7], a method of the enforcement of geolocation constraints that does not rely on a single point of failure using a TEE. D-GATE obtains location information based on the network latency, which is difficult to disguise, and performs usage control based on accurate location information.

The proposed framework uses taint analysis to verify the data processing. Even if the results of the taint analysis indicate that the provided data will not be output as is, it would be possible to infer the provided data from the processing results if the data were used in a branching condition. Therefore, it can be considered that when provided data are included in the branching condition, data should be analyzed as output data. Whether the branching condition should be included in the output data in this taint analysis is debatable.

## 8    Conclusion

In this paper, we proposed a data usage control method and a decentralized data processing framework that realize the method using TEE and DLT. This framework assumes data processing using personal data as provided data and ensures data confidentiality by executing data processing within a TEE enclave. In addition, the framework adheres to usage conditions agreed upon by a data consumer before data are provided to prevent data misuse and allows the verification of data processing by a data provider. This framework is characterized by using DLT for source code verification, which allows data providers to verify the usage control mechanism and data processing verification before providing data without relying on a single point of failure. The framework allows data processing apps implemented by data consumers to be verified within the framework, thus addressing not only scenarios where apps are pre-implemented and fixed, but also scenarios where there is a need to establish a dynamic trust relationship between data providers and consumers.

We evaluated the security of the proposed framework. The results of this evaluation showed that the proposed framework is able to resist adversaries who attempt to expose provided data and to ensure the confidentiality of provided data. In addition, we implemented a prototype of this framework and evaluated its performance. The results of the performance evaluation showed that the execution time of the app registration and application for data usage did not increase with the number of attempts. We also measured the execution time of the data processing phase when the number of data providers increased and showed that the execution time was realistic.

**Acknowledgement.** This work was supported by JSPS KAKENHI Grant Number JP22K17881 and was partially supported by JSPS KAKENHI Grant Number JP23K03847.

# References

1. Ayoade, G., Karande, V., Khan, L., Hamlen, K.: Decentralized IoT data management using blockchain and trusted execution environment. In: 2018 IEEE International Conference on Information Reuse and Integration (IRI), pp. 15–22 (2018). https://doi.org/10.1109/IRI.2018.00011
2. Basile, D., Di Ciccio, C., Goretti, V., Kirrane, S.: A blockchain-driven architecture for usage control in solid. In: 2023 IEEE 43rd International Conference on Distributed Computing Systems Workshops (ICDCSW), pp. 19–24 (2023). https://doi.org/10.1109/ICDCSW60045.2023.00009
3. Basile, D., Di Ciccio, C., Goretti, V., Kirrane, S.: Blockchain based Resource Governance for Decentralized Web Environments. Front. Blockchain **6** (2023). https://doi.org/10.3389/fbloc.2023.1141909
4. Eitel, A., et al.: Usage Control in the International Data Spaces. Aufl. IDS Association, Berlin (2021)
5. European Union: General Data Protection Regulation (GDPR) – Official Legal Text. https://gdpr-info.eu/ (2016), (Accessed 01 Mar 2024)
6. Felde, H.M.Z., Morbitzer, M., Schütte, J.: Securing remote policy enforcement by a multi-enclave based attestation architecture. In: 2021 IEEE 19th International Conference on Embedded and Ubiquitous Computing (EUC), pp. 102–108 (2021). https://doi.org/10.1109/EUC53437.2021.00023
7. Felde, H.M.Z., Reding, J.L., Lux, M.: D-GATE: decentralized geolocation and time enforcement for usage control. In: 2023 IEEE European Symposium on Security and Privacy Workshops (EuroS&PW), pp. 386–395 (2023). https://doi.org/10.1109/EuroSPW59978.2023.00049
8. Havur, G., Vander Sande, M., Kirrane, S.: Greater control and transparency in personal data processing. In: Furnell , S., Mori, P., Weippl, E., Camp, O. (eds.) Proceedings of the 6th International Conference on Information Systems Security and Privacy, pp. 655–662. SciTePress (2020). https://doi.org/10.5220/0009143206550662
9. Lei, H., Li, J., Li, S., Huang, M., Cheng, J., Bai, Y., Luo, X., Liu, C.: TrustControl: trusted private data usage control based on security enhanced TrustZone. Computers, Mater. Continua **73**(3), 5687–5702 (2022). https://doi.org/10.32604/cmc.2022.030995
10. Liang, H., Li, M.: Bring the missing Jigsaw Back: TrustedClock for SGX enclaves. In: Proceedings of the 11th European Workshop on Systems Security, pp. 1–6. No. 8 in EuroSec 2018. Association for Computing Machinery, New York (2018). https://doi.org/10.1145/3193111.3193119

11. Meta: Pyre - Pyre. https://pyre-check.org/, (Accessed 31 Dec 2023)
12. OASIS Standard: eXtensible Access Control Markup Language (XACML) Version 3.0. https://docs.oasis-open.org/xacml/3.0/xacml-3.0-core-spec-os-en.html (2013), (Accessed 11 July 2024)
13. Park, J., Sandhu, R.: The UCON$_{ABC}$ usage control model. ACM Trans. Inf. Syst. Secur. **7**(1), 128–174 (2004). https://doi.org/10.1145/984334.984339
14. Pearson, S., Casassa-Mont, M.: Sticky policies: an approach for managing privacy across multiple parties. Computer **44**(9), 60–68 (2011). https://doi.org/10.1109/MC.2011.225
15. Ramahlosi, M.N., Akanbi, Y.M.A.: A Blockchain-based Model for Securing Data Pipeline in a Heterogeneous Information System (2024). https://doi.org/10.48550/arXiv.2401.09240
16. Tsai, C.C., Porter, D.E., Vij, M.: Graphene-SGX: a practical library OS for unmodified applications on SGX. In: 2017 USENIX Annual Technical Conference (USENIX ATC 2017), pp. 645–658. USENIX Association, Santa Clara, CA (2017), https://www.usenix.org/conference/atc17/technical-sessions/presentation/tsai
17. Valadares, D.C.G., da Silva, M.S.L., Brito, A.E.M., Salvador, E.M.: Achieving data dissemination with security using fiware and intel software guard extensions (SGX). In: 2018 IEEE Symposium on Computers and Communications (ISCC), pp. 1–7 (2018). https://doi.org/10.1109/ISCC.2018.8538590
18. Wang, Y., Li, J., Zhao, X., Feng, G., Luo, X.R.: Using mobile phone data for emergency management: a systematic literature review. Inf. Syst. Front. **22**(6), 1539–1559 (2020). https://doi.org/10.1007/s10796-020-10057-w
19. Wheatley, S., Maillart, T., Sornette, D.: The extreme risk of personal data breaches and the erosion of privacy. Euro. Phys. J. B **89**(1), 1–12 (2016). https://doi.org/10.1140/epjb/e2015-60754-4
20. Xiao, Y., Zhang, N., Li, J., Lou, W., Hou, Y.T.: PrivacyGuard: enforcing private data usage control with blockchain and attested off-chain contract execution. In: Chen, L., Li, N., Liang, K., Schneider, S. (eds.) ESORICS 2020. LNCS, vol. 12309, pp. 610–629. Springer, Cham (2020). https://doi.org/10.1007/978-3-030-59013-0_30
21. Yabe, T., Jones, N.K., Rao, P.S.C., Gonzalez, M.C., Ukkusuri, S.V.: Mobile phone location data for disasters: a review from natural hazards and epidemics. Comput. Environ. Urban Syst. **94**, 101777 (2022). https://doi.org/10.1016/j.compenvurbsys.2022.101777
22. Zualkernan, I.A., Aloul, F.A., Sakkia, V., Noman, H.A., Sowdagar, S., Hammadi, O.A.: An IoT-based emergency evacuation system. In: 2019 IEEE International Conference on Internet of Things and Intelligence System (IoTaIS), pp. 62–66 (2019). https://doi.org/10.1109/IoTaIS47347.2019.8980381

# Malware Detection and Prevention

# You Can't Touch This: Detecting Typosquatting Packages for Enhanced Malware Prevention in Software Supply Chains

Minh Tien Truong[1] , Nils Gruschka[2(✉)] , and Luigi Lo Iacono[1]

[1] University of Applied Sciences Bonn-Rhein-Sieg, Sankt Augustin, Germany
minh.truong@smail.inf.h-brs.de, luigi.lo_iacono@h-brs.de
[2] University of Oslo, Oslo, Norway
nilsgrus@ifi.uio.no

**Abstract.** In recent years, typosquatting has become a significant threat to software supply chain systems, where malicious packages deceptively mimic legitimate ones. Attackers register these fraudulent packages with names strikingly similar to those of legitimate packages. As a result, developers can mistakenly download these malicious packages by mistyping the intended package name or selecting a package based on its convincing yet deceptive name.

In this paper, we assess the effectiveness of string-matching algorithms in identifying potential typosquatting candidates. We construct an open dataset comprising 394 typosquatting packages and evaluate the performance of these algorithms based on their ability to detect typosquatting packages. In addition, we introduce a novel string-matching algorithm, an extension of the Damerau-Levenshtein distance, demonstrating a notably higher true-positive rate than existing methods. Since our dataset contains features not previously considered, we also investigate how these new features affect the assignment accuracy of ML-based classifiers. Our results show an overall accuracy rate of 98.4% on our datasets and 96.0% and 93.5% accuracy on evaluating two other open datasets. These results provide valuable insights for researchers, package manager vendors, and developers to improve their understanding of malicious typosquatting packages and improve mediation strategies and technologies.

**Keywords:** Typosquatting · Malware Detection · Software Supply Chain · npm

## 1 Introduction

Since the first emergence of computer malware in the 1980 s, malicious programs have posed a significant cybersecurity threat. A notable example is the *WannaCry* ransomware, which infiltrated over 300,000 computers in more than 150 countries in May 2017 [7,42]. One reason malware remains problematic is its ability to constantly reinvent itself. Attackers continuously adapt their targets,

H. H. Song et al. (Eds.): NSS 2024, LNCS 15564, pp. 147–166, 2025.
https://doi.org/10.1007/978-981-96-3531-3_8

motivations, and distribution channels. Traditional email distribution is increasingly supplemented by alternative routes. In particular, attacks on software supply chains (SSCs) have significantly expanded in recent years [17]. Considering that open source software comprises about 80% of modern software stacks [11], encompassing everything from phones and cars to power grids and manufacturing plants, malware injected into an SSC can have critical impacts.

SSC refers to the components and procedures used in the creation, modification, and distribution of software products [18]. A critical element of SSC is the package manager, such as the well-known *npm* system for the JavaScript programming language. It enables developers to manage and integrate external software components from repositories into development, testing, or distribution. Because these repositories host many software packages without adequate origin authentication, they provide an ideal environment for malware infiltration. According to Sonatype, the number of malicious software packages within the *npm* ecosystem has increased on average by 742% per year over the past three years [1]. Sonatype's findings further suggest that one of the most common attack methods on SSC is *Typosquatting Packages*, as confirmed by Ohm et al. [26].

Furthermore, the paper [27] recommends additional research on typosquatting attacks due to the lack of existing literature and comparative evaluations. To counteract the high false positive rates in malware detection, the paper also suggests implementing a pre-filter that helps to quickly eliminate benign packages and focus on a smaller subset that is more likely to contain malicious packages. Typosquatting packages are one type of malicious package. Adding a pre-filter can improve efficiency and accuracy. Generally, malware detection does not yet sufficiently account for the different characteristics of various malware classes, contributing to high false-positive rates. This paper primarily investigates typosquatting attacks on software packages and examines whether pre-filtering and typosquatting package specifics lead to better detection accuracy.

## 1.1 Typosquatting Packages

Typosquatting is a type of social engineering and was initially applied within the Domain Name System (DNS) [2]. This technique deceives end users into accessing websites they did not intend to visit. It involves registering web addresses that mimic genuine ones through typos and misspellings, like `googl.com` instead of `google.com`.

In this paper, we study typosquatting in the context of SCC. Typosquatting attacks on package managers involve the introduction of software packages whose names are very similar to existing packages. This is done by selecting a suitable package, creating a new package containing malware, and slightly altering the original package name. Then, the attacker can register this typosquatting package and circulate it via the package manager. If developers accidentally make a corresponding typo, they download the malicious package.

In the stricter sense, typosquatting uses *typographical errors* to mimic package names [19,40]. The typical patterns are:

- Insertion of characters (adjacent keys): `angular` → `anguilar`
- Deletion of characters: `angular` → `angula`
- Transposition of characters: `angular` → `angulra`

If the change of package names goes beyond typographical errors, the typosquatting is called *confusion attack* [19,40]. Here, additional semantics are typically added to the name, e.g., `react` → `react-framework`. This paper will consider only the first type of typosquatting attacks that use typographical errors.

## 1.2   Contributions

In this work, we extend and evaluate different approaches for detecting typosquatting packages. As a basis, we constructed a dataset of typosquatting packages that were not previously available in this form. It contains the source code of the malware package and the target package as well as additional metadata. Using this dataset, we evaluate string matching algorithms known from the literature to detect typosquatting packages based on the similarity of the package names. We also introduce a new string matching algorithm. Furthermore, we derive new features for malware classifiers from our dataset and evaluate the classification properties that can be achieved with them. Our main contributions are:

**Typosquatting Dataset** As datasets of typosquatting packages for research and comparative evaluation are currently scarce [27], we construct a dataset of 394 typosquatting packages and make it available as an open dataset to encourage further research and enable the replication of our work.

**Extended Damerau-Levenshtein (EDL)** We present the EDL string matching algorithm, tailored for typosquatting package detection and built on previous work [37]. We also assess the effectiveness of five string matching algorithms, including EDL, for typosquatting package name detection as a prefilter.

**Extended Feature Set for ML Classifiers** We extend conventional feature sets for malware detection with new features extracted from our typosquatting package dataset, train a Random Forest (RF) model on our dataset, and evaluate its performance in identifying malicious content in typosquatting packages on external open datasets.

## 2   Related Work

As of now, *npm* states that it "[...] *can detect typosquat attacks*" [22]. However, the rise in typosquatting attacks necessitates further research [38]. In contrast, PyPI introduced a malware verification tool in 2020, benchmarked against tools like *Bandit4Mal* and *OSS Detect Backdoor (OSSGadget)* [41]. These tools detect over 85% of malicious packages but produce false positives for 68% to 96% of benign packages, posing challenges for automatic detection.

The most common metrics for string matching in identifying typosquatting packages are Levenshtein and Damerau-Levenshtein [6,39,40]. Additionally, Taylor [37] introduced a method to detect similarities among package names using triggers, which include the physical location of keys on an English keyboard. No other string matching algorithms besides these are discussed in the typosquatting context in the literature.

Classifying malicious and benign packages in open source repositories has been the subject of multiple studies [6,9,10,24,25,28]. Only a few publications provide classification reports allowing us to compare our model's performance with theirs – recent and relevant articles include [33] and [24].

The study by Ohm et al. [24] employs various machine learning techniques to detect malicious packages. They evaluated several models and selected the three most promising ones: Multi-Layer Perceptron (MLP), Support Vector Machines (SVM), and Random Forest (RF), with RF exhibiting the best performance. Furthermore, they created and evaluated various combinations of these models. The combination model demonstrated the highest precision, with the RF model achieving the highest recall rate on labeled data. When applied in real-world scenarios, models using some combination of the selected three proved most effective regarding true positive rate, though the number of correctly identified malicious packages dropped significantly. In contrast, techniques using a single model detected between 10 and 22 malicious packages, with the RF model detecting the most when excluding research-related packages.

Similar to Ohm et al., Sejfia and Schäfer [33] leveraged machine learning techniques to detect malicious packages. They introduced a system named *Amalfi*, comprising a machine learning based classifier, a reproducer, and a clone detector. The reproducer recreates the source code and compares it with the package, while the clone detector checks for equality with known malicious packages. The classifier, trained on labeled benign and malicious data, then classifies packages as malicious or benign. Their models, including Decision Trees, SVM, and Naive Bayes, showed the most promise with Decision Tree and SVM. Their SVM-based model performed best when evaluated on an external dataset provided by [9].

The above gaps in current research led to the following research questions, which we will address in this paper:

**RQ1** Which string matching algorithm is most effective in identifying potential typosquatting candidates by assessing the similarity of package names?

**RQ2** How can existing package classification methods be improved and typosquatting be determined more reliably?

## 3    Methodology

To answer our research questions, we follow a three-step process. First, we construct a suitable dataset since the available open datasets are neither specialized nor complete enough for our typosquatting research (see Sect. 4). This constructed typosquatting dataset forms the basis for our research in the following two steps. In the second step, we focus on the precision of identifying potential typosquatting candidates based on their name similarity with other packages (see Sect. 5). To achieve this, we evaluate the effectiveness of various string matching metrics proposed in the literature or used in practice. In addition, we introduce and evaluate a novel string matching algorithm based on the Damerau-Levenshtein distance, which we denote as *Extended Damerau-Levenshtein* (EDL). In the third step, we investigate how additional features affect the classification accuracy of ML-based models (see Sect. 6). To this end, we extract new features from our constructed dataset that previous studies have not used. We then evaluate the performance of models proposed in the literature based on these newly identified features. For this evaluation, we additionally draw on available open datasets that contain malicious packages.

## 4   Data Acquisition

Typosquatting research is currently impeded by the very limited amount of available open data [9, 26]. While the *Backstabbers Knife Collection* dataset [26] contains numerous malware packages, only about 100 can be attributed to typosquatting attacks. Additionally, the contained typosquatting packages lack relevant metadata, such as the number of downloads or, in some cases, the attack target. To address these limitations, we collected data from relevant vulnerability databases such as CVE [20] and Exploit DB [23]. Furthermore, we gathered data from three leading companies in malicious package detection—Sonatype [36], Snyk [35], and Phylum [31]—which had published lists of known typosquatting packages. Our data collection included information published by these companies up until the end of January 2023.

The process of data collection involved manual aggregation, categorization, filtering and input. In the first step, we identified a total of 426 typosquatting packages obtained from the sources mentioned above. These packages met two specific criteria: first, they were marked as typosquatting packages in the named sources and second, they contained a reference to the mimicked package. After forming a disjoint set of all typosquatting packages by their names across all sources and removing erroneous entries, 406 instances of typosquatting packages remained. Erroneous entries included, e.g., entries that pointed to legitimate packages. Among these, the source code for 397 typosquatting packages could be located on various *npm* mirrors. We excluded packages that had their source code deliberately made difficult to interpret, a process that extends beyond mere code minification. In our study, we identified three such packages, reducing our sample size to 394. These obfuscated codes were omitted because they obstruct analysis, complicate the assessment of potential threats, and can conceal the actual purpose and functionality of the packages. Such practices contradict the principles of openness and transparency that are fundamental to open-source projects. The following metadata of 272 packages was still obtainable from *npm* and added to our dataset:

– Release date of the typosquatting package
– Removal date of the typosquatting package

– Number of downloads obtained from npm

Note that *npm* 's current policy is to maintain typosquatting packages as empty placeholders to indicate that these malicious packages once existed and have since been removed. This means that downloads can still occur on these placeholder packages. To establish a replicable count of downloads, we consider the total number of downloads since the release date of the typo-squatted package.

Our dataset, consisting of 394 typosquatting packages, is publicly available[1]. For our analysis in Sect. 5, we focused on the 276 typosquatting packages with metadata to determine thresholds and assess the effectiveness of various string matching algorithms. In Sect. 6, we utilized all 394 typosquatting packages with source code, along with retrieving the source code of the target packages. Our dataset contributes a significant amount of new data, with only a minimal overlap of 3.06% with the Backstabber dataset [26] and 0.26% with the MalOSS dataset [9].

# 5   Identification of Typosquatting Candidates

A common method for detecting typosquatting packages includes using string matching metrics. However, this approach is often linked to a high rate of false positives [6,27,40], i.e., many legitimate packages are incorrectly classified as typosquatting. To further study this issue, we introduce a new string matching approach and compare the accuracy in detecting typosquatting packages with string matching metrics proposed in the literature and used in practice. To identify typosquatting packages with a particularly high effective spread, we use the *propagation potential* as a measure and define it as the number of package downloads in a given period. A low number of package downloads within a certain period means a low propagation potential and vice versa. The aim is to distinguish between very effective and less effective typosquatting names based on their propagation potential. In this way, we can identify the specific characteristics that contribute to the effectiveness of typosquatting names. Based on this understanding, we aim to effectively reduce false positives.

## 5.1   String Matching Algorithms

String matching algorithms compare the similarity between strings, crucial for tasks like spell checking, data deduplication, plagiarism detection, and identifying typosquatting candidates. The simplest, *Exact Matching*, considers strings identical only if all characters match. For more flexibility, *Approximate Matching* algorithms detect similarities despite minor variations. *Edit Distance Algorithms*, such as Levenshtein [16] and Damerau-Levenshtein [8], measure the minimal edits (insertions, deletions, substitutions) needed to transform one string into another. *Subsequence Matching Algorithms*, like Needleman-Wunsch [21]

---

[1] https://doi.org/10.5281/zenodo.14907785.

and Smith-Waterman [34], allow gaps or mismatches. *Fuzzy Matching Algorithms*, such as Soundex [32] and Metaphone [30], account for phonetic variations. *Token-based Algorithms* compare sets of words or $n$-grams using measures like Jaccard [13] and cosine [4] similarity.

For detecting typosquatting candidates, we use Levenshtein, Damerau-Levenshtein, Jaro-Winkler, and Gestalt-Pattern algorithms. Levenshtein and Damerau-Levenshtein are well-known for package name similarity detection [6, 19, 40]. We include Jaro-Winkler and Gestalt-Pattern due to their effectiveness in spell correction and record linking [12,14]. Additionally, we introduce a new algorithm specializing in intentional typos, hypothesizing that attackers craft malware package names to exploit likely typos by developers.

### 5.2   Extended Damerau-Levenshtein (EDL)

Existing string matching algorithms are typically designed for random errors. However, attackers introduce non-random errors to make their attacks more effective. We hypothesize that string matching metrics incorporating contextual information, such as keyboard layout, will better detect typosquatting packages. To test this, we integrated keyboard neighborhood relations into a string matching algorithm. The base idea was initially provided by [37].

We extended the Damerau-Levenshtein distance, which measures the similarity between two strings based on the minimum number of operations needed to transform one string into the other. The allowed operations, each with the same cost, are insertion, deletion, substitution, and transposition of characters. Our Extended Damerau-Levenshtein Distance adds the following rules:

- Insertion of neighboring keys reduces the cost: `react` → `reactr` results in a distance of 0.5.
- Insertion of non-neighboring keys increases the cost: `react` → `reacto` results in a distance of 2.
- Substitution of neighboring keys reduces the cost: `react` → `reqct` results in a distance of 0.5.
- Substitution of non-neighboring keys increases the cost: `react` → `regct` results in a distance of 2.
- Deletion of a single letter is reduced: `react` → `rect` results in a distance of 0.5.
- Transposition of two letters is set to a cost of 0.5.

The Damerau-Levenshtein distance was chosen for three main reasons. Firstly, it allows manual cost adjustment through a single variable, unlike the Jaro-Winkler and Gestalt-Pattern algorithms, which require significant equation changes for similar adjustments. Secondly, it directly supports the transposition of adjacent characters, a feature not directly available in the Levenshtein distance, which needs two operations for the same result. For example, the difference between `react` and `raect` often arises from a slight timing error when typing. Lastly, it inherently checks for letter equality and can be easily expanded to determine if two keys are neighbors on a keyboard, allowing for cost adjustments based on this proximity.

## 5.3    String Matching Threshold Determination

A string matching algorithm has a threshold that defines at which point two strings are considered a match. The threshold value must be carefully chosen to achieve a high true positive rate without compromising the finding of effective typosquatting packages. We conducted a statistical analysis of our constructed dataset to determine this threshold. In our study, the 'effectiveness' of a typosquatting package was quantified through the normalized number of downloads (daily downloads), designated as the dependent variable. To calculate the normalized downloads, the total number of downloads was divided by the number of days since the package's release. Conversely, the distance to its legitimate counterpart, measured by various string similarity metrics, was treated as the independent variable.

The scatter plots in Fig. 1 illustrate the number of daily downloads in relation to the distance between the typosquatting packages and its targets, with each plot representing a specific string matching algorithm. Typosquatting packages with distances greater than two from their targets consistently exhibit near-zero downloads in the Levenshtein and Damerau-Levenshtein distance graphs. The Jaro-Winkler scatter plot shows that packages with significantly higher download rates primarily begin with a similarity value of 0.95. Those below this threshold tend to have nearly zero daily downloads, except for minor outliers. Some typosquatting packages achieve a Jaro-Winkler similarity score of zero, highlighting challenges for short-named packages with this metric (e.g., 5rn vs. rn). The Gestalt-Pattern displays a similar but slightly broader distribution, while the EDL distance aligns closely with the original Damerau-Levenshtein and Levenshtein distances, offering finer granularity. Notably, packages initially categorized with Levenshtein and Damerau-Levenshtein distances of 2 and 1 are reclassified as 0.5, reducing dispersion among high-download packages and increasing it among low-download ones.

In this regard, Fig. 1 provides some initial indications of how the thresholds for the various metrics could be chosen. For instance, according to the graphs Levenshtein and Damerau-Levenshtein in Fig. 1, it is advisable to choose a Levenshtein and Damerau-Levenshtein distance of 2 since these cover all typosquatting packages that are downloaded at least once a day. Using a a bar chart, we can observe the characteristics from a different perspectives to further analyze how much of the downloads are covered by each distance class. Therefore, the bar chart in Fig. 2 depict the distribution of the download rate depending on the similarities between the typosquatting packages and their attack targets.

For the Levenshtein distance, e.g., it can be observed that the typosquatting packages with a Levenshtein distance of 1 account for about 60% of the total downloads. The Damerau-Levenshtein distance covers about 80% of the downloads starting from a distance of 1. Compared to the Levenshtein distance, the strictest Damerau-Levenshtein distance of 1 covers significantly more downloads than the strictest Levenshtein distance of 1. We assume that a stricter criterion reduces false positive rates, as it increases the requirements that a case must fulfill to be classified as positive, thus reducing potential misclassifications.

In contrast, however, a more strict criterion could decrease the number of true positives. Positive cases that are just below the defined threshold may not be recognized. It is important to find a good balance between the package to be detected and the strictness of the distance threshold. In this case, the Damerau-Levenshtein distance accounts for 80% of the downloads with its most strict criterion. This coverage should be our minimum requirement. For the bar of the Jaro-Winkler distance and the Gestalt-Pattern algorithm, the threshold was chosen to cover 80% of the downloads, following the minimum requirements set by the previous string matching algorithms. Thus, the threshold for such coverage is set to 0.95 for the Jaro-Winkler distance and 0.86 for the Gestalt-Pattern algorithm. The distribution of the EDL distance covers 84% of all downloads from a distance of up to 0.5. As with the original Damerau-Levenshtein distance, most downloads are covered by the least distance, 0.5. For the Levenshtein distance the threshold of 2 has been chosen. These values were selected to have equal coverage of at least 80% of the number of downloads while minimizing a possible false positive value.

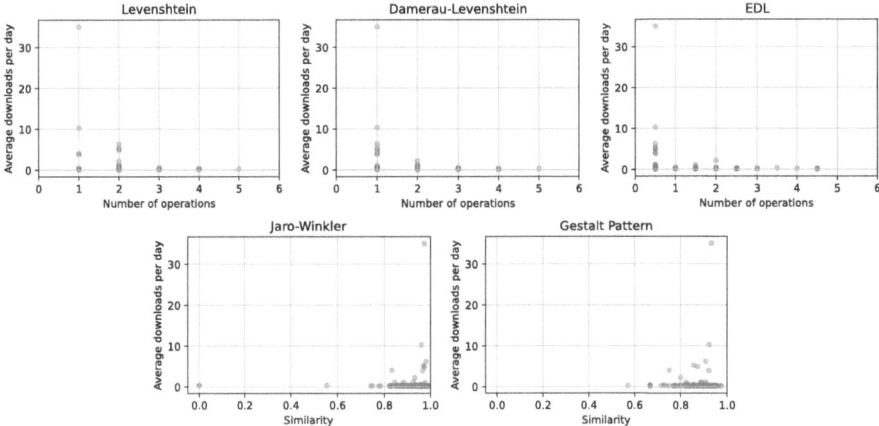

**Fig. 1.** Downloads per day in relation to the similarity between the names of the typosquatting package and its target package

## 5.4   Results and Discussion

During our examination of typosquatting packages, we noticed that 90% of them targeted packages listed among the 1,000 most used packages on *npm* [2]. Therefore, we evaluated various string metrics on the ten most popular libraries for precision, as these libraries are frequent targets for attackers. These libraries were then compared to the entire *npm* ecosystem to find matching candidates.

---

[2] https://gist.github.com/anvaka/8e8fa57c7ee1350e3491 - last accessed: 2024.04.25.

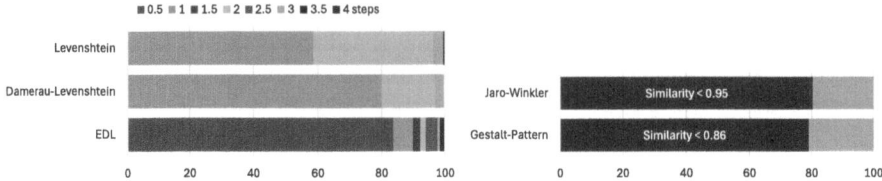

**Fig. 2.** Download distribution of similarity and distance classes for each analyzed string matching algorithm

Each found typosquatting candidate was checked to verify whether it was already confirmed by *npm* as a typosquatting package. Finally, we derived the ratio of the number of confirmed cases to the number of all typosquatting candidates for the respective target identified by the string matching algorithm. However, deriving a recall value is not possible without manual verification of the entire *npm* repository. The result of this process is displayed in Fig. 3. This figure represents the precision (percentage) of typosquatting candidates confirmed by *npm* as typosquatting packages depending on the used string metric.

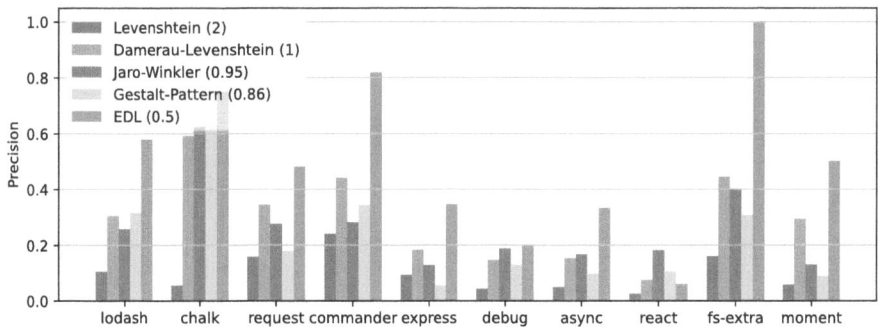

**Fig. 3.** Precision of each string matching algorithm analyzed in terms detection of typosquatting candidates based on package name similarity of the top 10 most downloaded *npm* packages (as of April 2024). The number next to the algorithm name in the legend is the threshold used in this experiment.

Various works have already been conducted regarding the string metric and detecting typosquatting candidates. Most papers used the Levenshtein distance or the Damerau-Levenshtein distance [6,37,39,40]. In the case of [40], the recommended Levenshtein distance of 2 was also identified in this work as an appropriate threshold. Additionally, based on the findings presented in Fig. 3, the utilization of Damerau-Levenshtein distance, incorporating insights from work by Taylor [37], consistently yields higher precision compared to the other four metrics in the majority of instances. A direct comparison with Taylor's approach was impractical due to the vague and interpretable triggers described only in words, without any algorithm or implementation provided. Furthermore the library `react` represents a single outlier in the results, i.e., EDL has a lower precision than the other string matching algorithms. Upon further investigation, we observed that the anomaly is attributed to several "defensive" typosquatting packages contained in the *npm* repository. Various users intentionally created these packages to safeguard the legitimate *react* library from typosquatting attacks and, therefore, were not marked by *npm* due to their benign characteristics.

> **Answer to RQ1:** The introduced EDL algorithm, which considers contextual information such as keyboard layout in a distance measure, shows significantly higher precision in identifying typosquatting candidates than the other commonly used and tested string matching algorithms.

> **Insight:** Introducing defensive typosquatting measures, such as adding empty packages with typosquatted names, significantly degrades this performance, making these mitigations mutually exclusive.

# 6    Classification of Typosquatting Candidates

Typosquatting candidates identified by package name similarity filtering may not necessarily contain malicious code, as name similarities can be coincidental. Thus, additional investigation is required to determine whether malicious intent can be identified. The presence of malicious intent becomes evident if a package's primary goal aligns with the primary goal groups mentioned in [26]. Attackers typically use tools such as modules, functions, or libraries for these goals [9,10, 26,33]. Identifying these tools, along with other indicators, can be used to train machine learning models, referred to as features.

## 6.1    Malicious Package Features

We manually examined the 394 typosquatting packages from our dataset and their source code to identify distinguishing features indicative of malicious intent. For this investigation, a detailed comparison was made between each typosquatting package and its respective targeted package. Code that was newly introduced by attackers often contained new libraries and special functions, such as the `eval` function or request functions to external systems. Our methodology involved the following steps:

1. **Manual Inspection**: We compared each typosquatting package's source code with the legitimate package to identify new or altered segments.
2. **Feature Identification**: We specifically looked for newly introduced libraries and special functions, flagging these as potential indicators of malicious behavior. For instance, functions that executed dynamic code or communicated with external servers were highlighted. If a feature, such as a new library

or special function, appeared more than once across different typosquatting packages, it was added to our feature set. This iterative process ensured that our feature set captured commonly used malicious tactics.

3. **Feature Set Establishment**: After examining all packages, we consolidated the identified features into a comprehensive feature set.

4. **Feature Extraction**: We extracted the defined features for each package, checking for their presence systematically.

5. **Mapping to Boolean Vector**: We mapped the libraries used by each package to a boolean feature vector.

The features we extracted were mostly consistent with previous literature, with the notable addition of explicitly imported libraries in our feature set [24, 33]. For the analysis, we assumed that the malicious intention of a package could be identified by the combination of the libraries used and several other characteristics known from previous literature. The complete feature set used to train the model is provided in the appendix in Table 3.

### 6.2   Malware Classifier

A total of 16 features were collected for each package. The typosquatting packages were labeled as malicious. The targets of the typosquatting packages were used as datasets for benign packages. The same features as for the typosquatting packages were extracted for these. A total of approximately 600 packages of malicious and benign samples were collected. Furthermore, a training dataset and a test dataset were created from these datasets. The ratio of training data to test data was set to 80:20, a ratio often used for splitting [15].

As indicated by [33] and [24], we assume and propose that the RF model is the strongest contender in detecting malicious packages as of the current state of art. Utilizing an RF model over Decision Trees offers numerous advantages. For instance, it mitigates the risk of overfitting and presents a more resilient approach, as highlighted by [5]. During the training of the RF model, multiple Decision Trees were generated using bootstrapping, where each tree is trained on a random subset of the training data. The out-of-bag sets are then used to evaluate the performance of each tree on the samples not included in its bootstrap sample. This helps to estimate the generalization performance of the model. Furthermore, a hyperparameter optimization using grid search was performed; the RF model was evaluated on the test dataset that was not included during the training phase. The model trained on our dataset was subsequently tested on datasets from the Backstabber's Knife Collection [26] and the MAL-OSS dataset [9] that were augmented with the 1000 most popular packages to ensure that the model was not specifically tailored to our dataset.

### 6.3   Results and Discussion

**Classification Results.** Table 1 shows the classification result. The terms *Malicious* and *Benign* are the classes of the data entries, and for the evaluation of

**Table 1.** Classification reports for different datasets: own dataset (top), MalOSS (middle), Backstabber's Knife Collection (bottom); WAM = Weighted arithmetic mean

|  |  | Precision | Recall | F1 Score | Support |
|---|---|---|---|---|---|
| *Own* | Benign | 0.978 | 0.978 | 0.978 | 46 |
|  | Malicious | 0.988 | 0.988 | 0.988 | 80 |
|  | Accuracy | – | – | 0.984 | 126 |
|  | WAM | 0.984 | 0.984 | 0.984 | 126 |
| *MalOSS* | Benign | 0.962 | 0.994 | 0.978 | 332 |
|  | Malicious | 0.931 | 0.675 | 0.782 | 40 |
|  | Accuracy | – | – | 0.960 | 372 |
|  | WAM | 0.959 | 0.960 | 0.957 | 372 |
| *B. Knife* | Benign | 0.858 | 0.991 | 0.920 | 979 |
|  | Malicious | 0.994 | 0.901 | 0.945 | 1610 |
|  | Accuracy | – | – | 0.935 | 2589 |
|  | WAM | 0.943 | 0.935 | 0.935 | 2589 |

each class, a precision, a recall, and an F1 score can be specified. The top row of the table shows the results for our dataset. A total of 126 records have been tested, 46 being true benign and 80 being true malicious. The RF model was able to classify 98.4% of the test data from our dataset correctly. The precision for the class Malicious is 0.988, meaning that if the model classifies a package as Malicious, it is correct 98.8% of the time. The recall value of the class Malicious with a value of 0.988 describes that the model could identify 98.8% of all true malicious packages.

Using our model and testing it on an external dataset (MalOSS) provided by [9] results in the classification report depicted in Table 1 (middle). For this, the ratio of benign to malicious packages used by [33] has been mimicked. Therefore, 40 malicious packages have been randomly selected from the whole dataset provided by [9]. For the benign packages, 332 packages have been randomly selected from the 1,000 most used packages.

Finally, the classification report of the test performed on the dataset from the Backstabber's Knife Collection [26] is depicted in Table 1 (bottom). For this, the top 1,000 most used packages serve as our dataset for benign packages.

**Performance Comparison.** To evaluate the performance of our model, we performed a comparison with the models presented in [33] and [24] (see Table 2).

The work by [33] leveraged Decision Trees, SVM, and Naive Bayes, with Decision Trees performing best on their data (basic corpus). However, the performance significantly dropped when applying their model to the MalOSS dataset, indicating overfitting. To reduce the possibility of overfitting, we utilized an RF model [5] and introduced additional features. Overall, using RF in combination with the proposed features yields notably improved performance, especially when

**Table 2.** Performance comparison between own model, Amalfi [33] and Ohm et al.'s model [24] on labeled datasets (BC = basic corpus, * = not further clarified in the paper)

|     | Model | Dataset | Precision | Recall | F1 Score | Size |
|-----|-------|---------|-----------|--------|----------|------|
| *Own* | RF | Own | 0.988 | 0.988 | 0.988 | 126 |
|     | RF | MalOSS | 0.931 | 0.675 | 0.783 | 372 |
|     | RF | B. Knife | 0.994 | 0.900 | 0.945 | 2589 |
| [33] | DT | BC | 0.98 | 0.43 | 0.60 | 179* |
|     | DT | MalOSS | 0.35 | 0.64 | 0.45 | 372 |
| [24] | SVM | B. Knife | 1.0 | 0.53 | 0.69 | 3136 |
|     | RF | B. Knife | 0.96 | 0.63 | 0.76 | 3136 |

tested on external datasets. For the MalOSS dataset, the recall value improved slightly, while the precision improved significantly.

The work by [24] evaluated various ML techniques, with SVM and RF being the most promising when tested on labeled data. Their SVM model achieved the highest precision score on labeled data, while their RF model attained the highest F1 Score and recall value. In practical real-world applications, their RF model detected the most malicious packages, although its true-positive rate was relatively low. In comparison, our RF model achieves a higher precision score than their RF model but a lower precision score compared to their SVM model. Notably, our model's recall value, which indicates how many true instances have been detected, is significantly higher. The overall performance, as indicated by the F1 Score, shows that our RF model outperforms both their SVM and RF models.

**Answer to RQ2:** Our RF-based model, trained on our extended feature set, outperforms the current best model in the literature, achieving high classification precision across different datasets. This highlights the importance of selecting and evaluating feature sets carefully. Further research is needed to better understand the features that influence classification precision.

**Insight:** Pre-filtering with dedicated methods and ML-based classification based on attack-specific features can reduce the false-positive rate and thus reduce the manual follow-up of suspected malware cases in specific malware classes.

# 7   Operationalization

Drawing from our findings, we introduce a specialized typosquatting detection scheme designed to address the characteristics of this particular malware class and its practical application by repository operators or researchers.

In the initial step 'Pre-Filter' of our approach to detect typosquatting in software repositories, we employ the EDL metric to focus on the most popular *npm* packages due to their high potential for propagation. By targeting these packages, we drastically reduce the number of string comparisons needed from approximately $3.645 \times 10^{12}$ comparisons for all packages in the repository to just $2.7 \times 10^9$ comparisons for the top thousand packages. This significant reduction makes the process more manageable and efficient. In the second step 'Classification', we use the proposed model to analyze the typosquatting candidates identified earlier, verifying whether they contain malicious code. The final step involves appropriate response measures for packages classified as potential typosquatting malware. Repository providers are advised to temporarily disable these packages and contact their authors for clarification, while researchers conduct further manual analysis to confirm any true positives. These confirmed cases are then reported back to the repository provider for necessary actions.

Once these steps are completed, only new packages need to be checked using this method. This enables iterative scanning of the entire repository by prioritizing target packages with high propagation potential.

## 8    Discussion and Limitations

While the results are promising, several important factors require further discussion. Handling obfuscated source code remains challenging for the current process and potentially affects model performance. Datasets like those from [9] and [26] were likely impacted by unverified obfuscated code, allowing malicious intent to evade detection by our model and increasing the difficulty of feature extraction. Possible solutions include leveraging abstract syntax trees (AST) for feature extraction, which are known for their resilience against code obfuscation [3], or using dynamic code analysis within a sandboxed environment [29]. Although AST offers some resistance to code obfuscation, they are not completely immune [3], making dynamic analysis potentially more effective. Furthermore, the inclusion of obfuscated code in open source repositories raises questions about its appropriateness, as it arguably contradicts the principles of transparency inherent in open source development.

While the model was tested on real-world typosquatting datasets, it has not undergone validation in a practical, real-world setting yet, potentially yielding different outcomes. Another consideration is that although the same data source was used, there may still be differences in the datasets, as the literature does not break down exactly which datasets were used for training and testing. After all, these data sources are enriched with additional datasets over time. Exact replication and comparability are, therefore, more difficult to achieve. The packages used here as benign samples comprise the most commonly used libraries. These libraries may differ in terms of several code characteristics like quality and size from usual libraries and, therefore, may contain a bias towards them. Last but not least, although the mentioned literature has successfully used Random Forest, it is worth considering testing other models, as the features and dataset differ. There may be other machine learning models that can perform better with our specific dataset and feature set as training data.

As pointed out by [24,27], the procedures developed by the various researchers, including this approach in malicious package detection, should not be viewed as complete solutions. Instead, each approach should be seen as a single step towards identifying malicious content to reduce the burden of manual review. Therefore, this method can and should be used in addition to other procedures. In the proposed operationalization in Sect. 7, the various procedures can be included in the steps *Pre-Filter* and *Classification*.

## 9   Conclusions

In this work, we provide an extension of the Damerau-Levenshtein metric, denoted as EDL, with additional characteristics based on the work of [37]. Testing this variation resulted in a significantly higher precision in detecting true typosquatting candidates. The primary purpose of this string matching algorithm is to narrow down the classifier's scope in the subsequent phase and, therefore, act as a pre-filter. It accomplishes this by providing a more manageable subset of potential malicious packages, namely typosquatting packages, instead of applying the classifier to the entire *npm* ecosystem containing 2.7 million packages. Additionally, we statistically examined our dataset and derived insights deemed helpful for further investigation. One is that most typosquatting packages in our dataset were inefficient, with nearly zero downloads per day. Only a minority of the packages were identified as effective typosquatting.

In addition to the usual features used in the classifier, we suggest including extra features that involve commonly used packages and how typosquatting attackers use them. To determine the introduced packages and modules, we examined a delta between a typosquatting package and its corresponding target. Testing our model on our own and the external datasets results in significantly higher precision and recall than current state-of-the-art models in this domain. The new proposed model and the additional features improved the performance of detecting malicious package behavior.

While our research has provided useful insights into typosquatting attacks in the *npm* ecosystem, some aspects remain unexplored for further research. The insights discovered here build on previous discoveries and expand the scope of understanding and mitigating the impact of typosquatting attacks on *npm* users and the broader software development community. Given the close relation to typosquatting in DNS, it might be interesting to test the EDL Distance in the context of DNS. In future work, we plan to benchmark this model against ensemble machine learning models, enhance the dataset and feature set for training, and extract additional libraries and features frequently introduced by attackers for further model refinement.

# Appendix

**Table 3.** Boolean feature vector for classifying packages with the new features identified and evaluated for the detection of typosquatting malware. (Note that specific information about the extracted features/libraries was not disclosed by [33] to prevent reverse engineering. If that was the case, we also assumed it to be a new feature.)

| Feature | Description | New |
|---|---|---|
| axios | Usage of the axios module | ● |
| child_process | Usage of the child_process module | ○ |
| crypto | Usage of the crypto module | ● |
| curl | Usage of curl, wget or ping in install script | ● |
| dns | Usage of the dns module | ● |
| entry_through_script | Using install hooks | ○ |
| eval | Usage of the eval function | ○ |
| fs | Usage of the fs module | ○ |
| has_binaries | Binaries, scripts and similar formats in package | ● |
| has_ip_or_address | IP or Address in package | ○ |
| http/https | Usage of the http or https module | ● |
| node-fetch | Usage of the node-fetch module | ● |
| node-serialize | Usage of the node-serialize module | ● |
| os | Usage of the os module | ● |
| path | Usage of the path module | ● |
| querystring | Usage of the querystring module | ● |

# References

1. Aklson, A., et al.: State of the software supply chain report: Sonatype's industry-defining research on the rapidly changing landscape of open source (2022). https://de.sonatype.com/state-of-the-software-supply-chain/introduction
2. Aldawood, H., Skinner, G.: Contemporary cyber security social engineering solutions, measures, policies, tools and applications: a critical appraisal (2019). https://f.hubspotusercontent30.net/hubfs/8156085/WhitePaper%20-%20IJS%20-%20Contemporary%20Cyber%20Security%20Social%20Engineering%20Solutions[1].pdf
3. Blanc, G., Miyamoto, D., Akiyama, M., Kadobayashi, Y.: Characterizing obfuscated javascript using abstract syntax trees: experimenting with malicious scripts. In: 2012 26th International Conference on Advanced Information Networking and Applications Workshops, pp. 344–351 (2012). https://doi.org/10.1109/WAINA.2012.140

4. Breese, J.S., Heckerman, D., Kadie, C.: Empirical analysis of predictive algorithms for collaborative filtering. In: Proceedings of the Fourteenth Conference on Uncertainty in Artificial Intelligence, UAI 1998, pp. 43–52. Morgan Kaufmann Publishers Inc., San Francisco, CA, USA (1998)

5. Breiman, L.: Random forests, pp. 5–32 (2001). https://link.springer.com/article/10.1023/A:1010933404324

6. Čarnogurský, M.: Attacks on Package Managers. Bachelor thesis, Masaryk University, Brünn, Tschechien (2019). https://is.muni.cz/th/y41ft/thesis_final_electronic.pdf

7. Chappell, B., Neuman, S.: U.s. says north korea 'directly responsible' for wannacry ransomware attack. NPR (2017-12-19), https://www.npr.org/sections/thetwo-way/2017/12/19/571854614/u-s-says-north-korea-directly-responsible-for-wannacry-ransomware-attack

8. Damerau, F.J.: A technique for computer detection and correction of spelling errors. Commun. ACM **7**(3), 171–176 (1964). https://doi.org/10.1145/363958.363994

9. Duan, R., Alrawi, O., Kasturi, R.P., Elder, R., Saltaformaggio, B., Lee, W.: Towards measuring supply chain attacks on package managers for interpreted languages. In: Sadeghi, A.R., Koushanfar, F. (eds.) Proceedings 2021 Network and Distributed System Security Symposium. Internet Society, Reston, VA (2021). https://doi.org/10.14722/ndss.2021.23055

10. Garrett, K., Ferreira, G., Jia, L., Sunshine, J., Kastner, C.: Detecting suspicious package updates. In: 2019 IEEE/ACM 41st International Conference on Software Engineering: New Ideas and Emerging Results (ICSE-NIER). pp. 13–16. IEEE (2019). https://doi.org/10.1109/ICSE-NIER.2019.00012

11. Hendrick, S., Mckeay, M.: Addressing cybersecurity challenges in open source software (2022). https://www.linuxfoundation.org/research/addressing-cybersecurity-challenges-in-open-source-software

12. Ilyankou, I.: Comparison of jaro-winkler and ratcliff/obershelp algorithms in spell check (2014). https://ilyankou.files.wordpress.com/2015/06/ib-extended-essay.pdf

13. Jaccard, P.: The distribution of the flora in the alpine zone.1. New Phytologist **11**(2), 37–50 (1912).https://doi.org/10.1111/j.1469-8137.1912.tb05611.x, https://nph.onlinelibrary.wiley.com/doi/abs/10.1111/j.1469-8137.1912.tb05611.x

14. Jaro, M.A.: Advances in record-linkage methodology as applied to matching the 1985 census of Tampa, Florida. J. Am. Stat. Assoc. **84**(406), 414 (1989). https://doi.org/10.2307/2289924

15. Joseph, V.R.: Optimal ratio for data splitting. Statist. Anal. Data Mining ASA Data Sci. J. **15**(4), 531–538 (2022). https://doi.org/10.1002/sam.11583

16. Levenshtein, V.I.: Binary codes capable of correcting deletions, insertions and reversals. Soviet Phys. Doklady **10**(8), 707–710 (1966)

17. Mayhew, B., et al.: State of the software supply chain 2021: the 7th annual report on global open source software development (2021). https://www.sonatype.com/hubfs/Q3%202021-State%20of%20the%20Software%20Supply%20Chain-Report/SSSC-Report-2021_0913_PM_2.pdf?hsLang=en-us

18. Mcbride, L.: Software supply chains: An introductory guide (2021). https://blog.sonatype.com/software-supply-chain-a-definition-and-introductory-guide

19. Meyers, J.S., Tozer, B.: Bewear! python typosquatting is about more than typos - in-q-tel (2020). https://www.iqt.org/library/bewear-python-typosquatting-is-about-more-than-typos

20. MITRE Corporation: Common vulnerabilities and exposures (cve) (2024). https://cve.mitre.org, Accessed: 17 Jan 2024
21. Needleman, S.B., Wunsch, C.D.: A general method applicable to the search for similarities in the amino acid sequence of two proteins. J. Mol. Biol. **48**(3), 443–453 (1970). https://doi.org/10.1016/0022-2836(70)90057-4
22. npm: Threats and mitigations. https://docs.npmjs.com/threats-and-mitigations (2023), Accessed 12 April 2024
23. Offensive Security: Exploit database (2024). https://www.exploit-db.com, Accessed 26 Feb 2024
24. Ohm, M., Boes, F., Bungartz, C., Meier, M.: On the feasibility of supervised machine learning for the detection of malicious software packages (2022). https://doi.org/10.1145/3538969.3544415, https://publica.fraunhofer.de/handle/publica/445251
25. Ohm, M., Kempf, L., Boes, F., Meier, M.: Supporting the detection of software supply chain attacks through unsupervised signature generation (2021). https://arxiv.org/pdf/2011.02235
26. Ohm, M., Plate, H., Sykosch, A., Meier, M.: Backstabber's knife collection: A review of open source software supply chain attacks (2020). http://arxiv.org/pdf/2005.09535v1
27. Ohm, M., Stuke, C.: Sok: practical detection of software supply chain attacks. In: Proceedings of the 18th International Conference on Availability, Reliability and Security, ARES 2023. Association for Computing Machinery, New York (2023). https://doi.org/10.1145/3600160.3600162
28. Ohm, M., Sykosch, A., Meier, M.: Towards detection of software supply chain attacks by forensic artifacts. In: Volkamer, M., Wressnegger, C. (eds.) Proceedings of the 15th International Conference on Availability, Reliability and Security, pp. 1–6. ACM, New York (2020). https://doi.org/10.1145/3407023.3409183
29. Ohm, M., Sykosch, A., Meier, M.: Towards detection of software supply chain attacks by forensic artifacts. In: Proceedings of the 15th International Conference on Availability, Reliability and Security. ARES 2020, Association for Computing Machinery, New York (2020). https://doi.org/10.1145/3407023.3409183
30. Philips, L.: Hanging on the metaphone (1990)
31. Phylum: Phylum blog (2024). https://blog.phylum.io, Accessed 26 Jan 2024
32. Russel, R.C.: Patent us1435663a (1922). https://worldwide.espacenet.com/patent/search/family/024063815/publication/us1435663a?q=pn%3dus1435663
33. Sejfia, A., Schäfer, M.: Practical automated detection of malicious npm packages (2022). https://doi.org/10.1145/3510003.3510104, https://arxiv.org/pdf/2202.13953
34. Smith, T., Waterman, M.: Identification of common molecular subsequences. J. Mol. Biol. **147**(1), 195–197 (1981). https://doi.org/10.1016/0022-2836(81)90087-5, https://www.sciencedirect.com/science/article/pii/0022283681900875
35. Snyk: Snyk security (2024). https://security.snyk.io/, Accessed 01 Mar 2024
36. Sonatype: Sonatype (2024). https://www.sonatype.com/, Accessed 26 Feb 2024
37. Taylor, M., Vaidya, R.K., Davidson, D., de Carli, L., Rastogi, V.: Spellbound: defending against package typosquatting (2020). http://arxiv.org/pdf/2003.03471v1
38. Team, P.R.: Q1 2023 evolution of software supply chain security (Jul 2023). https://blog.phylum.io/q1-2023-evolution-of-software-supply-chain-security/
39. Tschacher, N.P.: Typosquatting in Programming Language Package Managers. Bachelor thesis, University of Hamburg, Hamburg (2016). https://incolumitas.com/data/thesis.pdf

40. Vu, D.L., Pashchenko, I., Massacci, F., Plate, H., Sabetta, A.: Typosquatting and combosquatting attacks on the python ecosystem. In: 2020 IEEE European Symposium on Security and Privacy Workshops (EuroS&PW), pp. 509–514. IEEE (2020). https://doi.org/10.1109/EuroSPW51379.2020.00074

41. Vu, L.D., Newman, Z., Meyers, J.S.: Hunting malware on package repositories: interviews with pypi maintainers and a comparison of alternative approaches to pypi malware detection (2022)

42. Whittaker, Z.: Two years after wannacry, a million computers remain at risk. TechCrunch (2019-05-12). https://techcrunch.com/2019/05/12/wannacry-two-years-on/

# Towards a Malware Family Classification Model Using Static Call Graph Instruction Visualization

Attila Mester[1,3]($\boxtimes$)(iD), Zalán Bodó[1](iD), P. Vinod[2](iD), and Mauro Conti[2](iD)

[1] Babeş–Bolyai University of Cluj-Napoca, Cluj-Napoca, Romania
{attila.mester,zalan.bodo}@ubbcluj.ro
[2] University of Padua, Padua, Italy
{vinod.puthuvath,mauro.conti}@unipd.it
[3] Bitdefender, Cluj-Napoca, Romania

**Abstract.** This paper offers yet another static analysis method aimed at classifying malware families, by disassembling the executables with Radare2 and traversing the static call graph to train CNNs on instruction-based RGB images. The instruction-based family detection should have the potential to model common behavioral patterns, thus creating a profile for various families and actors. The experiments are carried out on the BODMAS, MalImg, and IBD (internal Bitdefender dataset). Our method's performance is compared to another static feature selection method – the EMBER features. Furthermore, we reveal proof of correlation between packers and malware families in all three datasets. Our conclusion states that the proposed model's accuracy does not reach the EMBER feature's performance due to the high number of packed files in these datasets. However, its stability still motivates its use since the instruction-based information cannot be altered easily as header-based features – our observations infer that while classifying malware families, ML methods which ignore unpacking the samples may overfit the data, learning packer traits instead of actual family behaviour, offering no explainability over the decision.

**Keywords:** static malware analysis · call graph · control flow graph · Radare2 · family classification · packer · BODMAS · EMBER · MalImg

## 1 Introduction

Attributing APT information to cyberattacks is a high priority of threat intelligence organizations. The attribution covers information about the attack's authors and the deployed malware families. This information can be leveraged to identify the attackers, reason their intentions, and prioritize certain security measures. Since manual analysts cannot process the vast amount of threats that appear on a global scale, automated analysis of malware samples is essential for real-time antivirus products.

Automated analysis may be dynamic – running the executable file in a virtual machine or sandbox, or static, meaning the application of various feature extraction techniques on the file's binary content. Due to practical reasons (e.g. the ability to process the incoming samples in real-time), this paper builds upon the idea of processing the static call graph image. Contrary to static analysis, dynamic analysis necessitates a robust sandbox environment, event tracking, hardware resources and also takes more time due to having to wait for payload activation – which may or may not happen in the case of more sophisticated malware that can detect the sandbox [52].

This paper proposes using deep learning architectures from computer vision (ResNet [20], MobileNetV3 [24], GoogleNet [60], EfficientNet [61], DenseNet [25]) to classify malware families. We achieve this by feeding the models with images representing the disassembled code of the malware samples. These CNN-based models will then classify the images into malware families. We hope that the models will learn patterns in the images that can later be traced back to the corresponding functionalities and instructions within the disassembled code. Our method aims to achieve real-time analysis of malicious files by disassembling them with Radare2 and creating the call graph using the r2 tool. Image-based malware analysis, specifically family classification is not a novelty, there have already been remarkable results in the field [7,14,30]. The originality of this work lies in how the images are created from an executable file, based on a specific depth-first-search (DFS) traversal on the static call graph nodes, organizing the instructions in a list that represents execution flow instead of simple function blocks. We also examine the problem of packed samples, and our findings indicate that machine learning techniques that skip unpacking these files may overfit the data by capturing packer features rather than genuine family behaviors, leading to non-explainable decisions.

This paper is structured as follows. Section 2 covers the literature regarding malware family analysis, methods based on creating visual features of an executable, and also the state-of-the-art public datasets, motivating our use of the BODMAS and MalImg datasets in Sect. 2.4. Our approach is conferred in Sect. 3, detailing various technical limitations and implementation details faced during the experiments, such as detecting packed samples, automating the unpacking process and generating RGB images and training CNN models. A comparison of our proposed method with the EMBER baseline is presented in Sect. 4, while a complementary analysis of the problem of packed files is discussed in Sect. 5, offering a possible explanation of the underperformance of our method compared to the EMBER baseline's classification accuracy. Our conclusion and future work ideas are detailed in Sect. 6.

## 2    Related Work

### 2.1    Call Graph-Based Features in Malware Analysis

The use of static call graphs as features for malware detection has been widely adopted in the automated malware analysis literature [63]. The analysis carried out can be static, relying solely on the binary file (e.g. byte sequences, opcode sequences, API calls, register usage, etc.), or dynamic, involving the execution of malware in a sandbox environment to observe its behavior, the most frequently used features being API calls, followed by byte sequences and API call graphs. The survey [44] contains more recent works as well, including, for example, models based on Graph Convolutional Neural Networks (GCN), tackling a considerably smaller set of papers than the survey mentioned above. According to the authors, the prerequisites for the effective use of Control Flow Graph-based (CFG) methods are the following: (i) efficient/correct disassembly and CFG extraction, (ii) robust and efficient machine learning methods, and (iii) explainability of the machine learning model.

In the context of working with API graph features, researchers have employed various methods for analyzing samples. Notably, graph matching algorithms and graph edit distances have been utilized to compare and analyze these features [11,50,56]. Additionally, some studies have focused on using graph-based n-gram features to enhance analysis [8,12,59]. In [16,22,29,51,67] the call graph-based features are obtained via node and graph embedding methods. Successful applications of GCNs can be seen in [35,49] for malware detection, or in [21] where the malware family classifier can also explain its decision by identifying the subgraph of the malware CFG that contributes the most to the prediction.

Dynamic analysis based on API and system call features was also experimented with promising classification results [22,62]; these features are also used in embedding and GCN methods [22,49]. However, the limitations of dynamic analysis cannot be overlooked: [49] reports 3000 h of runtime to process $40k$ samples and obtain 1.5TB data describing the dynamic API call sequences, making it impossible for real-time use cases. Another issue is packing, where malware obfuscates code to hinder proper disassembly and mislead analysis methods [1,37]. Conversely, if the disassembled code is correct, analyzing program behavioral patterns can provide a robust solution for detecting zero-day malware [2].

## 2.2    Analysis Based on Visualization Techniques

The first model using image-like representation was described in [47], the paper introducing also the widely used MalImg dataset. Here a grayscale 2D image is constructed from the binary file, each pixel representing one byte of the sample's binary. The authors also claim that malware belonging to the same family when packed with the same packer yields similar images, thus the method proposed can still produce high classification accuracy. The works [7,30] also carry out experiments using grayscale image representations of malware. In [14] the input file is split into sections, one channel representing the grayscale image of binary data, the other two being constant for one section, storing the section entropy and relative section size, respectively. The authors of [65] also consider section information, putting the grayscale image of the binary in colored frames to distinguish them from each other. Markov images also consist of a popular representation in malware analysis, where the transition probabilities between bytes, opcodes, etc. are visualized [72]. In [10] Markov images are extended to the RGB color space working with the disassembled code and taking the transition probabilities between characters, the first letters of the opcodes, and the last two letters of the opcodes, respectively. SimHash images are constructed by taking the locality-sensitive binary hash code generated by SimHash [6] for the opcode sequences, and converting it to a binary image [48]. The images are usually fed to Convolutional Neural Networks (CNNs) as inputs, the most popular architectures being AlexNet [34], VGG [58] and ResNet [20].

While visualization is often seen as a 2D image of data, the reason for the widespread use of 2D representation in the literature is unclear. Although convolutional networks typically interpret images by identifying local patterns of varying sizes and complexities, this technique can also be applied to any sequential data. Binary or program code is more of a 1D sequential structure rather than 2D. Despite this, only a few models in the literature use 1D convolutions to detect patterns in static opcode and dynamic syscall sequences for identifying malicious code [38,40,64]. Even though using pre-trained weights for deep CNN architectures is not advantageous, and the arbitrary choice of image width raises some questions, 2D models have proven effective, at least under the tested conditions [33].

## 2.3   Binary File-Based Approaches

Since disassembling the binary code of a program into source code/assembly instructions is a costly process [49], significant research effort is directed towards working directly with binary files, aiming to extract maximal information for predictive purposes. Besides the approaches working with binary file-based visualizations in Sect. 2.2, we mention binary n-gram features used in [32,39,45], while alternative solutions are focused on extracting API function calls and interpretable strings [69,71]. In [69], candidate interpretable strings are identified as sequences of ASCII, GB2312, Big5, and Unicode characters, and then refined using a natural language dictionary.

Other studies have shown promising results by leveraging features like the number of referenced DLLs and APIs, sections within the file, and symbols in the export table [5,55]. As the works mentioned above are only highlighted examples, rather than covering the entire literature, for a comprehensive list the reader is referred to the surveys [4,63,70].

The paper [3] introducing the EMBER (Endgame Malware BEnchmark for Research) dataset proposes a set of PE features for malware classification, and can be viewed as the aggregation of the features mentioned above. The features being extracted directly from the binary file are categorized as follows: (i) general file information (size, number of imports and exports, etc.), (ii) header information (machine, architecture, OS, etc.),(iii) imported and exported functions, (iv) section information (name, size, entropy, etc.), (v) byte histogram, (vi) byte entropy histogram, as described in [55], (vii) strings (paths, URLs, registry keys, etc.), (viii) data directories.[1] The resulting vector is a fully numeric one,

---

[1] The entire list of 2351 or 2381 features – depending on the version – can be found in the code provided by the authors: https://github.com/elastic/ember.

**Table 1.** Public malware datasets [68]. ○ = "not available", ● = "available", ◗ = "partially available", ✪ = "published by this work" (Sect. 3.5). The "Samples" column refers to the number of malicious files in the dataset – we are targeting family classification, hence benign samples are out of the scope of this table.

| Dataset | Published | Binaries | Families | Samples(mal.) | EMBER | Disasm. | Image |
|---|---|---|---|---|---|---|---|
| MalImg      [47] | 2011 | ○ | 25 | 9458 | ○  ✪ | ○  ✪ | ●  ✪ |
| MS BIG      [53] | 2015 | ○ | 9 | 10 868 | ○ | ● | ○ |
| EMBER       [3] | 2018 | ○ | ◗ | 800 000 | ● | ○ | ○ |
| UCSB-packed [1] | 2020 | ● | ○ | 232 415 | ○ | ○ | ○ |
| SOREL-20m [19] | 2020 | ● | ○ | 9 962 820 | ● | ○ | ○ |
| BODMAS    [68] | 2021 | ● | 581 | 57 293 | ● | ○  ✪ | ○  ✪ |
| **Malflow (this)** | **2024** | ○ | **47** | **18 756** | ✪ | ✪ | ✪ |

containing both integers and real values, applying the hashing trick in the case of nominal features. As EMBER features offer an efficient way to characterize samples, we will compare them to our call graph-based features in Sect. 4.

## 2.4   State-of-the Art Datasets: MalImg, BIG, EMBER, BODMAS

The malware analysis domain lacks the abundance of freely available public datasets with precise labels and annotation, due to the risk of publishing thousands of malicious files on the Internet, and the associated legal liability issues – that is why, although statistics and meta information are easier to access, most providers offer the binaries only upon request, or based on service membership fees (e.g. the VirusTotal Feed). This can also be concluded by analyzing the vast literature overview of [63], where the authors show that only a tiny percentage of research works offer the dataset on which the experiments were carried out. Certain vendors still offer malicious binaries to the public, such as Malware-Bazaar[2], exhibiting a remarkable database with over 700 thousand files – the problem is, only a fraction of them are assigned reliable – if any – family labels[2]. In this paper, we are focusing on malware family classification, thus we only take into consideration those datasets that offer family labels for the samples. Table 1 summarizes the properties of the publicly available malware datasets.

The popular MalImg dataset published in 2011 [47] contains $9.5k$ malicious samples' grayscale image based on their hex dump – categorized into 25 families. Several research works use this dataset [17, 18, 31, 46, 73].

The Microsoft Malware Classification Challenge dataset [53] (shortened as "Microsoft BIG 2015"), published in a Kaggle competition in 2015, contains $10k$ malware files, each assigned a family label from 9 different families. Note that the binaries are not published, only their headerless hex dump and an IDA Pro disassembly text file. Also, the files are anonymized, without MD5/SHA256 hash.

The EMBER dataset was first released in 2017 [3], and later updated in 2018. It is a significantly larger database than the former two, having $800k$ malicious

---

[2] https://bazaar.abuse.ch.

samples' SHA256 and feature vector, and in some cases family labels. A wide range of experiments use this dataset [9, 13, 15, 26, 28, 36, 52, 54, 66, 68].

UCSB-Packed [1] and Sorel-20 m [19] do not contain family labels, thus are incompatible with our research work.

BODMAS [68] represents the core of our experiments, with 57 923 malware binaries, each having a family label and the EMBER feature vector.

### 2.5   Our Contributions

Our previous work has all been concerned with static analysis of the code, fully aware of the drawbacks of this approach (e.g. possible code obfuscation by packers), the present research being a next piece of this. In [41] a signature-based approach was proposed, built on the premises that function call n-grams can properly describe the behavior of the program; locality sensitive-hashing was applied here as well to be able to catch similar instruction sequences. Graph-convolutional neural networks were employed to classify malware in [42] based on these features, while Radare2 and IDA Pro have been compared in several aspects in [43], two popular disassembler tools, essential instruments of our approaches. This work focuses on grasping malware family traits from visualized call graph instructions. This method achieves a relatively high family classification accuracy of nearly 0.88 micro $F_1$ on the filtered BODMAS dataset with 57 families. We are aware that this model does not overperform state-of-the-art malware family classification accuracy; rather, this work focuses on a model that ignores noise from the binary, learning from images based solely on instruction information. We conclude that while sections containing constants, parameters, and strings are useful for family classification, relying solely on instructions is also viable, albeit with a potential trade-off between classification accuracy and method stability. Unlike constants or other binary noise in a PE file, which attackers can easily modify, modifying instructions can potentially corrupt the binary file.

To sum up, our contribution has the following pillars:(i) offering a new, original method to generate RGB images for PE files based on disassembled call graph instruction flow, and training various CNN models to prove the method's usability; (ii) offering packer information, static call graph, images and instruction data for two well-known datasets, BODMAS and MalImg, on Kaggle; (iii) comparing our method to the state-of-the-art EMBER feature vector with baseline model training; (iv) publishing another dataset (IBD) on Kaggle.

## 3   Training CNN Models on Call Graph-Based Images

To experiment with behavior-based features in static analysis, we use static call graph instructions, as they are assumed to better represent the file's execution flow and behavior compared to header-based features. For accurate malware family classification, we propose mapping families to their common behavioral features based on patterns in their instruction images. We traverse the call graph's functions to compile a list of instructions, encoding each instruction into a pixel to generate the final RGB image. The pipeline of our work can be seen in Fig. 1.

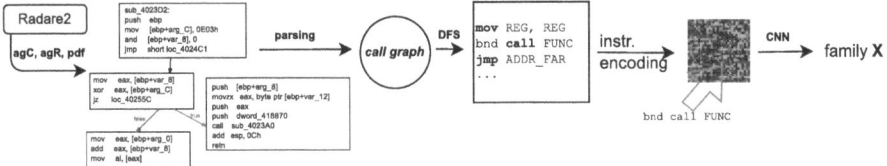

**Fig. 1.** Pipeline of our proposed method.

## 3.1 Creating the Static Call Graph

The static call graph generation necessitates a disassembler tool. We chose Radare2 (5.8.8 release) because of reasons detailed in [43]. IDA Pro is a viable alternative, however, its free-tier version's UNIX-based scripting capabilities are limited. Hereby we list the key steps of generating the static call graph of a PE file using Radare2 (details on GitHub[3]). By using the **r2pipe**[4] Python package, we apply the **agCd** and **agRd** commands to yield the global call and reference graph.[5] This latter is needed to obtain blocks which may not be included in the call graph in some cases. After traversing these graphs, we call for each function the **pdfj** command to obtain its instruction list. Our "CallGraph" object contains a dictionary mapping a node address (relative virtual address – RVA) to the node (i.e. function). One such node's properties are the following: label (e.g. "0x40012F" or "GetModuleHandleA"), RVA, type (subroutine, DLL or statically linked lib.), the instruction list, and the function call list. An instruction holds information about its bnd flag [27] and prefix (if any), its mnemonic and a list of parameters. We considered 11 prefixes (according to the Radare2 5.8.8 release), and 7 parameter types – this was our personal choice, categorizing parameters into constants (e.g. "0x5"), registers (EAX, ESI, etc.), addresses, far addresses, functions (an address having entry in the call graph registry), strings (an address to a string), and blocks (an address, but the RVA is not registered – typical case of jumps resulting from *if*, *else* or looping constructs). The structure of an instruction is as follows: **[bnd?] [prefix?] mnemonic [param1 [param2, ...]]**.

## 3.2 Analyzing Packed Samples

It has already been stated in the literature that packed samples may have a negative effect on training a classifier based solely on static features, since its binary code does not naturally reflect the payload's code – it is obfuscated, compressed, and will be transformed into the original code only in runtime, after the sample applies its unpacking routine [1,37]. We are using the open source tool *Detect-it-easy* – DIE[6], to determine the packer of each file in the

---

[3] https://github.com/attilamester/malflow.

[4] https://pypi.org/project/r2pipe.

[5] These stand for "analyze global call/reference graph", and return a graph with nodes marking function blocks and links representing calls or references between them.

[6] https://github.com/horsicq/Detect-It-Easy.

**Table 2.** Packer statistics obtained by DIE. Note that the number of actual vs. detected packed files may differ – these numbers show a lower estimate, see Sect. 3.2.

| | Total | Packed | | UPX | Petite | ASPack | DxPack | MPRESS | PEComp |
|---|---|---|---|---|---|---|---|---|---|
| BODMAS | 57 293 | 18 688 | (33%) | 9 676 | 3 795 | 1 771 | 1 654 | 1 174 | 580 |
| MalImg | 9 458 | 1 703 | (18%) | 1 686 | – | – | – | – | 4 |
| IBD | 18 756 | 2 195 | (12%) | 424 | 159 | 111 | 19 | 214 | 909 |

dataset, and also analyze the sections' entropy. As noted previously [37], DIE classifies a binary as packed if the average entropy of its sections exceeds 7.0.

As shown in Table 2, the majority of packed files are compressed with UPX – we managed to automatically unpack a relevant fraction of the files with "upx"[7].

### 3.3   Converting the Call Graph Into Image

We intended to grasp the static behavioral features and patterns in the call graph of an executable, by creating an image based on the instructions in the call graph. This way, the image does not reflect all bytes from each section, only the relevant instructions, by traversing the call graph in execution order – thus, eliminating the *noise*, compared to grayscale images based on hex dumps. We apply a depth-first-search traversal (DFS) of the call graph to obtain the list of nodes, i.e. functions – this list reflects the execution order of these functions. Instead of just appending these functions' instruction list after one another, we apply another DFS, now on the instruction level: in the order of these nodes e.g. *A-B-C*, we gather the instructions from *A*, but once we meet a *CALL*-like instruction, we jump to that address (let us presume in block *C*), and continue gathering the instructions from this block. After the recursive context finishes, we continue parsing the instructions in block *A*. Then, we move on to block *B*. If block *B* was already visited due to the recursive nature of this process, we just copy its instruction list again, now without following *CALL* jumps, in order to preserve the natural flow of the program execution. This type of call graph traversal should genuinely reflect the execution flow of a binary. Thus, images based on this traversal should exhibit patterns that reflect behavior – common, similar patterns presumably leading to common family traits.

The main question is, how do we encode one instruction into a pixel. For this task, we examined three distinct encoding schemes, differing in the amount of information it encapsulates. We note that the encoding involves assigning a three-byte value to each instruction, as we are creating three-channel RGB images.

**(FE) Full Encoding: Mnemonic, Prefix, Bnd, Two Parameters.** In our codebase we are tracking 2019 different mnemonics, ranging from general-purpose instructions to floating point operations, AVX, SSE, etc. We also keep

---

[7] The emulator-based unpacker "unipacker" was also examined, but due to technical limitations, we had to restrict the automated unpacking process to "upx" only.

track of 11 instruction prefixes, and 7 parameter types, as described in Sect. 3.1. An instruction can have a bnd flag [27], and in the case of mnemonics tracked by us, some of them may have up to 9 parameters (e.g. `encodekey256`). Thus, the instruction space so far has $2019 \times 11 \times 2 \times 7^9$ unique elements, which cannot be encoded into three bytes. Our solution is to encode the mnemonic – prefix – bnd information into the first two bytes, so the red–green channels ($2019 \times 11 \times 2 = 44\,418$ fits into two bytes), and truncate the parameters and keep the first two, encoded in the third byte, the blue channel ($7^2 = 49$, unfortunately, $7^3$ would not fit into one byte). Note that due to this encoding approach, most information is stored in the lower byte of the red–green channel, that is the green value – blue channel will be assigned a small number, max. 49. That is why our images with this encoding seem greenish, with red spots here and there, marking the presence of a prefix and/or bnd.

**(PE1) Partial Encoding: Mnemonic, Prefix, Bnd.** The motivation was to examine whether encoding instruction parameters into the image helps CNN models learn useful patterns and classify malware families. This encoding ignores the parameters and encodes the mnemonic, prefix, and bnd information into two bytes in the green and blue channels. Similar to the previous encoder, these images appear blueish, with green spots indicating the presence of prefix and/or bnd.

**(PE2) Partial Encoding: only Mnemonic.** To determine whether prefix and bnd information improve the model or not, we now ignore everything in the instruction and encode only the mnemonic, again, on two bytes, in the green–blue channels.

### 3.4   Training CNN Models

Once we generated images for the malware samples, the domain-specific problem turned into image classification, with target labels being families. Hence we can leverage any tool, model or technique that is used in training CNNs on images. Various deep convolutional neural networks are experimented with, as detailed in Sect. 3.4.

**Models.** We perform experiments on ResNet18, ResNet50 [20], Resnet1D [23], MobileNetV3 [24], GoogleNet [60], EfficientNet [61], and DenseNet [25]. The ResNet18 model is shallower and more lightweight compared to ResNet50, which likely explains the shorter training time observed for this model. Additionally, its performance metrics were better. As mentioned in Sect. 2.2, program code may be best represented by a 1D sequence, which is why we also experimented with a 1D ResNet architecture [23]. Table 3 presents a selection of the best model results.

| Simple hex dump | Encoding **FE** | Encoding **PE1** | Encoding **PE2** |
|---|---|---|---|

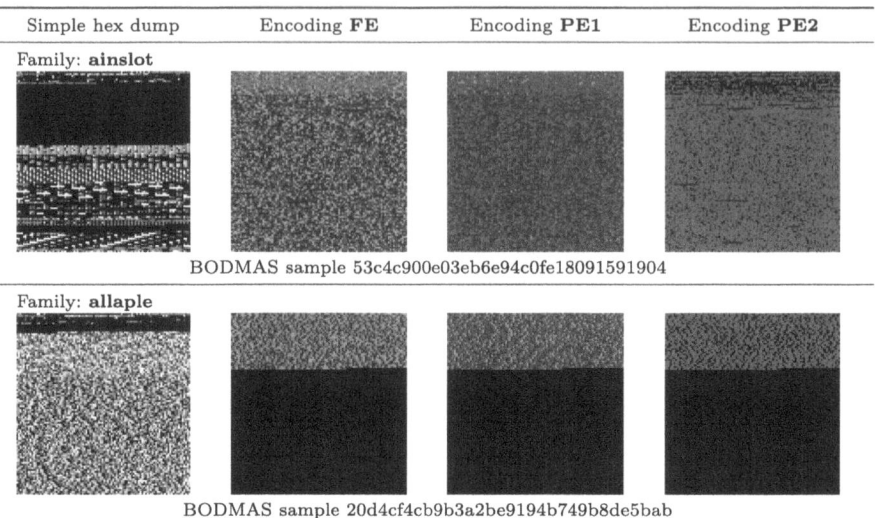

Family: **ainslot**

BODMAS sample 53c4c900e03eb6e94c0fe18091591904

Family: **allaple**

BODMAS sample 20d4cf4cb9b3a2be9194b749b8de5bab

**Fig. 2.** Comparing different instruction encodings (Sect. 3.3) and the simple hex dump image on different malware families.

**Image Formats.** Experiments were carried out on four different types of images: hex dump-based grayscale images (similarly to [47]), and the three different types of instruction encoding schemes presented in Sect. 3.3. Interestingly, we observed little to no difference in the performance of models trained on **FE** and **PE1** images – that is why we show results only according to **FE** scheme in Table 3. Applying **PE2** resulted in a 1–2% performance drop across all models. Although this change is statistically insignificant, we assume it may be due to the greater importance of prefix and bnd information compared to parameters in this type of call graph modeling.

**Hyperparameters.** Even though multiple hyperparametrization options were applied, in some cases negligible to no differences could be observed in the performance of the models, thus, in Table 3 only those parameters are included which affected the most the validation $F_1$ score: the CNN architecture and the image size – which also determined the batch size due to the GPU memory limits. We applied a random search on the hyperparameter space defined by the followings:

1. *CNN architecture* – as listed in Sect. 3.4 – **Models**.
2. *Pre-trained (Type:bool)* – in most CNN models, we could opt for pre-trained weights of the ImageNet dataset. In our case, though, the images are mostly pixelated, thus, it is natural that models using pre-trained weights did not perform better than the others, and the runtime was not faster as well.
3. *Min. samples per class (Type:int)* – We consistently set this parameter to 100 in Table 3. Due to the high dataset imbalance, we considered only families

**Table 3.** Performance of various models on BODMAS, MalImg and IBD.

| Model | Batch | Img. | Acc. | $F_1$ micro | $F_1$ macro |
|---|---|---|---|---|---|
| **BODMAS, 57 families** | | | | | |
| ResNet18 | 20 | $224 \times 224$ | 0.820 | 0.820 | 0.797 |
| ResNet18 | 20 | $100 \times 100$ | 0.887 | 0.887 | 0.859 |
| ResNet18 | 32 | $30 \times 30$ | 0.793 | 0.793 | 0.747 |
| ResNet50 | 32 | $100 \times 100$ | 0.812 | 0.812 | 0.786 |
| ResNet50 | 32 | $30 \times 30$ | 0.794 | 0.794 | 0.745 |
| ResNet1d | 20 | $100 \times 100$ | 0.784 | 0.784 | 0.727 |
| MobileNetV3 | 32 | $30 \times 30$ | 0.790 | 0.790 | 0.733 |
| GoogleNet | 32 | $30 \times 30$ | 0.790 | 0.790 | 0.731 |
| EfficientNet | 32 | $30 \times 30$ | 0.786 | 0.786 | 0.737 |
| DenseNet121 | 32 | $30 \times 30$ | 0.790 | 0.790 | 0.746 |
| **BODMAS, 57 families, hex dump images** | | | | | |
| ResNet18 | 20 | $100 \times 100$ | 0.881 | 0.881 | 0.873 |
| **MalImg, 23 families** | | | | | |
| ResNet18 | 20 | $100 \times 100$ | 0.722 | 0.744 | 0.737 |
| ResNet18 | 20 | $30 \times 30$ | 0.761 | 0.761 | 0.749 |
| **IBD, 47 families** | | | | | |
| ResNet18 | 20 | $100 \times 100$ | 0.872 | 0.872 | 0.784 |
| ResNet18 | 32 | $30 \times 30$ | 0.849 | 0.849 | 0.776 |

with at least $n$ samples. $n = 100$ seemed to be a good trade-off considering the family distribution of BODMAS.

4. *Batch size (Type:int)* – a good rule of thumb was to try batch sizes of $16, 32, 64, 128$. In the case of larger images, only smaller batches could be applied, which also implied a longer runtime. In most cases, this was set to 32.
5. *Augmentation (Type:bool)* – We applied augmentation on the level of malicious files, creating around 7000 augmented samples for the BODMAS, but did not observe significant improvements with the augmented train dataset – this may differ in case we created even more augmented samples.

Considering the various types of images and all three datasets, it is visible that the hyperparameter space is immense – we trained more than 200 models, with runtimes ranging from 30 min up to 26 h for the larger images.

## 3.5    Dataset

The CNN models were trained on three different datasets: BODMAS, MalImg, and an internal Bitdefender dataset (IBD). The IBD is private meaning that we

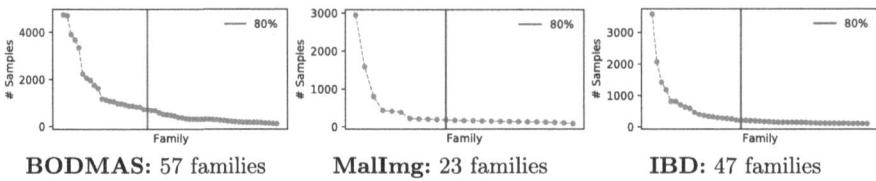

**BODMAS:** 57 families    **MalImg:** 23 families    **IBD:** 47 families

**Fig. 3.** Family distribution in the datasets (with min. 100 samples per family applied) used in the experiments of training CNN models on instruction images. The vertical lines show that only a few families make up the majority of the data.

publish only the list of MD5 hashes, but not the MD5 – family labeling as well. Since MalImg contains only MD5 hashes, we used the Bitdefender infrastructure to obtain the binary files. Figure 3 shows the distribution of families in the three datasets, demonstrating their high imbalance. The figures have linear scaling, showing the skewness of families: the largest few families make up nearly the entire dataset. We publish the IBD on Kaggle[8], together with all the auxiliary data we offer for all three datasets: callgraphs, images, packer information and instructions.

Due to the high imbalance of family labels in these dataset, we also tried data augmentation by invoking a metamorphic engine[9] to generate variations for small families – although this is not trivial, since altering an instruction must not change the register state, and must be the same size as the original instruction.

### 3.6   Results

In our experiments, we used Python3.8. with Radare2 5.8.8, and a GPU server with two RTX 2080 Ti graphics cards. Table 3 shows the result of the best models for each dataset. We conclude that the best classification accuracy in terms of $F_1$ score is reached by the ResNet18 architecture. Without surprise, we can observe that larger images perform better than the smaller $30 \times 30$ ones, due to the amount of information they contain. The $30 \times 30$ images in fact contain the first 900 instructions of the call graph, in the execution traversal order (Section 3), while the $100 \times 100$ images contain the first 10 thousand instructions – 10 times more information. It is however interesting that the largest images do not outperform the $100 \times 100$ images, presumably because at this size, a lot of the images tend to have few rows, thus the patterns may become distorted. We can formulate, that the best $F_1$ score achieved by these models is 0.887, performed by a ResNet18 on $100 \times 100$ images, using a batch size of 20 images, on the BODMAS dataset, and similarly on the IBD dataset as well. On the MalImg dataset, the winner was still a Resnet18 model, now with 0.744 $F_1$ score. It is also interesting to note that rather similar results have been obtained on the

---

[8] https://kaggle.com/datasets/amester/malflow.

[9] https://hub.docker.com/repository/docker/attilamester/pymetangine.

**Table 4.** Comparison between EMBER features and instruction-based histogram feature on different datasets. ($F_1$ m. and $F_1$ M. denote the micro- and macro-averaged scores)

| Model | EMBER (1) | | Mnem. hist. (2) | | (1) + (2) | |
|---|---|---|---|---|---|---|
| | $F_1$ m. | $F_1$ M. | $F_1$ m. | $F_1$ M. | $F_1$ m. | $F_1$ M. |
| **BODMAS, full dataset** – 51 974 **samples,** 57 **families** | | | | | | |
| DecisionTree | 0.907 | 0.886 | 0.172 | 0.058 | 0.904 | 0.877 |
| RandomForest | 0.924 | 0.905 | 0.174 | 0.056 | 0.924 | 0.900 |
| LinearSVC | 0.865 | 0.858 | 0.156 | 0.040 | 0.890 | 0.870 |
| SGD | 0.853 | 0.840 | 0.076 | 0.030 | 0.868 | 0.835 |
| LogReg | 0.892 | 0.876 | 0.154 | 0.033 | 0.897 | 0.880 |
| **BODMAS, only non-packed samples** – 33 807 **samples,** 44 **families** | | | | | | |
| DecisionTree | 0.930 | 0.917 | 0.879 | 0.831 | 0.932 | 0.922 |
| RandomForest | 0.945 | 0.938 | 0.884 | 0.839 | 0.944 | 0.939 |
| **MalImg, full dataset** – 9138 **samples,** 23 **families** | | | | | | |
| DecisionTree | 0.990 | 0.975 | 0.753 | 0.841 | 0.998 | 0.978 |
| RandomForest | 0.996 | 0.990 | 0.786 | 0.832 | 0.993 | 0.982 |
| **IBD, full dataset** – 18 756 **samples,** 47 **families** | | | | | | |
| DecisionTree | 0.923 | 0.862 | 0.897 | 0.838 | 0.923 | 0.870 |
| RandomForest | 0.961 | 0.936 | 0.924 | 0.877 | 0.963 | 0.940 |
| **IBD, only non-packed samples** – 16 088 **samples,** 41 **families** | | | | | | |
| DecisionTree | 0.922 | 0.866 | 0.892 | 0.828 | 0.916 | 0.867 |
| RandomForest | 0.960 | 0.938 | 0.918 | 0.866 | 0.961 | 0.941 |

BODMAS with hex dump images. It leads us to the conclusion that in this case, the binary files' structure, data section, offsets and such other "noise" is still useful, relevant information for family classification. Similarly, the information encapsulated in this "noise" coupled with its correlation with actual family labels (Sect. 5) is probably the reason why hex dump image-based classification on MalImg yields 0.98 accuracy [47] compared to the much lower score of only 0.72 with the instruction-based images.

## 4 Comparison with the EMBER Baseline

### 4.1 The EMBER Dataset and Features

The EMBER dataset [3] (described in Sect. 2.4) uses the LIEF[10] project to extract static features from executable files such as header, section, import and

---

[10] https://lief.re.

export information (see Sect. 2.3). Since our experiments first targeted the BOD-MAS [68] which also contains the EMBER feature vectors for each file, a good comparison metric of our call graph instruction-based RGB image classification model was to transform the images into vector representation. For this, we measured the instruction mnemonic histogram vector for each file – a 2019-dimensional integer vector, since we are tracking 2019 mnemonics.

## 4.2   Comparison Results

Based on the EMBER vectors and our mnemonic histogram vectors, several linear models have been trained: decision tree, random forest and SVM classifier, both on full size datasets, as well as on filtered datasets, containing only non-packed files, according to DIE (with our global filter of 100 samples/families). This was necessary to test our hypothesis that packed samples distort the model trained on the mnemonic histogram vector, but does not have so heavy effect on binary file-based features, i.e. the EMBER vector. This hypothesis was confirmed as shown in Table 4, comparing the micro and macro $F_1$ scores of different models trained on various datasets, using three different feature vectors: EMBER feature vectors, the mnemonic histogram vector, and the combination of them – i.e. a $2381 + 2019 = 4400$-long vector. We can observe that the mnemonic histogram vector has a strange behavior in the case of BODMAS: in its full size, it produces low $F_1$ performance, but once the packed samples are eliminated, this jumps from 0.174 to 0.884 – with random forest classifier. This is no longer valid in the IBD dataset. Considering the percentage of packed samples in these datasets (Table 2), we conclude that this interesting jump of $F_1$ score is a result of the mnemonic histogram model's sensitivity to packed samples. This, however, is not shown in the case of the EMBER vector, which seems to be unaffected by the presence or absence of packed samples. Another conclusion is that combining these two vectors gives hardly any improvement in the case of filtered datasets – meaning that the EMBER vector covers mostly all of the information that would be contained in the mnemonic histogram. This is somehow natural, since the EMBER's first 256 bytes represent a byte histogram, which highly correlates with the instruction histogram. The EMBER's great performance even on the datasets with packed samples led us to our final experiments: to examine the relation between packed samples and their family – presented in Sect. 5. If there is a correlation between these two variables, then this would explain why the EMBER vector works well on packed samples too – because of its byte histogram segment. This suspicion is also backed up by the fact that considering only the byte, and byte entropy histograms of EMBER (segments [0..255] and [256..511]), we obtain close classification performances on the BODMAS dataset – meaning that the family classification power of EMBER mostly comes from these byte histograms. Previous work [54] has also concluded that the features that carry the most information in EMBER are the import functions, section information, byte and byte entropy histograms.

The numeric results are shown in Table 5, where the classification $F_1$ scores are shown on BODMAS, using the EMBER vectors (the first pair of columns)

**Table 5.** Comparison between the full EMBER vector and its subsets, on BODMAS – the vector segments [0..255] and [256..511] represent the byte and byte entropy histogram, respectively, based on the EMBER feature extractor implementation [3].

| Model | [0..2381] | | [0..255] | | [256..511] | | [0..511] | |
|---|---|---|---|---|---|---|---|---|
| | $F_1$ m. | $F_1$ M. | $F_1$ m. | $F_1$ M. | $F_1$ m. | $F_1$ M. | $F_1$ m. | $F_1$ M. |
| **BODMAS, full dataset – 51 974 samples, 57 families** | | | | | | | | |
| DecisionTree | 0.907 | 0.886 | 0.864 | 0.829 | 0.887 | 0.852 | 0.889 | 0.850 |
| RandomForest | 0.924 | 0.905 | 0.906 | 0.880 | 0.914 | 0.891 | 0.914 | 0.895 |

**Table 6.** Cramér's V association score between malware family, packed status, and packer tool. The score ranges in [0, 1], a value of 1 indicating a perfect association between two categorical variables.

| | BODMAS | MalImg | IBD |
|---|---|---|---|
| Family – Packed | 0.755 | 0.981 | 0.736 |
| Family – Packer | 0.547 | 0.590 | 0.525 |

and its subsets: byte histogram only, presented in the second column tuple, byte entropy histogram only in the next tuple, and their combination in the last columns, which show slight increase in the classification accuracy, even though each subset in self produces close results when compared to the full EMBER.

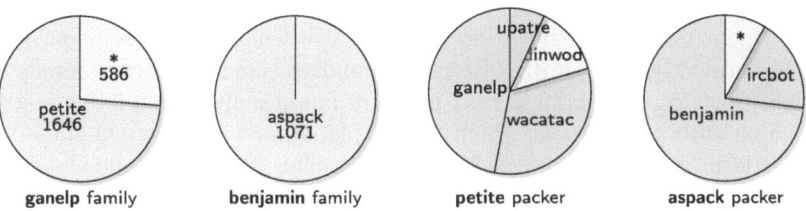

**Fig. 4.** BODMAS: packer-family association, showing the number of samples.

## 5   On Correlation Between Packers and Families

Inspired by the experiments presented in Sect. 4, we examined whether correlation exists between packed samples and their family. According to previous work [1], packers preserve useful information for malware classification – however, this is not rich enough to capture the behavior of the sample, to generalize family traits, or to be robust against adversarial attacks. Another study [37] shows that detecting packers may not be as simple as examining the entropy of the sections, because authors find a multitude of low-entropy packed files.

All of the above lead to the conclusion, that, while doing experiments presented in Table 4, filtering out packed samples based on DIE's verdict (which is based on an entropy threshold of 7.0) we probably still missed some packed files – which negatively affect the mnemonic histogram models.

Driven by the unchanged classification performance of the EMBER vector on BODMAS, regardless of filtering packed samples, led us to measure the correlation between families and packers. The correlation was measured using the association score between two pairs of three nominal variables, based on Cramér's V [57]: samples' family, their packed status and packer, as shown in Table 6.

In Fig. 4 we show two cases of interesting relation between the packer and the family in BODMAS. The first two charts represent the packer distribution within families *ganelp* and *benjamin*, while the last two charts show the family distribution of samples packed with *petite* and *aspack*, respectively. All 1071 files from *benjamin* family are packed with *aspack*, while this packer in only 25% of its apparition implies some other family. A similar relation can be seen in the first case, between *ganelp* family and *petite* packer.

Although the Cramér's V association scores presented in Table 6 are relatively high, we cannot infer a sample's family based on its packer, and vice-versa. However, this relation is constant in all three datasets, which cover nearly 15 years (MalIMG, BODMAS, IBD).

## 6   Conclusion and Future Work

This work proposes a malware classification method using call graph instruction-based RGB image model. Training various well-known CNN architectures on a multitude of image variations, the model's performance still not reached the state-of-the-art family classification $F_1$ score. We then examined why our model is outperformed by the EMBER baseline, and discovered the packer–family correlation (Sect. 5). Our claim is that malware families are in a relatively strong association with packer tools, which is an explanation why binary file-based features perform so well also on packed samples. This infers that one should pay additional attention to packed samples, otherwise, an ML model may overfit the data, learning the traits of packers instead of the actual behavior of the families, thereby failing to provide explainability for their decisions.

Our proposed model using instruction-based RGB images has the potential to map malware family behavioral traits to image patterns. The idea is backed up by our best model's family classification $F_1$ score of 0.88 on BODMAS.

Comparing our instruction-based model with the EMBER feature vector, we conclude that our model behaves significantly better in the case of filtered datasets, without packed files, since instruction information is strongly affected by packers. While the literature agrees that ML methods may not detect packed samples purely with static analysis, this may be a step in creating robust instruction-based models.

In this paper, the experiments are carried out on three datasets, BODMAS, MalImg, and IBD. We publish our results on Kaggle, offering for the first time disassembled objects of BODMAS and MalImg.

Future ideas include exploration of the instruction-based image generation, to facilitate mapping visual patterns to instruction patterns, leading to behavioral traits of malware families. Seeing the success of binary file-based features, fusing the two may lead to a model with better accuracy. It is also worth examining the robustness of the instruction-based features against adversarial attacks, compared to the EMBER vector.

**Acknowledgement.** The HORIZON Europe Framework Programme partly supported this work through the project "OPTIMA - Organization sPecific Threat Intelligence Mining and sharing" (101063107). Views and opinions expressed are however those of the author(s) only and do not necessarily reflect those of the European Union. Neither the European Union nor the granting authority can be held responsible for them. The project was partly funded by Babeş–Bolyai University. Experiments were run on Bitdefender servers. We thank the help of colleagues from Bitdefender and Babeş–Bolyai University in data curation and knowledge share.

**Funded by the European Union**

# References

1. Aghakhani, H., et al.: When malware is packin' heat; limits of machine learning classifiers based on static analysis features. In: NDSS (2020)
2. Alazab, M., Venkatraman, S., Watters, P.A., Alazab, M., et al.: Zero-day malware detection based on supervised learning algorithms of API call signatures. In: AusDM, vol. 11, pp. 171–182 (2011)
3. Anderson, H.S., Roth, P.: EMBER: an open dataset for training static pe malware machine learning models. arXiv preprint arXiv:1804.04637 (2018)
4. Aslan, Ö.A., Samet, R.: A comprehensive review on malware detection approaches. IEEE Access **8**, 6249–6271 (2020)
5. Bai, J., Wang, J., Zou, G.: A malware detection scheme based on mining format information. Sci. World J. **2014**(1), 260905 (2014)
6. Charikar, M.S.: Similarity estimation techniques from rounding algorithms. In: STOC, pp. 380–388. ACM (2002)
7. Cui, Z., Xue, F., Cai, X., Cao, Y., Wang, G.g., Chen, J.: Detection of malicious code variants based on deep learning. IEEE Trans. Indust. Inform. **14**(7), 3187–3196 (2018)
8. Dahl, G.E., Stokes, J.W., Deng, L., Yu, D.: Large-scale malware classification using random projections and neural networks. In: ICASSP, pp. 3422–3426. IEEE (2013)
9. Dener, M., Gulburun, S.: Clustering-aided supervised malware detection with specialized classifiers and early consensus. Comput. Mater. Continua **75**, 1235–1251 (2023)
10. Deng, H., Guo, C., Shen, G., Cui, Y., Ping, Y.: MCTVD: A malware classification method based on three-channel visualization and deep learning. Compu. Sec. **126**, 103084 (2023)
11. Elhadi, A., Maarof, M., Barry, B.: Improving the detection of malware behaviour using simplified data dependent API Call graph. Inter. J. Sec. Appli. **7**, 29–42 (2013)

12. Faruki, P., Laxmi, V., Gaur, M.S., Vinod, P.: Mining control flow graph as API call-grams to detect portable executable malware. In: SINCONF, pp. 130–137. ACM (2012)

13. Feng, Y., Anand, S., Dillig, I., Aiken, A.: Apposcopy: semantics-based detection of android malware through static analysis. In: SIGSOFT, pp. 576–587. ACM (2014)

14. Fu, J., Xue, J., Wang, Y., Liu, Z., Shan, C.: Malware visualization for fine-grained classification. IEEE Access **6**, 14510–14523 (2018)

15. Gao, Y., Hasegawa, H., Yamaguchi, Y., Shimada, H.: Malware detection by control-flow graph level representation learning with graph isomorphism network. IEEE Access **10**, 111830–111841 (2022)

16. Gascon, H., Yamaguchi, F., Arp, D., Rieck, K.: Structural detection of android malware using embedded call graphs. In: AISec, pp. 45–54. ACM (2013)

17. Gibert, D., Mateu, C., Planes, J., Vicens, R.: Using convolutional neural networks for classification of malware represented as images. J. Comput. Virol. Hacking Tec. **15**, 15–28 (3 2019)

18. Hai, T.H., Thieu, V.V., Duong, T.T., Nguyen, H.H., Huh, E.N.: A proposed new endpoint detection and response with image-based malware detection system. IEEE Access **11**, 122859–122875 (2023)

19. Harang, R., Rudd, E.M.: Sorel-20m: a large scale benchmark dataset for malicious pe detection. arXiv preprint arXiv:2012.07634 (2020)

20. He, K., Zhang, X., Ren, S., Sun, J.: Deep residual learning for image recognition. In: CVPR, pp. 770–778 (2016)

21. Herath, J.D., Wakodikar, P.P., Yang, P., Yan, G.: CFGExplainer: explaining graph neural network-based malware classification from control flow graphs. In: DSN, pp. 172–184. IEEE (2022)

22. Hong, J., et al.: Malware classification for identifying author groups: a graph-based approach. In: RACS, pp. 169–174. ACM (2019)

23. Hong, S., et al.: Holmes: health online model ensemble serving for deep learning models in intensive care units. In: SIGKDD, pp. 1614–1624 (2020)

24. Howard, A., et al.: Searching for mobilenetv3. In: ICCV, pp. 1314–1324 (2019)

25. Huang, G., Liu, Z., Van Der Maaten, L., Weinberger, K.Q.: Densely connected convolutional networks. In: CVPR, pp. 4700–4708 (2017)

26. Hussain, M.J., Shaoor, A., Baig, S., Hussain, A., Muqurrab, S.A.: A hierarchical based ensemble classifier for behavioral malware detection using machine learning. In: IBCAST, pp. 702–706 (2022)

27. Intel® 64 and IA-32 architectures software developer's manual (2024)

28. Jia, L., Yang, Y., Tang, B., Jiang, Z.: ERMDS: A obfuscation dataset for evaluating robustness of learning-based malware detection system. BenchCouncil Trans. Benchmarks, Standards Evaluations **3**, 100106 (2023)

29. Jiang, H., Turki, T., Wang, J.T.: DLGraph: malware detection using deep learning and graph embedding. In: ICMLA, pp. 1029–1033. IEEE (2018)

30. Kalash, M., Rochan, M., Mohammed, N., Bruce, N.D., Wang, Y., Iqbal, F.: Malware classification with deep convolutional neural networks. In: NTMS, pp. 1–5. IEEE (2018)

31. Kim, J., Paik, J.Y., Cho, E.S.: Attention-based cross-modal CNN using non-disassembled files for malware classification. IEEE Access **11**, 22889–22903 (2023)

32. Kolter, J.Z., Maloof, M.A.: Learning to detect and classify malicious executables in the wild. J. Mach. Learn. Res. **7**(12) (2006)

33. Kornish, D., Geary, J., Sansing, V., Ezekiel, S., Pearlstein, L., Njilla, L.: Malware classification using deep convolutional neural networks. In: AIPR, pp. 1–6 (2018)

34. Krizhevsky, A., Sutskever, I., Hinton, G.E.: ImageNet classification with deep convolutional neural networks. In: NeurIPS (2012)
35. Li, S., Zhou, Q., Zhou, R., Lv, Q.: Intelligent malware detection based on graph convolutional network. J. Supercomput., 1–17 (2021)
36. Maillet, W., Marais, B.: Neural networks optimizations against concept and data drift in malware detection. arXiv preprint arXiv:2308.10821 (2023)
37. Mantovani, A., Aonzo, S., Ugarte-Pedrero, X., Merlo, A., Balzarotti, D.: Prevalence and impact of low-entropy packing schemes in the malware ecosystem. In: NDSS (2020)
38. Martinelli, F., Marulli, F., Mercaldo, F.: Evaluating convolutional neural network for effective mobile malware detection. Proc. Comput. Sci. **112**, 2372–2381 (2017)
39. Masud, M.M., Khan, L., Thuraisingham, B.: A scalable multi-level feature extraction technique to detect malicious executables. Inf. Syst. Front. **10**, 33–45 (2008)
40. McLaughlin, N., Martinez del Rincon, J., Kang, B., et al.: Deep Android malware detection. In: CODASPY, pp. 301–308. ACM (2017)
41. Mester, A., Bodó, Z.: Validating static call graph-based malware signatures using community detection methods. In: ESANN, pp. 429–434 (2021)
42. Mester, A., Bodó, Z.: Malware classification based on graph convolutional neural networks and static call graph features. In: IEA/AIE. pp. 528–539. Springer (2022). https://doi.org/10.1007/978-3-031-08530-7_45
43. Mester, A.: Malware analysis and static call graph generation with Radare2. Studia Universitatis Babeş-Bolyai Informatica **68**(1), 5–20 (2023)
44. Mitra, S., Torri, S.A., Mittal, S.: Survey of malware analysis through control flow graph using machine learning. In: TrustCom, pp. 1554–1561. IEEE (2023)
45. Moskovitch, R., Feher, C., Elovici, Y.: A chronological evaluation of unknown malcode detection. In: Chen, H., Yang, C.C., Chau, M., Li, S.-H. (eds.) PAISI 2009. LNCS, vol. 5477, pp. 112–117. Springer, Heidelberg (2009). https://doi.org/10.1007/978-3-642-01393-5_12
46. Moussas, V., Andreatos, A.: Malware detection based on code visualization and two-level classification. Information **12**, 1–14 (3 2021)
47. Nataraj, L., Karthikeyan, S., Jacob, G., Manjunath, B.S.: Malware images: visualization and automatic classification. In: VizSec, pp. 1–7 (2011)
48. Ni, S., Qian, Q., Zhang, R.: Malware identification using visualization images and deep learning. Comput. Sec. **77**, 871–885 (2018)
49. de Oliveira, A.S., Sassi, R.J.: Behavioral malware detection using deep graph convolutional neural networks. Inter. J. Comput. Appli. **174** (2021)
50. Park, Y., Reeves, D., Mulukutla, V., Sundaravel, B.: Fast malware classification by automated behavioral graph matching. In: CSIIRW, pp. 1–4 (2010)
51. Pektaş, A., Acarman, T.: Deep learning for effective android malware detection using api call graph embeddings. Soft. Comput. **24**(2), 1027–1043 (2020)
52. Quertier, T., Marais, B., Morucci, S., Fournel, B.: MERLIN – Malware Evasion with Reinforcement LearnINg. arXiv preprint arXiv:2203.12980 (2022)
53. Ronen, R., Radu, M., Feuerstein, C., Yom-Tov, E., Ahmadi, M.: Microsoft malware classification challenge. arXiv preprint arXiv:1802.10135 (2018)
54. Sandor, M., Portase, R.M., Colesa, A.: Ember feature dataset analysis for malware detection. In: ICCP, pp. 203–210 (2023)
55. Saxe, J., Berlin, K.: Deep neural network based malware detection using two dimensional binary program features. In: MALWARE, pp. 11–20. IEEE (2015)
56. Shang, S., Zheng, N., Xu, J., Xu, M., Zhang, H.: Detecting malware variants via function-call graph similarity. In: MALWARE, pp. 113–120. IEEE (2010)

57. Sheskin, D.J.: Handbook of parametric and nonparametric statistical procedures. Chapman & Hall/CRC (2000)
58. Simonyan, K., Zisserman, A.: Very deep convolutional networks for large-scale image recognition. arXiv preprint arXiv:1409.1556 (2015)
59. Singh, A., Arora, R., Pareek, H.: Malware Analysis using Multiple API Sequence Mining Control Flow Graph. arXiv preprint arXiv:1707.02691 (2017)
60. Szegedy, C., et al.: Going deeper with convolutions. In: CVPR, pp. 1–9 (2015)
61. Tan, M., Le, Q.: EfficientNetV2: smaller models and faster training. In: ICML, pp. 10096–10106. PMLR (2021)
62. Tang, M., Qian, Q.: Dynamic api call sequence visualisation for malware classification. IET Inf. Secur. **13**(4), 367–377 (2019)
63. Ucci, D., Aniello, L., Baldoni, R.: Survey of machine learning techniques for malware analysis. Comput. Sec. **81**, 123–147 (2019)
64. Vinayakumar, R., Alazab, M., Soman, K., Poornachandran, P., Venkatraman, S.: Robust intelligent malware detection using deep learning. IEEE Access **7**, 46717–46738 (2019)
65. Xiao, M., Guo, C., Shen, G., Cui, Y., Jiang, C.: Image-based malware classification using section distribution information. Comput. Sec. **110**, 102420 (2021)
66. Yan, J., Jia, X., Ying, L., Yan, J., Su, P.: Understanding and mitigating label bias in malware classification: An empirical study. In: QRS, pp. 492–503 (2022)
67. Yan, J., Yan, G., Jin, D.: Classifying malware represented as control flow graphs using deep graph convolutional neural network. In: DSN, pp. 52–63. IEEE (2019)
68. Yang, L., Ciptadi, A., Laziuk, I., Ahmadzadeh, A., Wang, G.: BODMAS: an open dataset for learning based temporal analysis of PE malware. In: SPW, pp. 78–84 (May 2021)
69. Ye, Y., Chen, L., Wang, D., Li, T., Jiang, Q., Zhao, M.: SBMDS: an interpretable string based malware detection system using SVM ensemble with bagging. J. Comput. Virol. **5**, 283–293 (2009)
70. Ye, Y., Li, T., Adjeroh, D., Iyengar, S.S.: A survey on malware detection using data mining techniques. ACM Comput. Surv. (CSUR) **50**(3), 1–40 (2017)
71. Ye, Y., Li, T., Jiang, Q., Han, Z., Wan, L.: Intelligent file scoring system for malware detection from the gray list. In: SIGKDD, pp. 1385–1394 (2009)
72. Yuan, B., Wang, J., Liu, D., Guo, W., Wu, P., Bao, X.: Byte-level malware classification based on markov images and deep learning. Comput. Sec. **92**, 101740 (2020)
73. Zhan, D., Duan, Y., Hu, Y., Yin, L., Pan, Z., Guo, S.: AMGmal: adaptive mask-guided adversarial attack against malware detection with minimal perturbation. Comput. Sec. **127** (2023)

# Decoding Android Malware with a Fraction of Features: An Attention-Enhanced MLP-SVM Approach

Safayat Bin Hakim[1], Muhammad Adil[2], Kamal Acharya[1],
and Houbing Herbert Song[1(✉)]

[1] Department of Information Systems, University of Maryland, Baltimore County,
Baltimore, MD 21250, USA
{shakim3,kamala2}@umbc.edu, h.song@ieee.org
[2] Department of Computer Science and Engineering, University at Buffalo, Buffalo,
NY 14260, USA
muhammad.adil@ieee.org

**Abstract.** The escalating sophistication of Android malware poses significant challenges to traditional detection methods, necessitating innovative approaches that can efficiently identify and classify threats with high precision. This paper introduces a novel framework that synergistically integrates an attention-enhanced Multi-Layer Perceptron (MLP) with a Support Vector Machine (SVM) to make Android malware detection and classification more effective. By carefully analyzing a mere 47 features out of over 9,760 available in the comprehensive CCCS-CIC-AndMal-2020 dataset, our MLP-SVM model achieves an impressive accuracy over 99% in identifying malicious applications. The MLP, enhanced with an attention mechanism, focuses on the most discriminative features and further reduces the 47 features to only 14 components using Linear Discriminant Analysis (LDA). Despite this significant reduction in dimensionality, the SVM component, equipped with an RBF kernel, excels in mapping these components to a high-dimensional space, facilitating precise classification of malware into their respective families. Rigorous evaluations, encompassing accuracy, precision, recall, and F1-score metrics, confirm the superiority of our approach compared to existing state-of-the-art techniques. The proposed framework not only significantly reduces the computational complexity by leveraging a compact feature set but also exhibits resilience against the evolving Android malware landscape.

**Keywords:** Android · Malware Detection · Machine Learning · MLP · SVM · Cybersecurity

## 1 Introduction

The Android operating system, with over 3.9 billion active users as of 2024 [25], has become a predominant target for cybercriminals. Its open-source nature and

H. H. Song et al. (Eds.): NSS 2024, LNCS 15564, pp. 187–209, 2025.
https://doi.org/10.1007/978-981-96-3531-3_10

the ease of distributing apps through third-party stores make it particularly susceptible to malware attacks [7,28]. Traditional detection methods, primarily based on static analysis of application permissions, are increasingly ineffective against modern malware that employs advanced obfuscation techniques, dynamic code execution, and strategic evasions [3,6,21].

Deep learning has shown great promise in addressing these challenges due to its capability to unravel complex data patterns, significantly enhancing the accuracy of malware detection and classification [19,30]. However, the precise classification of malware families remains a nuanced and underexplored area. This classification is crucial for identifying attack vectors and devising targeted defenses. Additionally, the rise of adversarial attacks on deep learning models underscores the necessity for robust and resilient detection frameworks [9,20,27].

This paper proposes an innovative framework that integrates an attention-enhanced Multi-Layer Perceptron (MLP) for robust feature extraction with a Support Vector Machine (SVM) enhanced by a Radial Basis Function (RBF) kernel for precise malware family classification. Our approach leverages the CCCS-CIC-AndMal-2020 dataset, starting with an analysis of just 47 out of over 9,760 features. The attention mechanism within the MLP adaptively weights the significance of various features, enhancing the model's focus and interpretability. This enables the MLP to effectively perform representation learning, capturing the essential characteristics of the input data. The MLP is trained using these 47 features, and the trained MLP model is subsequently used to reduce the feature set by stripping down 95% of the features, ensuring that only the most informative features are retained. Linear Discriminant Analysis (LDA) is then applied to further refine these features to just 14 components, optimizing the feature space for classification. Despite this significant reduction in dimensionality, the SVM component, equipped with an RBF kernel, excels in mapping the 14 LDA-reduced components to a high-dimensional space, facilitating precise classification of malware into their respective families. This approach demonstrates remarkable performance across various metrics, achieving an accuracy of 99% in identifying malicious applications [15,23].

The feature reduction strategy plays a crucial role in enhancing computational efficiency and potentially improving the model's generalizability by mitigating the risk of overfitting. By focusing on the most informative features, the model can process data faster and more effectively, making it a scalable solution for real-world applications.

To ensure the transparency and interpretability of our model, we employ explainable AI (XAI) techniques, specifically SHAP (SHapley Additive exPlanations), to evaluate feature importance and provide insights into the decision-making process [24]. This not only enhances understanding but also ensures the robustness of our model against adversarial attacks.

Our framework addresses current methodological deficiencies by presenting a scalable, robust, and adversary-aware solution. Rigorous evaluations, including metrics such as accuracy, precision, recall, and F1-score, confirm the superiority of our approach compared to existing state-of-the-art techniques. By significantly reducing computational complexity through a compact feature set, integrating an attention mechanism for enhanced feature focus, employing XAI for model interpretability, and demonstrating adaptability to evolving malware, our research offers a potent solution for efficient Android malware detection and classification, setting a new standard in mobile cybersecurity.

The structure of this paper is organized as follows: Sect. 2 reviews the related literature on Android malware detection and deep learning applications in malware analysis. Section 3 details the proposed MLP-SVM framework, emphasizing its theoretical underpinnings and practical components. Experimental setup and performance evaluation metrics are outlined in Sect. 5. Section 6 presents a comprehensive analysis of the results, demonstrating the superior performance of our approach. Finally, Sect. 7 discusses the implications and future directions of our research, highlighting its potential impact on enhancing Android security measures.

## 2   Related Work

Significant advancements in Android malware detection employ diverse methodologies to counter sophisticated threats. Early detection efforts, like DREBIN, utilized static analysis to extract features such as app permissions and API calls, but faced limitations against evolving malware and obfuscation techniques [1]. The MaMaDroid Family enhanced detection by combining static and dynamic analysis, improving the understanding of application behavior [18]. Dynamic analysis frameworks like RevealDroid, which monitors runtime behaviors, addressed static analysis limitations by detecting anomalies indicative of malicious activities [8]. The integration of machine learning, as in MalScan, has shown promise for efficient and accurate malware detection through automated feature extraction and classification [29]. Ensemble approaches combining multiple detection methods have improved accuracy and stability, as evidenced by Daoudi et al. [5]. Deep learning techniques, particularly using CNNs and RNNs, have advanced the field by learning complex features directly from raw data, thus improving generalizability and detection accuracy in varied architectures [12,13,26].

Recent studies have demonstrated the potential of machine learning and deep learning techniques in advancing Android malware detection and classification. Notably, works by Islam et al. [11], Sayed et al. [22], and Li et al. [14] have employed various models, including ensemble methods and deep learning frameworks, leveraging the CCCS-CIC-AndMal-2020 dataset to achieve significant breakthroughs in malware identification and family classification. Hammood et al. [10] presented a machine learning-based adaptive genetic algorithm for Android malware detection in auto-driving vehicles, highlighting the importance of this domain in the context of connected and autonomous vehicles. Furthermore, Batouche and Jahankhani [2] provided a comprehensive review of the Android malware detection landscape, discussing the challenges and opportunities in this field. In our comparative analysis (Sect. 6.4), we evaluate the accuracy and efficiency of our proposed MLP-SVM model against these state-of-the-art approaches, demonstrating its superior performance in Android malware detection and classification.

## 3   Proposed Approach

### 3.1   Theoretical Foundations of MLP-SVM Integration with Attention Mechanism

This section elaborates on the theoretical underpinnings and practical implementation of our framework, which synergistically integrates Multi-Layer Perceptrons (MLPs), Support Vector Machines (SVMs) with a Radial Basis Function (RBF) kernel, an Attention mechanism, and Linear Discriminant Analysis (LDA). This integration capitalizes on the distinct yet complementary strengths of each component, resulting in a robust and efficient system for Android malware detection and family classification.

**Representation Learning with MLPs and Attention.** MLPs, with their deep feedforward neural network architecture, excel at learning complex, non-linear relationships within data, making them powerful tools for representation learning. Let $\mathbf{x} \in \mathbb{R}^d$ represent a $d$-dimensional input feature vector of an Android application. Our MLP, composed of $L$ layers, transforms this input through a series of non-linear transformations:

$$\mathbf{h}^{(l)} = \sigma^{(l)}(\mathbf{W}^{(l)}\mathbf{h}^{(l-1)} + \mathbf{b}^{(l)}), \quad l = 1, 2, ..., L, \tag{1}$$

where $\mathbf{h}^{(l)}$ denotes the hidden activations at layer $l$, $\mathbf{W}^{(l)}$ and $\mathbf{b}^{(l)}$ are the weight matrix and bias vector of layer $l$, respectively, $\mathbf{h}^{(0)} = \mathbf{x}$, and $\sigma^{(l)}(\cdot)$ is the activation function at layer $l$, typically a Rectified Linear Unit (ReLU).

The output of the final hidden layer, $\mathbf{h}^{(L)} \in \mathbb{R}^{512}$, serves as the learned feature representation of the input application.

To further enhance the discriminative power of these learned features, we introduce an attention mechanism. The attention layer dynamically weighs each feature in $\mathbf{h}^{(L)}$ based on its relevance to the classification task. The attention weights, denoted by $\mathbf{a} \in \mathbb{R}^{512}$, are computed as:

$$\mathbf{a} = \mathrm{softmax}(\tanh(\mathbf{h}^{(L)}\mathbf{W}_a + \mathbf{b}_a)), \tag{2}$$

where $\mathbf{W}_a$ and $\mathbf{b}_a$ are trainable parameters of the attention layer. The final feature representation, $\mathbf{z} \in \mathbb{R}^{512}$, is obtained by applying the attention weights:

$$\mathbf{z} = \mathbf{h}^{(L)} \odot \mathbf{a}, \tag{3}$$

where $\odot$ denotes element-wise multiplication. Figure 1 illustrates the integration of the attention mechanism within our model architecture.

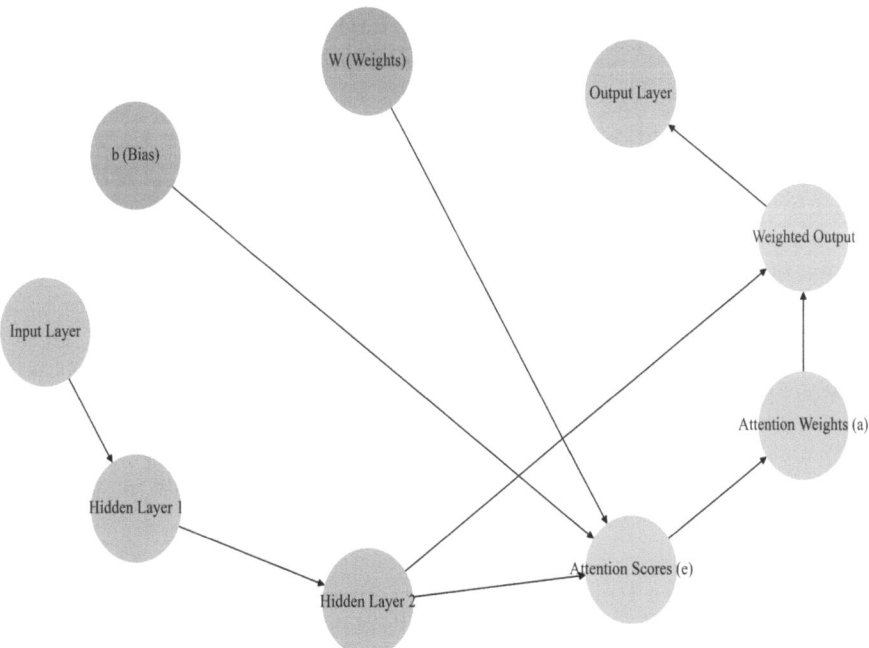

**Fig. 1.** Attention-Based Feature Weighting in the MLP-SVM Model for Android Malware Classification. This diagram illustrates the flow of data through various layers in the model, highlighting the integration of the attention mechanism for dynamic feature weighting.

**Dimensionality Reduction and Feature Enhancement with LDA.** Following feature extraction by the attention-enhanced MLP, we apply LDA to further refine the feature set. LDA seeks to find a projection matrix, $\mathbf{W}_{LDA} \in \mathbb{R}^{512 \times k}$, that maximizes the ratio of between-class scatter to within-class scatter, where $k$ is the desired number of output dimensions. This can be formulated as:

$$\mathbf{W}_{LDA} = \text{argmax}_{\mathbf{W}} \frac{\text{tr}(\mathbf{W}^T \mathbf{S}_b \mathbf{W})}{\text{tr}(\mathbf{W}^T \mathbf{S}_w \mathbf{W})}, \tag{4}$$

where $\mathbf{S}_b$ and $\mathbf{S}_w$ are the between-class and within-class scatter matrices, respectively, and $\text{tr}(\cdot)$ denotes the trace of a matrix.

The LDA-transformed features, $\mathbf{y} \in \mathbb{R}^k$, are obtained by projecting the attention-weighted features onto the LDA subspace:

$$\mathbf{y} = \mathbf{z}\mathbf{W}_{LDA}. \tag{5}$$

In our implementation, $k = 14$, resulting in a significant reduction in dimensionality while preserving information crucial for discriminating between malware families.

**Robust Classification with SVMs and RBF Kernel.** Finally, the refined features from LDA are used to train an SVM with an RBF kernel for malware family classification. The RBF kernel, defined as:

$$K(\mathbf{y}_i, \mathbf{y}_j) = \exp(-\gamma \|\mathbf{y}_i - \mathbf{y}_j\|^2), \tag{6}$$

implicitly maps the LDA features into a higher-dimensional space where linear separation between families is more achievable. The SVM learns a decision function of the form:

$$f(\mathbf{y}) = \sum_{i=1}^{n} \alpha_i y_i K(\mathbf{y}, \mathbf{y}_i) + b, \tag{7}$$

where $\mathbf{y}_i$ are the support vectors, $y_i$ their corresponding labels, $\alpha_i$ are the learned weights, and $b$ is the bias term.

By maximizing the margin between classes in this transformed feature space, the SVM achieves robust classification performance even in the presence of complex and potentially noisy data.

**Enhancing Feature Relevance with Attention.** The addition of an Attention layer aims to further enhance the model's ability to focus on salient features. The pseudocode for implementing the attention layer is outlined in Algorithm 1. This mechanism is crucial when dealing with complex data structures found in Android malware.

## 4   Overall Framework

In this section, we discuss the overarching framework of our system, focusing on how the layers of the MLP are aligned with the attention layer. We will then describe how the model, once trained, is utilized for representation learning before performing classification with an SVM equipped with an RBF kernel.

---

**Algorithm 1.** Attention Layer Pseudocode

---

1: **procedure** ATTENTION($x$)
2:     $input\_shape \leftarrow$ dimension of $x$
3:     $W \leftarrow$ trainable weight matrix of shape ($input\_shape, input\_shape$)
4:     $b \leftarrow$ trainable bias vector of length $input\_shape$
5:     $e \leftarrow \tanh(xW + b)$
6:     $a \leftarrow$ softmax($e$)                                    ▷ Compute attention weights
7:     $output \leftarrow x \odot a$                                   ▷ Apply attention weights
8:     **return** $output$
9: **end procedure**

---

## 4.1 Framework Overview

The MLP model serves as the primary detection mechanism, employing a deep neural network architecture that includes multiple fully-connected layers with Rectified Linear Unit (ReLU) activations. This configuration excels at learning complex interrelations among a diverse array of static and dynamic application features, such as app permissions, API calls, network traffic patterns, and suspicious strings, effectively distinguishing between benign and malicious applications.

The attention layer significantly enhances the MLP's capability to extract features more efficiently, focusing on the most informative parts of the input data which are critical for accurate classification.

Following the detection phase, LDA is employed to distill the features extracted by the MLP. LDA achieves this by identifying linear combinations of the original features that maximize the ratio of between-class scatter to within-class scatter, effectively separating different malware families while minimizing variance within each family. This step simplifies and reduces the complexity required for SVM training. After applying LDA, the feature set is reduced from 512 to just 14 components. These components are then utilized to train the SVM model, which is equipped with a Radial Basis Function (RBF) kernel. This SVM model performs fine-grained classification of the detected malware into distinct families. The SVM benefits from its ability to project features into a higher-dimensional space, thereby facilitating the creation of non-linear decision boundaries that adeptly separate various malware families based on their unique behavioral patterns.

The process of feature extraction using the attention-enhanced MLP can be viewed as representation learning. By learning to focus on the most salient features of the input data, the MLP effectively creates a robust representation of the application's behavior. This representation is less sensitive to noise and variations in the input, leading to a more robust and generalizable malware detection system.

## 4.2 Synergistic Model Integration

Our framework leverages the strengths of both MLP and SVM models by integrating them into a synergistic pipeline. The MLP, enhanced by the attention mechanism, learns robust feature representations from the raw application data, effectively performing initial malware detection. These representations are then refined by LDA, reducing dimensionality while simultaneously optimizing for class separability. This streamlined feature set is then fed into the SVM, which leverages its ability to construct non-linear decision boundaries for accurate malware family classification. This combination allows our system to benefit from the MLP's proficiency in feature extraction and the SVM's ability to handle complex, non-linear relationships between features and malware families.

## 4.3    Operational Flow

The operational flow of our framework is systematically organized into four key steps shown in Fig. 2, each integral to the detection and classification of Android malware:

1. **Feature Extraction:** Utilize the CCCS-CIC-AndMal-2020 dataset to extract a comprehensive set of static and dynamic features from Android applications.
2. **Malware Detection:** Employ the MLP model, enhanced with an attention layer, to analyze the extracted features and accurately differentiate between benign and malicious applications.
3. **Malware Classification:** Apply the SVM model with an RBF kernel, using the refined features from the MLP model's penultimate layer, to categorize the detected malware into specific families.
4. **Model Evaluation:** Assess the framework through both traditional performance metrics such as accuracy, precision, recall, and F1-score, and interpretative analysis using SHAP values to validate the model's efficacy in malware detection and classification.

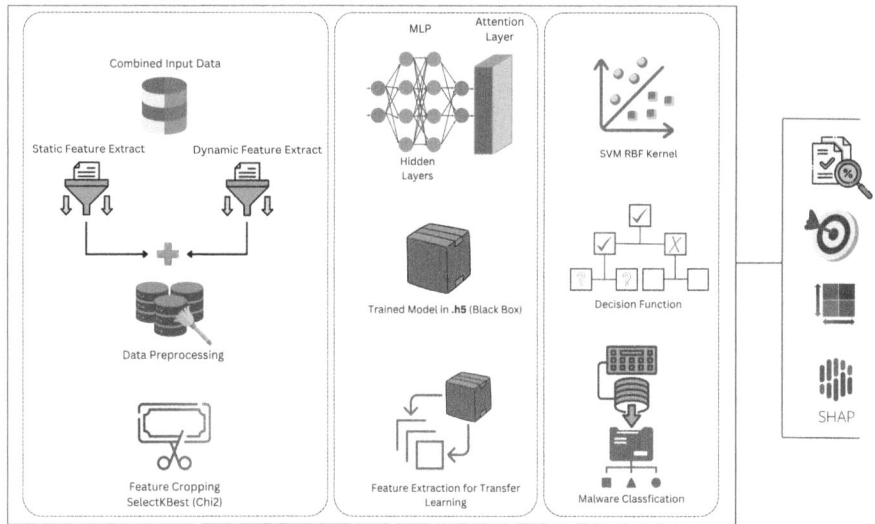

**Fig. 2.** Workflow of the integrated MLP-Attention and SVM model for Android malware classification. The diagram illustrates the sequential processing stages from input data through feature extraction, attention-based feature refinement, and SVM classification, culminating in malware classification, with a side panel detailing performance evaluation metrics including accuracy, precision, recall, F1-score, and Explainable AI (XAI) with SHAP.

# 5  Experimental Setup

## 5.1  Dataset

Our study leverages the comprehensive CCCS-CIC-AndMal2020 dataset to facilitate a nuanced analysis of Android malware [4]. This dataset, encompassing 400,000 apps equally distributed between benign and malicious categories, includes 14 malware types across 191 families, making it notable for its diversity and volume. It is instrumental in training and validating our proposed MLP-SVM model. Specifically, the "Dynamic" and "Static" analysis components offer a detailed view of app behaviors and characteristics, enabling precise feature extraction and model optimization. Dynamic analysis reveals runtime malware actions, while static analysis provides insights into the app's code structure without execution. Our methodology leverages both dynamic features, such as system calls and network traffic, and static features, like permissions and API calls, to craft a robust detection mechanism. This dual approach ensures comprehensive coverage of the Android malware landscape, promising significant advancements in detection accuracy and classification precision.

## 5.2  Implementation Details

**Data Preparation.** The dataset employed in this study, derived from the CCCS-CIC-AndMal-2020 collection, includes both static and dynamic features. Static features capture attributes such as application permissions and API calls, while dynamic features represent runtime behaviors, including network traffic and system logs. We extracted features using customized scripts to convert all relevant data points into a format suitable for machine learning models. Non-numeric columns were encoded using LabelEncoder, transforming categorical data into numerical format. The number of unique categories encoded for each non-numeric column varied, ranging from 669 to 77,741. The final combined dataset resulted in a feature space of 9,768 dimensions, with a total of 329,071 samples ready for further analysis and model training.

**Addressing Class Imbalance.** A significant challenge in the CCCS-CIC-AndMal-2020 dataset is class imbalance, as depicted in Fig. 3. This skewed distribution can lead to overfitting, where models may bias towards the majority class. To mitigate this and ensure a balanced learning process, we used adjusted class weights during model training. The class weights were computed using the `compute_class_weight()` function from the scikit-learn library, with the parameter `'balanced'` specified. This approach assigns higher weights to underrepresented classes, increasing their importance during training and improving the model's ability to generalize and accurately classify instances across all classes.

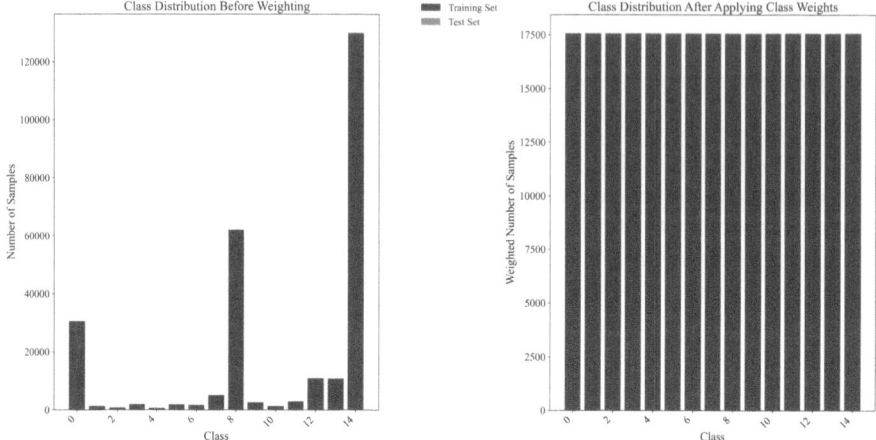

**Fig. 3.** Class distribution before and after applying class weights in the CCCS-CIC-AndMal-2020 dataset. The left subplot shows the original class distribution, indicating significant class imbalance. The right subplot demonstrates the adjusted class distribution, achieving a more balanced scenario through class weighting, critical for unbiased model training and evaluation.

**Integrated Feature Engineering and Preprocessing.** The raw data underwent a comprehensive feature engineering process to extract meaningful representations. Non-numeric columns were encoded using LabelEncoder, transforming categorical data into numerical format suitable for ML algorithms. Missing values were addressed using median imputation, chosen due to the observed skewed distribution of features, ensuring that missing data did not hinder the training process while minimizing bias. Subsequently, standardization normalized the features, scaling each to have zero mean and unit variance, preventing features with varying scales from disproportionately influencing the models.

Feature selection was performed using the SelectKBest method with the chi2 statistic, chosen for its efficiency in identifying features strongly associated with the target variable. Chi2 is well-suited for the mixed nature of the dataset, containing both categorical and numerical features. The SelectKBest method selected the top 47 features out of 9,768, significantly reducing dimensionality while retaining the most informative features for model training.

The dataset was split into training and test sets, with the training set comprising 263,256 samples and the test set consisting of 65,815 samples. This split allows for reliable evaluation of the model's performance on unseen data, providing an estimate of its generalization ability. While Recursive Feature Elimination (RFE) could offer a more refined subset of features by considering feature interactions, SelectKBest provided a faster solution, which was crucial given the high dimensionality of the initial feature space. This efficiency expedited the model development process without compromising performance, as demonstrated by the promising results achieved by both MLP and SVM models.

**Addressing Overfitting.** To combat overfitting, our approach encompasses a multi-faceted strategy designed to enhance the robustness and generalizability of our models. Initially, we employed the Optuna framework for feature selection to reduce the complexity of the model and focus on the most informative features. Furthermore, we implemented regularization techniques, specifically l1 and l2 regularization, to prevent our models from learning noise and memorizing the training data, which are essential for mitigating overfitting. Additionally, we used ensembling methods, particularly the RandomForestClassifier, known for its variance-reducing bagging properties, to further protect against overfitting.

Figure 4 below provides a visual representation of the effectiveness of these strategies. It illustrates the F1 scores before and after class weights were applied, revealing that the baseline model, despite achieving higher F1 scores, was likely overfitting to more frequently occurring classes. The adjusted model, with class weights, shows a moderated performance, indicative of a more balanced and generalized approach. This graphical evidence supports our comprehensive measures taken to defend against overfitting, demonstrating our commitment to developing robust predictive models.

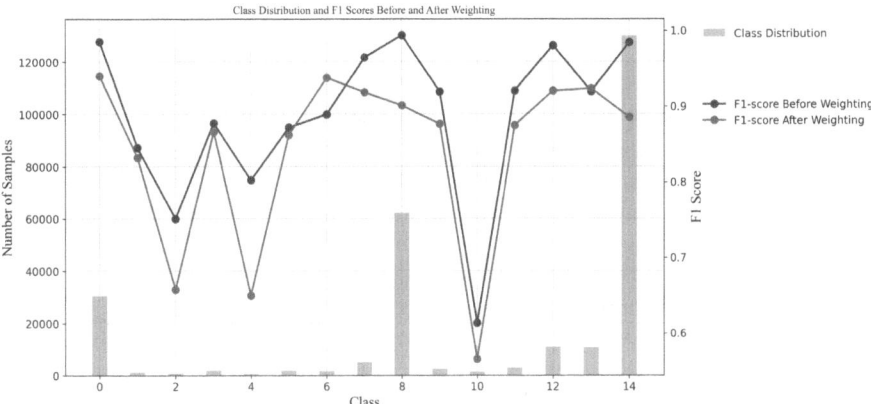

**Fig. 4.** Comparison of class distribution and F1 scores before and after class weighting. The graph clearly demonstrates that the baseline model, which exhibits higher F1 scores, may be overfitting to the majority classes, as shown by the significant fluctuations in F1 scores when class weights are adjusted.

**Model Architecture and Training.** The MLP model employed in this study was specifically designed to tackle the complexities associated with Android malware detection. Utilizing the hyperparameter optimization framework, Optuna, we conducted a systematic exploration to ascertain the most effective configurations of neural network layers, activation functions, and regularization methods.

The optimized architecture of the MLP model includes:

- **Input Layer:** This layer processes the optimized feature vector derived from extensive preprocessing of both static and dynamic data attributes.
- **Hidden Layers:** Comprises two densely connected hidden layers utilizing ReLU activation functions, pivotal for capturing the non-linear dynamics within the data.
- **Attention Mechanism:** Integrated subsequent to the hidden layers, this mechanism adaptively weights the significance of various features, thereby augmenting the model's focus and interpretability. It is mathematically defined as:

$$a = \text{softmax}(\tanh(\mathbf{W}\mathbf{x} + \mathbf{b}))$$

where $\mathbf{W}$ and $\mathbf{b}$ represent the trainable parameters.

- **Output Layer:** Implements a softmax activation function to output a probabilistic distribution over 14 malware families plus one benign category.

**Training Methodology**

To ensure accuracy and robustness in the training process, the Cosine Annealing with Warm Restarts learning rate scheduler was adopted [16]:

$$\eta_t = \eta_{\min} + \frac{1}{2}(\eta_{\max} - \eta_{\min})(1 + \cos(\frac{T_{\text{cur}}}{T_{\max}}\pi))$$

This method periodically resets the learning rate, effectively exploring the parameter space and helping to escape local minima.

In addition, strategies such as early stopping and trial pruning were implemented to optimize training and mitigate overfitting. Early stopping ceases training when there is no improvement in validation loss for a set number of epochs, while trial pruning discontinues less promising trials early based on intermediate outcomes to enhance computational efficiency.

The training was conducted over 20 trials with 30 epochs each, utilizing a rigorous 10-fold stratified cross-validation to maintain representativeness in each fold, ensuring consistency and reliability of performance across diverse data segments. The inner and outer folds further validated the model's generalizability on unseen data.

The parameters refined during the Optuna trials are documented in Table 1. These parameters were fine-tuned to ensure optimal model performance:

Following the optimization, the final model training was based on the best parameters identified, focusing on maximizing accuracy and preventing overfitting. This methodical approach ensures that the MLP model is not only customized to the specific requirements of the dataset but is also capable of effective generalization to new, unseen Android malware threats.

As shown in Fig. 5, the parallel coordinate plot provides a comprehensive view of the optimization process. It highlights how different parameter combinations, from activation functions to learning rates, affect the model's performance. Notably, variations in batch size and activation functions show significant impacts on the objective value, emphasizing their critical role in the model's effectiveness.

**Table 1.** Explored Hyperparameters in Optuna Optimization

| Hyperparameter | Values or Range |
| --- | --- |
| Hidden Layer Sizes | {'512,256', '512,512', '1024,512'} |
| Activation Functions | {'ReLU', 'Tanh', 'Leaky ReLU'} |
| $L1$ Alpha | $10^{-6}$ to $10^{-3}$ (log scale) |
| $L2$ Alpha | $10^{-6}$ to $10^{-3}$ (log scale) |
| Dropout Rate (First Layer) | 0.1 to 0.3 |
| Dropout Rate (Second Layer) | 0.1 to 0.3 |
| Initial Learning Rate | $10^{-5}$ to $10^{-2}$ (log scale) |
| Batch Size | {16, 32, 64, 128} |

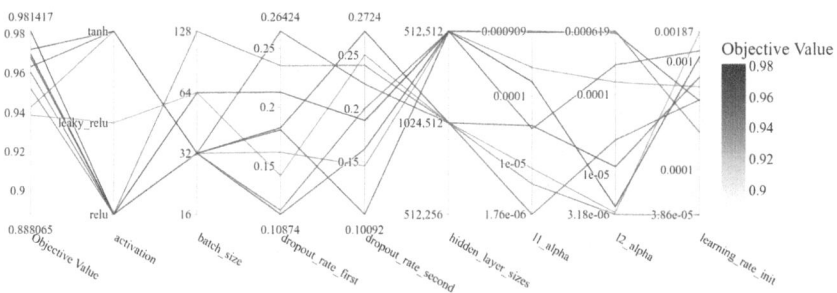

**Fig. 5.** Parallel coordinate plot illustrating the interdependencies and impact of various hyperparameters optimized during the study. Each line represents a trial, showing how hyperparameters like batch size, dropout rates, and learning rates interact to influence the objective value.

**SVM Model Configuration and Training.** Following the feature extraction process performed by a pre-trained MLP model, we employed LDA to reduce the dimensionality of the extracted features. LDA, a supervised dimensionality reduction technique, effectively projects the features onto a lower-dimensional space while maximizing class separability. This resulted in a reduction from 512 features to 14 LDA components, offering a streamlined yet discriminative feature space for subsequent classification.

We then utilized a Support Vector Machine (SVM) model for malware classification, exploring various kernel options to identify the most suitable configuration for our dataset. Hyperparameter optimization was conducted using the Optuna framework, which leverages efficient search algorithms like tree-structured Parzen estimators to explore the hyperparameter space effectively. The key hyperparameters we optimized included:

– **Kernel Type:** We tested both 'linear' and 'RBF' kernels to determine the optimal approach for capturing the relationships within our feature space.

– **Regularization Parameter (C):** This parameter was varied from $10^{-3}$ to $10^3$ on a logarithmic scale to control the trade-off between model complexity and training error.
– **Kernel Coefficient** ($\gamma$)**:** For the RBF kernel, we explored 'scale' and 'auto' options to adjust the influence range of individual support vectors.

To ensure robust evaluation and mitigate overfitting, we incorporated a 10-fold stratified cross-validation strategy within the hyperparameter optimization process. This allowed us to assess the generalization ability of different hyperparameter combinations across various data subsets and reflect the model's performance on unseen data. Our analysis revealed that the RBF kernel consistently provided high validation accuracy, often achieving optimal performance with higher C values, which suggests that a more complex decision boundary is beneficial for capturing the intricacies of the data. Finally, using the optimally tuned parameters identified by Optuna, we trained the final SVM model on the entire training dataset. This approach, combining LDA for feature reduction and Optuna for hyperparameter optimization, yielded a highly accurate and efficient SVM model for Android malware classification.

## 6    Results and Analysis

### 6.1    Training Outcomes and Model Performance

The MLP model, trained on 47 features from the CCCS-CIC-AndMal-2020 dataset and enhanced with an attention mechanism, achieved an impressive overall test accuracy of 99.85% (Table 2). The model's strong performance is supported by high precision, recall, and F1-scores across various malware categories, demonstrating its effectiveness in learning complex patterns and identifying discriminative features.

Table 2 presents the detailed classification performance for each malware category. While the model achieves high precision and recall for most classes, such as 'Adware' (Class 0), the performance for Class 10 (e.g., Scareware) is lower, with a precision of 0.65 and an F1-score of 0.77. These results suggest the need for further investigation into the factors contributing to the lower performance for specific classes.

Figure 6a to 6c further illustrate the MLP model's performance. The confusion matrix (Fig. 6a) shows a strong diagonal, indicating accurate classification for most classes, with some off-diagonal elements highlighting areas for improvement. For instance, the misclassification of some 'Dropper' samples (Class 3) as 'Adware' (Class 0) indicates areas where the model could be refined. The precision-recall curves (Fig. 6b) demonstrate high AUC-PR values across most classes, underscoring the model's effectiveness. The training accuracy, validation accuracy, and F1-score per trial (Fig. 6c) reflect the model's stability and consistent performance across multiple trials.

Following the MLP's feature extraction, the trained model was employed to reduce the original dataset to 5% of its initial size. LDA was then applied to

**Table 2.** Detailed Performance of MLP Model

| Class | Precision | Recall | F1-score | Support |
|---|---|---|---|---|
| 0 | 0.99 | 1.00 | 0.99 | 7610 |
| 1 | 0.95 | 0.98 | 0.96 | 320 |
| 2 | 0.93 | 0.93 | 0.93 | 182 |
| 3 | 1.00 | 0.81 | 0.89 | 458 |
| 4 | 1.00 | 0.90 | 0.95 | 136 |
| 5 | 0.98 | 0.82 | 0.89 | 473 |
| 6 | 0.99 | 0.86 | 0.92 | 409 |
| 7 | 0.99 | 1.00 | 0.99 | 1208 |
| 8 | 1.00 | 1.00 | 1.00 | 15666 |
| 9 | 0.97 | 0.96 | 0.96 | 641 |
| 10 | 0.65 | 0.94 | 0.77 | 311 |
| 11 | 0.94 | 0.93 | 0.93 | 675 |
| 12 | 0.99 | 1.00 | 1.00 | 2749 |
| 13 | 0.98 | 1.00 | 0.99 | 2680 |
| 14 | 1.00 | 1.00 | 1.00 | 32297 |
| **Overall** | 0.99 | 0.99 | 0.99 | 65815 |

**Table 3.** Detailed Performance of SVM Model

| Class | Precision | Recall | F1-score | Support |
|---|---|---|---|---|
| 0 | 1.00 | 1.00 | 1.00 | 7610 |
| 1 | 0.99 | 1.00 | 0.99 | 320 |
| 2 | 1.00 | 0.99 | 1.00 | 182 |
| 3 | 1.00 | 0.98 | 0.99 | 458 |
| 4 | 0.99 | 0.99 | 0.99 | 136 |
| 5 | 0.97 | 0.98 | 0.97 | 473 |
| 6 | 1.00 | 1.00 | 1.00 | 409 |
| 7 | 1.00 | 1.00 | 1.00 | 1208 |
| 8 | 1.00 | 1.00 | 1.00 | 15666 |
| 9 | 0.99 | 0.99 | 0.99 | 641 |
| 10 | 0.98 | 1.00 | 0.99 | 311 |
| 11 | 0.99 | 1.00 | 0.99 | 675 |
| 12 | 1.00 | 1.00 | 1.00 | 2749 |
| 13 | 1.00 | 1.00 | 1.00 | 2680 |
| 14 | 1.00 | 1.00 | 1.00 | 32297 |
| **Overall** | 1.00 | 1.00 | 1.00 | 65815 |

further reduce the feature set to 14 components, ensuring the most informative features were retained for distinguishing between malware families.

The SVM model, trained on these 14 LDA-reduced components and utilizing a Radial Basis Function (RBF) kernel, demonstrated superior performance compared to the MLP. Table 3 shows that the SVM achieved perfect precision, recall, and F1-scores for almost all classes. This improvement can be attributed to the RBF kernel's ability to effectively map the reduced feature space, enabling more accurate class separation.

Figure 6d to 6f illustrate the SVM model's performance. The confusion matrix (Fig. 6d) indicates perfect classification across all classes, while the precision-recall curves (Fig. 6e) show high AUC-PR values, confirming the model's robustness. The training accuracy, validation accuracy, and F1-score per trial (Fig. 6f) reflect the SVM model's consistent and high performance.

The comparison of MLP and SVM models reveals that the SVM model, despite using a significantly reduced feature set, outperforms the MLP in various metrics. This demonstrates the efficiency of using the SVM model for classification once the MLP has performed initial feature extraction and reduction. By leveraging the trained and saved MLP model, future malware detection tasks can save time and computational resources by directly utilizing the SVM for classification. The SVM's superior performance, despite using only 14 features, highlights the effectiveness of this hybrid approach in malware detection and family classification.

Moreover, the models exhibit stability and strong generalization ability, as evidenced by the consistent performance across train, validation, and test sets over multiple trials. The low gap between training and validation/test performance suggests the models are robust to overfitting, further emphasizing their

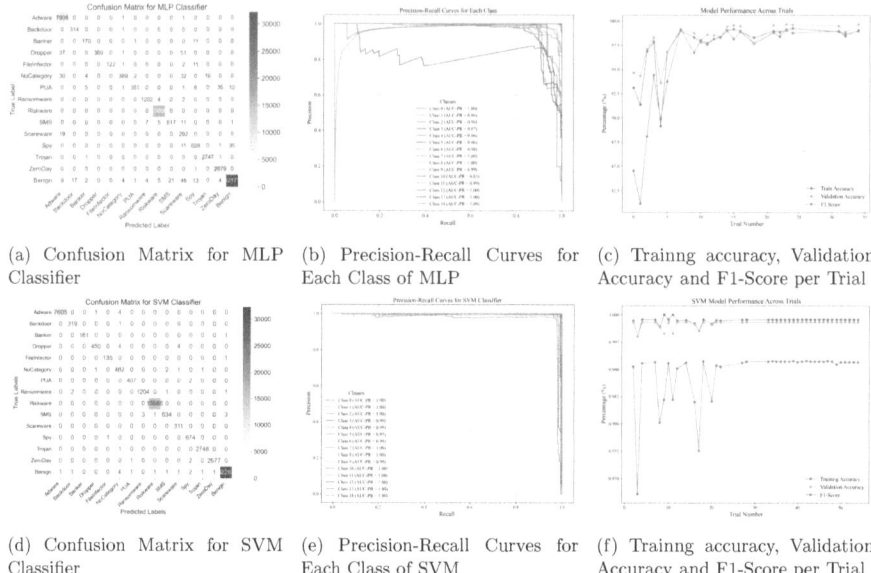

(a) Confusion Matrix for MLP Classifier

(b) Precision-Recall Curves for Each Class of MLP

(c) Trainng accuracy, Validation Accuracy and F1-Score per Trial

(d) Confusion Matrix for SVM Classifier

(e) Precision-Recall Curves for Each Class of SVM

(f) Trainng accuracy, Validation Accuracy and F1-Score per Trial

**Fig. 6.** Detailed Performance Visualization of the MLP and SVM Models: (a) Confusion matrix of MLP; (b) Precision-recall curves of MLP; (c) Training accuracy, Validation accuracy and F1-score per trial of MLP; (d) Confusion matrix of SVM; (e) Precision-recall curves of SVM; (f) Training accuracy, Validation accuracy and F1-score per trial of SVM.

reliability in real-world malware detection scenarios. This robustness is crucial for practical deployments, where models must handle diverse and evolving threats without degradation in performance.

### 6.2    Feature Importance Evaluation

Understanding the model's decision-making process is crucial for interpreting its predictions and assessing its reliability. To achieve this, we analyze the importance of features extracted from the CCCS-CIC-AndMal-2020 dataset, which includes both static and dynamic analysis features from a diverse set of Android malware and benign applications.

Figure 7 presents the top 20 most significant features based on their contribution to the model's performance. The visualization includes features from various categories, including memory usage, network activity, API calls, and file interactions. The prominence of memory-related features like Memory_PssTotal, Memory_PrivateClean, and Memory_PrivateDirty suggests that the model relies heavily on the memory footprint and allocation patterns of applications to distinguish between malicious and benign behavior. Similarly, network features such as Network_TotalReceivedBytes and Network_TotalTransmittedBytes highlight the importance of network communication patterns in identifying malware.

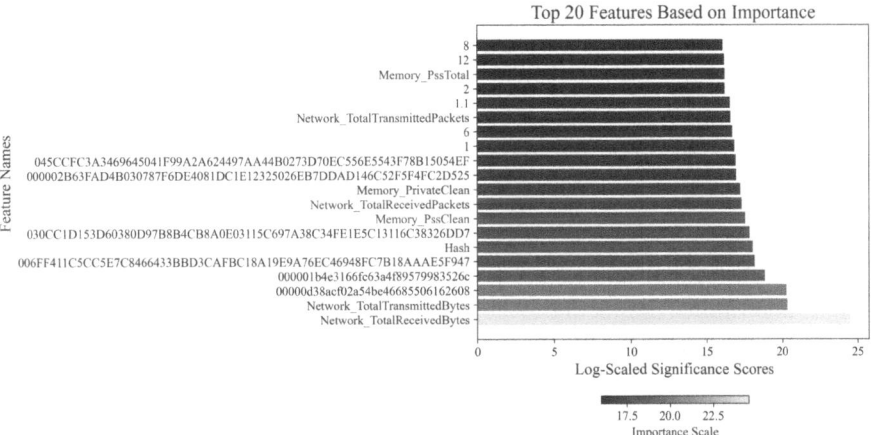

**Fig. 7.** Top 20 Features Based on Importance, displaying a full spectrum of feature contributions to the classification model's performance. This visualization highlights the model's dependency on specific attributes that significantly influence its decision-making process in detecting Android malware.

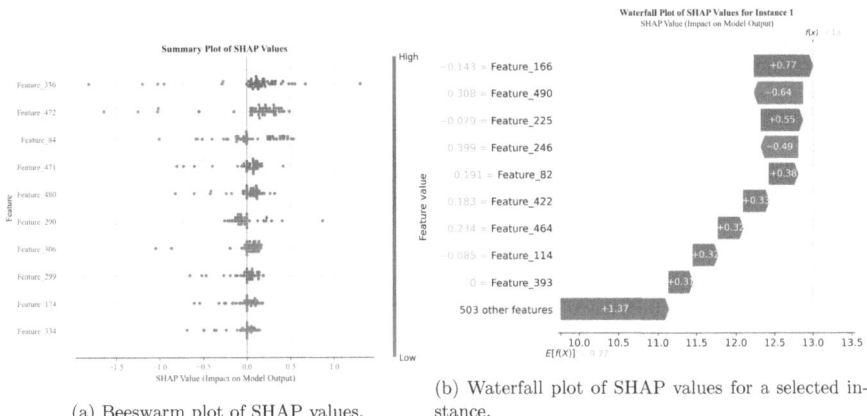

(a) Beeswarm plot of SHAP values.        (b) Waterfall plot of SHAP values for a selected instance.

**Fig. 8.** Visualization of SHAP values for the SVM model: (a) Beeswarm plot showing the distribution and impact of features; (b) Waterfall plot illustrating the sequential contribution of features to the final prediction outcome.

The presence of API call features like `API_Process_android.os.Process_start` and `API_JavaNativeInterface_java.lang.Runtime_loadLibrary` indicates that the model considers the usage of specific APIs, potentially related to process manipulation and native code execution, as indicative of malicious activity. Furthermore, the inclusion of static analysis features like application hashes demonstrates the model's ability to leverage unique identifiers and signatures for classification.

The log-scaled significance scores provide a clear visualization of the relative importance of features with varying magnitudes. This allows us to observe the full spectrum of feature contributions without obscuring the impact of features with smaller scores.

Additionally, this analysis informs the development of more targeted data preprocessing and feature engineering strategies. By understanding which features are most influential, we can optimize our data collection and processing pipelines to focus on the most relevant information, potentially reducing computational overhead and improving model efficiency. This targeted approach also helps in fine-tuning the model to be more sensitive to subtle variations in malware behavior, enhancing its ability to detect zero-day threats and advanced persistent threats (APTs) that often exhibit novel or minimally invasive behaviors.

### 6.3    Feature Importance Evaluation from Trained SVM Model Using SHAP Values

The use of SHAP (SHapley Additive exPlanations) values facilitates a deep understanding of the decision-making process within our SVM classification model. By quantifying the contribution of each feature to the prediction, SHAP values provide a powerful method for feature importance evaluation, ensuring model transparency and interpretability.

The beeswarm plot (Fig. 8a) illustrates the distribution and impact of each feature on the model's predictions with color coding indicating the feature value: red for higher and blue for lower values. This plot provides insights into which features are most influential and how their values affect the prediction outcomes. The waterfall plot (Fig. 8b) details the cumulative impact of the most influential features for a specific instance, demonstrating how each feature's contribution leads from the base value to the final prediction.

Both plots underscore the significant and nuanced roles of individual features, allowing for a detailed understanding that supports robust and transparent machine learning modeling.

### 6.4    Comparative Analysis

The comparative analysis of our Attention-enhanced MLP-SVM framework with state-of-the-art Android malware detection approaches, as summarized in Table 4, underscores the distinctive advantages and superior performance of our proposed method. Unlike the majority of prior studies that focused on either ML algorithms [2,10,11] or DL architectures [2,17,22], our approach synergistically combines MLP for feature extraction and SVM for malware family classification, achieving unparalleled accuracy and precision.

A key strength of our framework lies in its efficient utilization of the CCCS-CIC-AndMal-2020 dataset. While some studies employed subsets of the dataset

[10, 11] or focused on either static or dynamic features [14], our approach leverages the entire dataset, encompassing both static and dynamic aspects of malware behavior. This comprehensive analysis enables our model to capture a wider range of malware characteristics, contributing to its superior performance.

Computational efficiency is another area where our framework excels. By employing an attention mechanism in the MLP, our model achieves state-of-the-art performance using only 47 features, significantly fewer than the thousands of features used in other studies [10, 17]. This reduction in computational complexity, coupled with our model's ability to outperform the majority of the compared studies across various metrics (Table 4), highlights the effectiveness of our approach.

Overfitting is a common challenge in machine learning, and our study stands out by employing rigorous techniques in preprocessing, feature engineering, and MLP training to mitigate this issue. These measures, which are not consistently addressed in other studies, enhance the robustness and generalizability of our model.

The simplicity of our approach is another notable advantage. Once the attention-enhanced MLP model is trained, subsequent malware detection and classification can be efficiently performed by applying LDA and SVM. This streamlined process contrasts with the complex hybrid approaches used in some studies [10, 14], making our framework more accessible and adaptable for practical applications.

Moreover, our model's dynamic weighted voting mechanism offers an improvement over the simpler majority voting schemes employed in previous studies [22]. This enhancement, along with our framework's ability to handle both static and dynamic features, demonstrates its resilience against evolving malware threats and its superiority over narrowly focused approaches [14, 17].

The effectiveness of our MLP-SVM framework in categorizing complex malware behaviors into specific families is another significant advantage. By leveraging the RBF kernel, our approach demonstrates exceptional proficiency in navigating high-dimensional feature spaces, outperforming traditional ML and standalone DL models explored in prior works. This fusion of techniques not only improves accuracy but also enhances the generalizability of the malware detection and classification process.

The comparison of MLP and SVM models reveals that the SVM model, despite using a significantly reduced feature set, outperforms the MLP in various metrics. This demonstrates the efficiency of using the SVM model for classification once the MLP has performed initial feature extraction and reduction. By leveraging the trained and saved MLP model, future malware detection tasks can save time and computational resources by directly utilizing the SVM for classification. The SVM's superior performance, despite using only 14 features, highlights the effectiveness of this hybrid approach in malware detection and family classification.

**Table 4.** Comprehensive Comparison of Android Malware Detection Approaches Using CCCS-CIC-AndMal-2020 Dataset. Abbreviations used: **P1** for Islam et al. [11], **P2** for Li et al. [14], **P3** for Sayed et al. [22], **P4** for Hammood et al. [10], **P5** for Batouche and Jahankhani [2], **P6** for Musikawan et al. [17], and **Our Work** for Safayat et al.

| Aspect | Study Comparison | | | |
|---|---|---|---|---|
| | **\*\*Note:\*\*** Studies are referred to by their abbreviations (e.g., P1, P2) for brevity. Accuracy, Precision, Recall, and F1-score are presented as percentages unless otherwise specified. | | | |
| Dataset and Sampling (Static) | **P1**: 50% sampling, 70–30 train-test split; 141,000 training samples, 60,000 testing samples | **P2**: Full dataset (125,990 training samples, 53,998 testing samples) | **P3**: Full dataset (280,000 training samples, 120,000 testing samples) | **P4**: 5,600 training samples, 1,400 testing samples |
| Dataset and Sampling (Dynamic) | **P1**: 100% sampling, 70–30 train-test split; 280,000 training samples, 120,000 testing samples | **P6 and Our Work**: 357,805 total samples; Detailed sampling for static and dynamic not provided | **P3**: Full dataset (280,000 training samples, 120,000 testing samples) | **P5**: Full dataset (280,000 training samples, 120,000 testing samples) |
| Feature Engineering | **Feature Selection and Reduction: P1**: 56 features (with outlier handling), 125 features (without outlier handling), PCA (45 components explaining 99.9% of variance) **P3**: Recursive Feature Elimination (RFE) with Random Forest Classifier, 41 features removed, resulting in 99 features. **Our Work**: SelectKBest with chi-squared test, selecting the top 3,000 features. Further reduction using attention-enhanced MLP to 512 dimensions, then LDA to 14 components. | | **Features in Dataset: P2**: 220 static features selected using Gini Index. **P4**: 9,504 static features. **P5**: Static features from APK's manifest.xml file, including permissions, actions, categories, services (binary), and metadata, receivers, providers, activities (frequency). **P6**: 9,503 static features, 141 dynamic features. | |
| Modeling Approach | **ML Algorithms: P1** and **P5** explored RF, KNN, SVM, and NB classifiers. **P1** additionally used MLP and LR, while **P5** used DTC. **P4** investigated XGBoost, GB, ANN, and DNN. SVM kernels and DNN architectures were unspecified in some studies. | **DL Architectures: P3** utilized CNN, LSTM, GRU, and MLP architectures. **P5** employed a 3-layer DNN with 100 neurons each, implemented in TensorFlow. P6 introduced a custom DL architecture, AMDI-Droid. **Our work** focused on an MLP with 512/256 neurons, ReLU activation, softmax output, and an attention layer. | **Ensemble Techniques: P1** used weighted voting. **P2** implemented SynDroid with CTGAN-SVM. **P3** combined models using majority voting and dynamic weighted voting. **P4** employed XGBoost, RF, and NB using an adaptive genetic algorithm (AGA). | |
| Performance and Evaluation | **Best Model Performance: P1**: Weighted Voting ensemble (Accuracy: 95%) **P2**: SynDroid (Precision: 99.85%, F1-score: 99.82%) **P3**: Dynamic Weighted Voting (Accuracy: 92%) **P4**: XGB-AGA (Accuracy: 99.82%, Precision: 99.85%) **P5**: Random Forest (Accuracy: 89%, Weighted Avg. F1-score: 0.90) **P6**: AMDI-Droid (Performance metrics not directly comparable due to different evaluation methods) **Our Work**: Support Vector Machine (SVM) with RBF kernel (Accuracy: 100%, Precision: 100%, Recall: 100%, F1-score: 100%), Explainable AI using SHAP (SHapley Additive exPlanations). | | **Additional Contributions and Insights: P1**: Evaluates outlier handling in feature selection and its impact on classification performance. **P2**: Proposes KS-CIR test for class imbalance and uses CTGAN-SVM for synthetic data augmentation. **P4**: Focuses on minimizing False Positive (FP) and False Negative (FN) rates for autonomous vehicle security. **P5**: Analyzes Android malware detection datasets and discusses attack prediction for future research. **P6**: Introduces AMDI-Droid for efficient malware detection, highlighting faster training and detection speeds. **Our Work**: Achieves perfect classification accuracy with SVM. Enhances interpretability using SHAP analysis. | |

# 7   Discussion

## 7.1   Scalability Considerations

The scalability of the proposed MLP-SVM framework is crucial for its practical deployment in rapidly expanding Android ecosystems. By reducing the feature space from 9,760 to 14 components using an attention-enhanced MLP and LDA, our approach significantly decreases computational and memory overhead while maintaining classification accuracy. However, the framework's scalability must be evaluated with larger, more complex datasets. For extensive, high-dimensional data, techniques like Incremental Principal Component Analysis (IPCA) or Distributed LDA could be employed to maintain performance. To enhance scalability for real-time, large-scale malware detection, integrating distributed computing paradigms such as MapReduce or Apache Spark would enable horizontal scaling, mitigating latency and ensuring high throughput.

For deployment in resource-constrained environments like mobile or edge devices, model compression techniques such as knowledge distillation and network quantization should be explored. These optimizations would reduce the model's computational footprint without compromising detection efficacy, ensuring versatility across both high-performance cloud-based systems and low-resource devices. This approach would maintain operational efficiency and scalability while adapting to diverse deployment scenarios in the Android ecosystem.

## 8    Future Work

While our approach shows significant promise, further research is needed to address specific limitations and explore its full potential. Future work could focus on exploring alternative feature selection techniques to identify even more impactful features. Additionally, examining different deep learning architectures could further enhance performance. Evaluating the model's robustness against adversarial attacks is crucial to ensure its reliability in real-world applications. Moreover, investigating the feasibility of deploying this framework in a real-world setting is essential to assess its practical impact on enhancing mobile security. Expanding the dataset to include more diverse and recent malware samples could also improve the model's generalizability and effectiveness. Lastly, incorporating real-time detection capabilities could significantly enhance the framework's applicability in dynamic and rapidly evolving threat landscapes.

## 9    Conclusion

This research introduces an innovative and efficient framework for Android malware detection and classification, leveraging an attention-enhanced MLP coupled with an SVM. Our approach significantly outperforms existing state-of-the-art methods by achieving over 99% accuracy while analyzing only 47 out of 9,768 features from the CCCS-CIC-AndMal-2020 dataset. The MLP's attention mechanism focuses on the most discriminative features, leading to robust performance, and the subsequent application of LDA reduces the feature space to just 14 components. This dimensionality reduction, combined with the SVM's RBF kernel, facilitates precise and computationally efficient malware family classification, surpassing the accuracy and feature efficiency of previous studies. The proposed framework demonstrates resilience against the evolving landscape of Android malware by effectively identifying malicious applications with high precision and recall. The integration of explainable AI techniques, such as SHAP, further enhances the model's interpretability and transparency. These findings underscore the potential of combining attention mechanisms, dimensionality reduction, and support vector machines to create highly effective and efficient security measures for the mobile ecosystem.

**Acknowledgements.** This research was partially supported by the U.S. National Science Foundation through Grant No. 2317117 and Grant No. 2309760.

# References

1. Arp, D., Spreitzenbarth, M., Hubner, M., Gascon, H., Rieck, K., Siemens, C.: Drebin: effective and explainable detection of android malware in your pocket. In: Ndss, vol. 14, pp. 23–26 (2014)
2. Batouche, A., Jahankhani, H.: A comprehensive approach to android malware detection using machine learning. Inform. Sec. Technol. Controlling Pandemics, 171–212 (2021)
3. Bostani, H., Moonsamy, V.: Evadedroid: a practical evasion attack on machine learning for black-box android malware detection. Comput. Sec. **139**, 103676 (2024)
4. Canadian Institute for Cybersecurity (CIC): Cccs-cic-andmal-2020. Canadian Institute for Cybersecurity (CIC) Project in Collaboration with Canadian Centre for Cyber Security (CCCS) (May 2020), available online: https://www.unb.ca/cic/datasets/andmal2020.html Accessed 1 May 2024
5. Daoudi, N., Allix, K., Bissyandé, T.F., Klein, J.: A two-steps approach to improve the performance of android malware detectors. arXiv preprint arXiv:2205.08265 (2022)
6. Dong, S., et al.: Understanding android obfuscation techniques: a large-scale investigation in the wild. In: Beyah, R., Chang, B., Li, Y., Zhu, S. (eds.) SecureComm 2018. LNICSSITE, vol. 254, pp. 172–192. Springer, Cham (2018). https://doi.org/10.1007/978-3-030-01701-9_10
7. Faruki, P., et al.: Android security: a survey of issues, malware penetration, and defenses. IEEE Commun. Surv. Tutorials **17**(2), 998–1022 (2014)
8. Garcia, J., Hammad, M., Malek, S.: Lightweight, obfuscation-resilient detection and family identification of android malware. ACM Trans. Softw. Eng. Methodol. (TOSEM) **26**(3), 1–29 (2018)
9. Gopinath, M., Sethuraman, S.C.: A comprehensive survey on deep learning based malware detection techniques. Comput. Sci. Rev. **47**, 100529 (2023)
10. Hammood, L., Doğru, İA., Kılıç, K.: Machine learning-based adaptive genetic algorithm for android malware detection in auto-driving vehicles. Appl. Sci. **13**(9), 5403 (2023)
11. Islam, R., Sayed, M.I., Saha, S., Hossain, M.J., Masud, M.A.: Android malware classification using optimum feature selection and ensemble machine learning. Internet of Things Cyber-Phys. Syst. **3**, 100–111 (2023)
12. Kim, T., Kang, B., Rho, M., Sezer, S., Im, E.G.: A multimodal deep learning method for android malware detection using various features. IEEE Trans. Inf. Forensics Secur. **14**(3), 773–788 (2018)
13. Li, C., Zheng, J.: Api call-based malware classification using recurrent neural networks. J. Cyber Sec. Mobility **10**(3), 617–640 (2021)
14. Li, J., He, J., Li, W., Fang, W., Yang, G., Li, T.: Syndroid: an adaptive enhanced android malware classification method based on ctgan-svm. Comput. Sec. **137**, 103604 (2024)

15. Liu, Q., Chen, C., Zhang, Y., Hu, Z.: Feature selection for support vector machines with rbf kernel. Artif. Intell. Rev. **36**(2), 99–115 (2011)
16. Loshchilov, I., Hutter, F.: Sgdr: Stochastic gradient descent with warm restarts. arXiv preprint arXiv:1608.03983 (2016)
17. Musikawan, P., Kongsorot, Y., You, I., So-In, C.: An enhanced deep learning neural network for the detection and identification of android malware. IEEE Internet of Things J. (2022)
18. Onwuzurike, L., Mariconti, E., Andriotis, P., Cristofaro, E.D., Ross, G., Stringhini, G.: Mamadroid: detecting android malware by building markov chains of behavioral models (extended version). ACM Trans. Privacy Sec. (TOPS) **22**(2), 1–34 (2019)
19. Peiravian, N., Zhu, X.: Machine learning for android malware detection using permission and api calls. In: 2013 IEEE 25th International Conference on Tools with Artificial Intelligence, pp. 300–305. IEEE (2013)
20. Qiu, J., Zhang, J., Luo, W., Pan, L., Nepal, S., Xiang, Y.: A survey of android malware detection with deep neural models. ACM Comput. Surv. (CSUR) **53**(6), 1–36 (2020)
21. Rastogi, V., Chen, Y., Jiang, X.: Droidchameleon: evaluating android anti-malware against transformation attacks. In: Proceedings of the 8th ACM SIGSAC Symposium on Information, Computer and Communications Security, pp. 329–334 (2013)
22. Sayed, M.I., Saha, S., Haque, A.: Deep learning based malapps detection in android powered mobile cyber-physical system. In: 2023 International Conference on Computing, Networking and Communications (ICNC), pp. 443–449. IEEE (2023)
23. Scholkopf, B., et al.: Comparing support vector machines with gaussian kernels to radial basis function classifiers. IEEE Trans. Signal Process. **45**(11), 2758–2765 (1997)
24. Tallón-Ballesteros, A., Chen, C.: Explainable ai: using shapley value to explain complex anomaly detection ml-based systems. Machine Learn. Artifi. Intell. **332**, 152 (2020)
25. Turner, A.: How many android users are there? global and us statistics (2024). https://www.bankmycell.com/blog/how-many-android-users-are-there (2024), Accessed 4 Jun 2024
26. Vu, L.N., Jung, S.: Admat: a cnn-on-matrix approach to android malware detection and classification. IEEE Access **9**, 39680–39694 (2021)
27. Wang, Z., Liu, Q., Chi, Y.: Review of android malware detection based on deep learning. IEEE Access **8**, 181102–181126 (2020)
28. Wermke, D.: Security considerations in the open source software ecosystem (2023)
29. Wu, Y., Li, X., Zou, D., Yang, W., Zhang, X., Jin, H.: Malscan: Fast market-wide mobile malware scanning by social-network centrality analysis. In: 2019 34th IEEE/ACM International Conference on Automated Software Engineering (ASE), pp. 139–150. IEEE (2019)
30. Yuan, Z., Lu, Y., Xue, Y.: Droiddetector: android malware characterization and detection using deep learning. Tsinghua Sci. Technol. **21**(1), 114–123 (2016)

# System Security and Prevention

# RKPM: Restricted Kernel Page Mechanism to Mitigate Privilege Escalation Attacks

Hiroki Kuzuno[1]([✉])[iD] and Toshihiro Yamauchi[2][iD]

[1] Graduate School of Engineering, Kobe University, Kobe, Japan
kuzuno@port.kobe-u.ac.jp
[2] Faculty of Environmental, Life, Natural Science and Technology,
Okayama University, Okayama, Japan
yamauchi@okayama-u.ac.jp

**Abstract.** Kernel memory corruption attacks against operating systems exploit kernel vulnerabilities to overwrite kernel data. Kernel address space layout randomization makes it difficult to identify kernel data by randomizing their virtual address space. Control flow integrity (CFI) prevents unauthorized kernel code execution by verifying kernel function calls. However, these countermeasures do not prohibit writing to kernel data. If the virtual address of privileged information is specified and CFI is circumvented, the privileged information can be modified by a kernel memory corruption attack. In this paper, we propose a restricted kernel page mechanism (RKPM) to mitigate kernel memory corruption attacks by introducing restricted kernel pages to protect the kernel data specified in the kernel. The RKPM focuses on the fact that kernel memory corruption attacks attempt to read the virtual addresses around the privileged information. The RKPM adopts page table mapping handling and a memory protection key to control the read and write restrictions of the restricted kernel pages. This allows us to mitigate kernel memory corruption attacks by capturing reads to the restricted kernel page before the privileged information is overwritten. As an evaluation of the RKPM, we confirmed that it can mitigate privilege escalation attacks on the latest Linux kernel. We also measured that there was a certain overhead in the kernel performance. This study enhances kernel security by mitigating privilege escalation attacks through the use of software or hardware based restricted kernel pages.

## 1 Introduction

Kernel memory corruption is one of the most common vulnerabilities in operating system (OS) kernels. Such attacks lead to kernel data modification, enabling attackers to take control of a terminal by falsifying kernel data related to access control and administrator accounts, resulting in privilege escalation [1,2].

Countermeasures against kernel memory corruption attacks include KCoFI, which applies control flow integrity (CFI) [3] to the kernel to check the order of code calls. Kernel address space layout randomization (KASLR)

H. H. Song et al. (Eds.): NSS 2024, LNCS 15564, pp. 213–231, 2025.
https://doi.org/10.1007/978-981-96-3531-3_11

randomizes the virtual addresses of kernel code and data [4]. Additionally, using a CPU feature, memory protection key (MPK) can control kernel data writes to the page table entry (PTE) base [5]. These countermeasures mitigate the risks associated with vulnerable kernel code calls and kernel data modifications. However, privileged information can still be overwritten as follows:

**Privileged Information Due to Memory Corruption**
    KASLR makes it difficult to locate kernel data, and CFI makes it difficult to force kernel code calls but does not restrict kernel data writes. In addition, the write restriction of kernel data using hardware functions requires appropriate write control for each kernel data. If write restriction targets are omitted, privileged information may be modified by kernel memory corruption attacks that exploit kernel vulnerabilities, enabling attackers to conduct privilege escalation attacks.

This paper proposes a restricted kernel page mechanism (RKPM) to mitigate kernel data modification by introducing restricted kernel pages. The RKPM places these pages on top and bottom of adjacent memory location of privileged information in the kernel memory, serving as guard pages that trigger a page fault when a read or write occurs [6]. The RKPM targets the modification process of privileged information in memory corruption attacks, which are characterized by attempts to read adjacent virtual addresses of privileged information is overwritten [7]. By using KASLR and CFI, the RKPM improves the kernel's resistance to memory corruption attacks.

The RKPM has two implementations focusing on software and hardware approaches.

- **Implementation 1:** This general-purpose implementation handles the read and write restrictions of restricted kernel pages. It controls the mapping of restricted kernel pages from the page table to the kernel.
- **Implementation 2:** This implementation adopts the read and write restrictions of a CPU feature, specifically the Intel MPK protection keys for supervisor (PKS), to manage the restricted kernel pages. The MPK PKS is a lightweight method for protecting kernel pages.

The RKPM dedicates a kernel page (4KB) to the privileged information, prepared when the user process is created, with two restricted kernel pages reserved adjacent virtual addresses of this privileged information. Therefore, the RKPM introduces the memory layout that is the privileged information is arranged to be interposed among the restricted kernel pages. When an attacker attempts to overwrite the privileged information of a user process through a privilege escalation attack via memory corruption, it is possible to read the restricted kernel pages.

The RKPM detects a privilege escalation attack by catching a page fault that occurs when reading a restricted kernel page and halting the corresponding user process. This mechanism prevents privilege escalation attacks before privileged information is overwritten.

The research contributions of this paper are as follows:

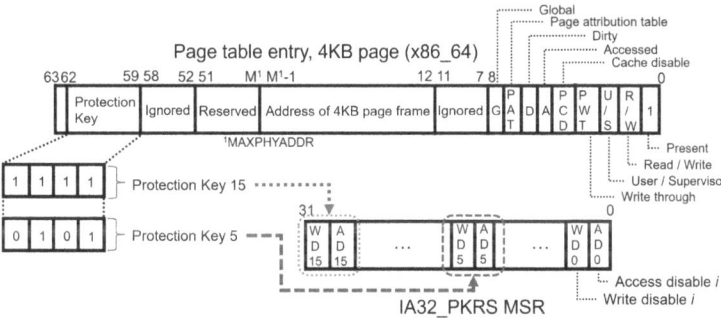

**Fig. 1.** Intel memory protection key [5]

**Table 1.** Effects of kernel vulnerability [8]

|        | Item                   | Description                                         |
|--------|------------------------|----------------------------------------------------|
| Effect | Memory corruption      | Modification of kernel data                        |
|        | Denial of Service      | Forcing kernel to stop running                     |
|        | OS information leakage | Information leakage from uninitialized data variables |

1. To mitigate memory corruption attacks, we designed and implemented a security mechanism that introduces the restricted kernel pages are placed top and bottom of adjacent memory location of privileged information. The RKPM provides two implementations for Linux. Implementation 1 handles the read and write permission to unmap restricted kernel pages, Implementation 2 adopts MPK PKS to prohibit read and write accesses to restricted kernel pages. Both implementations resist privilege escalation attacks involving memory corruption.
2. As an evaluation of the RKPM implementations, we confirmed that it can mitigate privilege escalation attacks by user processes. We also evaluated the performance of the RKPM and showed that it has only a 0.33% impact for Implementation 1 and 0.91% impact for Implementation 2 on the performance score of the Linux kernel.

## 2   Background

### 2.1   Memory Protection Key

Intel CPUs support MPK, which control read and write restrictions on a PTE [5]. The MPK includes PKS and IA32_PKRS_MSR registers (PKRS) for kernel mode. As shown in Fig. 1, the PTE has 16 protection keys (Pkeys), and a 32-bit flag (two bits per Pkey: write disable (WD) and access disable (AD)) controls the read and write restrictions for each Pkey.

```
1     // From Linux kernel v5.18.2 include/linux/sched.h
2     struct task_struct {
3        ...
4        const struct cred __rcu   *cred;
5        ...
6     }
7     struct cred {
8        ...
9        kuid_t    uid; /* real UID of the task */
10       kgid_t    gid; /* real GID of the task */
11       ...
12    }
13    // include/linux/uidgid.h
14    typedef struct {
15       // typedef __kernel_uid32_t uid_t;
16       // typedef unsigned int __kernel_uid32_t;
17       uid_t val;
18    } kuid_t;
19    typedef struct {
20       // typedef __kernel_gid32_t gid_t;
21       // typedef unsigned int __kernel_gid32_t;
22       gid_t val;
23    } kgid_t;
```

**Fig. 2.** Structures related to user ID in Linux [9]

## 2.2 Kernel Vulnerability

Kernel vulnerabilities involve modifications that can be used to attack kernels. Table 1 summarizes the effect of four types of attacks using kernel vulnerabilities [8]. A memory corruption attack attempts to write to an arbitrary virtual address in the kernel memory. If the memory area is rewritten, the attack target is overwritten.

## 2.3 Privileged Information

The attack target is kernel data related to privileged information. Figure 2 illustrates the structure definition of the user ID in Linux, which is kernel data for storing privileged information on user processes in the Linux kernel.

The kernel data of the privileged information are stored in the pointer of cred structure within the task_struct structure managed for each user process. The user ID is stored in the variable uid of the kuid_t structure on line 9, which is included in the cred structure on lines 7 to 12. The kuid_t structure is defined on lines 14 to 18. Similarly, the group ID is stored in the variable gid of the kuid_t structure on line 10, and its value is also defined in the kuid_t structure on lines 14 through 18, which the value of the kgid_t structure on lines 19 to 23.

## 2.4 Memory Corruption Attack

For privilege escalation attacks, a kernel vulnerability that takes privilege management omissions to forcibly call kernel code that performs privilege modification operations [10–12] and memory corruption attacks that exploit kernel vulnerabilities, arbitrary kernel code can be inserted and executed [7].

CVE-2017-16995 is an eBPF vulnerability that modifies the kernel data `cred` which stores privileged information through a memory corruption attack to change the user ID of a user process to an administrative user [7].

In a privilege escalation attack [7], the virtual address of the base point of the `task_struct` structure is first identified. Then, an attempt is made to identify the virtual address of the `uid` structure's `val` and the `gid` structure's `val`.

In the search, the values of the virtual addresses are added in order starting from the virtual address, which is the base of the `task_struct` structure to the virtual address that matches the value of the user ID, which is the privileged information of the attacker's user process.

When a match is found, it is determined that the user process privileged information is stored and rewritten to the root user ID (0) and group ID (0) values of uid structure and the gid structure.

## 3    Threat Model

As the threat model, the attack assumed by the RKPM is a privilege escalation attack through memory corruption.

### 3.1    Attack Target Environment

The attack target environment, as assumed by the threat model, is summarized as follows:

– **Attacker:** Executes a user process (hereafter referred to as the attacker's user process) with general user privileges. The attacker's user process invokes vulnerable kernel code. It causes memory corruption in the kernel memory.
– **Kernel:** Contains a kernel vulnerability that can be exploited for memory corruption to achieve privilege escalation attacks.
– **Kernel Vulnerability:** Allows identification of an arbitrary virtual address for privileged information and facilitates a memory corruption attack.
– **Attack Target:** The attack target is the privileged information of the attacker's user process stored in the kernel memory.

### 3.2    Attack Scenario

The attack scenario assumed by the RKPM is as follows:

– Attack Scenario: The attacker's user process executes a proof of concept (PoC) code that exploits the memory corruption of a kernel vulnerability to overwrite privileged information. The PoC code invokes kernel code containing the vulnerability via a system call to the kernel. The kernel code then searches for the virtual address of the privileged information to be attacked, identifies it, and attempts to overwrite the privileged information through memory corruption.

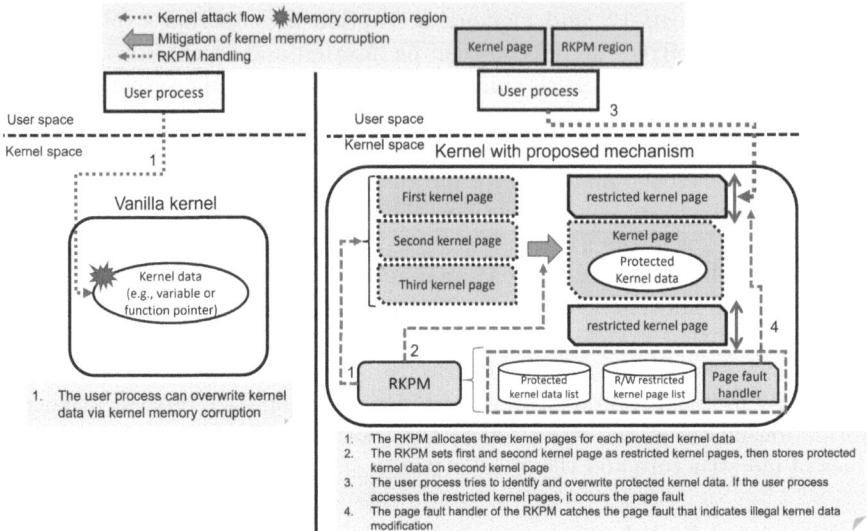

**Fig. 3.** Design overview of RKPM

# 4    Design of the Approach

## 4.1    Requirement

The RKPM introduces restricted regions to protect privileged information. Restricted regions are top and bottom adjacent memory locations of privileged information in the kernel memory.

In this design, we aimed to satisfy the following requirements:

**RQ1:** Ensure and make it difficult to overwrite protected kernel data of privileged information is transparent to user processes.

**RQ2:** Capture and judge read and write in restricted areas as behavior indicative of prior unauthorized writing of protected kernel data of privileged information.

## 4.2    Concept

The design concepts of the RKPM are defined as follows:

- **Concept 1:** Restricted kernel page handling is performed within the kernel as the countermeasure to user processing.
- **Concept 2:** The RKPM is designed to mitigate attacks on privileged information in a manner that does not affect user processes and kernel operations.

**Table 2.** Comparison of implementations of RKPM

| Item | Implementation 1 | Implementation 2 |
|---|---|---|
| Protected kernel data | Privileged information | Privileged information |
| Restricted kernel page | Page table mapping | MPK PKS |
| Overhead | Low | Low |
| Implementation | Software | Software & Hardware |
| Limitation | Stability | CPU depending |

### 4.3  Restricted Kernel Page Handling Challenge

Based on these design concepts, a design outline of the RKPM is presented in Fig. 3. To satisfy these requirements, restricted kernel pages are placed top and bottom adjacent memory location of privileged information in kernel memory. The RKPM manages the list of privileged information to be protected and a list of restricted kernel pages, and it provides a memory corruption attack detection feature.

The RKPM is applied to all user processes. When read access occurs on a restricted kernel page, the RKPM detects a memory corruption attack via a page fault and determines whether such an attack has occurred.

**Protected Kernel Data:** The protected kernel data managed by the RKPM consist of privileged information created at the time of user process creation, related to the access control of the user process.

**Restricted Kernel Page and Handling:** The RKPM automatically allocates multiple restricted kernel pages top and bottom adjacent memory location of privileged information. These restricted kernel pages are read and write prohibited in the kernel.

The restricted kernel pages in the RKPM are handled during user process creation. The RKPM allocates and places in the kernel memory area to protect kernel data with restrict kernel pages. These restricted kernel pages are placed adjacent memory location are consecutively allocated privileged information in the kernel memory.

## 5  Implementation

### 5.1  Implementation Overview

The environment for the RKPM implementation was Linux on an x86_64 CPU architecture. Table 2 presents the protected kernel data and the characteristics of restricted kernel page management for the implementations.

In both implementations, the privileged information of the user process constitutes the protected kernel data. Additionally, three kernel pages are allocated in the kernel memory as a range of contiguous virtual addresses to be restricted kernel pages. The first and third kernel pages are restricted kernel pages, while

**Table 3.** Kernel data to be protected in implementations

| Item | Description |
|------|-------------|
| Protected kernel data | User ID (e.g., uid, euid, fsuid, and suid) |
| | Group ID (e.g., gid, egid, fsid, and sgid) |

the second kernel page stores the privileged information. The RKPM implementations arrange the memory layout. It interposes privileged information among the restricted kernel pages. The following is an overview of the implementations overview of restricted kernel page management.

- **Implementation 1:** This software approach manages the mapping of restricted kernel pages from a page table. Restricted kernel pages are unmapped during user process creation to read and write accesses are prohibited. Even if a user process attempts privilege escalation, restricted kernel pages do not exist in the page table, and accesses to these pages lead to a page fault for attack detection. Although Implementation 1 moderate overhead for handling kernel page mapping, it can be applied to virtual OS without relying on hardware features.
- **Implementation 2:** This hardware approach manages the read and write permissions of restricted kernel pages using MPK PKS. Implementation 2 sets Pkeys for the restricted kernel pages and then disables the read and write flags of MPK at user process creation. Even if a user process attempts a privilege escalation, the CPU determines whether read or write access to restricted kernel pages is prohibited. These accesses automatically lead to a page fault for attack detection. Implementation 2 depends on the CPU hardware features of MPK. However, it manages the fast handling of restricted kernel page control through the PKey and PKRS register settings.

While processing the implementations, the kernel maintains a list that manages the range of virtual addresses of read restricted kernel pages, and a page fault handler to capture access to these pages. Additionally, Implementation 2 manages the Pkey and PKRS registers for restrictions.

## 5.2   Protected Kernel Data and Restricted Kernel Page

**Protected Kernel Data:** The implementations of the RKPM support the protection of privileged information to be protected as listed in Table 3.

In the implementations, each user process has a kernel page (4KB) that stores only the privileged information within the `cred` structure of the `task_struct` structure.

**Restricted Kernel Page:** In the implementations of the RKPM, the size of restricted kernel page is 4KB. Implementations 1 and 2 manage the restricted kernel page as follows:

– Implementation 1: Restricted kernel pages are removed from kernel memory to restrict read and write access. In Linux with Implementation 1, the `alloc_pages_exact` function is used to allocate kernel pages, and the `remove_pagetable` function is used to remove kernel pages, unmapping the kernel page from the kernel page table (the `pgd` variable of the `current`).

– Implementation 2: Restricted kernel pages are managed by the MPK to ensure read and write access restrictions. In Linux with Implementation 2, the `alloc_pages_exact` function is used for the allocation of kernel pages. Subsequently, Implementation 2 manages the Pkey $i$ of the PTE, and the WD$i$, and RD$i$ values of the PKRS register for MPK write and read restrictions. Restricted kernel pages share Pkey $i$ in Implementation 2. WD$i$ and RD$i$ are set to 1, restricting write and read access.

## 5.3   Restricted Kernel Page Handling

Restricted kernel pages and privileged information are handled as following:

1. User process creation.
2. Allocate three kernel pages using the `alloc_pages_exact` function.
3. Determine if the three kernel pages are in a contiguous virtual address range.
   (a) If the virtual addresses are not contiguous: Release the kernel page and perform reallocation processing. The trying max count of release is 10 times for implementations.
   (b) For consecutive virtual addresses: Continue storing privileged information and reading restriction processing.
4. Store in a range of virtual addresses that are restricted kernel pages in a managing list.
5. Store privileged information and set restricted kernel pages.
   (a) The second kernel page stores privileged information.
   (b) Implementation 1
      i. Remove the first kernel page from the kernel memory space as a restricted kernel page using the `remove_pagetabele` function.
      ii. Remove the third kernel page from the kernel memory space as a restricted kernel page using the `remove_pagetable` function.
   (c) Implementation 2
      i. Set Pkey $i$ to the PTE of first kernel page.
      ii. Set Pkey $i$ to the PTE of third kernel page.
      iii. Set WD$i$ and RD$i$ to 1 in the PKRS register to enable first and third kernel pages as a restricted kernel page.
6. Continue user process generation.

**Page Fault Handling:** In a Linux kernel with an RKPM, a page fault occurs when an attacker's user process reads a restricted kernel page during a privilege escalation attack, as this behavior involves searching for privileged information.

The Linux kernel provides a page fault handler, `handle_page_fault` that can determine the virtual address of the attempted read. In the implementation of the RKPM, the virtual address at the time a page fault occurs is within the range of the virtual address of a restricted kernel page. The differences between implementations 1 and 2 are as follow:

- **Implementation 1:** A page fault occurs due to read or write access to the restricted kernel page.
- **Implementation 2:** A page fault occurs due to a MPK PKS error during read or write access to the restricted kernel page.

The type of page fault can be distinguished by the error number of the bit flag. The RKPM determines that the attacker's user process is attempting to execute a privilege escalation attack. Subsequently, the RKPM sends a SIGKILL signal using the `force_sig_info` function to terminate the user process of the target attacker.

## 6    Evaluation

### 6.1    Evaluation Purpose

We evaluated the kernel with the RKPM to investigate the effectiveness of mitigation against privilege escalation attacks and to measure the overhead of the kernel. The evaluation contents are as follows:

1. Privilege escalation attack mitigation assessment
   We evaluated whether a kernel with RKPM implementations can mitigate privilege escalation attacks. For this evaluation, we introduced a memory corruptible vulnerability into the kernel.
2. Performance evaluation in the kernel operations
   The kernel performance overhead was measured using benchmark measurement software on kernels with RKPM implementations.

### 6.2    Evaluation Environment

A virtual machine was used to evaluate the effectiveness of the RKPM in mitigating privilege escalation attacks and to evaluate the performance of the kernel. The evaluation computer was an Intel(R) Core i5-13500 (1.8 GHz, 20 cores, 64 GB memory). The virtual machine infrastructure was ProxMox 8.1.4. For Implementation 1, the virtual machine had 4 CPUs and 8 GB memory, and OS is Debian 12.4 using the Linux kernel 6.1.73. We added 213 lines to six source files. For Implementation 2, QEMU 6.0.91 was used as the evaluation environment (QEMU Virtual CPU version 2.5+, 1 core, 100MB memory) with PKS support. It was executed on a virtual machine had 4 CPUs and 8 GB memory. The OS of QEMU was buildroot-2023.11. Implementation 2 required seven source files and 331 lines for Linux kernel 6.1.73. The kernel vulnerabilities that can be used for memory corruption were implemented in three files with an additional 32 lines of code and 134 lines of PoC code.

```
// PoC code running, process id is 2391          13.  // ex kernel pages' region
1.   user $ ./a.out                              14.  // ffff9abf82058000, ffff9abf82059000, ffff9abf8205a000
2.   uid=1000(user) gid=1000(user) groups=1000(user)   15.  [ 363.704204] uid virtual address: ffff9abf82059000
3.   [*] sys_kvuln01 system call invocation      16.  // Kernel memory corruption
4.   uid virtual address: ffff9abf82059000        17.  [ 363.704204] attack target virtual address: ffff9abf82058000
5.   [*] sys_kvuln02 system call invocation      19.  [ 364.216821] #PF: error code (0x0003), virtual address: ffff9abf82058000
6.   Killed user process                         20.  Page fault error code 3 (0b011)
                                                 21.  Page fault error code bits: from Linux v6.1.74 :
// Kernel log information                              arch/x86/include/asm/trap_pf.h
7.   // set kernel page of privilege at the user process creation   a.  bit 0 == 0: no page found 1: protection fault
8.   [ 363.704204] uid virtual address: ffff9abf82059000    b.  bit 1 == 0: read access 1: write access
9.   // start system call invocation             c.  bit 2 == 0: kernel-mode access 1: user-mode access
10.  [ 363.702116] sys_kvuln02 system call invocation   22.  // finish system call invocation
11.  [ 363.702179] sysnum: 0x6a  (352)           23.  // finish user process
12.  [ 363.702204] PID: user process 2391
```

Red text is the points of kernel memory corruption information

**Fig. 4.** Results of preventing privilege escalation attacks using Implementation 1

```
// PoC code running, process id is 1872          14.  [ 367.068469] uid virtual address: ffff88001d35fe40
1.   user $ ./a.out                              15.  // start system call invocation
2.   uid=1000(user) gid=1000(user) groups=1000(user)   16.  [ 367.068478] sys_kvuln02 system call invocation
3.   [*] sys_kvuln01 system call invocation      17.  [ 367.068478] sysnum: 0x6a  (352)
4.   uid virtual address: ffff88001d35fe40         18.  [ 367.068478] PID: user process 1676
5.   [*] sys_kvuln02 system call invocation      19.  // ex kernel pages' region
6.   Killed user process                         20.  // ffff888001d361000, ..., ffff888006370000
                                                 // Kernel memory corruption
// Kernel log information                         21.  [ 367.068479] attack target virtual address: ffff88001d35fe40
7.   [ 364.203309] PKS PRIV: enable pks currently   22.  [ 367.068479] #PF: error code (0x0002), virtual address: ffff88001d35fe40
8.   [ 363.713991] PKS PRIV: enable pks: pkey 1  23.  [ 367.204186] PKS: protection keys hw error code 35, pkey 1
9.   [ 363.714132] write_pkrs for CPU 0: 0x8     24.  HW error code 35 (0b100011)
10.  [ 363.714192] read_pkrs for CPU 0: 0x8      25.  Page fault error code bits:
11.  // set kernel page of privilege at the user process creation   from Linux v6.1.74 : arch/x86/include/asm/trap_pf.h
12.  [*] set protection key bit to PTE at the user process creation   a.  bit 0 == 1: protection fault, X86_PF_PROT
13.  [ 365.860037] PTE flags: 0x880000001d361000 pkey 1   b.  bit 1 == 1: write access, X86_PF_WRITE
     1.  bit 63-32: 1000 1000 0000 0000 0000 0000 0000 0000   c.  bit 5 == 1: protection keys block access, X86_PF_PK
     2.  bit 31-0: 0000 0110 0101 1001 1000 0000 0110 0011   26.  // finish system call invocation
     3.  bit 62-59 == 0001: protection key 1     27.  // finish user process
```

Red text is the points of kernel memory corruption information

**Fig. 5.** Results of preventing privilege escalation attacks using Implementation 2

## 6.3 Kernel Vulnerability

To evaluate the security functionality of the RKPM, we simulated CVE-2017-16995 [7] and introduced two vulnerable system calls to target a specified virtual address enabling a privilege escalation attack by a user process.

- **Vulnerable system call 1:** This system call specifies the virtual address of the privileged information of the user process and returns it to the user process.
- **Vulnerable system call 2:** This system call takes a virtual address as the first argument, overwrites the offset range as the second argument, and uses a read identifier as the third argument. This allows arbitrary data within an offset range from a specified virtual address to be overwritten, facilitating privilege escalation attacks through memory corruption.

## 6.4 Privilege Escalation Attacks Security Assessment

In the effectiveness evaluation of privilege escalation attack mitigation, we attempted a privilege escalation attack on a Linux kernel with the RKPM by exploiting a kernel vulnerability that allows an attacker's user process to cause memory corruption.

The attacker's user process uses the vulnerable system call 1 to identify the virtual address of privileged information, and then uses the vulnerable system call 2 to overwrite the virtual address with the offset range of the privileged information.

**Implementation 1:** Figure 4 shows the mitigation results of the RKPM when the attacker's user process launches a privilege escalation attack. The UID value is 1,000, indicating a normal user. The virtual address `0xffff9abf82059000` was identified. In line 4, vulnerable system call 2 is executed, it is the starting point of the privilege escalation attack. In the kernel, line 8 shows the virtual address of the privileged information of the attacker's user process.

In line 14, the first and last restricted kernel pages are located at the top and bottom memory layout of the privileged information, `0xffffff9abf82058000`, `0xffff9abf82059000`, and `0xffffff9abf8205a000`. In lines 17 and 18, an attempt is made to write to the virtual addresses `0xffffff9abf82058000` in the vulnerable system call 2. A page fault with error number 2 is captured in line 19. The virtual address included in the virtual address range of the restricted kernel page is `0xffff9abf82058000`. This indicates a write violation to address `0xffff9abf82058000`. After the RKPM catches the page fault, it identifies the virtual address to be written to as a restricted kernel page, and the corresponding attacker's user process is terminated.

**Implementation 2:** Fig. 5 shows the mitigation results of Implementations 2 of the RKPM. The UID value of the attacker's user process is 1,000, indicating a normal user. The virtual address of UID is `0xffff9abf82059000`.

Implementation 2 enables the MPK PKS to set the read and write disabilities to to PKRS for Pkey 1 in line 3. Subsequently, Implementation 2 sets Pkey 1 on the restricted kernel pages in line 13. The first and last restricted kernel pages are located at the top and bottom memory layout of the privileged information. The privilege escalation attack attempts to read the virtual address `0xffffff9abf82058000`, `0xffff9abf82059000`, and `0xffffff9abf8205a000` specified in the vulnerable system call 2. A page fault with an error number 35 is captured in line 23. The virtual address included in the virtual address range of the restricted kernel page is `0xffff9abf82058000`. This indicates a MPK read permission error at address `0xffff9abf82058000`. Implementation 2 of the RKPM captures the page fault in line 23. Subsequently, it identifies the virtual address to be written as a restricted kernel page, and the corresponding attacker's user process is terminated.

## 6.5   Overhead of Kernel Performance

To evaluate the performance of the kernel with the RKPM, the kernel benchmarking software UnixBench was run five times on the Linux kernel before and after applying the RKPM. Performance scores were calculated using the average value. UnixBench 5.1.3 provides performance scores for various kernel operations, such as numerical computation, file copying, process processing, and system calls. Linux kernel with Implementation 1 was natively executed on the vir-

**Table 4.** UnixBench comparison of performance

| (a) Implementation 1 | | | (b) Implementation 2 | | |
|---|---|---|---|---|---|
| | Vanilla kernel | RKPM (Overhead) | | Vanilla kernel | RKPM (Overhead) |
| Dhrystone 2 | 6211.54 | 6194.00 (0.28%) | Dhrystone 2 | 503.92 | 502.92 (0.20%) |
| Double-Precision Whetstone | 1963.02 | 1962.90 (0.01%) | Double-Precision Whetstone | 130.22 | 129.70 (0.40%) |
| Execl Throughput | 1574.78 | 1567.74 (0.45%) | Execl Throughput | 15.24 | 15.22 (0.13%) |
| File Copy 1024 bufsize | 2667.50 | 2629.54 (1.42%) | File Copy 1024 bufsize | 606.68 | 599.58 (1.17%) |
| File Copy 256 bufsize | 1687.64 | 1677.28 (0.61%) | File Copy 256 bufsize | 410.26 | 403.12 (1.74%) |
| File Copy 4096 bufsize | 6279.22 | 6232.02 (0.75%) | File Copy 4096 bufsize | 725.14 | 721.90 (0.45%) |
| Pipe Throughput | 964.88 | 955.90 (0.93%) | Pipe Throughput | 256.72 | 254.38 (0.91%) |
| Pipe-based Context Switching | 214.06 | 213.46 (0.28%) | Pipe-based Context Switching | 42.10 | 41.66 (1.05%) |
| Process Creation | 1443.14 | 1439.32 (0.27%) | Process Creation | 114.34 | 109.82 (3.95%) |
| Shell Scripts (1 concurrent) | 5297.38 | 5262.40 (0.66%) | Shell Scripts (1 concurrent) | 63.02 | 62.92 (0.16%) |
| System Call Overhead | 511.12 | 510.28 (0.16%) | System Call Overhead | 360.16 | 346.68 (3.74%) |
| System Benchmarks Index Score | 1736.62 | 1730.84 (0.33%) | System Benchmarks Index Score | 160.36 | 158.90 (0.91%) |

tual machine. Linux kernel with Implementation 2 was executed on the QEMU of the virtual machine. QEMU virtual CPU is low performance due to nested virtualization.

**Implementation 1:** Table 4a compares the vanilla Linux kernel and Linux kernel with RKPM implementations 1. The RKPM has the largest impact on the score at 1.42% for File Copy 1024 bufsize and the smallest impact on the score at 0.01% for Double-Precision Whetstone.

For user process creation, the impact of the RKPM was considered as follows: Process Creation: 0.27%, Shell Scripts (1 concurrent): 0.66%. Overall impact on the kernel performance score: 0.33%.

**Implementation 2:** Table 4b compares the vanilla Linux kernel and Linux kernel with RKPM implementations 2. The RKPM has the largest impact on the score at 3.95% for Process Creation and the smallest impact on the score at 0.13% for Execl Throughput. The overall impact on the kernel performance score is 0.91%.

## 7    Discussion

### 7.1    Evaluation Considerations

In the effectiveness evaluation of privilege escalation attack mitigation, the Linux kernel with RKPM implementations successfully mitigated privilege escalation attacks. The attacker's user process, which attempted to write to the restricted kernel page. It searches for privileged information targeted for modification, was identified. We confirmed that the privileged information was not modified, and that the attacker's user process could be stopped.

The performance evaluation results show that the implementations of the RKPM have minimal impact on numerical processing but introduce some overhead in processes related to file copying, pipe processing, and context switches. Implementation 1 increases the processing time. The overhead factor is the user process creation. It contains the allocation and unmapping of multiple kernel pages. Implementation 2, the overhead is related to the handling of the MPK PKS for restricted kernel pages during user process creation. The PKRS register is set at the kernel boot. Due to the software implementation of MPK PKS, Implementation 2 on the QEMU requires the emulation overhead of page table access at the process creation. Additionally, we confirmed that the performance overhead does not affect the stability of user processes and kernel operations.

For additional overhead evaluation, we must consider multiple-task situations that include a single task, multiple tasks, and parallel task processing. Additionally, it is necessary to evaluate a performance transition with memory consumption stressing on the running kernel with both implementations.

## 7.2 Approach Considerations

The RKPM places restricted kernel pages at top and bottom of adjacent memory location of privileged information in kernel memory at the time of user process creation. In our implementations, the protection of privileged information is transparent to user processes, and we believe that bypassing this security mechanism is challenging. When a user process reads or writes a restricted kernel page, it is quickly identified as an attempt at a privilege escalation attack and the user process is stopped to prevent such as attack.

The defeating of Implementations 1 requires the recovery of the mapping of restricted kernel pages to the page table. It is hard to find the unmapped kernel pages from the kernel memory space before the memory corruption. The defeating of Implementation 2 needs to modify the PKRS or Pkeys of PTE before the memory corruption. However, the monitoring kernel code of PKRS and Pkeys of PTE can be statically compiled at the kernel, then the sophisticated attack is necessary such as kernel behavior modification.

Protected kernel data can be generalized as an extension of the RKPM. When adding kernel data to be protected and dynamically allocating the restricted kernel pages, it is necessary to consider the complexity of implementation due to the large amount of kernel data in the kernel and the potential overhead on kernel performance due to kernel page allocation and deletion.

For the validity of the RKPM's security capability, it is necessary to analyze CVSS score to determine memory corruption as a prior type of vulnerability at a privilege escalation than other types of vulnerability (e.g., race condition).

## 7.3 Limitations

**Design and Implementation:** The RKPM prevents the searching process of privilege escalation attack that reads or writes the around memory rage of privileged information. If an attacker estimates the virtual address range of a restricted kernel page and writes to the virtual address range of the kernel page containing the privileged information, it will be overwritten.

The RKPM can be combined with other security mechanisms. KASLR achieves the randomization of kernel data placement making it difficult to identify, while the MPK enables the write limitations for each kernel data. We believe that dynamically protecting kernel data using MPK can improve the kernel's resistance to memory corruption.

**Protected Kernel Data and Restricted Kernel Page:** The RKPM requires the kernel data to be protected and adjusted according to the kernel page size (4KB). Additionally, the range of virtual addresses must be contiguous with the restricted kernel pages.

When protecting kernel data across multiple pages in a running kernel, it is necessary to consider the number of kernel pages required for the application of the RKPM, stable capture using page faults, and physical memory segmentation.

The RKPM requires the two restricted kernel pages for one protected kernel data. If the RKPM protects the user process, the number of restricted kernel pages twice increases by the number of user processes.

### 7.4   Portability

The portability of Implementation 1 of the RKPM to other OSes require that the kernel memory be built and managed using page tables. We also believe that the RKPM can be ported to a FreeBSD kernel [13]. Additionally, Implementations 2 of the RKPM requires MPK PKS, which requires the implementation of PTE in an OS that supports an Intel CPU.

## 8   Related Work

### 8.1   Running Kernel Hardening

**Kernel Memory Protection:** To mitigate memory corruption attacks in the kernel, KASLR randomizes the placement of kernel data and kernel code at kernel boot time, making attacks more difficult [4]. Moreover, methods for dynamically applying KASLR to device drivers [14] and applying KASLR to the guest OS at startup using a virtual machine monitor have been proposed [15]. Additionally, KDRM relocates kernel data of privileged information at the system call invocation to mitigate privilege escalation attacks [16].

**Prevention of Kernel Code Execution:**
To prevent malicious code execution in the kernel, KCoFI treats asynchronous processing in the kernel as an exception and applies kernel code invocation order checking to prevent illegal kernel code execution [3]. A practical method for kernel code invocation verification has also been proposed using pointer authentication based on ARM features [17].

**Kernel Data Protection using MPK:** To protect kernel data using MPK, libhermitMPK manages kernel code and kernel data with multiple Pkeys and provides read control on a per-Pkey basis to protect against unauthorized reads

[18]. xMP protects the kernel by dividing the kernel memory space into multiple domains and assigning Pkeys to each domain [19]. DOPE protects kernel data by assigning a Pkey to each kernel data type and appropriately controlling the reading privileges during kernel code execution [20].

**Guard Page and Protection of Privileged Information:** FreeGuard randomly allocates guard pages during memory allocation in the heap area to prevent heap-spread attacks [21]. PrivWatcher monitors privileged information written from outside the kernel [22]. PrivGuard stores privileged information in a separate area, such as the kernel stack, to detect whether privileged information has been modified before and after a system call [23].

**Table 5.** Comparison of kernel data protection methods

| Feature | FreeGuard [21] | PrivWatcher [22] | PrivGuard [23] | KDRM [16] | RKPM |
|---|---|---|---|---|---|
| Protection target | Heap | Kernel data | Kernel data | Kernel data | Kernel data |
| Implementation | Randomization | Outside kernel | Replication | Kernel page relocation | Kernel page fault |
| Limitation | Memory management | Kernel inspection | Kernel data variation | Kernel data handling | Kernel page handling |

### 8.2   Comparison

Table 5 shows a comparison of the RKPM with previous studies in terms of protection targets, implementation schemes, and limitations [16,21–23].

FreeGuard randomly inserts a guard page when heap memory allocated to prevent splay attacks that overwrite the heap area [21]. In the RKPM, after multiple kernel pages have been allocated to construct the memory layout that is the privileged information is arranged to be interposed among the restricted kernel pages. When combined with FreeGuard, which randomly allocates guard pages when allocating heap space, this provides a two-stage countermeasure against memory corruption attacks.

PrivWatcher manages the write access to privileged information [22]. It monitors privileged information writes from outside the kernel and prevents unauthorized modification of privileged information, effectively preventing privilege escalation attacks. However, appropriate allocation of kernel data is required for each protected kernel data, and the load increases with each external monitoring of kernel operations.

PrivGuard stores kernel data related to privileged information in the kernel stack in advance and detects the modification of privileged information before and after kernel code execution [23]. PrivGuard only requires a comparison of kernel stack operations and privileged information and can be applied to running kernels with low overhead.

KDRM forcibly relocates privileged information when user processes invoke system calls. It is difficult to execute a privilege escalation attack that identifies and overwrites the privileged information [16].

PrivWatcher, PrivGuard, and KDRM are designed to prevent and detect the modification attacking process of privileged information, but they do not prevent overwriting before it occurs. The RKPM restricts the modification attacking process of privileged information that is arranged to be interposed among the restricted kernel pages to detect and mitigate attacks, leading to privilege escalation attacks.

The RKPM does not perform any restricted operations on privileged information or kernel stack operations. We believe that the RKPM, PrivWatcher, PrivGuard, and KDRM do not conflict with each other and can be combined to protect privileged information before and after a privilege escalation attack occurs.

## 9 Conclusion

In this study, we proposed an RKPM to mitigate kernel memory corruption attacks by protecting privileged information in combination with restricted kernel pages. The RKPM consecutively allocates three kernel pages in the kernel memory. Subsequently, the RKPM sets first and third kernel pages as restricted kernel pages, then second kernel page stores privileged information. The RKPM focuses on the privileged information modification process in memory corruption attacks that attempt to read into top or bottom adjacent memory location of the privileged information to be overwritten [7].

Of the two implementations of the RKPM: Implementation 1 handles the mapping of the restricted kernel pages from the page table to manage read and write accesses. Implementation 2 manages the read and write restrictions of the restricted kernel pages using the MPK PKS in the running kernel. Both implementations enable the detection of page faults on the restricted kernel pages to mitigate the early stages of memory corruption in privilege escalation attacks.

From the evaluation results, we confirmed that the RKPM can mitigate privilege escalation attacks by detecting kernel memory corruption attacks on the implemented Linux kernel. The performance evaluation showed that the effects on the performance scores of the Linux kernel with Implementation 1 were 0.33% and 0.91% for Implementations. Neither implementation affected kernel operation stability.

**Acknowledgment.** This work was partially supported by the Japan Society for the Promotion of Science (JSPS) KAKENHI Grant Number JP23K24848, JP23K16882, the Telecommunications Advancement Foundation (TAF), and ACT-X Grant Number JPMJAX24M4, Japan.

## References

1. Exploit Database, Nexus 5 Android 5.0 - Privilege Escalation. https://www.exploit-db.com/exploits/35711/. Accessed 21 May 2019
2. grsecurity: super fun 2.6.30+/RHEL5 2.6.18 local kernel exploit. https://grsecurity.net/~spender/exploits/exploit2.txt. Accessed 21 May 2019

3. Criswell, J., Dautenhahn, N., Adve, V.: KCoFI: Complete control-flow integrity for commodity operating system kernels. In: Proceedings of the IEEE Security and Privacy, pp. 292-307. IEEE (2014). https://doi.org/10.1109/SP.2014.26

4. Shacham, H., Page, M., Pfaff, B., Goh, E., Modadugu, N., Boneh, D.: On the effectiveness of address-space randomization. In: Proceedings of the 11th ACM Conference on Computer and Communications Security, pp. 298-307, ACM (2004). https://doi.org/10.1145/1030083.1030124

5. Intel Corporation.: Intel(R) 64 and IA-32 Architectures Software Developer's Manual. https://www.intel.com/content/www/us/en/developer/articles/technical/intel-sdm.html. Accessed 18 August 2021

6. Song, D., Lettner, J., Rajasekaran, P., Na, Y., Volckaert, S., Larsen, P., and Franz, M.: SoK: sanitizing for security. In: Proceedings of 2019 IEEE Symposium on Security and Privacy, pp. 1275-1295. IEEE (2019). https://doi.org/10.1109/SP.2019.00010

7. CVE-2017-16995. https://cve.mitre.org/cgi-bin/cvename.cgi?name=CVE-2017-16995. Accessed 10 June 2019

8. Chen, H., Mao, Y., Wang, X., Zhow, D., Zeldovich, N., Kaashoek, F.M.: Linux kernel vulnerabilities - state-of-the-art defenses and open problems. In: Proceedings of the Second Asia-Pacific Workshop on Systems, pp. 1-5. ACM (2011). https://doi.org/10.1145/2103799.2103805

9. The Linux Kernel Archives. https://www.kernel.org/. Accessed 10 Jun 2019

10. CVE-2016-4997. https://cve.mitre.org/cgi-bin/cvename.cgi?name=CVE-2016-4997. Accessed 10 Jun 2019

11. CVE-2016-9793. https://cve.mitre.org/cgi-bin/cvename.cgi?name=CVE-2016-9793. Accessed 10 Jun 2019

12. CVE-2017-1000112. https://cve.mitre.org/cgi-bin/cvename.cgi?name=CVE-2017-1000112. Accessed 10 Jun 2019

13. FreeBSD architecture handbook. https://www.freebsd.org/doc/en_US.ISO8859-1/books/arch-handbook/. Accessed 8 August 2019

14. Nikolaev, R., Nadeem, H., Stone, C., Ravindran, B.: Adelie: continuous address space layout re-randomization for Linux drivers. In: Proceedings of the 27th ACM International Conference on Architectural Support for Programming Languages and Operating Systems, pp. 483–498. ACM (2022). https://doi.org/10.1145/3503222.3507779

15. Holmes, B., Waterman, J., Williams, D.: KASLR in the age of MicroVMs. In: Proceedings of the Seventeenth European Conference on Computer Systems, pp. 149-165. ACM (2022). https://doi.org/10.1145/3492321.3519578

16. Kuzuno, H., Yamauchi, T.: Mitigation of privilege escalation attack using kernel data relocation mechanism. Int. J. Inf. Secur. **23**, 3351–3367 (2024). https://doi.org/10.1007/s10207-024-00890-4

17. Yoo, S., Park, J., Kim, S., Kim, Y., Kim, T.: In-Kernel control-flow integrity on commodity OSes using ARM pointer authentication. In: Proceedings of the 31st USENIX Conference on Security Symposium, pp. 89-106. USENIX (2019)

18. Sung, M., Olivier, P., Lankes, S., Ravindran, B.: Intra-unikernel isolation with intel memory protection keys. In: Proceedings of the 16th ACM SIGPLAN/SIGOPS International Conference on Virtual Execution Environments, pp. 143-156. ACM (2020). https://doi.org/10.1145/3381052.3381326

19. Proskurin, S., Momeu, M., Ghavamnia, S., Kemerlis, P., V., Polychronakis, M.: xMP: selective memory protection for kernel and user space. In: Proceedings of the 2020 IEEE Symposium on Security and Privacy, pp. 563-577. IEEE (2020). https://doi.org/10.1109/SP40000.2020.00041

20. Lukas, M., Martin, S., Fabian, R., Daniel, G., Stefan, M.: DOPE: domain protection enforcement with PKS. In: Proceedings of the 39th Annual Computer Security Applications Conference, pp. 662–676 (2023). https://doi.org/10.1145/3627106.3627113

21. Silvestro, S., Liu, H., Crosser, C., Lin, Z., Liu, T.: FreeGuard: a faster secure heap allocator. In: Proceedings of the 24th ACM Conference on Computer and Communications Security, pp. 2389–2403. ACM (2017). https://doi.org/10.1145/3133956.3133957

22. Chen, Q., Azab, A.M., Ganesh, G., Ning, P.: PrivWatcher: non-bypassable monitoring and protection of process credentials from memory corruption attacks. In: Proceedings of the 2017 ACM on Asia Conference on Computer and Communications Security, pp. 167-178. ACM (2017). https://doi.org/10.1145/3052973.3053029

23. Qiang, W., Yang, J., Jin, H., Shi, X.: PrivGuard: protecting sensitive kernel data from privilege escalation attacks. IEEE Access **6**, 46584–46594 (2018). https://doi.org/10.1109/ACCESS.2018.2866498

# Auditing and Attributing Behaviours of Suspicious Android Health Applications

Muhammad Salman[1], I. Wayan Budi Santana[1,2], Muhammad Ikram[1(✉)], and Mohamed Ali Kaafar[1]

[1] Macquarie University, Sydney, Australia
{muhammad.salman,muhammad.ikram,dali.kaafar}@mq.edu.au
[2] Politeknik Negeri Bali, Badung, Indonesia
budisentana@pnb.ac.id

**Abstract.** Consumer mobile medical, health, and fitness apps, collectively known as mobile health or mHealth apps, monitor user activities such as steps, locations, and email. It seamlessly aggregates sensitive information to facilitate a wide range of functions, such as the management of health conditions and symptom checking. Although mHealth apps provide real-time health monitoring and easier access to healthcare resources, they may also pose serious risks to user safety. While the research community is primarily well aware of the user's exposure to several types of malware, there has not been a large-scale in-depth analysis of suspicious mHealth apps using a consistent methodology.

This study conducts a large-scale security and privacy analysis of 381 suspicious free mHealth apps (chosen from a corpus of 15,893 apps) available on "Google Play". We built a customized toolset to perform a comprehensive analysis of these apps. We explore the range of mechanisms used by mHealth apps to monitor users' activities, such as photos, text messages, and live microphone access, mainly through the injection of suspicious third-party libraries. In addition, we uncover the use of obfuscation methods employed by suspicious mHealth apps to hide their malicious codes. As mHealth apps are used by a large number of customers worldwide, we argue that patients, clinicians, technology developers, and policy-makers alike should be conscious of the hidden risks involved and weigh them carefully against the benefits.

**Keywords:** mobile health apps · google play · privacy · security

## 1 Introduction

With the steady growth in the population's access to smartphone devices, we have witnessed an explosion of mobile applications (in short, apps) available through various online marketplaces. As of late 2023, approximately 2.43 million apps [57] are available on Google Play alone. Breaking these by category, we note two popular, mutually exclusive categories of Medical and Health & Fitness apps. mHealth apps, these encompass a range of functions, from chronic condition management and symptom checkers to step/calorie counters and period trackers [32]. Reflecting the growth of this app segment, recent guidelines from the U.S. Food and Drug Administration (FDA) formalised the use of mHealth apps for healthcare and recommended considering those providing aid to patients or clinicians as medical devices [20].

As a result of recent advances in integrating new technologies, mobile phones are equipped with many useful sensors, which enable mHealth apps to offer a wide range of features and functionalities, such as recording users' health-related information and seamlessly monitoring users' behaviors and activities. Examples of such activities are weight, smoking or drinking trackers. Another class of such apps is used to contact your doctor, book appointments, vaccinations, medication and get e-prescriptions [49]. Moreover, health-related information collected and saved by these applications is of sensitive nature, and the security and privacy of health-related data are of particular importance [48].

mHealth apps by design track, manage and store the health data of users [55]. Mobile devices and apps used in health-related practice allow different forms of security and privacy threats [48] and dangers such as decentralised data storage systems, unwanted access to all the data at times and not enough regulations etc. So, several security and privacy challenges and relevant requirements need to be addressed [43]. In this study, we conducted the first large-scale analysis of suspicious mHealth apps available on Google Play with the goal of attributing the malicious behaviour, especially the behaviour related to user information harvesting and sharing, to the third party.

We developed custom-built test suites to analyze the source code and app's behaviour during the runtime of 381 suspicious mHealth apps on Google Play. Our analysis highlights a range of security and privacy audits from the characterisation of the malware family, attribution of malicious behaviour in mHealth apps that leads us to the finding of malicious third-party library and Online App Generator involvement from the perspective of the mHealth app's user. Our main findings are listed below:

- 75 (19.68%) of suspicious mHealth apps embed modified or malicious third-party libraries, including 14 apps detected to obfuscate their libraries.
- 114 (29.92%) suspicious mHealth developers conceal the malicious code inside of the apps built on the Online App Generator framework.
- 335 (88%) suspicious mHealth invoking methods to harvest user's information to be sent to third-party servers.
- 50 (13.12%) suspicious mHealth embedding library illegally harvested users' information through legitimate libraries such as Google and Facebook.
- 88 (23.09%) suspicious mHealth currently available and detected malicious by VirusTotal.

We believe this work further sharpens the understanding of suspicious mHealth apps, providing guidance for phone operating vendors and regulators in their efforts to undermine the use and accessibility of such applications.

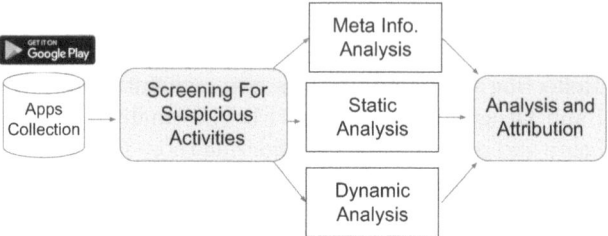

**Fig. 1.** Overview of our methodology for collecting and analysis suspicious mHealth apps on Google Play. Our analysis pipeline consists of three different types of analysis (meta info, static, and dynamic) to audit suspicious activities in the mHealth apps.

## 2   Overview of Mobile Health Application

The landscape of health-related apps is vast and comes with various advantages and disadvantages. In this section, we look at the state-of-the-art health applications available on Google Play.

**Apps for Doctors and Physicians.** This is a class of highly sophisticated applications that are not necessarily free. Nurses and health practitioners use these apps for drug referencing tools, clinical decision support tools, centralized health record system access, access to medical information materials, and updating and sharing patient records [10].

**Disease Specific Applications.** These mobile apps target specific health needs, such as "Eye Handbook" for eye care, "Outbreaks Near Me" for tracking disease outbreaks etc. [30,45].

**Applications for the General Public.** The most common types of mHealth apps are patient-centered apps. These applications are capable of performing comparatively trivial but a wide range of functions, helping consumers or users with managing exercise, keeping a record of how much a person walks, sleeps, or drinks water, managing chronic disease, weight, and smoking [50].

## 3   Data and Analysis Methodology

**Collecting mHealth Apps from Google Play.** Google Play does not provide a complete list of mHealth apps, and its search functionality does not yield all available apps. To address this, we developed a crawler that interacted directly with the store's interface. Starting from the top 100 apps in the Medical and Health & Fitness categories, the crawler systematically searched through other apps considered similar by Google Play (i.e., apps presented in the 'Similar apps' section). For each app, the crawler collected metadata including app category and price, availability locations, app description, number of installs, developer information, user reviews, and app rating.

Overall, we discovered 15,893 unique mHealth apps on the Google Play store as of Jan 1, 2022. Next, we use Raccoon [11] to download the APKs of the corresponding apps, which are then scanned with VirusTotal (VT) [62], as explained further in the following.

**Scanning mHealth apps with VirusTotal.** To identify suspicious mHealth apps, we inspected the APKs using the VirusTotal public API, which aggregates the scanning capabilities of over 70 antivirus tools. For each analyzed app, we obtained the malware label and several malware positives showing the class of malware, such as trojan or adware, and the agreement among the antivirus tools in classifying the app as malware. VirusTotal has been commonly used to detect malicious apps, executables, software, and domains [27–29,33]. As each of VirusTotal's antivirus tools may produce false positives, we computed the aggregate AV-Rank metric, i.e., the number of tools that flagged an APK as malicious, with the maximal score being 70. To minimize the occurrence of false positives and obtain a clear indication of malicious activity, we restricted our further analyses to apps having an AV-Rank $\geq 2$, in agreement with previous studies on Android app malware [7,29].

For each analysed mHealth app, VIRUSTOTAL generates a report that highlights whether any given AV tool has detected an app as malicious with a detection label. We aggregate labels for each mHealth app and leverage the [36,51] and EUPHONY, [19,26] to identify the types and families of malware present in its source code.

The results from VIRUSTOTAL revealed a number of apps that are exceptionally malicious in nature. Of the 381 apps analysed, 130 (34.2%) have an *AV-rank* $\geq 2$ The detection labels from VIRUSTOTAL showed that the apps consist of five main types of malware. Adware was detected in 45% (172) of the apps, followed by Trojan in 25% (97). Riskware, Malware, and Grayware combined were found in a total of 9% (34) of the apps. The remainder of the apps were either in an undefined category or returned a vague and undeterminable label from VIRUSTOTAL. Table 1 lists the Top 10 *suspicious* mHealth apps based on their respective *AV-rank*. We then use the scanning results to analyze the capabilities (explained below) and behavior of the 381 mHealth apps.

**Table 1.** List of *Suspicious* mHealth apps with *AV-rank* $\geq 18$.

| App Title | AV-rank | Installs | Rating |
|---|---|---|---|
| Urdu Best Totkays | 27 | 10,000+ | 3.8 |
| EEMCQ | 22 | 100+ | N/A |
| Nursing Care Plans List | 20 | 5,000+ | 4.6 |
| Nursing Diagnosis and Care Plans FREE | 20 | 10,000+ | 4.4 |
| Aapak Totkay | 20 | 100,000+ | 3.8 |
| Mental Health and Psychiatric Nursing Care Plans | 19 | 1,000+ | 4.1 |
| Fit Bites | 19 | 10,000+ | 4.1 |
| YOGA FOR DIABETES | 18 | 10,000+ | 3.4 |
| TritionRx: Tube Feeding | 18 | 1,000+ | 3.6 |

**Static Analysis.** We analyze the source code for each suspicious mHealth app using our custom-built toolset, focusing on sensitive permission requests and the presence of tracking libraries. The APKs are decompiled using `Apktool` [6], which converts Dalvik bytecode into Java bytecode and transforms `.dex` and `classes.dex` files into `.smali` using a smali disassembler. We access and parse the `AndroidManifest.xml` file to extract app permissions and services by examining the `uses-permission` and `service` tags.

We analyze the extracted permissions for potential illegitimate requests. While mHealth apps often require sensitive permissions to function effectively, permissions like `ACCESS_COARSE_LOCATION` and `ACCESS_FINE_LOCATION` may be appropriate in these apps to enhance step counting or pedometer accuracy, even though they might be questionable in non-mHealth apps. The permissions of the top 20 benign mHealth apps from Google Play's top 10 *Health & Fitness* and top 10 *Medical* apps are analyzed to determine if the requested permissions are due to malicious behavior or legitimate mHealth functionality. Different mHealth apps may require various dangerous permissions. For comparative analysis, suspicious mHealth apps are divided into *Health & Fitness* and *Medical* categories. To flag apps with potentially dangerous behaviors, the permissions sought by *suspicious* mHealth apps are compared to those typically requested by malicious apps [17].

To determine if apps' requested permissions are necessary, we map each app's permission to Android. To this end, we leverage method-to-permission mappings techniques proposed by PSCOUT [9] and Johnson et al. [31]. In particular, we examine the `smali` files to identify which calls launch permission-protected Android API calls, deeming any permissions not in the API calls as excessive. This helps determine which suspicious mHealth apps request necessary permissions and which request excessive ones. Once the API calls are mapped to the apps' permissions, we manually check their origin, disclosing whether the permissions are requested by the app itself or an embedded third-party library. Lastly, we establish a dictionary of malicious signatures, including malware domain URLs and known malware signatures [8], to detect the origin of suspicious app behavior by searching for malware signature calls or related methods.

`Apktool` expands third-party libraries in the apps, while Python's `os.walk` function extracts libraries and subdirectories. Apps with multiple `classes.dex` files are expanded into distinct directory trees, which are then traversed to extract third-party libraries. After collecting the libraries, they are compared to a dictionary of tracking libraries compiled from prior research [29]. The functioning of any libraries not listed in the dictionary was determined by manually analysing and researching them. Libraries identified as malicious or unknown were flagged as *suspicious* and their functionality was further investigated.

**Dynamic Analysis.** To perform dynamic analysis on the apps, we execute them in an observable environment. Android Studio supports virtual Android phones for this purpose. Most of the trials used a virtual Google Pixel running Android OS 8.0. However, due to varying app requirements, some were run on older Android phones and versions of Android OS. For behaviours to be triggered in the apps, their activities and components must be interacted with. To automate this procedure and increase the number of interactions, the input generator MONKEYRUNNER [41] was utilized. Moreover, `mitmproxy` (an interactive HTTPS proxy) [40] was used to monitor and record the content of each request. In particular, we analyze the content of POST requests as they are used to exfiltrate data to external servers. We examine POST requests to ascertain the exact data communicated between a given analyzed app and its external servers. We also examine whether the analyzed applications encrypt communications via services like HTTPS to protect against in-path attacks.

This investigation focused on whether apps communicated with malicious domains and what information was shared with third-party domains. The network packets were decoded in order to obtain the requested URLs and domains. Using VIRUSTOTAL's URL scanner, the security of each domain was evaluated to identify if apps transmitted or received data from malicious domains.

**Metadata Analysis.** We leverage metadata that we collected from the Google Play store to characterize the behaviors of suspicious mHeath apps. In particular, for each suspicious mHealth app, our crawler collects metadata, including name, description, version, category, size, latest update date, rating, number of ratings and installs, minimum Android version, and developer details. Using the app's description, we leverage CoreNLP (a natural language processing tool) [38] to determine the main declared functionality of the app on Google Play. Moreover, we use app's average rating and the number of installs to characterize the popularity of apps on Google Play. We also use user reviews text to characterize users' perceptions of suspicious mHealth apps.

# 4  Characterizing Malware Families

In this section, we characterize the malicious code presence in the analysed mHealth apps. First, we identify and classify the malware family of each suspicious mHealth app. Since the VirusTotal returns information based on each provider's standard, we then aggregate the malware families and types based on the machine learning aggregator for the malware family conducted by [36,51] and EUPHONY [19,26]. To increase the confidence of malicious behaviour, we only considered apps with an AV-rank $\geq 5$ in our analysis. The results for the malware family and type classification are provided in the Table 2.

Table 2 shows that the malware type is dominated by adware and Trojan. Antivirus tools in the VirusTotal report label with the string "a variant of" for a particular family name, indicating that the malware is modifying an original or a legit code or library. Our other result found that several malware family names returned by VirusTotal replicate the original or legit library and have the following characteristics.

**Airpush:** "A variant of Airpush" malware is leveraging the legitimate Airpush notification library, originally used for app monetization, by modifying it to display excessive ads. During runtime, it loads the `libjiagu-1004670200` dynamic library to harvest user location, device type, MAC address, and network operator information. It also sends the Android ID for ad monetization. Additionally,

Table 2. Malware families detected in *Suspicious* mHealth apps

| Family | Type | # of Apps | App Example | # of Install | AV Rank |
|---|---|---|---|---|---|
| Airpush | Adware | 77 | Uses for Coconut Oil | 100,000+ | 16 |
| Leadbolt | Adware | 8 | Aapak Totkay | 100,000+ | 20 |
| Revmob | Adware | 5 | Sleep Analyzer | 100,000+ | 13 |
| Autoins | Trojan | 4 | Simvalley PhoneWatch | 100,000+ | 8 |
| AppsGeyser | Adware | 2 | Clickpharmacy | - | 13 |
| SmsReg | Trojan | 2 | Madarsho | 50,000+ | 10 |
| Viser | Adware | 1 | Urdu Best Totkays | 10,000+ | 27 |
| Buzztouch | Trojan | 1 | EEMCQ | 100+ | 22 |

it taints temporary database transactions in `webview.db-journal`, indicating the use of an SQLite database in Webview. To protect its binary, the malware obfuscates its library and uses customized names, but analysis reveals them as obfuscated versions of the legitimate advertising library.

**Leadbolt:** Similar to Airpush, Leadbolt invokes geographical tagging methods such as `getCountry()`, `getLongitude()`, and `getLatitude()` enabled by the `ACCESS_FINE_LOCATION` permission. Additionally, Leadbolt requests access to device logs and executes shell scripts to harvest CPU frequency information. A tainted temporary SQLite transaction is found as a `ua.db-journal` file in the app's directory. As confirmed by [64], this malware can take over the device's display. Based on our observations and VirusTotal results, the malware's name resembles the Leadbolt monetizing library provided by [34], suggesting it may impersonate or modify the original library.

**Appsgeyser:** Originally, AppsGeyser is an Online App Generator (OAG) that allows non-programmers to create mobile apps [44]. However, in this study, we observed that a suspicious mHealth app developer has modified the original OAG platform for malicious activities. This variant of Appsgeyser malware is detected by Microsoft, ESET, and Quick-Heal antivirus engines, while NANO and Avira detect it as a Potentially Unwanted Application (PUA) or FakeApps variant. We found this malware injected into two apps, with network traffic analysis revealing communication with five different malicious domains and POST requests to domains like "adaranth.com," sharing device screen dimensions, country code, and geographic location.

**Revmob:** It is a Brazilian-based mobile ad network company that provided a service library for app monetization but is no longer supported due to operational issues. We traced the online code repository and found several GitHub repositories related to Revmob ad monetization library. We suspect that five suspicious mHealth apps contained Revmob malware, having duplicated and modified the library for use in their applications. Fortiguard labeled this malicious library as "adware" because it displays advertising content to users, typically as pop-up ads that take over the Android display without user consent [22].

**Autoins:** This malware was found in 4 suspicious mHealth apps and detected by eight antivirus engines. However, we could not find more detailed information about this malware from each antivirus repository. The eight antiviruses only mention that Autoins is a Trojan-type malware. Interestingly, we found several reports in [15,61] revealing that the Autoins variant was found in pre-installed apps on Android devices manufactured in East Asia and Europe. This trojan variant is an auto-updater known as `Android/PUP.Riskware.Autoins.Redstone`.

**SMSreg:** Fortiguard classifies this malware as a Trojan [21], while Microsoft flags it as a Potentially Unwanted Application (PUA) [39], and other engines mark it as Grayware or Riskware [18]. The debate continues on whether this library constitutes malware. Discussions on the Malwarebyte forum indicate that SMSreg is used for auto registration and billing via SMS, with some apps using it being whitelisted by Malwarebytes [37].

**Viser:** The app injected by Viser family malware requests six dangerous permissions, including `ACCESS_COARSE_LOCATION`, `ACCESS_FINE_LOCATION`, and `READ_PHONE_STATE`. The obfuscated folder name is found and contains *Vserv Mobi* sub-directory. The API call analysis shows that *Vserv Mobi* invokes numerous methods, including SMS-related activities and obtaining the device's exact coordinates, Device Type, ID, and MAC Address. Additional calls were found to invoke the `DownloadManager` of the `android.app` API to dynamically fetch additional app components. The network traffic analysis found multiple requests to the "vserv.mobi" domain and shared the user's Time Zone, Latitude, Longitude, Screen Dimensions, Advertising ID, Serial Number, and IMEI.

**Buzztouch:** Like AppsGeyser, Buzztouch is an Online App Generator (OAG). However, in this study, we found that a suspicious mHealth app containing Buzztouch malware was crafted using the Buzztouch OAG. Besides the *Facebook* third-party library, this app only included a main directory called *v1_4* with a sub-directory *eemcq*, matching the app's ID, indicating no embedded Buzztouch plugin library. Analysis of the app's API calls revealed that the *v1_4* directory invokes numerous calls to harvest device coordinates, Last Known Location, Device ID, Phone Number, and Serial Number. Further analysis showed that the library uses the `java.net` API to invoke the `openConnection()` method, sending an HTTP request to "www.buzztouch.com" with the device's ID, brand, model, and location details in the query.

## 5   Suspicious Behaviour Attribution

In this section, we leverage our analysis (cf. § 3) of the source code of each suspicious mHealth app to audit and attribute any suspicious behaviour. In particular, we report on the potential misuse of apps' capabilities exhibited by requested permissions and the integration of third-party libraries. We also present our analysis of suspicious mHealth apps piggybacking online app generators to generate malware at low development costs rapidly. We also elaborate on apps' abilities to harvest and exfiltrate users' sensitive health-related data to external servers and the mechanisms employed to hide their potentially suspicious behaviours. Finally, we present byte entropy analysis to validate the injection and integration of malware in the source.

### 5.1   Misusing Permissions for Potential Exploits

Due to the significant number of dangerous permissions requested by both the *suspicious* and benign mHealth apps, determining an app as *malicious* solely based on the dangerous permissions it requests was not feasible. As such, the permissions of *suspicious* apps were compared with permissions that are commonly found in malware. This also revealed which permissions have the potential for misuse. The apps can execute malicious code silently or take over the entire phone screen with permissions granted.

**Table 3.** Overview of permissions potentially misused by *suspicious* mHealth apps.

| Type | Name | # of Apps | Possible misuse |
|------|------|-----------|-----------------|
| *Dangerous* | WRITE_EXTERNAL_STORAGE | 244 | Store malicious data |
| | READ_PHONE_STATE | 129 | Tracking user devices |
| | CALL_PHONE | 40 | Make phone call without permission |
| *Normal* | INTERNET | 370 | Download malicious scripts |
| | WAKE_LOCK | 239 | Run malicious code continuously |
| | VIBRATE | 120 | Disable vibrator and notifications |
| | RECEIVE_BOOT_COMPLETED | 116 | Execute malicious code when booted |
| | GET_TASKS | 48 | Monitor and discover private info |
| *Signature* | SYSTEM_ALERT_WINDOW | 31 | Display ads over other apps |
| | READ_LOGS | 20 | Access sensitive data |

### 5.2   Abusing Third-Party Libraries Privilege

Guided by the results of the malware characterization in Sect. 4, we examined the mHealth apps directory more closely. We found similarities between names of the malware families and several popular commercial advertisement libraries used to monetize mobile apps, such as Revmob and Airpush. However, there were inconsistencies between the use of these advertisement libraries and VirusTotal's findings. For instance, we discovered that 27 mHealth apps embed Revmob libraries (see Table 4), but VirusTotal detected this malware in only five apps (see Table 2). This suggests that the five infected applications resulted from modifications of legitimate Revmob library. Further research revealed that the Revmob library is publicly available on GitHub,[1] making it easy to modify.

Another indication supporting our suspicion that mHealth apps modify legitimate libraries is the adoption of the Airpush library. Among the 77 apps containing the Airpush malware family, 16 were detected by more than ten antivirus engines. Detailed observation revealed that these 16 apps were obfuscated by renaming Smali files to shorter names such as `a.smali`, `a$1.smali`, `b.smali`, etc.. Despite unique names, analysis of their method headers and class structures indicated they were obfuscated versions of the same advertising library. Further analysis uncovered numerous method calls related to Airpush, including `getAirPushAppId()`, and URL constructions for the "ads.airpush.com" domain. Network traffic analysis showed frequent GET requests to "apportal.airpush.com." Additionally, ten apps shared critical device and user data with the "api.airpush.com" and "www.pushnotificationsender.com" domains. This data included the device's brand, model, IMEI, time zone, locale, country, and exact latitude and longitude.

**Table 4.** 3rd-party libraries cause suspicious behaviours (left) and Online App Generator (right) in *Suspicious* mHealth apps, ordered by number of apps injected.

| Modified Third-party Library | | | Online App Generator (OAG) | | |
|---|---|---|---|---|---|
| Name | #of Apps(%) | AV Rank | Name | #of Apps(%) | AV Rank |
| Revmob | 27 (7.07%) | 1 to 10 | Seattleclouds | 65 (17.06%) | 1 to 16 |
| Umeng | 16 (4.19%) | 1 to 4 | Appinventor | 25 (6.56%) | 1 to 16 |
| Airpush | 16 (4.19%) | 1 to 10 | AppsVision | 9 (2.36%) | 11 to 17 |
| Leadbolt | 8 (2.09%) | 1 to 10 | Mobincube | 9 (2.36%) | 1 |
| WQMobile | 2 (0.52%) | 14 | AppsGeyser | 6 (1.57%) | 1 to 10 |
| Qihoo | 2 (0.52%) | 16 | Buzztouch | 1 (0.26%) | 22 |
| Vserv Mobi | 1 (0.26%) | 27 | | | |
| Rever | 1 (0.26%) | 9 | | | |
| Gmobi | 1 (0.26%) | 8 | | | |
| **Total** | **75 (19.68%)** | | **Total** | **114 (29.92%)** | |

Originally, *Airpush* (rebrand into *Airnow*) is a legitimate advertising platform that assists Nissan, Walmart, KFC, and Huawei with advertising [3]. We believe that the suspicious mHealth developers have abused this library to gain the privilege of push notifications owned by this library, to excessively loading advertisement content to increase the monetization revenue of the apps.

Except for the `Qihoo` library, Table 4 shows all modified third-party libraries categorized as advertisement or analytics-supporting advertisement libraries.

---

[1] https://gist.github.com/revmob-sdk/3383267.

Qihoo is an internet security company that provides various protection services, including antivirus, binary protection, and security plugins for web and mobile applications [14,56]. Our API calls analysis revealed that the Qihoo library dynamically loads an additional library called Jiagu, which invokes the chmod native command on a file in the Jiagu library. This command changes the access permissions of file system objects to launch the Jiagu Packer platform. This finding aligns with the results from APKiD in Sub-section 5.6, where two mHealth apps were found to embed Packer to protect their binary files.

### 5.3    Piggybacking Online App Generators (OAGs)

During static analysis, we observe a particular naming pattern on several mHealth apps. Our further research find that the applications are created using Online App Generators (OAGs) or Online App Builders. The OAGs provide an online platform for the end-user with low-code to non-code skills to create their mobile apps [44]. An OAG provides various advantages, including support for multiple platforms so that the apps can run on iOS or Android, support for different monetizing components, and even the publishing pipeline.

To observe the existence of OAG used to create suspicious mHealth apps, we then conduct OAG fingerprinting through a specific indicator. Several platforms, such as Appsvision and Mobincube can be easily identified from the Package ID due to the package naming convention. While the others, such as Seattlecloud and Appsgeyser required more effort of decompilation and running through the app's directories. The result of OAG fingerprinting in Table 4 shows that Seattlecloud is dominating the OAG usage to build suspicious mHealth apps with 65 apps, followed by Appinventor with 25 apps.

Research in [44] discovered that OAG platforms are vulnerable to specific attacks, including reconfiguration and infrastructure attacks. In this study, we found real cases of how OAG platforms failed to protect their products, allowing them to be used for malicious activities. Table 4 shows that at least 114 suspicious mHealth apps leverage OAG platforms to conceal malicious code. We believe this malicious behavior is not inherited from the OAG platform, as each app exhibits non-uniform behavior. For example, tracing the existence of Appsvision, we found that at least 485 mHealth apps were built on this platform, but only nine were detected to contain malware by VirusTotal.

Moreover, the AV-rank of apps developed by the same platform also shows various numbers, indicating the non-uniformity of mHealth malicious behaviour. Another case of customized malicious behaviour of OAG-based apps is also shown by suspicious mHealth apps built on AppsGeyser, where only two apps (Table 2) were detected to contain Appsgeyser malware by VirusTotal out of 6 suspicious mHealth apps (Table 4) developed on the Appsgeyser OAG platform. In addition, we found that only 2 out of 65 apps leveraging Seattlecloud downgraded their connection protocol to plain HTTP, indicating that the flaw was not inherited from the original OAG platform.

Since the Android OS requires all applications to be packaged as APK files, piggybacking malware code into OAG platforms becomes more feasible. OAG platforms allow malware developers to package applications without developing them from scratch, as malicious code typically constitutes only a small part of the entire application package.

### 5.4  Information Harvesting and Sharing

Based on our methods to permission mapping (cf. § 5.1), we observe that suspicious mHealth apps massively harvested user and device information. As shown in Table 5, 88% (335) of mHealth apps invoke `getPhoneType()`, `getDeviceId()`, `getNetworkOperatorName()` and `getNetworkCountryIso()` methods under the `TelephonyManager` class to request such information through `android.telephony` API. We then trace the request's source and found that most of the methods are invoked by third-party libraries, such as Seattleclouds, Pollfish, Tencent, Startapp, Tappx, and Truene, categorized as Targeted Advertising Library by [29].

The harvested information is then sent to the associated third-party library's server. During the dynamic analysis, we found at least 32% (121) of the apps share the information with advertising domains through the use of POST requests. Analysis of the requested content revealed that the app shared information about the device, such as the device type, the screen dimensions, and the country code the phone is set to. Additionally, the exact latitude and longitude of the device were found in the URL query. Although this measurement result is considered to be lower bound due to technical issues such as SSL pinning adoption, this data harvesting and sharing are worrisome.

To check whether the information harvested is also shared with malicious domains, we tested all the domains accessed by mHealth apps against Virus-Total. As a result, we found that 21 apps shared the information with 22 domains flagged as malicious and phishing sites, including `adaranth.com`, `ds-club.ru`, `live.chartboost.com` and `cdn2.editmysite.com`. We also capture the request-response from `ds-club.ru` returned JavaScript which loads an Ad and sets its visibility to *hidden*.

### 5.5  Cross Library Data Harvesting

Due to massive method invocations related to user information harvesting, we were suspicious if the legit third-party library did not just trigger the invocation. Hence, in this study, we also figure out the appearance of third-party libraries that illegally collect users' information from the legit libraries installed on devices such as Facebook and Google. This type of data gathering mechanism is called Cross Library Data Harvesting (XLDH) [63]. This library actively monitors the package manager to find a targeted legit library installed on the device. Those libraries then illegally harvest the user's data by capturing the information flow during the information interchange via API. Due to this illegal and malicious operation, Facebook has taken legal action against the XLDH library provider [63].

**Table 5.** Dominant API calls, methods and class invocation detected in the source codes of suspected mHealth apps.

| API Call | Class | Method | # of Apps |
|---|---|---|---|
| android.media | MediaRecorder | | 107 (28%) |
| | AudioRecord | | 25(7%) |
| android.hardware | SensorManager | | 339 (89%) |
| | Camera | | 307 (81%) |
| android.telephony | TelephonyManager | getPhoneType() | 335 (88%) |
| | | getDeviceId() | 335 (88%) |
| | | getNetworkOperatorName() | 335 (88%) |
| | | getNetworkCountryIso() | 335 (88%) |
| | SmsManager | sendTextMessage() | 45(12%) |
| | | sendMultipartTextMessage() | 45(12%) |
| | PackageManager | getInstalledPackages() | 72(19%) |
| | | getInstalledApplications() | 103(27%) |
| java.util | Locale | getCountry() | 367 (96%) |
| | | getLatitude() | 334(88%) |
| | | getLongitude() | 334(88%) |
| | LocationManager | getLastKnownLocation() | 268(70%) |
| android.accounts | AccountManager | | 199 (52%) |

**Table 6.** Malicious Cross Library Data Harvesting (XLDH) library detected in suspicious mHealth apps.

| XLDH Library | Exfiltrated Data | Exfiltration Endpoints | # of Apps (%) |
|---|---|---|---|
| com.revmob | Facebook AccessToken | https://android.revmob.com | 27(7.08%) |
| com.umeng.socialize | Facebook/Twitter/Dropbox/Kakao/Yixin/Wechat/ QQ/Sina/Alipay/Laiwang/Vk/Line/Linkedin's AccessToken and user data (ID/name/link/photo) | http://plbslog.umeng.com/umpx_share | 6 (1.57%) |
| com.inmobi | Google activity | https://sdkm.w.inmobi.com/user/e.asm | 4 (1.05%) |
| com.appfireworks | goole id, android id | http://api.appfireworks.com/t/ | 3 (0.78%) |
| com.yandex.metrica | Google Advertising id, Android id | https://startup.mobile.yandex.net | 3 (0.78%) |
| cn.sharesdk | Bytedance | http://api.share.mob.com/log4 | 2 (0.52%) |
| com.ad4screen | Facebook appid, AccessToken | http://api.ad4s.local | 2 (0.52%) |
| com.appsgeyser | Google Advertising id, Android id, IMEI, Mac Address | https://ads.aerserv.com/as/sdk/v3/ | 2 (0.52%) |
| com.oneaudience | Facebook id, name, gender, email, link, Twitter user data | https://api.oneaudience.com/api/devices | 1 (0.26%) |
| | | Total | 50 (13.12%) |

Since we were struggling to intercept information flown in HTTPS tunnel and breaking the certificate authority of the SSL pinning mechanism, we traced the appearance of the XLDH library in mHealth apps by relying on previous research of [63]. Table 6 shows that 50 mHealth apps embed the XLDH library in their apps. The trace results of Revmob and Umeng XLDH libraries are aligned with the number of libraries found to be malicious in Table 4. Hence, we believe this XLDH library could be a source of malicious behaviour detected by VirusTotal.

## 5.6   Adopting Evasive and Obfuscation Methods

We determine whether an app uses any means of evading, obscuring, or disrupting the analysis of parties other than the application developers. In fact, malware developers rely on these techniques to evade primary analysis layers of application market stores such as Google Play [13]. The six different types of evasion techniques employed by mHealth apps are shown in Fig. 2. For each application, we use APKiD [12] tool to obtain a list of anti-analysis techniques including "manipulator", "anti-virtual machine", "anti-debug", "anti-disassembly", "obfuscator", and "packer" (cf. Appendix A).

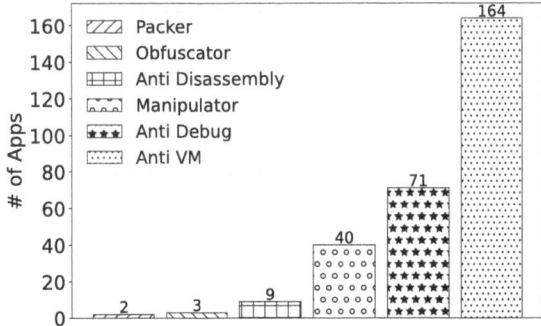

**Fig. 2.** Distribution of protection and hiding mechanims employed by the analysed suspicious mHealth apps.

## 5.7   Byte Entropy Analysis

The EMBER dataset, with nearly 1.1 million Windows PE samples, is a popular benchmark for malware research, using the LIEF framework to extract features like file and header information, imported/exported functions, and byte histograms [5]. Inspired by EMBER, we extend static analysis to APKs as follows:

1. Obtain VDEX and ODEX files by installing APK on Android devices. The VDEX and ODEX files were introduced by Google to optimise running time and boost time for APK apps in the Android environment.
2. Utilise the LIEF framework to extract raw features from VDEX and ODEX files [1].
3. Convert raw features into vectors for automated analysis and classification.

   To categorize samples by Binary Protection Type, we can analyze byte entropy (see Fig. 3). Malware authors often encrypt or compress applications to evade scanners, transforming the application body into random-looking data bytes. Calculating byte data variation in fixed block lengths (e.g., 256 bytes) effectively detects encryption or packer trails. Figure 3 shows that suspicious samples exhibit similar patterns with varying entropy at specific byte positions, confirming that these applications were built using a few common online app builders (see § 5.3). We found that 114 (29.9%) apps had malicious activities added manually after generation, and 14 apps had obfuscated activities, explaining the higher entropy in obfuscation bars.

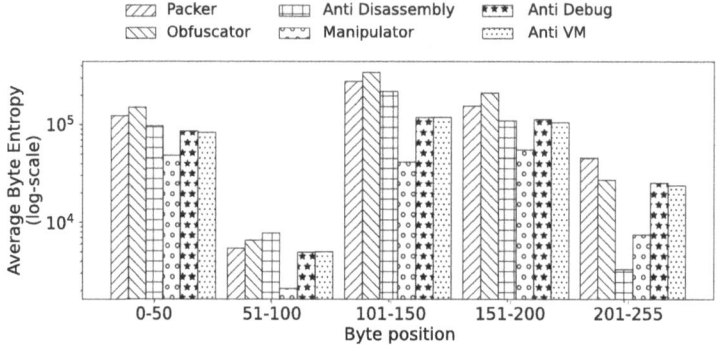

**Fig. 3.** Byte entropy comparison of evasive and obfuscation methods (cf. Appendix A) employed by suspicious mHealth apps.

## 6   Status Quo and User Awareness

**Status Quo.** In June 2022, Google restructured its Play Store, requiring developers to use Android App Bundle (AAB) formats instead of APKs, necessitating the sharing of private signing keys for app generation and integrity checks, enhancing security and remediation [54]. Additionally, Google updated its security and privacy policies, significantly altering the interface and mandating SDK alignment with Play Store policies. Another security measure by Google comes from improving Play's app-integrity tools. Google Play App Signing helps millions of apps on Google Play ensure that app updates can be trusted [35].

After all these security system improvements, we then retraced the existence of malicious mHealth on the Google Play Store. Out of a total of 381 malicious mHealth that we have, we found that 188 malicious apps are still on the Play Store. Then, to see the existence of malicious mHealth apps, we downloaded 188 apps and evaluated them against VirusTotal. As a result, 88 mHealth apps were detected as containing malware, with 16 having an AV-rank of 5 or above. This indicates that the security improvements of the Google Play Store did not detect and remove suspicious mHealth apps from their repository. Table 8 shows the Top-5 malicious mHealth currently on the Google Play Store.

To observe if the malicious behavior was obtained from the prolonged mHealth apps, we then compared the Hashed files of the mHealth apps with mHealth that existed after June 2022 policy updates and also with mHealth

**Table 7.** Sha256 hash comparison among 381 mHealth apps, 188 mHealth that still exist at Google Play (After June 2022 policy updates).

| Suspicious, Found before June 2022 | Apps after June 2022 | | | |
| --- | --- | --- | --- | --- |
| | Found | Updated | Suspicious | # of Apps(%) |
| ✓ | - | - | - | 381 (100%) |
| ✓ | ✗ | - | - | 193 (50.7%) |
| ✓ | ✓ | - | - | 188 (49.3%) |
| ✓ | ✓ | ✓ | - | 140 (36.7%) |
| ✓ | ✓ | ✗ | ✓ | 37 (19.7%) |
| ✓ | ✓ | ✓ | ✓ | 51 (27.1%) |
| ✓ | ✓ | ✓ | ✗ | 89 (47.3%) |

**Table 8.** Top-5 suspicious mHealth apps (# of installs > 1,000) that are still accessible (at time of writing, July 01, 2024) on Google Play. Here AV-rank shows the number of antivirus tools agreeing on flagging an mHealth app as suspicious.

| No | App Title | AV-rank | #of Install |
| --- | --- | --- | --- |
| 1 | Fit Bites [46] | 17 | 10,000+ |
| 2 | Calorie Calculator BMR BMI ads [24] | 14 | 1,000+ |
| 3 | BMI Calculator [23] | 13 | 1,000+ |
| 4 | 1byone Health [2] | 6 | 100,000+ |
| 5 | BodyMonitor [60] | 2 | 100,000+ |

that was still detected as malicious by VirusTotal. Table 7 lists that 140 of the 188 apps are new apps and the remaining 48 apps are apps that have not been updated. Even though they have been updated, 51 mHealth apps still inherit malicious behaviour from the previous version, while the remaining 89 have been whitelisted by VirusTotal.

**User Awareness** Analysis of the user awareness with respect to the presence of malware in the apps found that only 4% (15) of the apps have negative reviews, which correlates to the type of malware present in the apps. In 14 of these apps, the negative reviews relate to excessive advertising hindering the functionality of the app. Only one app has a review recognising a Trojan found through the use of antivirus software.

## 7 Related Works

Some research related to mobile health apps security and privacy analysis has been done previously, including a study conducted by [16], that focuses on the establishment of an overview of mHealth apps offered on iOS and Android with a particular focus on potential damage to users through information security and privacy infringements. Müthing et al., [42] conducted research that focused on identifying relevant security concerns on the server side of mHealth apps and comparing the servers used by mHealth apps with servers used in all domains. [59] conducted the first large-scale analysis of mobile health (mHealth) apps available on Google Play to provide a comprehensive view of mHealth apps' security features and gauge the associated risks for mHealth users and their data. While [58] investigated whether and what user data is collected by mHealth apps, characterised the privacy conduct of all the available mHealth apps on Google Play, and gauged the associated risks to privacy. [4] focuses on reviewing and analysing privacy policies, data sharing, and security policies of women's mHealth apps on the Apple Store and Google Play. [53] researched security and privacy analysis of apps that provide tracking and checking symptoms of health conditions or diseases through mobile devices. However, none of the mentioned research on the characterization and attribution of malicious behavior appears on mobile health apps, which becomes our focus in this study.

## 8    Discussion and Responsible Disclosure

Several studies have conducted security and privacy measurements of mHealth apps using standard parameters. However, none of these studies conducted an audit and attribution of the causes of maliciousness from mHealth apps. Our interesting finding begins when we characterize the malware found by VirusTotal, where there is a similarity in name between the malware family and the commercial advertising library that is circulated widely. Based on this fact, we observed further and found that 19.7% of the suspicious mHealth developers had abused the advertising library to gain privilege and massively invoked advertising content in order to monetize their apps. This coherent is considering that all of the mHealth apps in our corpus are free and require income for maintenance.

We also found a pattern in packages and directories naming based on the third-party libraries' analysis. Our further research found that 29.9% suspicious mHealth apps were built using the Online App Generator (OAG). This framework is a medium for suspicious mHealth app developers to insert malicious code, which is only a small proportion of the total code. This is supported by the results of the entropy measurement at the byte level code, where we did not find a significant delta among mHealth apps' entropy that embeds different binary protectors. This small entropy is caused by a small delta of code, considering that the malicious code is only a small part of the total APK package.

Our analysis of API calls and runtime revealed extensive user information being sent to third-party servers, with 20 mHealth apps communicating with domains flagged as malicious. Alarmingly, users appear to have a low level of awareness of this data harvesting, as indicated by the apps' average rating of above three, suggesting users maintain a positive perception of these suspicious mHealth apps. We suspect that users are either unaware of their data being harvested or indifferent to it. From a developer's perspective, many may be unaware that their apps are detected as malicious, especially since many apps are developed using OAGs and embed third-party libraries. Therefore, we believe this study highlights the severe problems that suspicious mHealth apps pose for both users and developers, offering a new perspective on the issue.

**Responsible Disclosure.** We contacted and shared our findings with the app developers of apps requesting sensitive permissions, apps that users negatively review, and apps with embedded third-party tracking libraries. We also contacted app developers, which our tests revealed as possibly containing malware in their APKs. We have disclosed and confirmed our findings to the mHealth developers mentioned in this paper. We have not yet received any responses from the contacted developers. We will update our paper according to the responses and the confirmations of the findings from the developers.

## 9    Conclusion

Despite being better aligned with security best practices than non-mHealth apps, suspicious mHealth apps are still accessible on Google Play and can potentially expose consumers to a wide range of security issues. App users, clinicians, technology developers, and policy-makers alike should be cognizant of the uncovered security issues and weigh them carefully against the benefits of mHealth apps. To this end, we performed the first comprehensive and in-depth analysis of mechanisms used by suspicious mHealth apps. This is the first study to conduct characterization and attribution of the mHealth apps' malicious behavior on the Google Play Store. The study revealed several types of malicious apps, including those that massively collect and share user information with third-party servers; apps that use modified and malicious libraries; and apps that embed libraries that illegally harvest user information from legit libraries. We believe that the toolset developed in this, in particular, the extraction of EMBER-like features, is a promising alternative way to complement the literature in analyzing Android applications. We aim to release our advanced toolset upon publication and share data with the research community.

## A    Evasive and Obfuscation Methods

**Manipulator.** We found that 40 (10.5%) apps contain a manipulator, as their Dalvik Executable (.dex) files were developed using the dexmerge compiler. The APKiD tool flags apps as containing a manipulator if the original .dex files are modified with libraries like dexmerge or created from reverse-engineered source code using dexlib [52].

**Anti Virtual Machine.** We detected 164 (43.04%) apps using anti-virtual machine (anti-vm) analysis to detect execution on an emulator or real device, hindering reverse-engineering. This is typically done by analyzing the *build.prop* file for Build API methods or checking fixed API values in the *Telephony manager* for Android emulators [47].

**Anti Debug.** We found 71 (18.63%) apps using anti-debugging techniques to disrupt reverse engineering, ensuring apps do not run under or change behavior in debugger mode. Identified by checking the *debuggable flag* in *ApplicationInfo* or using *ptrace* in Linux system calls, all mHealth apps activated the debug flag of `Debug.isDebuggerConnected()` check [47].

**Obfuscator.** App developers commonly use obfuscators to protect intellectual property and prevent reverse engineering. In this study, we found that APKID detected 3 (0.78%) apps leveraging obfuscator tools, where 2 of them were obfuscated using Low-Level Virtual Machine Tools (LLVM) such as Clang, and the rest are unidentified.

**Anti Disassembly.** Anti-disassembly techniques prevent reverse engineers from converting byte-code into higher-level code like Java or Smali. We found 9 (2.3%) apps using these techniques, often resulting in "Illegal class name" errors during decompilation.

**Packer.** In this research, we found that 2 (0.5%) mHealth apps leverage this technique.

Based on our analysis and the self-protection behavior claim in [25], we found that less than 50% of suspicious mHealth apps adopt binary protection mechanisms other than anti-VM. We suspect developers use mHealth apps to launch more ad-related libraries, as aligned with VirusTotal's detection of malicious libraries in Table 2. Note that APKId's results, particularly for obfuscation, might be lower-bound due to simple renaming techniques that evade its detection.

# References

1. Lief documentation - android formats and the API to use them. https://lief-project.github.io/doc/latest/tutorials/10_android_formats.html
2. 1byone: 1byone health. https://play.google.com/store/apps/details?id=com.quhwa.health
3. Airnow. https://airnowmonetization.com
4. Alfawzan, N., Christen, M., Spitale, G., Biller-Andorno, N.: Privacy, data sharing, and data security policies of women's mhealth apps: scoping review and content analysis. JMIR Mhealth Uhealth **10**(5), e33735 (2022). https://mhealth.jmir.org/2022/5/e33735
5. Anderson, H.S., Roth, P.: Ember: an open dataset for training static PE malware machine learning models (2018). arXiv preprint arXiv:1804.04637
6. Apktool. https://ibotpeaches.github.io/Apktool/
7. Arp, D., Spreitzenbarth, M., Hubner, M., Gascon, H., Rieck, K., Siemens, C.: Drebin: effective and explainable detection of android malware in your pocket. In: NDSS, vol. 14, pp. 23–26 (2014)
8. Arzt, S., et al.: Flowdroid: precise context, flow, field, object-sensitive and lifecycle-aware taint analysis for android apps. ACM Sigplan Notices **49**(6), 259–269 (2014)
9. Au, K.W.Y., Zhou, Y.F., Huang, Z., Lie, D.: PScout: analyzing the android permission specification. In: Proceedings of the 2012 ACM conference on Computer and communications security, pp. 217–228 (2012)
10. Boulos, M.N.K., Brewer, A.C., Karimkhani, C., Buller, D.B., Dellavalle, R.P.: Mobile medical and health apps: state of the art, concerns, regulatory control and certification. Online J. Public Health Inform. **5**(3), 229 (2014)
11. BouncyCastle: Raccoon – the APK donwloader. https://raccoon.onyxbits.de/

12. Case, J.: rednaga/apkid. https://github.com/rednaga/APKiD
13. Chau, N., Jung, S.: An entropy-based solution for identifying android packers. IEEE Access **7**, 28412–28421 (2019)
14. Chen, C.: Android community worried about presence of "chinese spyware" by qihoo 360 in samsung smartphones and tablets (2020). https://www.privateinternetaccess.com/blog/android-community-worried-about-presence-of-chinese-spyware-by-qihoo-360-in-samsung-smartphones-and-tablets/
15. Collier, N.: Pre-installed auto installer threat found on android mobile devices in Germany (2021). https://www.malwarebytes.com/blog/news/2021/04/pre-installed-auto-installer-threat-found-on-android-mobile-devices-in-germany. Accessed 01 July 2024
16. Dehling, T., Gao, F., Schneider, S., Sunyaev, A.: Exploring the far side of mobile health: information security and privacy of mobile health apps on iOS and android. JMIR Mhealth Uhealth **3**(1), e8 (2015)
17. Duc, N.V., Giang, P.T., Vi, P.M.: Permission analysis for android malware detection. In: The Proceedings of the 7th VAST-AIST Workshop "Research Collaboration: Review and perspective (2015)
18. F-Secure: F-secure -threat description - riskware:android/smsreg (2017). https://www.f-secure.com/sw-desc/riskware_android_smsreg.shtml
19. Fmind: fmind/euphony. https://github.com/fmind/euphony
20. Food, U., Administration, D.: Policy for device software functions and mobile medical applications (2019). https://www.fda.gov/media/80958/download
21. Fortiguard: Fortiguard labs - threat encyclopedia - android/smsreg.zi!tr. https://www.fortiguard.com/encyclopedia/mobile/7294379/android-smsreg-zi-tr (2017)
22. Fortinet: Fortiguard labs - threat encyclopedia - adware/revmob (2021). https://www.fortiguard.com/encyclopedia/mobile/7016460/adware-revmob. Accessed 01 July 2024
23. Grewenig, M.: BMI calculator. https://play.google.com/store/apps/details?id=de.grewe.android.bmi
24. Grewenig, M.: Calorie calculator BMR BMI ads. https://play.google.com/store/apps/details?id=de.grewe.android.caloriecalculatorfree
25. He, R., et al.: Beyond the virus: a first look at coronavirus-themed mobile malware (2020)
26. Hurier, M., et al.: Euphony: harmonious unification of cacophonous anti-virus vendor labels for android malware. In: MSR (2017)
27. Ikram, M., Kaafar, M.A.: A first look at mobile ad-blocking apps. In: NCA, pp. 1–8. IEEE (2017)
28. Ikram, M., Masood, R., Tyson, G., Kaafar, M.A., Loizon, N., Ensafi, R.: The chain of implicit trust: an analysis of the web third-party resources loading. In: The World Wide Web Conference, pp. 2851–2857 (2019)
29. Ikram, M., Vallina-Rodriguez, N., Seneviratne, S., Kaafar, M.A., Paxson, V.: An analysis of the privacy and security risks of android VPN permission-enabled apps. In: Proceedings of the 2016 Internet Measurement Conference, pp. 349–364 (2016)
30. Jenny, J.Y.: Measurement of the knee flexion angle with a smartphone-application is precise and accurate. J. Arthroplasty **28**(5), 784–787 (2013)
31. Johnson, R., Wang, Z., Gagnon, C., Stavrou, A.: Analysis of android applications' permissions. In: 2012 IEEE Sixth International Conference on Software Security and Reliability Companion, pp. 45–46. IEEE (2012)
32. Kay, M., Santos, J., Takane, M.: mhealth: new horizons for health through mobile technologies. World Health Org. **64**(7), 66–71 (2011)

33. Kharraz, A., Robertson, W., Balzarotti, D., Bilge, L., Kirda, E.: Cutting the Gordian knot: a look under the hood of ransomware attacks. In: Almgren, M., Gulisano, V., Maggi, F. (eds.) DIMVA 2015. LNCS, vol. 9148, pp. 3–24. Springer, Cham (2015). https://doi.org/10.1007/978-3-319-20550-2_1

34. Leadbolt: Leadbolt - high performance mobile advertising (2021). https://www.leadboltapps.com/. Accessed 01 July 2024

35. Lukashuk, I.: Google play store changes 2022: what to expect? (2022). https://appradar.com/blog/google-play-store-changes-2022. Accessed August 2022

36. Malicialab: malicialab/AVClass (2020). https://github.com/malicialab/avclass

37. Malwarebyte: Malwarebyte forum - android/pup.riskware.smsreg.wwpa (2019). https://forums.malwarebytes.com/topic/249727-androidpupriskwaresmsreg wwpa/

38. Manning, C.D., Surdeanu, M., Bauer, J., Finkel, J.R., Bethard, S., McClosky, D.: The Stanford CoreNLP natural language processing toolkit. In: Proceedings of 52nd annual meeting of the association for computational linguistics: system demonstrations, pp. 55–60 (2014)

39. Microsoft: Microsoft security intelligence - pua:androidos/smsreg.i!mtb (2021). https://www.microsoft.com/en-us/wdsi/threats/malware-encyclopedia-descriptio n?Name=PUA:AndroidOS/SMSReg.I!MTB&threatId=324027

40. mitmproxy. https://mitmproxy.org

41. MonkeyRunner: monkeyrunner: Android developers. https://developer.android.com/studio/test/monkeyrunner

42. Müthing, J., Brüngel, R., Friedrich, C.M.: Server-focused security assessment of mobile health apps for popular mobile platforms. J. Med. Internet Res. **21**(1), e9818 (2019)

43. Odeh, A., Keshta, I., Aboshgifa, A., Abdelfattah, E.: Privacy and security in mobile health technologies: challenges and concerns. In: CCWC (2022)

44. Oltrogge, M., et al.: The rise of the citizen developer: assessing the security impact of online app generators. In: 2018 IEEE Symposium on Security and Privacy (SP) (2018)

45. O'Neill, S., Brady, R.R.W.: Colorectal smartphone apps: opportunities and risks. Colorectal Dis. **14**(9), e530-4 (2012)

46. Orange, D.: Fit bites. https://play.google.com/store/apps/details?id=com.fit.bites

47. OWASP: Testing anti-debugging detection (mstg-resilience-2) - android anti-reversing defenses. https://mobile-security.gitbook.io/mobile-security-testing-guide/android-testing-guide/0x05j-testing-resiliency-against-reverse-engineering (2020), oWASP Mobile Security Guide. Accessed 18 Jan 2023

48. Papageorgiou, A., Strigkos, M., Politou, E., Alepis, E., Solanas, A., Patsakis, C.: Security and privacy analysis of mobile health applications: the alarming state of practice. IEEE Access **6**, 2169–3536 (2018)

49. Pinder, C., Vermeulen, J., Cowan, B.R., Beale, R.: Digital behaviour change interventions to break and form habits. TOCHI **25**(3), 1–66 (2018)

50. Schap, T.E., Zhu, F., Delp, E.J., Boushey, C.J.: Merging dietary assessment with the adolescent lifestyle. J. Hum. Nutr. Diet. **27**(Suppl 1), 82–88 (2014)

51. Sebastián, M., Rivera, R., Kotzias, P., Caballero, J.: AVCLASS: a tool for massive malware labeling. In: RAID (2016)

52. Security, R.: Detecting pirated and malicious android apps with APKID (2016). https://rednaga.io/2016/07/31/detecting_pirated_and_malicious_android_ apps_with_apkid/

53. Sentana., I.W.B., Ikram., M., Kaafar., M., Berkovsky., S.: Empirical security and privacy analysis of mobile symptom checking apps on google play. In: Proceedings of the 18th International Conference on Security and Cryptography - SECRYPT (2021)

54. Sha, A.: APK vs AAB (android app bundles): everything you need to know!. https://beebom.com/apk-vs-aab/. Accessed 18 June 2024

55. Smahel, D., Elavsky, S., Machackova, H.: Functions of mhealth applications: a user's perspective. HIJ **25**(3), 1065–1075 (2019)

56. Soylentnews.org: Samsung devices allegedly use qihoo 360 spyware to phone home to china (2020). https://www.newsbreak.com/news/1486552211048/samsung-devices-allegedly-use-qihoo-360-spyware-to-phone-home-to-china

57. Statista: Google play store: number of apps 2023. https://www.statista.com/statistics/266210/number-of-available-applications-in-the-google-play-store/

58. Tangari, G., Ikram, M., Ijaz, K., Kaafar, M.A., Berkovsky, S.: Mobile health and privacy: cross sectional study. BMJ **373**, n1248 (2021)

59. Tangari, G., Ikram, M., Sentana, I.W.B., Ijaz, K., Kaafar, M.A., Berkovsky, S.: Analyzing security issues of android mobile health and medical applications. J. Am. Med. Inf. Assoc. **28**(10), 2074–2084 (2021)

60. Technologies, S.: Bodymonitor. https://play.google.com/store/apps/details?id=com.senssun.bodymonitor

61. Townsend, K.: Threat from pre-installed malware on android phones is growing (2020). https://www.securityweek.com/threat-pre-installed-malware-android-phones-growing. Accessed 01 July 2024

62. VirusTotal: https://www.virustotal.com/gui/home/upload

63. Wang, J., et al.: Understanding malicious cross-library data harvesting on android. In: USENIX Security Symposium (2021)

64. Web, D.: Adware.leadbolt.24 technical information (2021). https://vms.drweb.com/virus/?i=24980493&lng=en. Accessed 01 July 2024

# Perceived Privacy Conflicts and Monitoring: A Study of Their Effects on Trust and Data Sharing in Social Networks

Yazan Alahmed[1]($\boxtimes$) iD, Reema Abadla[1] iD, and Mahmoud Khasawneh[2] iD

[1] College of Engineering, Al Ain University, Abu Dhabi, UAE
yazan.alahmed@aau.ac.ae
[2] Department of Computer Engineering, The University of Jordan, Amman 11942, Jordan

**Abstract.** As social networks become increasingly integrated into our digital lives, the tension between their claimed privacy policies and actual monitoring practices has brought about critical concerns about user trust and behaviour. In this paper, the perceived conflict between privacy policies and monitoring practices and its impact on trust in social networks, reputation management, and data-sharing behaviour amongst social network users is reviewed and examined. Through a quantitative study involving an online survey of 152 participants, the research explores the hypothesis that greater perceived conflict between privacy policies and monitoring negatively affects user trust, with potential moderation by reputation management practices. The findings present a weak positive correlation between perceived conflict and trust, which indicates that users may continue to trust social networks despite awareness of monitoring. By highlighting this unexpected revelation and contributing to a deeper understanding of the complex dynamics of user behaviour and trust in the digital age, this study provides valuable insights for researchers and practitioners in social networks and digital privacy.

**Keywords:** Social networks · privacy policies · monitoring · online reputation management · self-censorship · data sharing · trust · quantitative research

## 1 Introduction

Social networks have become an integral part of everyday life at a time when digital traces are just as important as physical ones. They have influenced how we interact as well as how we view online privacy and trust. Although social media platforms like Facebook, Instagram, and Twitter (X currently) present users with never-before-seen social engagement opportunities, they also present serious privacy risks. The recent rise of political censorship on social networks has awoken a strong sense of hesitation and realization of the tension between the privacy policies social networks publicly promote and the reality of platform monitoring practices. More than 85% of people's social networking activities across sixty different counties are monitored on the internet through social media surveillance programs [1]. This perceived conflict raises important questions about how users navigate trust, reputation management, and data sharing in these digital environments.

H. H. Song et al. (Eds.): NSS 2024, LNCS 15564, pp. 254–274, 2025.
https://doi.org/10.1007/978-981-96-3531-3_13

The use of social networks will not decrease any time soon. As indicated in Fig. 1, millions to billions of people use them worldwide. This large-scale utilization only escalates the need to investigate the factors affecting humans' perception of these networks from different aspects. An essential element of consumers' interaction with social networks is trust. Trust in social networks refers to users' belief that the platform will secure their personal information and adhere to its stated privacy regulations, impacting their willingness to participate and disclose data [2]. Users are more inclined to participate actively and provide information when they have confidence that the platform will protect their personal information and will follow its stated privacy standards. Users' confidence, however, may be jeopardized if there appears to be a disconnect between social networks' stated privacy standards and their real methods of data gathering and surveillance. Moreover, users' willingness to reveal sensitive information and how they maintain their online personas may be significantly impacted by this breakdown of trust.

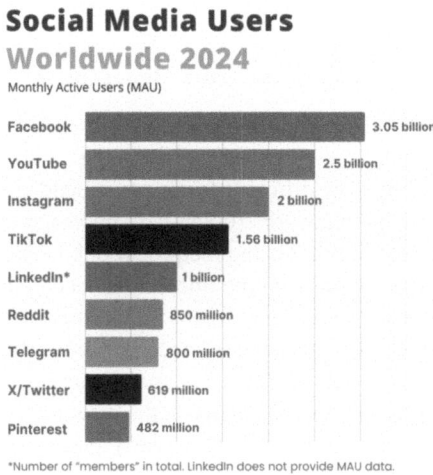

**Fig. 1.** Number of Social Media Users 2024 [5]

Another concept that has emerged and increased profoundly, particularly with the rise of the influencer age, is reputation management. Reputation management in social networks includes actively monitoring and changing how individuals or organizations are regarded by others online, influencing interactions, and maintaining the digital footprint to preserve a positive image [3]. Across all ages, people are becoming more conscious of how their online behavior and information sharing might affect their reputations in both their personal and professional spheres. They could thus take precautions to safeguard their online persona, such as changing privacy preferences, selecting what they post with excessive care, or even self-censoring their thoughts and opinions online, particularly if they fear that the platform or other users may be monitoring them. In 2024 alone, around 60% of social media users carried out modifications to their privacy settings, over 65% think social media businesses should do a better job of communicating their data privacy policies, and around 35% expressed their belief that the security of their data has decreased compared to the previous five years [4].

This study aims to investigate the link between the perceived conflict between the privacy regulations of social networks and the actual monitoring of the platform, focusing on how users' perceptions of this conflict affect their trust, reputation management, and data sharing. The research specifically attempts to test the hypothesis that increased perceived conflict between the privacy policies of social networks and the fact that platforms are monitored is negatively correlated with social network trust, with reputation management practices possibly moderating this relationship. By exploring these dynamics, this study contributes to a better understanding of how privacy concerns and reputation management tactics influence users' interactions with social networks. The findings are intended to give useful insights for both users and social network providers, particularly in the creation of more transparent and trustworthy platforms.

## 2  Literature Review

### 2.1  Perception of Privacy Policies and Trust Management

The perception of privacy policies and their influence on trust management is a crucial area of study, especially about social networks. In [6], the authors present a theoretical framework for understanding how different forms of embeddedness and social capital augmentation in Online Social Networks (OSNs) are impacted by different stages and sources of trust. The concept highlights the reciprocal link between social capital (i.e., resources & advantages users gain from the interactions and connections they have on the network) and trust, with trust serving as both a requirement and an outcome of social capital production in OSNs. A distinction is made between structural embeddedness, which refers to the network's structure (dense or sparse), and relational embeddedness, which refers to the strength of relationships inside the network. In sparse networks with weak ties or relationships, trust is critical in the early phases since it affects whether users would participate with the OSN or not. In this context, seeking out new knowledge and possibilities is critical, as is creating trust. On the other hand, dense networks with strong relationships are more suited for exploitation, as users rely on trust earned from previous experiences to increase their engagement and acquire, albeit possibly repetitive, information. Overall, the author contends that the kind of network structure and the form of ties impact the user's trust-building process and the mechanism of social capital augmentation (i.e., either through exploration of weak ties or exploitation and deepening of already-existing ones). Trust in OSNs is dynamic and context-dependent, influenced by the user's network position, relationship kinds, and mechanism of social capital improvement.

Privacy concerns play a significant role in shaping users' trust and their willingness to engage with online platforms. Detailed research on the usage of social media for e-government services in Pakistan sheds light on these dynamics [7]. The study used variance-based Partial Least Squares Structural Equation Modeling (PLS-SEM) using Smart PLS v.3.2.7 (software) to evaluate empirical data from Pakistani individuals to better understand the variables impacting their confidence in digital services. Key findings indicated that perceived privacy and security are strong determinants of trust. When individuals believe their privacy and data are safe, they are more inclined to trust and interact with e-government services via social media. This trust, in turn, encourages more personal information exchange and participation in government services online. In addition to privacy and security, the study highlights structural assurances, such as guarantees and safety nets given by government agencies, as significant variables in building confidence. These guarantees assist individuals believe that government bodies will follow laws and regulations. Furthermore, the quality of information available on social media platforms has been shown to have a substantial influence on trust, with high-quality, relevant, and easily accessible information increasing engagement with e-government services. The study also found that perceived simplicity of use is important in creating confidence, increasing perceived usefulness, and motivating individuals to participate in e-government services. When consumers believe that accessing social media platforms for e-government services is simple, they are more inclined to trust and value these services, leading to increased participation rates. Another important conclusion of the study is the effect of trust on individuals' willingness to participate in e-government services via social media. The findings indicate that higher levels of trust are directly connected with a greater propensity to use these services. Theoretical contributions are also noted by addressing a gap in the current literature on trust in social media-based e-government services. While earlier research has focused on e-government websites, this study offers new insights into the elements that influence trust in social media platforms. In practice, the findings have significant consequences for government institutions and politicians, particularly in developing nations such as Pakistan. According to the report, by concentrating on increasing privacy, security, information quality, and simplicity of use, government entities may increase public confidence and involvement in social media-based e-government services.

To explore the intersection of privacy concerns and trust management, particularly in the aftermath of privacy violations on social media platforms, [8] studies how corporations such as Facebook seek to restore user confidence following such occurrences by using apologies, an important component of crisis communication. The study takes a mixed-methods approach, integrating quantitative analysis with qualitative findings, and uses statistical estimating techniques to determine the influence of apologetic persuasiveness on user trust and privacy concerns. This work directly relates to the perception of privacy policies, as it examines users' responses to the alignment between an organization's public statements (apologies) and subsequent actions. The study emphasizes that, while apologies might build trust by displaying behavioural integrity, they frequently fail to address fundamental privacy issues, which is critical for understanding how users view trust management tactics. This is consistent with the wider debate in this section on how users' trust in social media platforms is impacted not just by the substance of privacy rules, but also by the perceived alignment between what the platforms promise and deliver. Moreover, the paper's results on the spillover effect, which occurs when one service's breach impacts trust in other linked services, highlight the need of consistent trust management across all elements of a platform's operations (although, such a reaction may be context-dependent and inapplicable to other platforms or scenarios). This is congruent with debates about the significance of comprehensive and consistent privacy rules that successfully manage trust across all aspects of a social media platform's services. While these findings offer insights into user perceptions of trust management strategies post-privacy breaches, enriching discussions on privacy policy effectiveness and user trust in social networks, its primary reliance on the persuasiveness of apologies as a mechanism for trust repair may potentially overlook other important factors like the role of long-term transparency and proactive privacy measures.

Another study involving Facebook users was done in [9] to observe how users' privacy and security perception of the platform impacts their precautionary, careful behavior. It identifies substantial differences in risk perception and preventative measures for a variety of dangers, including information exchange and account access. According to the study, privacy risks connected to information sharing are viewed as the most hazardous, resulting in more frequent cautious activity, whereas hazards related to the control of others' information sharing are perceived as less risky and induce less caution from users. The methods used include a comprehensive investigation of numerous dangers, as well as statistical tests to quantify perceived risk and preventive behaviour. Multi-level analysis was utilized to find predictors of risk perception and precautionary measures, distinguishing between hazard-specific (e.g., data breach-related threats) and subject-specific variables (e.g., individual privacy concerns). Significant determinants of perceived risk include the dread and catastrophic potential of the threat, as well as the length of Facebook sessions. Positive attitudes toward information sharing and perceived voluntariness were found to harm risk perception. In other words, people are more likely to perceive higher risks if they fear the consequences of sharing personal information, especially if they spend a lot of time on Facebook. On the other hand, if they feel good about sharing information and believe they have a choice in doing so, they tend to worry less about potential risks. Overall, the study concludes that perceived risk is a strong predictor of cautious behaviour, with users who perceive higher risk being more inclined to adopt preventative measures. However, feeling in control and spending more time on Facebook were found to be negative predictors of cautious activities. According to the findings, interventions to raise risk awareness should focus on specific dangers, highlight the dread and catastrophic nature of risks, and address the actions of both rookie and experienced users. It also recommends several interventions, such as educational, marketing, and design-based techniques, to enhance Facebook users' security and privacy behaviours.

## 2.2 Impact of Privacy Concerns on Data Sharing

The manner and degree to how much a person shares data on his/her online platforms is heavily influenced by their privacy views and concerns. In [10], the authors look at how contextual variables and privacy concerns influence privacy decisions in three countries: the United States, Korea, and China. The research proposes the term "perceived risk," which refers to users' subjective assessments of the potential negative repercussions of sharing personal information on social networking sites (SNSs). This perceived risk is impacted by a variety of contextual factors, including offline connections, mutual friends, shared college affiliations, and interesting content, which can all help to alleviate users' anxieties about possible privacy breaches. The study also discovers that these contextual elements considerably reduce perceived risk in all three nations, with the strongest impacts shown in the United States. Other contextual characteristics, such as being in the same social network group or city, do not consistently impact perceived risk across nations. In Korea and China, these characteristics have a smaller significance than in the United States, demonstrating cultural variations in how users estimate privacy threats. Moreover, the study also investigates the importance of privacy concerns, distinguishing between three categories of worries—information privacy issues, interactional privacy concerns, and psychological privacy concerns—and how they affect perceived risk. Information privacy issues concern the abuse or illegal access to personal data, whereas interactional privacy concerns concern the control over who may engage with or contact the user. Psychological privacy issues are about the mental or emotional consequences of privacy breaches, such as feeling watched or criticized. It was found that privacy concerns consistently raise perceived risk in all three nations, whereas interactional privacy concerns are especially important in the United States and Korea. As for psychological privacy concerns, it interestingly did not significantly affect privacy decisions in any of the countries studied, which suggests that people may prioritize tangible risks over more abstract psychological concerns. Overall, the findings suggest that in the U.S., social connections and shared affiliations have a stronger influence on privacy decisions compared to Korea and China. However, privacy concerns in the latter two countries can moderate these effects, leading to heightened privacy concerns even with favorable contextual factors. Cultural differences are crucial to understanding privacy behavior in SNSs, emphasizing the need for future research to differentiate between privacy concerns and contextual factors across different cultural contexts. According to these findings, the authors note the importance of transnational platforms customizing their privacy settings and "recommended friends" algorithms to account for the changing relevance of local elements and privacy concerns across nations. This strategy might boost user trust and engagement by matching platform features with culturally relevant privacy choices and risk assessments. In the context of privacy concerns, the authors provide vital insights into the behavioral repercussions of perceived surveillance on data sharing. The study highlights that users' knowledge of monitoring, particularly in the Chinese social media ecosystem, has a major impact on their data-sharing activities. The sense of being watched or monitored raises privacy concerns, prompting more cautious and selective data-sharing habits. Users frequently limit the information they post, engage in self-censorship, and use stricter privacy settings to manage their online visibility. The findings highlight the complex interplay between perceived monitoring, privacy concerns, and data-sharing practices, demonstrating how individuals deal with the tension between participating in social networks and preserving their personal information. However, one of the main drawbacks is the exclusive emphasis on the Chinese social media ecosystem, which may limit the findings' applicability to other cultural or national contexts. The special characteristics of Chinese social media platforms and government restrictions may imply that the observed behaviors are irrelevant in countries with distinct social media landscapes and privacy rules.

According to [11], having privacy concerns is insufficient to encourage protective actions unless users are additionally motivated and equipped with privacy management and customization tools. Protection Motivation Theory (PMT) is central to the study's exploration of the role of user-controllable privacy customization features and how these features affect self-disclosure behaviours on SNSs, specifically through the concepts of threat appraisal and coping appraisal. Threat appraisal involves assessing the sever-ity and likelihood of a perceived threat, such as potential privacy violations on SNSs. Coping appraisal, on the other hand, assesses the effectiveness of available strategies to mitigate the threat, including the use of privacy settings. The study finds that pri-vacy concerns (i.e., emotional responses to perceived threats) mediate the relationship between these two types of appraisals. This suggests that users' concerns about privacy can significantly influence how they evaluate and respond to potential risks on SNSs. After surveying around 315 SNS users (the majority of college students), the findings showed that privacy concern does not always lead to diminished self-disclosure; rather, it serves as a mediator between threat appraisal and coping appraisal. The study also identifies two opposing processes of protection motivation: it can inhibit self-disclosure by raising privacy concerns and promote it by advocating the usage of privacy cus-tomizing options. Overall, however, the effect of protection motivation is a decrease in self-disclosure. While privacy customization can provide users with a sense of security, the overall effect of protective motive is to diminish self-disclosure due to the increased awareness of potential threats.

In other work [12], a survey of over 500 people was conducted in Rwanda to study the links between corporate privacy guarantees and users' privacy concerns, perceptions, trust, and non-self-disclosure behaviour across various e-service utilizations (namely e-commerce, e-government, and social media). The study found that perceptions of privacy risk greatly affect the degree to which people share information across all e-services. Surprisingly, it was found that when users believe they have greater control over their privacy, they tend to withhold more personal information across all types of e-services. This suggests that users who feel they can manage their privacy settings may be more cautious and choose to share less information, rather than being more open. As for trust, while privacy risk perceptions significantly affect trust in e-government services, they do not majorly affect trust in social networking and e-commerce services. This discrepancy may be due to the formal and transactional nature of e-government platforms compared to other platforms. Furthermore, the study found that when users regard privacy regulations as effective and adequate, it increases their trust in the service, their proclivity to withhold personal information, and their perceptions of their capacity to control their privacy. This implies that well-implemented privacy policies may build user confidence and encourage users to keep their information private because they believe it is sufficiently protected. Views on self-regulation—how well a service administers and regulates its privacy practices—have a beneficial impact on the quantity of information users choose to keep private. This is true for all sorts of services except e-government, where self-regulation does not significantly impact trust or behaviour compared to e-commerce and social networking services. Overall, while users are typically concerned about privacy, their confidence in social networking sites is not primarily determined by the substance of privacy rules. Instead, trust is more heavily influenced by the transparency with which platforms reveal their surveillance techniques. The authors claim that clear, intelligible, and honest information about how user data is monitored and used can help reduce the detrimental effects of privacy concerns on trust. The study reveals that when users consider a platform to be open about its monitoring operations, they are more inclined to engage with it and contribute their data, despite underlying privacy concerns.

In a more niche study, [13] looks at the elements that impact users' trust in sharing travel-related information collected from SNS. The study focuses on the influence of perceived value, risk, and privacy concerns in shaping trust. A questionnaire of 266 students from three Greek colleges who had traveled at least once was and used social networking sites to arrange their trips conducted. The data was evaluated in two stages: first, a Structural Equation Model (SEM) was used to identify the determinants of trust, followed by a neural network model to assess the relevance of these determinants. The major findings indicate that perceived value is the most important element impacting consumers' confidence in sharing trip information via SNS. Users are more likely to trust and share information if they believe the material is valuable. Furthermore, while privacy issues had no significant impact on trust, the perceived risk did, with users demonstrating less trust in SNS when they considered the platform offered a larger risk. The study also emphasizes the significance of perceived enjoyment – the degree to which a user enjoys using and engaging with others in an SNS - which has been shown to favourably increase both perceived value and trust. The practical implications suggest that tourism managers should focus on enhancing the enjoyable and valuable features of their websites, such as integrating multimedia elements, to increase user trust and engagement. While the paper contributes to the theoretical understanding of how perceived value, enjoyment, and risk affect trust in SNS, particularly in the context of sharing travel information, its note of how privacy concerns don't significantly influence trust lies in contrast with many existing studies, some of which are previously discussed.

### 2.3  Reputation Management in Social Networks

You are what you post. In the age of social networks, a person's post – be it a picture, statement, or meme – has become a determinant of their reputation and presentation to the world. From celebrities to influencers to ordinary folk, people have become hyper-aware of the ever-lasting monitoring they're subjected to on social networks, both by the platform as well as others. How people manage their online identities and reputations across various social media platforms, with an emphasis on the balance between personal and professional life, is explored in [14]. The authors investigate how participants deal with self-censorship, selective sharing, and the different levels of professional and private information published on platforms such as Facebook, LinkedIn, and Twitter (now X). The main aspects emphasize the intersection of personal and professional domains, especially the difficulties participants have in selecting what is suitable to disclose and with whom. For example, whereas Twitter and Facebook allow for some professional crossover, LinkedIn is primarily a professional medium for most users. Participants were also concerned about how their knowledge would be received, and they often took precautions to maintain a positive reputation. The authors studied the personal experiences of 15 participants, all being of the age group Gen X, with information sharing and reputation management on social media. They were asked to reflect on their actions, particularly instances of self-censorship and how they manage their online relationships. Both interview responses and participants' social media diaries were considered, resulting in a combination of real-time activities and post-hoc thoughts. Interestingly, the study discovered that most individuals did not consciously evaluate their reputation management until pushed during the interviews, implying that these behaviours are frequently intuitive rather than deliberate. Furthermore, while participants are typically cautious about what they communicate, they are more tolerant in their assessments of others' reputations, particularly if they have an offline relationship with the individual in question. It was also found that, while participants understand the value of online presence, they are wary of anonymous profiles and cautious in their evaluations of others who use them. Moreover, the study challenges previous findings by showing that participants did not view second-level connections as significant for reputation evaluation and did not commonly use pseudonyms to experiment with online identities, instead focusing on reputation management within their real identities. Overall, the findings suggest that while participants engage in some level of reputation management, it is often subconscious and driven by an instinctual understanding of social norms rather than a deliberate strategy. In the same way, a person self-censors when discussing sensitive topics in public for their safety and reputation, they naturally tend to do so on online platforms as well.

On the other hand, the authors of [15] found that while users are aware of the essence of reputation in online SNS, little action is usually taken to properly manage it. To understand the motives for online reputation management (ORM), the authors conducted 22 face-to-face, semi-structured interviews with young adults in which flexibility while answering specified questions was facilitated. The sample consists of digital natives (i.e., those who grew up using digital technologies and are familiar with them) aged 18 to 30 with a variety of educational backgrounds. The data was collected in two phases and evaluated using a grounded theory technique. Open coding revealed main concepts, which were then developed into categories of drivers, inhibitors, and contextual elements influencing ORM motivation. The debate demonstrates that the individual environment influences how young adults view online reputation management (ORM), with drivers increasing motivation and inhibitors decreasing it. Most respondents use social media and maintain their accounts to some extent, but they only participate in ORM when driven by short-term intrinsic or extrinsic incentives, which are frequently linked to specific events (for instance, job applications or other special occasions). These motives, however, are insufficient for sustained ORM, and many participants are unaware of the long-term ramifications of ignoring their online reputation. Even though most interviewees believe ORM is essential, they rarely take regular action unless prompted. Moreover, a lack of personal experience with negative online content further decreases motivation, as many interviewees have not encountered reputational harm. While some participants express frustration with the difficulty of managing their online reputation, the challenges of removing content and the need for more accessible tools discourage them from participating in ORM. The introduction of the "right to be forgotten" law in Europe, where individuals can request that links to personal information be removed from search engine results if the information is obsolete, irrelevant, or potentially damaging to their privacy, is seen as a step forward, but its effectiveness is debated due to its limitations in fully removing content. The authors relate their findings to offline image management theories, noting that while certain aspects, such as intrinsic motivations, are shared, others, like the particular obstacles of maintaining digital reputations, are unique to the online environment. The anonymity and permanence of the internet provide substantial challenges to successful ORM. The study indicates that existing ORM solutions are insufficient, as inhibitors frequently outweigh drives, keeping individuals inert while understanding the value of their online reputation. However, these findings are confined to a sample of German digital natives and may vary among cultures or demographic groups.

The authors of [16] examine the relationship between online privacy, reputation management, and the role of Web search engines in shaping public perception. The author argues that search engines can inadvertently harm users' reputations by surfacing misleading or irrelevant information, especially in the absence of proactive reputation management. This raises concerns about how digital platforms, including search engines, influence users' reputations, a point that aligns with the exploration of how privacy policies and online monitoring affect reputation management. Methodologically, the paper discusses the use of investigative Web search engines and Fuzzy Cognitive Maps (FCMs) to enhance users' control over their online presence. These tools allow for a more interactive and iterative approach to managing one's reputation, reflecting the broader concern of how privacy policies - or rather the lack of them - might leave users vulnerable to misrepresentation. While the paper does not directly address privacy policies or monitoring, its emphasis on the need for tools that help users protect and manage their reputations online can be seen as a response to the broader context of inadequate privacy protections. The findings suggest that as the social Semantic Web evolves, the effectiveness of reputation management will increasingly depend on the availability of technological tools that allow users to assert control over how they are represented online. This is particularly relevant in the context of this paper, where the disconnect between privacy policies and actual online monitoring practices might undermine users' ability to manage their reputations effectively.

Given the challenges users face in effectively managing their online reputation (often unintentionally, as revealed in previous studies), there is a growing demand for tools that help users navigate these complexities more effectively. An innovative solution for addressing privacy concerns through reputation management is proposed in [17], where a tool that establishes and monitors social reputations, identifies social circles, and allows users to effortlessly group friends to safeguard their privacy is created. This method automatically groups users into social circles based on shared information or applications that other users should not access. The drive to create such a stool indicates how important reputation is in social networks and how it is intertwined with privacy concerns and trust.

## 2.4 Monitoring and Surveillance in Social Networks

There is no doubt that surveillance of social network users, whether conducted by the platform itself or external third parties, has become normalized. The experience of talking about something with your friend and seeing the topic appear on your social networks has become almost universal. This acceptance and normalization of data surveillance for the sake of engaging on social networks is highlighted in [18]. The authors review the historical evolution of data surveillance and how it's been re-defined over the years to "soft-sell" the idea of monitoring users' data and behaviour on social networks for their life enhancement, enabled by technological advances. In the 1990s, a corporate-centric approach to personal information triumphed, and privacy rules became obsolete and unenforceable. Data surveillance, particularly in secondary applications, lacked rigorous control, supporting the notion that surveillance is an unavoidable part of modern life. In terms of privacy, the paper emphasizes the dangers of social media data surveillance which affects users by exposing their personal information, creating significant privacy risks. One consequence is that individuals cannot easily leave their past behind, as personal details remain online and accessible. This issue extends beyond active users, as non-users can still be tagged in posts (such as on Facebook, Instagram, etc.), making them part of the digital footprint. The inability to escape one's past due to this constant online presence and surveillance can obstruct personal growth and development if one chooses to re-invent themselves.

The authors of [19] also brush up on how social networks like Facebook, Twitter, and Instagram have made once-private aspects of life publicly accessible, with users viewing this surveillance as a trade-off for social interaction and convenience, inevitably accepting surveillance as a normal part of daily life. Reasons for this adaptation include the desire for connectivity, convenience, and the self-imposed nature of social media surveillance, where users willingly share personal information. Not only have social networks led to a significant loss of privacy due to reforming what's considered private, but they have also become tools of surveillance for governments and third parties with minimal restrictions.

The issues with users' surveillance on social networks go beyond privacy concerns. Its effects can eventually reach users' personal, psychological, and/or professional lives. Recent examples of this include the Harvard student who was denied entry to the United States in 2019 due to social media posts his friends had shared [20]. This shows how surveillance of social media activity can impact immigration decisions. Another well-known fact is the surveillance conducted by law enforcement agencies, like the FBI, who use public posts on social networks for criminal and civil investigations, sometimes even monitoring private communications between users. The claim that this surveillance is done in the name of "counter-terrorism" and "security/safety checks" can be refuted by the fact that users' posts and activities on social networks can be easily misinterpreted (possibly intentionally by bias, racist, and corrupt authority figures), which can lead to harmful, incorrect allegations towards members of society. Not to mention the breach of privacy and hesitancy of users to openly engage on monitored social networks. Over the years, it has become evident that the motivation behind such surveillance is often more rooted in stereotypes and racial biases than in genuine protection, with recent examples being the surveillance and censorship conducted on Palestinian and Black Lives Matter activists [20–23].

[24–28] also explores the behavioural effects of social network surveillance on users and activists. According to the author, both democratic and authoritarian regimes are increasingly using social media surveillance to control opposition. This is part of a larger securitization trend that includes tighter control over protests, militarized police forces, and classifying protesters as domestic terrorists. Social media surveillance is intertwined with these strategies, resulting in self-censorship among users who are afraid of the consequences of partaking in political discourse. Drawing on Foucault's panopticon, the author contends that individuals are internalizing monitoring, and restricting their political speech. This is supported by a 2014 Pew Research survey, which found an increase in hesitancy to discuss politically sensitive issues online, especially government monitoring.

## 2.5 Research Gap

Existing research has shed light on the difficulties of data-sharing behaviour, trust, and privacy concerns in social networks. Researchers have investigated how individuals manage their online reputations, balance their personal and professional identities, and participate in selective self-presentation across various platforms. It has also revealed the subconscious nature of reputation management and the limited efforts that users frequently undertake to maintain their online presence unless motivated by urgent incentives such as job applications or public scrutiny. Furthermore, studies have looked at the impact of privacy concerns and surveillance in modelling user behaviour, with a focus on the normalization of data collection and its implications for personal freedom, psychological well-being, and even legal repercussions.

However, despite these contributions, there remains a significant gap in the literature concerning the perceived conflict between social network platforms' privacy policies and the reality of online monitoring. While many users are aware of the risks associated with data surveillance, there has been little investigation into how the perceived disconnect between what platforms promise in their privacy policies and the extensive monitoring that takes place influences user trust, reputation management, and data-sharing behaviour. Moreover, few studies have examined how this perceived conflict might drive self-censorship, particularly among younger users who are more likely to use social networks as part of their everyday lives. This gap is critical, as trust is fundamental to users' continued engagement with social networks, and any erosion of trust can have far-reaching consequences for both user behaviour and platform dynamics. By focusing on this perceived conflict, this research seeks to investigate how the inconsistency between privacy assurances and real-time surveillance impacts user trust in social networks, as well as how it influences their willingness to share data and manage their online reputations. This study will contribute to the broader discourse on privacy and surveillance in the digital age by providing empirical evidence on how social network users navigate these tensions and the potential long-term effects on their engagement with social platforms.

# 3 Methodology

## 3.1 Study Design

This study tests the following hypotheses:

- **H1**: Higher perceived conflict between the privacy policies of social networks and the reality of platform monitoring is negatively associated with trust in social networks.

A quantitative approach was employed, using an online survey to measure the key variables of perceived conflict between privacy policies and monitoring, trust in social networks, reputation management behaviours, and data-sharing practices.

Below is a summary of the main measures covered in the survey:

1- **Perceived Conflict:** Participants were asked about their perceptions of inconsistencies between privacy policies and platform monitoring, including questions on confidence in social networks adhering to their stated privacy policies and concerns about data usage.

2- **Trust in Social Networks:** Trust was assessed by asking participants how much they trusted social networks to protect their privacy and how perceived inconsistencies in privacy practices affected their trust.

3- **Reputation Management:** The survey explored how concerns about monitoring influenced participants' efforts to manage their online reputation, including adjustments in behaviour and content sharing.

4- **Data Sharing and Privacy Concerns:** Participants reported on the impact of potential surveillance on their willingness to share personal information and their comfort level in sharing under different privacy conditions.

5- **Awareness and Concern about Monitoring:** The survey assessed participants' awareness of monitoring practices on social networks and the extent of their concerns about being monitored.

6- **Demographics and Usage Patterns:** Basic demographic information, including age group and social network usage, was collected, along with questions about how frequently participants read privacy policies before signing up for social networks.

### 3.2  Data Collection

The participants consisted of 152 social network users recruited through online platforms, primarily WhatsApp, using a chain-referral method where respondents were encouraged to share the survey with others. The sample spanned various age groups, including Gen Z (14–27), millennials (28–43), and Gen X (44–59). Participants came from diverse educational and occupational backgrounds, including both students and professionals. They also represented a variety of nationalities, primarily from regions such as the Middle East, North America, and Europe. The gender composition included both male and female participants. Data was collected using an online survey, which included a mix of Likert-scale items and open-ended questions to capture perceptions, behaviours, and attitudes.

## 4  Results

We used Excel to interpret the results obtained by the survey. Firstly, we are examining the degree to which users of social networks trust these platforms to safeguard their privacy policies, despite being aware that their data and behaviour are monitored. We performed a linear regression analysis with perceived conflict as the independent variable and trust as the dependent variable to evaluate the hypothesis outlined in Sect. 1. The table below presents the results of this analysis (Table 1).

The slope of the regression line indicates how much trust (Y) is expected to change with a one-unit change in perceived conflict (X). Specifically, for each additional unit increase in perceived conflict, trust increases by approximately 0.2083 units. This small slope reflects a weak relationship, consistent with the weak correlation.

**Table 1.** .

| Measure | Value |
| --- | --- |
| Pearson Correlation coefficient | 0.17471316 |
| Slope | 0.20830923 |
| Intercept | 2.93126479 |
| r-squared | 0.03052469 |

The Pearson correlation coefficient gauges the strength and direction of the linear relationship between two variables. In this case, it shows a weak positive linear relationship between perceived conflict and trust. This means that as perceived conflict increases, trust in social networks tends to increase slightly, though the relationship is quite weak. This suggests that most social network users maintain a certain level of trust in these platforms, even if they are aware of monitoring practices.

The intercept represents the value of trust when perceived conflict is zero. When perceived conflict (X) is zero, the predicted trust (Y) is 2.9313. This value marks the starting point of the regression line on the Y-axis. R-squared measures the proportion of variance in trust explained by perceived conflict. In this case, only 3.05% of the variability in trust can be accounted for by perceived conflict.

Overall, these findings indicate that people continue to trust social networks to safeguard their privacy, despite awareness of monitoring practices. However, this does not support the hypothesis, as the relationship between perceived conflict and trust was weak and positive, rather than negative as expected. The potential reasons for this will be discussed in Sect. 5.

### 4.1 Perception of Privacy Policies

The pie chart illustrated in Fig. 2 shows the distribution of responses to the question of whether the perceived conflict between privacy policies and monitoring affects trust in social networks. The chart reveals that approximately 70% of respondents strongly believe that discrepancies between privacy policies and actual monitoring impact their trust in social networks.

As seen in Fig. 3, over 70% of respondents either never or rarely review these privacy policies before creating an account. Furthermore, it was found that only 11% of respondents feel confident that social networks follow their stated privacy policies, and 78% of users do not believe that their data is used according to the privacy policies of social networks. Hence, when studying the results regarding the concerned users' activities being monitored, it was no surprise that nearly two-thirds of users are worried, indicating a moderate level of awareness among social network users.

### 4.2 Reputation Management, Trust, and Self-censorship

In terms of reputation management out of concern of monitoring, 2/3 of users were found to alter their online behaviour or content, reflecting a high level of security awareness

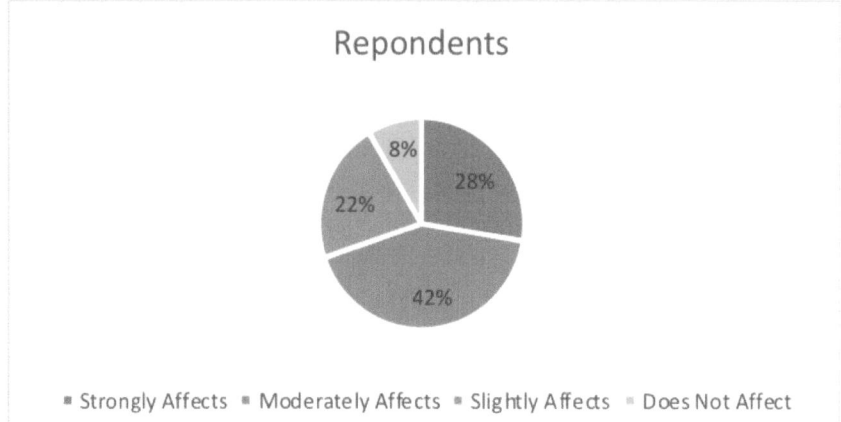

**Fig. 2.** Responses to the degree to which conflict between privacy policies and actual monitoring affect trust in social networks.

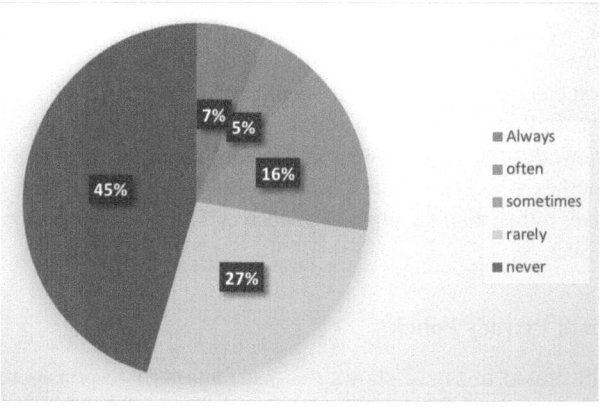

**Fig. 3.** Frequency of respondents reading privacy policies before signing up on social networks.

among social network users. Also, as shown in Fig. 4, 47% of users believe that increased reputation management (such as adjusting privacy settings or curating content) leads to greater trust in social networks. However, around 40% find that reputation management has no effect in their level of trust. This can be due to the aforementioned moderate awareness level of monitoring possessed by the users, rendering reputation management tools fruitless when it comes to increasing their trust in social platforms.

As for self-censorship, 75% of users were found to modify their activities or posts related to political issues on social networks out of fear that their privacy might be compromised or used against them. When asked whether they would be more likely to share personal information, including opinions and political views, if they were certain that the platform was not being monitored, the responses were nearly evenly split (as seen in Fig. 5), with the majority claiming they wouldn't. This suggests that factors

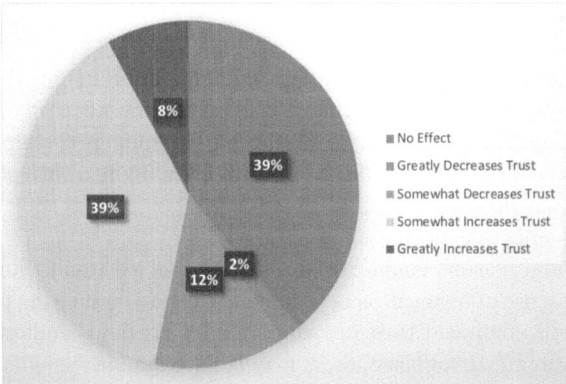

**Fig. 4.** Degree to which reputation management level affects trust in social networks.

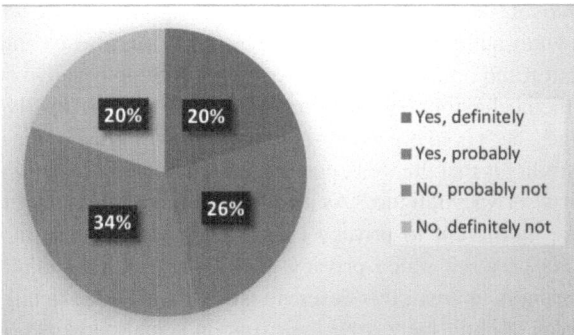

**Fig. 5.** Responses of social network users to the question of whether they would be more likely to share personal information, including opinions and political views if they were certain that the platform was not being monitored.

beyond monitoring influence users' willingness to share their opinions and political views on social networks. Some of these factors may stem from users' inherent privacy concerns, which go beyond surveillance by third parties or government bodies. For many, the need to maintain control over who can view their content (be it friends, family, or other users) shapes their sharing behaviour. The desire to preserve a certain public image, avoid personal conflicts, or protect sensitive information from unintended audiences may discourage them from openly sharing personal views, especially on controversial topics like politics. Moreover, concerns about long-term data permanence and the potential for their shared content to be misinterpreted in the future could be another factor that takes precedence over their fear of monitoring. In this context, self-censorship may reflect broader anxieties about reputation management, future consequences, and the general risks associated with digital exposure.

## 5  Discussion

The results of this study show an intriguing departure from the initial hypothesis. As opposed to the expectation that higher perceived conflict between privacy policies and platform monitoring would negatively impact trust, the findings revealed a rather weak positive correlation. This indicates that as users become more aware of the discrepancies between privacy policies and actual monitoring, their trust in social networks may increase slightly rather than decrease.

Several potential reasons could explain this unexpected result. Firstly, users may have developed a sense of resignation or acceptance toward monitoring practices, which is reflected in their continued trust (as supported by previous studies on this topic). Despite being aware of surveillance, users may believe that the benefits of using social networks, such as connectivity and access to information, outweigh privacy concerns. This could account for the weak positive correlation, where users maintain a certain level of trust in the platform's ability to safeguard their data, despite the presence of monitoring. Moreover, the likelihood of a person being affected by what they post is another factor that may build trust over time. For instance, a user who continuously shares personal information and opinions or sensitive topics with no negative consequences or repercussions to their behaviour (i.e., account blocked, authorities' involvement, stalkers, unwanted messages, etc.) is likely to continue to do so with trust in the platform.

Another possibility is that the weak positive correlation reflects a psychological phenomenon known as "privacy fatigue." As users grow accustomed to digital surveillance, they may become indifferent to privacy risks, developing a sense of desensitization toward the conflict between stated privacy policies and actual monitoring practices. Rather than lowering their trust, this desensitization may paradoxically result in users maintaining or even slightly increasing their trust in social networks, as they become less concerned with privacy issues over time. This could explain why the hypothesized negative association did not materialize in the data. Users might feel that since privacy violations have not significantly affected their experience so far, there is little reason to distrust the platform, even when aware of monitoring.

Furthermore, reputation management tactics, like adjusting privacy settings or curating content, may create a perception of control over one's online presence, which could encourage trust in social networks. However, the finding that 40% of respondents see no relationship between reputation management and trust suggests that for many users, these tactics may not be sufficient to influence their overall trust levels. This could indicate that reputation management alone is not a dominant factor in shaping trust, or that users do not fully trust the effectiveness of these tactics to protect them from potential risks.

Cultural factors could also contribute to this weak positive correlation. In some cultures, there may be a higher tolerance or even expectation of surveillance, especially in regions where government or institutional oversight is commonplace. Users in these contexts may be more accustomed to the idea of being monitored and, as a result, view social network surveillance as less of a threat to their personal privacy. Instead, they may perceive this monitoring as a necessary component of platform functionality or security, leading to an increased level of trust. On the other hand, users from cultures where privacy is highly valued might react differently, potentially showing less tolerance for platform monitoring and a greater decline in trust. Thus, cultural norms surrounding privacy, transparency, and trust could be an important moderating factor in explaining this weak positive relationship.

The concept of self-censorship also plays a critical role in understanding the dynamics between trust, privacy concerns, and monitoring. With 75% of users modifying their posts on sensitive topics like politics, it is clear that monitoring practices influence not just trust, but also behaviour on social networks. However, the nearly even split in responses regarding whether users would share more personal information if platforms were not monitored indicates that surveillance is only one of many factors influencing users' decisions. Concerns about audience control, public image, and long-term consequences of sharing personal information could be even more impactful than the fear of being monitored. For example, users might self-censor to maintain a positive reputation, which could, in turn, reinforce their trust in the platform by allowing them to feel more secure in managing their online persona.

Moreover, frameworks such as the European Union's General Data Protection Regulation (GDPR) and other national privacy regulations are crucial to consider in this discussion. The GDPR, for instance, mandates transparency and accountability in how organizations handle user data, which gives users greater control over their personal information. Hence, for users in regions where GDPR or similar data protection laws are enforced, the perceived conflict between privacy policies and monitoring might be lessened due to the trust placed in regulatory bodies to ensure compliance. On the other hand, the absence of a privacy law equivalent to the GDPR in other countries may leave users feeling more vulnerable to unchecked surveillance, which could worsen their sense of mistrust.

These results suggest that while privacy concerns and the awareness of platform monitoring shape user behaviour, the relationship between perceived conflict and trust is more complex than originally hypothesized. Trust may not be solely dependent on privacy policies or monitoring practices, but influenced by a range of factors including reputation management, perceived control, self-censorship, and cultural attitudes toward privacy and surveillance. Future research could further explore how these factors interact and whether other moderating variables, such as cultural differences, platform-specific features, or user demographics, play a role in shaping user trust in social networks.

# 6  Limitations

This research methodology has a few limitations that should be noted. Firstly, the reliance on self-reported data through an online survey due to potential bias (like social desirability bias, where participants might provide answers, they believe are more socially acceptable rather than reflecting their true perceptions or behaviours). However, to minimize this, the survey was designed with anonymity taken into consideration, encouraging participants to provide honest responses without fear of judgment. Secondly, the chain-referral sampling method (i.e., snowball method) may limit the generalizability of the results, as the sample may not fully represent the broader population of social network users. To reduce this limitation, efforts were made to distribute the survey widely across diverse social groups, and the sample includes participants from various age groups, nationalities, and educational backgrounds. Finally, the cross-sectional design prevents the establishment of causal relationships between the perceived conflict in privacy policies and trust in social networks. While this is a limitation, the survey results still offer valuable insights into the associations and correlation between these factors, and future research could not only explore longitudinal designs to address this, but also overcome the lack of generalizability and self-reporting bias due to snowball sampling.

## 7   Conclusion

The effect of perceived conflicts between social networks' privacy policies and actual monitoring practices on user trust, reputation management, and data sharing was studied in this paper. The study aimed to test the hypothesis that higher perceived conflict would negatively affect trust in social networks, with potential moderation by reputation management practices. Using a quantitative approach, an online survey with 152 participants to measure perceptions of privacy policy discrepancies, trust levels, reputation management behaviours, and data sharing practices was conducted. The analysis revealed a weak positive correlation between perceived conflict and trust, contrary to the hypothesized negative relationship. Although users are concerned about monitoring, they generally maintain their trust in social networks, likely due to the perceived value of these platforms and the limitations of reputation management practices in enhancing trust. The study also highlighted that self-censorship and reputation management are significant aspects of user behaviour, as many users were found to modify what they post or share online out of concern for privacy and monitoring. However, no strong correlation was shown between these practices and increased trust in social networks. The findings highlight the need for social network providers to improve transparency and address the gap between privacy policies and monitoring practices to build user trust. Future research should explore other additional factors that could potentially influence trust and user behaviour, given the dynamic nature of digital privacy.

## References

1. Shahbaz, A., Funk, A.: Social media surveillance. Freedom House (2019). https://freedo mhouse.org/report/freedom-on-the-net/2019/the-crisis-of-social-media/social-media-survei llance
2. Hsiao, K.-L., Chiou, J.-S.: The impact of online community position on online community participation: Trust, privacy concern, and social influence. Inf. Manag. **49**(1), 41–48 (2012)
3. Labrecque, L.I., Markos, E., Milne, G.R.: Online personal branding: processes, challenges, and implications. J. Interact. Mark. **25**(1), 37–50 (2011)
4. Lindner, J.: Alarming social media privacy statistics reflect lack of trust and control - WiFiTalents. In: 9th International Proceedings on Proceedings, pp. 1–2 (2024)
5. Tamblé, M.: [Infographic] Social Media Statistics 2018. Blog2Social Blog – Tips for social media marketing (2024). https://www.blog2social.com/en/blog/infographic-social-media-sta tistics/
6. Grabner-Kräuter, S., Bitter, S.: Trust in online social networks: a multifaceted perspective. Forum Soc. Econ. **44**(1), 48–68 (2013). https://doi.org/10.1080/07360932.2013.781517

7. Khan, S., Umer, R., Umer, S., Naqvi, S.: Antecedents of trust in using social media for E-government services: ZN empirical study in Pakistan. Technol. Soc. **64**, 101400 (2021). https://doi.org/10.1016/j.techsoc.2020.101400

8. Ayaburi, E.W., Treku, D.N.: Effect of penitence on social media trust and privacy concerns: the case of Facebook. Int. J. Inf. Manage. **50**, 171–181 (2020)

9. van Schaik, P., Jansen, J., Onibokun, J., Camp, J., Kusev, P.: Security and privacy in online social networking: risk perceptions and precautionary behaviour. Comput. Hum. Behav. **78**, 283–297 (2018). https://doi.org/10.1016/j.chb.2017.10.007

10. Li, Y., Rho, E.H.R., Kobsa, A.: Cultural differences in the effects of contextual factors and privacy concerns on users' privacy decision on social networking sites. Behav. Inf. Technol. **41**(3), 1–23 (2020). https://doi.org/10.1080/0144929x.2020.1831608

11. Mousavi, R., Chen, R., Kim, D.J., Chen, K.: Effectiveness of privacy assurance mechanisms in users' privacy protection on social networking sites from the perspective of protection motivation theory. Decis. Support. Syst. **135**, 113323 (2020). https://doi.org/10.1016/j.dss.2020.113323

12. Mutimukwe, C., Kolkowska, E., Grönlund, Å.: Information privacy in e-service: effect of organizational privacy assurances on individual privacy concerns, perceptions, trust, and self-disclosure behavior. Gov. Inf. Q. **37**(1), 101413 (2019). https://doi.org/10.1016/j.giq.2019.101413

13. Kitsios, F., Mitsopoulou, E., Moustaka, E., Kamariotou, M.: User-generated content behavior and digital tourism services: a SEM-neural network model for information trust in social networking sites. Int. J. Inf. Manag. Data Insights **2**(1), 100056 (2022). https://doi.org/10.1016/j.jjimei.2021.100056

14. Ryan, F., Cruickshank, P., Hall, H., Lawson, A.: Managing and evaluating personal reputations on the basis of information shared on social media: a generation X perspective. Inf. Res. **21**(4) (2016). https://napier-repository.worktribe.com/output/305045

15. Yang, S.: Understanding personal online reputation management: a grounded theory study. Association for information systems AIS electronic library (AISeL) (2015). https://core.ac.uk/download/pdf/301365271.pdf

16. Portmann, E., Pedrycz, W.: Fuzzy web knowledge aggregation, representation, and reasoning for online privacy and reputation management. Intelligent Systems Reference Library, pp. 89–105. Springer, Heidelberg (2013). https://doi.org/10.1007/978-3-642-39739-4_5

17. Yüksel, M.E., Yüksel, A.S., Zaim, A.H.: A reputation-based privacy management system for social networking sites. Turk. J. Electr. Eng. Comput. Sci. **21**, 766–784 (2013). https://doi.org/10.3906/elk-1110-30

18. van der Schyff, K., Flowerday, S., Furnell, S.: Duplicitous social media and data surveillance: an evaluation of privacy risk. Comput. Secur. **94**, 101822 (2020). https://doi.org/10.1016/j.cose.2020.101822

19. Odoemelam, C.E.: Adapting to surveillance and privacy issues in the era of technological and social networking. Int. J. Soc. Sci. Humanity **5**(6) (2015). https://www.ijssh.net/papers/520-H140.pdf

20. Panduranga, H., Mella Pablo, E.: Federal government social media surveillance, Explained I Brennan Center for Justice. Brennan center for justice (2022). https://www.brennancenter.org/our-work/research-reports/federal-government-social-media-surveillance-explained

21. Media, S.: Columbia undergraduate law review. Columbia undergraduate law review (2024). https://www.culawreview.org/journal/social-media-surveillance-of-the-black-lives-matter-movement-and-the-right-to-privacy

22. Human rights watch: Meta's broken promises. Human rights watch (2023). https://www.hrw.org/report/2023/12/21/metas-broken-promises/systemic-censorship-palestine-content-instagram-and

23. Ahmed, Y.A., Sharo, A.: On the education effect of CHATGPT: Is AI CHATGPT to dominate education career profession? In: 2023 International Conference on Intelligent Computing, Communication, Networking and Services (ICCNS), Valencia, Spain, 2023, pp. 79–84 (2023). https://doi.org/10.1109/ICCNS58795.2023.10192993

24. Owen, S.: Monitoring social media and protest movements: ensuring political order through surveillance and surveillance discourse. Soc. Identities **23**(6), 688–700 (2017). https://doi.org/10.1080/13504630.2017.1291092

25. Alahmed, Y., Abadla, R., Ameen, N., Shteiwi, A.: Bridging the gap between ethical AI implementations. Int. J. Membrane Sci. Technol. **10**(3), 3034–3046 (2023). https://doi.org/10.15379/ijmst.v10i3.2953

26. Alahmed, Y., Abadla, R., Badri, A.A., Ameen, N.: How does ChatGPT work" examining functionality to the creative AI CHATGPT on X's (Twitter) Platform. In: 2023 Tenth International Conference on Social Networks Analysis, Management and Security (SNAMS), Abu Dhabi, United Arab Emirates, 2023, pp. 1–7 (2023). https://doi.org/10.1109/SNAMS60348.2023.10375450

27. Alahmed, Y., Abadla, R., Ansari, M.J.A.: Exploring the potential implications of AI-generated content in social engineering attacks. In: 2024 International Conference on Multimedia Computing, Networking and Applications (MCNA), Valencia, Spain, pp. 64–73 (2024). https://doi.org/10.1109/MCNA63144.2024.10703950

28. Hesham, H., Al Ahmed, Y., Wael, B., Saleh, M.: Solar-powered smart bin: revolutionizing waste classification for a sustainable future. In: 2023 24th International Arab Conference on Information Technology (ACIT), Ajman, United Arab Emirates, pp. 1–8 (2023). https://doi.org/10.1109/ACIT58888.2023.10453850

# Network and Infrastructure Security

# Every Sherlock Needs a Watson: Practical Semi-realtime Attack Elaboration System

Zeya Umayya(✉) , Arpit Nandi , Amartyo Roy ,
and Sambuddho Chakravarty

IIIT Delhi, New Delhi, India
{zeyau,arpit20179,amartyor,sambuddho}@iiitd.ac.in

**Abstract.** Security Operations Center (SOC) analysts work with both types of network intrusion detection systems (NIDS). These include signature based-NIDS (SNIDS) and ML/AI-based NIDS (MNIDS). User-studies involving SOCs highlight that false-alarms of SNIDS causes alert-fatigue to SOC analysts. User-studies focused on MNIDS highlight that although they are efficient in spotting malicious traffic, they have still not matured enough to be deployed in SoCs for providing benefits in realtime. Such benefits include specific attack classification in realtime, that help analysts prevent, mitigate or send appropriate responses for studying the attackers' behaviour, via honeypots.

Thus, keeping in mind the realtime deployability aspects which involve studying the effect of packet losses and attacks with varied speeds, we present *Watson*, a modular system that works in conjunction with a MNIDS. Watson classifies the traffic into specific attack classes and types, using its modules. We prototype and implement Watson for three threat classes, *viz.,* password guessing attacks, active reconnaissance, and denial-of-service attacks. Collectively, Watson has modules covering 11 types of attacks with varying speed from 10Mbps to 10Gbps. We test Watson in-lab, using public datasets and on a live university network. It reported F1-scores of upto 0.98 and FPRs close to zero.

**Keywords:** Network Security · Intrusion Detection · SOC

## 1 Introduction

Given the plethora of solutions for NIDS available, recently, some researchers took a very important step of finding the actual usability of those by interviewing the SOC analysts directly [2,49]. Their studies present very practical pictures about the actual deployment challenges of these NIDS. As per the first study, 19 out of 21 analysts using SNIDS were dissatisfied, citing high-false alarms ($\approx$ 99%), resulting in alert-fatigue. On the other hand, in the second study involving SOC analysts using ML-based NIDS (MNIDS), suggests that MNIDS should be used along with rule-based. As per them, although ML can learn subtle patterns, it is prone to false positives. While this is well known [67], the feedback from analysts suggest the requirement for amalgamation of rule-based and MNIDS.

H. H. Song et al. (Eds.): NSS 2024, LNCS 15564, pp. 277–300, 2025.
https://doi.org/10.1007/978-981-96-3531-3_14

The practical drawbacks of both types of NIDS prevents the development of appropriate and efficient intrusion prevention or mitigation systems which can work in real time. Apart from mitigation, SOC analysts might also want to learn the attackers' behaviour by redirecting the traffic to honeypots and sending appropriate responses back. Active observation, prevention and mitigation requires solutions which present details of ongoing attacks, by classifying them and also providing their types *e.g.*, distributed attacks from multiple sources (like DNS amplification or floods). Developing such solutions which can handle high speed traffic while still providing attack classes with low FPRs (unlike SNIDS) is a challenging task. Several proposals for attack classification work primarily on datasets (*i.e.*, mostly PCAPs) [4,43,74]. Since real world deployments were not a focus of these works, several aspects and challenges of actual enterprise-level attack detection, were not considered.

As already demonstrated by Fu *et al.* [25], making a readily deployable solution requires a different type of feature selection and extraction process, than used for offline solutions. Also, their performance should be tested thoroughly in scenarios that mimic real world deployments, involving variable attack traffic speeds. Changes in attack traffic speed are useful for observing packet drops and thus their impact on detection performance. This observation will have a ripple effect on the algorithm building and feature extraction process. Hence, we stress that solutions merely using datasets, may not be able to address these dynamics, and might not be considered in actual deployments.

We present *Watson*, which tries to solve exactly these issues *i.e., the absence of synergy between ML and rule-based systems, lack of online attack elaboration modules*. The synergy requires designing heuristic based algorithms which work in tandem with MNIDSs. Watson is a modular system consisting of various attack detection heuristics which have been designed to work in an online fashion. Thus, Watson, along with MNIDS engines, provides a finer classification of attacks and their types while discarding the false positives detected by the MNIDS. ML algorithms used by NIDS are relatively more resilient against evasion attacks, compared to heuristic-based ones [49]. This combination works at scales, inspecting large volume of malicious traffic in an online manner, by leveraging NIDS (*e.g.*, Whisper [25,73]).

Watson's modules classify threats using protocol-level behavior observed during an attack. The modules are designed to identify the specific type of attacks launched on individual applications, *e.g.*, SSH or DNS. The protocol-level behaviors of an application show similar patterns, regardless of the network where it is used. To detect attacks, Watson employs heuristics for such patterns, corresponding to the threat class in consideration. These heuristics depend on the victim network.

We tested Watson's prototype with modules corresponding to attacks of three threat classes, *viz.* password guessing, active reconnaissance, and denial of service. For the proof of concept, we developed 4 modules, *i.e.*, for SSH brute-force, port scan, DNS floods, and DNS amplification considering the above classes. These attacks are common when advanced persistent threats (APTs) are launched [41]. Watson processes packets at a high speed that are delivered through a packet transmission/reception library (*viz.*, Intel DPDK [39]). This makes Watson fit for identifying attacks with semi-realtime latencies[1]. Section 3.2 presents guidelines for designing modules for attacks of similar classes.

We tested Watson in controlled and realistic scenarios and observed high accuracy across various attack traffic speeds. We aimed to evaluate Watson's efficiency, F1-score and accuracy in classifying attacks. In general, in controlled setups, we observed very high F1-score ($> 98\%$) even when attack packets were transmitted very fast (*e.g.*, for flooding attacks, like DNS amplification, at 20Gbps). Further, even upon testing with public data sets, Watson detected attacks with high enough F1-score (*e.g.*, $\approx 98\%$ to detect SSH brute-force for CICIDS-2017 [14,21] dataset[2]).

Finally, to gauge Watson's applicability in the wild, we tested it in a real organizational environment[3], juxtapositioned with *Enidrift*, an adaptive ensemble-based NIDS. Next, we generated our own attack traffic from cloud machines targeted to victim hosts under our control, in the organization. Enidrift took about 35 s to process one thousand packets and accurately classify them with high accuracy ($\approx 97\%$). Thereafter, Watson identified the attacks and their details in under 2 s with over 96% F1-score. Thus, with this experiment, we were able to test Watson as a part of the complete detection pipeline *i.e.,* from attack generation, to passing it through NIDS, and then to Watson. The outcomes suggest that SOCs could use MNIDSs augmented with Watson.

The following summarizes our contributions:

1. Design and implementation of a modular system, Watson, that detects different types of attacks by observing malicious network traffic received from a NIDS.
2. Empirical evaluation of Watson:
   (a) Tested under various scenarios – controlled, live network, and on publicly available attack data sets, while varying the attack traffic speeds.
   (b) Augmented with a state-of-the-art NIDS, *i.e., Enidrift*, to show its usefulness. We tested it with real network traffic by passing the university's traffic through Enidrift and then through Watson. Traffic marked malicious by Enidrift were further classified by Watson accurately ($> 98\%$) and efficiently (in under 2 s for all attack types).
   (c) Compared to a SNIDS *i.e.,* Snort in similar scenarios, Watson performs better.
3. Guidelines to add new detection modules for attacks in similar class of threats.

Lastly, we did a qualitative user study with 4 members of a SOC, where got positive feedback and suggestions on increasing Watson's usability (ref. Sect. 5.2).

---

[1] Semi-realtime since there will always be the latency of the first stage *i.e.*, NIDS.
[2] We used the updated version of CICIDS-2017 dataset [21].
[3] Refer to Appendix A.3 for ethical considerations.

## 2    Background and Related Work

### 2.1    Background

In 2023 Cloudflare reported [10] that multiple organizations suffer from DDoS attacks (DNS based) with traffic speeds ranging from 100Gbps to 1.3Tbps. Further, a technical report [9] by Cloudflare talks about the impacts of large DDoS attacks on DNS resolvers, which could incur losses worth about \$2M. SSH botnets are also reported to be on the rise [18,28]. Such reports highlight the importance of NIDS. NIDSs are very important to an organization for securing public-facing networks from external attacks.

**Importance of Real-World Deployments and Incident Response:** An important task of a SOC analyst is to perform incident response once an attack is detected. However, most SOCs usually turn-off the automated response, *e.g.,* blocking malicious IPs, since most of these alarms are false alerts [2]. Thus, blocking these IPs could lead to collateral damage. Moreover, the reported intrusions often require further analysis to make sense. Further, Ramanathan *et al.* [60] emphasized the disadvantages of blacklisting IP addresses due to their heavy reuse in the real world.

In 2021, SANS report [57], describes the ubiquity of honeypots in SOCs, and the challenges that are faced while deploying them. Programming honeypots to launch automated responses, requires analyzing and accurately identifying the types of intrusions reported. Our solution, an adoptive system to identify specific attacks by inspecting malicious traffic, attempts to solve such issues.

### 2.2    Related Work

**Network Traffic Based Solutions** Solution working on network traffic can be further classified into two categories.

1. **Realtime** NIDS like *Enidrift* [73], *Kistuse* [50], *Whisper* [25] use ML/DL-based approaches and are trained to distinguish between benign and malicious traffic in an online manner. Among the current NIDS, Whisper can work at high traffic throughput of 13.69Gbps. Watson has been designed to use such online solutions available til day. Apart from ML/AI based NIDS, there are SNIDS as well *e.g.,* Snort [62] and Suricata [36]. But user-studies involving SOCs highlight that most of the alarms produced by such systems are 99% false alerts. The analysts spend most of their time validating such alarms causing alert fatigue [27,64].
2. **Non-realtime** A plethora of solutions work in an offline fashion on datasets [3,4,26,34,35,47,59]. Solutions like ActDetector [40] proposes a framework to detect multi-stage attacks. It receives inputs from Suricata. However, ActDetector's efficacy relies on the adequacy of signatures in Suricata; they were curated from multiple datasets (*i.e.* DARPA2000 [75] and ISCXIDS2012 [66]). Finally, the belief that such solutions would work in (quasi-)real-time situations, is unfounded.

**Non-network traffic solutions** There is yet another category of threat monitoring systems – *viz.*, SIEMs [46,48,68]. These systems log all the security-related events, but lack capabilities of contextual analysis of alerts collectively. Solution like *DeepCase* [71] try to ameliorate the situation. It clusters similar events for individual devices, based on what the SIEMs provide. Its authors reported up to 90.53% workload reduction for SOC analysts. Lanvin *et al.* [43] propose similar methods of clustering the explanations of anomalies flagged malicious by the anomaly detectors. However it relies on an expert to manually inspect and label the clusters. Also, their method primarily focuses on explaining the outcomes of NIDS to make them trustworthy, while Watson elaborates them into their respective types for fast mitigation and incident response. Similarly important works like Unicorn [33], R-CAID [29] and Kairos [8] which are host-based IDSs should also be not compared with Watson.

**Interpreting Anomalies.** On the other hand, researchers have produced potential systems like *DeepAID* [32], *xNIDS* [74] and many more [6,44,52] to interpret and explain the ML/AI based security solutions. For example, DeepAID present frameworks for interpreting the anomalies specifically in DL-based NIDS (*e.g.,* Kitsune, Deeplog *etc.*). It requires an expert to manually add interpretations. Although, these works are contributing greatly towards reducing the skepticism of SOCs to deploy ML based solutions, but we argue that these works are orthogonal to what Watson is built for.

**Summary.** All such solutions either directly work with the security event produced by the network monitoring tools, or try to interpret and explain the anomalies spotted. But Watson does not rely on the security event logs/notification. Rather, it directly works on the malicious network traffic flagged by the ML/DL-based NIDS (*e.g.,* Whisper [25] *etc.*) in semi real-time. Since Watson works in semi-realtime settings, it should not be compared with research that involves employing attack detection algorithms [4,21,45,65] directly on datasets, in an offline manner (*i.e.,* non-realtime).

## 3    System Architecture

We propose Watson to augment learning-based NIDS. Our main goal is to add elaboration and specific type of attack conformance once the traffic is flagged malicious by the NIDS. It can be used to detect several attack variants of an individual attack type. We demonstrate this through modules that involve detecting the following types of threat classes – password bruteforce, active reconnaissance, and flooding. We selected some very prevalent real-world attacks corresponding to each of these classes, *viz.* SSH bruteforce, TCP port scanning, DNS flood and DNS amplification [10,28,38]. Port scan and SSH brute force are often used for persistent asset discovery in APT pipelines and taking control of SSH servers used by network admins [28,38]. SNIDS generate a lot of alerts (including false ones) for traffic similar to these attacks (ref. Sect. 2.2).Thus, we keep the design of Watson modular in nature to develop solutions for these attacks and their variants.

**Premise:** SOC analysts would deploy Watson in a manner that it has access to the traffic flagged malicious by a NIDS. We assume that analysts work closely with the target organization and know the systems which need protection and thus configure Watson accordingly. Notably, Watson will receive packets from NIDS positioned before it.

### 3.1  Overall System Design

Figure 1 shows the over-all design of Watson and its placement in the net-work where the Internet traf-fic enters the internal net-work via an edge-router and a firewall. As per Fig. 1, we assume that the NIDS receives the network traf-fic *via* port mirroring. The malicious packets output from

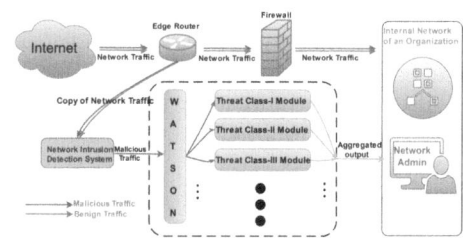

**Fig. 1.** *Overall design & positioning of Watson.*

a NIDS (*e.g.,* Whisper [25]) are then fed to Watson which processes them par-allelly using the four deployed modules, *i.e.,* port scan, SSH brute-force, DNS flood, and DNS amplification module. Each module classifies attacks using dif-ferent heuristics. For Watson, a new detection module would result in a new thread that receives copies of malicious packets to work on (details in Sect. A.2). We now describe the working of Watson through the specific modules, mentioned above.

**Port Scan Module (PSM).** Attackers launch reconnaissance on target orga-nizations to know about the various services running. Port scans [23] are one such method. They can be of different types – TCP-SYN, TCP-Connect, TCP-FIN, UDP scan *etc.* In general, port scans have a sequence of TCP packets with different flags enabled. We designed a PSM that observers multiple packets to identify possible (types of) port scans.

*Possible Attack Sequences:* All types of port scans are collections of packets with certain TCP flags occurring in a specific sequence. To categorize these port scans, we rely on various packet-level features, *viz.,* inter-arrival time (IAT), packet direction (*i.e.,* src → dst or vice versa), flags (*i.e.,* SYN, ACK, FIN, RST, PSH, URG), packet length, window size, and port numbers. Thus, a sequence is represented with the above set of features extracted from the TCP packet headers. We collected traces of all scan types using Sect. 4.1's setup.

**Detection Method:** To detect a particular type of scan in incoming network traffic, Watson needs to compare it with all possible sequences that were collected earlier. This can be done using the *Dynamic Time-Warping (DTW)* algorithm [63]. DTW, originally was designed to compare two time-series data of different lengths, with the assumption that the first and last packets of the two sequences are same. In our case, this assumption does not hold since we can not predict the attributes of the incoming packets. But at the same time, our objective is to determine whether the incoming packets are similar to a known scan sequence. Thus, Watson uses a modified DTW for such scenarios. In our case, we compare the incoming batch with multiple scan sequences to find a closest match.

Watson compares the attributes of each packet of an incoming batch, to those of known scan sequences. The comparison involves the calculation of the Euclidean distance between the respective feature values. We explain this with an example. Consider an input batch of packets, *B1*. For batch *B1*, PSM maintains one array for scores and another for the count of unique ports per IP (that receives the packets). These scores represent the distances between the incoming batch and known scan sequences. The values of each array for an incoming batch *B1* is calculated as follows:

- *Step 0:* Initialize an array `score`, large enough to maintain the scores for each type of scan, to all zeroes.
- *Step 1:* Calculate Euclidean distance between the features of the currently observed packet, with corresponding features of every packet in a stored scan sequence.
- *Step 2:* Select the minimum of all calculated distances (in the above step) and add it to *score*, at offset corresponding to the currently tested scan sequence.
- *Step 3:* Repeat step1 & 2 for all packets in batch *B1*. Increment the array position for to the current packet's IP by number of unique destination ports seen in *B1*.
- *Step 4:* Repeat step1 to 3 and store the score values for all types of sequences for batch *B1*. For each IP being scanned, calculate the confirmation score by dividing the corresponding unique port count by the total number of packets in batch *B1*.

Finally, the batch *B1* is labeled with the type of scan sequence having the minimum score. The same procedure is followed on all batches in incoming traffic. To log the scan, Watson produces the list of IPs under attack, their respective scan types, and the confirmation score. The confirmation score is an indication that the IP under attack is actually being scanned. Moreover, if the underlying NIDS is falsely logging benign traffic, the confirmation score will indicate a lower value as compared to an actual attack scenario. We set the threshold value for the confirmation score by observing the benign traffic of the organization (details in Sect. 3.3).

**SSH Bruteforce Module (SBM).** SSH burteforce, as the name suggests, involves attackers gaining remote shell access on vulnerable machines inside the organization by brute forcing with a list of username and password combinations [51]. Technically, each SSH connection starts with a TCP SYN packet and ends with a FIN packet. After establishing the initial socket connection over TCP, both parties negotiate secret keys for communication. Thereafter, the user authentication and all the subsequent messages are encrypted with the secret key. Thus, detecting SSH brute force is not trivial since all the messages, including authentication failures, are encrypted.

**Detection Method:** SBM's objective is to monitor short-lived SSH connections initiated by either a single or multiple IPs. We consider the connection duration to be the delay between the first SYN packet and the last FIN packet. This is because the traffic is encrypted after the key negotiation, and SBM cannot observe whether the login succeeded or failed. Since attackers use tools like `Hydra` [72], `Medusa` [24], and `NCrack` [55] to launch such attacks, we profiled the duration of each login attempt, at different network speeds. Generally, SNIDSs like Snort count the number of SYN packets within a time window and raise an alert if it crosses a threshold. But these can include benign user connections, and thus it may lead to false alerts.

To detect SSH brute-force attacks, Watson maintains a set of unique IPs, a counter per IP (called `Bfscore`), and two threshold values (`TH1` and `TH2`). `TH1` is the upper bound of the time between a connection attempt and user authentication failure, *observed when using brute-force tools*. `TH2` is the number of acceptable connection attempts with a duration less than `TH1`. If this is exceeded, Watson logs an alert. Watson tracks every SSH/TCP session by noting the duration between the TCP SYN and the corresponding TCP FIN packet. If the duration is under `TH1`, Watson logs its source IP, and the correlated `Bfscore` is incremented by one. If `Bfscore` (cumulatively, for all IPs) exceeds `TH2`, Watson logs an alert (with these IPs).

**DNS Flood Module (DFM).** Domain Name Services (DNS) are required to map domain names to their corresponding IPs. Attackers, positioned outside the trusted network of the organization, may try to choke the organization's authoritative name servers to prevent genuine users from accessing services [12,37].

**Detection Method:** In case of DNS flood, attackers generate DNS queries using a list of random subdomain names for the domain of the target organization. Most of these queries arrive at the authoritative name server of the organization and evoke NXDOMAIN (NXD) responses. This attack surges the NXD responses observed in the organization's traffic. To detect DNS floods, DFM counts the number of requests that evoke NXD for every incoming batch of packets. If DFM notices that the count exceeds a threshold (*say,* `TH3`), it logs an alert with all the attacker IPs.

An organization's network traffic may contain NXD responses especially due to mistyped URLs. The frequency of these needs to be accounted for and considered in the detection method, to remove false alerts. Watson's thresholds need to be fine-tuned by profiling the organization's DNS traffic (ref. to Sect. 3.3).

**DNS Amplification Module (DAM).** In DNS amplification attack, attackers target an individual system (of an organization) and overwhelm it with a large volume of DNS traffic [11]. Generally, To increase the traffic volume, these attacks are performed in a distributed fashion where attackers deploy an army of bots. All these bots send DNS query messages with the target's IP as their source address. This in turn evokes a lot of DNS response messages directed towards the target, thereby overwhelming it. Attackers often exploit open DNS resolvers on the Internet.

**Detection Method:** In case of DNS amplification attack, DAM monitors the DNS traffic of the organization, and keeps track of DNS response messages to spot those that do not have a corresponding query. Once the number of such query-less responses reaches a certain threshold (*say,* TH4), an alert is logged for each IP that seems to be attacked. Watson requires continuous tuning of the threshold value as per the target network's benign traffic (ref. Sect. 3.3).

### 3.2   Guidelines for Incorporating New Modules per Threat Class

We now describe guidelines to add new attack detection modules to Watson with an example. Our detection algorithm has been designed keeping in mind the protocol's behavior and not on any specific attack modalities. Thus, to design a new module for detecting brute force against an unexplored protocol like FTP, SMB, MySQL, VNC, RDP *etc..*, one only needs to understand how it works and find out its response packets seen in case of authentication failures. There are two possible scenarios. The

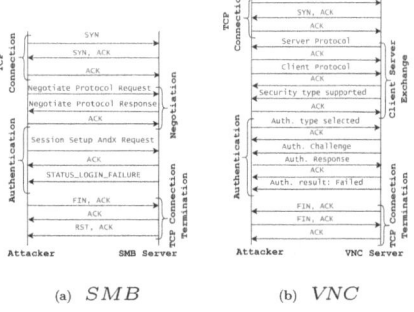

(a) *SMB*          (b) *VNC*

**Fig. 2.** *Sequence of packets in different application protocols.*

response, bearing the authentication failure message(s), could be encrypted (in case the protocol uses its secure version), or it could be exposed in plaintext. We now explain how to add new modules for an attack class.

- *Step 1:* Setup attacker and victim machines and use suitable tools to launch the attack on victim machine to collect samples of the traffic.
- *Step 2:* Study packet sequences to observe how the protocol works.
- *Step 3:* From Step 2, find the response that attacker machine receives on password failure. One may observe either of the two things:
    - *Case I:* Un-encrypted – Search for the error codes corresponding to authentication failures and keep a count.
    - *Case II:* Encrypted – Use heuristics similar to that used to detect SSH bruteforce (see Sect. 3.1). The only observable difference while studying unexplored protocols may be how TCP connections end (*i.e.,* FIN or RST).
- *Step 4:* Determine the thresholds by observing organizational traffic as explained in Sect. 3.3 for the specific protocol.

- *Step 5:* Set the thresholds and error-codes/connection close methods (FIN/RST) in the new detection module, similar to what is done for SSH.
- *Step 6:* The front-end should be updated to send the malicious traffic to the newly added backend module (Fig. 5a). Watson should now be able to detect new attacks related to the protocol under study.

**Example:** We can apply previously mentioned steps for protocols in Fig. 2. In Fig. 1a packet sequences, we observe that packets after `Client Server Exchange` step are encrypted and failed authentication results in TCP connection termination. Thus here case II applies from above guidelines (see results in Sect. 4.4).

### 3.3    Tuning Watson's Modules

To fine-tune the thresholds, SOC analysts may require the benign profile of the target organization. For **port scan**, Watson needs to periodically count the number of unique destination ports on which the public-facing servers receive connections. Next, it selects the threshold to be greater than the number of said unique port numbers.

For **SSH brute-force**, Watson needs to set two thresholds, `TH1` and `TH2`. While generating attack traffic using tools mentioned in Sect. 4.1, we found `TH1` to be 12 s on average. To set `TH2`, Watson observes the duration of regular SSH connection for the organization and counts the number of short-lived ones (*e.g.*, ones shorter than `TH1`). Let this be denoted by $sl_{max}$. `TH2` is set to a value greater than $sl_{max}$.

Counting $sl_{max}$ required to account for human typing errors leading to authentication failures. These attempts shouldn't contribute to the count, `TH2`. In our university setting, this was usually 22% of all benign SSH sessions.

For **DNS flood**, Watson relies on the threshold `TH3`. If the number of NXD responses in the organization exceeds `TH3`, then Watson logs an alert. A network may see NXD responses as a result of misspelled URLs. Thus, Watson observes the organization's benign traffic and counts the occurrence of such responses. Then it chooses `TH3` to be greater than the number of NXD responses the network traffic usually sees. In our university setting, we found it to be 21% in all benign DNS traffic.

For **DNS amplification**, Watson uses a threshold `TH4`. The system keeps track of the number of DNS responses with no corresponding queries. If ever this number crosses the threshold `TH4`, Watson logs an appropriate alert. The number `TH4` is chosen to be greater than the number of such "query-less" DNS responses the network usually sees. In our university setting, we found it to be 0.007% in all DNS traffic.

## 4    Empirical Evaluation

**Testing Watson with diverse data sources** We have tested Watson under three settings: in a controlled (in-lab) setup, on publicly available attack datasets, and under a realistic university setting along with a NIDS (*i.e., Enidrift*). Next, we present the details of these tests and their outcomes.

**Evaluation parameters** We selected F1-score, accuracy, false positive rate, the time taken by individual modules to log, per-packet processing latency, throughput, and how packet losses impact them. Throughput values give an idea about how much traffic Watson is capable of handling in realtime. Further, the effect of packet loss on accuracy and throughput tests the robustness of Watson.

## 4.1 Testing in Controlled Setup(s)

Our first evaluation was done in a controlled lab setup. For this, we generated attack traffic using commonly used tools. It had two server machines, one acting as an attacker and the other as a victim. Here, Watson is positioned on the same machine as victim. The setup is shown via Fig. 5a. Initially, we kept all modules running, and replayed the attack traffic from "attacker" to the victim machine. Further, we also tested Watson by keeping only one module running at a time. We vary the number of running modules so as to determine the maximum efficiency of each module individually. The results of these tests are presented in section (b) and (c)).

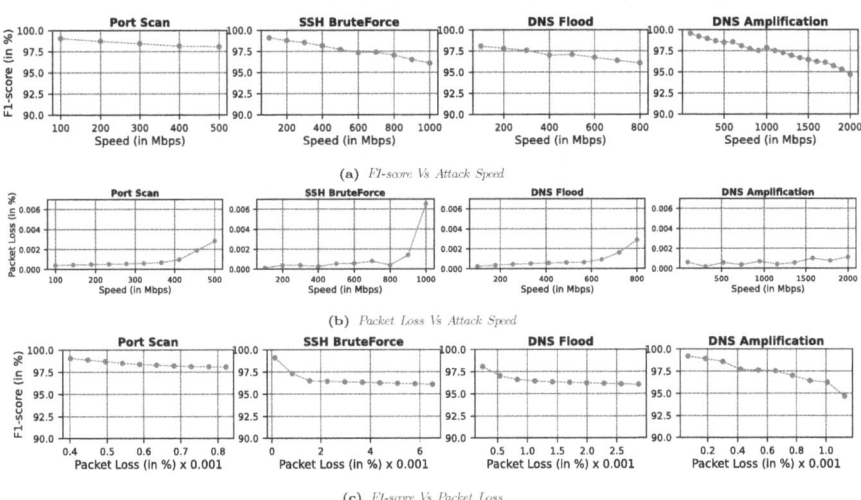

(a) *F1-score Vs Attack Speed*

(b) *Packet Loss Vs Attack Speed*

(c) *F1-score Vs Packet Loss*

**Fig. 3.** *Trends between F1-scores, attack speeds, and packet losses for all modules in controlled setup.*

(a) **Setup to generate datasets:** In order to test Watson, we created our own dataset for the four types of attacks and their variations. All the setups used multiple virtual machines (VMs). We provide details about the tools and setup as follows:

- *Port scan:* We used popular port scanners [30,54,56] and launched all the available scans, from one VM to another VM.
- *SSH bruteforce:* To emulate SSH bruteforce, we used `Hydra`, `Medusa` as well as `NCrack` tools, with their default speeds and other options, only varying the duration of the attack. These tools are specifically designed for launching brute-force attacks.
- *DNS flood:* To launch DNS flood we used `NCat` [54] tool, and wrapped it with our own multi-threaded C program. This C program generated DNS queries for random subdomains to trigger NXD responses from the target DNS server. The victim machine ran `BIND9` [19] DNS server with a few fake DNS records.
- *DNS amplification attack:* For DNS amplification, we wrote a multi-threaded python script to craft the malicious packet, spoofing the IP address of the target machine. For this, we deployed three machines – the attacker's host, the DNS server from the DNS flood experiment, and a victim machine whose IP was spoofed in the DNS request packet so that it gets the replies from the DNS server.

(b) **Results when running all the modules:** We evaluated Watson by replaying the above-generated attack traffic from the "attacker" to the "victim" machine (see Sect. A.1). We launched the attack at 10Mbps and gradually increased the speed to adjudge the maximum efficacy of the modules. It is noteworthy that attackers usually spread attacks like port scan and SSH brute-force over several hours or even days [42]. This may reduce the overall speed of these attacks (in comparison to the DNS flood or amplification attack [61]). Recent NIDS' proposals [25,50] have considered these attacks' speeds from 100Kbps to 50Mbps; we chose the maximum speeds accordingly. While performing one type of attack, we also checked if unrelated modules mistakenly classified the corresponding packets (none of the modules produced any false positives). We present Watson's results for each type of attack at different speeds.

**Port Scan Module (its different types):** Watson achieved 99.05% F1-score with *no* packet loss on port scan attack. This module, on average, spent 54 $\mu$s processing one packet (*i.e.*, step-0 to step-2 in Sect. 3.1). The trend of F1-score vs speed is presented in Fig. 3a. Watson was over 98% accurate, even when the packets were transmitted at about 300Mbps.

Further, as expected, increasing packet transmission rates, also lead to an increase in packet losses (Fig. 3b). But our design ensures that this increase in packet losses is negligible at best. *E.g.*, at 100Mbps, we observed 0.0004% of packet loss. We controlled the packet losses and optimized the port scan module by parallelizing the detection algorithm for all possible scans. Also we also observed that the other (unrelated) modules did not misclassify these packets as attacks that they were themselves designed for (*i.e.*, **zero false positives**).

Apart from an overall alert for port scans, Watson also classified them into their specific types (*e.g.*, SYN or ACK scan). The corresponding port scan traffic contained $\approx$ 2M packets. Figure 4a reports the individual accuracy scores of each type of scan. The column represents the ground truths in the attack traffic, and the corresponding row shows the scans logged by Watson. The diagonal values represent the scores of actual attack detected. *E.g.*, Watson accurately detected FIN, XMAS, Maimon attacks. For the rest of scan types, Watson selected the attack identified with the highest confidence score as the type of actual scan[4]. *E.g.*, SYN scan can be considered a subset of Connect and Version scan. Thus Connect and Version scans were also logged as SYN scans. Similarly, ACK and Window scans are detected to be of the same kind. It is noteworthy that even though a particular scan matches other kinds with some accuracy, it matches itself the most. *E.g.*, Version scan matches SYN(0.60), Connect (0.60) and FIN (0.09), but matches with itself closely (0.71).

**SSH Brute-force Module:** Watson achieved 99.09% F1-score with no packet loss while detecting SSH brute-force. The variation of detection accuracy with increasing brute-force attempts can be seen in Fig. 3a. Evidently, the F1-score falls from 99.09% to 96.08% while varying transmission rates from 100Mbps to 1Gbps. SSH brute force module, on average, spent $10\mu s$ for processing each packet. This resulted in about 0.006% packet losses for attack packets transmitted at 1Gbps (ref. Figure 3b).

**DNS Flood Module:** DFM achieved 98.07% F1-score with no packet losses. Variations in detection accuracy, for different attack speeds can be seen from Fig. 3a. Watson achieved $\approx 97.07\%$ F1-score even at 500Mbps. While further increasing the attack speeds, packet losses increased since the module takes $\approx 8.2\mu s$ to process each packet. Thus due to packet losses, F1-score dropped a bit.

**DNS Amplification Module:** Watson achieved 99.54% F1-score with no packet losses for DNS amplification attack. It took around $4.27\mu s$ to process a packet on average. Watson achieved over 95.14% F1-score even for 900Mbps attack speeds. Beyond that, F1-score suffered slightly due to increasing packet drops. Even then, Watson identified the attack transmitted at 2Gbps, with over 89.86% F1-score (while suffering $\approx 0.001\%$ packet-losses). Figure 3a and Fig. 3c present these trends.

(c) **Results for Individual Modules:** To test modules individually, we kept only one module running at the time. Here, our main focus was to test the processing throughput and detection accuracy of each module. We present the results in 4b.

In this experiment, we varied the attack traffic speeds starting from 100Mbps to 10Gbps, and monitored each modules' performance. For instance in Fig. 4b, we observed that SSH brute-force module achieved 79.15% accuracy when attack traffic was sent at 10Gbps, with 48% packet losses. WE can observer that all modules have accuracy above 80% for attacks sent at 2Gbps. Thus, the SOC analyst might deploy each module independently as per the urgency of a specific type of attack detection.

---

[4] Since some of the scans are actually subsets of other types, Watson often identified them to be the latter kinds.

(d) **Processing latency of different components:** Watson's modules process each incoming packet and logs attacks as soon as detected. To study the overall processing latency of different components (ref. Fig. 5a), we monitored Watson by increasing the number of packets gradually from the "attacker" machine. Figure 5b shows the delay due to the frontend, *i.e.,* the DPDK capture program receiving the packets from the NIC and sending them to all the modules.

While, by itself, the latency of the frontend for capturing packets was constant, the backend modules, with their respective processing delays, throttle the frontend from sending packets to the backend. The additional waiting delay varies depending upon the module and the traffic load it is processing. Thus, frontend latency T1 in Fig. 5a incorporates both packet sending and waiting time for each module. The variation of the waiting delay on T1 can be observed from the line-hatched bars in Fig. 5b. In Fig. 5b, the X-axis represents the increasing number of packets from 5k to 100k in attack traffic and Y-axis represents the time taken by each component. The second component in each bar represents the time taken to process the incoming packets, and thus module latency. We can see that port scan module takes the highest and DNS flood/amplification takes the lowest time.

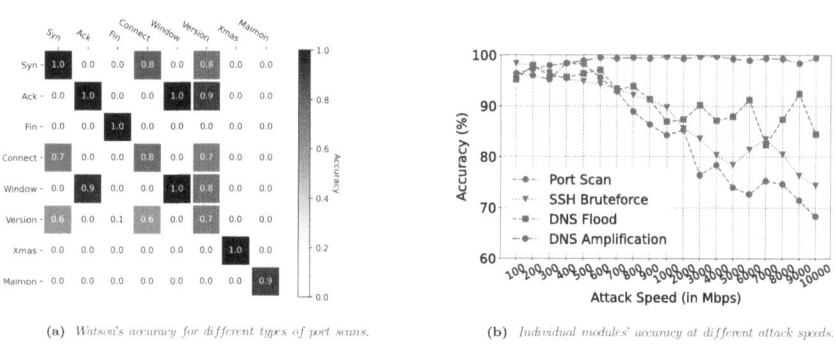

(a) *Watson's accuracy for different types of port scans.*    (b) *Individual modules' accuracy at different attack speeds.*

**Fig. 4.** *(a) Heatmap for port scans. (b) Accuracy trend with increasing traffic speed.*

## 4.2    Testing with Publicly Available Attack Datasets

Watson's modules are designed by observing the behaviour of attack traffic, which should ideally be the same across all networks [13–15,17,31,53]. The difference lies in the nature of the benign traffic across organizations. This is why we believe that Watson should work well to specifically categorize the malicious packets present in these datasets. Thus, we tested the modules on publicly available datasets. From these datasets, we selected packet traces of port scan and

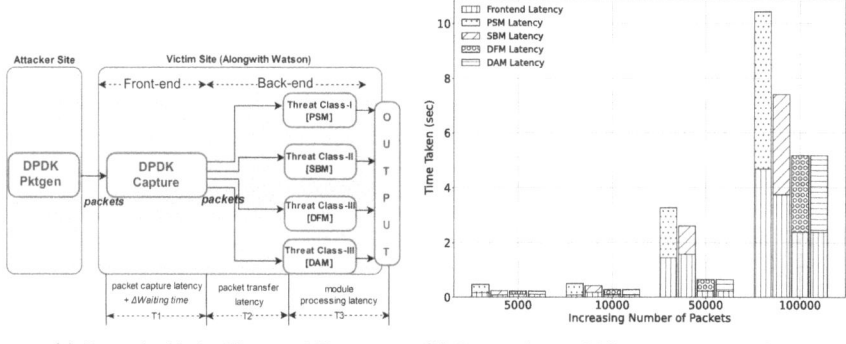

(a) *Front-end and back-end functions of Watson.*    (b) *Processing latency of different components in each module.*

**Fig. 5.** *In (b), X-axis shows increasing number of packets. Frontend (T1): DPDK module receiving packets + different Δ waiting time for each module, back-end(T2+T3):packet copying and module processing latency, (ref. to Figure 5a). Note:T2 << T1 & T2; thus not visible in above bars.*

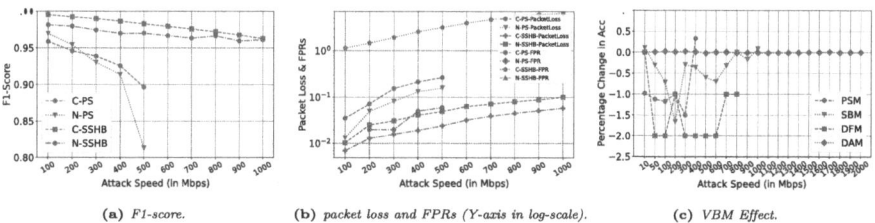

(a) *F1-score.*    (b) *packet loss and FPRs (Y-axis in log-scale).*    (c) *VBM Effect.*

**Fig. 6.** *(a) & (b) shows evaluation results for public datasets. C:CICIDS-2017, N:NDSec-1, PS:Port Scan, SSHB:SSH Bruteforce. (c) shows the effect of VBM module over others modules accuracy.*

SSH brute-force attack[5]. Each dataset was generated in a completely different network setting and thus adds diversity to the inputs. We describe these datasets, and the test results as follows:

(a) **Datasets:** The modules in Watson are developed to identify attacks by observing their nature (in terms of their traffic packets/patterns). Thus, Watson detects the attacks in a variety of publicly available datasets [14,53] out of different public datasets (*e.g.*, [16,17,22]). For our evaluation, we only selected those datasets that include the raw `pcap` files (corresponding to Watson's modules). Thus, we considered CICIDS-2017 [14] (Revised by [21]) and NDsec-1 [53].

(b) **Results:** We replayed the traffic in datasets through Watson by changing attack speeds, like earlier (Sect. 4.1). Figures 6a 6b show the results for these. We varied the attack speed from 100Mbps to 500Mbps for port scan and 100Mbps to 1Gbps for SSH brute-force attack (as done in controlled

---

[5] There were no properly labeled pcaps for DNS flood and amplification attacks.

**Table 1.** *Watson's performance against real organization data along (when used with Enidrift). Enidrift flags the malicious traffic but also ends up capturing some of the benign packets.*

| Complete Pipeline - (80/20 Benign/Malicious) | | | | | |
|---|---|---|---|---|---|
| | Enidrift | | | Watson | |
| Network Traffic (Attack+Benign (Number of packets)) | Time taken (s) | Acc. (%) | Attack packets flagged (%) | Time taken (s) | F1-score (%) |
| Port Scan (14k) | 602.26 | 99.23 | 95.11 | 0.71 | 99.05 |
| SSH Brute-force (24k) | 836.72 | 97.11 | 95.22 | 0.57 | 96.64 |
| DNS Flood (75k) | 2468.90 | 97.14 | 97.11 | 0.71 | 98.23 |
| DNS Amplification (34k) | 2001.41 | 96.22 | 94.99 | 1.69 | 98.75 |

tests). Initially, the port scan module's F1-score was 96.95% (less than that observed in Sect. 4.1) for the CICIDS-2017 dataset. After inspecting the pcap, corresponding to the timestamps, we found that it strangely contained some benign packets also. This led to lower F1-scores (causes further drop *i.e.,* 91.36% to 81.31%). Similarly, there are some benign packets present among the SSH brute-force traces of CICIDS-2017, which led to FPR of 1.14% and 6.37% for port scan module at 100Mbps and 1Gbps, respectively.

### 4.3   Testing on Real Network Traffic Along with Enidrift

We also tested Watson under realistic scenarios, besides controlled and public datasets experiments (Sec. 4.14.2. We chose our university as the target organization, where the traffic usually reaches 2Gbps at peak hours. We juxtapositioned Watson with *Enidrift* [73], a state-of-the-art NIDS. We trained Enidrift with benign traffic and tested with an admixture of benign and attack packets.
**Attack and Detection Pipeline**:

(a) **Attacker and victim sites:** In our setup, we hosted two cloud VMs, designated as the attackers. These launched attacks on specific public-facing machines of the university, designated as victims. One of the victim machines acted as the victim DNS server which had dummy entries as DNS records. The other port had 22 open, besides others, for SSH brute-force.

(b) **Enidrift and Watson:** Enidrift was placed near the edge-router of the university and obtained traffic via port mirroring. It received the traffic and flagged them as malicious or benign. Then, a separate program identifies the corresponding malicious packets (from the capture) and sends them to Watson's frontend, which relays them to the backend modules (ref. Fig. 5a). We customized Enidrift only with respect to how it presents the output to find the flagged packets.

(c) **Enidrift training:** We collected the university's traffic for 5 different days, each for a short duration (for 5 min). Enidrift is trained on the first 4 days collected pcap (around 2GB). First, the pcap are converted into CSV files containing features as described in Enidrift. These files are then fed to

Enidrift. For training Enidrift we used the same setup as earlier (in Fig. 1) with attacker machines positioned on the cloud server, targeting deliberately installed systems under our control.

(d) **Results:** We present the evaluation results in Sect. 1 for each type of attack performed on the live network. For testing, we performed attacks on the 5th day and collected the packets (*i.e.*, benign+attack), and fed them to Enidrift. The outcomes of the tests are elaborated in Sect. 1. We note that Enidrift is able to detect at least 94% of the attack traffic, but spends the most amount of time processing the input test data[6]. Once Enidrift identifies the malicious packets, another program sends those packets to Watson at the rate of 0.34ms (per packet) for further processing. Watson is able to process the packets under 2 s with F1-score of above 96% with 0% FPR in all modules (except 0.42% in port scan module in case of SSH brute force attack). Thus, through this experiment, we conclude that Watson can work in conjunction with NIDS and hence facilitate their adoption in SOCs.

**Ethical Consideration:** Given the type of experiments involved in Watson, we applied for IRB from the university board and got the approval from it. We followed ethics as per the Belmont report [5] (refer to Appendix A.3 for more details).

### 4.4  Effect of New Threat Class-II Module on Watson's Performance

Following the guidelines in Sect. 3.2, we designed a new module for VNC brute force attack (VBM). For VBM, TH1 is 1 s and TH2 is below 1% of benign VNC traffic. TH1 duration is observed while using Hydra as a VNC attack tool and TH2 is observed in the collected 1-day organizational traffic. VBM performs similar to SBM module as shown in Table 2.

**Table 2.** *VMB Performance.*

| Attack (Mbps) | Speed | F1-score (%) | Packet Loss (%) |
|---|---|---|---|
| 100-300 | | 99.11 | 0.0004 |
| 400-600 | | 98.42 | 0.0021 |
| 700-1000 | | 97.55 | 0.0041 |

*Effect on Other Modules:* To find out the effect of adding a new module on existing ones, we repeated the in-lab experiments as mentioned in Sect. 4.1. Figure 6c presents the percentage change in the accuracy of each existing module. Evidently, all modules are able to maintain their accuracy with a maximum loss of upto 2%. For PSM, SBM and DFM accuracy loss is below 1.5%.

### 4.5  Comparison with Snort

Watson's modules are designed using the protocol-level behavior of each attack type. Each module has tunable thresholds based on the organizational needs (see Sect. A.1). However, rule-based systems *e.g.*, Snort, and Suricata, need specific signatures to handle variants of an attack. *E.g.*, to detect bruteforce attack, Snort monitors incoming traffic and flags them if the count of TCP connections

---

[6] Enidrift is not GPU-accelerated and likely the reason for high processing time.

crosses a threshold. Lack of protocol level heuristics (*e.g.*, connection durations and frequency of errors), makes it susceptible to false positives. We thus repeated some experiments from Sect. 4 to compare Watson against Snort (v3.0.0)[7].

Overall, Snort is able to detect **SSH brute force** attack with accuracy ranging from 98–91% in controlled and public datasets with attacks ranging from 100Mbps-1Gbps (packet loss up to 10%). But with real setup, its accuracy falls to 59%, with an FPR of 21.25% (falsely logging port scans). For **DNS flood** attack, Snort is only able to detect the attack in controlled setup with accuracy and packet loss trends similar to SSH brute force. On real setup, although its accuracy is 81% it also falsely alerts the packets as port scan (*i.e.*, 41.46% FPR) and SSH bruteforce (*i.e.*, 13.35%) attack. Further, Snort is unable to detect **port scan** attacks in controlled and public evaluation setups. Instead, it falsely alerts them as SSH brute force attack (*i.e.*, FPR ranging from 4 to 11% at increasing network speeds). It only detects port scan in case of real setup (with 69% FPR). Lastly, Snort was able to detect **DNS amplification** with only 21% accuracy in real setup and could not detect in controlled setup at all. We conclude that Snort requires specific signatures for the same attack in different networks, despite which it produces high FPR and cannot substitute Watson.

## 5    Discussion

### 5.1    Batch Size Vs per Packet Processing Time

In Sect. 3.1, the PSM module uses DTW which involves a calculation of Euclidean distance (ED) between packets of stored sequences and the incoming batch of traffic. One may argue that ED calculation may scale quadratically with increasing number of packets. Nonetheless, we empirically observed the trend between per packet processing time (in milliseconds) and increasing batch size from 1 to 10k. Figure 7 establishes that batch size should be below 6k for low processing times.

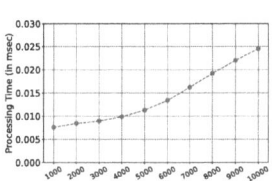

**Fig. 7.** *Batch size Vs per packet processing time.*

### 5.2    Qualitative User-Study

To get an initial feedback on Watson, we involved members of a (small scale) SOC and performed semi-structured interviews by following the already accepted structure provided by Alahmadi *et al.* [2]. We chose $N = 4$ participants, all with at least 6 years of experience ($min = 6, max = 15$), all having taken undergraduate computer science courses. All participants were given a copy of Watson paper to read. We asked questions specific to its pipeline and its usefulness to guage their understanding.

---

[7] We used signatures from default rules available in Snort and from [1].

Overall, all participants were positive, *w.r.t.* realtime deployment factors *e.g.*, fast mitigation and modularity. All gave Watson a rating of 4(/5) while stating that such proof of concepts should be tested in organizations. We infer that SOC analysts would prefer solutions considering real-world deployment setups rather than those tested offline (*e.g.*, on datasets).[8] All participants stressed again that organizations with high-speed access, hosting several services would certainly benefit from Watson.

### 5.3   Future Work

We shall test Watson in an SOC along with efficient NIDS such as Whisper. Whisper is designed to work in networks with large volumes of benign traffic. We believe that Watson can be deployed since it was tested on a live network where the peak traffic exceeds 3Gbps, with deliberately generated attack traffic transmitted at about 1Gbps. The high accuracy in such scenarios shows promise for it to be deployed in much larger organizations where traffic of diverse nature.

## 6   Conclusion

We present Watson, a modular system to detect attacks and their variants in real time. Watson is designed to receive malicious traffic from any MNIDS. We prototyped Watson with four modules corresponding to major network threat classes. Watson can detect port scans and its variants generally seen in the wild. It achieves over 98% F1-score in all modules and is able to identify the scan type with an accuracy of 100% for 5 (out of 8) scans. Similarly, the detection accuracy is over 90%, for attacks with speeds up to 2Gbps (*e.g.*, in DNS amplification). Watson's performance is consistent across the three different setups – controlled, public datasets, and real-world attack traffic of an organization. Also, it performs better than Snort in all setups.

**Acknowledgments..** This work was funded by NSCS SRP-158 grant to IIIT Delhi, India.

## A   Appendix

### A.1   Experimental Setup and Implementation

We used two Dell PowerEdge R530 (2.30GHz) running Ubuntu 20.04 (Linux kernel v5.4). One acted as a traffic generator, and the other ran an implementation of Watson (packet receiver/capturer) (Fig. 5a). DualPort 40G Intel XL710 ethernet cards were installed on both machines (connected back-to-back with optical SFP connectors). One of the machines was used to replay traffic at high speeds. To avoid kernel level bottlenecks [7], we relied on Intel's Data Plane Development

---

[8] Additionally, P2 and P4 suggested to consider Watson to be deployed for protecting the local network as well.

Kit (`DPDK v19.11.8`) [39] utility `Pktgen v22.04.1` [20]. The other host ran one traffic-capturing process and the four detection modules[9]. The traffic capture program used `PcapPlusPlus` library [58] that uses DPDK to receive packets. This program sends the captured packets to the four modules using a zero-copy IPC (*i.e.*, `vmsplice()`). Finally, Enidrift was trained and tested on one of the servers.

*Resources Used:* The packet-generator machine used two CPU cores for `Pktgen`. Both machines (generator as well as receiver) reserved at least 60GB of `huge-pages` for running DPDK and DPDK-based applications. The receiver-side server used a total of 36 cores to run all four modules and the DPDK capture program. Individually SBM, DFM and DAM modules used eight cores each, PSM used nine cores per batch of input packets, and the traffic capturer program uses three cores.

### A.2    Limitations and Challenges

- **Zero-day threats:** Watson has been designed to assist the analysts for known attack detection and thus will not classify zero-days. However, if the zero-day is a modification of an existing attack, it may flag it to its closest form of the said attack.
- **Dependence on the target organization's data & periodic updation of Watson's thresholds:** SOCs need to know about the internal network structure of an organization and have access to traffic destined to the public-facing services that need to be defended. Such information is very crucial for SOCs since the distribution and type of benign traffic may vary from one organization to another [2]. Thresholds in modules must be updated whenever the profile changes over time because of various reasons (*e.g.*, addition of infrastructure and/or (human) resources).

### A.3    Ethical Considerations

Our research involves capturing traffic of a section (VLAN) of our university's network that sees heavy use, mostly for research and academic purposes. It also involves generating attack traffic to machines we control (only for a few minutes of each attack type, so that it does not disrupt normal university services) to evaluate the efficacy of Watson to identify attacks in the malicious flow. We took utmost care to first anonymize it using tools like [69] before using it for our analysis. The data collection and the involved process has been approved by our university's IRB committee.

## References

1. Adiwal, S., Rajendran, B., et al.: DNS intrusion detection (did)–a snort-based solution to detect DNS amplification and DNS tunneling attacks. Franklin Open **2**, 100010 (2023)

---

[9] Our code is public on [70].

2. Alahmadi, B.A., Axon, L., et al.: 99% false positives: a qualitative study of SOC analysts' perspectives on security alarms. In: Proceedings of the 31st USENIX Security Symposium, Boston, MA, USA, pp. 10–12 (2022)

3. Alaidaros, H., Mahmuddin, M., et al.: An overview of flow-based and packet-based intrusion detection performance in high speed networks. In: Proceedings of the International Arab Conference on Information Technology, pp. 1–9 (2011)

4. Apruzzese, G., Laskov, P., et al.: SOK: pragmatic assessment of machine learning for network intrusion detection. In: 2023 IEEE 8th European Symposium on Security and Privacy (EuroS&P), pp. 592–614. IEEE (2023)

5. Beauchamp, T.L.: The belmont report. The Oxford textbook of clinical research ethics, pp. 149–155 (2008)

6. Bhusal, D., Shin, R., et al.: SOK: modeling explainability in security analytics for interpretability, trustworthiness, and usability. In: Proceedings of the 18th International Conference on ARES, pp. 1–12 (2023)

7. Cai, Q., Chaudhary, S.: et al.: Understanding host network stack overheads. In: Proceedings of the 2021 ACM SIGCOMM 2021 Conference, pp. 65–77 (2021)

8. Cheng, Z., Lv, Q., et al.: Kairos: practical intrusion detection and investigation using whole-system provenance. In: 2024 IEEE Symposium on Security and Privacy (SP), pp. 3533–3551. IEEE (2024)

9. Cloudflare: Cloudflare white paper: DNS and the threat of DDOS. https://www.cloudflare.com/static/c14f1244a3b819345f92da3e4f59846e/DNS_and_the_Threat_of_DDoS_Whitepaper.pdf

10. DDOS threat report for 2023 q1 (2023). https://blog.cloudflare.com/ddos-threat-report-2023-q1/

11. DNS amplification attack (2024). https://www.cloudflare.com/learning/ddos/dns-amplification-ddos-attack/

12. DNS-flood DDOS attack. https://www.cloudflare.com/learning/ddos/dns-flood-ddos-attack/, 2024

13. Datasets, C.: Cidds 2017 dataset. https://www.hs-coburg.de/forschung/forschungsprojekte-oeffentlich/informationstechnologie/cidds-coburg-intrusion-detection-data-sets.html#c6121

14. Datasets, C.-I.: Cic-ids 2017. https://www.unb.ca/cic/datasets/ids-2017.html

15. Iscxids-2012 dataset. http://www.unb.ca/cic/datasets/ids.html

16. Datasets, K.: Kitsune network attack dataset data set. https://archive.ics.uci.edu/ml/datasets/Kitsune+Network+Attack+Dataset

17. Datasets, U.: Unsw-nb15. https://www.unsw.adfa.edu.au/unsw-canberra-cyber/cybersecurity/ADFA-NB15-Datasets/

18. Decipher: Linux botnet targets weak SSH server credentials. https://duo.com/decipher/linux-iot-botnet-targets-weak-ssh-server-credentials

19. Docs, B.: Bind9. https://bind9.readthedocs.io/en/v9_18_4/chapter1.html

20. Docs, P.: Pktgen. https://pktgen-dpdk.readthedocs.io/en/latest/

21. Engelen, G., Rimmer, V., et al.: Troubleshooting an intrusion detection dataset: the cicids2017 case study. In: IEEE Security and Privacy Workshops (SPW), pp. 7–12 (2021)

22. Fontugne, R., Borgnat, P., et al.: MAWIlab: combining diverse anomaly detectors for automated anomaly labeling and performance benchmarking. In: Proceedings of the 6th International COnference, Co-NEXT 2010 (2010)

23. Fortinet: What is a port scan? https://www.fortinet.com/resources/cyberglossary/what-is-port-scan (2024)

24. Forum, F.A.S.S.: Medusa. http://foofus.net/?page_id=51, 2024

25. Fu, C., Li, Q., et al.: Realtime robust malicious traffic detection via frequency domain analysis. In: Proceedings of the 2021 ACM SIGSAC Conference on Computer and Communications Security, pp. 3431–3446 (2021)
26. Garcia-Teodoro, P., Diaz-Verdejo, J., et al.: Anomaly-based network intrusion detection: techniques, systems and challenges. Comput. Security 28(1-2), 18–28 (2009)
27. George Sandford, G.T.N.: SOC burnout is real. https://www.helpnetsecurity.com/2021/06/23/soc-burnout-is-real/
28. Goodin, D.: After lying low, SSH botnet mushrooms and is harder than ever to take down. https://arstechnica.com/information-technology/2022/02/after-lying-low-ssh-botnet-mushrooms-and-is-harder-than-ever-to-take-down/
29. Goyal, A., Wang, G., et al. R-Caid: embedding root cause analysis within provenance-based intrusion detection (2024)
30. Graham, R.D.: Masscan. https://github.com/robertdavidgraham/masscan
31. Group, M.W., et al.: Traffic archive. *http://mawi.wide.ad.jp/mawi/*, 2024
32. Han, D., Wang, Z., et al.: Deepaid: interpreting and improving deep learning-based anomaly detection in security applications. In: Proceedings of the 2021 ACM SIGSAC CCS, pp. 3197–3217 (2021)
33. Han, X., Pasquier, T., et al.: Unicorn: runtime provenance-based detector for advanced persistent threats. arXiv preprint arXiv:2001.01525 (2020)
34. Hellemons, L., Hendriks, L., Hofstede, R., Sperotto, A., Sadre, R., Pras, A.: SSHCure: A Flow-Based SSH Intrusion Detection System. In: Sadre, R., Novotný, J., Čeleda, P., Waldburger, M., Stiller, B. (eds.) AIMS 2012. LNCS, vol. 7279, pp. 86–97. Springer, Heidelberg (2012). https://doi.org/10.1007/978-3-642-30633-4_11
35. Hsu, Y.-F., He, Z., et al.: Toward an online network intrusion detection system based on ensemble learning. In: 2019 IEEE 12th International Conference on Cloud Computing (CLOUD), pp. 174–178. IEEE (2019)
36. IDS, S.: Suricata- open source ids / ips / nsm engine. https://suricata-ids.org/
37. Imperva: DNS-flood. https://www.imperva.com/learn/ddos/dns-flood/
38. Institute, I.: Anatomy of an apt attack: Step by step approach. https://resources.infosecinstitute.com/topic/anatomy-of-an-apt-attack-step-by-step-approach/
39. Intel: Intel data plane development kit. https://www.dpdk.org/
40. Kang, J., Yang, H., et al.: ActDetector: a sequence-based framework for network attack activity detection. In: 2022 IEEE Symposium on Computers and Communications (ISCC), pp. 1–7. IEEE (2022)
41. Kaspersky: What is an advanced persistent threat (apt)? https://www.kaspersky.com/resource-center/definitions/advanced-persistent-threats
42. Labs, L.: Groundhog botnet rapidly infecting cloud. https://www.lacework.com/blog/groundhog-botnet-rapidly-infecting-cloud/
43. Lanvin, M., Gimenez, P.-F., et al.: Towards understanding alerts raised by unsupervised network intrusion detection systems. In: The 26th International Symposium on Research in Attacks, Intrusions and Defenses (RAID 2023) (2023)
44. Li, R., Li, Q., et al.: Interpreting unsupervised anomaly detection in security via rule extraction. In: Thirty-seventh Conference on Neural Information Processing Systems (NeurIPS) (2023)
45. Liu, H., Lang, B., et al.: CNN and RNN based payload classification methods for attack detection. Knowl. Based Syst. 163, 332–341 (2019)
46. LogRhythm. https://logrhythm.com/
47. Maseer, Z.K., Yusof, R., et al.: Benchmarking of machine learning for anomaly based intrusion detection systems in the CICIDS2017 dataset. IEEE Access 9, 22351–22370 (2021)

48. Milajerdi, S.M., Gjomemo, R., et al.: Holmes: real-time apt detection through correlation of suspicious information flows. In: 2019 IEEE Symposium on Security and Privacy (SP), pp. 1137–1152. IEEE (2019)
49. Mink, J., Benkraouda, H., et al.: Everybody's got ml, tell me what else you have: Practitioners' perception of ml-based security tools and explanations. In: 2023 IEEE Symposium on Security and Privacy (SP), pp. 2068–2085 (2023)
50. Mirsky, Y., Doitshman, T., et al.: Kitsune: an ensemble of autoencoders for online network intrusion detection. In: NDSS (2018)
51. MITRE: Brute force. https://attack.mitre.org/techniques/T1110/001/
52. Nadeem, A., Vos, D., et al.: SOK: explainable machine learning for computer security applications. arXiv preprint arXiv:2208.10605 (2022)
53. NDSec: Ndsec-1 dataset. https://www2.hs-fulda.de/NDSec/NDSec-1/Files/
54. NMAP: Ncat. https://nmap.org/ncat/
55. Ncrack. https://nmap.org/ncrack/
56. NMap-the network mapper. https://nmap.org/
57. Org, S.: A sans 2021 survey: Security operations center (SOC) (2021)
58. PcapPlusPlus. https://pcapplusplus.github.io/
59. Rajadurai, H., Gandhi, U.D.: A stacked ensemble learning model for intrusion detection in wireless network. In: Neural Computing and Applications, pp. 1–9 (2020)
60. Ramanathan, S., Hossain, A., et al.: Quantifying the impact of blocklisting in the age of address reuse. In: Proceedings of the ACM Internet Measurement Conference (IMC), pp. 360–369 (2020)
61. Report, I.: 2021 global DNS threat report. https://www.efficientip.com/wp-content/uploads/2021/06/2021-IDC-DNS-Threat-Report-Infobrief-final_compressed.pdf
62. Roesch, M., et al.: Snort: lightweight intrusion detection for networks. Lisa **99**, 229–238 (1999)
63. M.T.D. Science: Dynamic time warping. https://towardsdatascience.com/dynamic-time-warping-3933f25fcdd
64. Secureworks: How to decrease alert fatigue while increasing SOC efficiency. https://www.secureworks.com/blog/how-to-reduce-alert-fatigue
65. Sharafaldin, I., Lashkari, A.H., et al.: Toward generating a new intrusion detection dataset and intrusion traffic characterization. ICISSp **1**, 108–116 (2018)
66. Shiravi, A., Shiravi, H., et al.: Toward developing a systematic approach to generate benchmark datasets for intrusion detection. Computers & Security **31**(3), 357–374 (2012)
67. Sommer, R., Paxson, V.: Outside the closed world: on using machine learning for network intrusion detection. In: 2010 IEEE Symposium on Security and Privacy (SP), pp. 305–316. IEEE (2010)
68. Splunk: Siem, Aiops, application management, log management, machine learning, and compliance. https://www.splunk.com/
69. Turner, A.: Tcpreplay (2011). http://tcpreplay.synfin.net/trac/
70. Umayya, Z., Nandi, A.: Watson. https://github.com/zeya2u9/Watson/
71. van Ede, T., Aghakhani, H., et al.: DeepCase: semi-supervised contextual analysis of security events. In: IEEE Security and Privacy (2022)
72. van Hauser: Hydra. https://github.com/vanhauser-thc/thc-hydra
73. Wang, X.: ENIDrift: a fast and adaptive ensemble system for network intrusion detection under real-world drift. In: Annual Computer Security Applications Conference (ACSAC), pp. 785–798 (2022)

74. Wei, F., Li, H., et al.: XNIDS: explaining deep learning-based network intrusion detection systems for active intrusion responses. In: 32nd USENIX Security Symposium (USENIX Security 23), Anaheim, CA, USA (2023)
75. Zissman, M.: Darpa intrusion detection scenario specific data sets (2000)

# Sharing Is (S)caring: Security and Privacy Issues in Decentralized Physical Infrastructure Networks (DePIN)

Maurantonio Caprolu[1]([envelope]) [ORCID], Simone Raponi[2] [ORCID], and Roberto Di Pietro[1] [ORCID]

[1] King Abdullah University of Science and Technology (KAUST),
Thuwal 23955, Saudi Arabia
{maurantonio.caprolu,roberto.dipietro}@kaust.edu.sa
[2] Equixly S.r.l. Firenze, Firenze 50124, Italy
simone.raponi@equixly.com

**Abstract.** Decentralized Physical Infrastructure Networks (DePIN) have emerged as a promising paradigm, offering numerous benefits across various domains. For instance, DePIN allows to share (and monetize) excess resources, such as computing capacity and network bandwidth, enabling the provisioning of a wide range of services, including anonymous navigation, data acquisition, and computation, in exchange for cryptocurrency. The above examples are just the tip of the iceberg of the dematerialization, distribution, and democratization capabilities of the DePIN paradigm. However, in addition to their potential advantages, the decentralized nature of DePIN applications also introduces significant security and privacy concerns that must be carefully addressed.

In this paper, we analyze the security and privacy implications of the DePIN infrastructure focusing on two domains: *Network Services* and *Computation for AI-based Tasks*. By examining the major active projects within each domain, we identify common security and privacy issues that require urgent attention from the community. Specifically, vulnerabilities related to the sharing of resources with unknown entities pose significant risks to the integrity and reliability of DePIN networks. In addition, concerns related to the handling of sensitive data, such as personal information and financial transactions, underscore the importance of robust security measures. Furthermore, inherited cybersecurity challenges from the underlying blockchain technology, including Sybil attacks and consensus vulnerabilities, exacerbate the security landscape of DePIN networks. To bridge this gap, we propose several directions for future research aimed at addressing security issues common to the DePIN paradigm.

**Keywords:** DePIN · Security · Privacy · Blockchain · IoT · Tokenomics

H. H. Song et al. (Eds.): NSS 2024, LNCS 15564, pp. 301–318, 2025.
https://doi.org/10.1007/978-981-96-3531-3_15

# 1   Introduction

The emergence of the DePIN sector marks a significant variation from the traditional Web2-based online service model. To fully grasp the innovation introduced
by this new paradigm, it is useful to recall the evolution of Internet technologies
and service models, as illustrated in Fig. 1. Although Web2 enabled end-users
to generate and share content, its centralized architecture granted major tech
companies full control over users' data and identities. In contrast, the user-
centric Web3 model, on which the DePIN architecture is implemented, allowed
users to share physical resources, e.g., bandwidth, storage, and computation,
in a zero-trust environment, giving them ownership of their data [8]. In Web2,
dominant big tech companies, such as Facebook, Google, and Amazon, exercise
significant control over user data and interactions [7]. These platforms act as
intermediaries, collecting large amounts of user data to fuel targeted advertising
and other monetization strategies. In this model, users often sacrifice privacy
and autonomy in exchange for access to free services. For example, social media
platforms track users' online activities, preferences, and interactions to deliver
personalized content and advertisements in exchange for free access to their platforms and services [6,13]. On the contrary, Web3 embraces decentralization with
the aim of allowing users to regain control over their data. Blockchain technology plays a central role in Web3, enabling decentralized applications (DApps),
which operate without centralized servers. Users retain ownership of their data
and can interact with DApps in a peer-to-peer manner without relying on intermediaries. For example, decentralized social media platforms, such as Steemit
and Minds, reward users for their contributions and allow them to monetize
their content directly, bypassing traditional intermediaries [7]. The concept of
value exchange is, in fact, one of the key differences between Web2 and Web3. In
Web2, a few big companies extract value from users' data and attention, often
without adequately compensating them. On the contrary, Web3 leverages tokenomics methodologies and decentralized finance (DeFi) protocols, where users
can earn and exchange tokens for their contributions. For example, platforms like
Uniswap and Compound enable users to participate in decentralized exchanges
and lending/borrowing protocols, earning tokens in exchange for liquidity or borrowing assets [19]. Following the Web3 revolution, the DePIN model emerged
as a response to the limitations and drawbacks of centralized infrastructure and
services in traditional Internet of Things (IoT) and networking architectures. His-
torically, IoT frameworks have operated primarily in two modes: cloud-centric,
where data from physical devices is routed through IoT gateways to centralized
cloud servers for processing and storage, or edge-centric, which involves processing data closer to the source by specialized edge servers [14]. Although these
approaches have been prevalent in IoT applications, they tend to be centralized or hybrid in nature. In contrast, DePIN introduces a pioneering approach
by integrating three core concepts: Blockchain, IoT, and Tokenomics, following
the Web3 model. This integration enables the creation of decentralized systems
that are not only efficient but also transparent and economically incentivized,
enabling community-driven development and resource management. In the last

few years, several common use cases have risen for DePIN, showcasing the versatility and potentialities of this model. Some of the most common DePIN use cases include decentralized Internet access, supply chain management, energy grid, and finance, just to name a few.

Although DePIN applications offer numerous benefits, they also pose several security concerns that need to be addressed. Unfortunately, as usually happens during the development of new technologies, both academic and industrial research focus more on designing and implementing new platforms that enable innovative use cases, often neglecting crucial security considerations.

**Contributions.** To address the cited gaps, in this paper we analyze the novel DePIN infrastructure from both the security and privacy perspectives. In this regard, we first selected two domains, based on the popularity and capitalization of their prominent projects. Then, for each of the two domains, we discuss the major active projects and identify security and privacy concerns that need to be addressed by the community. Finally, we present several security issues that are horizontal to DePIN use cases and propose several directions for future research on possible countermeasures. In more detail, the main contributions of this paper can be summarized as follows:

- After discussing the DePIN technological pillars, we summarize and synthesize the general DePIN architecture providing a unified reference framework—contrary to the partial and scattered information available in the literature.
- We analyze two different DePIN domains, *Network Services* and *Computation for AI-based tasks*, identify the major related active projects, and discuss their peculiar security and privacy issues.
- We outline several security challenges idiosyncratic to the DePIN paradigm, while also suggesting potential directions for future research aimed at developing effective countermeasures.

## 2   Related Work

Research into Decentralized Physical Infrastructure Networks (DePIN) is still in its infancy, with a few key studies setting the initial groundwork for understanding and developing these complex systems. This section reviews some of the seminal works that address the architecture, classification, and foundational protocols of DePIN, focusing on how these studies frame the current landscape and identify the primary challenges of these networks. Fan et al. position paper [5] discusses the potential to scale DePIN through the use of rollup-centric architectures. They propose the integration of off-chain transaction aggregation and on-chain data commitment as a solution to the scalability limitations of traditional blockchain systems. This approach is suggested to significantly improve transaction throughput, which is essential for DePIN applications that demand high transaction volumes and swift processing. The insights from the paper provide a preliminary look at how DePIN systems can be made more efficient and

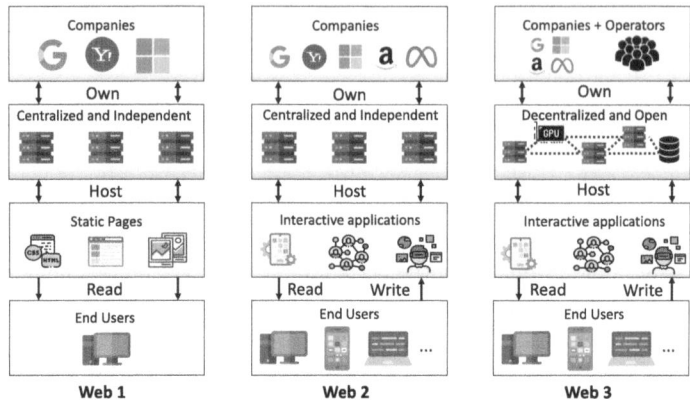

**Fig. 1.** Evolution of Internet technologies, from Web1 to Web3.

scalable. Ballandies et al. [2] offer one of the first categorizations of the emerging field of DePIN through a comprehensive taxonomy. Their work organizes DePIN systems based on the underlying technologies, operational mechanisms, and applications. This taxonomy is valuable for systematically identifying and understanding the diverse aspects of DePIN systems. Sarkar [15] has introduced a generalized protocol framework aimed at standardizing the core functionalities of DePIN. His framework outlines the critical components and interactions within DePIN systems, aiming to support the development of modular and interoperable applications across different sectors. Sarkar's framework contributes to the foundational efforts in promoting a cohesive approach to DePIN development, highlighting the need for standards and consistency in these decentralized systems.

These early studies are pivotal in shaping the initial conceptual and technical understanding of DePIN. However, they also reveal a significant gap in the literature, particularly in addressing security and privacy challenges that are critical to the robust and safe deployment of DePIN systems. Our research builds upon these preliminary findings, focusing specifically on enhancing security and privacy mechanisms, key elements for the broader adoption of DePIN technologies.

## 3   DePIN Architecture

The concept of DePIN is strictly related to Decentralized Applications (DApps), a novel software paradigm that leverages blockchain technology to run applications on decentralized networks rather than centralized servers. The architecture and implementation details of a DePIN application strictly depend on the underlying blockchain environment. In the following, we generalize an architectural design, common to any DePIN project, which consists of technologies and methods combined to enable decentralized infrastructure management and operations. The core technological pillars include blockchain, which implements smart contracts and powers *DApps* technologies, as well as IoT, *tokenization*, and novel methodologies like *tokenomics*.

DePIN applications leverage blockchain technology to establish a decentralized and tamper-proof public ledger to record data exchanges within the system. This decentralized infrastructure eliminates the need for centralized intermediaries, enabling transactions between participants in a trustless environment. The blockchain infrastructure also provides smart contracts, a crucial component in DePIN applications. Smart contracts are self-executing pieces of code that implement agreements between parties with predefined rules and conditions. Directly deployed on the blockchain platform, smart contracts enable efficient and transparent operations within the network, implementing several functions, such as asset management, data sharing, incentive mechanisms, and many others.

DePIN applications, typically built as *DApps* on top of a blockchain infrastructure, leverage a Layer 1 blockchain to facilitate seamless interactions with the underlying system. This enables users to manage shared resources, view real-time data, and participate in network governance. Once deployed, these applications operate autonomously through smart contracts, executing tasks according to predefined rules without human intervention. Their decentralized nature ensures that no single entity controls them, relying instead on distributed consensus mechanisms to maintain transparency and security.

Another crucial concept for DePIN is *tokenization*, that is, the process of converting assets into digital tokens on a blockchain. These tokens can represent different types of assets, including physical assets, e.g., real estate or commodities [12], financial assets[1], e.g., stocks or bonds, or digital assets, e.g., cryptocurrency or digital collectibles. A critical feature provided by *tokenization* is to enable *fractional ownership* by dividing assets into smaller, tradable units usually managed by smart contracts within DePIN applications. In the context of *DApps*, and particularly in the *DeFi* and DePIN domains, *tokenization* plays a crucial role in creating fungible or non-fungible tokens that represent ownership or rights to specific assets or utilities within the ecosystem.

Providing end-users with economic incentives to boost active participation and maintain adherence to the protocol is imperative for the security and success of any decentralized project. In this context, *tokenomics*, which studies the economic incentives that make a crypto-based project valuable, assumes a pivotal role in DePIN applications. Typically, *DApps* use either the native token of the underlying blockchain network or a customized one to encourage participation, reward contributions, and facilitate value exchange. These tokens may represent ownership rights, access to network resources, or voting power within the governance framework of the system. A popular component of tokenomics, relevant but not exclusive to DePIN, are airdrops: quantities of tokens distributed to active users (typically, if some conditions are verified) in order to start aggregating a community that could possibly foster interest in the project [9].

---

[1] https://www.coindesk.com/markets/2024/03/20/blackrock-enters-asset-tokenization-race-with-new-fund-on-the-ethereum-network/.

A general DePIN infrastructure is shown in Fig. 2. At the core of the network are physical devices, owned by users participating in the protocol, often called *operators*. This layer can include any device, ranging from personal computers to small sensors embedded with IoT capabilities, shared by operators to end-users. Physical devices are deployed across the infrastructure network to provide particular services related to the main goal of the implemented application, such as collecting, processing, or storing data, handling network packets, and managing green energy production and distribution, just to name a few [3]. Operators connect their physical resources to the DePIN application, which leverages smart contracts, tokenization, and tokenomics to create the market. End-users make an offer according to their needs, use the resources, and pay a rental fee. Finally, the transaction is stored on a Layer 1 blockchain, and the operator receives the benefit according to the platform rules and conditions.

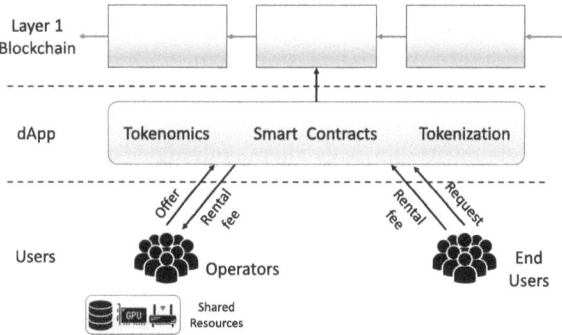

**Fig. 2.** A generic high-level DePIN architecture

## 4   Decentralization of Network Services

DePIN technologies have introduced novel approaches to the provision and management of network services, offering distinct advantages in terms of resilience, scalability, and economic efficiency. Wireless connectivity and VPN services stand out as domains that are undergoing a substantive transformation thanks to the DePIN paradigm, generating use cases that, other than being interesting on their own, also epitomize the added value of DePIN and show further possible applications in different domains as well. In this section, we discuss the most popular projects related to *decentralized VPN* (dVPN) and *decentralized wireless* (deWI). Then, we analyze the security and privacy aspects of these two use cases from the perspective of both the users participating in the protocol, i.e., the ones who share their resources, and the end-users, i.e., the ones who utilize the shared resource.

## 4.1   Decentralized VPN (dVPN)

Virtual Private Networks (VPNs) play a crucial role in ensuring secure and private communications over the Internet, especially in particular contexts, such as public networks and areas under censorship. Traditional VPN services are centralized and operated by commercial providers, raising concerns about data privacy, software vulnerabilities, and potential regulatory restrictions. In this scenario, DePIN applications seek to address these limitations by offering decentralized alternatives to traditional VPN services, leveraging blockchain technology and distributed infrastructure to improve security, privacy, and user control.

In a DePIN-based VPN ecosystem, participants deploy decentralized VPN nodes (dVPNs), creating a distributed network of exit points for the VPN service. Using blockchain-based identity management and encryption protocols, dVPNs ensure secure and private communication, protecting user data from surveillance, censorship, and unauthorized access. These applications leverage tokenomics to incentivize node operators and users. The system rewards operators with native tokens for providing bandwidth and maintaining infrastructure, while users access services by staking tokens or paying fees.

dVPNs offer several advantages over centralized VPN providers. First, dVPNs encrypt user packets and mix them with network traffic of other users, making online activities harder to trace. Without centralized servers, dVPNs reduce the risk of data breaches, logging, and surveillance, making censorship and blocking difficult. These advantages make dVPNs particularly suitable for regions with restricted internet access. Additionally, dVPNs leverage residential IP addresses, since exit nodes are operated by retail users, unlike centralized VPNs that use data center IPs. Residential IPs usually have better reputations, resulting in fewer restrictions, and provide greater access to geo-restricted content. They also reduce the risk of IP blocking, offering a smoother browsing experience and enhanced online freedom.

It is worth noting that dVPN is not a novel concept. One of the first proposals for a fully distributed VPN system over P2P networks, called Everywhere Local Area network (ELA) [1], dates back to 2005. Although the rationale is the same, the lack of incentives for participants, as well as a reliable underlying technology layer, prevented the wide diffusion of this technology. However, the advent of the DePIN paradigm, that is, blockchain and smart contracts combined with novel tokenomics methodologies, fueled the revival and rapid spread of dVPN services, demonstrating the power of DePIN infrastructures. Although dVPN is still in its infancy, the provided solution is attracting numerous operators and end-users, also fueling research into optimal monetization strategies [18] and novel architectures [16,17].

### Major Active Projects
**Deeper Network.** This project aims to integrate cybersecurity, network sharing, and blockchain technology to create an innovative internet infrastructure inspired by the Web3 paradigm, adhering to the principle "Of the Users, By the Users, For the Users," which aims to return internet infrastructure ownership

to end-users. Deeper Network operates a decentralized infrastructure powered by proprietary hardware devices running an open-source operating system, *atomOS*. Users connect these plug-and-play devices to their home routers, becoming network exit nodes and gaining free access to Deeper Network's dVPN service in exchange for sharing their bandwidth. The network is governed by a Proof-of-Credit (PoCr) consensus algorithm. In addition, users can stake the native token, Deeper Network (DPR), to participate in mining and earn rewards. The underlying blockchain, Deeper-chain, is built on the Substrate framework to support essential network functionalities. A key advantage of this project is the versatility and user-friendliness of its devices. Although traditional dVPNs are often complex and suited only for tech-savvy users, Deeper Network's devices simplify setup, making the network accessible to users regardless of their technical expertise.

**Mysterium Network.** Mysterium Network is an open-source ecosystem offering several privacy-focused tools and services, including a dVPN. Participants join by running the free MystNodes software, which connects their device to the network as an exit node. In return for sharing bandwidth and routing other users' traffic, node owners earn the native token, MYST, based on connection time and data volume. The network's tokenomics model allows node runners and token holders to stake MYST in the delegation pool, participate in the consensus protocol, and earn additional tokens. Networking functionalities are built on the WireGuard protocol, and the micropayment system uses *Hermes*, a proprietary protocol that allows pay-as-you-go transactions. *Hermes* operates on a Layer 2 solution backed by the Ethereum blockchain. One major advantage of Mysterium Network is its purely software-based approach, allowing users worldwide to join without setup costs; in contrast, Deeper Network requires purchasing proprietary hardware. MystNodes is lightweight and can run on budget devices, such as the Raspberry Pi, enabling continuous operation with minimal hardware and energy costs. The Mysterium network boasts over 22,000 nodes in 155+ countries, routing 1.83 PB of traffic monthly, according to the official website.

**Security and Privacy Issues of dVPN**
While dVPNs offer unique advantages in terms of architecture, provided services, and monetization model, they also present certain challenges and limitations that users and operators should carefully consider before adopting them as their preferred VPN solution. Some disadvantages stem from technical aspects, e.g., potential speed reduction due to routing through many different heterogeneous nodes, and setup complexity. Although these challenges can be addressed by developing and implementing more robust and user-friendly protocols, others arise from the distributed and permissionless nature of the network, posing risks to the security and privacy of both users and operators. In fact, the volunteer-based model of any DePIN application means trusting nodes operated by unknown entities, as well as sharing resources with unknown users.

Furthermore, in the particular case of dVPNs, regulatory ambiguity is also a big concern. In fact, the legal status of these services can be unclear or vary by region, potentially putting operators at risk of unknowingly violating local laws. In the following, we discuss some potential security and privacy issues peculiar to dVPN applications that involve both operators, who serve as exit nodes, and end-users, who utilize dVPN services (the attack target is reported within the squared bracket).

**Privacy Attacks [end-users].** By design, dVPN end-users route their traffic through exit nodes operated by the community. For this reason, they may be exposed to various privacy attacks, with one particularly concerning issue being the threat posed by malicious exit nodes. These attacks can compromise user privacy in several ways. First, malicious nodes could try to analyze network traffic, monitoring the patterns and volume of data that passes through the network. By analyzing traffic patterns, attackers can infer sensitive information about users' browsing habits, interests, and online activities, even if the content of the data packets is encrypted. This kind of attack is particularly difficult to detect, as the attacker passively analyzes the traffic without further interaction with the victim. With the same goal and methodology, malicious nodes may log and retain user internet traffic and meta-data, compromising their privacy and trying to infer their identities.

Among active attacks, we can cite DNS spoofing, where the malicious node redirects users' DNS requests to malicious servers controlled by the attacker. This allows the attacker to control the resolution of domain names, redirect users to any external website, possibly containing phishing software, or intercept sensitive information transmitted over insecure connections. Similarly, malicious end nodes may attempt to intercept and manipulate users' Internet traffic, acting as intermediaries between the user and their intended destination, i.e., man-in-the-middle attack. In this case, the attacker can intercept communications, modify or inject malicious content into data packets, and impersonate legitimate websites or services, leading to data theft, phishing, or malware infection.

**Legal Issues [perators].** Participants who agree to serve as exit nodes in a dVPN infrastructure share their Internet connection with unknown and untrusted end-users. As the final exit point from the VPN network to the public internet, the exit node is responsible for decrypting and forwarding end-users' data packets to their intended destinations. This means that the exit node operator's IP address will be tied to end-users internet traffic, making them potentially liable for any illegal activities conducted through their node. Although operators may argue that they are merely providing a technical service and are not responsible for the actions of individual users, legal authorities may hold them accountable as facilitators of illegal activity. Additionally, some jurisdictions impose legal obligations on network operators to monitor and prevent illegal activities, further increasing the potential liability for exit node owners. Potential legal problems may arise from different perspectives, including:

i) *Generic Illegal Activities:* If users engage in illegal activities, such as hacking, distributing malware, or accessing illicit content, through the VPN service, exit node operators may be held responsible for aiding and abetting such activities. Depending on the jurisdiction, this could result in criminal charges or civil lawsuits against the operator;

ii) *Copyright Infringement:* Exit node operators may face legal liability for copyright infringement if users utilize the VPN service to access copyrighted content without authorization. Although the operator may not be directly responsible for the infringement, they could be held liable for facilitating the transmission of copyrighted material;

iii) *Government Surveillance and Interception Orders:* In some jurisdictions, governments may issue surveillance or interception orders requiring exit node operators to monitor or intercept users' Internet traffic. Compliance with such orders could raise legal and ethical concerns, particularly if they infringe on users' privacy rights or violate the principles of net neutrality. These orders are usually directed at ISPs and centralized VPN providers. However, they could be extended to dVPN operators, as they are performing the same operations.

**Illicit Use [External Targets].** Whenever a platform enables users to share resources in exchange for benefits, such as monetary compensation, malicious actors can exploit third-party resources without authorization to make a personal profit. This behavior, known as sponge attack [4], has been observed across several domains, particularly in crypto mining and residential proxies [4,10]. In this type of attack, the victim remains unaware that a resource-sharing protocol operates on their infrastructure, resulting in the unauthorized use of resources for the attacker's gain. This attack vector extends to the realm of dVPN in various forms. For instance, malicious users may embed dVPN code within other software, such as Android SDKs or malware, and distribute it to unwilling users. Additionally, unethical employees may stealthily install a dVPN within a company's infrastructure without authorization, making a personal profit while drawing the company's resources.

Some of the above-mentioned problems, such as legal issues for operators and privacy leakage for end-users, are not idiosyncratic of dVPN but shared with similar software, such as centralized VPNs and ToR. However, in the case of centralized VPNs, the problem is slightly different, as end-users know the company name and reputation and are free to decide whether to trust it or not. In the case of ToR, instead, the problem is the same, i.e., exit nodes are operated by unknown and potentially malicious entities [11], but with a smaller impact. In fact, the vast majority of the ToR community is composed of experienced users, with more knowledge on the risks related to the particular technology. In contrast, dVPNs sport fast-growing communities, with all kinds of user joining the protocol attracted by the possibility of monetizing their unused bandwidth, completely unwilling of related threats.

## 4.2   Decentralized Wireless (DeWI)

Wireless technology is essential in modern communication systems, providing seamless connectivity for a wide range of devices and applications. Decentralized wireless is a novel concept of wireless communication that aims to democratize access to wireless networks while ensuring robustness and reliability. Unlike the classic centralized architecture, DeWI deploys a decentralized infrastructure of nodes equipped with IoT-enabled devices, such as Wi-Fi routers or mesh networking devices, creating distributed wireless networks that are resilient to single points of failure and more robust to external disruption. As a DePIN application, DeWI leverages blockchain technology to establish transparent and tamper-proof ledgers to manage access rights, bandwidth allocation, and service agreements within the network. Usually, smart contracts govern the automated execution of network transactions, allowing participants to share their Internet access, and end-users to easily access and use wireless connectivity. Additionally, tokenomics mechanisms incentivize users to contribute to the network in exchange for a reward, e.g., native tokens or user rights, fostering community-driven network growth and sustainability.

**Major Active Projects**

**Helium**. The Helium project represents a pioneering project in the realm of DePIN, with the ambition of revolutionizing wireless communication and connectivity. At its core, Helium leverages blockchain technology and a peculiar incentive mechanism to create a decentralized network of hotspots that provide wireless connectivity coverage. Hotspot owners are incentivized to contribute to the network by sharing wireless connectivity and routing data, earning the native token of the project, called HNT, in return for their bandwidth. Initially based on a proprietary Layer 1 Helium blockchain, the project migrated to the Solana chain in April 2023, in an attempt to improve the scalability, reliability, and functionality of its ecosystem. The Helium infrastructure employs a distinctive consensus algorithm known as "Proof-of-Coverage" (PoC) to validate the accurate representation of Hotspots' location, configuration, and wireless coverage. This mechanism is designed to facilitate the deployment of hotspot devices in under-served regions and report their installations honestly.

**Wicrypt.** Wicrypt is an innovative project focusing on providing decentralized Internet access through a peer-to-peer network. Embracing blockchain technology and smart contracts, Wicrypt enables users to share their Internet bandwidth with others in exchange for cryptocurrency rewards. The infrastructure is built on top of *Minima*, a Layer 1 blockchain ecosystem specifically designed to support DePIN applications. The network is powered by operators, who run routers with the custom Wicrypt firmware, and end-users who utilize connectivity services.

### Security and Privacy Issues of DeWI

**Legal Issues [operators].** This issue has been previously addressed within the context of dVPN and holds equal relevance in the DeWI domain.

**Security Concerns [operators].** Sharing the Internet connection with unknown users promotes the expansion and accessibility of the network. However, it also introduces the risk of malicious users connecting to the operator's local area network (LAN). In fact, unknown users who gain access to the LAN can exploit vulnerabilities in other devices, launch attacks such as malware infections or unauthorized access attempts, and compromise the integrity and security of the entire network.

**Service Level Agreement (SLA) [operators, end users].** Auditing SLA is a critical issue in many systems. In DeWI applications, this problem is particularly difficult to address. In fact, verifying whether operators actually share the promised bandwidth is not trivial, especially in an open-source, permissionless, and trustless environment. Similarly, ensuring that end-users accurately report their resource consumption presents another challenge, as they may attempt to understate usage to reduce costs. For this reason, any DeWI application must implement a mechanism to resolve possible disputes between operators and end-users regarding service quality and resource usage.

**Privacy Attacks [end-users].** This issue has been previously addressed within the context of dVPN, and holds equal relevance in the DeWI domain.

## 5  Decentralized Computation for AI-Based Tasks

As Artificial Intelligence technologies proliferate across various sectors, the demand for computational resources escalates, often surpassing the capabilities of traditional centralized systems. Decentralized computation presents a novel paradigm, harnessing blockchain technology to distribute computational tasks across a network of peer-contribute resources, thus increasing accessibility, reducing costs, and enhancing the scalability of AI applications. This section delves into the evolution and operational dynamics of major active projects in this domain, examining their impact on the AI landscape and their contribution to the advancement of decentralized computing solutions. In addition, it presents some of the security and privacy issues inherent to these decentralized systems, highlighting the challenges and solutions that define their implementation and use.

**Major Active Projects**

**Render** . The Render Network emerges as an innovative decentralized platform that leverages blockchain technology to address the growing demand for GPU computing power in the fields of AI. By enabling individuals and organizations to contribute their idle GPU resources, Render enables a distributed ecosystem that significantly enhances and eases the accessibility and efficiency of computational resources for AI-related tasks. This approach, other than democratizing high-performance computing, introduces an economic model wherein contributors are rewarded with cryptocurrency tokens, incentivizing the participation of GPU owners worldwide. For AI computations and intense rendering tasks, Render offers substantial benefits, including (i) scalability, where the network can dynamically adjust resources based on demand; (ii) cost efficiency, achieved through reduced operational and infrastructure expenses; and, (iii) sustainability.

**Fetch.ai.** Fetch.ai is a decentralized AI-based project that aims to create an open economic framework for autonomous machine-to-machine (M2M) interactions. The Fetch.ai platform is designed to facilitate the creation of autonomous agent systems, with the aim of delivering efficient, secure, and scalable solutions across various industries, including finance, logistics, and energy. By integrating AI and multi-agent systems with distributed ledger technology, Fetch.ai enables the creation of a decentralized network of agents that can perform tasks autonomously, such as data sharing, transactions, and complex decision-making processes without human intervention. This network is built to be adaptive and self-organizing by design, enabling agents to learn and evolve over time through interaction with the environment (and other agents).

**SingularityNET.** SingularityNET emerges as a pioneering platform in the intersection of AI and blockchain technology, aiming to democratize access to AI services. Its core mission is to facilitate a decentralized marketplace for AI algorithms, enabling developers, businesses, and AI enthusiasts to buy and sell AI services at scale. This innovative approach aims to mitigate a critical bottleneck in the traditional AI industry: the centralization of AI technologies and resources in the hands of a few major corporations, which limits access and reduces innovation. One of SingularityNET's distinctive features is its commitment to interoperability and open standards. The platform is designed to support AI services developed in various programming languages and running on different operating systems, making it an agnostic ecosystem for AI technologies.

**Security and Privacy Issues of Decentralized Computation**

The innovative integration of blockchain and AI technologies promotes a new era in computing, promising enhanced decentralization, efficiency, and access to computational resources. However, the deployment of such decentralized networks for AI-based tasks, exemplified by platforms like Render, Fetch.ai, and

SingularityNET, introduces subtle security and privacy threats. This section explores these challenges, emphasizing the new complexities introduced.

**Data Provenance and Integrity Concerns.** Data provenance involves tracking the origin, movement, and history of data within the network, ensuring that the information used and generated by AI algorithms can be verified and trusted. Integrity, on the other hand, ensures that data remains genuine, i.e., unaltered, from its source to its destination. The decentralized nature of platforms involving distributed computation, while offering robustness against centralized points of failure, complicates the enforcement of data provenance and integrity. Malicious actors or compromised nodes could potentially inject corrupted, falsified, or malicious data into AI computations, leading to inaccurate and harmful outcomes. For example, a compromised node in the Render network could manipulate computational results or inject malicious data, affecting the reliability and trustworthiness of rendered outputs. Similarly, in Fetch.ai's ecosystem, tampered data could mislead autonomous agents, resulting in erroneous decisions or transactions.

**Unverified Contributor Risks.** The democratization of computational resources, a key concept in DePIN systems, also poses significant security risks for end-users. By allowing contributions from a broad array of sources, platforms could inadvertently integrate compromised or insecure hardware into their ecosystem. This issue is compounded by the fact that individual contributors' hardware does not undergo rigorous security checks, making the network vulnerable to a range of attacks. For example, an attacker could leverage compromised hardware to perform malicious activities, from snooping on sensitive computational tasks to disrupting network operations through Denial of Service (DoS) attacks.

**Integrated System Vulnerabilities** . In the complex and dynamic ecosystem of DePIN, integration among heterogeneous systems and collaborations between different projects are commonplace. For example, an imminent merge between Fetch.ai, SingularityNET, and Ocean Protocol has recently been announced[2]. The integration of these distinct platforms–each with its architecture, smart contract protocols, and security frameworks–into a single ecosystem amplifies the risk of generating system vulnerabilities. The complexity of harmonizing different technologies can lead to new, unforeseen security loopholes and privacy concerns, especially in areas where their systems overlap. This complexity is compounded by the need to merge potentially divergent governance models, data management protocols, and cryptographic standards. Possible security and privacy concerns that are worth mentioning include cross-platform compatibility and legacy vulnerabilities, data privacy and integrity across merged platforms, as well as governance and smart contract coordination.

---

[2] https://fetch.ai/blog/superintelligence-alliance-token-merge-asi.

# 6   Common Security and Privacy Issues

In this section, we report the security and privacy issues that, although emerging from the above-explored domains, are shared by any DePIN application, stemming from their reliance on blockchain technology.

**Smart Contract Vulnerabilities.** Smart contract vulnerabilities arise from flaws in their design or code, which can be exploited by attackers to manipulate contract outcomes, drain funds, or compromise sensitive information. Given the immutable nature of blockchain, once a smart contract is deployed, it can be extremely difficult to rectify any vulnerabilities without consensus mechanisms or hard forks, both of which can be disruptive and contentious within the community. For instance, a vulnerability in a smart contract used by the Render network to handle transactions for GPU resource contributions could potentially allow an attacker to redirect payments or access computational resources without proper compensation. Similarly, in Fetch.ai and SingularityNET, vulnerabilities could compromise the integrity of autonomous agent interactions or AI service transactioned, leading to loss of funds or unauthorized access to proprietary AI technologies.

**Governance Complexities.** The governance of decentralized networks introduces additional layers of complexity in ensuring security and privacy. Effective governance structures are essential for the establishment of security protocols, privacy policies, and compliance with regulatory requirements. However, the decentralized nature of these networks often means that governance is distributed among a wide array of participants, each with varying interests and levels of commitment to security practices. This can lead to inconsistencies in the application of security measures and difficulties in responding cohesively to security incidents.

**Insufficient Contractual Safeguards.** Service Level Agreements (SLAs) in decentralized networks often fail to provide robust security and privacy protections. The intrinsic challenge lies in the decentralized architecture, which distributes control and authority across a wide network rather than centralizing it. This dispersion complicates the enforcement of SLAs, as ensuring compliance and accountability becomes significantly more difficult. The lack of centralized oversight means that breaches of privacy or security may not be promptly identified or rectified.

# 7   Countermeasures

In this section, we propose a set of countermeasures and research directions that can be universally applied to mitigate the security issues discussed above. These strategies aim to mitigate the vulnerabilities inherent in decentralized systems, ensure robust defense mechanisms, and enhance user trust.

**Smart Contract Vulnerabilities.** To minimize the risk of smart contract vulnerabilities, it is critical to implement thorough testing and auditing protocols before contracts are deployed on the blockchain. This includes both automated testing, such as static code analysis and dynamic analysis, as well as manual peer reviews by experienced developers. Developing and using formal verification tools can provide mathematical assurances on the correctness of the smart contracts' behavior, ensuring that they act as intended under all foreseeable conditions. These tools help in identifying and eliminating bugs or security loopholes that could be exploited by attackers. Furthermore, adopting a modular approach to smart contract development can improve security. By isolating different functionalities into separate contracts and limiting interactions between them, the potential impact of a vulnerability in one module can be contained, preventing it from compromising the entire system.

**Governance Complexities.** Addressing governance complexities in decentralized networks involves creating inclusive, transparent, and accountable governance structures. These structures should be designed to facilitate equitable participation from all stakeholders, ensuring that no single entity has undue influence over the network. Implementing Decentralized Autonomous Organizations (DAOs) can provide a democratic framework for managing governance, where decisions are made based on consensus among participants rather than centralized power. This approach can help manage the diverse interests and levels of commitment to security practices within the network. Additionally, regular governance audits and the recording and validation of governance actions on-chain can enhance transparency and trust among participants, ensuring that governance practices are consistently applied and maintained across the network.

**Insufficient Contractual Safeguards.** Improving the robustness of Service Level Agreements (SLAs) in decentralized networks requires innovative approaches to contract design, monitoring, and enforcement. Smart contracts can play a crucial role here, automating the enforcement of SLAs and ensuring transparency. These contracts can be programmed to automatically execute agreed-upon terms and conditions, reducing reliance on manual oversight and increasing efficiency. However, any DePIN project must develop a mechanism to verify off-chain events and assess their compliance with SLAs. The "Proof-of-Coverage" developed by Helium to verify whether participants accurately report their shared resources is a good example in this direction, although still in its infancy and far from being an optimal solution.

**Unverified Contributor Risks.** To mitigate the risks associated with unverified contributors, it is essential to establish a rigorous vetting process. This could involve performing security audits on the hardware and software used by contributors before they are approved to join the network. Such audits can be automated to some extent using AI-driven security tools that scan for known vulnerabilities and compliance with security best practices. Additionally, implementing hardware attestation mechanisms can provide further assurance of the integrity of contributing devices. These mechanisms ensure that only hardware configurations that meet specific security criteria are allowed to participate in the network, significantly reducing the risk of introducing compromised devices.

## 8  Conclusion

In this paper, we provided a comprehensive exploration of the emerging paradigm of Decentralized Physical Infrastructure Networks (DePIN). Starting our analysis from flagship applications, we have focused on the security and privacy challenges inherent in such systems. Through detailed investigation of two major domains–*Network Services* and *Computation for AI-based Tasks*–we have identified key security issues and proposed both remedial and potential directions for future research and development. Our findings highlight that while DePIN offers significant innovations and advantages over traditional centralized models, such as enhanced user autonomy, economic incentivization through tokenomics, and increased resilience against central points of failure, it also introduces complex security vulnerabilities and privacy concerns. These issues range from smart contract vulnerabilities to the risks associated with unverified contributors and the complexities of managing decentralized governance structures. To address these challenges, we presented several research directions and operational guidelines that include developing more robust security protocols, improving smart contract design and verification, and establishing stronger governance frameworks that can effectively enforce security and privacy standards across decentralized networks. In conclusion, our paper underscores DePIN's transformative potential and security challenges, proposing key research directions to drive the development of more secure and resilient decentralized infrastructures.

**Acknowledgements.** We acknowledge the use of AI-based tools, such as *Grammarly* and *ChatGPT*, to refine the writing and proofread the final draft of this paper.

## References

1. Aoyagi, S., Takizawa, M., Saito, M., Aida, H., Tokuda, H.: Ela: a fully distributed vpn system over peer-to-peer network. In: The 2005 Symposium on Applications and the Internet, pp. 89–92 (2005)
2. Ballandies, M.C., Wang, H., Law, A.C.C., Yang, J.C., Gösken, C., Andrew, M.: A taxonomy for blockchain-based decentralized physical infrastructure networks (depin) (2023)
3. Benisi, N.Z., Aminian, M., Javadi, B.: Blockchain-based decentralized storage networks: a survey. J. Netw. Comput. Appl. **162**, 102656 (2020)
4. Caprolu, M., Raponi, S., Oligeri, G., Di Pietro, R.: Cryptomining makes noise: Detecting cryptojacking via machine learning. Comput. Commun. **171**, 126–139 (2021). https://doi.org/10.1016/j.comcom.2021.02.016, https://www.sciencedirect.com/science/article/pii/S0140366421000797

5. Fan, X., Xu, L.: Towards a rollup-centric scalable architecture for decentralized physical infrastructure networks: A position paper. In: Proceedings of the Fifth ACM International Workshop on Blockchain-Enabled Networked Sensor Systems, pp. 9–12. BlockSys '23, Association for Computing Machinery, New York, NY, USA (2024)

6. Johnson, M., Egelman, S., Bellovin, S.M.: Facebook and privacy: it's complicated. In: Proceedings of the Eighth Symposium on Usable Privacy and Security. SOUPS '12, Association for Computing Machinery, New York, NY, USA (2012)

7. Li, C., Palanisamy, B.: Incentivized blockchain-based social media platforms: A case study of steemit. In: Proceedings of the 10th ACM Conference on Web Science, pp. 145–154. WebSci '19, Association for Computing Machinery, New York, NY, USA (2019)

8. Liu, W., Cao, B., Peng, M.: Web3 technologies: Challenges and opportunities. IEEE Network pp. 1–1 (2023)

9. Makridis, C.A., Fröwis, M., Sridhar, K., Böhme, R.: The rise of decentralized cryptocurrency exchanges: evaluating the role of airdrops and governance tokens. J. Corp. Finan. **79**, 102358 (2023)

10. Mi, X., Tang, S., Li, Z., Liao, X., Qian, F., Wang, X.: Your phone is my proxy: Detecting and understanding mobile proxy networks. In: 28th Annual Network and Distributed System Security Symposium, NDSS 2021, virtually, February 21-25, 2021. The Internet Society (2021)

11. Minárik, T., Osula, A.M.: Tor does not stink: use and abuse of the tor anonymity network from the perspective of law. Comput. Law Secur. Rev. **32**(1), 111–127 (2016)

12. Moriarty, C.: Is realt reality? investigating the use of blockchain technology and tokenization in real estate transactions. Minn. JL Sci. Tech. **24**, 471 (2022)

13. Rader, E.: Awareness of behavioral tracking and information privacy concern in facebook and google. In: 10th Symposium On Usable Privacy and Security (SOUPS 2014), pp. 51–67. USENIX (2014)

14. Raponi, S., Caprolu, M., Di Pietro, R.: Intrusion detection at the network edge: Solutions, limitations, and future directions. In: Zhang, T., Wei, J., Zhang, L.J. (eds.) Edge Computing - EDGE 2019, pp. 59–75. Springer International Publishing, Cham (2019)

15. Sarkar, D.: Generalised depin protocol: A framework for decentralized physical infrastructure networks (2023)

16. Varvello, M., Azurmendi, I.Q., Nappa, A., Papadopoulos, P., Pestana, G., Livshits, B.: Vpn-zero: A privacy-preserving decentralized virtual private network. In: 2021 IFIP Networking Conference (IFIP Networking), pp. 1–6 (2021)

17. Wolinsky, D.I., Lee, K., Boykin, P.O., Figueiredo, R.: On the design of autonomic, decentralized vpns. In: 6th International Conference on Collaborative Computing: Networking, Applications and Worksharing (CollaborateCom 2010), pp. 1–10 (2010)

18. Xiao, Y., Varvello, M., Kuzmanovic, A.: Monetizing spare bandwidth: the case of distributed VPNs. Proc. ACM Measure. Anal. Comput. Syst. **6**(2), 1–27 (2022). https://doi.org/10.1145/3530899

19. Xu, J., Paruch, K., Cousaert, S., Feng, Y.: SoK: Decentralized Exchanges (DEX) with Automated Market Maker (AMM) protocols. ACM Comput. Surv. **55**(11), 1–50 (2023). https://doi.org/10.1145/3570639

# VoIP Vanguard: A Practical Front Line Defense Against VoIP Identification Attacks in Tor

S. Jithin$^{(\boxtimes)}$, Richa Gupta, Reeshabh Kumar Ranjan, Shreyansh Nagpal, Mukulika Maity, and Sambuddho Chakravarty

IIIT Delhi, Delhi, India
{jithins,richa,reeshabh17086,shreyansh17109,mukulika,
sambuddho}@iiitd.ac.in

**Abstract.** Tor serves as a widely adopted anonymous communication network, highly valued by privacy advocates, journalists, and whistleblowers seeking to maintain anonymity. While its primary use is for anonymous website access, recent research has revealed the feasibility of anonymous Voice over IP (VoIP) calls over Tor. However, due to the distinctive characteristics of VoIP and Tor's inability to conceal its metadata, VoIP traffic remains *vulnerable to detection*. We address this challenge by proposing a defense to effectively conceal VoIP flows from detection. We begin by showing a simple throughput-based heuristic is sufficient to detect VoIP traffic through Tor. To counter this vulnerability, we initially attempted to obscure VoIP's identifiable throughput characteristics by interspersing VoIP packets with HTTP traffic over the same Tor circuit. However, this approach proved inadequate against advanced machine learning (ML) and deep learning (DL) detection techniques.

Consequently, we developed an advanced defense mechanism that manipulates timing and throughput-related features to make VoIP traffic resemble regular HTTP downloads. We also developed and deployed multiple ML and DL models to test and validate this defense rigorously. Notably, this defense strategy successfully evaded detection by these models (*viz.*, detection rate dropped from 95% to 20%) without significantly degrading VoIP call quality, as verified by PESQ (Perceptual Evaluation of Speech Quality) measurements (Average PESQ $\approx$ 2.5). Our findings indicate that this approach provides a robust solution for safeguarding VoIP communications on Tor against sophisticated traffic analysis attacks, ensuring voice quality.

**Keywords:** VoIP · Tor · Identification · Defense

## 1 Introduction

Voice over Internet Protocol (VoIP), is a group of protocols and technologies that facilitates voice communication over the Internet. The usage of VoIP has

H. H. Song et al. (Eds.): NSS 2024, LNCS 15564, pp. 319–346, 2025.
https://doi.org/10.1007/978-981-96-3531-3_16

increased significantly in last decades. Over past few years, several governments, apart from Internet surveillance, have engaged in dedicated VoIP surveillance programs [26,31,61]. Detecting VoIP calls is known as VoIP identification
attacks. A mere VoIP identification can reveal a lot of meta-data *viz.* caller identity, number of calls, call timestamps, call duration. In addition, once VoIP calls
are detected, even the encrypted VoIP traffic can undergo VoIP re-identification
attacks such as identifying the speaker [39], language-detection [71], identifying
the key phrases [70,72]. Thus, we consider the VoIP identification as a significant
threat for privacy-conscious individuals *viz.* whistle-blowers, journalists, activists
*etc.*.

Previously, Sharma *et al.* [56] and Bromberg *et al.* [6] show that Tor could
be a viable solution for placing untraceable VoIP calls. Tor [12] is a low latency,
anonymous communication network with 3 million daily users [65]. It operates by
sending the client's traffic through a cascade of relays with telescopic encryption
that hides the IP addresses of the communicating peers. The network consists of
$> 6500$ [62] volunteer-operated relays. For a long time, Tor has been considered
unsuitable for real-time protocols like VoIP. However, the aforementioned studies have demonstrated the feasibility of anonymous VoIP calls using Tor. The
paper [56] evaluated the performance of voice calls over Tor by considering factors such as latency, packet loss, and jitter, which are essential for maintaining
good call quality. The longitudinal study showed that Tor supports good voice
quality (PESQ $> 3$ and one-way delay $<400$ ms) in more than 85% of 0.5 million
measurements.

VoIP flows bear a distinctive pattern, that can be used to differentiate from
HTTP. VoIP packets are transmitted at relatively low (and constant) throughputs, unlike HTTP that is bursty. Using this feature, it becomes relatively easy
to spot VoIP even if tunneled via Tor. Further, attempts to hide such observability may significantly impact performance, and the flows may still be vulnerable
to advanced traffic analysis (*e.g.* involving learning techniques).

There exists a plethora of research that explores traffic analysis attacks [14,
17,20,28,38,40,43,47,48,59,67]. Some of these deal with either deanonymizing
Tor clients' traffic by inspecting the traffic at the Tor *entry* and *exit nodes*. Others
involve identifying which website a user is visiting even when traffic decryption is
not possible. Additionally, traffic analysis can be used for detecting the category
of traffic under investigation, *i.e.* *traffic classification* or *identification* [9,21,32,
45]. It involves examining the traffic metadata, to look for patterns that help
determine their type. Few studies have explored the feasibility of realtime traffic
classification over Tor, likely because it predominantly transports HTTP [27,37].
The proven feasibility of transporting VoIP (over Tor), may motivate adversaries
to classify traffic (maybe as a part of their surveillance activities), and study their
access behavior (*e.g.* studying when the targets browse websites or make VoIP
calls).

We observed that the aforementioned throughput based patterns was indeed
sufficient to spot VoIP flows, tunneled through Tor circuits. Thus, we devised
a preliminary defense that obscures the throughput pattern of VoIP flows. This

defense involves interspersing VoIP flows with those of other types, in the same Tor circuit. This makes it hard for a passive observer relying on the throughput heuristic, to differentiate between the flow types. This naïve defense succeeded in hiding the throughput of the VoIP flows. It might be still possible to detect flows bearing VoIP, as there might be other revealing parameters like packet lengths and interarrival times. Leveraging learning techniques, and drawing from existing research on traffic classification [32], we employed pattern recognition tools to spot flows containing VoIP. Our investigation show that even when VoIP flows are interspersed with flows of other types, it is still possible to discover them. We employed algorithms like k-Nearest Neighbor (k-NN), Naïve Bayes, Support Vector Machine (SVM), and Random Forest, and achieved high accuracy in detecting the VoIP-containing flows.

Subsequently, our objective was to build a defense mechanism resistant to the detection by the ML classifiers. Along with evading detection, such a defense should maintain call quality. The existing website fingerprinting defenses might add delays to packet transmission, potentially affecting call quality. Defenses like [7,8,35] intentionally introduce delays, whereas those without inherent delays [11,18] may do so inadvertently either due to fragmentation of packets [11] or partitioning them to route through multiple networks [18]. In addition, some defenses [16] against website fingerprinting are too specific to such attacks. To build a defense hiding the VoIP flows, we identified timing and volume-based features that contribute to the detection of VoIP flows and developed a defense that modifies these features of VoIP-containing flows, to evade the classifiers. We modified the revealing features of VoIP flows to make them look like HTTP flows. The defense mechanism effectively misled the machine learning classifiers, resulting in a notable decrease in their detection accuracy.

Further, we evaluated the robustness of our solution against deep learning (DL) based attacks. We used a CNN-based model using the raw values of the top-ranked features (discovered using Random Forest) contributing to the the detection of VoIP. The CNN model detected the defended VoIP flows with an accuracy of 4% which shows that our defense was resilient against deep learning models. The overall contributions of this paper are as follows:

1. **On the observability of VoIP calls through Tor:** In this study, we prove that the VoIP calls placed through Tor are *observable*, leaving them vulnerable to surveillance. We explored various possibilities for identifying VoIP flows over Tor. Typically, VoIP flows are transmitted at low throughput (with low variance), unlike regular HTTP traffic. We applied this and detected these VoIP flows with high accuracy.

2. **Naïve solution and its ML-based analysis:** We propose a Naïve defense method that would obscure the throughput patterns of VoIP by interspersing them with HTTP flows. This neutralized the throughput-based attack. However, by applying ML-models derived from classifiers like k-NN, Naïve Bayes, SVM, and Random Forest, we were able to detect VoIP in the interspersed flows with high accuracy(>90%) in both balanced and unbalanced testing scenarios. The unbalanced set represents the infrequent occurrence of VoIP

flows in Tor. These models were trained using 6000 data points, collected across seven geographic locations (using cloud VMs).

3. **Defense against ML-based and DL-based classifiers:** Having identified the revealing features that led to ML-based identifications, we propose a defense mechanism to counter such attacks. It involves smartly sending cover traffic to befuddle the ML models. We were able to bring down the VoIP detection accuracy to around 20%, without significantly impacting the call quality (Avg. PESQ: 2.5 ⇒ 2.4 (with defense)). Further, we evaluate the efficiency of our solution in the face of DL-based attacks. We tested our defense in both balanced and unbalanced settings and the VoIP detection accuracy remained low in both cases.

## 2   Background and Motivation

This section outlines the concepts of VoIP, VoIP quality assessment, Tor and anonymous VoIP. At the end, we elucidate the motivation of our research.

*VoIP:* is an Internet telephony framework that enables voice calls over networks, involving protocols such as the session initiation protocol (SIP) for session management and the real-time protocol (RTP) for voice payload transmission via UDP. Various audio codecs, such as G.711, G.722, G.729, Speex, GSM, and Opus, encode voice signals with differing bandwidth requirements based on their sampling rate, bit depth, and compression algorithms. VoIP quality is assessed using metrics such as the *Mean Opinion Score (MOS)*, latency, jitter, and packet loss. We utilize the *Perceptual Evaluation of Speech Quality (PESQ)* metric, based on ITU-T P.862, to objectively predict call quality by comparing the original and degraded speech signals, providing a score from 1 (worst) to 5 (best).

*Tor:* [12], The Onion Router, is a low-latency overlay network providing anonymity by routing traffic through volunteer-operated relays, ensuring that no single relay knows the complete data path. Tor was deemed to be unsuitable for VoIP traffic for a long time [34,36]. Sharma *et al.* [56] showcased that, contrary to popular belief, it is indeed feasible to establish voice calls over Tor with acceptable call quality. The paper evaluated the performance of voice calling over Tor by considering factors such as latency, packet loss, and jitter, which are essential for maintaining good call quality. The longitudinal study portrayed that Tor supports good voice quality (PESQ > 3 and one-way delay <400 ms) in more than 85% of 0.5 million measurements. The analysis indicated that the contentions due to cross-traffic were low enough to support VoIP calls, that are anyways transmitted at low rates (<120 Kbps). In other words, the observed throughput of the VoIP through Tor is not affected due to insufficient bandwidth or latency.

**Motivation:** In the past decade, several governments engaged in Internet surveillance [30,58,60]. Prior research shows that Tor is a suitable solution for anonymous VoIP calls. However, Tor is not impervious to surveillance as well. As outlined in Sect. 7, sophisticated adversaries can glean important information about traffic through statistical analysis. This motivated us to explore the possibilities of detection of VoIP flows in Tor. We consider the mere detection of VoIP flows in Tor to be risky to its users, as it can lead to a collection of call metadata of vital importance [69] (*viz.*caller identity, number of calls, length of the call). In addition, once VoIP calls are detected, even the encrypted VoIP traffic can undergo *VoIP re-identification attacks* such as identifying the speaker [39], language-detection [71], identifying the key phrases [70,72]. Thus, we consider the VoIP identification as a significant threat for privacy-conscious individuals *viz.* whistle-blowers, journalists, activists *etc.*. So it is imperative to safeguard the privacy of VoIP users in Tor. Hence, we propose a defense mechanism to counter the detection methods of the adversaries.

## 3   Problem Statement and Threat Model

**Problem Statement:** Anonymous and confidential VoIP communication is crucial to whistle-blowers, journalists, hacktivists and other privacy-conscious users. Tor provides anonymity to users by hiding their IP addresses. Recent studies show that Tor is viable for anonymous VoIP communication. But we ponder whether VoIP (over Tor) is absolutely resilient against adversaries that could surveil Tor traffic to determine hidden communication. Unlike, regular web browsing, VoIP exhibits different characteristics *viz.* duration, throughput, and volume of traffic. Keeping these facts in mind we try to answer the following questions:

1. Can VoIP flows through Tor be detected accurately?
2. Is it possible to hide the unique characteristics of the VoIP flows?
3. Can we use pattern recognition methods like machine learning to reveal the presence of the VoIP flows even after hiding the unique characteristics?

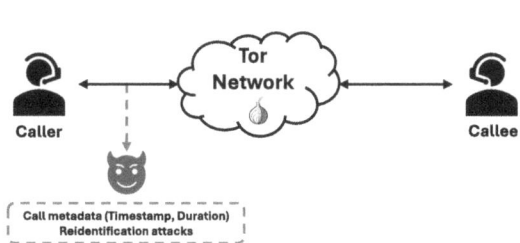

**Threat Model.** The threat model of our study is shown in the Fig. 1. We consider a passively eavesdropping, local adversary who is capable of observing and recording network traces between the client and the entry node of the Tor. In addition, the attacker can also rigorously extract features from the network flows, and train machine learning algorithms to identify the underlying patterns of the

**Fig. 1.** Threat Model: A passive, local adversary between the client and the entry node.

flows. Once identified, the adversary can learn call information such time stamps and length and perform re-identification attacks to identify the speaker [39], language spoken [71], or voice reconstruction [70,72]. An adversary might be an Internet Service Provider (ISP), a government agency, *etc.* [22,30,58,60].

## 4    Spotting VoIP over Tor and How to Obfuscate It

As we mentioned earlier, Tor is suitable for anonymous calls. In accordance with the problem statement, our current focus is on detecting VoIP flows passing through the Tor network. To establish the ground truth of detection of VoIP flows in Tor, we first collect a comprehensive dataset of VoIP-containing network traffic, accurately labeled and representative of real-world scenarios. This section describes step-by-step methodology for data collection, analysis strategy, and a heuristic for VoIP flow detection and ends with a basic obfuscation technique.

### 4.1    Spotting VoIP Traffic over Tor

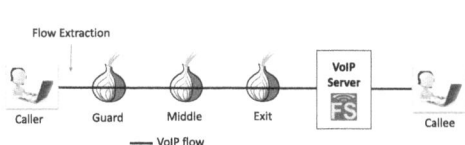

**Fig. 2.** Data Collection Setup: Caller connects to the VoIP server through Tor.

To validate the ground truth of VoIP detection, it is crucial to contrast the characteristics of VoIP traffic with those of another type of traffic. In the Tor network, HTTP is the most prevalent traffic [27,37]. We chose HTTP for this comparison. We gathered throughput data for a range of VoIP and non-VoIP flows from network traces containing the pertinent traffic. Following the collection of network traces containing the traffic, we tried to analyze the throughput of the flows and developed a simple heuristic to detect the VoIP flows.

**Experimental Setup.** A schematic of the experimental setup is shown in Fig. 2. In the setup, there are two communicating peers (caller and callee) whose VoIP sessions are facilitated by a VoIP server. The caller is connected to the VoIP server through the public Tor network. An overview of the system configuration is as follows:

1. **Caller and callee:** We placed VoIP calls between two endpoints, namely the caller and callee, which had similar system configurations. We used pjsip [49] stack which is a multimedia communication library supporting protocols like SIP and RTP to facilitate VoIP calls between peers. Since Tor does not support UDP (RTP), we tunneled VoIP traffic encapsulated through an unencrypted TCP-based OpenVPN tunnel that can be transported through Tor. For placing the calls, we played a voice clip at both ends and recorded the voice transmitted between the peers on both sides for assessing quality. We did not use a diverse set of voice clips because they would not contribute to the diversity of the metadata. Tor segments the data into fixed-size cells, rendering variations in the voice clips irrelevant. Note, that while we never interfered with Tor's circuit creation, we made sure that circuits were never reused as we explicitly deleted them after every call.

2. **VoIP server**: We used `FreeSWITCH` [15] (a free, open-source application), as the VoIP server, to facilitate VoIP calls between endpoints. FreeSWITCH accommodates numerous VoIP protocols and offers an extensive selection of audio codecs. We used G.711, codec for our experiments. We employed `FreeSWITCH` to establish calls between two peers registered as separate users. Additionally, we had option to choose codecs used for our calls.
3. **Web Server**: We used Apache [3] web server to generate the HTTP download traffic. We hosted files of different sizes, *viz.*, 1MB, 10MB and 100 MB for the client to download and generate suitable traffic flows.

In our setup, the caller ran on a 1-core/1GB RAM machine, running Linux Kernel v5.4 OS. Another machine with the same configuration ran the callee, the web server (`Apache 2.4`) and the `FreeSwitch 1.10.3` [15] server. The setup was first used to generate and collect VoIP and HTTP network traces. We now describe how we did the same.

**VoIP Data Generation:** To collect data, we ran the following steps iteratively:

1. The caller initiates VoIP calls through Tor to the callee. The voice traffic (RTP), being UDP, is encapsulated inside an unencrypted TCP-based Open-VPN tunnel, whose packets are converted to Tor cells and transported via TLS connection through the Tor network.
2. Once a VoIP session is established, we played audio recordings on both caller and callee ends. We also captured audio received at each endpoint to assess call quality.
3. At the client, we identified the IP address of the guard node through which connection the tunnel's TCP stream is attached and we ran `tcpdump` on the physical interface to record the network traces to the specified guard node.
4. After data generation, the VPN connection, and the Tor circuit, were explicitly torn down.

We utilized a 30-second recorded audio segment to enable PESQ measurement, as also used by previous researchers [56].

**HTTP Data Generation:** For the generation of HTTP traffic, we followed similar steps as that of VoIP. We used `wget` to download a large file from an Apache web server under our control. Like in VoIP, we ran `tcpdump` and recorded the network traces.

**Throughput Heuristics.** VoIP detection experiments are conducted using single-blind setup. One experimenter, $E_1$, generated 2,000 VoIP and HTTP flows, while another, $E_2$, who was unaware of ground truth, analyse network traces to identify flows using throughput patterns.

To capture diverse data, we varied the locations of caller and callee using VPSs from a cloud service provider. $E_2$ examined forward (caller to callee) and backward (callee to caller) throughput of VoIP and HTTP flows. VoIP flows showed consistent throughput in both directions after session establishment, while HTTP flows exhibited higher, variable throughput in server-to-client direction.

$E_2$ accurately identified VoIP flows 95% of the time, using the throughput criteria outlined in Table 1. The figures show the differences in throughput patterns between VoIP and HTTP, confirming the distinct characteristics of each. According to the criteria outlined in Table 1, $E_2$ identified VoIP flows with an accuracy of 95%. According to the criteria outlined in Table 1, $E_2$ identified VoIP flows with an accuracy of 95%.

## 4.2  Naïve Defense

**Table 1.** Throughput variation of VoIP flows.

| Direction | Throughput(kbps) |
|-----------|------------------|
| Forward | 130.15 ± 93.61 |
| Backward | 77.48 ± 55.14 |

We demonstrated that VoIP flows can be detected using throughput heuristics. Thwarting VoIP traffic identification would require disrupting the unique throughput pattern. One method to achieve this is by mixing VoIP traffic with other traffic types in a manner that prevents adversaries from detecting the consistent throughput patterns of VoIP. To do so, the throughput at the adversary's observation point should no longer be in its original form. In our threat model, the adversary is positioned between the client and the guard node. To disrupt the unique throughput pattern of VoIP, it should be obscured with cover traffic. We accomplished this by sending VoIP and regular HTTP traffic through the *same* Tor circuit. This makes both flows go through the same TCP/TLS connection (via the same guard node). This should ideally make the HTTP throughput pattern subsume the VoIP throughput pattern. In practice, we initiated a file download at the exact point when the caller initiated the call and this continued throughout the duration of the call.

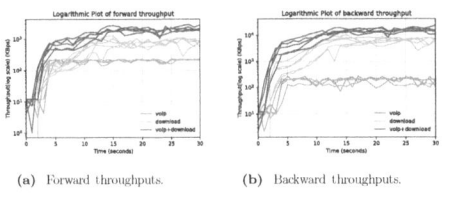

(a) Forward throughputs.          (b) Backward throughputs.

**Fig. 3.** Throughput variations for VoIP, downloads and interspersed traffic (for forward and backward traffic).

We generated 2000 flows of interspersed traffic and repeated the single-blind approach of experiments. This time, the second experimenter who had no knowledge of ground-truth couldn't distinguish between the HTTP flows and the VoIP-bearing interspersed flows. The mean and the standard deviation of such interspersed flows closely resembled that of download. We illustrate the throughput patterns of VoIP, HTTP downloads and the interspersed traffic in Fig. 3. The graphs reveal VoIP's distorted throughput pattern, making it difficult for an adversary to fingerprint VoIP based on throughput.

# 5    Advanced Attack

We successfully averted throughput-based detection of VoIP flows by interspersing VoIP with HTTP traffic. But throughput might not be the only factor that detects VoIP flows. There exist traffic classification studies [9,21,32,33,45] using machine learning, employing time and volume-based features. We explore the possibility of detecting VoIP-bearing Tor flows using these advanced methods. We now discuss the features used for building classification models, the training procedure, evaluation metrics, and classification results.

## 5.1    Features

As mentioned, researchers have proposed attacks on Tor, ranging from simple statistical analysis to advanced DL techniques, involving a variety of features. Our aim is to defeat VoIP detection based on any such feature. Various features considered with potential applicability for distinguishing VoIP/VoIP-containing flows from regular HTTP ones, are as follows.

**Traffic-Direction Based Statistics:** The direction of flow of packets can be a valuable feature for spotting covert traffic. Previously, others [17,57] have successfully used such features to defeat WF defenses. Hence, we have also used traffic direction for building detection models against VoIP-containing flows in Tor.

**Packet-Timing Based Statistics:** Inter Arrival Time (IAT) of packets, in network flow, refers to time elapsed between arrivals of consecutive packets. Different types of traffic (VoIP, HTTP, streaming) have distinct IAT patterns. VoIP traffic often has regular, small IATs due to its real-time nature, whereas HTTP may have more variable IATs due to request-response nature of web browsing. We have considered derived features of IATs in detecting VoIP flows.

**Packet Size Based Statistics:** These features rely on packet sizes to characterise and identify traffic tunneled through Tor. Tor generates fixed 512-byte segments carrying TCP payload. Original packet sizes are largely modified when packets are segmented into cells. We consider such features to see if it provide insights in detecting VoIP flows.

**Throughput-Based Features:** §4.1 shows that throughput plays a significant role in distinguishing VoIP flows from web traffic. We thus used the derived features of throughput for building models. We used statistical features like mean, standard deviation, minimum, and maximum of the dataset to train our ML models.

## 5.2   Dataset, Preprocessing, Training and Testing

**Dataset:** We used the dataset consisting of earlier mentioned features extracted from `pcaps` collected (outlined in §4.1 and §4.2). Our dataset comprises 24,000 data points collected from four distinct geographic locations of both callers and callees, utilizing various codecs.

*Geographic Locations:* Categorically, we chose four caller–callee pairs, *i.e.* (1) Bangalore (BLR), Amsterdam (AMS), (2) Amsterdam (AMS), Frankfurt (FRA) (3) Singapore (SGP), San Francisco (SFO), and (4) New York (NYC) and Sydney (SYD). Then, we generated three different types of traffic between them (via regular Tor circuits): (i) VoIP calls ($V$), (ii) HTTP download ($D$) and (iii) VoIP and HTTP download, interspersed through the same Tor circuit ($VD$).

*Codecs:* We used four popular codecs [42] *viz.* G.711, GSM, SPEEX, and OPUS for data collection in generating VoIP calls. G.711, GSM, and SPEEX are constant bit-rate (CBR) codecs. OPUS [46] a variable bit-rate (VBR) codec, is widely used in today's telecommunication systems. GSM and SPEEX are lossy codecs, which means they achieve compression by discarding some audio data. These codecs exhibit varying properties in terms of packet sizes, packetization intervals, and packets per second, which significantly affect meta-data properties like throughput and inter-arrival times.

We collected 6000 network traces for each codec, with 2000 each for $V$, $D$ and $VD$, attributing 24000 data points. These were later used to build models involving k-Nearest Neighbors (k-NN), Naïve Bayes, Support Vector Machine (SVM), and Random Forest [5,41].

**Preprocessing:** We initially applied two pre-processing steps, *i.e.* outlier removal and scaling the data. Outlier removal tries to ensure robustness of the models by eliminating data points that could potentially skew the results. Feature scaling standardizes the features by removing mean and scaling to unit variance. We performed this using StandardScaler. These steps are crucial for k-Nearest Neighbors (k-NN) and Support Vector Machine (SVM) models as they are sensitive to the magnitude of feature values.

**Train and Test:** After preprocessing the data, we tuned hyperparameters for various models. For kNN, we tuned hyperparameters using GridSearchCV, which yielded the best performance with 'metric': 'Euclidean', 'k': 3, and 'weights': 'distance'. In contrast, Gaussian Naïve Bayes classifier required minimal preprocessing, focusing only on outlier removal, as it is less sensitive to variations in feature scales. With SVM, we normalized the dataset and performed hyperparameter tuning using GridSearchCV, ultimately choosing Gaussian RBF kernel for the best performance. Finally, we used Random Forest and tuned its hyperparameters using GridSearchCV, maintaining default Gini impurity measure as the criterion.

The dataset was divided into training and testing using an 80–20 split, with 80% of data used for training and 20% reserved for testing. This stratified split ensures that the distribution of target variable remains consistent across both subsets. The training set was used to train the models, while the testing set was used to evaluate their performance. We trained our classifiers on data collected from various geographic locations acting as caller callee pairs, across various codecs as mentioned above. All these steps were implemented in `Python3` using the library `scikit-learn 1.2.0` [53].

**Testing using Deep Learning:** To show the efficacy of our VoIP defense, which is explained in §6, we buiild DL models using features of interest. Inspired from previous work [43,50,55,57], we adopted CNN based deep learning model to test against the defense. CNNs have proven to be widely deployed in various applications [4,10,52]. It consists of a set of layers, each designated to perform a different task for feature identification. CNN usually works on data structured in a grid-like topology. In this research, we chose ResNet18 [2], a CNN-based architecture having 18 deep layers. This has been popularly used in similar Website Fingerprinting defenses [57] and proven to be performant. We tailor fit ResNet18 for our requirements as shown in the architecture diagram in the **Appendix**(Figure 9).

*Dataset and Pre-processing:* We selected the raw values of two features: IAT and directions. We used IAT as it was a top contributing feature in detecting VoIP flows. The other feature was the direction of flow of packets, which is a significant feature in undermining defenses similar to ours. Thus, following the methodology of *Deep Fingerprinting* [57], we simplified the raw traffic traces by labeling them '-1' or '+1' depending upon their direction (*i.e.* client $\rightarrow$ server or vice-versa). These features were then used for training the DL models.

*Training:* The training process for the model utilized raw features derived from 24000 trace files, encompassing three categories: $V$, $D$, and $VD$ as explained in §4.1. Hyperparameter tuning was conducted within a specified search space. Details of specific hyperparameters and their ranges are presented in Table 4 located in Appendix B.

**Evaluation Metrics:** We used precision, recall and False Positve Rate (FPR) to evaluate performance of models under different testing conditions. These metrics are crucial for models. For a specified class, *precision* denotes ratio of accurately predicted positives to all predictions labeled as positive for that class. *Recall* or *True Positive Rate* indicates how many of actual positives the model captures by labeling it as positive (True Positive). *False Postive Rate (FPR)* represents proportion of actual negatives that get incorrectly marked as positive. To evaluate performance of our classification model, we focus on following key metrics:

– **Precision for Class** $D$: This metric measures the accuracy of predictions for class 'd'. It is crucial to ensure that instances classified as $D$ are truly $D$.

- **Recall for Classes $V$ and $VD$**: This ensures that actual instances of $V$ and $VD$ are correctly identified, minimizing false negatives.
- **False Positive Rate (FPR) for Class $D$**: This metric measures the proportion of $V$ and $VD$ instances incorrectly classified as $D$, which we aim to minimize. We use the FPR for assessing the models in unbalanced testing.

## 5.3   Classification Results

We implemented high-performing classifiers to distinguish VoIP and non-VoIP flows. We also explain the results of classification using balanced and unbalanced datasets.

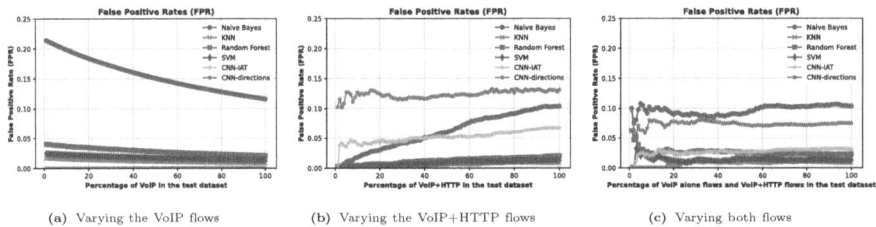

(a) Varying the VoIP flows          (b) Varying the VoIP+HTTP flows          (c) Varying both flows

**Fig. 4.** Performance of various models on unbalanced datasets: FPR of HTTP flows was considered as evaluation metrics. NB showed a rise in FPR when the proportion of vd is increased.

**Testing on Balanced Dataset:** Firstly, as mentioned earlier, we trained our models using datasets from three distinct caller:callee pairs and then tested them on a fourth. This method not only validated the models' reliability but also assessed their performance on unseen data from a different geographical context. Our test data maintained a balanced distribution across labels: $V$, $D$, and $VD$. After testing across the four sites, each classifier yielded four sets of metrics of precision, and recall for each label.

The analysis revealed that NB, while generally maintaining high precision ($\approx 98\%$) and recall ($\approx 98\%$) in most categories, experienced a noticeable drop in performance, particularly in the 'vd' category. In contrast, SVM and RF exhibited consistently high precision ($\approx 96\%$) and recall ($\approx 96\%$) across all categories. The CNN-IAT and CNN-dir classifiers also performed well, with precision ranging from 92% to 95% and recall from 92% to 97%, though they did not suffer the same drop as NB. Overall, SVM and RF were the most stable classifiers, while NB showed vulnerability in mixed traffic scenarios. In summary, all classifiers adeptly identified VoIP ($V$) and interspersed traffic ($VD$) in a balanced dataset.

**Testing on Unbalanced Dataset:** As Tor was considered to be unsuitable for VoIP calls until recently, it's likely that users seldom choose Tor for anonymous VoIP communication. This suggests that VoIP calls over Tor might be infrequent. To emulate a realistic scenario, it's crucial to assess classifiers' effectiveness in detecting VoIP flows under unbalanced conditions.

For this, we combined datasets from all regions. 75% of this combined dataset was used for training and the remaining 25% for testing. Each category $V$ $D$, and $VD$ contained 500 data points in the testing dataset. Then, we introduced imbalance in three distinct ways:

1. Imbalance in $V$: We started with 1% of 2400 VoIP ($V$) flows. We then gradually increased the proportion of VoIP flows until a balance was achieved (*i.e.* all the VoIP flows).
2. Imbalance in $VD$: Analogous to the first approach, we began with 1% of 2400 interspersed ($VD$) flows, incrementally raising proportion until equilibrium was reached.
3. Combined Imbalance in $V$ and $VD$: Here, we induced imbalance simultaneously in both v and vd categories. Like earlier, we commenced with 1% from both VoIP ($V$) and interspersed ($VD$) flows, subsequently incrementing until the balance was reached.

This methodology enabled us to discern the classifiers' performance trends. To evaluate them, we leaned on the false positive rate (FPR) for downloads. *Note that for an attacker, detecting all VoIP-containing flows is crucial. Thus, achieving high precision and recall for V and VD signifies the exemplary performance of the classifiers. Furthermore, a low FPR for D is equally meritorious, as it indicates fewer misclassifications of V or VD as D. The FPR for d across different situations is depicted in Figure 4.*

In every scenario, the FPR for kNN, SVM, and RF remained notably low and stable compared to the NB. Specifically, when changing the proportion of v, the FPR peaked at 25% but then steadily decreased, settling around 10%. On the other hand, with a varied proportion of interspersed vd traffic, there was a consistent rise in FPR, rendering the model less effective. Interestingly, when v and vd were jointly adjusted, the FPR trend mirrored that observed with v alone. For all other classifiers, the FPR remained consistently below 0.8%.

The CNN models based on IAT and directions did not have any false positives, while varying the proportion of Class $V$, as evident in Fig. 4a. In Fig. 4b, CNN-Dir showed a relatively higher FPR, while varying the instances of $VD$. It started at 10% and settled at around 13%, while CNN-IAT showed a variation between 0 and 6%. A similar pattern can be seen (4c) while varying the proportions of $V$ and $VD$ together. CNN-Dir exhibited varying FPR between 5% and 7%, while CNN-IAT showed a variation between 0% and 3%. In all the cases, DL models performed well while detecting VoIP flows.

The subpar performance of the Naïve Bayes classifier can be attributed to the high correlation present among some of the features. This contradicts the classifier's underlying assumption of feature independence. Thus the model tends to inflate probability estimates, leading to erroneous classifications. Despite these shortcomings, Naïve Bayes classifier remains a part of our ensemble of attack models as it exhibits a fair performance in detecting VoIP flows. Note that it has 99% precision and recall in detecting VoIP alone flows. In addition, it has a distinct operational principle compared to models like SVM, kNN, or Random Forest. Hence, it's imperative to assess its resilience in detecting defended VoIP flows as well.

## 6    Defense

Hitherto, we showed how traffic analysis combined with machine learning models can be used to detect VoIP flows over Tor even when they are interspersed with HTTP traffic. We presented the accuracy of well-known machine learning algorithms such as k-NN, Naïve Bayes, SVM, and Random Forest classifiers in detecting VoIP containing flows. We now describe a defense strategy capable of concealing VoIP flows from these machine learning classifiers.

Before we describe the details, we list how our work differs from WF attacks' defenses: (1) We focus on detecting the presence of VoIP flows, while WF attacks aim to determine the websites being visited in both *open* and *closed-world* settings [47,48,67]. (2) A multitude of WF defenses exist, but none specifically designed for real-time protocols like VoIP, unlike ours. (3) We transform VoIP's flow features, so that they resemble HTTP. WF defenses on the other hand focus on obfuscating traffic features to prevent detection of websites a client visits. (4) To defend VoIP calls, we require engaging both the caller and callee in a manner that traffic patterns resemble those of HTTP. Unlike WF defenses, which require modification in relays, the VoIP defense can be setup without any participation from Tor relays. (5) Delays in WF defenses (impacting HTTP traffic) can be tolerated. But even a slight delay introduced by our defense could compromise the call quality.

To devise a defense to counteract the attack models, it's crucial to comprehend how these classifiers are able to identify VoIP flows. This requires pinpointing the features that may be instrumental in flow detection. The Random Forest classifier provides generalized and multicollinearity resilient feature importance scores [5,41]. So we based our understanding of the feature importance on it. This classifier determines feature importance by calculating the Mean Decrease in Impurity (MDI), also referred to as Gini Importance [54]. we observe that nearly 55% of the importance is attributed to the combination of derived features from inter-arrival times. Approximately 35% of the importance is associated with throughput-related features, while size-related features contribute less than 10% to the overall importance. This aligns with expectations, as Tor transmits data in fixed-byte cells.

We now aim to develop a defense strategy to counteract the classifiers' ability to detect VoIP-containing flows. To achieve this, we will adjust the revealing time and volume features of VoIP-carrying flows to resemble those of download flows. This defense modifies the statistical features of VoIP flows in a way that mimics HTTP downloads. As the original statistical features of VoIP flows are altered to appear like HTTP, we refer to this defense as *Transformation Defense*. We first describe the design and requirements of the defense, next implementation, and finally, evaluate the performance of the proposed defense strategy.

### 6.1   Design: Transformation Defense

We discuss the requirements and design for the transformation defense. As previously discussed, our aim is to adjust the characteristics of VoIP carrying flows to resemble those of HTTP download flows. The requirements of such a defense technique are as follows:

1. When an adversary tries to classify the defended VoIP flows by extracting the aforementioned features the classifiers should misclassify them as HTTP downloads.
2. It is important that any defense technique for VoIP flows should not degrade the quality of the VoIP calls beyond a certain tolerable limit. The defense techniques for the real time protocols will bear this additional burden of maintaining the quality.

We design the defense by satisfying these two requirements. We identified the important features that distinguish VoIP flows. To modify time and volume based features, we propose a packet generator which would generate dummy packets and a padder which would add extra bytes to the packets. The functioning of both is as follows:

– **Dummy Packet Generator:** A dummy packet generator is used for generating random packets with a given payload length. These packets have valid TCP and IP headers along with random bytes as application data. These dummy packets are inserted in between RTP packets and sent to other side. We use this mechanism to adjust the timing and volume of the flows. We simply ignore the dummy packets and do not process them at receiving end.
– **Padder:**   The purpose of the padder is to pad some extra bytes to the packets to increase the volume of the traffic. As we mentioned before, we try to make the VoIP flows look like HTTP downloads. In a typical client-server architecture, there will be large volume of traffic from the server to the client. To mimic this behaviour, we assume that the callee to behave as server and we pad extra bytes to the packets sent from the callee to the caller. It is to be noted that, we pad these extra bytes to the RTP packets as well as to the dummy packets sent from the callee. At the caller, we discard the dummy packets and we extract the RTP payload from the extra padded bytes.

Using aforementioned operations, we explain the operation of our defense. Figure 5 shows how packets sent from caller and callee sides are transformed. Let superscripts $+$ and $-$ denote forward and backward directions, $l$ denotes length of the packet and $\delta$ denotes inter-arrival time between packets. Subscripts $v$ and $d$ denote the VoIP and download flows respectively. *E.g.*, $\delta_v^-$ denotes the inter-arrival time of the packets flowing in the backward direction.

**Transforming Inter-Arrival Times:** In our defense we try to make $\delta_v^+ \approx \delta_d^+$ and $\delta_v^- \approx \delta_d^-$. We observed that the inter arrival time of the RTP packets is always higher than that of the download packets. To reduce the IAT of the RTP flow we insert dummy packets between successive RTP packets. This operation was performed at both the sides of caller and callee.

**Transforming Volume of Flows:** As discussed earlier, the flow rate of VoIP packets flowing in both the directions is low and relatively constant. To mimic high throughput data transfer of downloads, we alter length of packets wherever required.

As per the threat model, an adversary should see a large volume of data flowing from callee to caller so that it should look like the caller (or client) is downloading some large files using Tor. From caller to callee, we don't have to do this as a download client only sends ACKs to the server. This should effectively mimic the traffic pattern akin to downloads.

To mimic the behavior, at the callee side, we set the size of dummy packets to be Maximum Transmission Unit (MTU) of the interface (as seen in download packets) and RTP packets are padded with extra bytes ($l_v^- = l_d^-$). However, we make sure that the dummy packets and the RTP packets have different lengths so that it can be distinguished at the callee side. At the caller side, we just send the IP and TCP headers of the dummy packets without any application payload ($l_d^+ = 0$) and we do not pad any bytes to the RTP packets ($l_v^+$).

Figure 5 shows how the defended VoIP flows and how the above parameters are transformed.

## 6.2    Implementation: Transformation Defense

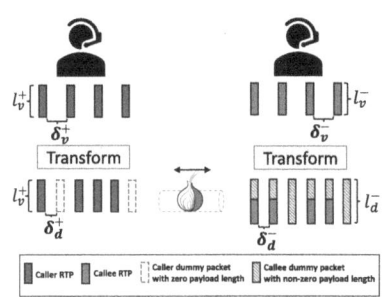

**Fig. 5.** Figure shows the undefended flows(top) and the defended VoIP flows(bottom) after modifying the IAT and packet lengths.

We now discuss the implementation and the internal workings of the defense mechanism in detail. As we mentioned earlier, the purpose of the defense is to make the VoIP flows look like HTTP download flows, to an observing adversary. We accomplish this by transmitting dummy and modified RTP packets in both directions based on the aforementioned design. The defended VoIP calls, bears the following types of packets with the mentioned attributes:

*From caller to callee,* (1) Dummy packets with IAT $\delta_d^+$ and length $l_d^+ = 0$, (2) RTP packets with IAT $\delta_v^+$ and length $l_v^+$. *From callee to caller,* (1) Dummy packets with IAT $\delta_d^-$ and length $l_d^-$, (2) RTP packets with IAT $\delta_v^-$ and length $l_d^-$

The inter-arrival times $\delta_d^+$ and $\delta_d^-$ of the dummy packets are selected from a normal distribution. This distribution's values are derived by calculating the mean and standard deviation of IAT of HTTP downloads from the dataset employed for training our machine learning models. Figure 6 shows the schematic diagram of the defense implementation. We describe the detailed functioning of the defense as follows:

1. On execution, the defense app starts sending dummy packets from caller to callee with an inter-arrival time $\delta_d^+$ and length $l_d^+ = 0$. The latter is for mimicking ACK packets sent from the client to the server, while downloading.
2. The caller side RTP packets, generated from VoIP application, are redirected to the defense app. (using Linux `iptables`).
3. The defense application temporarily halts the sending dummy packets and promptly receives the RTP packet without delay. It doesn't modify their time and size parameters.
4. The received RTP packets are placed inside the dummy packets and sent. Note that the dummy packets containing RTP packets have distinct lengths to identify them by the peer. The difference in packet sizes is not visible to an observing adversary as the traffic is sent through Tor which fragments the data into fixed-sized cells, that are encrypted with TLS.
5. The packets received at the callee side are redirected to the defense program (using `iptables`) that discards the dummy packets (based on their lengths) and forwards the RTP packets to the callee application.
6. The defense mechanism at the callee side is similar to that of caller. At the callee side, the defense app starts sending dummy packets to the caller with an inter-arrival time of $\delta_d^-$ and length $l_d^-$. These are redirected to the defense application using Linux `iptables`.
7. The callee's defense application temporarily halts the sending of the dummy packets and forwards the RTP packet *after* padding extra bytes so that the length of the packet becomes $l_d^-$. This is to mimic the high throughput behaviour of HTTP flows.
8. The packets are then transmitted to the caller.
9. At the caller side, these packets are redirected to the defense application that removes the extra bytes padded and forwards the original RTP packets to the caller application.

The defense program was written in C and tested on a 1-core machine with 1GB RAM, running Linux kernel v5.4.

## 6.3    Results: Transformation Defense

To assess the robustness of our defence, we implemented and deployed it, and placed 1000 defended calls, capturing the network traces and voice recordings to gauge the quality. To assess the defense's effectiveness, we extracted features from the network traces as detailed in Section §5.1. Using the attack models previously described in Section §5, we attempted to classify these defense instances. Our evaluation comprised two methods: utilizing both a balanced and an unbalanced dataset. A balanced setting, helps evaluate how a generalized model can

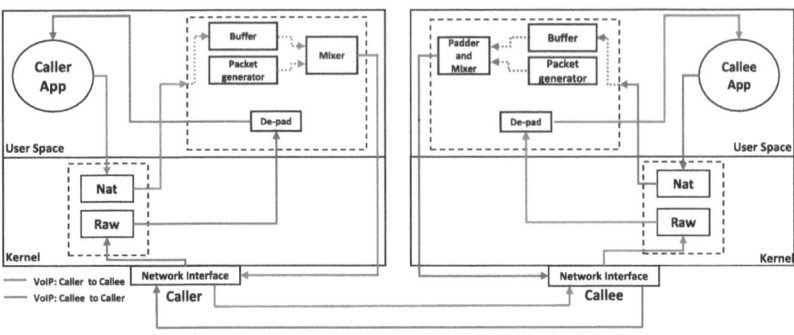

**Fig. 6.** A system-level schematic showing the implementation of transformation defense.

perform when class distributions are unpredictable. On the other hand, unbalanced set represents the infrequent occurrence of defended VoIP flows in Tor which is a more realistic scenario. As a measure of success, we introduced the 'VoIP detection rate'. This rate represents the proportion of defense points classified as either $V$ or $VD$ relative to the overall count of defense points. This metric was applied in both balanced and unbalanced testing scenarios. Also note that, although we initially hypothesized that the participants' locations might influence network features, it did not seem to have much impact on the detection rate.

**Testing on a Balanced Dataset:** Our test set included an equal distribution of $V$, $D$, $VD$, and defense instances. The outcomes can be seen in Table 2. When protected by our defense strategy, the classifiers struggled to identify VoIP flows. The most adept classifiers only managed VoIP detection rates of 16% and 12.2%. Without defense, our attack models consistently identified VoIP flows with a True Positive Rate (TPR) exceeding 95%. This underscores the efficacy of our defense approach in concealing VoIP flows.

**Table 2.** Classification results for Transform defense.

| Classifier | VoIP detection rate |
|---|---|
| Naïve Bayes | 12.2 |
| k-NN | 0.7 |
| SVM | 0.08 |
| Random Forest | 8.9 |
| CNN-Dir | 16 |
| CNN-IAT | 3 |

**Testing on an Unbalanced Dataset:** As previously noted, VoIP calls over Tor might be infrequent, as are defended VoIP flows. Thus, assessing VoIP classification performance in an unbalanced testing scenario becomes vital. To assess robustness of our defense, we used the earlier attack models (see § 5) on the unbalanced set of data. In this experiment, we kept an even distribution between $V$, $D$, and $VD$ (with 1000 data points each) and adjusted the proportion of defended flows in test set until a balanced condition was achieved. The fluctuation in VoIP detection rates is depicted in Fig. 7. Notably,

SVM classifier almost entirely missed the VoIP-containing flows. When the defended VoIP flows constitute less than 20%, detection rates varied among the three classifiers. Random Forest started with a detection peak at 17%, which then decreased and stabilized around 5%. Naïve Bayes began with a detection rate of 15%, later settling below 10%. Initially, kNN achieved an accuracy of up to 12%, but this dwindled to nearly 1%, as the proportion of defended VoIP flows increased. These outcomes prove that attackers fails to identify defended VoIP flows, mistaking them mostly as downloads.

*Results:* Similar to the approach what we described in §5, we assessed our defense data points under two distinct scenarios: balanced and unbalanced testing. In balanced testing, we evaluated the model using raw features of IAT and backward throughput, which were extracted from 1000 defense network traces. This resulted in only 4% of the defense data points being identified as VoIP, as detailed in Table 2. For unbalanced testing, we emulated our previous method by gradually altering the proportions of defense data points under examination, ranging from 1% to 100%, while maintaining an even distribution across $V$, $D$, and $VD$ categories. The outcomes of this are depicted in Fig. 7. Similar to the results observed with Random Forest, the detection rate initially was 20%, then experienced a sharp decline to 2.5%, before stabilizing at approximately 5%.

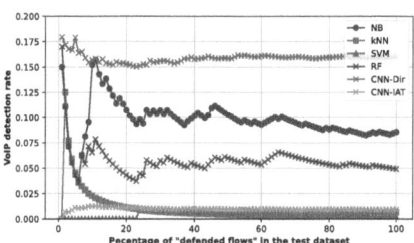

**Fig. 7.** Classification of "defended flows" across different classifiers in an unbalanced setting.

The direction based CNN model is performing relatively well in detecting the defense. A consistent output of around 16% can be observed for this model. However, IAT based CNN is performing poor compared to the ML models. Thus our defense was resistant against CNN and our defense mechanism to make VoIP appear like HTTP is well enough to defend multiple types of learning based attack models.

**Quality of Defended VoIP Calls:** Figure 8 shows the PESQ of calls for both undefended and defended calls. The highest recorded PESQ in both cases was > 3.9. The average PESQ value for both cases was ≈ 2.25. As evident, the defended and undefended calls had comparable PESQ. Almost 70% of undefended calls had PESQ ≈ 2.1. This number modestly drops to 2.0 for the defended calls. This is considered *fair* as per ITU-T standards and prior research [25,56]. Thus the defense does not dramatically degrade the call quality.

# 7   Related Work

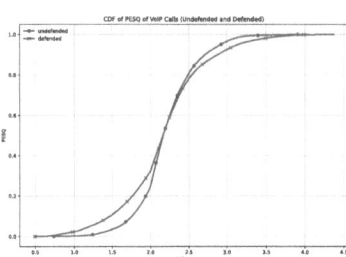

**Fig. 8.** CDF of PESQ of defended and undefended calls.

**VoIP over Tor:** Recent research has demonstrated feasibility of VoIP calls through Tor [6,56]. This development might attract attention of adversaries interested in identifying type of traffic routed through Tor circuits, making traffic classification a crucial concern within Tor network. Though Sharma *et al.* [56] confirmed that VoIP is indeed viable over Tor, they did not explore the aspects of traffic analysis and traceability of VoIP within this framework. Bromberg *et al.* [6] introduced *Donar*, to enable high-quality VoIP calls by scheduling VoIP packets via various fast Tor circuits. The system facilitates VoIP calls by duplicating and sending packets through multiple Tor circuits. But each of these circuits bears characteristics of single VoIP flows, and thus does not prevent adversaries from detecting them.

**Traffic Analysis attacks on Tor:** There exists a plethora of research that explores traffic analysis attacks on Tor, like traffic correlation [43,59], and *website fingerprinting (WF)* [17,47,48,67]. The former deals with correlating multiple ingress and egress flows to deanonymize clients' connections through Tor. The latter deals with identifying the website visited by client, by inspecting network traces captured between client and guard node. However, there exist very few studies that explored feasibility of traffic classification over Tor. This may be because HTTP is the predominant protocol that is transported over Tor [27,37].

**Traffic Analysis Defenses on Tor:** There are several defenses against WF attacks [8,29]. They employ strategies such as padding, modifying IAT, and incorporating dummy packets. However, when developing a defense tailored for VoIP, it's crucial to maintain the call quality. This is particularly vital because the RTP protocol, responsible for delivering VoIP payload, is highly sensitive to time lags. Even slight delays in transmission can significantly compromise quality of a VoIP call. To better understand how WF defenses impact VoIP, we've classified these defenses into two primary categories: Delaying defenses and Non-delaying defenses.

*Delaying Defenses:* This category of defense involves intentionally adjusting the IAT of HTTP packets. This is a deliberate measure to thwart website fingerprinting attacks. Such alterations can notably impact jitter, leading to potential degradation in call quality, if applied to VoIP protocol. Past WF defenses like

**Table 3.** Comparison of WF defenses and their Suitability for VoIP. Although these defenses are not designed to hide or transform VoIP traffic, we compare their features with ours to evaluate their potential applicability.

| Defense | Description | Year | Latency impact | Tor relay support | Why unsuitable for VoIP? |
|---|---|---|---|---|---|
| BuFLO [13] | Fixed-size, fixed-interval padding, adding regular dummy packets. | 2012 | Yes | Yes | Introduces jitter, affecting real-time communication quality. |
| CS-BuFLO [7] | Congestion-sensitive variant of BuFLO, adjusts padding based on congestion levels. | 2012 | Yes | Yes | High latency, not suitable for latency-sensitive applications like VoIP. |
| Tamaraw [8] | Improved BuFLO with non-uniform padding intervals. | 2014 | Yes | Yes | High latency, not suitable for latency-sensitive applications like VoIP. |
| WTF-PAD [29] | Adaptive padding based on histograms to obscure traffic patterns. | 2015 | No | Yes | Relies on sending dummy packets during the burst mode and gap mode. |
| Walkie-Talkie [68] | Uses half-duplex communication and burst molding to obscure traffic patterns. | 2017 | Yes | Yes | Introduces significant latency and indistinguishability based on decoy burst sizes has no role on VoIP. |
| BiMorphing [1] | Bi-directional bursting defense using statistical sampling and optimization techniques. | 2019 | No | Yes | Focuses on web traffic bursts, potential for bandwidth overhead, and may not align with VoIP's regular packet intervals. |
| FRONT & GLUE [16] | Obfuscates the trace front of web traffic by injecting randomized dummy packets. | 2020 | No | Yes | VoIP lacks an identifiable trace front, and its regular packet intervals render FRONT ineffective for VoIP hiding. |
| TrafficSilver [11] | Splits user traffic across multiple Tor entry nodes to limit data visibility and distort patterns. | 2020 | No | Yes | Splitting traffic introduces variability in packet delivery of VoIP RTP packets. May result in increased jitter and potential delays. |
| RegulaTor [19] | Regularizes the size and shape of packet surges, uses decaying rates and dummy packets. | 2022 | No | Yes | The approach of linking upload traffic rates to download traffic and using decaying rates does not align well with the consistent, bidirectional packet flow needed for high-quality VoIP communication. |
| *VoIP Vanguard* | *Modify IAT, packet padding, throughput to transform the flow to look like HTTP.* | *2024* | *No* | *No* | *Our defense doesn't modify the real VoIP-RTP packet timings. Simply use dummies to manipulate the timings and packet paddings to manipulate metadata.* |

\* While WTF-PAD might adapt to defend VoIP, it wasn't designed for this purpose and remains vulnerable to direction-based detection attacks [57]. Our defense, however, effectively protects VoIP.

*BuFLO* [7], *Tamaraw* [8], and *DynaFlow* [35], made modifications to the IAT, aiming to maintain a steady packet transmission rate. In contrast, our method aims to diversify IAT of VoIP packets. We manage this by introducing dummy packets, ensuring no additional transmission delays for the primary VoIP packets.

*Non-delaying Defenses:* These defenses do not alter the Inter-Arrival Time (IAT) of protocol packets. We highlight three recent defenses in this category: *Traffic-Silver* [11], *HyWF* [18], and *FRONT and GLUE* [16]. Although these defenses don't intentionally adjust the IAT of the packets, their mechanisms might inadvertently introduce delays. TrafficSilver [11], relies on fragmenting and merging packets, either at the network or application layer. This leads to packet reordering, which could potentially modify IAT and impact VoIP call quality. Implementing this technique also necessitates changes to the existing Tor source code. HyWF [18] employs a similar strategy, partitioning traffic to route it across various networks using multipath TCP. Routing through multiple networks incurs additional transmission and queuing delays, that could negatively impact call quality. Wang *et al.* proposed FRONT and GLUE [16]. This paper introduced two techniques: FRONT, which masks initial loading features critical for WF classification, and GLUE, which sends consecutive packets to counteract WF attacks that rely on noticeable time lapses between page visits. However, these strategies are not suitable for concealing VoIP traffic, as they are very specific to webpage loading traffic patterns and they were never tested for concealing VoIP like traffic. A summary of potential WF defenses is given in the Table 3.

**Special note on WTF-PAD:** WTF-PAD [29] is another website fingerprinting defense with zero latency overhead. It uses an adaptive padding mechanism following log-normal distributions while choosing IAT of dummy packets. Our mechanism, even if somewhat similar, tries to transform VoIP flow to appear as HTTP, altogether, making VoIP identification attacks difficult. Also WTF-PAD is implemented in Tor source code [44,63]. Although not enforced by default, relay operators and clients can enable WTF-PAD by configuring and recompiling source for experimentation. It requires participation from a middle node. In contrast, our defense does not need cooperation from Tor relays, as it is deployed directly at calling peers. Additionally, WTF-PAD is vulnerable to detection when directional features are used [57]. But our defense is not vulnerable to such a detection as explained in §6.3.

## 8    Discussion

Our method could play a crucial role in preserving communication privacy, especially for Tor users in restrictive environments. However, our work has certain limitations, and there is scope for further improvements, which we will describe in this section.

One of the drawbacks of our defense is the significant data overhead. To replicate the behavior of HTTP downloads, we had to send MTU-sized dummy packets more frequently than VoIP RTP packets, leading to a steep increase in throughput and inefficient bandwidth usage ($\approx 2Mbps$). In future work, we aim to optimize the defense to minimize the additional throughput required while still effectively deceiving classifiers.

Another limitation of our VoIP quality measurements is that we tested only short, 30-second calls due to our reliance on the PESQ metric. In future work, we plan to evaluate longer calls and assess the defense's long-term performance under varied network conditions. We will also incorporate additional metrics such as jitter, one-way delay, and packet loss, along with advanced assessments like *POLQA* [23] and the *E-model* [24], for a more comprehensive analysis of VoIP performance. Furthermore, we will gather qualitative feedback from users to better understand perceived call quality. Additionally, we aim to adapt the defense to emerging VoIP technologies (e.g., codecs) and enhance its resilience against evolving traffic analysis techniques by exploring new obfuscation methods or adaptive mechanisms.

Finally, we also plan to conduct more rigorous testing by incorporating additional features and learning models. Our future work will involve evaluating the defense mechanism against a wider range of attack scenarios, including various learning models and adversarial attacks, to better assess its robustness in diverse conditions.

## 9    Conclusion

In this paper, we show that even though VoIP can be anonymized through systems like Tor, there are little to no ways to ensure that such calls can be safeguarded against detection. By carefully manipulating timing and throughput characteristics, we were able to make VoIP traffic resemble standard HTTP downloads, significantly reducing its detectability by both machine learning and deep learning models. This approach provides a strong layer of protection against traffic analysis attacks, while maintaining an acceptable level of VoIP call quality, as confirmed by PESQ evaluations. Our solution offers a promising direction for enhancing the anonymity and security of VoIP communications within the Tor network.

## A    Ethical Considerations

Our experiments involved analyzing network traffic between two peers during phone calls. We did not use human subjects to make the calls; instead, we used recorded voices of the researchers involved or copyrighted speech samples obtained from the internet. [51,66]. We never collected any personally identifiable information at any stage of our experiments.

We captured the network traces of the VoIP calls that were routed through Tor, at the clients themselves and did not record any other Tor packets (header and/or payload) from the network. Initial tests were conducted on a test Tor network, with public network experiments only following successful results.

Our proposed defense mechanism increased VoIP traffic throughput from around 320 Kbps to 2 Mbps due to added dummy packets and padding. Given that Tor now supports higher throughput, as noted by Tor metrics [64], our methodology posed no security or anonymity risks. Public Tor network tests were staggered over weeks to minimize relay node load.

## B    Deep Learning

The CNN architecture for detecting VoIP flows is shown in Fig. 9. It consists of four blocks, each with a convolutional layer using ELU activation and a Max Pooling layer with ReLU activation. Hyperparameter tuning was conducted, and the final hyperparameters are listed in Table 4.

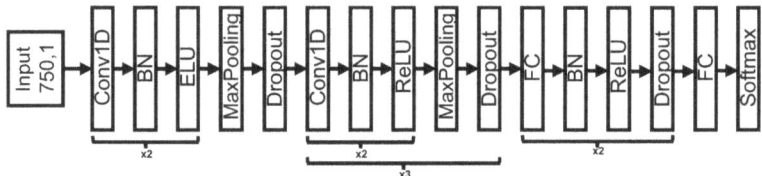

**Fig. 9.** CNN Architecture diagram.

**Table 4.** Hyperparameter Tuning.

| Hyperparameters | Values |
|---|---|
| Input Dimension | (750,1) |
| Optimizer | Adamax |
| Learning Rate | 0.002 |
| Training Epochs | 50 |
| Mini Batch Size | 30 |
| Filter, Pool, Stride Sizes | (2,2), (2,2), 4 |
| Activation Functions | ELU, ReLU |
| Number of Filters | [32,64,128,256] |
| Pooling Layers | Max |
| Number of FC Layers | 2 |
| Hidden Units (each FCs) | [512, 512] |
| Dropout [Pooling, FC1, FC2] | [0.1, 0.7, 0.5] |

## References

1. Al-Naami, K., El-Ghamry, A., et al.: BiMorphing: a Bi-directional bursting defense against website fingerprinting attacks. IEEE Trans. Dependable Secure Comput. **18**(2), 505–517 (2019)
2. Vidhya, A.: ResNet — Understand and Implement from scratch. https://medium.com/analytics-vidhya/resnet-understand-and-implement-from-scratch-d0eb9725e0db (2011)

3. Apache Software Foundation. Apache Web Server. https://httpd.apache.org/ (2023)
4. Ayyachamy, S., et al.: Medical image retrieval using Resnet-18. In: Medical Imaging 2019: Imaging Informatics for Healthcare, Research, and Applications, vol. 10954, pp. 233–241. SPIE (2019)
5. Bishop, C.M.: Pattern Recognition and Machine Learning (Information Science and Statistics). Springer-Verlag, Berlin, Heidelberg (2006) 0387310738
6. Bromberg, Y.-D., et al.: Donar: anonymous {VoIP} over tor. In: 19th USENIX Symposium on Networked Systems Design and Implementation (NSDI 22), pp. 249–265 (2022)
7. Cai, C., et al.: CS-BuFLO: a congestion sensitive website fingerprinting defense. In: Proceedings of the 13th Workshop on Privacy in the Electronic Society, pp. 121–130 (2014)
8. Cai, X., et al.: A systematic approach to developing and evaluating website fingerprinting defenses. In: Proceedings of the 2014 ACM SIGSAC Conference on Computer and Communications Security, CCS '14, pp. 227–238 (2014)
9. Cheng, J., et al.: MATEC: a lightweight neural network for online encrypted traffic classification, vol. 199, p. 108472. Elsevier (2021)
10. Choudhury, S.H., Kumar, A., et al.: Adaptive management of multimodal biometrics–a deep learning and metaheuristic approach. Appl. Soft Comput. **106**, 107344 (2021)
11. De la Cadena, W., et al.: TrafficSliver: fighting website fingerprinting attacks with traffic splitting. In: Proceedings of the 2020 ACM SIGSAC Conference on Computer and Communications Security, CCS '20, pp. 1971–1985 (2020)
12. Dingledine, R., Mathewson, N., et al.: Tor: the second-generation onion router. In USENIX Security Symposium, vol. 4, pp. 303–320 (2004)
13. Dyer, K.P., et al.: Peek-a-boo, i still see you: why efficient traffic analysis countermeasures fail. In: 2012 IEEE Symposium on Security and Privacy, pp. 332–346. IEEE (2012)
14. Edman, M., Syverson, P.: As-awareness in tor path selection. In: Proceedings of the 16th ACM Conference on Computer and Communications Security, pp. 380–389 (2009)
15. FreeSWITCH. FreeSWITCH. https://signalwire.com/freeswitch (2023)
16. Gong, J., Wang, T.: Zero-delay lightweight defenses against website fingerprinting. In: 29th USENIX Security Symposium (USENIX Security 20), pp. 717–734 (2020)
17. Hayes, J., Danezis, G.: k-fingerprinting: a robust scalable website fingerprinting technique. In: 25th USENIX Security Symposium (USENIX Security 16), pp. 1187–1203 (2016)
18. Henri, S., et al.: Protecting against website fingerprinting with multihoming. In: Proceedings on Privacy Enhancing Technologies (2020)
19. Holland, J.K., Hopper, N.: Regulator: a straightforward website fingerprinting defense. arXiv preprintarXiv:2012.06609 (2020)
20. Hopper, N., Vasserman, E.Y., et al.: How much anonymity does network latency leak? ACM Trans. Info. Syst. Secur. (TISSEC) **13**(2), 1–28 (2010)
21. Hoque, M.A., et al.: Context-driven encrypted multimedia traffic classification on mobile devices, vol. 88, p. 101737. Elsevier (2023)
22. India Today Tech. Rising surveillance risk . https://www.indiatoday.in/technology/news/story/report-says-india-sniffing-internet-traffic-passing-through-undersea-cables-raises-surveillance-risk-2429311-2023-08-31 (2023)
23. ITU-T. POLQA: ITU-T Standard. http://www.polqa.info/ (2008)

24. ITU T. E-model: ITU-T Standard. https://www.itu.int/ITU-T/2005-2008/com12/emodelv1/tut.htm (2010)
25. ITU-T. ITU-T Standards Interpretation. https://www.itu.int/rec/dologin_pub.asp?lang=f&id=T-REC-P.863.1-201906-I!!PDF-E&type=items (2019)
26. Lynch, J.: VoIP surveillance. https://ecfr.eu/publication/iron-net-digital-repression-in-the-middle-east-and-north-africa/ (2022)
27. Jansen, R., Johnson, A.: Safely measuring tor. In: Proceedings of the 2016 ACM SIGSAC Conference on Computer and Communications Security, CCS '16, pp. 1553–1567 (2016)
28. Johnson, A., et al.: Users get routed: traffic correlation on tor by realistic adversaries. In: Proceedings of the 2013 ACM SIGSAC Conference on Computer and Communications Security, CCS '13, pp. 337–348 (2013)
29. Juarez, M., et al.: Toward an efficient website fingerprinting defense. In: Computer Security–ESORICS 2016: 21st European Symposium on Research in Computer Security, Heraklion, Greece, September 26-30, 2016, Proceedings, Part I 21, pp. 27–46. Springer (2016)
30. Shubber, K.:. Tempora Surveillance. https://www.wired.co.uk/article/gchq-tempora-101 (2013)
31. Poireault, K.: VoIP surveillance. https://www.infosecurity-magazine.com/news/lightspy-iphone-spyware-linked/ (2023)
32. Kim, H., et al.: Internet traffic classification demystified: myths, caveats, and the best practices. In: Proceedings of the 2008 ACM CoNEXT Conference, pp. 1–12 (2008)
33. Lashkari, A.H., et al.: Characterization of tor traffic using time based features. In: International Conference on Information Systems Security and Privacy, vol. 2, pp. 253–262. SciTePress (2017)
34. Le Blond, S., et al.: Herd: a scalable, traffic analysis resistant anonymity network for VOIP systems. In: Proceedings of the 2015 ACM Conference on Special Interest Group on Data Communication, pp. 639–652 (2015)
35. Lu, D., et al.: DynaFlow: an efficient website fingerprinting defense based on dynamically-adjusting flows. In: Proceedings of the 2018 Workshop on Privacy in the Electronic Society, pp. 109–113 (2018)
36. R. M.: A Study of VoIP performance in anonymous network-The onion routing (Tor) - PhD thesis (2012)
37. Mani, A., Sherr, M.: Historε: differentially private and robust statistics collection for tor. In: Network and Distributed System Security Symposium, NDSS '17 (2017)
38. Mittal, P., Khurshid, A., et al.: Stealthy traffic analysis of low-latency anonymous communication using throughput fingerprinting. In: Proceedings of the 18th ACM conference on Computer and Communications Security, pp. 215–226 (2011)
39. Moore, W.B., Tan, H., et al.: Multi-class traffic morphing for encrypted voip communication. In: Financial Cryptography and Data Security: 19th International Conference, FC 2015, San Juan, Puerto Rico, January 26-30, 2015, Revised Selected Papers 19, pp. 65–85. Springer (2015)
40. Murdoch, S.J., Zieliński, P.: Sampled traffic analysis by internet-exchange-level adversaries. In: International Workshop on Privacy Enhancing Technologies, pp. 167–183. Springer (2007)
41. Murphy, K.P.: Machine Learning: A Probabilistic Perspective. The MIT Press (2012). ISBN 0262018020
42. Unuth, N.: Common VoIP Codecs. https://www.lifewire.com/voip-codecs-3426728 (2021)

43. Nasr, M., Bahramali, A., et al.: DeepCorr: strong flow correlation attacks on tor using deep learning. In: Proceedings of the 2018 ACM SIGSAC Conference on Computer and Communications Security, CCS '18, pp. 1962–1976 (2018)
44. Nick, M.: Tor New Release. https://blog.torproject.org/new-release-tor-0401-alpha/ (2019)
45. Oh, S., Lee, M., et al.: AppSniffer: towards robust mobile app fingerprinting against VPN. In: Proceedings of the ACM Web Conference, vol. 2023, pp. 2318–2328 (2023)
46. Opus Info. Opus Info. https://opus-codec.org/ (2021)
47. Panchenko, A., Lanze, F., et al.: Website fingerprinting at internet scale. In: Network and Distributed System Security Symposium, NDSS '16 (2016)
48. Panchenko, A., Niessen, L., et al.: Website fingerprinting in onion routing based anonymization networks. In: Proceedings of the 10th Annual ACM Workshop on Privacy in the Electronic Society, pp. 103–114 (2011)
49. PJSIP. PJSIP Stack. https://www.pjsip.org/ (2023)
50. Rimmer, V., Preuveneers, D., et al.: Automated website fingerprinting through deep learning (2018)
51. SampleSwap. SampleSwap. https://sampleswap.org/index.php (2023)
52. Sarwinda, D., Paradisa, R.H., et al.: Deep learning in image classification using residual network (ResNet) variants for detection of colorectal cancer. Procedia Comput. Sci. **179**, 423–431 (2021)
53. Scikit-Learn. sklearn. https://scikit-learn.org/stable/index.html (2022)
54. Scikit Learn. Mean Decrease in Gini Impurity: Feature Importance Calculation. https://scikit-learn.org/stable/auto_examples/inspection/plot_permutation_importance.html (2023)
55. Shapira, T., Shavitt, Y.: FlowPic: encrypted internet traffic classification is as easy as image recognition. In: IEEE INFOCOM 2019-IEEE Conference on Computer Communications Workshops (INFOCOM WKSHPS), pp. 680–687. IEEE (2019)
56. Sharma, P.K., Chaudhary, S., et al.: The road not taken: Re-thinking the feasibility of voice calling over tor. In: Proceedings on Privacy Enhancing Technologies, vol. 4, pp. 1–20 (2020)
57. Sirinam, P., Imani, M., et al.: Deep fingerprinting: undermining website fingerprinting defenses with deep learning. In: Proceedings of the 2018 ACM SIGSAC Conference on Computer and Communications Security, CCS '18, pp. 1928–1943 (2018)
58. Sottek. PRISM Surveillance. https://www.theverge.com/2013/7/17/4517480/nsa-spying-prism-surveillance-cheat-sheet (2013)
59. Sun, Y., Edmundson, A., et al.: {RAPTOR}: Routing attacks on privacy in tor. In: 24th USENIX Security Symposium (USENIX Security 15), pp. 271–286 (2015)
60. Telegraph India. VPN ban in India. https://www.telegraphindia.com/business/vpns-shut-india-based-servers-blame-invasive-government-rules/cid/1888380 (2022)
61. The Verge. VoIP surveillance. https://www.theverge.com/2013/6/7/4407782/phone-spying-and-prism-internet-surveillance-whats-the-difference (2013)
62. Tor–Project. Tor Metrics. https://metrics.torproject.org/networksize.html (2023)
63. Tor Documentation. Circuit Padding Developer Documentation. https://gitlab.torproject.org/tpo/core/tor/-/blob/HEAD/doc/HACKING/CircuitPaddingDevelopment.md (2022)
64. Tor Project. Tor bandwidth. https://metrics.torproject.org/bandwidth.html (2023)
65. TorProject. Tor User base. https://metrics.torproject.org/userstats-relay-country.html (2023)

66. University of Hawaii. University of Hawaii. https://library.wcc.hawaii.edu/c.php?g=35279&p=4005956 (2023)

67. Wang, T., Cai, X., et al.: Effective attacks and provable defenses for website fingerprinting. In: 23rd USENIX Security Symposium (USENIX Security 14), pp. 143–157 (2014)

68. Wang, T., Goldberg, I.: {Walkie-Talkie}: an efficient defense against passive website fingerprinting attacks. In: 26th USENIX Security Symposium (USENIX Security 17), pp. 1375–1390. (2017)

69. Washington Post. Importance of Call meta-data. https://www.washingtonpost.com/politics/full-text-of-president-obamas-jan-17-speech-on-nsa-reforms/2014/01/17/fa33590a-7f8c-11e3-9556-4a4bf7bcbd84_story.html?tid=a_inl_manual (2014)

70. White, A.M., Matthews, A.R., et al.: Phonotactic reconstruction of encrypted VoIP conversations: Hookt on Fon-iks. In: 2011 IEEE Symposium on Security and Privacy, pp. 3–18. IEEE (2011)

71. Wright, C.V., Ballard, L., et al.: Language identification of encrypted VoIP traffic: Alejandra y roberto or alice and bob? In: USENIX Security Symposium, (USENIX Security 07), pp. 43–54 (2007)

72. Wright, C.V., Ballard, L., et al.: Spot me if you can: uncovering spoken phrases in encrypted VoIP conversations. In: 2008 IEEE Symposium on Security and Privacy (SP 2008), pp. 35–49. IEEE (2008)

# Blockchain and Smart Contracts

# PQS-BC: Comparative Analysis of NIST Post-quantum Signatures for Blockchain

Wan Kai Wong, Naipeng Dong$^{(\boxtimes)}$, and Cong Minh Dinh

The University of Queensland, St Lucia QLD 4072, Australia
{wankai.wong,c.dinh}@uq.net.au, n.dong@uq.edu.au

**Abstract.** Blockchain technology is increasingly important across various sectors with cryptography, particularly digital signatures, playing a crucial role in ensuring transparency, trust and security. However, current digital signature algorithms in blockchain are vulnerable to the impending advancements in quantum computing, anticipated to compromise these algorithms by 2030. Such vulnerabilities could result in substantial financial losses, given the significant market value of cryptocurrencies. Thus, it is essential to identify digital signature algorithms capable of withstanding quantum threats, known as post-quantum signatures, that are best suited for various blockchain applications.

This project evaluates 43 NIST post-quantum digital signature algorithms, including 3 finalist algorithms and 40 new submissions for the current round, as they represent the most viable candidates for adoption. We conduct performance testing based on a comprehensive set of 6 criteria and perform data analysis to provide an in-depth comparison of these algorithms, contributing significantly to post-quantum cryptography. The findings recommend 6 promising algorithms for 4 types of blockchains, enhancing blockchain security against quantum threats.

**Keywords:** Quantum Threats · Post-Quantum Crypto · NIST · Blockchain

## 1 Introduction

Blockchain is experiencing a surge in market size across various sectors, including financial transactions, supply chain management, healthcare, government, and real estate, due to its potential to enhance security, efficiency, and transparency [1]. Cryptography is fundamental to these benefits, among which, digital signatures play a particularly important role to maintain the principles of trust, security, and non-repudiation in relationship between Blockchain transactions [32]. Currently, the most widely used digital signature algorithms in blockchain belong to the family of Elliptic Curve Cryptography (ECC) that are approved by the National Institute of Standards and Technology (NIST) [12], including the ECDSA e.g., used in Bitcoin [40] and EdDSA e.g., used in Solana [53].

Nonetheless, a significant concern is the rapid development of quantum computing technology. Proos and Zalka demonstrated in [43] that breaking ECC

H. H. Song et al. (Eds.): NSS 2024, LNCS 15564, pp. 349–369, 2025.
https://doi.org/10.1007/978-981-96-3531-3_17

requires 2500 qubits. And the Quantum Risk Calculator from QByte [44] suggests that, even with a pessimistic forecast, we could see quantum computers equipped with around 2000 qubits by 2030. This has brought to light the alarming possibility that in the not too-distant future, blockchain network security may be seriously compromised.

Being aware of the potential threats posed by quantum computing, a considerable amount of effort has been dedicated to developing digital signature algorithms that can withstand quantum attacks, leading to the field of post-quantum digital signatures (PQS). There have been notable achievements in this field, such as *NTRUSIGN* [23], *Rainbow* [15], *CRYSTALS-Dilithium* [16], and *MAYO* [9], each representing a key contribution to the advancement of post-quantum cryptography (PQC). Central to these efforts is NIST's PQC Standardization Project [11], which plays a pivotal role in consolidating the most promising algorithms to set the stage for future standards. To date, there are 3 PQS algorithms selected by NIST [5] and an additional 40 submissions under consideration [34].

Given NIST's history of standardizing widely-used algorithms like RSA, ECDSA, EdDSA, these 43 algorithms are poised to be front runners in the next generation of blockchain technologies. Therefore, our project evaluates all these 43 PQS algorithms with the goal of migrating blockchain to be quantum safe. To do so, we collected a comprehensive set of evaluation metrics of PQS that are suitable in the context of blockchain. The evaluation process involves performance testing on these metrics to collect data, followed by data analysis to generate rankings and comparison analysis. The results provide a comprehensive view of each algorithm's performance. On top of that, we classified blockchain into 4 types and recommended a total of 6 PQS algorithms suitable for these blockchain categories. Furthermore, we provide insights on adopting PQS in blockchain, for instance, the need for customization as different blockchains may prioritize the criteria differently. In summary, this project contributes significantly in advancing blockchain technology by identifying the most promising PQS suitable for various types of blockchains. Additionally, it makes a significant contribution to the field of PQC by offering valuable feedback to NIST's selection process, thereby contributing to the future of cryptographic standards.

## 2 Background

### 2.1 Digital Signatures

Digital signatures are crucial for authenticating communications, documents, and transactions [47], allowing the sender of a message or the writer of a document to clearly identify themselves as the original source [41], and guarantee data integrity during transmission. They are widely adopted in various applications, underscoring the need to develop a comprehensive understanding of their mechanisms and the quantum threats they face.

Digital signatures play an essential role in ensuring the blockchain's benefits of data authentication, integrity, non-repudiation, and immutability [18]. To add a transaction to the blockchain, entities must sign the transactions and broadcast to every node in the blockchain network [32]. Each node verifies transactions, confirming authenticity. Only valid transactions are added to the blockchain, proving that the sender is the legitimate owner, preventing denial of involvement and unauthorized transactions, crucial in blockchain's trustless environment.

Digital signatures rely on the use of key pairs [41], with the public key accessible to all and the private key securely held by its owner. Their security is based on the formidable computational challenges presented by mathematical problems such as integer factorization (in the case of RSA) and the discrete logarithm problem (as seen in ECDSA and EdDSA) [31], which make deriving of the private key from the corresponding public key extremely difficult. When signing data, the senders use their private key to perform a mathematical operation, generating an unique digital signature that has a complex connection to both the data and the private key [41]. The afterwards verification involves using the sender's public key to perform a mathematical operation on the signature.

## 2.2 Quantum Threats and Post-quantum Signatures

The security of digital signature algorithms is increasingly threatened by the advancements in quantum computing. Shor's algorithm significantly accelerates the solving of both the integer factorization and discrete logarithm problems, reducing their time complexity from exponential to polynomial [2]. Shor's algorithm [49] consists of two parts: a classical part that reduces the factorization problem to a period-finding problem, and the quantum part that uses the quantum computational power to solve the period-finding problem, ultimately solving the target problem. Given the imminent threat posed by quantum computing [2], PQS adoption has become critical to withstand quantum attacks. These algorithms e.g., [15,16,23], and [9] designed to resist both classical and quantum attacks [8], relying on hard problems unsolved by current quantum algorithms.

## 2.3 NIST Post-quantum Signatures

Of significance, NIST initiated the PQC Standardization Process in 2016, where 20 PQS algorithms were submitted [4]. After three rounds of evaluation and analysis, in July 2022, three PQS algorithms were announced to be the standard [5], namely *FALCON*, *SPHINCS+*, and *CRYSTALS-Dilithium (Dilithium)*. While the selected algorithms possess strengths across various domains, diversity concerns persist regarding their future standardization. FALCON and Dilithium rely on lattice-based algorithms [7,21], their security depend on the complexity of solving hard problems within expansive lattice dimensions. If a novel quantum algorithm emerges capable of resolving such challenges, the security of both algorithms could be compromised simultaneously. Conversely, SPHINCS+ is a Hash-based algorithm [6], which exhibits clear efficiency drawbacks. Therefore, in October 2022, NIST requested more submissions for PQS [36]; another 40 candidates were submitted by July 2023. These 43 PQS are categorized into seven distinct classes based on their fundamental hard problems, shown in Fig. 1.

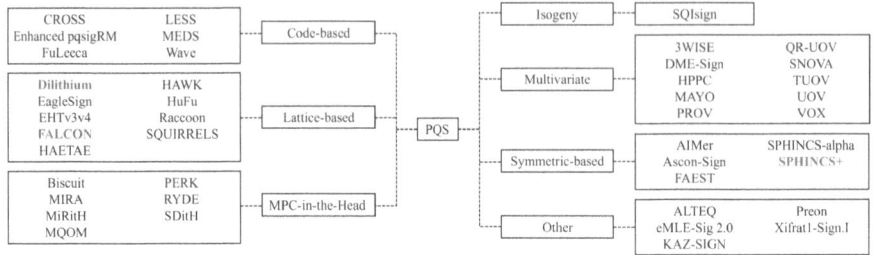

**Fig. 1.** Classification of 43 post-quantum digital signature.

**Table 1.** Summary of Related Works: Targets, Platforms, and Metrics.

| Reference | Testing Targets | Platforms | Metrics |
|---|---|---|---|
| [46] | Dilithium and Kyber | Constrained Devices | pk sm |
| [48] | 5 types of PQS | Constrained Devices | pk sk sm sg sv |
| [20] | NIST Round 4 KEM, selected PQC | Constrained Devices | kg sg sv |
| [22] | Dilithium, SPHINCS+, Rainbow, GeMSS | Constrained Devices | pk sm sv |
| [29] | NIST Additional Round PQS | Constrained Devices | kg sg sv |
| [13] | NIST Round 2 PQC | Hardware | pk sk sm kg sg sv |
| [51] | qTESLA and Dilithium | Hardware | kg sg sv |
| [19] | NIST Round 2 PQC | Hardware | pk sk sm kg sg sv |
| [50] | NIST Round 2 PQC | TSL | pk sk sm sg sv |
| [45] | Dilithium, FALCON, Rainbow, GeMSS | TSL | pk sm kg sg sv |
| [24] | NIST selected PQS | / | pk sk sm |

pk, sk, and sm are length (byte) of public key, private key, and signature; kg, sg, and sv are speed (time/cycle) of key generation, signature generation, and verification.

## 3   Related Work

We conducted a comprehensive review of academic publications released since 2016, coinciding with the year that NIST launched its call for proposals. Google Scholar was used to explore various keyword combinations, synonyms, and variations, such as "Digital Signature," "Blockchain," "Benchmark," "NIST," and "Post-Quantum." These studies, particularly those emphasizing the benchmarking and evaluation of NIST's PQS algorithms in various environments, are summarized in Table 1.

### 3.1   Evaluation Metrics

The above benchmarking research revealed a common thread: despite the diversity in testing criteria, they universally focus on keys and signature lengths, as well as the computational time or cycles required for key generation, signature generation, and verification. These factors are crucial in determining the efficiency of signature algorithms. For instance, computational time or cycles directly influence the algorithm's operational speed, while data length impacts storage requirements, transaction velocity, and more. Consequently, our project embraces these six pivotal criteria: *Key Generation Time*, *Signature Generation Time*, *Signature Verification Time*, *Signature Length*, *Public Key Length*, and *Private Key Length*, with the objective of identifying algorithms that are both rapid and compact according to these metrics.

## 3.2    Evaluation of NIST PQS

Among the above related works, only one study [29] focus on similar targets like us, but only evaluating 15 out of the 40 candidate algorithms. This limitation was due to the study being conducted on pqm4, a platform with constrained capabilities. Motivated by the limitations encountered in [29], we have opted for a measurement platform that prioritizes accessibility and simplicity. This decision stems from the recognition that the 40 candidate schemes, being relatively new, lack tailored implementations for specific devices, making the creation of 40 distinct implementations both resource-intensive and challenging. Considering this is the initial phase of the current rounds, our priority is to furnish comprehensive testing data for all algorithms, ensuring a thorough evaluation.

Furthermore, while several studies have benchmarked NIST algorithms on different platforms, few have assessed their suitability for blockchain applications. Only one study [19] provided recommendations for blockchain applications, focusing solely on NIST round 2 candidates. Another study [24] examined whether NIST-selected algorithms meet blockchain suitability based on length criteria but lacked performance testing results. Inspired by the findings of [24], we acknowledge that the current NIST-selected PQS algorithms may be too large for blockchain applications. This insight further supports our motivation to test all schemes comprehensively and draw comparisons, particularly focusing on the potential of additional round candidates for future blockchain signatures.

As a results, given the unique objectives of our project, including the comprehensive survey of the current round algorithms and making blockchain-specific recommendations, our literature search revealed no prior work with identical testing and recommendation goals. This absence of directly comparable studies is likely due to the novelty of NIST's announcement, which occurred merely a year prior to the drafting of this paper.

# 4    Project Design

The aim of this project is to identify the optimal PQS algorithms for blockchain. As the most viable candidates for adoption, we evaluate the current 43 NIST PQS algorithms including 40 current submissions and 3 finalist. A key focus is on evaluating the performance of these algorithms in different aspects, like the speed of generating key pairs and signatures. This exploration aims to uncover whether any of the new algorithms are optimally suited for blockchain application. Additionally, we are interested in comparing the performance of algorithms selected by NIST with these newer contenders to identify which ones are best suited for different blockchain types. These considerations shape the research goal: to identify the optimal PQS algorithms for blockchain.

## 4.1    Assumptions

To ensure a fair comparison of all algorithms, only the *Reference Implementations* were being tested, that is the Optimized Implementations were not included in the testing. This decision was driven by the diverse optimizations used, the lack of optimizations in some algorithms, and the incompatibility of certain optimizations with all devices. Recall that the aim of this project is to provide developers and researchers with a broad understanding of the performance and resource usage of different algorithms for their suitability for various blockchain systems. If an algorithm performs optimally in its Reference Implementation, it possesses a higher potential to perform well and efficiently after blockchain-specific optimizations. Therefore, even by testing only the Reference Implementation, this approach offers valuable insights.

This paper aims to rank the 43 algorithms, highlighting that testing on the same device minimizes variations, regardless of the device type or computational power. Hence, all tests were executed on a single computer system equipped with an Intel(R) Core(TM) i7-9750H CPU @ 2.60GHz 2.59 GHz, a 64-bit operating system, and a x64-based processor. Additionally, considering that all algorithms are implemented in C and compatible with a Linux environment, Ubuntu 22.04.3 LTS was chosen as the platform for executing the testing scripts. This setup ensures a controlled and consistent testing environment.

**Table 2.** Classification of Security Levels by NIST.

| Security Level | Security Strength | Any attack require computational resources $\geq$ |
| --- | --- | --- |
| 1 | 128 | key search on AES128 |
| 2 | 128 | collision search on SHA256 |
| 3 | 192 | key search on AES192 |
| 4 | 192 | collision search on SHA384 |
| 5 | 256 | key search on AES256 |

Different PQS algorithms may present diverse parameter setups to satisfy various security levels. For a balanced comparison, it is essential to categorize all parameters into different security levels. Given the unpredictable advancements in quantum computing and the potential for new quantum algorithms [39], estimating the security strengths of these PQS algorithms involves considerable uncertainties. As a result, NIST has based its classification on the range of security strengths provided by the existing NIST standards in symmetric cryptography. The security level classification provided by NIST is presented in Table 2. It is important to note that all claimed security levels were assumed to be accurate and met without any additional testing. In our experiments, security strengths of 128-bit, 192-bit, and 256-bit were categorized respectively as NIST-1/2, NIST-3/4, and NIST-5.

## 4.2   Methodology

To achieve the project objectives, the initial step is performance testing to gather data with respect to the six criteria. This data is then being analyzed to generate rankings and comparison tables, ultimately leading us to recommend the most suitable algorithms for blockchain. This section provides an overview of our performance testing framework, as shown in Fig. 2, covering our Data Collection strategies, Automation processes, and Data Analysis methodology.

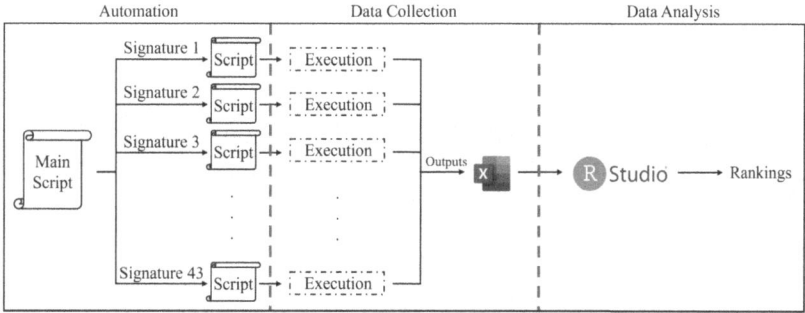

**Fig. 2.** The complete infrastructure of the performance testing approach.

**Data Collection.** To evaluate all the algorithms in terms of execution time and length, benchmarking files are typically the most effective tool. However, upon reviewing all the algorithms, it was observed that while some algorithms provide their own benchmarking executables, their measurement methods and output styles vary significantly. More importantly, most of the algorithms do not provide benchmarking executables at all. Initially, it was anticipated that custom benchmarking files would need to be created for each algorithm to ensure consistent format and output. However, this would require modifying each algorithm's unique Makefile or CMake to include the compilation of the new benchmarking files. To address these challenges, the Known Answer Test (KAT) files provided by NIST were used [35]. These files include test vectors that verify the accuracy of algorithm implementations, and were universally included with submitted packages, along with compile and execution instructions.

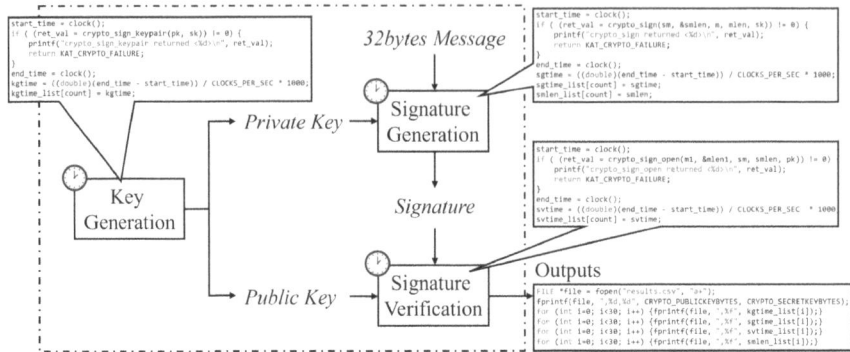

**Fig. 3.** The data collection framework using the `PQCgenKAT_sign.c`.

The data was collected primarily by modifying the `PQCgenKAT_sign.c` within the KAT files, as shown in Fig. 3. Among the six criteria, the lengths of the public and private keys are directly available as input to `PQCgenKAT_sign.c`, eliminating the need for extra testing. The code was specifically modified in the segments concerning the key generation, signature generation, and signature verification functions by integrating time stamping and data collection mechanisms both prior to and subsequent to each function's execution. This modification facilitated the collection of signature lengths and enabled the precise calculation of the running times for each respective function. Additionally, the modified `PQCgenKAT_sign.c` performs 30 iterations using a fixed message length of 32 bytes, assuming the use of a 256-bit hash function (e.g., SHA-256) prior to the signature process. The selection of 30 iterations is grounded in the principles of the Central Limit Theorem [17], while the decision for 32-byte messages aligns with standard signature practices that typically hash inputs before signing. Finally, all the results were automatically recorded into an Excel files.

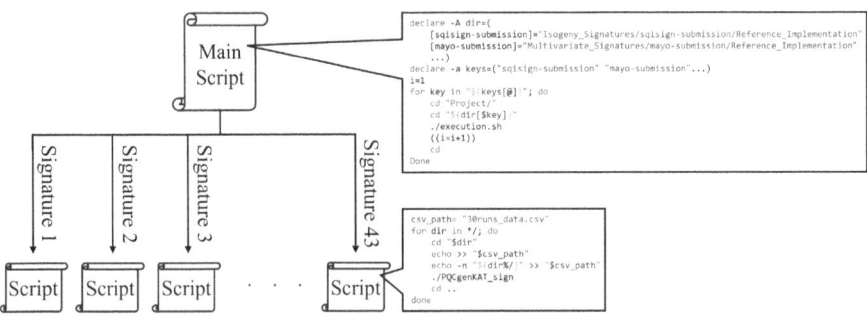

**Fig. 4.** The automation framework.

**Automation.** To streamline the execution process, a script named execution.sh was developed. This script was stored within the implementation folder of their respective algorithms. Their role is to automatically navigate through each parameter folder, executing PQCgenKAT_sign with the corresponding parameters, where the parameter name matches the folder name. Additionally, a master script, execution_main.sh, was created to automate the execution of execution.sh across all algorithms. This automation framework is shown in Fig. 4.

Prior to utilizing these execution scripts, it is necessary to replace the original PQCgenKAT_sign.c file and compile the modified version. It's important to note that this process lacks a straightforward method due to the varied maintenance and compilation approaches adopted by the submissions. To address this, we have provided two scripts on GitHub [3] to simplify the process, although individual modifications to these scripts may be required for each signature algorithm.

While these scripts generally perform well, certain algorithms encounter issues related to compilation or execution. For instance, the algorithms CROSS and LESS require downloading additional libraries not included in their submission packages. Moreover, some algorithms may experience extended run times. To assist with these challenges, we have made the necessary extra libraries available on GitHub [3]. Additionally, we modify the PQCgenKAT_sign.c to include a function to estimate and display the running time for each parameter setup.

**Data Analysis.** After the collection of all testing results, the mean and standard deviation of each criteria were computed in Excel. Then, the results were imported into R-studio. Within R-studio, the 95% Confidence Intervals (CIs) and its bounds were computed. Following that, the rankings for each criterion were assigned based on mean values and CIs. In cases where two parameters had overlapping CIs, they were given identical ranks, as shown in Fig. 5.

| Signature Parameters | Signature Generation Time | | | | |
|---|---|---|---|---|---|
| | mean | 95%CI | CIL | CIU | Rank |
| mayo_1 | 1.058 | 0.015 | 1.043 | 1.073 | 25 |
| sphincs-sha256-128s-simple | 1.06 | 0.016 | 1.044 | 0.076 | 25 |

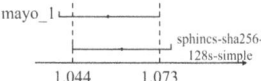

**Fig. 5.** The demonstration of ranking based on overlapping CI.

The data analysis process resulted in the exportation of three results tables, each corresponding to a different security level category. An example is provided in Table 3, with the complete tables accessible on GitHub [3]. These tables include all values and rankings for each parameter across the six criteria.

**Table 3.** Partial testing results for NIST-1/2.

| Signature Parameters | Key Generation Time ms | rank | Signature Generation Time ms | rank | Signature Verification Time ms | rank | Signature Length byte | rank | Public Key length byte | rank | private Key Length byte | rank |
|---|---|---|---|---|---|---|---|---|---|---|---|---|
| falcon512 | $22.971 \pm 2.174$ | 37 | $7.167 \pm 0.011$ | 18 | $0.062 \pm 0.002$ | 4 | $689.033 \pm 0.687$ | 24 | 897 | 18 | 1281 | 22 |
| hawk512 | $6.663 \pm 0.832$ | 32 | $0.166 \pm 0.003$ | 3 | $0.168 \pm 0.002$ | 9 | $587 \pm 0$ | 23 | 1024 | 21 | 184 | 14 |
| dilithium2 | $0.143 \pm 0.003$ | 6 | $0.592 \pm 0.153$ | 6 | $0.157 \pm 0.004$ | 8 | $2452 \pm 0$ | 31 | 1312 | 24 | 2544 | 27 |
| haetae2-kat-sign-main | $0.955 \pm 0.281$ | 12 | $4.685 \pm 1.319$ | 14 | $0.197 \pm 0.008$ | 10 | $1495 \pm 0$ | 30 | 992 | 19 | 1408 | 23 |
| mayo_1 | $1.189 \pm 0.025$ | 13 | $2.46 \pm 0.093$ | 9 | $1.058 \pm 0.015$ | 17 | $353 \pm 0$ | 19 | 1168 | 23 | 24 | 2 |
| SNOVA-28-17-16-2-ssk | $4.795 \pm 0.152$ | 31 | $5.031 \pm 0.189$ | 15 | $1.293 \pm 0.007$ | 20 | $138 \pm 0$ | 7 | 9842 | 32 | 48 | 4 |

# 5 Results and Discussion

This section aims to fulfill the primary goal of this project: to recommend the most suitable algorithms for various blockchain types. We begin by examining the insights derived directly from our data analysis.

## 5.1 Analysis Observations

The analysis of our results allows us to evaluate the compatibility of different algorithms with specific blockchains. For instance, Solana [53], known for its high-speed transactions, mandates that all verifiers submit their signature verification results within 500 ms. This requirement necessitates that the verification time must be less than 500 ms, enabling us to eliminate algorithms that do not meet this criterion for Solana. Moreover, Solana boasts a throughput of up to 710k tps on a 1 gbps network with a minimum transaction size of 176 bytes. This implies that the combined length of the signature and public key must be significantly less than 176 bytes to maintain Solana's high-speed feature.

Our data shown in Fig. 6 reveals that even within the NIST-1/2 category, only KAZ-SIGN, with a verification time of $3.68 \pm 0.114$ ms, a signature length of 77 bytes and a public key length of 62 bytes, meets these requirements. While other algorithms may fulfill some of the criteria, they often fall short on the other. Given the variety of criteria influencing the selection of suitable algorithms for a particular blockchain, and considering that no PQS algorithms may offer the speed and compactness of current blockchain algorithms, it becomes clear that recommending a universally optimal algorithm is not feasible. The diverse nature of blockchains, each with its unique set of priorities, further complicates this task. Therefore, we have categorized the features of different blockchains into four distinct types. This classification, detailed in the subsequent subsection, allows us to rank algorithms based on the criteria prioritized by these blockchain types, ultimately leading to recommendations of the best algorithms for each category.

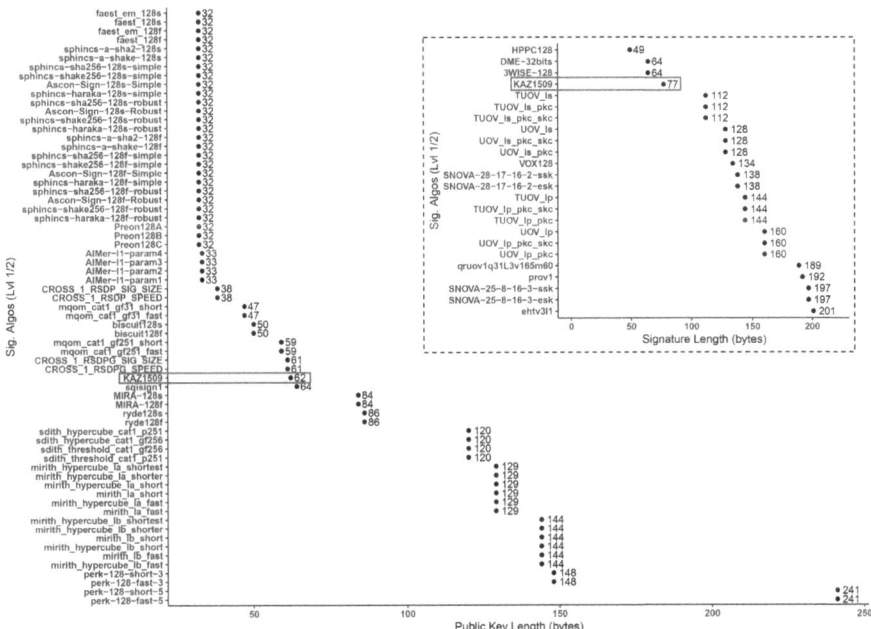

**Fig. 6.** The scatter plots of signature length and public key length for NIST-1/2.

## 5.2    Blockchain Classification

Algorithms ideal for blockchains often prioritize signature verification time, public key length, and signature length. This prioritization facilitates the recommendation of algorithms by re-ranking them based on these three criteria. However, given the wide array of blockchains, each with its unique real-world applications, it is unlikely for a single algorithm to be universally optimal. For instance, FALCON might rank highly based on the three criteria and be generally optimal for blockchains, but it might not be the best choice for a specific type of blockchain that necessitates frequent key generation. To provide more customized recommendations, blockchains were categorized into four types, as shown in Fig. 7.

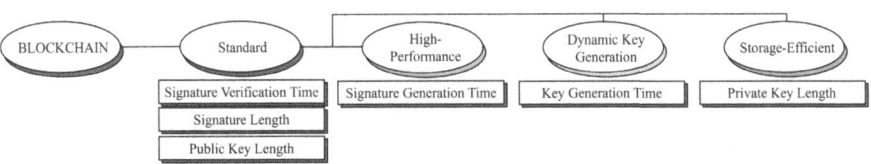

**Fig. 7.** Classification of blockchains based on the six criteria.

**Standard Blockchain (SBC)** primarily requires efficient signature verification time, public key length, and signature length. This category typically includes blockchains without specialized use cases. Taking Bitcoin as an example, with a mining speed of approximately 10 min [32], the time taken for key generation and signature generation becomes less significant in comparison. Moreover, devices that access standard blockchain like Bitcoin usually have enough storage, eliminating the need for a small private key. These factors cause the blockchain to prioritize only the remaining three criteria, classifying it as a Standard Blockchain.

**High-Performance Blockchain (HPBC)** places a strong focuses on signature generation time, in addition to the previously mentioned three criteria. This category typically contains blockchains that prioritize rapid transaction speeds. Taking Solana as an example, with block times of approximately 0.4 s [53] and the capacity to scale to around 700k tps, the execution time at which signatures are generated directly influences the rate at which they can be added to a block. Consequently, the execution time of signature generation could significantly impact transaction speeds.

**Dynamic Key Generation Blockchain (DKGBC)** places a strong focuses on key generation time, in addition to the previously mentioned three criteria. This category represents blockchains that necessitate frequent key generation for each transaction. For instance, Zcash uses zero-knowledge proofs to safeguard privacy [25], consistently generating new keys to update addresses. Consequently, the execution time of key generation directly influences the speed of transactions.

**Storage-Efficient Blockchain (SEBC)** places a strong focuses on private key length, in addition to the previously mentioned three criteria. This category is representative of blockchains that work with devices that operate with limited storage space. An example of this is IOTA, which handles transactions among devices interconnected within the IoT ecosystem [42], which frequently have constrained storage capacity. Consequently, the length of the private key directly impacts the usability of blockchain in IoT devices.

### 5.3   Rankings Based on Blockchain Types

To rank the algorithms according to the blockchain classification, equal weightage was applied to all criteria of each blockchain type. For instance, to rank the algorithms for the SBC, the ranking values of signature verification time, signature length, and public key length were summed. These sums were then ranked to obtain the new rankings for the SBC. Using Table 4 as an example, the sum of the rank of verification time, signature length, and public key length for falcon512 is 46 and hawk512 is 53, hence falcon512 ranks higher than hawk512 in SBC. The complete ranking results are presented in GitHub [3].

**Table 4.** Demonstration of ranking based on blockchain type.

| Signature Parameters | Ranks of criteria | | | | | | Ranks of blockchain types | | | |
|---|---|---|---|---|---|---|---|---|---|---|
| | Key Generation Time | Signature Generation Time | Signature Verification Time | Signature Length | Public Key Length | Private key Length | SBC | HPBC | DKGBC | SEBC |
| falcon512 | 37 | 18 | 4 | 24 | 18 | 22 | 4 | 8 | 13 | 8 |
| hawk512 | 32 | 3 | 9 | 23 | 21 | 14 | 6 | 4 | 15 | 7 |

## 5.4   Results Based on Security Level

For each security level, we generated the top 30 testing setups i.e., the PQS algorithm together with specific parameters, for each blockchain type. Figure 8 presents these rankings for NIST-1/2, while Fig. 10 and 11, located in the Appendix, display the rankings for NIST-3/4 and NIST-5, respectively. Consider the security level definitions provided by NIST [37], levels 1 to 3 are considered "likely/probably secure for the foreseeable future," while levels 4 to 5 are viewed as "likely excessive". Consequently, algorithms and their parameters in NIST-1/2 will likely be used in the foreseeable future. Therefore, our discussions will primarily focus on NIST-1/2, with NIST-3/4 and NIST-5 mentioned only in the "Overall Recommendations" section without further discussion.

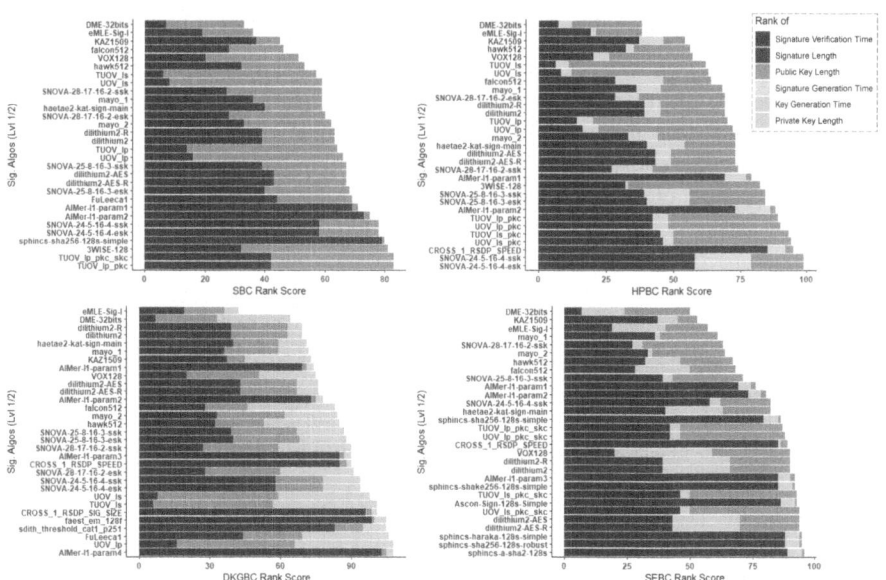

**Fig. 8.** Top 30 PQS with specific parameters for each blockchain type in NIST-1/2.

From Fig. 8, DME-SIGN, eMLE-Sig 2.0, and KAZ-SIGN emerged as notably strong contenders across at least three blockchain types, securing top three rankings. However, vulnerabilities have been identified for each of these algorithms as reported in [33]: DME-SIGN was susceptible to an efficient key recovery attack, eMLE-Sig 2.0 to a full key recovery attack, and KAZ-SIGN to a signature forgery attack. The uncertain status of these top three algorithms led to an in-depth analysis of the top five algorithms, focusing on Dilithium, HAWK, VOX, HAETAE, MAYO, SNOVA, and FALCON. Among these, VOX was found to be vulnerable to a rectangular attack [33]. The practical consequences of exploiting vulnerabilities can be severe. For instance, a successful attack on DME-Sign could allow an adversary to recover private keys, compromising the integrity of transactions and user data on the blockchain. Such breaches could undermine trust in blockchain systems, lead to significant financial losses, and threaten the overall security posture of the network. Therefore, despite the impressive performance of DME-SIGN, eMLE-Sig 2.0, KAZ-SIGN, and VOX, their recommendation is withheld until further verification of their security robustness.

An important observation is that among the top-performing algorithms yet to be identified with vulnerabilities, they can be categorized into two distinct PQS types. Specifically, Dilithium, HAWK, HAETAE, and FALCON belong to the Lattice-based Signature, whereas MAYO and SNOVA are classified under Multivariate Signature. Consequently, the discussion is structured into two parts, each dedicated to one of these PQS types. The foundational security principles inherent to each PQS category are examined first. Following this, the specific attributes of the algorithms are explored, with a focus on their parameters, performance strengths, and adaptability to various blockchain environments.

**Lattice-Based Signatures** stand out for their efficient computation, using vectors and matrices defined by the public key and the signature, a process well-documented in sources like [30, 38], and [26]. Their robust security is based on the complexity of lattice problems, such as finding the shortest or a close vector in a lattice. These problems are considered straightforward in practice because the processes of creating and verifying signatures involve relatively simple operations, such as matrix multiplications and additions. These operations are not only computationally lightweight but also highly parallelizable, enabling lattice-based signatures to be fast both in signature generation and verification. The top algorithms from the performance test employed distinct lattice-based problems: Dilithium and HAETAE use the Module Learning with Errors and Module Short Integer Solution problems, as detailed in [7, 10]. HAWK is built on the Ring Learning with Errors problem, incorporating Gaussian and rejection sampling techniques for enhanced security [27]. FALCON adopts the Gentry-Peikert-Vaikuntanathan framework, integrating NTRU lattices and fast Fourier sampling to achieve its goals [21].

Performance metrics in Table 5 for these top algorithms reveal exceptional verification speeds, all under 0.2ms, indicating the capability for over 5000 verifications per second. Among these, FALCON stands out, being approximately three times faster than its counterparts, making it the preferred choice for SBC. In terms of signature generation time, HAWK and Dilithium lead, with Dilithium

**Table 5.** The testing results of the top parameters in Lattice-based Signature.

| Signature Parameters | Key Generation Time | | Signature Generation Time | | Signature Verification Time | | Signature Length | | Public Key Length | | Private Key Length | | Ranks of block chain types | | | |
|---|---|---|---|---|---|---|---|---|---|---|---|---|---|---|---|---|
| | ms | rank | ms | rank | ms | rank | byte | rank | byte | rank | byte | rank | SBC | HPBC | DKGBC | SEBC |
| falcon512 | 22.971±2.174 | 37 | 7.167±0.011 | 18 | 0.062±0.002 | 4 | 689.033±0.687 | 24 | 897 | 18 | 1281 | 22 | 4 | 8 | 13 | 8 |
| hawk512 | 6.663±0.832 | 32 | 0.166±0.003 | 3 | 0.168±0.002 | 9 | 587±0 | 23 | 1024 | 21 | 184 | 14 | 6 | 4 | 15 | 7 |
| haetae2-kat-sign-main | 0.955±0.281 | 12 | 4.685±1.319 | 14 | 0.197±0.008 | 10 | 1495±0 | 30 | 992 | 19 | 1408 | 23 | 8 | 15 | 5 | 12 |
| dilithium2 | 0.143±0.003 | 6 | 0.592±0.153 | 6 | 0.157±0.004 | 8 | 2452±0 | 31 | 1312 | 24 | 2544 | 27 | 14 | 10 | 3 | 18 |

being three to four times faster than HAWK, making HAWK the preferred choice for HPBC. For key generation time, HAETAE and Dilithium emerge as top performers, recommended for DKGBC. However, when considering the length criteria, all algorithms present comparatively large sizes, with HAWK showing the best performance among the evaluated parameters. Due to none of the algorithms excelling in length criteria, none is specifically recommended for SEBC.

**Multivariate Signatures.** are based on the NP-hard challenge of solving systems of multivariate quadratic polynomial equations over a finite field [14,28] [11]. The core of the signature involves equations that are nonlinear and involve multiple variables. Since the relationship among variables can be expressed concisely, smaller representations of the equations can be used, enabling multivariate signatures to be shortest in private key length. The top algorithms in performance testing are both based on the Oil and Vinegar signature scheme, a prominent approach within this category. The Oil and Vinegar scheme categorizes variables into two sets: "oil" variables and "vinegar" variables. It constructs quadratic equations in such a way that each equation includes at least one vinegar variable, ensuring nonlinearity and complexity. Notably, SNOVA is an Unbalanced Oil and Vinegar Signature Scheme makes use of a non-commutative ring structure for enhanced security [52], while MAYO introduces a variant with reduced public key sizes [9], offering a more efficient solution.

**Table 6.** The testing results of the top parameters in Multivariate Signature.

| Signature Parameters | Key Generation Time | | Signature Generation Time | | Signature Verification Time | | Signature Length | | Public Key Length | | private Key Length | | Ranks of block chain types | | | |
|---|---|---|---|---|---|---|---|---|---|---|---|---|---|---|---|---|
| | ms | rank | ms | rank | ms | rank | byte | rank | byte | rank | byte | rank | SBC | HPBC | DKGBC | SEBC |
| mayo_1 | 1.189±0.025 | 13 | 2.46±0.093 | 9 | 1.058±0.015 | 17 | 353±0 | 19 | 1168 | 23 | 24 | 2 | 8 | 9 | 6 | 4 |
| SNOVA-28-17-16-2-ssk | 4.795±0.152 | 31 | 5.031±0.189 | 15 | 1.293±0.007 | 20 | 138±0 | 7 | 9842 | 32 | 48 | 4 | 8 | 19 | 18 | 5 |

The performance metrics presented in Table 6 highlight the efficiency of these algorithms, particularly in terms of private key length, with both being under 50 bytes. This compact key size is advantageous for applications in SEBC, where resource constraints are a significant consideration. While both algorithms perform well across various metrics, MAYO exhibits superior performance in five out of six criteria, excluding signature length. Consequently, MAYO is more recommended for SEBC applications, offering a balance of efficiency and security.

**Overall Recommendations.** The evaluation process was consistently applied to both NIST-3/4 and NIST-5 categories, yielding similar outcomes. Table 7 presents the top five parameters for each category, highlighting algorithms with identified vulnerabilities in red.

**Table 7.** Top five algorithm with specific parameters for each blockchain type.

| Ranking | SBC | | | HPBC | | |
|---|---|---|---|---|---|---|
| | NIST-1/2 | NIST-3/4 | NIST-5 | NIST-1/2 | NIST-3/4 | NIST-5 |
| 1 | DME-32bits | DME-48bits | DME-64bits | DME-32bits | DME-48bits | DME-64bits |
| 2 | eMLE-Sig-I | eMLE-Sig-III | eMLE-Sig-V | eMLE-Sig-I | eMLE-Sig-III | eMLE-Sig-V |
| 3 | KAZ1509 | KAZ2321 | KAZ3241 | KAZ1509 | KAZ2321 | KAZ3241 |
| 4 | falcon512 | VOX192 | falcon1024 | hawk512 | VOX192 | hawk1024 |
| 5 | VOX128 | Xifrat1-Sign.I | hawk1024 | VOX128 | Xifrat1-Sign.I | falcon1024 |

| Ranking | DKGBC | | | SEBC | | |
|---|---|---|---|---|---|---|
| | NIST-1/2 | NIST-3/4 | NIST-5 | NIST-1/2 | NIST-3/4 | NIST-5 |
| 1 | eMLE-Sig-I | eMLE-Sig-III | eMLE-Sig-V | DME-32bits | DME-48bits | KAZ3241 |
| 2 | DME-32bits | dilithium3 | DME-64bits | KAZ1509 | KAZ2321 | DME-64bits |
| 3 | dilithium2 | dilithium3-R | haetae5 | eMLE-Sig-I | eMLE-Sig-III | eMLE-Sig-V |
| 4 | dilithium2-R | haetae3 | KAZ3241 | mayo_1 | mayo_3 | hawk1024 |
| 5 | haetae2 | DME-48bits | dilithium5-R | SNOVA-28-17 -16-2-ssk | SNOVA-43-25 -16-2-ssk | SNOVA-61-33 -16-2-ssk |

Despite the fact that a significant portion of the top-performing algorithms were found to have vulnerabilities, updates have been implemented to address these issues [33]. The algorithms DME-Sign and eMLE-Sig 2.0 received updates in February 2024, while KAZ-SIGN and VOX were updated in April 2024. These updates were aimed at patching the security weaknesses identified, but further testings are required to confirm their robustness. The algorithm Xifrat1-Sign.I, however, has not been updated since its vulnerabilities were discovered, which limits its immediate applicability. Consequently, recommendations are made in Fig. 9, excluding these algorithms. It is important to note that while these are the top-performing algorithms without currently known vulnerabilities, there remains a possibility that new vulnerabilities may be discovered in the future.

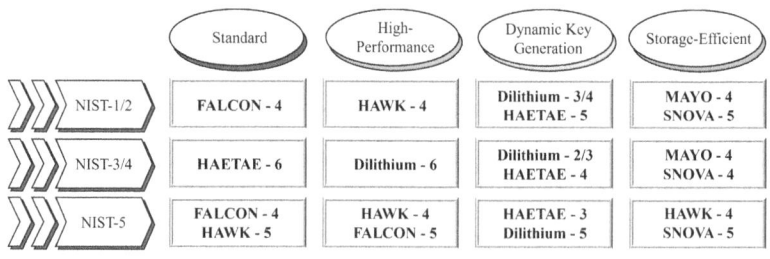

**Fig. 9.** Recommended algorithms and their rankings for different blockchain types.

# 6 Limitations

**Customization.** This project ranked algorithms for blockchain types without customizing for specific blockchains, assuming equal importance for all criteria. However, blockchains may value these criteria differently. A potential solution is to develop a tool that allows developers to adjust the weightings of these criteria for more tailored recommendations. This tool would take the target platform and custom weightings as inputs, filter out algorithms that do not meet size constraints, and then generate a new ranking based on the adjusted weightings. Such a tool would provide more specific recommendations for each blockchain's unique requirements.

**Implementation Comparisons.** Reference Implementations were used for algorithm comparisons due to the inconsistency and challenges of comparing Optimized Implementations. However, Reference Implementations may not fully reflect the performance in actual blockchain environments, particularly when deployed on platforms such as mobile devices, IoT devices, or low-power environments, which are increasingly important in blockchain use cases. These environments may introduce resource constraints such as limited processing power, memory, or energy efficiency, which could significantly impact the performance of the algorithms tested in this paper. Developing and testing blockchain-specific implementations for the most promising algorithms is a promising future work.

**Security Levels.** The chosen security levels of the algorithms follow NIST standards, which mainly consider protection against brute force attacks. However, other security threats, such as side-channel attacks, were not evaluated in this study. As these attacks may pose significant risks in practical applications, future work should focus on assessing the algorithms' resistance to side-channel attacks to provide further assurance of their security robustness.

# 7 Conclusion and Future Works

This project is a proactive initiative aimed at addressing the quantum threat through a comprehensive evaluation of the 43 most recent NIST PQS algorithms. It offers precise recommendations for different blockchain types, supported by thorough analyses of each suggested algorithm. This project advances PQC research by being the first study to test all latest NIST PQS algorithms on a unified platform. The comparative analysis provides valuable insights for NIST's ongoing PQS selection process. Furthermore, this work provides insights on selection criteria of PQS prioritized by blockchain. The detailed recommendation pave the way for future research on refining blockchain-specific PQS solutions. Therefore, our future plan is twofold: practical evaluation in real-world blockchain environment and blockchain-specific implementations for leading PQS algorithms.

# Appendices

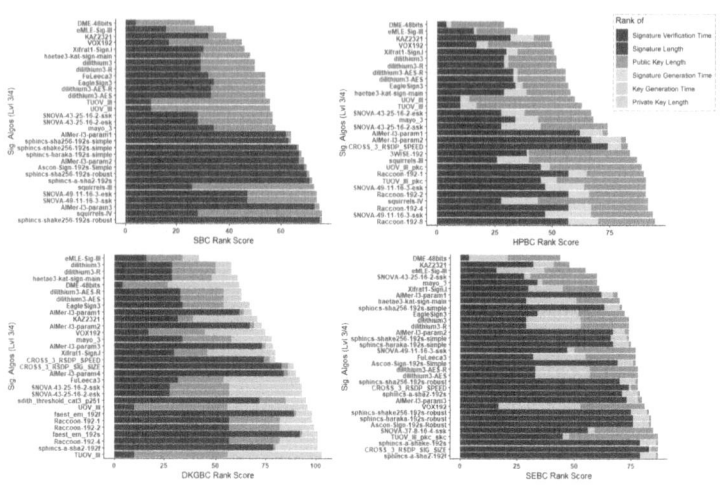

**Fig. 10.** Top 30 PQS with specific parameters for each blockchain type in NIST-3/4.

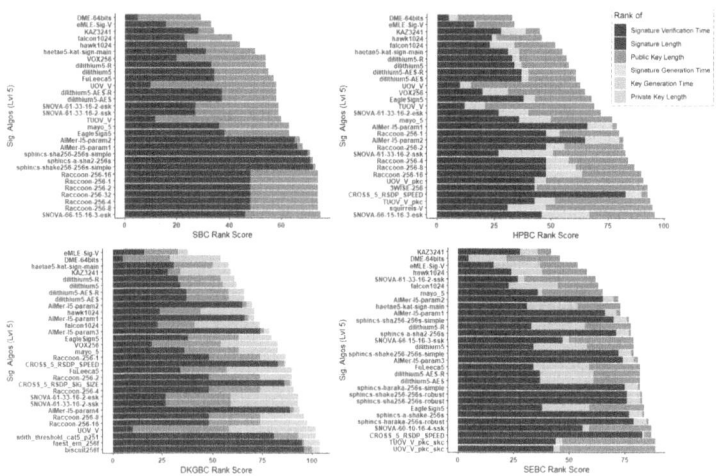

**Fig. 11.** Top 30 PQS with specific parameters for each blockchain type in NIST-5.

# References

1. Blockchain technology market size, share and industry anslysis, by component, by type, by application, by deployment, by industry and regional forcast, 2024-2032. https://www.fortunebusinessinsights.com/industry-reports/blockchain-market-100072
2. The quantum computer and its implications for public-key crypto systems. Tech. rep. (2020). https://www.entrust.com/-/media/documentation/whitepapers/sl20-1026-001-ssl_quantumcomputers-wp.pdf
3. PQC-blockchain-assessment    (2024).    https://github.com/pqc78999/pqc-blockchain-assessment.git. Accessed 01 Jul 2024
4. Alagic, G., et al.: Status report on the first round of the NIST post-quantum cryptography standardization process (2019)
5. Alagic, G., et al.: Status report on the third round of the NIST post-quantum cryptography standardization process. US Department of Commerce, NIST (2022)
6. Aumasson, J.P., et al.: Sphincs. Tech. rep., Stanford Univ., Tech. Rep (2019)
7. Bai, S., et al.: CRYSTALS-Dilithium: Algorithm specifications and supporting documentation (version 3.1). NIST Post-Quantum Cryptography Standardization Round **3** (2021)
8. Bernstein, D.J., Lange, T.: Post-quantum cryptography. Nature **549**(7671), 188–194 (2017)
9. Beullens, W.: Mayo: practical post-quantum signatures from oil-and-vinegar maps. In: International Conference on Selected Areas in Cryptography, pp. 355–376. Springer (2021)
10. Chen, C., et al.: Algorithm Specifications and Supporting Documentation. Brown University and Onboard security company, Wilmington USA (2019)
11. Chen, L., et al.: Report on Post-Quantum Cryptography, vol. 12. National Institute of Standards and Technology, US Department of Commerce (2016)
12. Chen, L., Moody, D., Regenscheid, A., Robinson, A.: Digital signature standard (DSS) (2023)
13. Dang, V.B., Farahmand, F., Andrzejczak, M., Mohajerani, K., Nguyen, D.T., Gaj, K.: Implementation and benchmarking of round 2 candidates in the NIST post-quantum cryptography standardization process using hardware and software/hardware co-design approaches. Cryptology ePrint Archive: Report 2020/795 (2020)
14. Dey, J., Dutta, R.: Progress in multivariate cryptography: systematic review, challenges, and research directions. ACM Comput. Surv. **55**(12), 1–34 (2023)
15. Ding, J., Schmidt, D.: Rainbow, a new multivariable polynomial signature scheme. In: International Conference on Applied Cryptography and Network Security, pp. 164–175. Springer (2005)
16. Ducas, L., et al.: CRYSTALS-Dilithium: a lattice-based digital signature scheme. IACR Transactions on Cryptographic Hardware and Embedded Systems, pp. 238–268 (2018)
17. Dudley, R.M.: Central limit theorems for empirical measures. The Annals of Probability pp. 899–929 (1978)
18. Fang, W., Chen, W., Zhang, W., Pei, J., Gao, W., Wang, G.: Digital signature scheme for information non-repudiation in blockchain: a state of the art review. EURASIP J. Wirel. Commun. Netw. **2020**(1), 1–15 (2020)
19. Fernandez-Carames, T.M., Fraga-Lamas, P.: Towards post-quantum blockchain: a review on blockchain cryptography resistant to quantum computing attacks. IEEE access **8**, 21091–21116 (2020)

20. Fitzgibbon, G., Ottaviani, C.: Constrained device performance benchmarking with the implementation of post-quantum cryptography. Cryptography **8**(2), 21 (2024)
21. Fouque, P.A., et al.: Falcon: fast-fourier lattice-based compact signatures over NTRU. Submission NIST's Post-Quantum Crypt. Stand. Process **36**(5), 1–75 (2018)
22. Gonzalez, R., et al.: Verifying post-quantum signatures in 8 kB of RAM. In: Post-Quantum Cryptography: 12th International Workshop, PQCrypto 2021, Daejeon, South Korea, July 20–22, 2021, Proceedings 12. pp. 215–233. Springer (2021)
23. Hoffstein, J., Howgrave-Graham, N., Pipher, J., Silverman, J.H., Whyte, W.: NTRUSign: digital signatures using the NTRU lattice. In: Cryptographers' track at the RSA conference, pp. 122–140. Springer (2003)
24. Holmes, S.A.: Impact of post-quantum signatures on blockchain and DLT systems (2023)
25. Hopwood, D., Bowe, S., Hornby, T., Wilcox, N., et al.: Zcash protocol specification. GitHub: San Francisco, CA, USA **4**(220), 32 (2016)
26. Howe, J., Pöppelmann, T., O'neill, M., O'sullivan, E., Güneysu, T.: Practical lattice-based digital signature schemes. ACM Trans. Embed. Comput. Syst. (TECS) **14**(3), 1–24 (2015)
27. Huang, T.P., Postlethwaite, E.W., Prest, T., Pulles, L.N., van Woerden, W.: Hawk version 1.0.1 https://hawk-sign.info
28. Ikematsu, Y., Nakamura, S., Takagi, T.: Recent progress in the security evaluation of multivariate public-key cryptography. IET Inf. Secur. **17**(2), 210–226 (2023)
29. Kannwischer, M.J., Krausz, M., Petri, R., Yang, S.Y.: pqm4: Benchmarking NIST additional post-quantum signature schemes on microcontrollers. Cryptology ePrint Archive (2024)
30. Liu, F., et al.: A survey on lattice-based digital signature. Cybersecurity **7**(1), 7 (2024)
31. Naik, A., Yeniaras, E., Hellstern, G., Prasad, G., Vishwakarma, S.K.L.P.: From portfolio optimization to quantum blockchain and security: A systematic review of quantum computing in finance. arXiv preprint arXiv:2307.01155 (2023)
32. Nakamoto, S.: Bitcoin: A peer-to-peer electronic cash system (2008)
33. National Institute of Standards and Technology: Post-quantum cryptography (PQC) forum. https://groups.google.com/a/list.nist.gov/g/pqc-forum
34. National Institute of Standards and Technology: Post-quantum cryptography: Round 1 additional digital signature schemes. https://csrc.nist.gov/Projects/pqc-dig-sig/round-1-additional-signatures
35. National Institute of Standards and Technology: PQC – known answer tests and test vectors. https://csrc.nist.gov/CSRC/media/Projects/Post-Quantum-Cryptography/documents/example-files/kat.pdf
36. National Institute of Standards and Technology: Round 1 additional signatures (2023). https://csrc.nist.gov/Projects/pqc-dig-sig/round-1-additional-signatures
37. National Institute of Standards and Technology: Post-quantum cryptography FAQs (2024). https://csrc.nist.gov/Projects/post-quantum-cryptography/faqs
38. Nejatollahi, H., Dutt, N., Ray, S., Regazzoni, F., Banerjee, I., Cammarota, R.: Post-quantum lattice-based cryptography implementations: a survey. ACM Comput. Surv. (CSUR) **51**(6), 1–41 (2019)
39. NIST CFP: Submission requirements and evaluation criteria for the post-quantum cryptography standardization process (2016)
40. Okupski, K.: Bitcoin developer reference. Eindhoven, pp. 3–4 (2014)
41. Pooja, M., Yadav, M.: Digital signature. Int. J. Sci. Res. Comput. Sci., Eng. Inf. Technol. (IJSRCSEIT) **3**(6), 71–75 (2018)

42. Popov, S.: The tangle. White Pap. **1**(3), 30 (2018)
43. Proos, J., Zalka, C.: Shor's discrete logarithm quantum algorithm for elliptic curves. arXiv preprint quant-ph/0301141 (2003)
44. QByte: Qbyte quantum risk calculator. https://qbyte.btq.com/
45. Raavi, M., Wuthier, S., Chandramouli, P., Balytskyi, Y., Zhou, X., Chang, S.Y.: Security comparisons and performance analyses of post-quantum signature algorithms. In: International Conference on Applied Cryptography and Network Security, pp. 424–447. Springer (2021)
46. Ravi, P., Sundar, V.K., Chattopadhyay, A., Bhasin, S., Easwaran, A.: Authentication protocol for secure automotive systems: benchmarking post-quantum cryptography. In: 2020 IEEE International Symposium on Circuits and Systems (ISCAS), pp. 1–5. IEEE (2020)
47. Rivest, R.L., Shamir, A., Adleman, L.: A method for obtaining digital signatures and public-key cryptosystems. Commun. ACM **21**(2), 120–126 (1978)
48. Shim, K.A.: A survey on post-quantum public-key signature schemes for secure vehicular communications. IEEE Trans. Intell. Transp. Syst. **23**(9), 14025–14042 (2021)
49. Shor, P.W.: Algorithms for quantum computation: discrete logarithms and factoring. In: Proceedings 35th Annual Symposium on Foundations of Computer Science, pp. 124–134. IEEE (1994)
50. Sikeridis, D., Kampanakis, P., Devetsikiotis, M.: Post-quantum authentication in TLS 1.3: a performance study. Cryptology ePrint Archive (2020)
51. Soni, D., Basu, K., Nabeel, M., Karri, R.: A hardware evaluation study of NIST post-quantum cryptographic signature schemes. In: Second PQC Standardization Conference. NIST (2019)
52. Wang, L.C., Tseng, P.E., Kuan, Y.L., Chou, C.Y.: A simple noncommutative UOV scheme. Cryptology ePrint Archive (2022)
53. Yakovenko, A.: Solana: A new architecture for a high performance blockchain v0. 8.13. Whitepaper (2018)

# SPVPC: Smart Contract Based Publicly Verifiable Polynomial Computations

Partha Sarathi Chakraborty[ID] and Somanath Tripathy[✉][ID]

Department of Computer Science and Engineering, Indian Institute of Technology
Patna, Patna, India
{partha_1921cs26,som}@iitp.ac.in

**Abstract.** The desire to delegate computation to the cloud arises from the proliferation of small, computational restrained devices. However, to ensure the security and privacy of the stored data in the cloud, data owners always encrypt their sensitive data before outsourcing it. Nonetheless, computation outsourcing proves beneficial only when the returned result is trustworthy. Moreover, it must ensure the security and confidentiality of the computation and data during execution. Thus, the challenge lies in efficiently verifying the correctness of computation results generated over encrypted data and maintaining practical computational time for verifying results. Blockchain emerges as a trustworthy entity, enabling fairness and transparency in the scheme. We propose a secure and efficient smart contract based publicly verifiable polynomial computation with an incentive mechanism to protect confidentiality. In the proposed scheme, the smart contract is a verifier that ensures trusted verification and manages incentive transfer. We demonstrate the proposed scheme's effectiveness through security proofs and performance analysis, significantly reducing verifier computational costs and enhancing overall efficiency.

**Keywords:** Outsourcing Computation · Publicly Verifiable · Encrypted Data · Multivariate Polynomial · Homomorphic Encryption

## 1 Introduction

Cloud computing emerges as an attractive option for weak computational clients to access on-demand computational resources with minimal economic overhead and achieve great efficiency by delegating their computation and data. However, outsourcing resources to the cloud raises concerns about security issues, data confidentiality, and potential misbehaviour by cloud servers. Even during data processing, security and privacy threats persist, such as ensuring result integrity, preventing disclosure of data contents, and safeguarding data privacy. Moreover, clients rely on third parties for output verification, and conventional payment protocols may suffer from unfairness.

Researchers have introduced a solution for verifiable outsourced computation to tackle the challenge of result verification. This approach ensures that

H. H. Song et al. (Eds.): NSS 2024, LNCS 15564, pp. 370–386, 2025.
https://doi.org/10.1007/978-981-96-3531-3_18

clients not only receive correct results but also obtain *cryptographic proof* that validates the accuracy of the outsourced execution. The cryptographic proof upholds classical security requirements such as *correctness*, *completeness*, and *soundness*. Furthermore, it prioritizes generating result verification with significantly less computational effort compared to the effort required for computing results. Verifiable computation effectively reduces the risk of dishonest cloud servers returning false results to clients without executing the tasks as intended. To protect data privacy, input and output data is encrypted.

Blockchain is an open, traceable, and immutable technology that can be used to build an adaptable alternative trustworthy platform among untrusted participants. Using blockchain and verifiable computing enables a new paradigm to establish fairness, transparency, dispute resolution among entities, and a consistent environment. In engineering and scientific problems, polynomial evaluation is a fundamental and crucial type of computation with widespread application. Thus, the clients often need to evaluate different polynomials over the outsourced encrypted data, such as linear, univariate, quadratic, sparse, and multivariate. Therefore, clients aim to validate the correctness of results produced by the cloud after polynomial evaluation.

Researchers have proposed various solutions in verifiable computation, including references [4,8,11,16,18,21] to address this issue. However, designers of most existing schemes tailor them to a specific operation and have rigid designs. It makes these existing schemes difficult to adapt to another framework.

**Table 1.** Comparison of blockchain based verifiable computation schemes

| Models | VA | DU | IE | VT | PV | C | CO | | | Security | | | | F | B | BO | Verification | | | IN | TE | IM |
|---|---|---|---|---|---|---|---|---|---|---|---|---|---|---|---|---|---|---|---|---|---|---|
| | | | | | | | I | II | III | IV | V | VI | VII | | | | VE | VT | PT | | | |
| Dong *et al.*[9] | ▲ | $\mathcal{P}$ | F | ◎ | ✓ | × | × | ✓ | × | ✓ | ✓ | × | ✓ | ✓ | □ | ℘ | S | ∴ | ∴ | ✓ | × | ◐ |
| Reddy *et al.*[10] | △ | $\mathcal{P}$ | F | ◎ | ✓ | ✓ | ✓ | × | × | × | × | × | × | ✓ | □ | ℘ | S | ∴ | ∴ | ✓ | × | ○ |
| Avizheh *et al.*[3] | ▲ | $\mathcal{P}$ | F | ◎ | ✓ | ✓ | ✓ | × | × | × | × | ✓ | ✓ | ✓ | □ | ℘ | S | ∴ | ∴ | ✓ | × | ◐ |
| VeriBlock[14] | △ | $\mathcal{P}$ | $\mathbb{P}$ | ◎ | ✓ | × | × | × | × | × | × | × | × | ✓ | ■ | ℘ | S | ♦ | ◇ | ✓ | ✓ | ● |
| Emrah *et al.*[17] | △ | $\mathcal{P}$ | $\mathbb{P}$ | ◎ | ✓ | ✓ | ✓ | × | × | × | × | × | × | ✓ | □ | ≠ | S | ♦ | ◇ | ✓ | × | ● |
| Guan *et al.*[12] | △ | $\mathcal{P}$ | $\mathbb{P}$ | ◎ | ✓ | × | × | × | × | × | × | × | × | ✓ | □ | ℘ | S | ♦ | ♦ | ✓ | × | ● |
| Fides[15] | ▲ | $\mathcal{P}$ | F | ◎ | ✓ | ✓ | ✓ | × | × | × | ✓ | ✓ | ✓ | × | □ | ℘ | S | ∴ | ∴ | × | × | ○ |
| Lee *et al.*[13] | △ | $\mathcal{E}$ | F | ◎ | ✓ | × | ✓ | ✓ | ✓ | ✓ | ✓ | ✓ | ✓ | ✓ | □ | ℘ | S | ∴ | ∴ | ✓ | × | ○ |
| Cao *et al.*[6] | △ | $\mathcal{E}$ | L | ◎ | ✓ | ✓ | ✓ | ✓ | ✓ | ✓ | ✓ | ✓ | ✓ | × | □ | ≠ | C | ⊕ | ⊕ | × | × | ● |
| SPVPC | △ | $\mathcal{E}$ | $\mathbb{P}$ | ◎ | ✓ | ✓ | ✓ | ✓ | ✓ | ✓ | ✓ | ✓ | ✓ | ✓ | □ | ℘ | S | ♦ | ♦ | ✓ | × | ● |

**VA**: Verifiable Computing Approach (△: Cryptography based, ▲: Replication based), **DU**: Data Used ($\mathcal{E}$: Encrypted, $\mathcal{P}$: Plaintext), **IE**: Input Equation (F: Function, $\mathbb{L}$: Linear Equation, $\mathbb{P}$: Polynomial Equation), **VT**: Verifiable Computing Technique (◎: Interactive, ◎: Zero-Knowledge Proof), **PV**: Public Verifiability, **C**: Correctness, **CO**: Confidentiality, **I**: Data, **II**: Input, **III**: Computation, **IV**: Output, **V**: Entities Behaviour Analysis, **VI**: Unforgeability, **VII**: Privacy Preserving, **F**: Fairness, **B**: Blockchain (□: Permissioned less, ■: Permissioned), **BO**: Blockchain Operation (℘: Verify On-Chain & Transactions in Blockchain, ≠: Verify Off-Chain & Transactions in Blockchain), **VE**: Verifier (S: Smart Contract, C: Client), **PT**: Prover Time, **VT**: Verifier Time, **IN**: Incentive Mechanism, **TE**: Trusted Execution Environment, **IM**: Implementation (○: Theoretical, ◐: Partial, ●: Implemented); ✓: consider in this scheme, ×: not consider in this scheme; ♦: Practical, ⊕: Acceptable, ◇: Impractical, ∴ Not measured;

Many existing schemes based on blockchain [3,6,9,10,12–15,17] are also tailored to specific operations, lacking flexibility and inflexible designs. Additionally, the majority of these schemes do not facilitate public verification over encrypted data [3,9,10,12,14,15,17], relying instead on users' confidential information for the verification process. Even their prover time is impractical and makes inefficient verification. In an outsourced computation mechanism, two primary security concerns are data privacy and confidentiality, and efficient verification of computed results, ensuring computation integrity. Another concern is enabling fairness and a trustworthy environment among participating entities. However, Chakraborty *et al.* [7] introduced a scheme to address these issues except an incentive mechanism. It achieves data privacy during computation, preserves input and output data confidentiality, and shows a significant advantage in verification efficiency. Thus, we aim to design a fair and efficient outsourced computation scheme using blockchain.

*Contribution*: A blockchain-based verifiable computation mechanism is described as:

- This paper proposes a secure, efficient, **S**mart contract based **P**ublicly **V**erifiable **P**olynomial **C**omputations, named SPVPC. It performs arbitrary polynomial computations over encrypted data in the cloud while ensuring accuracy through the smart contract as a public verifier and protecting data privacy.
- The proposed work SPVPC demonstrated security and resistance against forging attacks.
- To enable fairness in SPVPC uses incentive mechanism. It facilitates rewards for each successful verification and fines the entity for each unsuccessful verification or attempted forgery, as well as compensation to the victim.
- Evaluate its performance, thereby demonstrating its efficiency and feasibility that highlight significant advantages to reducing the workload of the verifier through efficient verification and polynomial evaluation capability upon encrypted data at the cloud.

*Organization*: The remainder of the paper follows the following organization: Sect. 2 discusses the related works in blockchain-based verifiable computation. Section 3 presents the useful information on Preliminaries. Section 4 presents the system model, threat model, and design goals. Section 5 elaborates on the proposed scheme and its correctness proof. Security analyses are presented in Sect. 6. Section 7 presents a performance analysis by evaluating experiment results to test the effectiveness and efficiency of the proposed scheme. Finally, Sect. 8 concludes this work.

## 2  Related Work

The earlier works on secure verifiable outsourced computation and its application with privacy preservation can be found in [2,19,20]. These existing techniques are based on *replication* or *cryptography* mechanisms. The replication mechanism alleviates concerns regarding overhead in computing proof and pre-computation, where the actual cost exceeds the verified computation. However, concerns about overhead arise in the replication mechanism due to the utilization of multiple replicas across clouds [9]. Typically, three replicas are required, resulting in a tripling of the total cost. With a minimum of two replicas, like [5], the scheme introduces an overhead equivalent to approximately 10 to 20 times the verified computation. Moreover, all the replication-based schemes rely on the condition that the entities do not collude with each other to function correctly, but in reality, this assumption may not always hold.

Recently, researchers have developed new schemes [3,6,9,10,12–15,17] for verifiable outsourced computation by utilizing blockchain to promote transparency, incentivize financial fairness, and foster trust among participating entities. Smart contracts used in blockchain further enrich the functionality. The schemes [3,9,15] are based on a replication mechanism and focus on establishing fairness using a game-based approach while analyzing the behaviour of participating entities. The schemes [3,15] adapt the refereed delegation of computation model of Canetti *et al.* [5]. The verifier is the smart contract and resolves disputes [3,15] or performed by a trusted third party [9]. However, [3,15] diminish data confidentiality and privacy-preserving concerns, while [9] have limits. Reddy *et al.* [10] aims to design a fair protocol for verifiable computation of the GCD function using the delegator and worker model. It concerns fast verification and payment while eliminating data integrity, confidentiality, and privacy-preserving issues. Here, smart contracts validate the payment and establish fairness.

Authors in [14] and [17] presented different polynomial function computation and its verification. Maddali *et al.* [14] proposed a method that uses permissioned blockchain and a trusted execution environment (TEE) for fast and secure verification. However, their approach suffers from high proof generation time, making it impractical, and also raises data confidentiality concerns. Emrah *et al.* [17] address these shortcomings by proposing a framework that leverages a public blockchain platform and a cryptographic mechanism. Their solution additionally supports execution for matrix multiplication, image matching, and shortest path computation without relying on a TEE. While [17] achieve very fast verification time, their overall efficiency is hampered by high prover time. Furthermore, their work does not consider security and confidentiality issues.

Guan *et al.* [12], proposed verifying arbitrary polynomial outsourcing computation to guarantee fairness and minimize computational costs. Their proposal achieves fast public verifiability, high efficiency, and fairness but does not address data security issues. Both Lee *et al.* [13] and Cao *et al.* [6] prioritized data security and confidentiality and thus used encrypted data. Lee *et al.* [13] proposed a theoretical approach that executes functions directly on encrypted datasets. Their method leverages Fully Homomorphic Encryption (FHE) and Fully Homomorphic Signatures (FHS) for verifiable computation, but it lacks practical implementation. However, their scheme incorporates an incentive mechanism to ensure fair payment. In contrast, Cao *et al.* [6] restricted their work to evaluating linear polynomials and verifying the results. They utilize blockchain technology for record-keeping and dispute resolution. While their approach achieves acceptable overall efficiency due to client-side verification, it sacrifices fairness within the scheme. Table 1 presents a comparative analysis of blockchain-based verifiable computation schemes.

## 3    Preliminaries

### 3.1    Homomorphic Encryption

Homomorphic Encryption (HE), specifically the CKKS (Cheon-Kim-Kim-Song) [1] scheme bases its homomorphism[1] on the Ring Learning With Errors (RLWE) encryption scheme. Its flexibility, efficiency, and applicability to real-world use cases make it a promising technology for advancing privacy-preserving computations over sensitive data, particularly in fields such as cloud computing, data analysis, machine learning, and medical research.

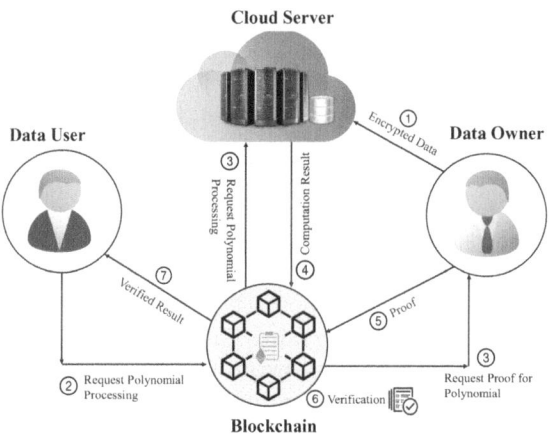

**Fig. 1.** System Model

### 3.2    Euclidean Algorithm for Multivariate Polynomials

It has been proven [7] that the Euclidean algorithm can be applied over multivariate polynomials in Theorem 1.

**Theorem 1.** *Let $P(\mathbf{x}) = P(\mathbf{x}_1, \mathbf{x}_2, \ldots, \mathbf{x}_n) \in Z_p[\mathbf{x}]$ be a multivariate polynomial with n-variable and $\mathbf{g}(\mathbf{x}) = \mathbf{g}(\mathbf{x}_1, \mathbf{x}_2, \ldots, \mathbf{x}_m) \in Z_p[\mathbf{x}]$ be a multivariate polynomial with m-variable where $\{\mathbf{x}_1, \mathbf{x}_2, \ldots, \mathbf{x}_m\} \subset \{\mathbf{x}_1, \mathbf{x}_2, \ldots, \mathbf{x}_n\}$ such that there always*

---

[1] A mapping $f : \mathcal{R} \to \mathcal{S}$ between rings is termed a ring homomorphism if it satisfies the properties $f(x + y) = f(x) + f(y)$ and $f(xy) = f(x)f(y)$ for all $x, y \in \mathcal{R}$.

*exists multivariate polynomial* $a(\mathbf{x}) = a(\mathbf{x}_1, \mathbf{x}_2, \ldots, \mathbf{x}_v)$, $b(\mathbf{x}) = b(\mathbf{x}_1, \mathbf{x}_2, \ldots, \mathbf{x}_s)$ *and* $d(\mathbf{x}) = d(\mathbf{x}_1, \mathbf{x}_2, \ldots, \mathbf{x}_t)$ *where* $d(\mathbf{x}) = gcd(P(\mathbf{x}), \mathbf{g}(\mathbf{x}))$ *and*

$$\{\mathbf{x}_1, \ldots, \mathbf{x}_v\}, \{\mathbf{x}_1, \ldots, \mathbf{x}_s\}, \{\mathbf{x}_1, \ldots, \mathbf{x}_t\} \subseteq \{\mathbf{x}_1, \ldots, \mathbf{x}_n\}, \tag{1}$$

*would satisfy*

$$a(\mathbf{x}) \cdot P(\mathbf{x}) + b(\mathbf{x}) \cdot \mathbf{g}(\mathbf{x}) = d(\mathbf{x}). \tag{2}$$

## 4   System and Security Model of SPVPC

### 4.1   System Model

Figure 1 shows the SPVPC system model. There are four entities as follows.

- *Data Owner* [DO]: Having computational resources and storage space, the DO delegates its own data to the cloud server and agrees to verify result accuracy.
- *Data User* [DU]: It is a computationally weak system. It may request various processes, including data accessing, performing heavy computations, requesting the correctness of the computed result, depositing the initial credit, paying rewards, and receiving compensation.
- *Cloud Server* [CS]: It offers extensive storage space and powerful computational assets, fulfilling user requests and earning incentives in return.
- *Blockchain* [BC]: It keeps the record of each scheme transaction in the ledger and assists in resolving disputes to uphold fairness and foster trust among entities. Smart contracts [SC$_{\mathrm{BC}}$] serve as verifiers for the correctness of the results computed by the CS and facilitate the transfer of rewards or imposition of fines to entities.

In the proposed scheme, the DO aims to outsource its sensitive data in encrypted form to the CS. The CS is tasked with computing a polynomial function ($P \in Z_p^{\mathbf{n}}[x]$) using the encrypted data set ($\mathcal{D}_1, \mathcal{D}_2, \ldots, \mathcal{D}_i$), where ($\mathcal{D}_i \in Z_p$) (with $p$ being a large prime number). The DU, as the entity seeking the final computation result provided by the CS, faces the potential risk of manipulation or provision of inaccurate results by the CS. To guarantee computation accuracy, the DO engage in a role that validates the results provided by the CS. DO is a trusted entity with a computation facility to support this verification without revealing the plaintext of input and output. We assume no collusion between the DO and CS; the CS does not possess the secret keys used for data encryption by the DOs and thus prevents access to information related to the original data except during computations on the encrypted data.

### 4.2   Threat Model

In SPVPC, CS is responsible for storing the encrypted data, performing polynomial function computations, and returning the computation result to DU. The proposed work aims to guarantee that CS performs correct computation, validated by the smart contract. However, CS malicious behaviour or potential security threats from adversaries can occur are

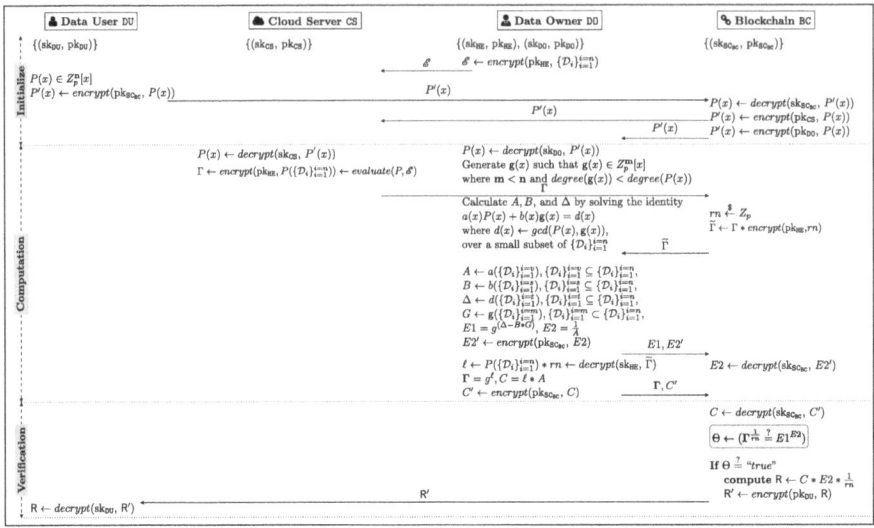

**Fig. 2.** Schematic Diagram

- *Corrupt Data*: The CS may corrupt outsourced data, and it's used for polynomial computation, potentially yielding incorrect results.
- *Incorrect Result*: The CS fails to complete designated computations over all inputs, generates random results, or dispenses previously computed results to conserve computational resources due to financial considerations.
- *Forge Attack*: The adversaries may forge proof and deceive verifiers.

### 4.3 Design Goal

- *Data Confidentiality*: No participant entity in the protocol can learn about the data had by the data owner.
- *Input Privacy*: No participant entity in the protocol can learn or know the input data used for computation.
- *Output Privacy*: No participant entity in the protocol can learn or have knowledge of output data except the data user who requests for computation.
- *Transparency*: The protocol doesn't rely on privately generated randomness during setup, which needs to remain confidential. Maintain a ledger for each transaction in the scheme and use it for dispute resolution if any occurs among entities.
- *Feasibility & Efficiency*: It guarantees that the client can verify the proof using significantly fewer resources compared to those required for computing polynomial $P$ (including communication and computation). The prover can generate the proof in less overhead time.
- *Public Verification*: Anyone can independently verify the correctness of the result without knowing the individual inputs or the intermediate computations returned by the cloud server without accessing the secret key.

– *Fairness*: Fair Payment delivery to each entity. It should ensure that the data user can get a correct computed result if paid. The cloud and the prover can be rewarded if they follow the protocol correctly. The corresponding data owner received a fee for the used data. The smart contracts are executed automatically and faithfully on blockchains, which realize fairness if the computed result can be verified publicly.

### 4.4   Fairness

To hold fairness, all the participating entities deposit initial credit while joining to avail themselves of the services. It motivates the rational cloud server to execute the task faithfully, providing the data user with the correct answer and ensuring payment of the reward in return or fine imposed if verification is unsuccessful.

– *No deposit, No Services*: No services will be available if the participating entity does not make the initial deposit while joining.
– *Verified Execution*: If the cloud server executes correctly, it receives payment from the DU or vice versa.
– *Compensation*: The smart contract checks the computation is valid and independent of the original data. So, the entity that tries to deviate from the underlying scheme will face punishment. If CS returns an incorrect result, a fine will be imposed, and compensation will be given to DU. The incentive mechanism is shown in Algorithm 1.

## 5   SPVPC: The proposed Model

The schematic diagram of the proposed scheme is shown in Fig. 2. Each procedure is described as follows.

1. **KeyGen**() $\to (pk, sk)$: Let $\mathbb{G}$ be a group of order $p$, where $p$ is a large prime number selected by DO, and the generator is $g$. DO choose a random number $\text{sk}_{\text{DO}} \in Z_p$ as a secret key and computes public key $\text{pk}_{\text{DO}}$ and FHE key pairs $[(\text{sk}_{\text{HE}}, \text{pk}_{\text{HE}})]$ using the function. Similarly, other entities also execute the function to generate public key pairs, for CS $[(\text{sk}_{\text{CS}}, \text{pk}_{\text{CS}})]$, DU $[(\text{sk}_{\text{DU}}, \text{pk}_{\text{DU}})]$, and $\text{SC}_{\text{BC}}$ $[(\text{sk}_{\text{SC}_{\text{BC}}}, \text{pk}_{\text{SC}_{\text{BC}}})]$. Then, the public keys are shared within the system.
2. **OutsourceData**($\mathcal{D}$,$\text{pk}_{\text{HE}}$) $\to \mathcal{E}$: To ensure the privacy of data, DO encrypts data $\{\mathcal{D}_i\}_{i=1}^{i=n}$ using $\text{pk}_{\text{HE}}$ and gets $\mathcal{E}$. Then, outsource $\mathcal{E}$ to CS.
3. **OutsourceFuntion**($\text{pk}_{\text{DU}}$,$P(x)$) $\to P'(x)$: DU wants to evaluate a multivariate polynomial $P(x)$. Consider $P(x) = P(x_1, x_2, x_3, ..., x_n)$ such that, $P(x) \in Z_p^n[x]$ equivalent to any arithmetic circuit. Thus, DU delegates $P(x)$ to $\text{SC}_{\text{BC}}$ using $\text{pk}_{\text{SC}_{\text{BC}}}$ such that $P'(x) = encrypt(\text{pk}_{\text{SC}_{\text{BC}}}, P(x))$. Then, $\text{SC}_{\text{BC}}$ decrypt $P(x)$ and delegate it to the CS and the DO, using respective public keys.
4. **Compute**($P'(x)$,$\mathcal{E}$) $\to (\tilde{\Gamma}, rn')$: When CS receives data and polynomial function, then computes $P(x)$ over $\mathcal{E}$ and obtains an encrypted result $\Gamma$, *i.e.* $\Gamma \leftarrow encrypt(\text{pk}_{\text{HE}}, P(\{\mathcal{D}_i\}_{i=1}^{i=n})) \leftarrow evaluate(P, \mathcal{E})$. Then, CS sends $\Gamma$ to $\text{SC}_{\text{BC}}$.

5. **ProofRequest**$(P'(x)) \rightarrow (E1, E2')$: After gets $P'(x)$, DO decrypts it. Then, DO randomly generates a different $m$-variate polynomial $\mathbf{g}(x)=\mathbf{g}(x_i, x_j, ..., x_l)$ such that $\mathbf{g}(x) \in Z_p^{\mathbf{m}}[x]$ where $\mathbf{m}<\mathbf{n}$ and degree of $\mathbf{g}(x)<$ degree of $P(x)$ and set $\{x_i, x_j, ..., x_l\} \subset \{x_1, x_2, x_3, ..., x_n\}$ and $|\{x_i, x_j, ..., x_l\}|=m$. Then, computes the multivariate polynomial $a(x), b(x)$ and $d(x)$ such that $a(x)P(x) + b(x)\mathbf{g}(x) = d(x)$ holds true, where $d(x) = gcd(P(x), \mathbf{g}(x))$. Next, DO finds $A, B, \Delta$ by computing $a$ over sample data $\{\mathcal{D}_i\}_{i=1}^{i=v}$, $b$ on sample data $\{\mathcal{D}_i\}_{i=1}^{i=s}$, $d$ on sample data $\{\mathcal{D}_i\}_{i=1}^{i=t}$ respectively, such that $\{\mathcal{D}_i\}_{i=1}^{i=v} \subseteq \{\mathcal{D}_i\}_{i=1}^{i=n}$, $\{\mathcal{D}_i\}_{i=1}^{i=s} \subseteq \{\mathcal{D}_i\}_{i=1}^{i=n}$ and $\{\mathcal{D}_i\}_{i=1}^{i=t} \subseteq \{\mathcal{D}_i\}_{i=1}^{i=n}$. Now, DO evaluates $\mathbf{g}$ on sample data $\{\mathcal{D}_i\}_{i=1}^{i=m} \subset \{\mathcal{D}_i\}_{i=1}^{i=n}$ to find $G$. Further, DO computes $E1 = g^{(\Delta-B*G)}$, $E2 = \frac{1}{A}$ and encrypts $E2' \leftarrow encrypt(\text{pk}_{\text{SC}_{\text{BC}}}, E2)$. Finally, sends $E1, E2'$ to $\text{SC}_{\text{BC}}$.

6. **RequestDecryptResult**$(\Gamma) \rightarrow \widetilde{\Gamma}$ : $\text{SC}_{\text{BC}}$ hides $\Gamma$ from DO by using a random number $rn \xleftarrow{\$} Z_p$ and obtains $\widetilde{\Gamma}$, i.e. $\widetilde{\Gamma} \leftarrow encrypt(\text{pk}_{\text{HE}}, P(\{\mathcal{D}_i\}_{i=1}^{i=n}) * rn) \leftarrow \Gamma * encrypt(\text{pk}_{\text{HE}}, rn)$. Then, $\text{SC}_{\text{BC}}$ sends $\widetilde{\Gamma}$ to DO.

7. **SendDecryptResult**$(\widetilde{\Gamma}) \rightarrow (\Gamma, C')$: Now, DO decrypts the inputs $\widetilde{\Gamma}$ using $\text{sk}_{\text{DO}}$ and obtains $\ell$. Next, computes $\Gamma = g^{\ell}, C = \ell * A$ and encrypts $C' \leftarrow encrypt(\text{pk}_{\text{SC}_{\text{BC}}}, C)$. Then, DO sends $\Gamma, C'$ to $\text{SC}_{\text{BC}}$.

8. **VerifyCompute**$(E1, E2', \Gamma, C') \rightarrow$R: $\text{SC}_{\text{BC}}$ decrypts the parameters and obtains $C, E2$. Now, apply proof parameters $E1, E2$ to verify Eq. 3 to check whether it holds *true*. If *true*, then the original result is the correct evaluated outcome by CS *i.e. accepted*; otherwise, reject it. Computes original result $(C * E2 * \frac{1}{rn})$ and stores the verified result in R, then send encrypted R using $\text{pk}_{\text{DU}}$ to DU.

$$\Theta \leftarrow (\Gamma^{\frac{1}{rn}} \overset{?}{=} E1^{E2}) \tag{3}$$

## 5.1   Correctness Proof

In SPVPC, the smart contract can verify the computation result done by CS if the following Eq. 3 holds. Simplification of R.H.S of the verification Eq. 3 is followed

L.H.S.

$$=\Gamma^{\frac{1}{rn}} = (g^{\ell})^{\frac{1}{rn}} = g^{\frac{\ell}{rn}} = g^{\frac{P(\{\mathcal{D}_i\}_{i=1}^{i=n})*rn}{rn}} = g^{P(\{\mathcal{D}_i\}_{i=1}^{i=n})} = g^{\text{R}}$$

$$\text{R.H.S.} = E1^{E2} = (g^{(\Delta-B*G)})^{\frac{1}{A}} = g^{\frac{(\Delta-B*G)}{A}}$$

$$= g^{\frac{d(\mathcal{D}_1, \mathcal{D}_2, ..., \mathcal{D}_t)-b(\mathcal{D}_1, \mathcal{D}_2, ..., \mathcal{D}_s)*\mathbf{g}(\mathcal{D}_1, \mathcal{D}_2, ..., \mathcal{D}_m)}{a(\mathcal{D}_1, \mathcal{D}_2, ..., \mathcal{D}_v)}}$$

$$= g^{P(\mathcal{D}_1, \mathcal{D}_2, ..., \mathcal{D}_n)} \qquad \text{Using Equation } 1, 2$$

$$= g^{(P(\{\mathcal{D}_i\}_{i=1}^{i=n})*\frac{rn}{rn})} = g^{(decrypt(\text{sk}_{\text{HE}}, \widetilde{\Gamma})*\frac{1}{rn})}$$

$$= g^{decrypt(\text{sk}_{\text{HE}}, encrypt(\text{pk}_{\text{HE}}, P(\{\mathcal{D}_i\}_{i=1}^{i=n})*rn))*\frac{1}{rn}}$$

$$= g^{P(\{\mathcal{D}_i\}_{i=1}^{i=n})*rn*\frac{1}{rn}} = g^{P(\{\mathcal{D}_i\}_{i=1}^{i=n})}$$

$$= g^{\text{R}} = \text{L.H.S.} \qquad \qquad \therefore \text{L.H.S.} = \text{R.H.S.}$$

## 5.2 Completeness Proof

**Theorem 2.** *SPVPC satisfies the completeness property requirement for the polynomial delegation.*

*Proof.* To demonstrate the completeness property, let's assume that CS and DU honestly adhere to the protocol. Referring to the correctness proof provided in Sect. 5.1, we can readily observe that the verifier Eq. 3 authenticates $\Gamma$ by employing a data set specimen with a fixed number of field operations.

Initially, DU sends encrypted $P'(x)$ to $SC_{BC}$. Then, $SC_{BC}$ delegates $P'(x)$ to CS and DO for computation. When DO receives the polynomial $P'(x)$, decrypts it and randomly generates multivariate polynomial $g(x) \in Z_p^m[x]$ such that $\mathbf{m} < \mathbf{n}$ and degree of $g(x)<$ degree of $P(x)$. The $g(x)$ computes over the small fragment $\{D_i\}_{i=}^{i=m} \subset \{D_i\}_{i=1}^{i=n}$, and finds the value of $G$ on computing $g(\{D_i\}_{i=1}^{i=m})$ in $\mathcal{O}(m)$ at DO. Likewise, $\langle A, B, \Delta \rangle$ are evaluated over distinct small fragment of $\{D_i\}_{i=1}^{i=n}$ as shown in correctness proof in Sect. 5.1. DO further evaluates the proof value $E1 = g^{(\Delta - B*G)}$, $E2 = \frac{1}{A}$ and sends it to $SC_{BC}$. DO also computes $\Gamma = g^{\ell}, C = \ell * A$ where $\ell \leftarrow P(\{\mathcal{D}_i\}_{i=1}^{i=n}) * rn \leftarrow decrypt(sk_{HE}, \widetilde{\Gamma})$ to hide result $\ell$ and sends $\Gamma, C$ to $SC_{BC}$. At last $SC_{BC}$ determines a output $=$ "true" (*accept*) or "false" (*reject*) after executes verification. Thus, $SC_{BC}$ accepts $\Gamma$ (result computed by CS), if $\Gamma^{\frac{1}{rn}} = E1^{E2}$ holds true; else, reject.

Therefore, our constructions hold completeness only if each computation's sample data set is a part of an actual data set. This ensures the authenticity and uniqueness of $E1, E2$ computed over $\langle A, B, \Delta, G \rangle$.

## 5.3 Soundness Proof

**Theorem 3.** *SPVPC satisfies the soundness property requirement for the polynomial delegation.*

*Proof.* Demonstrating the soundness of SPVPC's verification mechanism involves proving that when CS generates a random $\Gamma$, the verifier $SC_{BC}$ is inclined to reject it with high probability.

Let's consider that CS maliciously behaves and generates $\hat{\Gamma}$ randomly. Then, send it to $SC_{BC}$. So, $SC_{BC}$ decrypts it by sending a request to DO and receives results $\hat{\Gamma}$ and $C$.

Verifier $SC_{BC}$ requests proof message $E1, E2$ for verifying the output $\hat{\Gamma}$ using parameters $P'(x)$ from DO. In SPVPC, DO is a trusted entity and sends the accurately computed proof $E1, E2$ over $\langle A, B, \Delta, G \rangle$ to $SC_{BC}$.

When $SC_{BC}$ receives the proof messages $E1$ and $E2$, the smart contract $SC_{BC}$ performs the verifying Eq. 3 and test for $\hat{\Gamma}^{\frac{1}{rn}} \overset{?}{=} E1^{E2}$. However, CS generates $\hat{\Gamma}$ randomly, not possessing proof messages $E1$ and $E2$. Consequently, $\hat{\Gamma} \neq E1^{E2}$, and the smart contract $SC_{BC}$ catches the forged output $\hat{\Gamma}$ and rejects it.

Drawing from the analysis above, if CS randomly generates $\Gamma$, soundness guarantees integrity and authenticity of SPVPC verification equation, preventing CS from fraudulent attempts to ensue verification Eq. 3 successfully.

# 6   Security Analysis

## 6.1   Confidentiality

**Theorem 4.** *The SPVPC achieves the confidentiality requirement of results at computation and during verification and preserves the confidentiality of data, assuming the secure FHE technique.*

*Proof. Computation Confidentiality at CS*: We establish the validity of the computation confidentiality at CS assuming the secure FHE technique, through a security game that tests the adversary $\mathscr{A}$'s capacity to compromise the SPVPC model with a non-negligible advantage. The security game unfolds as follows:

- Challenger $\mathfrak{C}$ executing an algorithm to initiate the game and providing public key $pk_{HE}$ to the adversary $\mathscr{A}$ and preserves secret key $sk_{HE}$.
- Thereafter, $\mathscr{A}$ generates equal length messages $m_0$ and $m_1$, then sends them to $\mathfrak{C}$.
- Now, challenger $\mathfrak{C}$ toss a coin to ascertain the value of $b \in (0, 1)$. Then, $\mathfrak{C}$ generates a ciphertext $c$ for the message $m_b$ that encrypts using the public key $pk_{HE}$ and sends it to the adversary $\mathscr{A}$.
- Finally, $\mathscr{A}$ tries to determine $b' \in (0, 1)$ for $b$. If $b$ equal to $b'$, then $\mathscr{A}$ wins the game.

The SPVPC security depends on the constitutive *FHE* problem. The $\mathfrak{C}$ conducts the above-defined game. Let $\mathsf{p}$ represent the probability for $\mathscr{A}$ to accurately predict $b'$ when $b$ equals $b'$. Then, due to the homomorphic encryption property, $|\mathsf{p} - \frac{1}{2}| < \epsilon$.

*Confidentiality of result preserves in CS*: The CS computes polynomial function $P(x)$ over $\mathscr{E}$ , *i.e.* a homomorphically encrypted data outsourced by DO, resulting in the generation of a homomorphically encrypted result $\Gamma$. Consequently, the probability for CS to discover an original evaluated result from $\Gamma$ is potentially less than $\epsilon$.

*Confidentiality of result preserves in DO*: The DO receives an encrypted form of computed result $\tilde{\Gamma}$ from $SC_{BC}$. Upon decryption, DO discovers $P(\{D_i\}_{i=1}^{i=n}) * rn$ as a randomized form (using an unknown value $rn$, where $rn \in \mathbb{Z}_p$ employed by smart contract $SC_{BC}$). Consequently, DO cannot retrieve the original encrypted result $\Gamma$ without knowledge of $rn$. Therefore, the probability of correctly guessing $rn$ by DO is $\frac{1}{2^t}$ (where $t$ represents the bit length of $rn$), which is exceedingly negligible.

*Confidentiality of result preserves during verification*: Let's assume adversary $\mathscr{A}$ tries to attack the proposed scheme and conducts as follows: a challenger $\mathfrak{C}$ randomly select some plain dataset $\mathscr{D} = (d_1, d_2, \cdots, d_n)$ and encrypt it $\mathscr{D}' = (c_1, c_2, \cdots, c_n)$. Then, send it to $\mathscr{A}$ and perform outsourced polynomial function $P$ over it. $\mathscr{A}$ uses a subset $\hat{\mathscr{D}}'$ of $\mathscr{D}'$ for $P$ and determine $\hat{\Gamma} = P(\hat{\mathscr{D}}')$. Next, suppose $\mathscr{A}$ send $\hat{\Gamma}$ to $\mathfrak{C}$. To achieve success in this game, $\mathfrak{C}$ must determine

$\hat{\Gamma} \stackrel{?}{=} E1^{E2}$. The success probability of this condition is at least than that of guessing randomly $\hat{\Gamma} = \Gamma$. Therefore, $\mathscr{A}$ is unsuccessful in such a situation.

*Confidentiality of data preserves in CS*: The CS only stores the encrypted data $\mathscr{E}$ that outsourced by DO. Outsourced data is encrypted using HE over the original data $\{D_i\}_{i=1}^{i=n}$. So, it is computationally infeasible for CS to determine any plaintext information of original data from $\mathscr{E}$ without using the corresponding HE secret key. Thus, the probability of retrieval would be much less than $\epsilon$.

## 6.2  Privacy Preserving

**Theorem 5.** *For adversaries, finding the actual data while exchanging information for computation verification to preserve data privacy is computationally infeasible.*

*Proof.* The SPVPC ensures data privacy by preventing the verifier or adversaries $\mathscr{A}$ from discovering DO's plaintext based on messages received from CS and DO for verification. The CS only stores the encrypted data $\mathscr{E}$.

*Case 1*: To ensure data privacy, considering the messages, the result $\Gamma$, proof messages $E1, E2$ and decrypt result message $\mathbf{\Gamma}, C$ that is required for verification. The result $\Gamma$ is computed by CS and its HE encrypted result. So, without secret key $\text{sk}_{\text{HE}}$, it is impossible for adversaries $\mathscr{A}$ to discover any information from it. So, the probability that $\mathscr{A}$ discover the original data would be less than $\epsilon$. Next, the proof messages $E1, E2$ compute over $\langle A, B, \Delta, G \rangle$ and do not contain any DO's data. The hardness of the DL problem makes it hard for adversaries $\mathscr{A}$ to predict the value of $E1$. $E2$ is an encrypted message, so it is impossible for adversaries $\mathscr{A}$ to discover any information without a secret key. Lastly, decrypt result message $\mathbf{\Gamma}$ preserves under the hardness of the DL problem, so adversaries $\mathscr{A}$ has very less probability to predict the value of $\mathbf{\Gamma}$ and $C$ is an encrypted message that cannot reveal any information to adversaries $\mathscr{A}$ without a secret key. Thus, the probability of discovering DO's plaintext by $\mathscr{A}$ based on proof messages and decrypt result messages is less than $\epsilon$.

*Case 2*: At blockchain, to ensure data privacy, analyse miners can identify any information leaked from proof message $E1, E2$, the result $\Gamma$ message, and decrypt result message $\mathbf{\Gamma}, C$. From the above case 1 analysis, SPVPC also ensures that miners' probability of discovering DO's plaintext based on the proof message, result message and decrypt result messages are less than $\epsilon$.

**Table 2.** HE Computation Time (in seconds)

| Method | Enc | Dec | Add | Mul |
|---|---|---|---|---|
| BGV used in [7] | 0.0285 | 0.0139 | 0.0026 | 0.0419 |
| CKKS used in SPVPC | 0.0197 | 0.0097 | 0.0018 | 0.0325 |

## 7   SPVPCPerformance Evaluation

The performance analysis of the proposed scheme over an experimental platform which utilizes an Intel(R) Core(TM) i7-4790 CPU @ 3.60GHz processor
with 12GB RAM, operating on the Ubuntu 21.04.6 LTS OS and simulates DO
and DU procedures. The simulation employs the CKKS FHE scheme. The computation times of each homomorphic operation with 64-bit input are presented in
Table 2, comparing BGV and CKKS. We evaluate the efficiency of our outsourced
computation scheme by simulating the system using Python. The verification
contract is developed using Solidity. The smart contracts are deployed on a local
simulated network, Ganache and SepoliaRPC (official Ethereum testnet), showing the practicality of SPVPC. Here, the Amazon EC2 platform acts as a cloud
environment. Next, Table 3 analyses the communication cost among each participating party in SPVPC. We exclude the proposed scheme's initial setup and
communication costs for only once performed. The communication costs are only
analysed over the communication channel of the proposed scheme. It includes
the additional communication cost of requests and queries such as encryption,
decryption, or share keys with fixed sizes. In Table 4, compare the computation
cost of SPVPC and Yu *et al.* [21] with respect to the *degree* (de) and *number of
variables* (nv) of a polynomial. Our scheme has a significant advantage in reducing the total verification time used to check the correctness of results generated
by CS.

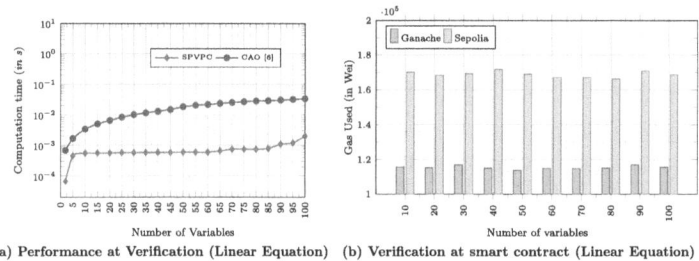

(a) Performance at Verification (Linear Equation)    (b) Verification at smart contract (Linear Equation)

**Fig. 3.** Performance and Gas Cost Analysis for Linear Equation.

Figures 3 and 4 represent the result verification of polynomial computation
analysis and gas used during verification at blockchain. The address of the smart
contract deployed at Ganache is 0x79E93365094A184A0F140C596910FC051b2b
B72D, and 0xA5fA40cF95baF02e1338223Be75980CBF49621BD is the account
created at sepoliaRPC. The gas cost for deployment of smart contracts at Ganache is 268704 wei, and at SepoliaRPC is 342402 wei ($9.0623 \times 10^{-4}$ ETH). The
gas price is 9 Gwei as per Etherscan (https://sepolia.etherscan.io/), which costs
reasonable when deploying a smart contract once. Figure 3(a) for total verification time for linear polynomial computation and compare proposed scheme with
existing scheme Cao *et al.* [6] by varies the nv from 10 to 100. Figure 3(b) shows

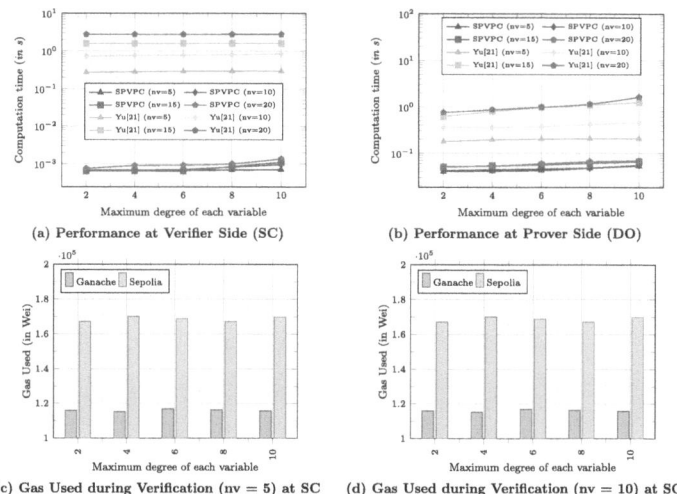

(a) **Performance at Verifier Side (SC)**    (b) **Performance at Prover Side (DO)**

(c) **Gas Used during Verification (nv = 5) at SC**    (d) **Gas Used during Verification (nv = 10) at SC**

**Fig. 4.** Performance and Gas Cost Analysis for Multivariate Polynomial

---

**Algorithm 1** SPVPC Incentive Mechanishm

---

**Input:** $\Theta$, $DO_{Acc}$, $CS_{Acc}$, $DU_{Acc}$
**Output:** $DO_{Acc}$, $CS_{Acc}$, $DU_{Acc}$
1:  $CS_{Acc} = CS_{Acc}$ - $Deposit_{CS}$                          ▷ "Initialization and Deposit"
2:  $DO_{Acc} = DO_{Acc}$ - $Deposit_{DO}$
3:  $DU_{Acc} = DU_{Acc}$ - $Deposit_{DU}$
4:  Verify each entity deposit. There is no service if no deposit is made.
5:  **if** $\Theta \stackrel{?}{=}$ "*true*" **then**
6:      $CS_{Acc} = CS_{Acc}$ + {$Deposit_{DU}$ - ServiceCharge}
7:      $DO_{Acc} = DO_{Acc}$ + {$Deposit_{DU}$ - ServiceCharge}
8:  **else**
9:      $DU_{Acc} = DU_{Acc}$ + {$Deposit_{CS}$ - CompensateCharge}
10:     $DO_{Acc} = DO_{Acc}$ + {$Deposit_{CS}$ - ServiceCharge}
11: **end if**
12: **return** $DO_{Acc}$, $CS_{Acc}$, $DU_{Acc}$

---

total gas consumption for verification at Ganache and SepoliaRPC for SPVPC. The gas cost is 166313 to 171718 wei in SepoliaRPC. The Fig. 4 analysis of the multivariate polynomial computation verification of SPVPC with Yu *et al.* [21]. Figure 4(a) shows performance analysis of schemes at the verifier side (SC), and Fig. 4(b) shows performance analysis of schemes at the prover side (DO). Both show graphs with varying nv from 5 to 20 and polynomial de from 2 to 10. It reflects SPVPC not affected by the polynomial's de and nv. In contrast, the changes in nv impact Yu *et al.* [21] scheme that raises verification time. Figure 4(c) and Fig. 4(d) shows gas consumption for SPVPC verification with nv=5 and nv=10 at Ganache and SepoliaRPC. The gas cost is reasonable for verifiable multivariate polynomial computation, which requires only 167104 to 170113 wei for nv=5 and 167427 to 170071 wei for nv=10 in SepoliaRPC.

**Table 3.** Cost of communication among each participating party.

| Communication Channel | Cost | Communication Channel | Cost |
|---|---|---|---|
| DO to CS $[\mathscr{E}]$ | $\mathcal{O}(n)$ | DU to BC $[P'(x)]$ | $\mathcal{O}(n)$ |
| BC to CS $[P'(x)]$ | $\mathcal{O}(n)$ | BC to DO $[P'(x)]$ | $\mathcal{O}(n)$ |
| CS to BC $[\Gamma]$ | $\mathcal{O}(1)$ | BC to DO $[\tilde{\Gamma}]$ | $\mathcal{O}(1)$ |
| DO to BC $[E1, E2']$ | $\mathcal{O}(1)$ | DO to BC $[\mathbf{\Gamma}, C']$ | $\mathcal{O}(1)$ |
| BC to DU $[\mathsf{R}']$ | $\mathcal{O}(1)$ | | |

**Table 4.** Computation Cost

| Scheme | Initialization | | Verification |
|---|---|---|---|
| | DO | OC | Verifier |
| Yu [21] | $\tilde{\mathcal{O}}(\lambda^2)$ | $\tilde{\mathcal{O}}(n \times \lambda \times d^3)$ | $\tilde{\mathcal{O}}(n' \times \lambda \times d'^3)$ |
| SPVPC | $\tilde{\mathcal{O}}(\lambda^2)$ | $\tilde{\mathcal{O}}(n \times \lambda \times d^3)$ | $\mathcal{O}(n \times \mathcal{D}^2)$ |

**DO**: Data Outsourced, **OC**: Outsourced Computation; **Note**: $\mathcal{O}(n) \ll \tilde{\mathcal{O}}(n)$, $n' < n$, $d' < d$, where $n$ is nv and $d$ is polynomial de. $\mathcal{D}$ is de of ideal.

# 8   Conclusion

This paper proposed SPVPC that enables polynomial computation over encrypted data and establishes fairness through blockchain, fostering trust in the cloud computing environment. SPVPC is assessed by comparing the computed results with the existing scheme and performing gas analysis by deploying a smart contract at Ganache and SepoliaRPC to show its effectiveness and efficiency. It consumes reasonable gas during the verification process, which reflects its cost-effectiveness. Moreover, the proposed scheme implements efficient prover computations to reduce the total result verification time generated by CS. Thus, we achieve a significant advantage in variable polynomial computation. Future work will investigate the function privacy mechanisms and incorporate reputation mechanisms for players to enhance entity trustworthiness.

# References

1. Agrawal, R., Joshi, A.: CKKS FHE Scheme. In: On Architecting Fully Homomorphic Encryption-based Computing Systems, pp. 19–48. Springer (2023)
2. Ahmad, H., et al.: Primitives towards verifiable computation: a survey. Front. Comp. Sci. **12**(3), 451–478 (2018). https://doi.org/10.1007/s11704-016-6148-4
3. Avizheh, S., Nabi, M., Safavi-Naini, R., Venkateswarlu K., M.: Verifiable computation using smart contracts. In: Proceedings of the 2019 ACM SIGSAC Conference on Cloud Computing Security Workshop. London, pp. 17–28. CCSW'19, ACM (Nov 2019), https://doi.org/10.1145/3338466.3358925

4. Backes, M., Fiore, D., Reischuk, R.M.: Verifiable delegation of computation on outsourced data. In: Proceedings of 2013 ACM SIGSAC Conference on Computer & Communications Security (CCS '13). Berlin, pp. 863–874 (Nov 2013). https://doi.org/10.1145/2508859.2516681

5. Canetti, R., Riva, B., Rothblum, G.N.: Practical delegation of computation using multiple servers. In: Proceedings of the 18th ACM Conference on Computer and Communications Security. Melbourne, Australia, pp. 445–454. CCS '11, ACM, New York, NY, USA (2011)

6. Cao, C., Zhu, X.: Secure and verifiable outsourced computation based on blockchain. In: Proceeding of 2023 4th Information Communication Technologies Conference (ICTC). Nanjing, China, pp. 327–331 (2023). https://doi.org/10.1109/ICTC57116.2023.10154879

7. Chakraborty, P.S., Gavhane, O.S., Tripathy, S.: SEVCOD: secure and efficient verifiable computation on outsourced data. Cluster Comput. **27**, 4725–4739 (Dec 2023). https://doi.org/10.1007/s10586-023-04190-9

8. van Dijk, M., Gentry, C., Halevi, S., Vaikuntanathan, V.: Fully homomorphic encryption over the integers. In: Gilbert, H. (ed.) EUROCRYPT 2010. LNCS, vol. 6110, pp. 24–43. Springer, Heidelberg (2010). https://doi.org/10.1007/978-3-642-13190-5_2

9. Dong, C., Wang, Y., Aldweesh, A., McCorry, P., van Moorsel, A.: Betrayal, distrust, and rationality: Smart counter-collusion contracts for verifiable cloud computing. In: Proceedings of the 2017 ACM SIGSAC Conference on Computer and Communications Security. Dallas, USA, pp. 211–227. CCS '17, ACM (2017). https://doi.org/10.1145/3133956.3134032

10. Dorsala, M.R., Sastry, V.N., chapram, S.: Fair protocols for verifiable computations using bitcoin and ethereum. In: Proceedings of 2018 IEEE 11th International Conference on Cloud Computing. San Francisco, CA, USA, pp. 786–793 (2018). https://doi.org/10.1109/CLOUD.2018.00107

11. Gong, X., Hu, B., Xiong, Y., Zhao, X.: Practical verifiable computation on encrypted data. In: Proceedings of 2022 IEEE 8th International Conference on Big Data Security on Cloud (BigDataSecurity). Jinan, China, pp. 67–74 (2022). https://doi.org/10.1109/BigDataSecurityHPSCIDS54978.2022.00022

12. Guan, Y., Zheng, H., Shao, J., Lu, R., Wei, G.: Fair outsourcing polynomial computation based on the blockchain. IEEE Trans. Serv. Comput. **15**(5), 2795–2808 (Sep-Oct 2022). https://doi.org/10.1109/TSC.2021.3054772

13. Lee, H.L., Au, M.H.A., Sun, S.F.: Blockchain-based trustless fair payment protocol for verifiable confidential outsourcing computation. In: Proceedings of 2023 IEEE International Conference on Blockchain. Ocean Flower Island, Hainan, China, pp. 221–228 (Dec 2023). https://doi.org/10.1109/Blockchain60715.2023.00045

14. Maddali, L.P., Thakur, M.S.D., Vigneswaran, R., Rajan, M.A., Kanchanapalli, S., Das, B.: Veriblock: A novel blockchain framework based on verifiable computing and trusted execution environment. In: Proceedings of 2020 International Conference on COMmunication Systems & NETworkS (COMSNETS). Bengaluru, India, pp. 1–6 (2020). https://doi.org/10.1109/COMSNETS48256.2020.9027414

15. Nabi, M., Avizheh, S., Safavi-Naini, R.: Fides: A system for verifiable computation using smart contracts. In: Proceedings of 2022 International Conference on Financial Cryptography and Data Security (FC 2022). Tokyo, Japan. Lecture Notes in Computer Science, vol. 13412, pp. 448–480. Springer (2023)

16. Nayak, S.K., Tripathy, S.: SEMKC: secure and efficient computation over outsourced data encrypted under multiple keys. IEEE Trans. Emerg. Top. Comput. **9**(1), 414–428 (2021)

17. Sariboz, E., Kolachala, K., Panwar, G., Vishwanathan, R., Misra, S.: Off-chain execution and verification of computationally intensive smart contracts. In: Proceedings of 2021 IEEE International Conference on Blockchain and Cryptocurrency (ICBC). Virtual Conference, pp. 1–3 (2021)
18. Setty, S., Mcpherson, R., Blumberg, A., Walfish, M.: Making argument systems for outsourced computation practical (sometimes). In: Proceedings of 2012 NDSS Symposium, pp. 1–20 (Feb 2012)
19. Yang, Y., et al.: A comprehensive survey on secure outsourced computation and its applications. IEEE Access 7, 159426–159465 (2019). https://doi.org/10.1109/ACCESS.2019.2949782
20. Yu, X., Yan, Z., Vasilakos, A.V.: A survey of verifiable computation. Mobile Netw. Appl. 22(3), 438–453 (2017)
21. Yu, X., Yan, Z., Zhang, R.: Verifiable outsourced computation over encrypted data. Inf. Sci. 479, 372–385 (2019)

# Identifying the Origins of Business Data Breaches Through CTC Detection

Gayle L. Frisbier[1], Omar Darwish[1] ⓘ, Anas Alsobeh[2](✉) ⓘ,
and Abdallah Al-shorman[1]

[1] Eastern Michigan University, Ypsilanti, MI, USA
{gfrisbie,odarwish}@emich.edu, aalshorm@eich.edu
[2] Southern Illinois University Carbondale, Carbondale, IL, USA
anas.alsobeh@siu.edu

**Abstract.** The frequency of cybersecurity events and data breaches is escalating, resulting in substantial financial liabilities for businesses. Contemporary organizations rely heavily on network connections to facilitate efficient operations in diverse locations. Covert timing channels (CTCs), a sophisticated cyber threat, involve the surreptitious embedding of sensitive information into regular network traffic, thus establishing concealed communication pathways that are difficult to detect. This study proposes a novel approach for detecting CTCs using machine learning (ML), which significantly advances the state-of-the-art in data breach detection and information leakage through CTC. Our approach introduces a unique integration of Unicode transformation and ML that enhances the detection capability by analyzing inter-packet timing data. In particular, our findings indicate that the Gradient Boost Classification model yields an accuracy rate ranging from 73% to 78%, while the Random Forest model (RF) also exhibits significant accuracy.

**Keywords:** Covert Timing Channel (CTC) · Machine Learning (ML) · Binary Translation · Data Type Origin Detection · Cybersecurity · cyber-attacks · Supervised Learning

## 1 Introduction

Covert Timing Channels (CTCs) constitute a complex and advancing cyber threat, enabling malevolent entities to secretly convey sensitive information by embedding data inside the timing fluctuations of standard network traffic. These covert channels depend on meticulous synchronization and manipulation of packet timings, utilizing delays to convey data undetected [1]. Conventional cybersecurity measures frequently neglect these temporal abnormalities, making CTCs especially perilous. The capacity to control these time gaps allows attackers to establish covert communication channels that can circumvent traditional security measures across multiple layers—network protocols, system processes,

H. H. Song et al. (Eds.): NSS 2024, LNCS 15564, pp. 387–406, 2025.
https://doi.org/10.1007/978-981-96-3531-3_19

or hardware components. The intrinsic stealth of CTCs renders them a significant hazard, particularly in intricate network contexts like cloud computing [2].

The rising incidence of data breaches, which has escalated by over 24% since 2019, with 95% of breaches being financially motivated, highlights the urgent necessity for enhanced detection and identification systems [3]. CTCs are crucial in these breaches as they provide the clandestine distribution of sensitive information while circumventing conventional detection techniques. The integration of clandestine communications with normal network traffic exacerbates the difficulty, necessitating that businesses implement sophisticated detection methods to identify these anomalies.

Prior investigations into CTCs have primarily concentrated on broad detection methodologies [4] and augmenting the complexity of hidden channels to circumvent current detection strategies [5]. Numerous studies have focused on enhancing detection capabilities for diverse covert channels and network traffic formats [6]. Nonetheless, a substantial gap persists in identifying both the presence of covert channels and comprehending the nature and provenance of the exfiltrated data. Furthermore, the majority of traditional solutions depend on either static rule-based systems or standalone ML applications, both of which exhibit limits in varied corporate settings.

This work presents an innovative and thorough methodology for CTC detection that markedly enhances the current standards in two principal aspects: This study introduces an innovative application of Unicode transformation to corporate data before to its conversion into binary for discreet transmission. This modification not only conceals the data but also improves the machine learning model's capacity to identify timing abnormalities by diversifying data representation. In contrast to conventional CTC detection techniques that concentrate just on packet timing, our approach employs several Unicode transformations (e.g., Unicode 50, Unicode 100, Unicode 150) to create unique signatures that enhance the detection precision of covert channels. The utilization of machine learning algorithms, including Gradient Boosting (GB) and Random Forest (RF), transcends the sole identification of circulating tumor cells (CTCs). These models characterize the type of data being compromised, so offering essential insight into the nature of the danger. This work rectifies a significant deficiency in contemporary research, which frequently fails to distinguish between categories of exfiltrated material. This technique enhances the practical application of CTC detection in business environments by identifying both the presence and type of stolen data, offering a proactive security solution rather than a reactive measure. This dual capability is a substantial enhancement over existing methods, which generally do not emphasize the classification of extracted content.

Our methodology combines Unicode-based alterations with advanced machine learning algorithms, resulting in a more refined understanding of CTCs compared to traditional detection methods. This comprehensive method enhances the standard by enabling organizations to not only identify CTCs but also determine the nature of the data at risk, so increasing both preventive and reactive cybersecurity measures.

## 2   Literature Review

ML is one of the techniques employed to identify CTCs. It is essential in research for detecting and evaluating patterns within datasets. ML enables the training of models to identify and categorize patterns in network data, facilitating the effective identification of CTCs. This enables us to devise novel and potent detection techniques for CTCs that are precise and effective.

The k-nearest Neighbor (kNN) algorithm is a form of supervised learning, which retains a labeled training dataset to categorize new unlabeled data according to its resemblance to the labeled data. A novel detection approach utilizing the kNN algorithm was proposed in a paper by [7]. This approach employed statistical data concerning time intervals and payload length to train the machine learning model. The authors performed testing and determined that the kNN algorithm attained an accuracy of 0.96 during 10-fold cross-validation, hence enhancing the model's performance. A separate study [8] revealed that kNN achieved the greatest precision rate of 98% in identifying covert channels. In this research, the authors developed a dataset to evaluate multiple machine learning methods, including Support Vector Machines (SVM), k-Nearest Neighbors (kNN), and Deep Neural Networks (DNN). The efficacy of kNN was illustrated in its capacity to effectively identify and categorize covert channels.

A study by Zander [9] employed decision trees to identify concealed communication, particularly a novel kind of CTC. The authors indicated that decision trees offer an advantage to researchers due to the human interpretability of the final classifier. Additionally, in a separate study by [10], the authors investigated the application of SVM as an alternative supervised learning model. SVM seek to identify an ideal hyperplane that distinguishes data classes or forecasts continuous values, aiming to maximize the margin between support vectors. Their work concentrated on the identification of CTCs via Long-Term Evolution Advanced (LTE-A) technology. The model was trained utilizing 1,000,000 data packets from an overt channel and 500,000 from covert channels. The supervised training model effectively identified CTCs using LTE-A. The researchers in [11] concentrated on identifying CTCs through deep machine learning in a Software Defined Network (SDN). Their suggested ML model comprised the network layer, the ANN layer, and the classification layer. This approach can be implemented in a software-defined network to identify and eliminate covert channels during live communication. The authors showcased that the approach successfully identified and halted covert channels in the course of real-time communication.

In a different investigation, Sun et al. [12] utilized a recurring neural network (RNN) to introduce a novel model aimed at identifying covert networks through machine learning. The model employed a recurrent neural network with a memory capability, integrating both standard and atypical network data for its training process. Furthermore, Long-Short-Term Memory (LSTM) was incorporated into the RNN model for enhanced optimization. The researchers utilized publicly accessible data sets for training and attained an F1 score of 95% during the evaluation of their proposed detection method. A recent study by [13] presented an innovative neural network known as Fedona CNN. This advanced model incorporates layers designed to process input through a systematic approach, utilizing a sliding window technique to examine the data effectively. Following this, interconnected layers analyze the complete dataset to detect possible recurring patterns. Additionally, [14] employed ML in an unsupervised approach to identify zero-day attacks within the covert channels of domain name servers (DNS). Their investigation revealed a minimal occurrence of false positives.

In some studies, researchers combine different ML methods to create new approaches. In a particular study by [15], the authors used spectrograms of inter-arrival packet delays in a CTC with an image-based deep ML framework to develop a detection method. The spectrograms were generated by converting the inter-packet delays using the short-time Fourier transform and then normalizing them between 0 and 1. The ML techniques utilized included Decision Tree, Naïve Bayes, and ANNs. Two modified schemes, named Squeeze Net and VGG-16, were proposed. The VGG-16 method was found to outperform conventional approaches in detecting CTCs in e-health transmissions, achieving an f-measure of 0.929, a recall of 0.930, and a precision of 0.928.

Similarly, the study referenced in [16] also utilized the technique in their work. The authors of the research paper introduced a framework based on SVM to identify CTCs. This model involved a network monitor passing traffic through a traffic filter, and then a fingerprint extractor sending the traffic through the SVM framework. To test the reliability of their classifier, the authors selected four popular CTC algorithms. The authors reported that the framework was able to accurately detect the CTCs across generic channels without being specific to a particular type, unlike other research. The authors [17] incorporated SVM in their work and proposed an ensemble model that combined SVM, RF, and Naive Bayes ML techniques into a single detection method. The output from the three ML techniques was combined using the logical regression classifier to create a meta-classifier. The accuracy of the ensemble model with ML was reported to be 98.5%.

In a study by [18], various ML methods were employed to develop a new technique for accurately identifying CTCs. This technique, called SnapCatch, involved processing images and utilizing ML methods to classify CTCs. The study compared different classifiers for SnapCatch, including ANNs, Naive Bayes, SVM, and Decision Trees. According to [19,20], the significance of ML in detecting covert channels for the security and privacy of applications is evident. However, it was noted that ML algorithms struggle to effectively address multiple covert channels. Furthermore, it was suggested that the ML approach should be used in the early stages of development to assess vulnerability.

## 3  Methodological

Figure 1 shows the research design, including data collection, system setup, evaluation, experiment steps, statistical and ML setup, statistical tests and models, statistical and ML evaluation, and Unicode accuracy evaluation.

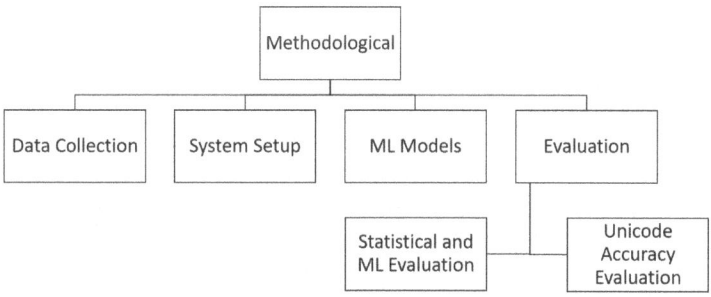

**Fig. 1.** Methodological

### 3.1  Data Collection and Rationale

The dataset strategy aimed to simulate normal language interactions commonly exchanged over an organization's email system, which could potentially be leaked across a network. This involved curating three distinct classifications of data typically communicated via email within an organization: Human Resources, Financial, and Marketing data. These classifications were selected due to their prevalence in corporate communications and their high risk for data leaks, making them an ideal subject for CTC detection [21]. To compile this dataset, a comprehensive approach was adopted, drawing on industry expertise, marketing reports from reputable sources [22–25], publicly available financial reports (such as those from [26] in 2022), and template data [27]. The final dataset encompasses 1020 records, with each data classification containing 340 records (Tables 1 and 2).

The dataset was divided into three sets based on its classification: Human Resources, Financial, or Marketing data. Each set was then converted into Unicode and subsequently translated into binary data. The experiment used four different translations of Unicode with a multiplier, as presented in Table 3.

Table 3 shows each Unicode transformation was chosen to introduce variability in the data representation, providing diverse features for ML analysis. The rationale behind the different levels of Unicode transformation was to generate distinct timing signatures that could potentially improve detection accuracy by making CTC anomalies more distinguishable.

**Table 1.** Data Sample with Original Text

| Class | Original Text |
| --- | --- |
| Human Resources | Efforts shall be made to fill the vacant positions internally. |
| Financial | Payroll costs for this month are now $734,210. |
| Marketing | This represents an increase of 34%. |

**Table 2.** Binary Data Representation of Each Class

| Class | Binary Representation |
| --- | --- |
| Human Resources | – 01000101 01100110 01100110 01101111 01110010 01110100 01110011 00100000 01110011 |
| | – 01101000 01100001 01101100 01101100 00100000 01100010 01100101 00100000 01101101 |
| | – 01100001 01100100 01100101 00100000 01110100 01101111 00100000 01100110 01101001 |
| | – 01101100 01101100 00100000 01110100 01101000 01100101 00100000 01110110 01100001 |
| | – 01100011 01100001 01101110 01110100 00100000 01110000 01101111 01110011 01101001 |
| | – 01110100 01101001 01101111 01101110 01110011 00100000 01101001 01101110 01110100 |
| | – 01100101 01110010 01101110 01100001 01101100 01101100 01111001 00101110 |
| Financial | – 01010000 01100001 01111001 01110010 01101111 01101100 01101100 00100000 01100011 |
| | – 01101111 01110011 01110100 01110011 00100000 01100110 01101111 01110010 00100000 |
| | – 01110100 01101000 01101001 01110011 00100000 01101101 01101111 01101110 01110100 |
| | – 01101000 00100000 01100001 01110010 01100101 00100000 01101110 01101111 01110111 |
| | – 00100000 00100100 00110111 00110011 00110100 00101100 00110010 00110001 00110000 |
| | – 00101110 |
| Marketing | – 01010100 01101000 01101001 01110011 00100000 01110010 01100101 01110000 01110010 |
| | – 01100101 01110011 01100101 01101110 01110100 01110011 00100000 01100001 01101110 |
| | – 00100000 01101001 01101110 01100011 01110010 01100101 01100001 01110011 01100101 |
| | – 00100000 01101111 01100110 00100000 00110011 00110100 00100000 01110000 01100101 |
| | – 01110010 01100011 01100101 01101110 01110100 00101110 |

**Table 3.** Dataset Version with Unicode Conversion

| Dataset Version | Unicode Conversion | Name |
|---|---|---|
| 1 | Normal Unicode | Normal Unicode |
| 2 | (Unicode * 50) + Unicode | Unicode 50 |
| 3 | (Unicode *100) + Unicode | Unicode 100 |
| 4 | (Unicode *150) + Unicode | Unicode 150 |

### 3.2   System Setup for CTC Simulation

Initially, the experiment involved using the system setup for four different data versions with Unicode conversion. These versions are detailed in Table 3. The first run included normal Unicode conversion for all three data type datasets (Human Resources, Financial, and Marketing data), transmitting information from the Server PC to the Client PC, while the resulting network traffic was logged into WireShark. This initial run produced three result files, including network timing information. Subsequently, the experiment was carried out using Unicode 50 conversion for all three data types, followed by runs using Unicode 100 and Unicode 150. This led to a total of 12 result files containing recorded network traffic and timing information. The result files were then sorted based on data type classification and data version and were prepared for evaluation.

To simulate a CTC within an organizational setting, a laboratory setup was used involving two Windows 10 Pro personal computers connected via a local area network. Figure 2 shows the system setup included, on the client installed with Wireshark Version 4.2.0 for capturing network traffic, and NetBeans IDE 8.2 to facilitate JavaScript execution for CTC creation. On the Server, we installed NetBeans IDE 8.2 to create and execute the CTC. The server transmitted the dataset converted into binary over the network to the client. The network connection between the server and client PCs was facilitated through a wired Ethernet gigabit switch, providing a controlled environment for the experiment. The JavaScript program designed for this experiment transmitted binary '1' and '0' by implementing inter-packet delay times of 20,000 microseconds and 10,000 microseconds respectively, as illustrated in Fig. 3.

### 3.3   ML Models Implementation

The experiment was conducted for all four Unicode conversions (Normal Unicode, Unicode 50, Unicode 100, Unicode 150). Each dataset version was transmitted from the Server PC to the Client PC over the network. The network traffic, including packet timing information, was captured using Wireshark, resulting in 12 sets of result files across the three data classifications and four dataset versions.

We use SVM, RF, GB, and Gaussian Naive Bayes (GNB) to detect CTCs. SVM is a robust supervised learning algorithm that operates by identifying decision boundaries between data points based on the classes they have been trained

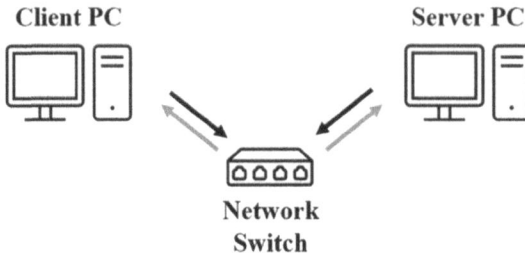

**Fig. 2.** Lab setup of Server and Client PCs

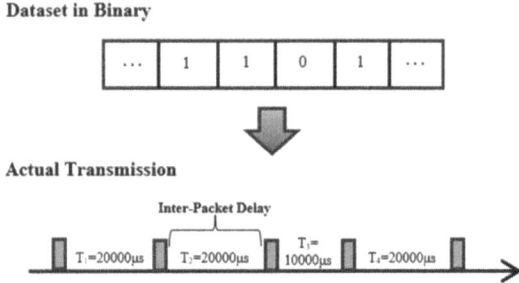

**Fig. 3.** Dataset representation of transmission controlled inter-packet delay time

with. This makes it effective for both classification and regression analysis. Utilized with a linear kernel and a regularization parameter (C) of 1.0. The model was chosen due to its ability to identify decision boundaries effectively for classification tasks. RF Classification is a supervised learning algorithm that utilizes an ensemble of decision trees to iteratively split data, eventually converging on a singular result. It is widely applied in predictive modeling and classification tasks due to its ability to handle large datasets and minimize overfitting. Selected for its robustness against overfitting and effectiveness in handling high-dimensional datasets. GB is a form of ML that leverages a series of decision trees to optimize the subsequent tree, ultimately minimizing the loss function. This iterative approach enhances the predictive accuracy and resilience of the model, making it suitable for a wide range of applications, including ranking, classification, and regression problems. Chosen due to its iterative approach to minimizing errors and enhancing prediction accuracy, particularly in capturing subtle timing differences. GNB applies the Gaussian distribution to the dataset while assuming independence between the features of the data. Renowned for its simplicity and efficiency, it is widely used in text classification, spam filtering, and recommendation systems due to its ability to handle large feature spaces and adapt well to online learning scenarios. These models were trained on the timing feature set, which included metrics such as minimum, maximum, mean, median, standard deviation, entropy, and variance of inter-packet arrival times. Implemented to assess its performance in classification tasks where feature independence could be assumed. This model is often effective for text classification and was adapted here for packet timing analysis.

## 3.4 Evaluation

The datasets, originally written in English, were converted into binary format to facilitate transmission over a CTC. The average length of a function word in English is 3.13 letters, and for a content word, it is 6.47 letters [28]. The packets were subsequently divided into groups of 32, 64, 96, and 128 packets for each data version to analyze the detection of content types. Each packet represented one bit of data, and different group sizes were used to evaluate whether detection occurred at one, two, three, or four words. For example, one English word equates to 4 characters on average, which translates to 8 bits per character, resulting in a total of 32 bits. Consequently, 64 packets represented two English words, 96 packets represented three words, and 128 packets represented four words. Subsequently, these packet groups were evaluated using statistical and ML models to analyze the inter-packet arrival time of the network packets.

Prior to training the ML models, a comprehensive series of statistical tests were conducted on the results files. The subsequent section provides an in-depth overview of the methodologies employed for statistical analysis and the ML models utilized:

- **Minimum**: This refers to the lowest value in a list of numbers or the largest negative number present within the dataset.
- **Maximum**: Denoting the highest value in a list of numbers, or the least negative number if the dataset comprises entirely of negative numbers.
- **Mean**: Representing the average or central value of the set of numbers.
- **Median**: Defined as the middle number of a data set when arranged from least to greatest, providing insight into the central tendency of the dataset.
- **Standard Deviation**: A measure of the amount of variation or dispersion of a set of values from the mean, helping to gauge the consistency of the dataset.
- **Entropy**: This metric signifies the measure of randomness and uncertainty within the dataset, offering valuable insights into the overall distribution and predictability of the data.
- **Variance**: This quantifies the spread or dispersion of the dataset, providing essential information about the data distribution and enabling a deeper understanding of its characteristics.

**Statistical and ML Evaluation.** Performance metrics were utilized to assess the efficacy of each ML model, encompassing accuracy, precision, recall, and F1-Score. The initial evaluation was conducted on a one-word or 32-packet group, which served as input for the ML algorithms. Figure 4 depicts the process of dataset generation and subsequent input into the ML models. Subsequently, this methodology was replicated for two-word, three-word, and four-word packet groups in consecutive experiments.

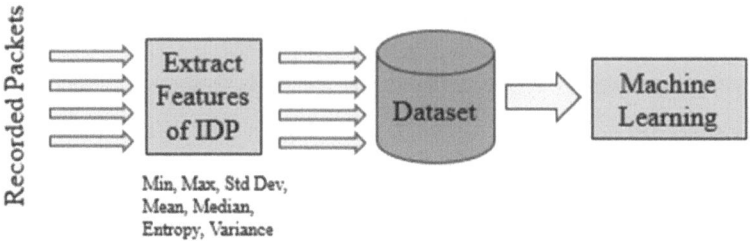

**Fig. 4.** The production of a dataset and feeding it to the ML algorithm

The data evaluations primarily focused on the assessment of F1-Score and accuracy. Accuracy holds paramount importance in evaluating ML models for predicting true positives and true negatives, especially when dealing with similar class distributions. An optimal accuracy score is 100%. The F1-Score plays a critical role in determining the likelihood of the ML model to predict false negatives and false positives, particularly in cases of wide-ranging or imbalanced class distributions. It represents the average of precision and recall, with the optimal F1-Score standing at 1.0.

Figure 5 shows the Confusion Matrix for SVM, Random Forest, GB, and GNB, where the Unicode equation is 100, and the number of packets is 128 as a group. Moreover, Table 4 shows statistical evaluation metrics:

**Table 4.** Statistical

| # | Mean | Median | Min | Max | STD | Entropy | Variance |
|---|---|---|---|---|---|---|---|
| 0 | 0.045522 | 0.046639 | 0.000456 | 0.061401 | 0.046639 | 5.0000 | 7.259691e−05 |
| 1 | 0.046563 | 0.046513 | 0.041880 | 0.051102 | 0.046513 | 5.0000 | 1.635901e−06 |
| 2 | 0.046432 | 0.046453 | 0.041477 | 0.051811 | 0.046453 | 5.0000 | 2.129335e−06 |
| 3 | 0.046402 | 0.046536 | 0.044529 | 0.049307 | 0.046536 | 5.0000 | 1.141736e−06 |
| 4 | 0.046399 | 0.046420 | 0.043730 | 0.047651 | 0.046420 | 5.0000 | 4.942697e−07 |

**Unicode Accuracy Evaluation.** The accuracy of the normal Unicode conversion to binary was evaluated. In Fig. 6 below, the accuracy of each Unicode conversion method is plotted for various ML models. Table 5 displays the percentage accuracy for each Unicode conversion method per data packet group size for each type of ML model. The normal Unicode conversion exhibited an accuracy range of 37.88% to 57.66%, slightly better than 50% at its highest accuracy. Unicode 50 achieved an accuracy range of 30.42% to 78.9%, Unicode 100 had an accuracy range of 35.51% to 78.92%, and Unicode 150 had an accuracy range of 34.38% to 68.55%.

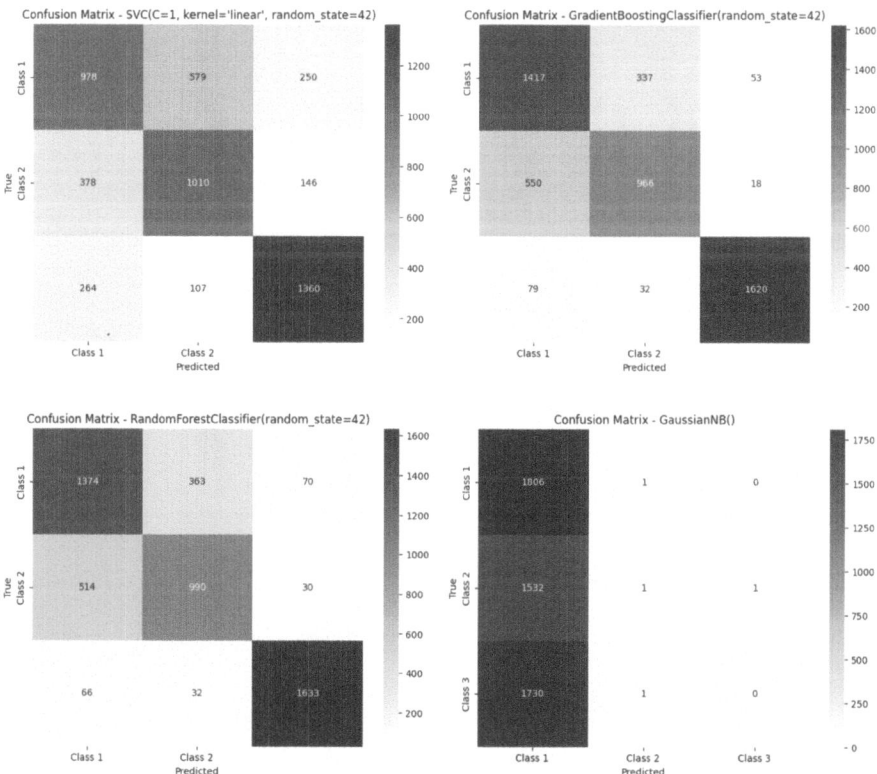

**Fig. 5.** Confusion Matrix for SVM, Random Forest, GB, and GNB, where the Unicode equation is 100, and the number of packets is 128 as a group

From the data, it is evident that the normal Unicode and Unicode 150 were less accurate compared to the conversion to Unicode 50 or Unicode 100. Furthermore, when comparing the range of Unicode 50 and Unicode 100, it is clear that Unicode 100 has a higher minimum accuracy, thus making it more accurate than Unicode 50. The data also indicates that there is not a significant disparity between the data groups when comparing the Unicode conversion against the accuracy for each ML model.

The study involved an evaluation of Unicode conversions based on their F1-Scores. Initially, the F1-Scores were examined with respect to data packet sizes or the number of words in a group. Figure 7 illustrates the F1-Scores for each Unicode conversion method across different ML models. Normal Unicode conversion yielded an F1-Score range from 0.0 to 0.70, while Unicode 50 had a range from 0 to 0.86. Additionally, Unicode 100 showed a range from 0 to 0.95, and Unicode 150 had a range from 0 to 0.80.

The data depicted that normal Unicode and Unicode 150 were comparatively less accurate than Unicode 50 and Unicode 100. Furthermore, Unicode 100 demonstrated higher precision when compared to Unicode 50. Consequently,

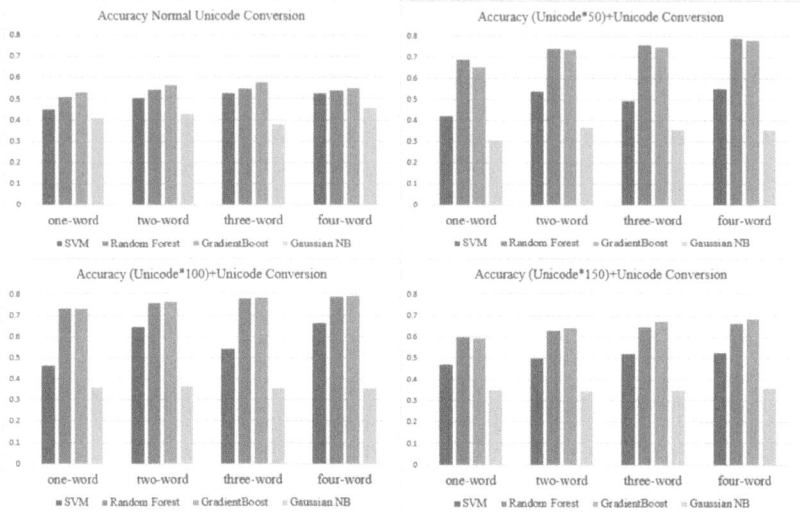

**Fig. 6.** Accuracy of ML models per the data group sizes and Unicode conversion

**Table 5.** Accuracy of Unicode Conversions Based on Data Group Size Across the ML Models

| Conversion Type | Data Group Size | SVM | RF | GradientBoost | Gaussian NB |
|---|---|---|---|---|---|
| Normal Unicode | one-word | 44.60% | 50.78% | 53.08% | 40.83% |
| | two-word | 50.45% | 54.44% | 56.43% | 42.48% |
| | three-word | 52.50% | 54.73% | 57.66% | 45.80% |
| | four-word | 52.75% | 53.77% | 55.14% | 45.80% |
| Unicode 50 | one-word | 41.79% | 68.94% | 65.13% | 30.42% |
| | two-word | 53.78% | 74.16% | 73.81% | 36.53% |
| | three-word | 49.30% | 75.18% | 75.12% | 35.40% |
| | four-word | 54.99% | 78.90% | 78.10% | 35.40% |
| Unicode 100 | one-word | 46.49% | 72.99% | 73.01% | 36.01% |
| | two-word | 64.24% | 75.99% | 75.29% | 35.63% |
| | three-word | 53.99% | 78.16% | 78.16% | 35.51% |
| | four-word | 66.01% | 78.81% | 78.92% | 35.63% |
| Unicode 150 | one-word | 46.49% | 72.99% | 73.01% | 36.01% |
| | two-word | 64.24% | 75.99% | 76.25% | 36.39% |
| | three-word | 53.99% | 78.16% | 78.16% | 35.40% |
| | four-word | 66.01% | 78.81% | 78.92% | 35.63% |

due to their underperformance, normal Unicode, Unicode 50, and Unicode 150 will not be further evaluated in this study.

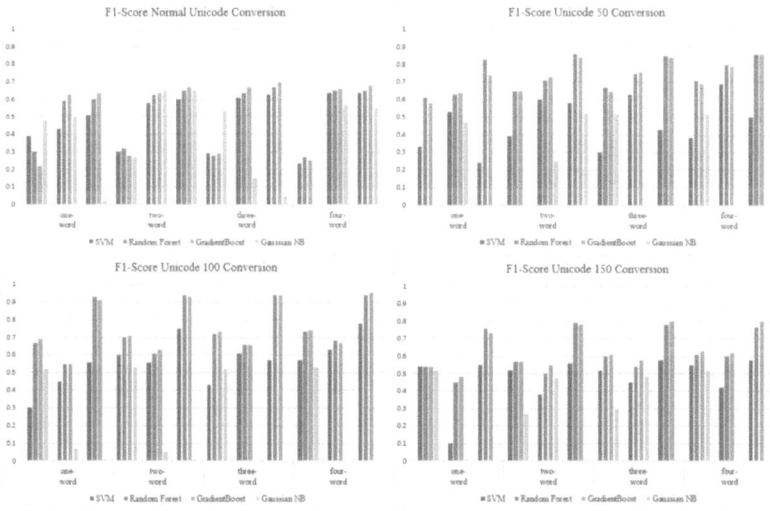

**Fig. 7.** F1-Score of ML models per the various data group sizes and Unicode conversion

## 4    Result and Discussion

The performance of the models is assessed in terms of accuracy and F1-Scores across different packet groups, providing a comparative analysis to illustrate the effectiveness of each model. We also discuss the implications of the findings and how they compare to existing literature in this domain. GNB model has an accuracy range of 35.51% to 36.39%. The lowest accuracy for this model was observed with the 32-packet group or one-word detection, and the highest was at two-word detection.

The accuracy of each ML model for different Unicode conversion methods is presented in Fig. 6. Each graph illustrates the results for normal Unicode, Unicode * 50, Unicode * 100, and Unicode * 150 conversions. The evaluation was conducted on one-word, two-word, three-word, and four-word packet group sizes, with accuracy results presented across all ML models—SVM, Random Forest, GB, and GNB.

GB model consistently outperformed the other models, showing the highest accuracy across most packet group sizes and data types. For instance, in the Unicode 100 conversion, the Gradient Boost model achieved the highest accuracy, particularly in the four-word packet group, where it reached approximately 78.92%. This consistent performance can be attributed to Gradient Boost's ensemble nature, which combines multiple weak learners to minimize bias and variance. This adaptive mechanism enables GB to capture complex features that are instrumental in detecting CTCs, especially as the size of the packet groups increases.

On the other hand, the RF model demonstrated an accuracy that closely matched Gradient Boost, with values ranging from approximately 72.9% to

78.81%. Despite having a similar ensemble-based approach, RFutilizes bagging, which diversifies the training process, making it effective for the dataset used in this study. However, its performance slightly trailed behind Gradient Boost, especially in more complex packet groups, due to its inability to minimize bias as effectively as Gradient Boost's boosting technique.

The SVM displayed moderate performance, with accuracy values ranging from approximately 46.49% to 66.01%. The SVM's linear kernel struggled to fully capture the non-linear relationships present in the inter-packet timing data, which resulted in lower performance when compared to ensemble-based models like GB and RF. GNB, with an accuracy range of 35.51% to 36.39%, exhibited the lowest performance across all models, primarily due to its inherent assumption of feature independence, which is often violated in packet timing data.

**F1-Score of ML Models.** The F1-Score analysis, as illustrated in Figs. 7 and 8, provided additional insights into the overall performance of the models. The F1-Score takes both precision and recall into account, offering a balanced view of model performance in detecting covert channels.

The GB classification model showed F1-Scores ranging from 0.55 to 0.95 across different data types and packet groups, indicating its superior ability to maintain a high balance of precision and recall. Particularly, the model showed excellent performance in marketing data classification, achieving F1-Scores of up to 0.95 for larger packet groups. This can be attributed to the more straightforward nature of marketing data, where timing variations can be more consistently captured and classified.

RF exhibited a similar trend, with F1-Scores ranging from 0.55 to 0.94 across different data types. RF demonstrated slightly better results in the Human Resources category compared to Gradient Boost, particularly in smaller packet groups, which suggests its robustness and ability to handle variance effectively when the available data is more limited.

The SVM model, with F1-Scores ranging from 0.30 to 0.78, struggled primarily in the financial category, indicating its lower effectiveness in distinguishing between legitimate and covert timing patterns. The Gaussian NB model showed poor F1-Scores across all categories, ranging from 0 to 0.53, due to its inability to handle complex, non-linear relationships in the data.

To provide a clearer view of the subtle differences between GB and Random Forest, Fig. 9 presents a comparative analysis of their F1-Scores for different data types. Both models displayed high F1-Scores for Financial and Marketing data, with GB slightly outperforming Random Forest. In contrast, RFhad a slight edge over GB for Human Resources data. This indicates that both models are highly capable of capturing timing anomalies, but their relative effectiveness can depend on the data type and complexity of the communication patterns.

Based on our findings, Gradient Boost Classification has shown higher accuracy and F1-Scores when compared to other ML models. We conducted an evaluation of the packet grouping size and its relationship to the data type. As depicted in Fig. 10, we observed that the precision of data detection based on

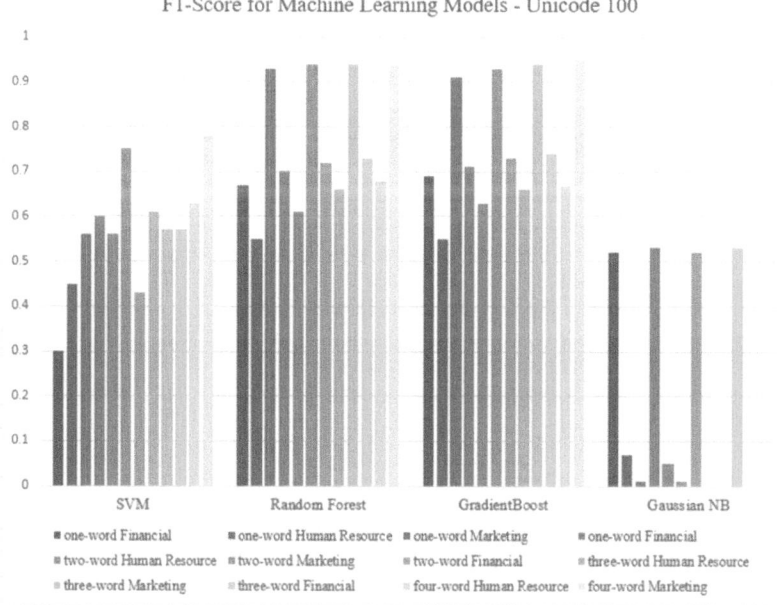

F1-Score for Machine Learning Models - Unicode 100

Legend:
- one-word Financial
- two-word Human Resource
- three-word Marketing
- one-word Human Resource
- two-word Marketing
- three-word Financial
- one-word Marketing
- two-word Financial
- four-word Human Resource
- one-word Financial
- three-word Human Resource
- four-word Marketing

**Fig. 8.** F1-Score of ML Models for Unicode 100

the number of words—one, two, three, or four—corresponds to higher F1-Scores. This can likely be attributed to the additional characters used in training and detection, which ultimately results in better precision in detection. Moreover, marketing and financial data exhibit better F1-Scores, possibly due to their numerical communication being more prevalent and less reliant on character-driven communication.

The results of this study shows the importance of ensemble methods, particularly GB and Random Forest, in detecting CTCs. Both models excelled in handling the diverse data types used in this research, with GB slightly outperforming RFdue to its iterative approach that reduces bias and variance effectively. Compared to existing rule-based detection methods, the ML models used in this study demonstrate significant advancements in detection capabilities. Traditional rule-based approaches rely heavily on predefined patterns and struggle to adapt to subtle timing variations, making them less effective against sophisticated attacks. In contrast, ensemble models like GB and RFlearn from the data, enabling them to adaptively identify covert patterns that may not follow any static rule. The implications of these findings are considerable for organizations aiming to bolster their cybersecurity defenses. Implementing ML models, particularly ensemble techniques, can substantially improve the detection of covert channels in real-time network monitoring systems. Organizations are encouraged to consider using GB and RF as part of their intrusion detection systems, especially for environments with diverse communication patterns.

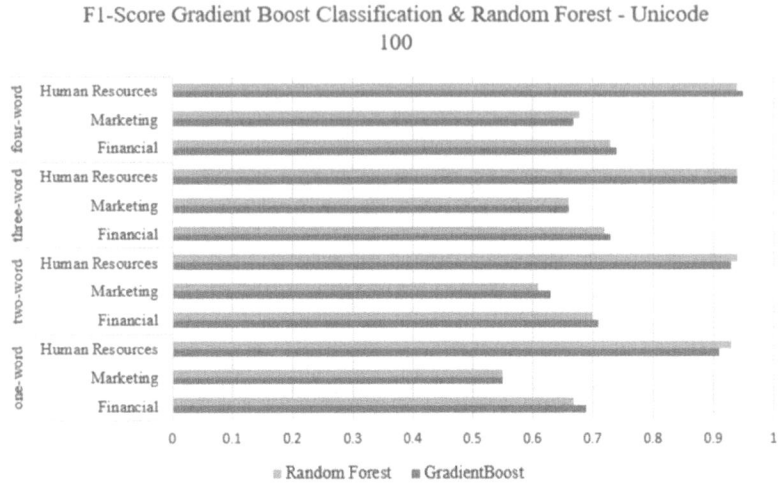

**Fig. 9.** F1-Score of GB Classification and RF for Unicode 100

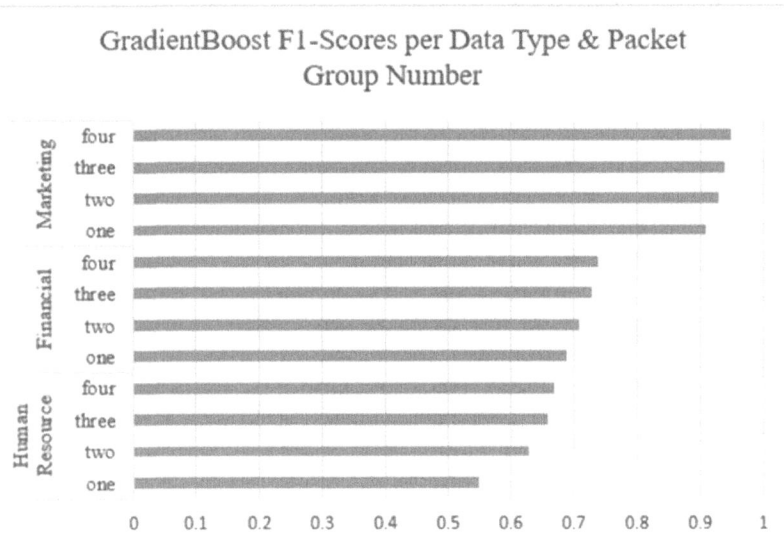

**Fig. 10.** GB Classification F1-Scores per Data Type and Packet Group Number

## 5    Conclusion and Future Work

In previous experiments, a wide variety of statistical and ML techniques have been employed to study the detection of CTCs. This paper introduced an approach that integrates ML techniques for identifying the source of data leaks within organizations using CTC detection. Specifically, the proposed method leverages inter-packet timing information along with ML models to classify the type of leaked data. The results demonstrated that Gradient Boost Classification achieved an accuracy range of approximately 73% to 78%, with RF (RFM) also achieving similarly high accuracy across different packet group sizes. These results indicate that ensemble-based ML models, such as Gradient Boost and Random Forest, are highly effective in identifying and classifying CTCs, thereby highlighting the applicability of ML techniques in augmenting traditional cybersecurity measures. Moreover, the study underscores the importance of leveraging more sophisticated models for detecting intricate covert channels that evade static detection methods. By utilizing interarrival time information as a core feature, the methodology presented in this research offers a novel and promising direction for determining the origins of data leaks with improved precision. Compared to existing rule-based approaches, ML-based detection proved to be more adaptable and capable of learning from complex patterns, making it well-suited for identifying sophisticated data leak mechanisms. However, there are still several avenues for improvement and future work. Future research should focus on further refining the ML models to enhance their generalizability and robustness. Expanding the dataset to include more realistic and diverse data types, including real-world network traffic, would be beneficial in increasing the reliability of the models. Additionally, exploring deep learning models, such as recurrent neural networks or transformers, could potentially provide enhanced performance by capturing temporal relationships more effectively. Our work provides foundational insights into the detection of CTCs using ML and presents a viable pathway for the proactive prevention of organizational data leaks. The results suggest that adopting ML techniques for CTC detection can significantly improve the accuracy and adaptability of intrusion detection systems, thereby helping organizations mitigate sophisticated data breaches.

### 5.1    Limitations and Future Directions

Despite the promising results, this study has several limitations that should be acknowledged. One major limitation is the use of synthetic data generated using Unicode conversions to simulate CTCs. While this approach provides a controlled environment to evaluate model performance, it may not fully replicate the complexity of real-world network traffic. Future research should focus on evaluating these models with real-world network data to determine their practical applicability and robustness.

Another limitation is the restricted number of ML models evaluated in this study. The inclusion of deep learning models, such as recurrent neural networks (RNNs) or transformer-based architectures, could provide further insights into whether these models could outperform traditional ensemble methods in detecting CTCs.

Future research should also consider the impact of additional data types, such as medical or legal information, which may exhibit different characteristics compared to the categories considered in this study. Such an expansion would allow for a more comprehensive understanding of the capabilities and limitations of ML models in detecting covert channels across various domains.

**Acknowledgments.** The authors would like to thank their collaborators for their invaluable support and contributions throughout the research process. Special thanks are extended to the Southern Illinois University Carbondale and Eastern Michigan University research groups for providing the infrastructure necessary for data collection and analysis. This work is a collaborative effort conducted under the supervision of faculty from Eastern Michigan University.

**Disclosure of Interests.** The authors declare no competing interests relevant to the content of this article. All authors contributed to this work and have no financial or personal relationships that could influence the results reported in this paper.

# References

1. Okhravi, H., Bak, S., King, S.T.: Design, implementation and evaluation of covert channel attacks. In: 2010 IEEE International Conference on Technologies for Homeland Security (HST), pp. 481–487. IEEE, November 2010
2. Venkataramani, G., Chen, J., Doroslovacki, M.: Detecting hardware covert timing channels. IEEE Micro **36**(5), 17–27 (2016)
3. Verizon, Arcila, C., Pritam, N., Rowntree, L.: 2023 Data Breach Investigations Report: Frequency and cost of social engineering attacks skyrocket (2023). https://www.verizon.com/about/news/2023-data-breach-investigations-report?msockid=3d0759a516106c310e284caf175f6de6
4. Goher, S.Z., Javed, B., Saqib, N.A.: Covert channel detection: A survey based analysis. In: High Capacity Optical Networks and Emerging/Enabling Technologies, pp. 057–065. IEEE, December 2012
5. Liu, Y., Ghosal, D., Armknecht, F., Sadeghi, A.R., Schulz, S., Katzenbeisser, S.: Hide and seek in time-robust covert timing channels. In: Computer Security-ESORICS 2009: 14th European Symposium on Research in Computer Security. Saint-Malo, France, September 21–23: Proceedings 14, pp. 120–135. Springer, Heidelberg (2009)
6. Classen, J., Schulz, M., Hollick, M.: Practical covert channels for WiFi systems. In: 2015 IEEE Conference on Communications and Network Security (CNS), pp. 209–217. IEEE, September 2015
7. Han, J., Huang, C., Shi, F., Liu, J.: Covert timing channel detection method based on time interval and payload length analysis. Comput. Secur. **97**, 101952 (2020)
8. Chourib, M.: Detecting selected network covert channels using machine learning. In: 2019 International Conference on High Performance Computing & Simulation (HPCS), pp. 582–588. IEEE, July 2019
9. Zander, S., Armitage, G., Branch, P.: Stealthier Inter-packet Timing Covert Channels. In: Domingo-Pascual, J., Manzoni, P., Palazzo, S., Pont, A., Scoglio, C. (eds.) NETWORKING 2011. LNCS, vol. 6640, pp. 458–470. Springer, Heidelberg (2011). https://doi.org/10.1007/978-3-642-20757-0_36

10. Xu, G., Yang, W., Huang, L.: Supervised learning framework for covert channel detection in LTE-A. IET Inf. Secur. **12**(6), 534–542 (2018)
11. Kumar, M.A., Pai, A.H., Agarwal, J., Christa, S., Prasad, G.M., Saifi, S.: Deep learning model to defend against covert channel attacks in the SDN networks. In: 2023 Advanced Computing and Communication Technologies for High Performance Applications (ACCTHPA), pp. 1–5. IEEE, January 2023
12. Sun, Y., Zhang, L., Zhao, C.: A study of network covert channel detection based on deep learning. In: 2018 2nd IEEE Advanced Information Management, Communicates, Electronic and Automation Control Conference (IMCEC), pp. 637–641. IEEE, May 2018
13. Peña, T. A. (2020). A deep learning approach to detecting covert channels in the domain name system. Capitol Technology University
14. Saeli, S., Bisio, F., Lombardo, P., Massa, D.: DNS covert channel detection via behavioral analysis: a machine learning approach (2020). arXiv preprint arXiv:2010.01582
15. Massimi, F., Benedetto, F.: Deep learning-based detection methods for covert communications in E-health transmissions. In: 2022 45th International Conference on Telecommunications and Signal Processing (TSP), pp. 11–16. IEEE, July 2022
16. Shrestha, P.L., Hempel, M., Rezaei, F., Sharif, H.: A support vector machine-based framework for detection of covert timing channels. IEEE Trans. Dependable Secure Comput. **13**(2), 274–283 (2015)
17. Elsadig, M., Gafar, A.: Packet length covert channel detection: an ensemble machine learning approach. J. Theor. Appl. Inf. Technol. **100**(23), 7035–7043 (2022)
18. Al-Eidi, S., Darwish, O., Chen, Y., Husari, G.: SnapCatch: automatic detection of covert timing channels using image processing and machine learning. IEEE Access **9**, 177–191 (2020)
19. Elsadig, M.A., Gafar, A.: Covert channel detection: machine learning approaches. IEEE Access **10**, 38391–38405 (2022)
20. Darwish, O., Al-shorman, A., AlSobeh, A., Tashtoush, Y.: A Survey Analysis of Internet of Things (IoT) Education Across the Top 25 Universities in the United States. In: International Conference on Advanced Information Networking and Applications, pp. 497–510. Springer, Cham, April 2024
21. Darwish, O., Al-Eidi, S., Al-Shorman, A., AlSobeh, A., Maabreh, M., Tashtoush, Y.: LinguTimeX: Explainable AI of Natural Language Detection in Leakage Information with Covert Timing Channels (2024)
22. Allied Market Research. Utility Vehicle Market Statistics 2030 (2022). https://www.alliedmarketresearch.com/utility-vehicle-market-A12422
23. Willoughby, C., Early, E., Holcomb, R., Reed, K.: Market Research Study: Organic Fruit, Vegetable and Herb Production. FAPC-152, Oklahoma State University, June 2017. https://extension.okstate.edu/fact-sheets/print-publications/fapc-food-and-agricultural-products-center/market-research-study-organic-fruit-vegetable-and-herb-production-fapc-152.pdf
24. Grand View Research. Electric Vehicle Market Size, Report Overview (2023). https://www.grandviewresearch.com/industry-analysis/electric-utility-vehicle-market-report
25. Grand View Research. Paper Straw Market Size & Trends (2023). https://www.grandviewresearch.com/industry-analysis/paper-straw-market
26. Lululemon. Annual Report (2022). https://corporate.lululemon.com/~/media/Files/L/Lululemon/investors/annual-reports/lululemon-2022-annual-report.pdf

27. Postelnyak, M.: Top 10 Sample HR Emails to Employees. Contact Monkey, 12 Feb 2024. https://www.contactmonkey.com/blog/sample-hr-email-to-employees
28. AlSobeh, A.M., Gaber, K., Hammad, M.M., Nuser, M., Shatnawi, A.: Android malware detection using time-aware machine learning approach. Cluster Computing, 1–22 (2024)

# Data Security

# VulMatch: Binary-Level Vulnerability Detection Through Signature

Zian Liu[1(✉)], Shigang Liu[1,2(✉)], Lei Pan[3], Chao Chen[4], Ejaz Ahmed[2], Jun Zhang[1], and Dongxi Liu[2]

[1] Swinburne University of Technology, Melbourne, Australia
{zian.liu,shigangliu,junzhang}@swin.edu.au
[2] Data 61, CSIRO, Canberra, Australia
{Shigang.liu,ejaz.ahmed,dongxi.liu}@data61.csiro.au
[3] Deakin University, Melbourne, Australia
l.pan@deakin.edu.au
[4] Royal Melbourne Institute of Technology, Melbourne, Australia
chao.chen@rmit.edu.au

**Abstract.** Vulnerabilities often recur in software due to code reuse, particularly with widely used third-party libraries. Detecting such vulnerabilities, including 1-day and N-day types, is crucial for cybersecurity. Current methods struggle with poor performance as they focus on detecting patch existence rather than actual vulnerabilities and derive signatures directly from binary code. We propose VulMatch, which generates precise vulnerability signatures by analyzing both source and binary code. Our method outperforms existing tools like Asm2vec and Palmtree and provides better explainability in detection. Tested on over 1,000 vulnerabilities across seven open-source projects and commercial firmware, VulMatch demonstrates superior fine-grained detection capabilities.

**Keywords:** vulnerability detection · software patch · source code · binary code · code signature

## 1 Introduction

Detecting vulnerabilities is essential for software quality, as they often persist due to delayed patches. Learning from existing vulnerabilities helps identify similar issues. While human analysts can manually find bugs by reviewing code, automation is needed due to the vast amount of code and the spread of vulnerabilities through code reuse [1,2,2]. Detecting vulnerabilities in binary code is crucial. This paper explores efficient methods for finding similar vulnerabilities.

Automated detection methods offer significant advantages over manual analysis due to the inherent complexity of binary code, which is notoriously difficult for humans to read and comprehend. Mainstream research can be categorized into three areas: binary code similarity detection [3–8], patch existence detection [3,9–11], and vulnerability signature detection [12–14]. However, similarity-based

© The Author(s), under exclusive license to Springer Nature Singapore Pte Ltd. 2025
H. H. Song et al. (Eds.): NSS 2024, LNCS 15564, pp. 409–427, 2025.
https://doi.org/10.1007/978-981-96-3531-3_20

methods are coarse-grained, producing results at a broad level (e.g., function level). Given that function-level binary code is typically large in scale and vulnerabilities often pertain to just a few instructions, this approach fails to pinpoint the specific instructions that indicate a vulnerability. Patch existence detection generally focuses on kernel binaries with debugging symbols, such as function names, to filter query functions and identify patch signatures. However, this approach is insufficient for determining the presence of vulnerabilities, as the absence of patches does not necessarily indicate a vulnerability. Furthermore, the process of vulnerability signature detection—extracting signatures directly at the binary level—may introduce irrelevant instructions due to compiler optimizations, such as instruction substitution and function inlining. This challenge drives our research into *how to effectively and efficiently identify similar vulnerabilities or bugs based on existing ones.*

We propose a novel approach to generate accurate, fine-grained vulnerability-related signatures to address existing research gaps. We manually preprocess data to include comprehensive CVE information, affected functions, and source code versions. Unlike previous work [12–14] that directly compares binary versions, we generate source-code-level signatures and align them with binary-level signatures using debugging information, allowing us to exclude irrelevant binary code. Our method, VulMatch, processes source code to prevent inlining of vulnerable functions and locates binaries accurately. The source code is only needed for signature generation, not for matching.

To match binary-level signatures, we introduce three signature types (add, delete, and change) and use local control-flow information for fine-grained matching, enhancing signature uniqueness. VulMatch also provides a user interface to help users understand its decisions by displaying matched signatures and scores.

We evaluated VulMatch using seven popular open-source projects with 906 CVEs and 1281 vulnerable functions. VulMatch outperformed state-of-the-art tools Asm2vec and Palmtree by 9% and 6% in top-1 score, and reduced mismatch scores by 80% and 79%, respectively. We also demonstrated VulMatch's practical application in detecting real-world vulnerabilities in commercial firmware and its ability to help users interpret detection results.

This paper makes the following contributions:

- We proposed a novel approach that addresses the key limitations of existing vulnerability signature generation methods by leveraging source-code-level and precise binary signatures. Extensive experiments were conducted to evaluate the effectiveness of our scheme, and the results demonstrated that it outperforms the baseline methods.
- We proposed a novel approach to extract, store, and match the vulnerability-related signatures. We have implemented the approach into a tool called Vul-Match that is open-source and publicly accessible on GitHub[1]. It is capable of detecting real-world similar vulnerabilities.

---

[1] The source code is available upon request and will be made public after the paper is accepted. .

## 2   Related Work

We review related work in three areas: 1) code similarity detection, 2) patch analysis, and 3) vulnerability detection.

### 2.1   Code Similarity Detection

**Binary-Code-Level Similarity Detection.**   Binary-code-level similarity methods can be divided into:

**Learning-Based Methods:** These methods encode binary code into embeddings for comparison. Gemini [15], Vulseeker [16], and Genius [17] use graph embeddings, while Safe [18], InnerEye [19], αDiff [20], Kam1n0 [21], and Asm2Vec [22] generate block or function embeddings.

**Program-Analysis Based Methods:** Methods like Binsequence [23] and Tracy [24] use sequence alignment, SIGMA [25], FOSSIL [26], and Beagle [27] rely on instruction semantics, and Bingo [28] and IMF-SIM [29] use input-output relations. Expose [30], Binhash [31], Binhunt [32], CoP [33], ESH [4], GITZ [5], and XMATCH [8] use symbolic execution for comparison.

**Limitations:** Similarity-based methods assess entire functions, but vulnerabilities may only involve a few lines of code. Thus, while these methods can identify similar functions, they cannot reliably detect vulnerabilities.

### 2.2   Patch Identification and Analysis

FIBER [9] detects patches in Linux kernel binaries using symbolic execution. PDiff [10] also uses symbolic execution and memory status to identify patches, accounting for customizations and build configurations. Spain [3] identifies patches through binary-level semantics and summarizes patch and vulnerability patterns. Patchscope [11] uses memory-object-centric methods and dynamic execution for patch detection.

**Limitations:** These methods assume function names are known or that similar functions have been pre-selected. They focus on detecting patches rather than vulnerabilities, as the absence of a patch does not necessarily indicate a vulnerability.

### 2.3   Vulnerability Detection

VMPBL [12] uses a database of vulnerable and patched functions to differentiate between pre-patch and post-patch functions. VIVA [13] compares binaries from before and after a patch to retrieve vulnerability signatures and uses pre-filtering and instruction clustering for detection. BINXRAY [14] analyzes both pre-patch and post-patch binaries to identify and store vulnerability-related instructions as signatures, then queries functions against these signatures.

**Limitations:** These methods often misinterpret differences between binary versions as vulnerabilities, leading to the inclusion of irrelevant instructions in signatures.

# 3  Methodology

This section presents the design of VulMatch. VulMatch's four components are shown as Fig. 1.

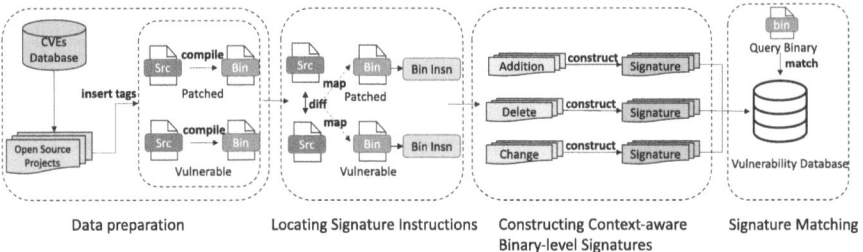

**Fig. 1.** VulMatch consists of four steps: Data Preparation, Locating Signature Instructions, Constructing Context-aware Binary-level Signatures, and Signature Matching. *Src* is short for source code. *Bin* is short for binary code. *Insn* is short for instruction.

## 3.1  Data Preparation

We collect many already well-studied vulnerabilities from several publicly-available open source projects to build the vulnerability database. According to [13], vulnerabilities tend to be fixed in new versions of software releases. Thus, the vulnerability-related versions consist of the last pre-patching and the first post-patching versions. The last pre-patching and the first post-patching version will be used later to extract the signatures. We download all the vulnerability-related versions for each project and record each CVE's information. Specifically, for each CVE, we record its related vulnerable source code file name and the vulnerability-related functions within them. We also record each CVE's affect versions for later preparing testing binaries for evaluation.

**Challenges:** Not all vulnerability-related functions exist in the compiled binary code due to the automatic function-inlining behavior. Automatic function-inlining refers to merging a function `FuncA` into another function `FuncB` that calls back `FuncA`. If vulnerable functions are inlined, it would be challenging to locate them in the binary code. This case holds even if we manually turn off the function-inline option during compilation. Hence, it is challenging for us to generate binary signatures.

**Solution:** We need to ensure that the database contains no inlined functions in the compiled binaries. VulMatch automatically analyzes the source code files and edits the functions in the source code files to inform the compiler not to inline the function. Technically, VulMatch inserts a non-inline tag `__attribute__((noinline))` before each vulnerable function in all related versions to preserve the tagged functions in the compiled binary code. For each CVE,

VulMatch loads the CVE's information to retrieve its vulnerable source code files along with the corresponding vulnerable functions. Then for each related version (i.e., the last pre-patching version and the first post-patching), VulMatch analyzes the vulnerable source code file to locate the vulnerable functions and automatically insert no-inline tags. Finally, we compile these versions into binaries with the same default compilation options.

### 3.2   Locating Signature Instructions and Challenges

We generate signatures related to vulnerabilities and patches using the source codes and compiled binary codes. For each vulnerable function, we generate its signatures in two steps—1) generate source-level vulnerability-related instructions, 2) locate vulnerability-related binary instructions through mapping.

**Generating Source-Level Vulnerability-Related Instructions.** We prepare the last pre-patching and the first post-patching versions using the information we retrieved in Subsect. 3.1. Subsequently, we generate vulnerability and patch-related signatures on the source code level. We use the `diff` tool[2] to extract source-code-level patched instructions. There are three types of source-code-level patches in the `diff` outputs. 1) Added instructions that are used in the patched version and absent in the vulnerable version, as shown in Fig. 3a. 2) Deleted instructions that are removed from the vulnerable version and absent in the patched version as shown in Fig. 3b. 3) Changed instructions that are updated from the vulnerable version to the patched version, as shown in Fig. 3c. The changed instructions usually share the same context instructions among the two versions.

**Locating Vulnerability-Related Binary Instructions Through Mapping.** We use the source-to-binary mapping with the binary's debugging information to locate the source code's corresponding assembly instructions. Although VulMatch employs the simple idea, there are practical challenges primarily in two aspects.

1. Asymmetric source-binary mapping: it is challenging to map source line changes in the source code files (e.g., .cpp or .c file) to the corresponding binary file,
2. Identification of vulnerability-specific source lines.

**Two Challenges to Map Source Code Files:**

- **Challenge1: Asymmetric source-binary mapping.** Not all the source code lines have a matching binary code instruction. For example, Fig. 2 shows an example of missing mapping between source code and binary code. Lines 1226 and 1228 declare new variables but do not map to any binary instructions

---

[2] https://man7.org/linux/man-pages/man1/diff.1.html.

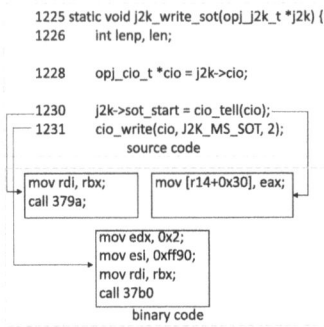

**Fig. 2.** An example of a missing match between source code and binary code. The first two lines 1226 and 1228 do not have any mapping instructions in binary code because the assembly code does not need to specify the type information for functions and variables. Line 1230 maps to two different basic blocks. Line 1231 maps to one basic block. This example is extracted from openjpeg version 1.5.0.

because the variables at the binary level are directly used without explicit type declaration due to the binary code convention.

- **Solution1:** Generally, the source code lines declaring new variables (e.g., line 1226 and 1228 in Fig. 2) do not have a mapping binary code because of binary code convention. However, it does not affect finding the binary signatures. We further elaborate on the following two cases: 1) If a new variable declaration is added, it must be used later in some other source code lines, implying that the correlated source lines still exist after diffing source codes of the patched and vulnerable functions. 2) If a variable's name is changed, the source code referring to that variable must change, which is detected by diffing the source codes. For a variable with type change (e.g., change from a defined structure `structA` to an updated structure `structA'`), source code lines using that variable tend to change because of different type usage (e.g., defining different fields in the different structure type).

- **Challenge2: Identification of vulnerability-specific source lines.** The add type signature is challenging to represent. Because the add type signature only exists in patched versions, the added instructions imply the existence of a patch rather than the vulnerability itself. Therefore, there are no direct vulnerable instructions from the vulnerable version. For example, Fig. 3a shows an example of the add type signature in the source-code level. Green lines (lines B2 to B6 on the right-hand side) are the added lines in the patched version, and grey lines are the unchanged lines across the two versions. The absence of the green lines in the vulnerable version implies a vulnerability. However, other random functions may lack added instructions without the same vulnerability. Therefore, the lack of added instructions cannot be directly used as the vulnerable signature. We need to infer the vulnerability signature in the vulnerable version to detect vulnerability existence.

– **Solution2:** To represent add type vulnerability signature, our solution is to focus on the context. For example, lines A1 and B1 in Fig. 3a are unchanged in the two versions. A1 flows to A2 in the vulnerable version, while B1 flows to B2 in the patched version. The control flow from the unchanged instruction A1 to the following instruction A2 is regarded as the vulnerability signature in VulMatch. Conversely, the control flow from B1 to B2 is regarded as a patch signature. Since the added instructions are inserted at some point within the function, they must have identical context instructions (e.g., A1 and B1 in the example) with different subsequent instructions (e.g., A2 and B2). For simplicity, we explain this concept at the source code level. But we extract add type signatures at the binary level. For more details refer to Subsect. 3.3.

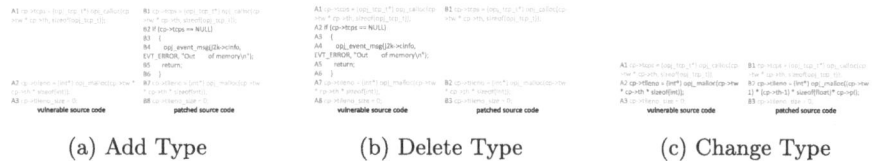

|  (a) Add Type  |  (b) Delete Type  |  (c) Change Type  |

**Fig. 3.** Examples of add, delete and change types. Green lines are the newly added or changed instructions in the patched version. Red lines are the deleted or changed lines in the vulnerable version. Grey lines are the intact lines. (Color figure online)

### 3.3   Constructing Context-Aware Binary-Level Signatures

We construct the binary-code-level signatures before storing them in the database for signature matching. Simply storing the sets of instructions in the database as vulnerable signatures and detecting those signatures' existence in the query binary code may not be beneficial. As mentioned in Subsect. 3.2, added instructions in the patched binary cannot directly be used to form a vulnerability signature because it only indicates patches. The term *context* refers to the adjacent blocks' instructions of the vulnerable binary instructions. The vulnerable binary instructions are usually short. If we generate signatures by simply concatenating those instructions into a sequence, the signature may carry inadequate information to prevent false positives. Therefore, we propose to form new structures by combining the context and the vulnerable instructions. Our newly combined structure gives the signature adequate uniqueness to boost the performance of signature matching. We propose to build the context around the vulnerable signature instructions through generalization to reduce false positives. For instance, the extracted signature instructions size is small (e.g., only 3 instructions). Checking the existence of signature instructions without context information makes the signature not unique enough, leading to excessive mismatches (false positives).

Since the added instructions in the patched version have blocks directly preceding them, the counterpart preceding blocks in the vulnerable version should have different instructions following them. Therefore, we capture local control flows around the preceding blocks in the vulnerable version to represent the vulnerability signature.

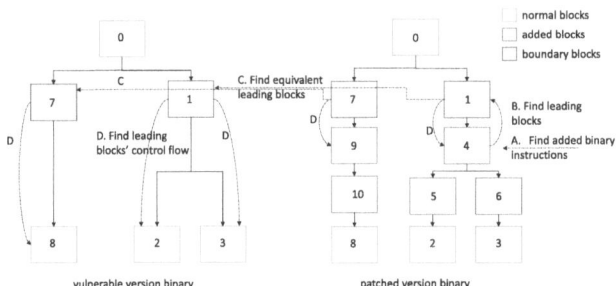

**Fig. 4.** An example of binary-code-level add signature and the steps to extract the corresponding binary signature.

We propose to generate the binary-level signature with control-flow information. Firstly, we define several terms.

- **Add Batch**. When newly added source code snippets are mapped to binary code blocks, the newly added blocks could either be directly connected to each other (e.g., block 4 and 5 in Fig. 4) or separate from each other (e.g., block 4 and 9 in Fig. 4). An **add batch** is made up of the added blocks that are strongly connected to each other. As shown in Fig. 4, block $(4, 5, 6)$ and block $(9, 10)$ are two add batches.
- **Leading Blocks**. The **leading block** is the unchanged block immediately preceding an added batch. As shown in Fig. 4, blocks 1 and 7 are two leading basic blocks because they immediately precede two add batches.
- **Parents-children Structure**. We define a parents-children structure to store the control flow and literal information for add and change signatures. Specifically, in one parents-children structure, we have an initial block from the function as the parent. We include the chosen block's children blocks in the function into the parents-children structure. Conversely, we can select a child block before including its parents to establish a parents-children structure.
- **Block List Structure**. We define a block list structure to store only the literal information when control-flow information is not available or unnecessary. In one block list structure, we store all the vulnerable binary instructions grouped by blocks.

We store both vulnerable and patch signatures. Vulnerability signatures are generated from the instructions in the vulnerable version. This signature type consists of parents-children structures or block list structures. Patch signature consists of the instructions that only exist in the patched version and only consists of the block list structure. Patch signature is used to reduce the false positives further. Despite the vulnerability match score, the patch signature directly implies a patch. The vulnerable signatures contain three types: 1) add, 2) delete, and 3) change. Those signatures have different structures to capture different information because different signature type has different nature. We capture various information for different signature types to enrich the signature information.

For the **add type signature**, to locate the add type binary signatures, we **A)** retrieve the added binary instructions in the patched version (i.e., the output of the operations in Subsect. 3.2). **B)** We find the leading basic blocks in the patched version binary. **C)** We find its counterpart leading basic block in the vulnerable version binary. **D)** We include the vulnerable binary's leading basic blocks' children blocks as a parents-children structure in the signature.

For the **delete type signature**, we directly locate the mapping binary instructions and store those instructions into block list structures as delete signatures since the deleted instructions usually map to multiple blocks. Since the mapped blocks are usually sufficient in amount, lexical information already makes the signature unique for matching. If we record their control-flow information we will use excessive parents-children structures. We exclude any patch signature for this signature type because the patched version does not have any unique instruction that does not exist in the vulnerable version.

The **change type signature** has two categories, including one-block-change and many-blocks-change. Many-block-change means the changed instructions are distributed in multiple blocks (i.e., distributed in neighbor blocks or blocks that are not directly connected). One-block-change is the case if all the changed instructions are accommodated in one block in the binary code.

**Many-Block-Change:** If the change is many-block-change, we will need to record both control-flow and lexical information in the database since the change sites are usually small in size. This category of signature provides rich information as it contains adequate lexical information (i.e., binary instructions) from multiple blocks or control-flow information between those blocks. Therefore, for each block in a many-block-changes structure, if its neighbor (i.e., either predecessor or successor block) is a change block, we include this neighbor to form a parents-children structure. If none of its neighbor blocks is changed, all changed instructions are grouped as a block in the signature. Note that if the many-block-change contains a deeper level other than two levels (i.e., the level of parents-children structure), we use multiple parents-children structures to cover all the strongly connected blocks. For example, if block $A$ flows to block $B$, and block $B$ flows to block $C$, we will have two parents-children structures to cover the flow from $A$ to $B$ and from $B$ to $A$ respectively.

**One-Block-Change:** Conversely, if the change is a one-block-change, the information is limited because we only have lexical information without control flow information. Thus, we need to add more control flow information to enhance the signature and reduce potential mismatch. We include its parent blocks in a parents-children structure to enhance the signature. We include the children blocks in the parents-children structure if it has no parent block.

**Patch Signatures:** We generate signatures for patches. After we generate vulnerable signatures as above, we diff the vulnerability-related sites in both versions. We identify the instructions that only exist in the patched version and store it using a block list structure as the patch signature.

### 3.4   Signature Matching

We detect the vulnerability's existence by using both vulnerability and patched signatures. For the add signature, we search for each vulnerable parents-children structure in the query binary code. Then, we check for the existence of a patch signature. If a patch is found, the function is directly considered patched. For the delete signature, we search for the existence of the blocks from the block list structures. We do not match patch signatures for the delete type because the delete type does not has unique instructions in the patched version. For the change signature, we search for the existence of each parents-children structure or block list structure in the query binary code. Subsequently, we check the existence of the patch signature. If the patch is found through a query, the function is considered patched (denoted by $P = 1$); otherwise, $P = 0$.

We propose a measurement of the vulnerability existence score ($Sim$) to demonstrate the probability of the query function containing a given vulnerable signature. Specifically, a final score of vulnerability existence is calculated as follows:

$$Sim = \begin{cases} \dfrac{\Sigma_{i=1}^{len(S)} Matched(S[i])}{\Sigma_{i=1}^{len(S)} Total(S[i])} & \text{if } P = 0 \\ 0 & \text{if } P = 1 \end{cases}$$

where $Sim$ represents the result similarity score to the vulnerable signature. $S$ represents one vulnerable signature. A signature consists of one or multiple structures (a structure is either parents-children structure or block list structure). $len()$ calculates the number of structures regarding an input signature. $S[i]$ represents a structure. $Matched()$ calculates the number of instructions matched between the input structure and the given query binary function. If the structure is parents-children structure $PS$, $Matched()$ searches through the query binary to find the similar parents-children structure $PS'$ with the maximum similarity. Then $Matched()$ counts the instructions shared between $PS$ and $PS'$. If the structure is a block list structure, $Matched()$ finds all the blocks with the maximum similarity to each block in the block list structure before $Total()$ aggregates the total instruction number of the input structure.

## 4   Evaluation

### 4.1   Experimental Setup

**Data Collection:** We collected source code for seven open-source projects, including OpenSSL, OpenJPEG, FFmpeg, TCPDUMP, LibTIFF, cURL, and

LibPNG. These projects are selected from diverse domains like communication protocols, image processing tools, and network traffic analyzers. After manual analysis, we extracted 906 CVEs corresponding to 1,281 vulnerable functions. Table 3 in the Appendix section lists the versions, application domains, CVE information, vulnerability, and code-related information.

**Baseline Tool Selection and Testbed:** We prepared two state-of-the-art baseline tools Asm2Vec [22] and PalmTree [34], because of their popularity and excellent performance in vulnerability detection. We ran VulMatch and Asm2vec on an Intel NUC kit (NUC8i5BEH) with an i5-8259U processor and 16 GB memory. Since Palmtree is a deep learning-based approach and requires intensive GPU power, we ran it on an accelerator cluster of high-performance computer (HPC) systems with 456 NVidia Tesla P100, 114 Dual Xeon 14-core E5-2690, and 256 GB memory.

**Project Compilation:** As mentioned in Subsect. 3.1, we compile all the versions relating to each vulnerability (i.e., the last version before patching and the first version after patching) of the project to generate binary code instances. Depending on the project, we use the projects' default compiling flags, either -O2 or -O3. For each project, we use identical compiling flags for building. So when we diff the compiled binary code to generate vulnerability and patch signatures, the compiling options are the same. This minimizes the differences in binary codes and is the common practice as [13,14] to help find vulnerable instructions. At compile time, we set the debugging symbol option to acquire source-binary instructions mapping that will serve as ground truth.

**Research Questions:** In the first experiment, we compare VulMatch with two state-of-the-art baseline tools to evaluate how well they find known binary code vulnerabilities. In the second experiment, we test how VulMatch interprets the found similar vulnerabilities and how VulMatch assists humans in understanding the reason it considers the query binary vulnerable. In the third experiment, we match vulnerabilities in real-world firmware binaries to test how VulMatch work in a real-world application. In the fourth experiment, we investigate how diverse types of proposed vulnerability signatures (i.e., add, delete, and change) distribute.

## 4.2   Performance Metrics

**Top-1 Score:** Each vulnerable function was patched after a certain version. And all the versions or a range of function versions are vulnerable before that specific version. Therefore, we select a vulnerable binary function $f$ from binary code $\mathcal{B}$ to test how the tools discover similar vulnerabilities. We construct the vulnerable and patch signature of $f$ from the last pre-patch version and the first post-patch version and store the signature in the database. To test how well the signature in the database can be matched, we prepare a binary version (denoted by $\mathcal{B}_v$) containing the vulnerable version of $f$ (denoted as $fv$), and a patched version binary (denoted by $\mathcal{B}_p$) containing the patched version of $f$ (denoted as $fp$) for testing purpose.

$\mathcal{B}_V$ and $\mathcal{B}_P$ should differ from the versions that generate the binary signature. $\mathcal{B}_v$ and $\mathcal{B}_p$ contain many functions, including the vulnerable and patched version of $f$, and other functions. For vulnerable function $f$, we inspect each function $fi$ in both $\mathcal{B}_v$ and $\mathcal{B}_p$ to derive a match score indicating the percentage that $fi$ is similar to $f$'s vulnerable signatures. $fv$ in $\mathcal{B}_v$ should have the highest score among all other functions; conversely, $fp$ and all other functions in $\mathcal{B}_p$ should have low match score. It is reasonable for $fp$ in $\mathcal{B}_p$ to have a higher score than other functions in $\mathcal{B}_p$ since $fp$ is patched from $f$. Nevertheless, $fp$ should be lower than $fv$'s score. We use the top-1 score to measure the rate of ranking ground truth vulnerable function in the first place.

We provide a simple example of how the top-1 score works in VulMatch. Suppose there are ten vulnerable functions, each with a vulnerable and a patched binary version $B_v$ and $B_p$. $B_v$ contains $fv$. $B_p$ contains $fp$. Both $B_v$ and $B_p$ also contain many other functions. We match the vulnerable signature of $f$ in the database with each function in both $B_v$ and $B_p$. If vulnerable function $fv$ has the highest score, we rank $fv$ at the top-1 place. If 8 out of 10 vulnerable functions rank their testing vulnerable version $fv$ in the top-1 place, then the top-1 score is 0.8.

**Mismatch Score:** Merely referring to the top-1 score partly reflects how accurately the tools distinguish ground truth vulnerable functions from other functions. However, the top-1 score cannot well demonstrate how the tools consider the non-ground-truth vulnerable function as non-vulnerable. A tool that identifies vulnerable functions well with a high top-1 score may not identify non-vulnerable functions as not vulnerable well. If non-vulnerable functions have extremely close match scores to vulnerable functions, this leads to a high mismatch score.

For instance, some tools may output a similarity score of the ground truth vulnerable function as 0.98, while the score for the ground truth patched function or another random function is 0.97. In this case, even though the ground truth function is ranked first, the two scores are too close to reaching the final verdict. The ground truth vulnerable function should have a significantly higher score than any other function. If any non-ground-truth vulnerable function has a score close to or higher than the ground-truth vulnerable function, the function receives a non-zero **mismatch score**.

The mismatch score indicates the reliability of the top-1 score. To keep track of the mismatch score of each vulnerable function, the $\alpha$ parameter is a threshold to activate the mismatch score. We consider it a mismatch for any non-vulnerable function with a threshold above $S_{GV} - \alpha$, where $S_{GV}$ denotes the ground-truth vulnerable function score. If $S_{GV}$ has an extremely low score (e.g., near zero), any non-vulnerable function having a score close to or above $S_{GV}$ is not considered a mismatch. Because the root failure occurs in detecting a vulnerability function rather than non-vulnerable functions, we set $S_{GV} < 0.6$ as an extremely low score.

## 4.3   Vulnerability Detection

Since VulMatch aims to find replicated known vulnerabilities, and the two baseline tools Asm2vec and Palmtree find vulnerabilities based on binary code similarity, we compare VulMatch with those two baseline tools to test their performance on the first objective—finding replicate vulnerabilities. Moreover, the query binary is non-deterministic in real-world scenarios since it could be either a vulnerable or patched version. Thus, it is vital to the second objective—differentiate vulnerable functions from other non-vulnerable functions. Therefore, we design this experiment to test these two goals concurrently.

**Vulnerable Function Detection Accuracy:** Table 1 lists top-1 scores of VulMatch, Asm2vec, and Palmtree on the seven selected projects. Regarding the top-1 score, VulMatch outperforms both baseline methods in six projects and is marginally lower than Palmtree on OpenSSL. VulMatch ranks multiple testing vulnerable functions at the top after it extracts accurate vulnerability signatures and matches vulnerable and patched signatures. It is because VulMatch matches the fine-grained vulnerability-related instruction (signature) rather than coarsely matches the whole function. Since the vulnerability signature tends to be small snippets of instructions, matching the whole function similarity fails to detect such fine-grained information.

**Table 1.** Top-1 scores of seven open-source projects.

| Project | Openjpeg | FFmpeg | Tcpdump | Libtiff | curl | LibPNG | OpenSSL |
|---------|----------|--------|---------|---------|------|--------|---------|
| Asm2vec | 0.673 | 0.643 | 0.702 | 0.675 | 0.821 | 0.815 | 0.536 |
| Palmtree | 0.573 | 0.643 | 0.702 | 0.779 | 0.840 | 0.837 | **0.691** |
| VulMatch | **0.791** | **0.714** | **0.786** | **0.825** | **0.872** | **0.859** | 0.673 |

**Non-vulnerable Function Detection Accuracy:** Table 2 lists mismatch measurements of VulMatch, Asm2vec, and Palmtree with respect to different $\alpha$ values. In the mismatch score perspective, VulMatch achieved the best result with the lowest mismatch score, indicating that VulMatch differentiates the vulnerable version and patched versions with the highest confidence level. Conversely, Asm2vec and Palmtree had high mismatch scores, indicating that many decisions between vulnerable and patched versions were made with low confidence. Since $\alpha$ denotes the threshold distance to the vulnerable version and $S_{GV} < 0.6$, we vary $\alpha$ between 0.1 and 0.4 to obtain positive mismatch scores. Our evaluation results empirically suggest that $alpha = 0.1$ yields the best result.

For FFmpeg, VulMatch achieved mismatch scores as 0 compared with baseline methods' mismatch scores of approximately 1. For other projects, there are huge contrasts between VulMatch and baseline tools. VulMatch outperforms two baseline tools because VulMatch derives vulnerable signatures from the vulnerable and patched versions. Another reason is VulMatch matches the fine-grained vulnerability signature rather than the coarse whole function similarity. Therefore, subtle vulnerability-related differences are accurately identified, which is superior to whole-function-level similarity matching.

### 4.4 Interpretability

When finding vulnerable functions, a tool's interpretability is as important as its high accuracy. In practice, vulnerability-detecting tools assist human experts in making a final verdict. Therefore, a good tool should clearly explain why a query result is considered vulnerable. Unfortunately, the state-of-the-art baselines fail to provide good interpretation functionality. Palmtree outputs only the overall similarity score between the query function and the functions stored in its database. In addition to the overall similarity score, Asm2vec lists similar instructions for the query. Asm2vec fails to highlight the vulnerability-related instructions; instead, it highlights the whole function as different or similar.

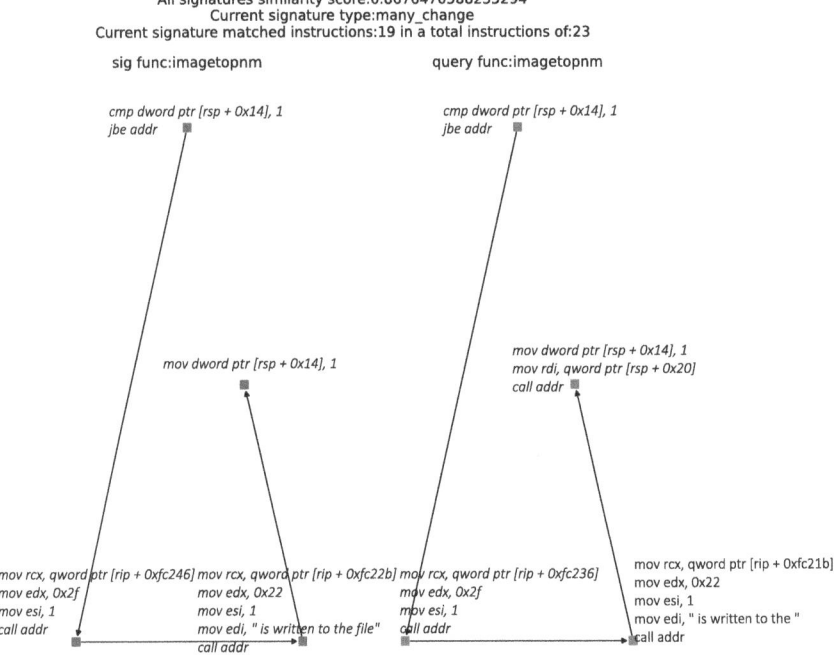

**Fig. 5.** Interpreting a `many-block-change signature` matching. The left-hand side is the generated vulnerable signature, and the right-hand side is the matched instructions in the query binary.

Figure 5 demonstrates an example of VulMatch's interpretability. This example is a `many-block-change` vulnerable signature matching selected from CVE-2016-9117. The signature (left-hand side) was extracted from the `imagetopnm`

**Table 2.** Mis-match scores of seven open-source projects. A stands for Asm2vec, P for Palmtree, and V for VulMatch. A lower score indicates a better performance.

| $\alpha$ | Project | Openjpeg | FFmpeg | Tcpdump | Libtiff | curl | LibPNG | OpenSSL |
|---|---|---|---|---|---|---|---|---|
| 0.1 | A | 0.700 | 0.929 | 0.881 | 0.968 | 0.949 | 0.924 | 0.945 |
| | P | 0.909 | 0.821 | 0.905 | 0.955 | 0.750 | 0.946 | 0.936 |
| | V | **0.091** | **0.000** | **0.190** | **0.162** | **0.038** | **0.098** | **0.118** |
| 0.2 | A | 0.836 | 0.964 | 0.988 | 1.000 | 1.000 | 1.000 | 1.000 |
| | P | 0.982 | 1.000 | 0.940 | 1.000 | 0.885 | 1.000 | 0.955 |
| | V | **0.127** | **0.000** | **0.286** | **0.260** | **0.103** | **0.152** | **0.127** |
| 0.3 | A | 0.900 | 1.000 | 1.000 | 1.000 | 1.000 | 1.000 | 1.000 |
| | P | 0.991 | 1.000 | 0.940 | 1.000 | 0.974 | 1.000 | 0.955 |
| | V | **0.155** | **0.000** | **0.429** | **0.312** | **0.147** | **0.163** | **0.182** |
| 0.4 | A | 0.962 | 1.000 | 1.000 | 1.000 | 1.000 | 1.000 | 1.000 |
| | P | 1.000 | 1.000 | 0.976 | 1.000 | 1.000 | 1.000 | 0.964 |
| | V | **0.173** | **0.000** | **0.500** | **0.383** | **0.224** | **0.196** | **0.218** |

function with versions 2.1.2 and 2.2.0. The matched instructions (right-hand side) in the query binary are from version 2.1.1. For the selected signature, there are 23 instructions in all structures, and 19 of them are matched. The unmatched instructions mov rcx, qword ptr [rip + 0xfc246], mov rcx, qword ptr [rip + 0xfc22b] on the left-hand side and the instructions mov rcx, qword ptr [rip + 0xfc236], mov rcx, qword ptr [rip + 0xfc21b] on the right-hand side have different offsets due to structure fields are changed. Note that this vulnerable function has multiple signatures, and we omit others for clarity. The overall match score combining all signatures exceeds 0.867, indicating VulMatch's high confidence level for the verdict.

## 4.5  Real-World Vulnerability Detection

Since IoT devices' firmware reuse open-source projects, they often contain 1-day vulnerabilities. In this experiment, we evaluate how effectively VulMatch detects a real-world 1-day vulnerability in an IoT device's firmware. We select four IoT devices' firmware instances (i.e., DCS-3511, DCS-6517, DCS-7517, and DCS-6915) collected in the wild. We manually analyze the firmware and prepare 36 ground-truth 1-day vulnerabilities, including 52 vulnerable functions. We generate the vulnerability binary code signatures and store them in the database. For each vulnerable signature in the database, we detect it against each function $Fi$ in the firmware and assign a matching score for $Fi$. If the $Fi$ with the top score is the ground-truth vulnerable function, a vulnerable function is correctly detected. VulMatch correctly detects 40 out of 52 (77%) vulnerable functions. Again, the high accuracy in finding real-world replicate vulnerabilities is due to VulMatch's concentration on the fine-grained vulnerable instructions along with the local control-flow information. We manually analyzed the failed case and found two main failure causes: 1) The binary code contains other function(s) with high similarity to the vulnerable one. 2) The testing binary code contains different structure fields thus at the binary level, the offsets of the structures are different from the signature in the database. For example, [esi+0x40] changed to [esi+0x48] where esi is the memory address of the structure. The same field changed from offset 0x40 to offset 0x48 because of adding or deleting other fields in the structure.

## 5    Discussion

**Require Source Code:** Unlike three state-of-the-art tools [12–14] that claim to work with binary code alone, we require both source and binary code to extract signatures. These tools need all vulnerability-related binary versions and must be compiled with identical optimization flags, which is impractical for binaries collected from different sources. Thus, they also rely on source code to ensure consistency in binary compilation.

**Cross Architecture:** VulMatch operates within the same architecture but does not address matching signatures across different architectures (e.g., ARM, x32, PowerPC). Solutions such as translating instructions to an intermediate language or extracting signatures for various architectures are potential approaches but are not covered in this paper.

**Differences Introduced by Compilation:** Instruction differences due to varying compiler optimizations, versions, or settings pose challenges. This paper uses default optimization and compiler settings, but real-world binaries may vary. To address this, symbolic execution could mitigate differences but is time-consuming. An alternative is expanding training data by compiling projects with multiple optimization levels or compilers to improve signature detection across different settings.

Patch and vulnerability detection often use assembly instructions for signatures. Data-driven methods, such as Asm2vec [22] and Palmtree [34], convert assembly to vectors to handle differences introduced by compilation. Combining vectorized signatures with fine-grained methods could enhance detection and efficiency, with potential extensions involving graph-based embeddings [15,16].

## 6    Conclusion

In this paper, we proposed a novel approach called VulMatch to extract and match binary-level vulnerability-related signatures. VulMatch consists of four steps: 1) data preparation, 2) locating signature instruction, 3) constructing context-aware binary-level signatures, and 4) signature matching. Compared to previous work, VulMatch accurately locates vulnerability-related instructions and detects vulnerability within functions. Through our empirical studies, Vul-Match outperformed two state-of-the-art similarity-based vulnerability detection tools—Asm2vec [22] and Palmtree [34]. Specifically, VulMatch achieved the most accurate results on six out of seven projects with the least ambiguities while providing reasons for vulnerable functions. Hence, VulMatch effectively facilitates human understanding of its decision process during vulnerability detection. Our experiment on real-world firmware vulnerability detection indicates VulMatch is practical to find vulnerabilities in real-world scenarios. Our analysis of vulnerability distributions confirmed that VulMatch is a versatile detector with good potential for future extension.

# A    Appendix

**Table 3.** Information of the seven selected open-source projects. V stands for versions. B stands for Binary flies. .c represents .c files. .h represents .h files. VF stands for vulnerable functions. # represents **number of**.

| Project | V(#) | B(#) | .c(#) | .h(#) | CVEs(#) | VF(#) | Avg Size |
|---------|------|------|-------|-------|---------|-------|----------|
| Tcpdump | 20 | 152 | 167 | 78 | 192 | 213 | 20.45 |
| Curl | 67 | 315 | 419 | 197 | 111 | 231 | 44 |
| OpenSSL | 51 | 755 | 903 | 243 | 114 | 220 | 205 |
| Openjpeg | 15 | 104 | 205 | 139 | 94 | 187 | 24.50 |
| LibPNG | 63 | 39 | 36 | 14 | 52 | 50 | 6.90 |
| Libtiff | 30 | 69 | 102 | 24 | 142 | 169 | 12.30 |
| FFmpeg | 104 | 1206 | 1591 | 629 | 201 | 211 | 584 |
| **Total** | 350 | 2640 | 3423 | 1324 | 906 | 1281 | 897.15 |

Table 3 lists the versions, application domains, CVE information, and other details related to vulnerabilities and code. The projects span various domains: Tcpdump is a network packet analyzer, Curl is a data transfer tool, OpenSSL is a cryptographic protocol. Openjpeg, LibPNG, and Libtiff are focused on image processing. And FFmpeg is used for multimedia processing.

# References

1. Heffley, J., Meunier, P.: Can source code auditing software identify common vulnerabilities and be used to evaluate software security? In: Proceedings of the 37th Annual Hawaii International Conference on System Sciences, pp. 21:1–10. IEEE (2004)
2. Haefliger, S., Von Krogh, G., Spaeth, S.: Code reuse in open source software. Manage. Sci. **54**(1), 180–193 (2008)
3. Xu, Z., Chen, B., Chandramohan, M., Liu, Y., Song, F.: Spain: security patch analysis for binaries towards understanding the pain and pills. In: Proceedings of the 2017 IEEE/ACM 39th International Conference on Software Engineering (ICSE), pp. 462–472. IEEE (2017)

4. David, Y., Partush, N., Yahav, E.: Statistical similarity of binaries. ACM SIG-PLAN Notices **51**(6), 266–280 (2016)
5. David, Y., Partush, N., Yahav, E.: Similarity of binaries through re-optimization. In: Proceedings of the 38th ACM SIGPLAN Conference on Programming Language Design and Implementation, 2017
6. Lakhotia, A., Preda, M.D., Giacobazzi, R.: Fast location of similar code fragments using semantic 'juice'. In: Proceedings of the 2013 ACM SIGPLAN Program Protection and Reverse Engineering Workshop (2013)
7. Pewny, J., Schuster, F., Bernhard, L., Holz, T., Rossow, C.: Leveraging semantic signatures for bug search in binary programs. In: Proceedings of the Annual Computer Security Applications Conference, pp. 406–415 (2014)
8. Feng, Q., Wang, M., Zhang, M., Zhou, R., Henderson, A., Yin, H.: Extracting conditional formulas for cross-platform bug search. In: Proceedings of the 2017 ACM on Asia Conference on Computer and Communications Security, pp. 346–359 (2017)
9. Zhang, H., Qian, Z.: Precise and accurate patch presence test for binaries. In: Proceedings of the 27th USENIX Security Symposium (USENIX Security 18), pp. 887–902 (2018)
10. Jiang, Z.., et al.: Pdiff: semantic-based patch presence testing for downstream kernels. In: Proceedings of the 2020 ACM SIGSAC Conference on Computer and Communications Security, pp. 1149–1163 (2020)
11. Zhao, L., Zhu, Y., Ming, J., Zhang, Y., Zhang, H., Yin, H.: Patchscope: memory object centric patch diffing. In: Proceedings of the 2020 ACM SIGSAC Conference on Computer and Communications Security, pp. 149–165 (2020)
12. Liu, D., Li, Y., Tang, Y., Wang, B., Xie, W.: Vmpbl: identifying vulnerable functions based on machine learning combining patched information and binary comparison technique by lcs. In: Proceedings of the 2018 17th IEEE International Conference On Trust, Security And Privacy (TrustCom/BigDataSE). IEEE, pp. 800–807 (2018)
13. Xiao, Y., et al.: Viva: binary level vulnerability identification via partial signature. In: Proceedings of the 2021 IEEE International Conference on Software Analysis, Evolution and Reengineering (SANER), pp. 213–224. IEEE (2021)
14. Xu, Y., Xu, Z., Chen, B., Song, F., Liu, Y., Liu, T.: Patch based vulnerability matching for binary programs. In: Proceedings of the 29th ACM SIGSOFT International Symposium on Software Testing and Analysis, pp. 376–387 (2020)
15. Xu, X., Liu, C., Feng, Q., Yin, H., Song, L., Song, D.: Neural network-based graph embedding for cross-platform binary code similarity detection. In: Proceedings of the 2017 ACM SIGSAC Conference on Computer and Communications Security, pp. 363–376 (2017)
16. Gao, J., Yang, X., Fu, Y., Jiang, Y., Sun, J.: Vulseeker: A semantic learning based vulnerability seeker for cross-platform binary. In: Proceedings of the 2018 33rd IEEE/ACM International Conference on Automated Software Engineering (ASE), 2018, pp. 896–899
17. Feng, Q., Zhou, R., Xu, C., Cheng, Y., Testa, B., Yin, H.: Scalable graph-based bug search for firmware images. In: Proceedings of the 2016 ACM SIGSAC Conference on Computer and Communications Security, pp. 480–491 (2016)
18. Massarelli, L., Luna, G.A.D., Petroni, F., Baldoni, R., Querzoni, L.: Safe: self-attentive function embeddings for binary similarity. In: Proceedings of the 2019 International Conference on Detection of Intrusions and Malware, and Vulnerability Assessment, pp. 309–329. Springer (2019)

19. Zuo, F., Li, X., Zhang, Z., Young, P., Luo, L., Zeng, Q.: Neural machine translation inspired binary code similarity comparison beyond function pairs. In: Proceedings of the 2022 Network and Distributed System Security Symposium (NDSS) (2022)
20. Liu, B., et al.: αdiff: cross-version binary code similarity detection with dnn. In: Proceedings of the 33rd ACM/IEEE International Conference on Automated Software Engineering, pp. 667–678 (2018)
21. Ding, S.H.H., Fung, B., Charland, P.: Kam1n0: mapreduce-based assembly clone search for reverse engineering. In: Proceedings of the ACM SIGKDD International Conference on Knowledge Discovery and Data Mining (2016)
22. Ding, S.H., Fung, B.C., Charland, P.: Asm2vec: boosting static representation robustness for binary clone search against code obfuscation and compiler optimization. In: Proceedings of the 2019 IEEE Symposium on Security and Privacy (SP), pp. 472–489. IEEE (2019)
23. Huang, H., Youssef, A.M., Debbabi, M.: Binsequence: fast, accurate and scalable binary code reuse detection. In: Proceedings of the 2017 ACM on Asia Conference on Computer and Communications Security, pp. 155–166 (2017)
24. David, Y., Yahav, E.: Tracelet-based code search in executables. ACM SIGPLAN Notices 49(6), 349–360 (2014)
25. Alrabaee, S., Shirani, P., Wang, L., Debbabi, M.: Sigma: a semantic integrated graph matching approach for identifying reused functions in binary code. Digital Investigation, pp. S61–S71 (2015)
26. Alrabaee, S., Shirani, P., Wang, L., Debbabi, M.: Fossil: A resilient and efficient system for identifying foss functions in malware binaries. ACM Trans, Privacy Secur (2018)
27. Lindorfer, M., Di Federico, A., Maggi, F., Comparetti, P.M., Zanero, S.: Lines of malicious code: Insights into the malicious software industry. In: Proceedings of the ACM Annual Computer Security Applications Conference, pp. 349–358 (2012)
28. Chandramohan, M., Xue, Y., Xu, Z., Liu, Y., Cho, C.Y., Tan, H.B.K.: Bingo: Cross-architecture cross-os binary search. In: Proceedings of the ACM SIGSOFT International Symposium on Foundations of Software Engineering (2016)
29. Wang, S., Wu, D.: In-memory fuzzing for binary code similarity analysis. In: Proceedings of the 2017 32nd IEEE/ACM International Conference on Automated Software Engineering (ASE), pp. 319–330. IEEE (2017)
30. Ng, B.H., Prakash, A.: Expose: discovering potential binary code re-use. In: Proceedings of the IEEE Annual Computer Software and Applications Conference, pp. 492–501 (2013)
31. Jin, W., et al.: Binary function clustering using semantic hashes. In: Proceedings of the 2012 International Conference on Machine Learning and Applications, pp. 386–391 (2012)
32. Wang, S.-C., Liu, C.-L., Li, Y., Xu, W.-Y.: Semdiff: finding semtic differences in binary programs based on angr. In: Proceedings of the 2017 ITM Web of Conferences (2017)
33. Luo, L., Ming, J., Wu, D., Liu, P., Zhu, S.: Semantics-based obfuscation-resilient binary code similarity comparison with applications to software plagiarism detection. In: Proceedings of the 22nd ACM SIGSOFT International Symposium on Foundations of Software Engineering, pp. 389–400 (2014)
34. Li, X., Qu, Y., Yin, H.: Palmtree: learning an assembly language model for instruction embedding. In: Proceedings of the 2021 ACM SIGSAC Conference on Computer and Communications Security, 2021, pp. 3236–3251 (2021)

# Revisiting Binary Code Authorship Analysis

Saed Alrabaee[1][(✉)], Mousa Al-kfairy[2], Mohammad Bany Taha[3],
Omar Alfandi[2], Fatma Taher[2], and Jie Tang[4]

[1] Department of Information Systems and Security, CIT,
United Arab Emirates University, Al Ain, UAE
salrabaee@uaeu.ac.ae
[2] College of Technological Innovation, Zayed University, Abu Dhabi, UAE
{mousa.al-kfairy,omar.alfandi,fatma.taher}@zu.ac.ae
[3] Department of Data Science and Artificial Intelligence,
American University of Madaba, Amman, Jordan
m.taha@aum.edu.jo
[4] Department of Computer Science, Tsinghua University, Beijing, China
jietang@tsinghua.edu.cn

**Abstract.** Binary authorship analysis is a crucial step in malware reverse engineering, but the volume and complexity of the code exacerbate the challenge of this manually intensive task. Consequently, efforts have been made to develop reliable automated tools to facilitate malware authorship analysis; however, many challenges are associated with automated approaches. For instance, the compilation process may remove stylistic features present in the source code. This paper evaluates the features used in existing approaches by utilizing various datasets, including programs written for the Google Code Jam programming competition, student projects from programming courses at multiple universities, and content from GitHub repositories. Additionally, we examined the impact of statistical features on precision, recall, and the false positive rate of these methodologies. The evaluation results reveal that the accuracy of these approaches varies across different application domains and datasets, and some of the selected features appear unrelated to the author's style, indicating that careful consideration is needed when applying this approach. Finally, using statistical features enhanced the precision and recall of existing approaches while reducing the false positive rate by 10–15%.

**Keywords:** Reverse Engineering · Binary Code Analysis

## 1 Introduction

Binary authorship attribution is the process of identifying the author of an anonymous binary code by analyzing its stylistic characteristics. This is a valuable tool for security applications, as the source code for malware is often

H. H. Song et al. (Eds.): NSS 2024, LNCS 15564, pp. 428–449, 2025.
https://doi.org/10.1007/978-981-96-3531-3_21

unavailable. There are two main challenges to automating binary authorship attribution. First, many stylistic features, such as variable names, are lost when code is compiled into binary form. Second, analyzing binary code is more time-consuming and resource-intensive than analyzing source code [9–14,16,17,19,22,23,25,31,44]. Existing automated binary authorship attribution methods typically rely on stylistic features that are likely to survive the compilation process. These features include naming conventions for variables and functions, control and data flow structures, comments, and whitespace. Despite these challenges, binary authorship attribution is a promising area of research with the potential to improve the security of computer systems.

Software authorship has many practical applications, such as copyright infringement and malware analysis. For example, by attributing the authorship of program binaries, important insights can be gained to facilitate other mitigation strategies (e.g., technical and legal responses). To this end, several approaches have been suggested for binary authorship attribution [33,40–43], typically employing machine learning techniques to identify unique features for each author. These features are then used to match a specific binary to its author. Nevertheless, these strategies encounter several obstacles: the selected features usually pertain to functionality rather than the author's style, the accuracy declines notably in scenarios involving multiple authors, and the methods are easily undermined by refactoring or code transformation techniques.

In this paper, we empirically re-evaluate the following approaches: (i) Rosenblum et al. [33], (2) Caliskan et al. [40], Alrabaee et al. [41], Meng et al. [42], and Alrabaee et al. [43]. Our goal is twofold. First, we would like to evaluate the techniques' effectiveness when applied to different software domains or applications. Second, we would also like to assess the impact of statistical features when used with the existing features. Both aspects will be critical for an authorship analysis technique to produce reliable and convincing results in practical applications. We re-implement and evaluate the method using real-world program binaries to achieve those goals.

Our main contributions are threefold.

- First, we discover that many top-ranked features obtained using the approaches above are unrelated to the authors' programming styles. While apparently unrelated to author styles, such features are highly ranked by the machine learning approaches because of a strong correlation with authorship (i.e., those features are often unique for each author). This finding indicates that the correlation with authorship alone is insufficient to be used as a stylistic feature.
- Second, we discover the accuracy varies between the software domains and applications. Specifically, the accuracy of the method decreases quickly as the population of authors increases, and the accuracy usually reaches a meaningless level (around 40%, which is expected for a random assignment of authorship) for just 25 authors. This finding indicates that, even without considering the presence of the features discussed in the preceding bullet point, the low accuracy of such features may render them impractical for many applications.

– Third, we discover adding statistical features of authorship styles may improve the accuracy and reduce the false positive rate. The key observation is that, as indicated by our above findings, features based on individual instances of patterns may not be as reliable as their statistical aggregations for capturing authors' styles. We demonstrate the potential of this approach through a case study in which experimental results show that the proposed method may provide more accurate results with a more meaningful connection to author styles.

## 2  Binary Authorship Attribution Existing Approaches

To make this paper self-contained, we now summarize the existing binary authorship existing techniques [33,40–43]. Table 1 presents a comparison of binary authorship attribution approaches.

**Table 1.** A comparison of binary authorship attribution approaches. (•) indicates that the proposal is affected by the corresponding obfuscation technique. Otherwise, it is empty.

| Work | Author Identification | | Features | | | | Obfuscation | | | Availability |
|------|--------|----------|----------|----------|------------|-------------|----|----|-----|-------------|
| | Single | Multiple | Syntactic | Semantic | Structural | Statistical | RR | IR | DCI | |
| [33] | ✓ | ✗ | ✓ | ✓ | ✓ | ✗ | • | • | • | Public |
| [40] | ✓ | ✗ | ✗ | ✓ | ✓ | ✗ | | • | | GitHub |
| [41] | ✓ | ✗ | ✓ | ✓ | ✗ | ✗ | • | • | • | Private |
| [42] | ✓ | ✓ | ✓ | ✓ | ✗ | ✗ | • | • | • | Private |
| [43] | ✓ | ✓ | ✗ | ✓ | ✓ | ✗ | | | • | Private |

### 2.1  Rosenblum [33]

Rosenblum et al. aimed to introduce authorship attribution techniques for program binaries, with applications to malware, based on the assumption that certain programming styles may be preserved throughout the compilation process [33]. The authors first defined a collection of so-called feature templates in order to capture code details at instruction and control flow levels. They then employed a machine learning approach to rank the features and select those most closely correlated to authorship. The high-level workflow of this approach is described as follows:

1. A set of binary codes with similar functionality and known authorship (e.g., code written by different authors at a programming competition or from an academic course assignment) is collected as the training data from which stylistic features are to be extracted and ranked.

2. Features are extracted using pre-defined templates, such as sequences of consecutive commands or subgraphs in the call graphs, using existing software tools (e.g., IDA Pro [28]).
3. The mutual information between those extracted features and the known authorship is computed for each program and author in the training dataset to rank and select features.
4. Authorship classifiers are built using the support vector machine method based on the selected features. The most likely author of each target program is decided based on the classification results.
5. A clustering analysis is also performed over the collection of programs assuming no known authorship. Knowledge obtained in the supervised domain is borrowed and applied to the unsupervised domain to avoid selecting the wrong features representing program functionality instead of author styles.

In [33], Rosenblum et al. employed a large program corpus from the Google Code Jam programming competition (http://code.google.com/codejam/) and another from an undergraduate student programming project as the training data. Their experiments showed relatively high accuracy in identifying programs' authorship.

### 2.2   Caliskan et al. [40]

They perform programmer de-anonymization from a machine learning perspective, utilizing a feature set that includes those derived from decompiling the executable binary back to source code. By adopting a potent suite of techniques from the realm of source code authorship attribution, coupled with stylistic elements embedded in assembly, they successfully de-anonymize a large group of programmers. Their approach significantly surpasses the previous attempt at programmer de-anonymization by Rosenblum et al. [33]. While Rosenblum et al. [33] extracted structures like control-flow graphs directly from executable binaries, this study is the first to demonstrate that automated decompilation of executable binaries provides additional useful feature categories. Specifically, they generate abstract syntax trees from decompiled source code, finding that syntactical properties derived from these trees enhance the accuracy of executable binary attribution techniques. Additionally, they illustrate that employing multiple disassembly and decompilation tools simultaneously boosts de-anonymization accuracy by generating diverse code representations that encapsulate various aspects of a programmer's style.

### 2.3   OBA2 [41]

They introduce a layered method for Binary Authorship Attribution, dubbed the Onion Approach, or OBA2. This approach incorporates three complementary layers: preprocessing, syntax-based attribution, and semantic-based attribution. The initial layer, referred to as the Stuttering Layer (SL), employs a signature-based technique that can automatically detect software library functions or other functions known to be unrelated to an author's style. The second layer introduces a method for constructing a syntax dictionary, which helps create an author profile by correlating binary code syntax with identified source codes. For the final layer, they develop a model known as the register flow graph, which captures semantic-based features that represent patterns in register manipulations. The experimental results indicate that OBA2 yields more accurate outcomes and provides a meaningful link to the authors' coding styles.

## 2.4   Meng et al. [42]

They suggest a system designed to identify multiple authors within a binary code. This includes fine-tuned methods to tackle the more challenging task of identifying the author of each basic block. The decision to attribute authors at the basic block level stems from an empirical study of three large open-source software projects. This study revealed that a significant portion of basic blocks could be confidently attributed to a single author. They introduce a set of core features that encapsulate programming style at the basic block level, propose an approach for identifying external template library code, and devise a method to capture correlations between the authors of basic blocks in a binary. These techniques were evaluated on a dataset derived from the open-source projects used in the empirical study, comprising 147 C binaries and 22 C++ binaries. These binaries, compiled with GCC 4.8.5 and $-O2$ optimization, contained 284 authors and 900,583 basic blocks. Overall, the techniques achieved a 65% accuracy rate in classifying 284 authors, a significant increase from the 0.4% accuracy achieved by random guessing.

## 2.5   BinChar [43]

This research aims to create an automated tool capable of handling the complex and error-prone task of binary authorship characterization - determining the indications related to a binary code's author(s). Software code written by human programmers mirrors the author's educational background, expertise, and unique coding styles. These can be profiled by identifying significant features and analyzing them. Binary authorship characterization uncovers information that is invaluable for security applications, such as digital forensics, malware triage, and binary vulnerability tracking. They introduce a system, BinChar, designed to capture various aspects of an author's style, encompassing code trait features, code structure features, and code behavior features. A Convolutional Neural Network (CNN) is utilized for detection, further refining the results through Bayesian calibration. BinChar was tested for its ability to identify the characteristics of binary program authors. They employed it on malware samples from the Kaggle Microsoft Malware Classification Challenge, demonstrating BinChar's suitability as a tool for characterizing malware families.

# 3   Binary Authorship Attribution Methodology

In contrast to source code, program binaries lack meaningful details, which may be selected as features for capturing authors' styles.

## 3.1   Features Engineering

Here, we summarize the features used in existing approaches [33, 40–43].

**Idioms.** In a programming context, idioms are used to pinpoint precise code patterns. These idioms represent the specific, lower-tier details of program instructions. They are brief instruction sequences that define the technical and formal characteristics embedded within the assembly files generated by disassembly tools.

**Byte n-Grams.** Byte n-grams have been utilized in malware analysis, as cited in sources. This method involves viewing a file as a succession of bytes. By focusing on every unique set of 'n' contiguous bytes, byte n-grams are obtained and considered distinct features.

**Graphlets.** A graphlet intermediates assembly instructions and the Control Flow Graph (CFG). It's classified as a subgraph of the CFG, consisting of every trio of nodes. Each node within the graphlet corresponds to a basic block that maintains a roster of neighboring blocks. To be precise, it's a basic block that links to other basic blocks via a branch instruction.

**SuperGraphlets.** Supergraphlets can be created by combining and condensing neighboring nodes of a Control Flow Graph (CFG). These graphlets operate analogously to the node collapsing algorithm, utilizing an equal canonical representation. As these nodes collapse, the outcome might include a modification in the edge type or the emergence of a new color.

**CallGraphlets.** They are composed solely of nodes that carry a call instruction. These graphs are designed around the function names that come from imported libraries. For instance, they might call ds:printf.

**Register Flow Graph.** A register graph identifies the dependencies among the registers. These interconnected relationships offer crucial insights into the binary code. The vitality of a register quantifies the management of variables during operation and determines if local or global variables ought to be engaged.

**Opcode.** This refers to operational codes. It is characterized as a textual explanation or description. A single mnemonic can correspond to many opcodes. Instances of opcode include commands like move, push, etc.

**Context Features.** Context features encapsulate the loops and the functions that a basic block is a part of. This may include quantifying loops' nesting levels and sizes to portray loop contexts. For the context of a function, the breadth and depth of a function's CFG using a breadth-first search (BFS) is computed, where each basic block is assigned a BFS level.

**Author Style Graph.** The Annotated Flow Graph (ACFG) is a semantic control flow graph. This is an abstracted version of the CFG, with various criteria guiding the extraction of certain feature types from the CFG. The construction process for the ACFG is outlined. The system inputs a CFG and computes the frequency of opcode appearances in the instruction groups. It then classifies assembly instructions into one of six groups. The generated ACFG describes structural features. The next phase involves augmenting it with the Data Flow Graph (DFG). Subsequently, data flow dependencies can be integrated, enabling coarse analysis of program control flow and data dependencies to deduce how the author manages program variables and establishes variable relationships. Recognizing the complementary perspectives the ACFG and DFG offer about how a specific task is implemented - highlighting different facets of the underlying authorship traits - these two graphs merged into the Author Style Graph (ASG).

Table 2 presented the Features used in existing binary authorship attribution approaches.

**Table 2.** Features used in existing binary authorship attribution approaches.

| Features | Approach | | | | |
|---|---|---|---|---|---|
| | [33] | [40] | [41] | [42] | [43] |
| Idioms | ✓ | ✗ | ✓ | ✓ | ✓ |
| Byte n-grams | ✓ | ✗ | ✗ | ✓ | ✗ |
| Graphlets | ✓ | ✗ | ✗ | ✗ | ✗ |
| SuperGraphlets | ✓ | ✗ | ✗ | ✗ | ✗ |
| CallGraphlets | ✓ | ✗ | ✗ | ✗ | ✗ |
| Register Flow Graph | ✗ | ✗ | ✓ | ✗ | ✓ |
| Opcode | ✓ | ✓ | ✓ | ✗ | ✓ |
| Context Features | ✗ | ✓ | ✗ | ✓ | ✗ |
| Author Style Graph | ✗ | ✗ | ✗ | ✗ | ✓ |

### 3.2 Statistical Authorship Analysis

Statistical authorship analysis relies on statistics computed over binary code as features. Informally speaking, a statistical analysis of binary code may provide a profile that can capture author habits exhibited in the source code. For example, such habits may be reflected as the more frequent use of the *IF arguments* (other examples may include the register assignment, the abstraction patterns, *simple loop definition, nested loop definition, loop data flow, types of encryption algorithms*, and the *level of author's skills and experiences*, etc.). A statistical analysis on binary code may capture such habits or properties of authors, e.g., using the *IF* statements more frequently than using *SWITCH* statements. This may be captured in terms of an increased percentage of jump instructions.

**Statistical Signatures.** In this subsection, we introduce the equations that represent the statistical signatures.

$$\mu = \frac{\Sigma x_j}{N-1}. \qquad (1)$$

$$V = \frac{\Sigma (x_j - \overline{x_j})^2}{N-1}. \qquad (2)$$

$$MSE_j = (x_j - \overline{x_j})^2. \qquad (3)$$

$$SD = \sqrt{V} \qquad (4)$$

In addition to the statistical signature, we verify the signature by calculating the *distance* between the mean and the variance by using equation (2). As shown in equation (2), there are two means and two variances. For each count (e.g. jmp), the first variance is in the different programs for the same author, and the second is in the same programs among the same instruction family type (e.g. jnz).

$$D_j = \frac{(\mu_j - \overline{\mu_j})^2}{\left(\sigma_j{}^2 + \overline{\sigma_j}{}^2\right)}. \qquad (5)$$

where $\mu_j$ is the mean of the opcode among the other opcode from the same family (e.g. jmp, jle, jg), $\overline{\mu_j}$ is the mean of opcode among the same opcode but from different programs for the same author. However, $\sigma_j$ and $\overline{\sigma_j}$ are the variance. The benefit of using the above equation is measuring the distance between features and athe uthor's behavior. The values of V-jmp, V-REG1, and MSE1 are obtained as follows: to find the variance of jmp, we use Eq. (2) (Table 3).

**Table 3.** Symbols used in statistics analysis example

| Symbol | Description | Symbol | Description |
|--------|-------------|--------|-------------|
| JFN | The number of jump functions | MSE1 | Mean Square Error of each instruction |
| NC | The number of calls | Variance | Variance of each category |
| JIN | The number of jump instruction | SD | Standard deviation for each category |
| VAS | The virtual address size | jge | Jump if greater or equal |
| V-REG1 | The variance of register 1 (ebp) and it the same for the registers | jg | Jump if greater |
| V-jmp | The variance of jmp instruction and the same for the other branch instructions | jle | Jump if less or equal |
| Nlogic | Nlogic The number of the logic operations (and, or, xor, etc.) | jl | Jump if less |
| Stack | Stack The number of stack operations (push and pop), and load effective address (lea) instruction | jz | Jump if zero |
| Math | Math The mathematics instructions (add, sub, imul, idiv, etc.) | jnz | Jump if not zero |
| Normal | Normal The other instructions (e.g. mov) | jb | Jump on below/less than |
| s-jmp | The standard deviation for the jump instruction among the jump instruction category | jbe | Jump if below or equal, $CF = 1$ or $ZF = 1$ |

### 3.3   Features Ranking

In the feature ranking phase, it was assumed that each wrote a known set of program authors and a set of programs of those authors. The feature ranking algorithm was then designed to order the features by their correlation with authorship. Many extracted features may be familiar to most programs, even though different authors write those programs. The feature ranking algorithm aims to lower such common features so they will not be selected later. The feature ranking algorithm was based on mutual information between the feature and known authorship.

$$Mutual\ Information = \Sigma\Sigma p(m,n)log_2\frac{(p(m,n))}{p(m)p(n)} \tag{1}$$

where $p(m,n)$ is the joint probability distribution function of a feature and an author, and $p(m)$ and $p(n)$ are the marginal probability distribution functions of a feature and an author respectively. The mutual information measures the information that a feature and an author share, i.e., this calculates the degree to which identifying one of these variables decreases the others' ambiguity. However, if there are two independent variables (for instance, feature m and author n), identifying the former does not provide information on the latter.

To calculate the marginal probability of a specific feature, the algorithm calculates the number of its occurrences and the total number of existing features. Using this algorithm, all the features mentioned above may be ranked based on their mutual information.

### 3.4   Authorship Classification

This method of classifying authorship assumes that an identified set of authors and their program samples are gathered. Following the extraction and ranking of the features (as detailed earlier), a classifier is constructed according to the top-ranked features. This generates a design function that is capable of allocating a label, i.e., authorship, to any new program based on the set of identified authors. The following are the general stages of authorship classification:

1. Initially, every program is represented as an integral-valued feature vector that details the features encompassed in the program.
2. The features are sorted via the previously discussed ranking algorithm based on the shared information and identified author labels. Certain top-ranked features are chosen, and others are excluded to decrease the training expenses and risk of excess data.
3. Cross-validation is carried out on the top-ranked features. Together, these features can generate a practical decision function for the authorship classifier.

### 3.5   Authorship Clustering

Since training data with known authorship may not always be available, especially for malware binaries, it was considered desirable to form clusters of malware programs based on common authorship. For this purpose, the authors rely on unsupervised learning algorithms and perform authorship clustering by following the steps:

1. The clustering algorithm is designed to form clusters of programs based on relative distances in a $d$-dimensional space. Specifically, a $d\times d$ distance metric $A$ is defined such that the distance between two feature vectors is:

$$D_A(X_a, X_b) = \sqrt{(X_a - X_b)^T A(X_a - X_b)} \tag{2}$$

2. To ensure that the clustering is based on author styles, instead of other properties, such as functionality, a two-part algorithm is designed for transferring knowledge learned from labeled data to unlabeled data.
3. The authors use the large margin nearest neighbors (LMNN), DBSCAN, and k-mean algorithms for the clustering.

To make this paper self-contained, we now summarize the existing binary authorship existing techniques [33,40–43]. Table 1 presents a comparison of binary authorship attribution approaches.

Table 4 presented a binary authorship attribution classification and clustering approach.

**Table 4.** Binary authorship attribution classification and clustering approaches.

| Work | Authorship Attribution | |
|------|------------|----------------|
|      | Clustering | Classification |
| [33] | ✓ | ✓ |
| [40] | ✗ | ✓ |
| [41] | ✗ | ✓ |
| [42] | ✗ | ✓ |
| [43] | ✓ | ✓ |

# 4   Evaluation

In this section, we first evaluate existing works [33,40–43]. We then provide details on our choice of datasets and their implementation. Next, we present experimental results on the method's accuracy, examples of misleading features, and the percentage of such misleading features. Finally, we conclude the evaluation results and propose potential improvements.

## 4.1   The Choice of Data Sets

The first step towards the evaluation is to select appropriate datasets to be utilized in the authorship attribution training and testing phases. Obtaining representative datasets is a fundamental problem as no standard one is available for the authorship attribution problem. For our evaluation purposes, we have gathered programs written for the Google Code Jam programming competition and from student projects in a programming course at the first author's university.

**Google Code Jam.** Google Code Jam is a global programming competition run by Google. It entails several rounds in which competitors have a specific amount of time to solve sets of algorithmic problems. There are typically between three and six problems in each set, and competitors are tasked with writing a program to solve them using any programming language or development setting. In this evaluation, contest data from 2008 and 2020 is employed. Table 5 summarizes the binary code feature templates and the number of each represented in a typical Google Code Jam corpora.

**Table 5.** Number of feature templates for Google Code Jam corpus of program binaries. Each template captures one or more features at different levels such as Ins: Instructions. BB: basic block. Lib: Library

| Features | # | Code Level | | |
|---|---|---|---|---|
| | | Ins | BB | Lib |
| N-grams | 483,211 | * | | |
| Idioms | 65,843 | * | | |
| Graphlets | 59,370 | * | * | |
| Supergraphlets | 11,265 | * | * | |
| Callgraphlets | 1,980 | | * | * |
| Library calls | 124 | | | * |
| Opcode | 211,914 | * | | |
| Code context | 10,956 | * | * | |
| Attribution graph | 421 | | * | |
| Statistical signatures | 300 | * | * | * |

**University Projects.** Our second corpus consists of programs written by graduate students enrolled in a course at our university. The students completed seven programming assignments during the course. Those programs are written in the same language and for the same functionality in each assignment. Table 6 summarizes binary code feature templates and the number of each instantiated one in a typical corpus for academic projects. The two different data sets differ significantly in the distribution of program sizes and the number of programs written by each author. The evaluation against such diverse data sets will provide a clear picture of the method is dependence on the software domains. The application differs from Table 6 in that it refers to academic projects. The data sets also greatly contrast the distribution of program sizes and each author's number of diverse programs. Evaluating with such disparate data sets will facilitate a comprehensive determination of the methods' level of reliance on the software domains and applications.

**Table 6.** Number of feature templates for University Projects corpus of program binaries. Each template captures one or more features at different levels, such as Inst: Instruction, BB: basic block, Lib: external library. AG: Attribution graph, SS: Statistical signatures

| Features | # | Code Property | | |
|---|---|---|---|---|
| | | Inst. | BB. | Lib. |
| N-grams | 440,365 | * | | |
| Idioms | 155,980 | * | | |
| Graphlets | 44,023 | * | * | |
| Supergraphlets | 7,838 | * | * | |
| Callgraphlets | 2,463 | | * | * |
| Library calls | 215 | | | * |
| Opcode | 300,250 | * | | |
| Code context | 18,114 | * | * | |
| AG | 609 | | * | |
| SS | 428 | * | * | * |

## 4.2 Testing Environment

For the evaluation purpose, our prototype relies on both (1) the ParseAPI library of the Paradyn project [25] compiled for Windows and (2) IDA Pro [29], to obtain control flow graphs and the underlying assembly, respectively. The feature extraction comes after a preprocessing phase where many binary functions are filtered. This step is necessary to remove the code that is unrelated to the user. All the feature types listed in Table 5 are automatically extracted. The mutual information is computed using their frequencies and known author labels, and each feature is automatically ranked. We perform both cross-validation and random subset testing to evaluate classification accuracy. Thus, we randomly draw authors and use their programs to test accuracy.

## 4.3 Accuracy Results

We assess every feature in terms of its contribution to the overall accuracy of author ascription and the level of precision it offers in deducing an author's identity using existing feature templates. The findings indicate that as the number of authors increases, the complexity of distinguishing between them also rises.

Table 7 depicts the cross-validation accuracy of two models; the first is trained with different numbers of features from each sort of feature, and the second is trained with all types of features. From the Google Code Jam data set, the classifier accomplished an 82% accuracy level for ten separate authors. The experimental results confirm that the accuracy of authorship classification decreases very quickly for larger populations. Table 7 shows the classifier performance as a function of the number of authors included in a subset of the data; classifier accuracy decreases as the author population size grows. Clearly, the accuracy is almost meaningful in many cases, considering the fact that a 10% accuracy can be expected from a completely random assignment of authorship.

**Table 7.** Accuracy results for the used features with different sets of authors based on Google Code Jam

|  | Number of Authors | | |
| --- | --- | --- | --- |
| Features | 500 | 1000 | 15000 |
| Idioms | 40% | 32% | 29% |
| N-grams | 35% | 24% | 21% |
| Graphlets | 31% | 21% | 20% |
| Supergraphlets | 30% | 20% | 19% |
| Call-graphlets | 15% | 10% | 11% |
| Libcalls | 28% | 20% | 17% |
| Opcode | 61% | 50% | 48% |
| Code Context | 81% | 74% | 69% |
| AG | 75% | 62% | 51% |
| SS | 85% | 82% | 81% |
| All together | 90% | 84% | 82% |

Table 8 lists cross-validation accuracy for authorship classification on university projects corpus. The university project data present a significantly harder challenge for authorship attribution because it has fewer programs per author compared to the Jam Code data set. Moreover, each program in this data set is not necessarily written by a single programmer since there are project groups assigned for the course projects. Another challenge is that the students need to follow the rigid specifications provided by the professor in completing the projects, and such common specifications may hinder the extraction of significant stylistic characteristics from the data set.

Experiments on university projects also confirm that the classifier performance quickly decreases to unsatisfactory accuracy as the population increases in size. We also observe that the original claims about author classification may critically depend on the application domain since different domains may imply different skills and habits of the programmers or different requirements for the programming tasks, which may all lead to different difficulties of authorship attribution.

**Table 8.** Accuracy results for the method of Rosenblum et al. with different set of authors based on University Projects

|  | Number of Authors | | |
|---|---|---|---|
| Features | 250 | 500 | 750 |
| Idioms | 51% | 40% | 25% |
| N-grams | 42% | 31% | 22% |
| Graphlets | 37% | 28% | 19% |
| Supergraphlets | 31% | 25% | 15% |
| Call-graphlets | 35% | 24% | 21% |
| Libcalls | 28% | 22% | 13% |
| Opcode | 76% | 65% | 54% |
| Code Context | 89% | 80% | 74% |
| AG | 90% | 80% | 67% |
| SS | 91% | 88% | 87% |
| All together | 94% | 90% | 87% |

### 4.4   Misleading Features

Further deteriorating the situation, upon reevaluation, it was highlighted that there is no correlation between many top-ranked features and the authors' styles. For instance, at the binary level, the names of many of the source-code level functions remain unidentified, meaning that IDA Pro allocates a name with a "sub" prefix, and the compiler randomly generates numbers with which the source-code level functions are then post-fixed. Testing has found that by calculating the shared information, the functions with random numbers are pivotal in features becoming top-ranked. This finding indicates that this method may choose features connected to other properties like the compiler-generated functions rather than the author styles. Figure 1 shows the percentage of functions that certainly are not related to styles, which is increasing towards the ranked features, meaning that a significant portion of the features selected for author attribution by this method may be mistakenly assumed as about author styles.

Moreover, some extracted features turn out to be unique for an author while not being related to the author's programming style. To illustrate this, we consider a common software requirement to check the existence of a single program instance running at a given time. The following piece of code is highly representative of the academic code set.

```
#include<stdio.h>
#define student_ID 12345 // 0x3039

int checkSingleInstance(int);
```

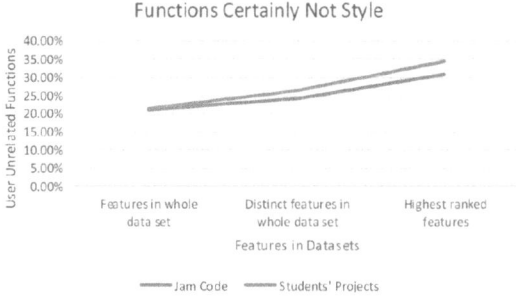

**Fig. 1.** Percentages of misleading features

```
// returns instances

int main() {
if(!checkSingleInstance(student_ID))
printf("multiple instances detected \n");
else
printf("single instance detected");
// [...]
return 0;
}

int checkSingleInstance(int foo) {
// count the program instances
// if one:
return 1;
}
```

Many programmers (in this case, students) preferred to use a unique value, i.e., the student_ID, to perform the task. As a result, several features related to unique student_ID are easily identifiable as unique for an author without reflecting the programming style. For example, there are several idioms containing the hexa value of the student ID, e.g., `push 3039h`, or n-grams like `68 39 30`. If the mentioned requirement is to be met by all programs written by an author, it becomes clear that authorship will be assigned based on such unique features.

### 4.5  Discussion

Our evaluation shows that, although programmer style may likely be preserved in program binaries, the existing technique may not be satisfactory in selecting the right stylistic features to capture the authorship. The classifier may not be able to identify an author out of ten candidates with good enough accuracy, and many selected features are unrelated to author styles. In addition, we have the following observations and suggestions.

**Functionality or Styles.** During the evaluation, it was noticeable that the features chosen by current methods are more intimately linked with the program's functionality than with the author's stylistic elements. This viewpoint can be backed by the fact that a simple, shorter program possesses fewer features than larger programs that are focused more on functionality. This suggests that the number of features is directly proportional to the program's size, which typically illustrates functionality [?], but not necessarily the author's style, as indicated by the studies of [33, 40, 41]. To mitigate this, utilizing specific existing systems as a preprocessing phase could be beneficial, as recommended by [42, 43], which involves various steps.

**Feature Pre-processing.** In our analysis, we have come across high-ranking features associated with the compiler, like the stack frame set-up operation. Therefore, it becomes crucial to exclude non-relevant functions, such as those of the compiler, to better spotlight sections of code related to the author, as suggested by [33]. A filtering approach that employs FLIRT technology for library identification and a system for filtering compiler functions should be implemented to counteract this issue. Successfully differentiating between these two categories of functions - library/compiler functions and user functions - would result in significant time savings and would allow the analysis to focus more on pertinent functions [33].

**Application Type.** Our findings indicate that the precision of current methods, as highlighted by [33, 40], is significantly contingent on the application's context. For instance, as depicted in Table 5, the Google Code Jam dataset displays a notably high accuracy rate, averaging 57%. This can be attributed to Rosenblum et al.'s method of extracting SysCalls, which proves more beneficial for academic or competition codes compared to other cases. This is likely due to the authors' consistent dependence on external libraries and their implementation of MFC APIs, for example. Furthermore, the results reveal that Alrabaee et al.'s accuracy is application-dependent, as their technique extracts how the author manages branches; for example, the accuracy decreases dramatically from 88% to 75% when using the Google Code Jam dataset. Upon examination of the source code, it is evident that the number of branches is relatively small, which further complicates the task of attribution.

**The Source of Features.** Caliskan et al. [40] employ a decompiler to convert the program into C-like pseudo-code using Hex-Ray. This code is then subjected to a fuzzy parser, which results in an abstract syntax tree from which features are extracted. However, there are not only limitations associated with Hex-Ray, but also significant differences between the C-like pseudo-code and the original code. This disparity extends to variables, branches, and keywords. For example, in the source code, we observed a function containing the following keywords: (1-do, 1-switch, 3-case, 3-break, 2-while, 1-if), and 2 variables. Upon inspecting the same function post-decompilation, it comprised the following keywords: (1-do, 1-else/if, 2-goto, 2-while, 4-if), with the number of variables increasing to 4. This variance will undoubtedly lead to the extraction of potentially misleading features.

## 4.6    Applying Existing Works to Malware Binaries

We apply established methodologies to various real malware sets, including Ramnit, Lollipop, Kelihos, Vundo, Simda, Tracur, Obfuscator.ACY, and Gatak, selected for their availability. These samples comprise different variants of the same malware, leading us to presume that the same individual or team authors these variants. Given the absence of an absolute reference, we manually compare the results of each approach to ensure they belong to the same family. Further information on the malware dataset is provided in Table 9.

**Table 9.** Characteristics of malware datasets. (BF): binary functions, (CF): compiler functions, (LF): library function.

| Malware | # of variants | # of BF | # of CF | # of LF |
|---|---|---|---|---|
| Ramnit | 4 | 5285 | 1601 | 50 |
| Lollipop | 3 | 3510 | 1054 | 100 |
| Kelihos | 2 | 1924 | 847 | 74 |
| Vundo | 4 | 7923 | 2410 | 219 |
| Simda | 2 | 2100 | 689 | 105 |
| Tracur | 2 | 1657 | 787 | 100 |
| Obfuscator.ACY | 3 | 2762 | 986 | 310 |
| Gatak | 2 | 2054 | 860 | 174 |

The number of compiler functions is determined based on IDA Pro, while the fifth column indicates the number of library functions procured by F.L.I.R.T technology. As per Table 9, it's evident that the proportion of compiler functions is relatively high, thus necessitating a pre-processing step prior to applying authorship attribution methods. For example, the Lollipop family has 30% compiler functions. We apply existing methodologies and group functions based on their features using standard $k-means$ clustering. Subsequently, we manually analyze the resulting clusters to categorize them into correct or incorrect clusters, as detailed in Table 10.

**Table 10.** Clustering results based on the features used in existing systems. (TC): the total number of clusters, (CC): the percentage of correct clusters, (WC): the percentage of wrong clusters.

| Malware | OBA2 [41] | | | Caliskan-Islam [40] | | | Rosenblum [33] | | | Meng [42] | | | BinChar [43] | | |
|---|---|---|---|---|---|---|---|---|---|---|---|---|---|---|---|
| | TC | CC | WC | TC | CC | WC | TC | CC | WC | TC | CC | WC | TC | CC | WC |
| Ramnit | 145 | 60% | 30% | 110 | 47% | 50% | 208 | 18% | 70% | 210 | 71% | 21% | 140 | 79% | 12% |
| Lollipop | 90 | 75% | 14% | 185 | 59% | 38% | 220 | 21% | 67% | 190 | 44% | 40% | 89 | 80% | 14% |
| Kelihos | 41 | 88% | 8% | 17 | 90% | 4% | 75 | 34% | 55% | 100 | 84% | 11% | 56 | 77% | 14% |
| Vundo | 200 | 62% | 14% | 89 | 28% | 68% | 384 | 39% | 48% | 250 | 88% | 10% | 160 | 88% | 7% |
| Simda | 52 | 49% | 50% | 41 | 92% | 5% | 109 | 42% | 51% | 70 | 80% | 10% | 39 | 70% | 19% |
| Tracur | 44 | 89% | 9% | 53 | 83% | 12% | 124 | 51% | 40% | 85 | 66% | 10% | 20 | 85% | 14% |
| Obfuscator.ACY | 30 | 78% | 21% | 45 | 74% | 24% | 89 | 29% | 70% | 80 | 55% | 22% | 23 | 76% | 18% |
| Gatak | 29 | 57% | 34% | 51 | 87% | 12% | 79 | 38% | 62% | 77 | 44% | 40% | 33 | 74% | 14% |

## 5   Conclusion

The issue of authorship attribution in binary code has received less attention compared to source code level attribution, due to several factors such as the time-intensive nature of reverse engineering and the limited preservation of features during the compilation process. This paper initially provides a comprehensive review of literature pertinent to authorship identification in both binary and source code. Following this, we elucidate the process of binary feature extraction. We then thoroughly analyze and evaluate existing research in various contexts, including scalability. Ultimately, we apply these studies to a genuine set of malware binaries. It is apparent that numerous features could potentially aid in identifying the authorship of malware. However, the greater challenge lies in confirming their practicality through empirical studies. Special attention must be accorded to the following considerations when addressing binary authorship attribution: 1) A small amount of training set code might not be sufficient to make a good identification and a precise comparison unless very unusual indicators are present. 2) The identification of authors in the case of multiple authors will be more challenging, since we have first to identify code fragments that are written by the same author.

**Acknowledgement.** This work was supported by grant number 12R170.

## References

1. Deyannis, D., Papadogiannaki, E., Kalivianakis, G., Vasiliadis, G., Ioannidis, S.: Trustav: practical and privacy preserving malware analysis in the cloud. In: Proceedings of the Tenth ACM Conference on Data and Application Security and Privacy, pp. 39–48 (2020)
2. D'Elia, D.C., Coppa, E., Palmaro, F., Cavallaro, L.: On the dissection of evasive malware. IEEE Trans. Inf. Forens. Secur. **15**, 2750–2765 (2020)

3. Saed, M.D., Wang, L.: CPA: accurate cross-platform binary authorship characterization using LDA. IEEE Trans. Inf. Forens. Secur. (2020)

4. Alrabaee, S., Shirani, P., Wang, L., Debbabi, M., Hanna, A.: Decoupling coding habits from functionality for effective binary authorship attribution. J. Comput. Secur. (Preprint), 1–36 (2019)

5. Caliskan, A., et al.: When coding style survives compilation: de-anonymizing programmers from executable binaries. In: NDSS 2018 (2015)

6. Marquis-Boire, M., Marschalek, M., Guarnieri, C.: Big Game Hunting: The Peculiarities in Nation-State Malware Research. Black Hat, Las Vegas (2015)

7. Moran, N., Bennett, J.T.: Supply chain analysis: from quartermaster to sunshop (Vol. 11). FireEye (2013)

8. Meng, X., Miller, B.P., Jun, K.-S.: Identifying multiple authors in a binary program. In: Foley, S.N., Gollmann, D., Snekkenes, E. (eds.) ESORICS 2017. LNCS, vol. 10493, pp. 286–304. Springer, Cham (2017). https://doi.org/10.1007/978-3-319-66399-9_16

9. Krsul, I.: Authorship analysis: identifying the author of a program, Technical report CSD-TR-94-030, Department of Computer Sciences, Purdue University, West Lafayette, Indiana (1994)

10. Krsul, I., Spafford, E.H.: Authorship analysis: identifying the author of a program. Comput. Secur. **16**(3), 233–257 (1997)

11. MacDonell, S.G., Gray, A.R., MacLennan, G., Sallis, P.J.: Software forensics for discriminating between program authors using case-based reasoning, feed-forward neural networks and multiple discriminant analysis. In: the Sixth International Conference on Neural Information Processing, Perth, Australia, pp. 66–71. IEEE Computer Society Press (1999)

12. Ding, H., Samadzadeh, M.H.: Extraction of Java program fingerprints for software authorship identification. J. Syst. Softw. **72**(1), 49–57 (2004)

13. Frantzeskou, G., Gritzalis, S., MacDonell, S.G.: Source code authorship analysis for supporting the cybercrime investigation process. In: the First International Conference on E-business and Telecommunication Networks, Setubal, pp. 85–92. Kluwer Academic Publishers (2004)

14. Frantzeskou, G., Stamatatos, E., Gritzalis, S., Katsikas, S.: Source code author identification based on n-gram author profiles. In: Artificial Intelligence Applications and Innovations, New York City, NY, pp. 508–515. Springer (2006)

15. Frantzeskou, G., Stamatatos, E., Gritzalis, S., Chaski, C.E., Howald, B.S.: Identifying authorship by byte-level n-grams: the source code author profile (SCAP) method. Int. J. Digit. Evid. **6**(1) (2007)

16. Kothari, J., Shevertalov, M., Stehle, E., Mancoridis, S.: A probabilistic approach to source code authorship identification. In: The Fourth International Conference on Information Technology, Las Vegas, NV, pp. 243–248. IEEE Computer Society Press (2007)

17. Lange,R.C., Mancoridis, S.: Using code metric histograms and genetic algorithms to perform author identification for software forensics. In: The Ninth Annual Conference on Genetic and Evolutionary Computation, London, pp. 2082–2089. ACM Press (2007)

18. Burrows, S., Tahaghoghi, S.M.M.: Source code authorship attribution using n-grams. In: Proceedings of the 12th Australasian Document Computing Symposium, Melbourne, Australia, pp. 32–39 (2007)

19. Burrows, S., Uitdenbogerd, A.L., Turpin, A.: Application of information retrieval techniques for source code authorship attribution. In: the Fourteenth International Conference on Database Systems for Advanced Applications, Brisbane, pp. 699–713. Springer (2009)

20. Kilgour, R.I., Gray, A.R., Sallis, P., MacDonell, S.G.: A fuzzy logic approach to computer software source code authorship analysis. In: The Fourth International Conference on Neural Information Processing – The Annual Conference of the Asian Pacific Neural Network Assembly (ICONIP'97), Dunedin, New Zealand (1997)

21. Chen, R., Hong, L., Lu, C., Deng, W.: Author identification of software source code with program dependence graphs. In: The 34th Annual IEEE Computer Software and Applications Conference Workshops, Korea, Seoul, pp. 281–286 (2010)

22. Burrows, S.: Source code authorship attribution. Ph.D. Thesis, School of Computer Science and Information Technology, RMIT University, Melbourne, Australia (2010)

23. Burrows, S., Uitdenbogerd, A.L., Turpin, A.: Comparing Techniques for Authorship Attribution of Source Code. John Wiley and Sons (2012). https://doi.org/10. 1002

24. Palmer, G.: A road map for digital forensic research. Technical Report DTR- T001-01, Digital Forensics Research Workshop (DFRWS) (2001)

25. The Paradyn project. http://pages.cs.wisc.edu/~paradyn/

26. Bilar, D.: Opcodes as predictor for malware. Int. J. Electron. Secur. Dig. Forens. 1(2), 156–168 (2007)

27. Santos, I., et al.: Opcodesequence- based malware detection. Lecture Notes in Computer Science, vol. 5965, pp. 35–43 (2010)

28. Santos, I., Brezo, F., Ugarte-Pedrero, X., Bringas, P.G.: Opcode sequences as representation of executables for data-mining-based unknown malware detection. Inf. Sci. (2011)

29. IDA Pro multi-processor disassembler and debugger. http://www.hexrays.com/ products/ida/index.shtml

30. Brucker, F.: Modèles de classification en classes empiétantes. Ph.D. Thesis, Dép. IASC de l'École Nationale Supérieure des Télécommunications de Bretagne, France (2001)

31. Bai, J., Yang, Y., Mu, S., Ma, Y.: Malware detection through mining symbol table of Linux executables. Inf. Technol. J. 12(2), 380–383 (2013)

32. Rosenblum, N.E., Miller, B.P., Zhu, X.: Recovering the toolchain provenance of binary code. In: Proceedings of International Symposium on Software Testing and Analysis (2011)

33. Rosenblum, N.E., Xiaojin, Z., Miller, P.: Who wrote this code? Identifying the authors of program binaries. In: Sixteenth European Symposium on Research in Computer Security (ESORICS), Leuven, Belgium (2011)

34. Authorship Attribution (SUPPLEMENTARY MATERIALS). http://pages.cs. wisc.edu/~nater/esorics-supp/

35. Frantzeskou, G., Gritzalis, S., MacDonell, S.: Source code authorship analysis for supporting the cybercrime investigation process, In: 1st International Conference on eBusiness and Telecommunication Networks - Security and Reliability in Information Systems and Networks Track (ICETE04), pp. 85–92 (2004)

36. Caballero, J., Poosankam, P., McCamant, S.: Input generation via decomposition and re-stitching: finding bugs, In: Malware 17th ACM Conference on Computer and Communications Security, pp. 413–425 (2010)

37. Wang, X., Pan, C.-C., Liu, P., Zhu, S.: SigFree: a signature-free buffer overflow attack blocker. IEEE Trans. Depend. Secure Comput. (2010)

38. Knuth, D.E.: Backus normal form vs. backus naur form. Commun. ACM **7**(12) (1964)

39. Kruegel, C., Kirda, E., Mutz, D., Robertson, W., Vigna, G.: Polymorphic worm detection using structural information of executables. In: RAID (2005)

40. Caliskan, A., Yamaguchi, F., Dauber, E., Harang: When coding style survives compilation: de-anonymizing programmers from executable binaries. In: NDSS (2018)

41. Alrabaee, S., Saleem, N., Preda, S., Wang, L., Debbabi, M.: Oba2: an onion approach to binary code authorship attribution. Digit. Investig. **11**, S94–S103 (2014)

42. Meng, X., Miller, B.P., Jun, K.-S.: Identifying multiple authors in a binary program. In: Foley, S.N., Gollmann, D., Snekkenes, E. (eds.) ESORICS 2017. LNCS, vol. 10493, pp. 286–304. Springer, Cham (2017). https://doi.org/10.1007/978-3-319-66399-9_16

43. Alrabaee, S., Debbabi, M., Wang, L.: On the feasibility of binary authorship characterization. Digit. Investig. **28**, S3–S11 (2019)

44. Focus on Source Code. http://ec.europa.eu/internal_market/copyright/docs/studies/etd2005imd195recast_report_2006.pdf

45. Microsoft Malware Classification Challenge. https://www.kaggle.com/c/malware-classification/data

# Author Index

H. H. Song et al. (Eds.): NSS 2024, LNCS 15564, pp. 451–452, 2025.
https://doi.org/10.1007/978-981-96-3531-3

The manufacturer's authorised representative in the EU is Springer
Nature Customer Service Centre GmbH, Europaplatz 3, 69115 Heidelberg,
Germany. If you have any concerns regarding our products, please
contact ProductSafety@springernature.com

Printed and bound by CPI Group (UK) Ltd, Croydon, CR0 4YY
27/04/2026
02097586-0016